Nathaniel Hawthorne

A Literary Reference to His Life and Work

SARAH BIRD WRIGHT

Facts On File
An imprint of Infobase Publishing

To my husband, Lewis Wright,
and my son, Alexander Grant Wright,
who have welcomed Hawthorne into their lives
and illuminated my work in countless ways.

Critical Companion to Nathaniel Hawthorne: A Literary Reference to His Life and Work

Copyright © 2007 by Sarah Bird Wright

Facts On File, Inc.
An imprint of Infobase Publishing
132 West 31st Street
New York NY 10001

Library of Congress Cataloging-in-Publication Data

Wright, Sarah Bird.
Critical companion to Nathaniel Hawthorne: a literary reference to his life and work / Sarah Bird Wright.
p. cm.
Includes bibliographical references and index.
ISBN 0-8160-5583-1 (acid-free paper)
1. Hawthorne, Nathaniel, 1804–1864—Handbooks, manuals, etc.
2. Authors, American—19th century—Biography—Handbooks, manuals, etc.
I. Title.
PS1881.W75 2006
813'.3—dc22   2005034648

Text design by Erika K. Arroyo
Cover design by Cathy Rincon/Dorothy Preston

Printed in the United States of America

VB Hermitage 10 9 8 7 6 5 4 3 2 1

This book is printed on acid-free paper.

CONTENTS

INTRODUCTION

In his book on Nathaniel Hawthorne, Henry James wrote that Hawthorne was "the most valuable example of the American genius" he knew, offering "the most vivid reflection of New England life that has found its way into literature." Although Hawthorne wrote only a handful of novels, in addition to his volumes of tales, various sketches, and children's books, his works are among the most widely read and taught in the canon of American literature. His writing endures today because it deals with such universal experiences as birth, death, love, toil, heartache, and guilt. His novels and tales often begin with what appear to be provincial scenes but then widen in breadth, achieving a profound exploration of human nature and society as a whole. Hawthorne is regarded as the principal chronicler and interpreter of the spiritual history of his native New England.

This book is intended as a comprehensive guide to Hawthorne's life and work, with particular attention paid to the tales and novels that students read most often in high school and college classes. Part I provides a concise biography of Hawthorne. Part II provides detailed entries on his works, major and minor, in alphabetical order. Entries on the most important tales and novels contain a synopsis of the work, critical analysis, information on its reception by scholars and reviewers, and subentries on characters in the work. Part III contains entries on related people, places, and topics. Part IV contains appendices, including chronologies of Hawthorne's life and of his works, a bibliography of secondary sources, the texts of some of the major reviews of Hawthorne's works (including reviews by Edgar Allan Poe and Henry Wadsworth Longfellow), a section entitled "Melville and Hawthorne" (giving the text of a letter from Herman Melville to Hawthorne and Melville's essay "Hawthorne and His Mosses"), and a section entitled "Henry James on Hawthorne" (giving extracts from James's masterful book-length study of Hawthorne).

Any reference to a work by Hawthorne that is the subject of an entry in Part II or to a person, place, or topic that is the subject of an entry in Part III is given in SMALL CAPITAL LETTERS the first time it appears in a particular entry.

ACKNOWLEDGMENTS

I am greatly indebted to my earliest and closest friend, Mary Ann Caws, whose prodigious scholarship has provided inspiration and an enduring, if unattainable, model for my own efforts. Elsa Nettels and Jean Blackall offered wise counsel and practical assistance, as did Mary Suzanne Schriber. Margaret Rorison of Wilmington, N.C., has, as Henry James might say, seen the project through and offered her support in countless ways.

My colleagues at the School of Continuing Studies, University of Richmond, including Martha Edmonds, Elizabeth Scott, Virginia Schmitz, and Elisabeth Wray, have encouraged me at every stage in the preparation of this work. I am also greatly indebted to Janet Schwarz, who has alerted me to new books and articles about Hawthorne, and to Rosemary Dietrick, with whom I have had many discussions about the challenges and rewards of writing. I am also grateful to Dr. Beverly Peterson of Penn State University, Uniontown, Pennsylvania, for her friendship and support, and for informing me of new Hawthorne publications.

My brother, Richard Oscar Grant, and his wife, Jane Irby Grant, of Wrightsville Beach, N.C., provided welcome havens for reading and writing, both in their home and aboard their Hatteras motor yacht, *Southern Accent*. Their children, my nephew Rick Grant and niece Louise Grant, have followed the progress of the book with a lively interest, as have my nephews Ashley Grant and Charlie Grant, sons of my beloved late brother Martin Grant.

My cousin Rose Martin King and her husband, Wallace Eric King, of Bozeman, Montana, encouraged my progress in every way and alerted me to new publications about Hawthorne. Rose and I also enjoyed long walks at Wrightsville Beach, N.C., discussing the legacy of our grandfather, Robert Moody Martin, who founded and edited the *Liberty County Herald* in Georgia, unwittingly setting us both on the path of writing and research.

While visiting Rock Ferry, across the Mersey River from Liverpool, in the summer of 2003, I had a fortuitous encounter with Mary and Simon Petris, who are the de facto custodians and librarians of Hawthorne memorabilia and artifacts surviving from his years as American consul in Liverpool. They were instrumental in saving the gatepost when the Hawthorne home in Rock Ferry was demolished to allow construction of a motorway, and they hospitably shared their extensive Hawthorne archives with me.

I would like to express my gratitude to Mr. Barry Smith, chair, The Friends of Kensal Green Cemetery, London, and to the Friends of Kensal Green Cemetery for information about the remains of Sophia Hawthorne and her daughter Una. I am profoundly indebted to Mr. Saf Meah, Superintendent of Kensal Green Cemetery, London, who, in 2003, drove me to the graves of Sophia Hawthorne and Una Hawthorne, which I was able to photograph. Their remains have now been moved to Sleepy Hollow Cemetery, Concord, Massachusetts, but Barry Smith has kindly informed me that the headstone for Sophia remains in the Kensal Green Cemetery. The Sisters of Mercy have donated it to the Friends of Kensal Green Cemetery, which will preserve it for the future. The headstone for Una and a footstone were returned to Sleepy Hollow Cemetery.

Leslie Shen contributed a great deal to my work, for which I am extremely grateful. I take particular pleasure in thanking my Facts On File editor, Jeff Soloway, for his resourcefulness, valuable suggestions, and patience. Cam Dufty of Facts On File provided a close reading of the text as well as many valuable suggestions. Jeanne Fredericks, my agent, was tireless in offering support and wise counsel throughout the course of the book, from inception to publication.

PART I

Biography

Nathaniel Hawthorne

(1804–1864)

Nathaniel Hawthorne once called himself the "obscurest man in American letters." Nevertheless, his remarkable achievements as a novelist and short-story writer have given him a lasting reputation in American letters. In his study of Hawthorne, Henry James wrote that he was "the most valuable example of the American genius" he knew, offering "the most vivid reflection of New England life that has found its way into literature."

Hawthorne did not attain fame at first, however. Slowly, with his publication of short stories in many influential periodicals, and with his novels, he claimed a central place in American letters. He figured in the artistic development of Herman Melville, Henry James, and many others. He focused on the nation's past, especially the Puritan era. He was also much concerned with the social and psychological aspects of human behavior and undertook the mission of exploring the darker side of humanity.

Nathaniel Hawthorne was born on July 4, 1804, in Salem, Massachusetts, to Nathaniel Hathorne and Elizabeth Clarke Manning. Born Nathaniel Hathorne, he later added a *w* to the family name. He had two sisters, Elizabeth and Louisa. Elisabeth was born in 1802, and Louisa in 1808. The Hathornes were an old Salem family, descendants of Thomas Hawthorne of Bray, Berkshire, England. Thomas Hawthorne was the earliest paternal ancestor of Nathaniel Hawthorne who has been authoritatively identified. He is thought to have been born in the 15th century. In the 16th century, the family name came to be spelled "Hathorne." The brothers William and John Hathorne emigrated to Massachusetts in the early 17th century, settling first in Dorchester, and then moving to Salem. The earliest Hathornes took part in the persecution of Quakers and those thought to be witches.

Hawthorne's father, Nathaniel Hathorne, was a shipmaster. He died in 1808, at the age of 28, when his son was only four, on a voyage to Dutch Guiana. Hawthorne's mother, Elizabeth Manning, was the daughter of a blacksmith. She was greatly impoverished when her husband died and could not afford to maintain her own household. She moved her family from the Hathorne home on Union Street, Salem, to the home of her parents on Herbert Street in Salem. She was forced to rely on her Manning relatives for support. Something of a recluse, she never remarried, but lived in Salem except for the years she and her family resided in Raymond, Maine, where one of her brothers built her a house. In Maine, Nathaniel ran "quite wild" as he skated, fished, and hunted.

When Hawthorne was seven or eight, his uncles Robert and Samuel Manning took him on a trip into New Hampshire. Robert began planting trees on the property the Mannings owned in Raymond, Maine, on the shores of Lake Sebago. Hawthorne was, meanwhile, being tutored by Joseph Emerson Worcester. In December 1816, Robert Manning took Hawthorne to a boarding school at Stroudwater, Maine, run by the Reverend Caleb Bradley, but he was there for only about two months.

Nathaniel Hawthorne *(Courtesy of the Library of Congress)*

Engraving of Captain Nathaniel Hathorne, Hawthorne's father, by S. A. Schoff *(Courtesy of the Peabody Essex Museum)*

At the age of nine, Hawthorne sustained a serious leg injury while playing ball, an event that resulted in two years of invalidism. He passed the time in extensive reading. Later he reflected that these two years resulted in his acquiring his "cursed habits of solitude." After he recovered, he spent a great deal of time on family property on Lake Sebago, Maine, which fostered his love of nature. Always a voracious reader, as a boy he read the works of Shakespeare, Milton, John Bunyan, and James Thomson. The first book he bought as a boy with his own money was Spenser's *The Faerie Queen.* It is said that he often read while lying on the floor.

In order to prepare her son for college, Mrs. Hawthorne sent him back to Salem. There he lived with his Manning relatives and studied with a lawyer, Benjamin Lynde Oliver. There he began a small newspaper, *The Spectator,* in which he imitated the journal of the British 18th-century writers Richard Steele and Joseph Addison. He published the newsletter himself and served as his own writer

and editor. He was also his own printer, a process he managed by careful and diligent hand lettering. The paper included family gossip, brief essays, and poetry. He included an amusing classified notice intended to find a husband for his aunt Mary.

While publishing the newsletter, he also worked as secretary and bookkeeper for his uncle William Manning, the proprietor of a stagecoach office. In addition, he continued his studies in preparation for college. He told his sister "Ebe" (Elizabeth), "No man can be a Poet and a Book Keeper at the same time." This statement proved prophetic: When he later held down jobs in the Salem Custom-House, he was unable to produce any creative writing.

Little is known of Hawthorne's friendships with other boys until he entered Bowdoin College. He seems to have passed a somewhat reclusive childhood. He chose Bowdoin, a frontier institution near Portland, Maine, because of its closeness to his mother and sisters, which was a decided advantage. He enrolled there in 1821. His college education was funded by his maternal uncle Robert Manning. He spent four formative years at Bowdoin, graduating in 1825. Although he studied Latin, Greek, mathematics, philosophy, and natural science, it is thought that he was not instructed in modern languages, literature, or history. It is possible that Hawthorne began writing stories and sketches at Bowdoin, but he apparently destroyed these early manuscripts.

At Bowdoin, his closest friends were Jonathan Cilley, Henry Wadsworth Longfellow, Franklin Pierce, and Horatio Bridge. In a letter to his mother, he pondered various professional paths open to him as a career: "I do not want to be a doctor and live by men's diseases, nor a minister to live by their sins, nor a lawyer to live by their quarrels. So, I don't see that there is anything left for me but to be an author." He considered being a minister "out of the Question," for it was a "dull way of life." Moreover, he informed his mother that he was not born "to vegetate forever in one place, and to live and die as calm and tranquil as . . . a puddle of water." Lest she recommend the profession of law, he forestalled her, saying there were too many lawyers already, and some were in a "state of actual starvation." As for his being an author, the "illegibility" of his handwriting would certainly be an advantage. Moreover, his mother would be proud to see his works "praised by the reviewers, as equal to proudest productions of the scribbling sons of John Bull." Nonetheless, he realized that authors were always "poor devils."

While still at Bowdoin, Hawthorne began to write some stories he titled "Seven Tales of My Native Land." He also began his first novel, *Fanshawe*, published in 1828. When he graduated from college, he was 18th in a class of 35. He left with

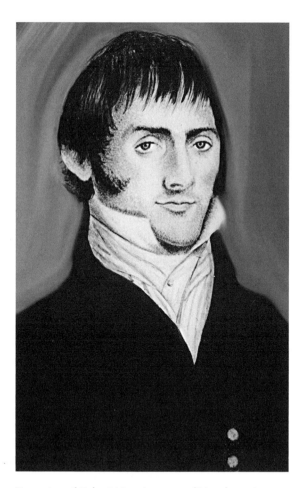

Engraving of Robert Manning, one of Hawthorne's maternal uncles, ca. 1818. After the death of Hawthorne's father, Manning served as his nephew's guardian and took a keen interest in his progress. *(Courtesy of the Peabody Essex Museum)*

the intention of becoming a writer, although he was uncertain how he would go about it. Before his graduation, his mother and sisters had moved back to Salem. He joined them there in 1825 and spent the ensuing decade in a "dismal and squalid chamber" as he endeavored to launch his writing career. He spent much of his time reading and writing, although from time to time he traveled within New England. According to library records, he borrowed at least 1,200 works of nonfiction from the Salem Athenaeum.

While living with his mother and sisters, he wrote historical sketches and allegorical tales, but was unable to publish them and decided to burn them. He then offered *Fanshawe,* the romance that he had initially begun at Bowdoin College, to a number of publishers, but, unfortunately, none of them expressed an interest. He finally undertook to print it at his own expense. The title was taken from the principal character, a student at a fictional institution called Harley College. Roughly patterned after the novels of Sir Walter Scott, *Fanshawe* has the merits of variety of characters, a plot centered on romantic love, and various dramatic deeds of heroism and villainy. In the words of the critic Stanley Williams, the characters are "thin and two-dimensional, the dialogue pretentious; but a contemporary was right in declaring that in *Fanshawe* we may detect the weak and timid presence of all of Hawthorne's peculiar powers" (*Literary History of the United States,* ed. Robert E. Spiller et al., vol. 1, 421–422). *Fanshawe* was not altogether ignored by critics, despite Hawthorne's poor opinion of his first novel. William Leggett, writing in *Critic: A Weekly Review of Literature, Fine Arts, and the Drama,* noted that the novel was not the first attempt of the author and should not be his last. He declared prophetically that the "mind that produced this little, interesting volume, is capable of making great and rich additions to our native literature." The influential literary editor Sarah Josepha Hale, the founder of *Godey's Lady's Magazine,* recommended the book and declared it "worth buying and reading." Hawthorne was, nevertheless, discouraged by the reception and sales of the novel and tried his best to acquire all copies and

Nathaniel Hawthorne, portrait by Henry Inman, 1835
(Courtesy of the Peabody Essex Museum)

destroy them. He succeeded to the extent that the volume is now one of the most valuable and rare titles in American literature.

Hawthorne then published various tales and sketches anonymously, but made very little money from them. His friend Horatio Bridge persuaded him to publish a collection of tales under his own name. Titled *Twice-told Tales,* the volume came out in 1837 and enjoyed immediate success. In 1838, Hawthorne made several journeys to Maine, to see his friend Bridge, and to North Adams, Massachusetts, where he kept a descriptive journal of people he met.

Late in the year 1838, he met Sophia Peabody, daughter of a Salem dentist, Dr. Nathaniel Peabody. She had endured a difficult childhood. Sickly as a small child, she had been sent to the home of her grandmother during the War of 1812. She was forced to eat all food placed before her, made to read the Bible aloud, and mistreated by her aunts. In time she developed the temperament of an invalid, with vivid nightmares. She was given strong drugs such as opium for her headaches. Eventually, she

was taught to paint by the artist Thomas Doughty. Slowly, her health improved.

Despite Sophia's progress, her mother convinced her that, since she had no physical strength, she should be "strong in faith" and accept the probability that she would never marry. Sophia was hidden away and watched over. In 1833, she and her sister Mary, who was also believed to have very poor health, sailed to Cuba to try to improve the nervous condition from which both suffered. They lived on a sugar plantation owned by family friends, the Morrells, and tutored the Morrell children. Both Sophia and Mary enjoyed improved health thanks to the climate in Cuba and their long walks. Sophia kept diaries of her Cuban experiences, which were later of interest to Hawthorne. After two years in the Tropics, the sisters returned to Salem.

When Sophia and Mary returned to Massachusetts, they, along with their sister Elizabeth, became acquainted with Hawthorne's sisters and, in time, Hawthorne himself. He soon became intensely interested in Sophia. She was well read and a talented artist. She also knew Latin, Greek, and Hebrew. Before long, she and Hawthorne were secretly engaged.

Sophia's sister Elizabeth Palmer Peabody became the champion of *Twice-told Tales.* She reviewed it for the *New-Yorker* in March 1838 and recommended it to her many Boston and Concord friends, including Ralph Waldo Emerson. She encouraged Hawthorne to focus on writing historical accounts of New England's past for children. As a result, he wrote *Grandfather's Chair: A History for Youth* (1841), *Famous Old People: Being the Second Epoch of Grandfather's Chair* (1841), and *Liberty Tree: With the Last Words of Grandfather's Chair* (1841). All of these books were published by Elizabeth Peabody and sold in her bookshop. Another volume by Hawthorne, *Biographical Stories for Children* (1842), provided accounts of the colonial American painter Benjamin West, Benjamin Franklin, Sir Isaac Newton, Oliver Cromwell, Samuel Johnson, and Queen Christina of Sweden. Unfortunately, these biographies did not sell well in the marketplace. Ticknor and Fields later published a collection of them that found a wider readership.

Between 1825 and 1835, Hawthorne wrote a number of manuscripts and submitted them to publishers. Unfortunately, he received many rejection notices and, in moments of frustration, burned some of his manuscripts. He took long evening strolls, went on occasional hiking trips, and frequently walked along the seashore but, in general, saw little of the world. In January 1836, he accepted an appointment as editor of *The American Magazine of Useful and Entertaining Knowledge,* a magazine published in Boston. He and his sister Elizabeth wrote most of the copy themselves. But when the publisher became bankrupt in June 1836, Hawthorne was forced to return to Salem. He wrote to Henry Longfellow to explain what he had been doing since their last meeting. He remarked, "I have secluded myself from society; and yet I never meant any such thing, nor dreamed of the sort of life I was going to lead. I have made a captive of myself and put me in a dungeon; and now I cannot find the key to let myself out." He wanted the tales he had written to reach a wide audience, but this had not yet happened.

In 1837, Hawthorne was invited to contribute to a new journal, founded by Louis O'Sullivan, the *United States Magazine and Democratic Review.* O'Sullivan told Hawthorne it was a journal designed, as he expressed it, "to be of the highest rank of magazine literature," modeled on first-class magazines in England. When the first issue appeared in October 1837, Hawthorne's short story "The Toll-Gatherer's Day" was included. O'Sullivan himself was the son of an American consul. He had been born in 1813 in the harbor at Gibraltar, aboard a British man-of-war. His father had perished in a shipwreck when his son was only

The Peabodys' home at 53 Charter St., Salem *(Courtesy of the Peabody Essex Museum)*

10 years of age. O'Sullivan was later able to attend Columbia College and earned degrees in the law as well as in the arts. He did practice law from time to time, but his talents were too varied and his personality too vibrant for him to be content with a career as an attorney. He coined the well-known term "Manifest Destiny" and organized an ill-fated expedition to seize Cuba for America. For this he was forced to stand trial, but he was acquitted. He has been described as "flamboyant, charismatic, energetic but with a restless attention span," a person with "great potential," but one who also had "easy recourse to convenient expediences" because he always needed money (Miller, Edwin, *Salem Is My Dwelling Place,* 150). O'Sullivan was much taken with the young Hawthorne and was later invited to be the godfather for Hawthorne's first child, Una. Hawthorne wrote to Sophia that he had a "genuine affection" for O'Sullivan and a "confidence in his honor." However, Hawthorne also thought O'Sullivan sometimes had "foul companions" forced upon him by his career in politics.

In 1838, Elizabeth Peabody, sister of Sophia Peabody, became convinced that Hawthorne needed a position that would allow him enough time to write. She wrote to her friend Orestes Brownson, who was steward of the Chelsea Marine Hospital, who, in turn, contacted George Bancroft. At the time, Bancroft was collector of the Port of Boston and had assisted Orestes Brownson in obtaining his post. Bancroft offered Hawthorne the post of inspector in the Boston Custom-House, at an annual salary of $1,100 (Turner, Arlin, *Nathaniel Hawthorne: A Biography,* 117).

Hawthorne sent Bancroft a letter of acceptance in early 1839, although he was actually uncertain about his qualifications for inspecting incoming vessels and controlling their cargo. He hoped, however, to have time to continue his writing. He was highly capable in performing his duties and remained in the post until January 10, 1841.

In November 1840, he and Sophia Peabody had decided their future lay in the Brook Farm communal society that was being established by George Ripley in West Roxbury, just outside Boston (Turner, *Nathaniel Hawthorne: A Biography,* 129 130). Hawthorne knew that he wanted to

marry Sophia and hoped that, by residing at Brook Farm, he might be able to save enough money to succeed. In January 1841, he resigned from the Boston Custom-House. He then invested a thousand dollars in the farm and, in April 1841, joined the Brook Farm Institute of Agriculture and Education, a farm of 200 acres that had become a transcendentalist cooperative community in West Roxbury, Massachusetts.

The Brook Farm pilgrims, both young and middle-aged, believed, according to the critic Edwin Miller, that it would be easy to return to a "simple agrarian life and to simple Christian principles." They planned to become self-sufficient and to reject the "money-oriented, industrialized society" they saw developing around them. They would rely on "wisdom and purity" and bestow the "benefits of the highest, physical, intellectual and moral education in the present state of human knowledge" on the community (Miller, *Salem Is My Dwelling Place,* 187–188). The disillusioned Unitarian clergyman George Ripley was the founder of the Brook Farm community. Others included Lloyd Fuller, brother of the American essayist, editor, teacher, and writer Margaret Fuller. The aesthete Charles King Newcomb was also a shareholder in Brook Farm. Hawthorne bought two shares at $500 each, a large sum for him. Ralph Waldo Emerson called the experiment "a perpetual picnic, a French Revolution in small, an Age of Reason in a patty pan." Women wore skirts with matching knickerbockers, wide-brimmed hats, and berry, vine, and flower wreaths. The men wore blue frocks, sack trousers, and thick boots. There were eight cows, but Hawthorne was too inexperienced to be allowed to milk them (Miller, 188–191).

This experiment in utopianism continued only until 1847; Hawthorne stayed less than a year. His experience figures in his novel *The BLITHE-DALE ROMANCE.* Margaret Fuller is thought to have been the model for the character of Zenobia. Both Zenobia and Margaret Fuller were writers, gifted conversationalists, and strong advocates of women's rights. In April 1841, when he was living at Brook Farm, Hawthorne wrote to Sophia that Margaret Fuller's cow was at the farm, and that she "hooks the other cows, and has made herself ruler of the herd, and behaves in a very tyrannical manner" (*Letters*, 15, 528). Hawthorne's description of Zenobia's beauty, however, was probably based on another Brook Farm resident, Mrs. Amelia Barlow (Turner, *Nathaniel Hawthorne: A Biography*, 239). Hawthorne departed from Brook Farm in November 1841 but kept up his ties with many of the residents he had come to know.

Hawthorne had noted in an early letter to Sophia that his youthful life at home, in his "haunted chamber," was meaningless. He wondered whether the world would ever know him. When he began to gain recognition, he still found nothing in the outside world that was preferable to his old "solitude"—until a "certain Dove" was revealed to him. He continued with an account of their developing relationship. He had drawn nearer and nearer to the Dove and opened his "bosom to her, and she flitted into it, and closed her wings there—and there she nestles now and forever, keeping my heart warm and renewing my life with her own" (Martin, Terence, *Nathaniel Hawthorne*, 27).

Hawthorne's sister Elizabeth ("Ebe") was adamantly opposed to the marriage, an opposition many critics attribute to her possessiveness of her brother. On one occasion, she appropriated flowers that Sophia Peabody's sister, Elizabeth Peabody, had sent to Nathaniel. They had been delivered by Sophia. Ebe imagined that they were a gift to her, pretending that Nathaniel considered a love of flowers to be a "feminine taste." Hawthorne's son Julian, writing about the incident many years later, declared that Ebe was jealous, and that his father was certainly "sensible" of the "beauty and charm of flowers." Ebe always believed that Hawthorne's writing suffered after the marriage, although Hawthorne himself was firmly convinced that Sophia "rescued him from a life of alienation" (Erlich, Gloria, *Family Themes and Hawthorne's Fiction: The Tenacious Web*, 88–90).

None of the Peabodys attended Sophia's wedding to Hawthorne on July 9, 1842, a few days after his 38th birthday. By all accounts Sophia and Hawthorne were extraordinarily happy together. They had three children, Una, Julian, and Rose. Sophia was a devoted wife throughout his life, arranging their housing, accompanying him on all his trav-

Sophia (Amelia) Peabody Hawthorne, 1847. From an etching by S. A. Schoff. *(Courtesy of the Peabody Essex Museum)*

els, and, at one time, helping the family financially by making lampshades. She was also an excellent painter and a good copyist. She illustrated Hawthorne's story "The Gentle Boy," which he dedicated to his wife. The story was published in a separate volume by Weeks & Jordan in Boston and by Wiley & Putnam in New York and London in 1839.

Hawthorne formally resigned as an associate of the Brook Farm Institute on October 17, 1842. At that time, he wrote that he did not feel "entirely disconnected" from the community but knew that he would not return. He promised, however, to take the "warmest interest" in the progress of the experiment and believed in its ultimate success (Miller, 199).

The Hawthornes rented the Old Manse, in Concord, for the next three years. Concord was then a rural settlement by the winding Concord River. Hawthorne valued the Old Manse and regarded it as a retreat and place of privacy. The house was set back from the street, the Concord River ran past the apple orchard at the rear, and there was deep snow throughout the winter. Ellery Channing and Henry Thoreau were both neighbors, whose company Hawthorne enjoyed.

Hawthorne then published *Biographical Stories for Children*. This was a collection of biographies of interest to children, first published in Boston by Tappan and Dennet, 1842. It included biographies of Benjamin West, Sir Isaac Newton, Samuel Johnson, Oliver Cromwell, Benjamin Franklin, and Christina, queen of Sweden.

The Hawthornes' first child, Una, was born March 3, 1844, at the Old Manse. Hawthorne then set about editing and improving a manuscript by his Bowdoin friend Horatio Bridge, titled *The Journal of an African Cruiser*. Meanwhile, he had accepted employment in the Salem Custom-House. The Hawthornes' only son and second child, Julian, was born June 22, 1846, in Boston. Rose, their last child, was born May 20, 1851, in the Berkshires. Hawthorne described the birth of Rose in a letter to his sister Louisa: "She made her appearance this morning at about three o'clock, and is a very promising child—kicking valiantly and crying most obstreperously."

Hawthorne often read to Sophia in the evenings: Shakespeare, Macaulay, Spenser, and other writers. The family suffered from poverty, however. Sophia wrote to her mother that her husband and Una were her "perpetual Paradise," but she "besieged heaven with prayers" that they might not be forced to separate, "whatever privations" they might suffer in order to remain together (Woodberry, 114–158, passim). It was from this period that some of Hawthorne's most noted sketches and tales date, including "The Celestial Rail-road," "The Bosom Serpent," "The Minister's Black Veil," "The Birth-Mark"," "Rappaccini's Daughter," and "The Artist of the Beautiful."

In the summer of 1849, Elizabeth Clarke Manning Hawthorne, Hawthorne's mother, died. As Brenda Wineapple describes the scene, his "desolate sisters" hovered over their mother's bedside. Hawthorne occasionally tiptoed in, shocked to see how she had shrunken. She begged him to take

The Old Manse, Concord, Massachusetts. After the Hawthornes were married in July 1842, they were conveyed by carriage to the Old Manse, which had been filled with flowers by neighbors. *(Courtesy of the Peabody Essex Museum)*

care of his sisters. In his journal, Hawthorne wrote about his tears: "I tried to keep them down . . . but it would not be—I kept filling up, till, for a few moments, I shook with sobs." Later he wrote, "Surely it is the darkest hour I ever lived." He wrote in his journal, "I love my mother . . . but there has been, ever since boyhood, a sort of coldness of intercourse between us, such as is apt to come between persons of strong feelings, if they are not managed rightly." Wineapple observes that Hawthorne and his mother "remained afraid of one another" even when he was an adult. Sophia, however, was aware of the strong affection between them: "'There was the deepest sentiment of love & reverence on both sides," she observed. Two days before his mother died, Hawthorne happened to look out of the window and see his daughter playing outside and then turned his gaze back to his mother. "And then I looked at my poor dying mother; and seemed to see the whole of human existence at once, standing in the dusty midst of it" (Wineapple, *Hawthorne: A Life*, 206–207).

Because Hawthorne had no job and no income, his friend Horatio Bridge came to his rescue by asking John Jay, the attorney for *Blackwood's Magazine*, whether Hawthorne might contribute articles to the publication. Sophia, in addition, had saved some of the Custom-House salary that Hawthorne had earned and was able to afford at least such staples of their diet as bread and rice. She accepted donations from friends, including Ann Hooper and Francis and Anna Shaw; sometimes these donations were in cash, and at other times they took the form of clothes. She also began selling the lampshades she had painstakingly decorated, and she painted mythological scenes based on illustrations by John Flaxman. Unfortunately, the lampshades could be sold for only five or 10 dollars apiece, and her enterprise did not generate enough money to feed the family. The Hawthornes' friend George Hillard appealed to other friends of the family and managed to collect enough to be of real help. However, he realized that Hawthorne would be unwilling to accept charitable donations. Hillard wrote to him, "It is only paying, a very imperfect measure, the debt we owe you for what you have done for American Literature" (Wineapple, *Hawthorne: A Life*, 207). Hawthorne was still very reluctant to accept assistance. He remarked, "It is something else besides pride that teaches me that ill-success in life is really and justly a matter of shame."

Hawthorne secretly began writing *The Scarlet Letter*. His friend James T. Fields wanted desperately to help him and made a special trip to Salem in order to see him. However, Hawthorne declared he had written nothing. At the same time, Sophia told her mother, "He writes immensely." He worked on the novel for hours every day yet refused to admit it. As Fields finally started down the steps of the Hawthorne home, Hawthorne rushed after him and pressed a roll of manuscript in his hand. It was *The Scarlet Letter*, nearly finished. Fields read it on the train as he traveled back to Boston. Then he turned and went back to Salem, convinced that the work he held in his hand was spellbinding and would be far easier to sell than "another tale about the Puritans." As Wineapple puts it, "*The Scarlet Letter* would secure both Hawthorne's and Fields's respective reputations as eminent writer and purveyor of eminent writers." Sophia, however, stated that Fields was not solely responsible for the publication of *The Scarlet Letter*, and that it was "entirely a mistake" to credit him alone. She declared, "It was Mr. Whipple, the clever critic and really literary man of careful culture, who came to Salem with Mr. Fields and told him what a splendid work it was—and then Mr. Fields begged to be the publisher of it." When Hawthorne read the novel to Sophia, she realized she had "just heard a powerful piece of literature." Henry James would later declare the novel to be "the finest piece of imaginative writing yet put forth in this country."

Hawthorne provided an introductory essay for the novel called "The Custom-House," describing the debilitating effect his civil service job had had on his writing. "My imagination was a tarnished mirror. It would not reflect, or only with miserable dimness, the figures with which I did my best to people it." He tried to determine how much longer he could stay in the Custom-House, "and yet go forth a man." He was then, fortuitously, fired from the Custom-House. Determined to become a writer, he began work "as if the devil" were within him (Wineapple, *Hawthorne: A Life*, 210–211).

Salem Custom-House, where Hawthorne was employed from 1846 to 1849. He held a position there as Surveyor for the port of Salem. He lost this job following the Whig victory in the election of 1848, but later drew upon his surveyor experiences for scathing descriptions of civil servants in *The Scarlet Letter*. *(Courtesy of the Peabody Essex Museum)*

The novel was based on his experiences in the Custom-House. In his introduction, Hawthorne imagines his descendants' view of him: "A writer of story-books! What kind of a business in life,—what mode of glorifying God, or being serviceable to mankind in his day and generation,—may that be? Why, the degenerate fellow might as well have been a fiddler!" He is, nevertheless, confident about his work: "Let them scorn me as they will, strong traits of their nature have intertwined themselves with mine." The story of Hester Prynne was inspired by his own Puritan ancestry, which he needed both to affirm and to resist. He had long been haunted by the tale of a woman forced to wear an A on her breast as an advertisement for her sinfulness. The novel he wrote about Hester Prynne, however, both mocks the creative process and, as Miller puts it, "accepts

and questions the tenets" of romanticism and the romantic artist (Miller, *Salem Is My Dwelling Place*, 279). Hawthorne intended to reflect the dour Puritans who were dedicated to God, and to discipline and duty. He himself, however, as he wrote, was "happier, while straying through the gloom of those sunless fantasies, than at any time since he quitted the Old Manse." The actual writing of the novel, though, was more complex than he admitted.

Miller observes that "The Custom-House" is actually a romance itself, as much so as *The Scarlet Letter*. In his notebooks, Hawthorne reveals that he had been haunted for more than a decade by a tale he had read about a woman who had committed adultery and who had undergone the extraordinary punishment of wearing an A on her breast in order to indicate her sinfulness. This type of punishment was not unheard of. In fact, Hawthorne had discovered that his 17th-century Manning ancestors had included two sisters who had been forced to sit in the meeting house at Salem with bands about their foreheads. The bands were emblems of their incestuous conduct with their brother, Captain Nicholas Manning, who, at the time, had fled to the Maine woods, where he was hiding (Miller, *Salem Is My Dwelling Place*, 278).

Hawthorne did not altogether trust the assessment of his publisher, James T. Fields, that *The Scarlet Letter* would be an important addition to the canon of American literature. He originally planned to include the novel as the centerpiece of a collection of other tales he had published, in addition to some that he had not published. He wrote to Fields: "Is it safe, then, to stake the fate of the book entirely on this one chance? A hunter loads his gun with a bullet and several buck-shot; and, following his sagacious example, it was my purpose to conjoin the one long story with half a dozen shorter ones; so that, failing to kill the public outright with my biggest and heaviest lump of lead, I might have other chances with the smaller bits, individually and in the aggregate" (Miller, 280).

William Dean Howells, one of Hawthorne's most perceptive critics, remarked that Europeans expected American fiction to be "aesthetically responsive" to the country's immense spaces and powerful impetus toward their development for "the use of man." They supposed native American novels would be "rude" and "shapeless." In his opinion, however, Hawthorne's novel was of a "verity so robust" that it was all but impossible to see how it could ever be surpassed. The characters were "all there to speak and act for themselves," and they did not need the help of the reader's fancy ("Hawthorne's Hester Prynne," *Heroines of Fiction* [New York: Harper's, 1901], 161–174).

The first edition, of 2,500 copies, was published in March 1850 by Ticknor, Reed, and Fields, Boston, and sold out within 10 days. The second edition, of 2,500 copies, was published in April 1850, and a third edition of 1,000 copies was published in September 1850 (Clark, Jr., C. E. Frazer, *Nathaniel Hawthorne: A Descriptive Bibliography*, 140–148). The book found a wide audience in Salem as well as farther afield. The *Salem Gazette* termed the book "thrilling." Edwin Whipple wrote that the introductory essay was like the work of Joseph Addison and Charles Lamb, and added that the novel pierced "directly through all externals to the core of things" (Wineapple, *Hawthorne: A Life*, 217).

The novel, though widely praised, failed to produce sufficient funds to allow the Hawthornes to continue living in Salem. In any case, Hawthorne wanted very much to leave the town. Sophia was finding it hard to make enough lampshades to fill the orders she received, and she suffered an attack of pleurisy soon after publication of *The Scarlet Letter*. Her husband felt they might be much happier in western Massachusetts. He wrote to his friend Horatio Bridge, "I detest this town so much that I hate to go into the streets, or to have people see me." The family searched for a home near Portsmouth, New Hampshire, which would have the advantage of being near Bridge, but they were unable to find any residence that would be suitable.

Sophia had a wealthy friend, Caroline Sturgis, who was staying with her husband, William Aspinall Tappan, in the Berkshire mountains. They were near Lenox, occupying the estate of Anna and Samuel Ward while they built their own "cottage" (the local word for mansion) on the acreage called Tanglewood. (Tanglewood is now the summer home of a noted music festival.) There were a number of noted literary and artistic figures living in or near Lenox. The writer Catharine Maria Sedgwick lived in Stockbridge, the actress Fanny Kemble lived in a cottage near Lenox, and Herman Melville and his large family were living in nearby Pittsfield.

The Hawthornes decided that it would be wise to move to Lenox. Sophia wrote, "To give up the ocean caused rather a stifling sensation, but I have become used to the mountains now" (Wineapple, *Hawthorne: A Life*, 218–219). In May 1850, the Hawthorne family moved to a rented farmhouse, the "red house," in Lenox, Massachusetts, situated in the Berkshire mountains. At the time, they had two children, Una and Julian. Rose Hawthorne was born in May 1851 in Lenox.

Hawthorne then embarked on *The House of the Seven Gables,* which he considered a "romance."

In his preface to the work, he distinguished between a romance and a novel. The romance, he suggested, offered more latitude to the writer than the novel, yet it was necessarily subject to certain laws as a work of art and must not swerve from the "truth of the human heart." The writer, however, might "so manage his atmospherical medium as to bring out or mellow the lights and deepen and enrich the shadows." In *The House of the Seven Gables*, Hawthorne aimed to "connect a bygone time" with the present that is continually disappearing.

This novel was a more cheerful tale than *The Scarlet Letter;* Hawthorne intended to shape it so that it would have a happy ending. The story concerns events that stem from evil deeds committed by the earliest member of the Pyncheon family, who forced the Maule family from their land in order to build a grand home on the site, considered desirable because of its proximity to a natural spring. The current descendant of the Pyncheon family, Miss Hepzibah Pyncheon, occupies a home on property originally owned by Matthew Maule. Hepzibah's ancestor, Colonel Pyncheon, had been instrumental in convicting Maule of witchcraft and having him hanged, as a result of which a curse was associated with the house. The natural spring became polluted when the new house was built. The present family occupying the house is proud of its ancestry but has gradually lost position and sunk into near poverty. Hepzibah is destitute and regarded as pathetic by the town. The novel turns on the conflict between forces representing the past and other forces directed toward living within the present. As the novel opens, Hepzibah's beloved brother, Clifford, falsely imprisoned for most of his life for a crime he did not commit, has been released, although he has been much impaired emotionally. He hopes to rejoin humanity but sometimes is almost suicidal about his wasted life; he becomes very close to leaping from an upperstory window. The fall and redemption of the Pyncheon family are the central theme of the novel. By the end of the story, the evil Judge Pyncheon, who had caused Clifford to be imprisoned, has died, and Hepzibah, Clifford, her young cousin, Phoebe, and her lodger, Holgrave, are liberated. They are then able to leave the dilapidated house and move to the judge's country estate.

Ticknor, Reed, and Fields of Boston published 1,690 copies of the first edition, first printing, of the novel on April 9, 1851. By September 1851, there had been four printings. The original manuscript that served as the printer's copy is located in the Houghton Library at Harvard (Clark Jr., *Nathaniel Hawthorne: A Descriptive Bibliography,* 168–169). Critics were delighted by the novel. George Ripley, writing in *Harper's New Monthly Magazine,* praised the characters as having "the air of old acquaintance," one "managed with admirable artistic skill." He declared the novel "unsurpassed" by Hawthorne's other writings (Idol and Jones, *Nathaniel Hawthorne: The Contemporary Reviews,* 167–168). Hawthorne advised against connecting the "imaginary events" in the story with a particular locality, but, despite this warning, visitors have long flocked to Salem in order to tour the house that is reputed to be the original "House of the Seven Gables."

Hawthorne's third novel, *The Blithedale Romance,* which he began planning in Lenox, Massachusetts, was written largely in 1851, when he and his family lived in the home of the Horace Manns in West Newton, Massachusetts. It was published in 1852. The novel is essentially a "satire against social reformers," as Louise DeSalvo observes (*Nathaniel Hawthorne,* 97). It was loosely based on the period Hawthorne spent in 1841 at the transcendentalist Brook Farm Institute of Agriculture and Education, in West Roxbury, Massachusetts. This community had been founded by the American editor, reformer, and literary critic George Ripley, a Unitarian minister in Boston. In April 1841, Ripley and 20 other members of the Transcendental Club moved to Brook Farm's 200 acres, about nine miles from Boston, on the Charles River. Ripley hoped that the community would embody "Christ's idea of society." The residents' time would be divided between manual and mental labor (Hoeltje, *Inward Sky: The Mind and Heart of Nathaniel Hawthorne,* 168). Hawthorne lived there from April until November 1841 but ultimately found communal living unappealing.

The novel has had, to many critics, a fatal flaw: the disjunction between its apparent polemical purpose, an exploration of the Brook Farm experiment, and its actual theatrical focus on performance, in the form of mesmerism, masquerades, dancing, and veils. Even if it is considered solely as a satire against social reform, the events are marked with a dualism that puzzles many readers. Some of Hawthorne's practical experiences at Brook Farm figure in the novel. For instance, he drove to the Brighton Cattle Fair with the head farmer, William Allen, to buy baby pigs and sell a calf (Hoeltje, *Inward Sky: The Mind and Heart of Nathaniel Hawthorne,* 176). In the novel itself, however, the baby pigs and the cattle fair seem as shrouded and shaded as the Veiled Lady. The reader who is expecting a sober account of the daily lives of the participants and the working out of problems inhibiting and promoting the experiment may be frustrated by the paucity of detail that George Eliot, Thomas Hardy, Honoré de Balzac, or Charles Dickens might have supplied.

Instead, Hawthorne veers off into masked identities and the world of theater, several times shifting the scene back to Boston, which the reformers have fled to establish their experimental community. He seems aware of this difficulty at the outset. In his preface to the novel, he states that he does not wish to deny that he had the community in mind, but declares that he considers the institution "as not less fairly the subject of fictitious handling, than the imaginary personages whom he has introduced there." His "fictitious handling," however, is frequently meager. With more conviction, he emphasizes that he is not trying to "illustrate a theory, or elicit a conclusion, favourable or otherwise, in respect to Socialism," but rather to "establish a theatre . . . where the creatures of his brain may play their phantasmagorical antics, without exposing them to too close a comparison with the actual events of real lives." He insists that he has not sketched the "likenesses" of any persons at Brook Farm, such as the "self-concentrated Philanthropist," the "high-spirited Woman," the "weakly Maiden," or the "Minor Poet" (Preface, *The Blithedale Romance*). The "phantasmagorical antics" have puzzled many readers ever since the novel was published.

After *The Blithedale Romance* was published, an important national event took place that would have a substantial impact on Hawthorne and his family during his last years. In 1852, Franklin Pierce, his longtime friend from Bowdoin College, became the Democratic nominee for president. He was unexpectedly chosen by the party on the 49th ballot after the front runners—Lewis Cass, Stephen A. Douglass, and James Buchanan—all failed to secure sufficient backing to attain the nomination. Hawthorne had met Pierce through the Athenaean Society at Bowdoin College. Although he was one class ahead of Hawthorne, Pierce had become one of his closest friends.

Pierce was not very well known at the time. He had been elected to the New Hampshire legislature in 1828; he then served in the United States Congress as a representative. He served one term in the U.S. Senate and, during the Mexican War, had been a brigadier general. His nomination led Hawthorne to become a biographer again. Working rapidly in order to boost the candidate's chances, he embarked on a campaign biography of Pierce. He launched appeals for materials he needed. He was able to glean some information from conversations with Pierce and made good use of Pierce's journal, which had been kept during his military service. Other pertinent data were collected from letters, documents, and newspaper clippings. However, in addition to Pierce's relative newcomer status, he was handicapped by the stand he had decided to take on the question of slavery. Pierce had voted for the Compromise of 1850, and he had little sympathy at the time for the measures some abolitionists were more than willing to take in order to free slaves. Hawthorne, as well as Pierce, believed that slavery would eventually end, and both men were convinced that the nation would be spared a bloodbath. They agreed with George Washington, who had expressed the hope that slavery would eventually be abolished in America. That belief, or hope, colored Hawthorne's presentation of Pierce's own views on slavery. Years later, Hawthorne's stand adversely affected his reputation, when he dedicated his book on his travels in England, *Our Old Home: A Series of English Sketches* (published in 1863), to Pierce.

The campaign biography, titled *The Life of Franklin Pierce,* was published in 1852 by Ticknor, Reed, and Fields. It was available in two formats. The cloth edition sold for 50 cents; a paperback edition was sold for 37.5 cents. The Whigs, on the whole, denounced the biography. The Democrats, however, approved of it. A reviewer for the *Springfield Republican* wrote in a rather dismissive fashion: "This is Hawthorne's last fiction, and has been considered by competent judges to be his best, at least, as one indicating a greater degree than any of his previous works. The author's disclaimer of political partisanship is one which we do not receive or believe in for a moment."

Initially, Hawthorne did not expect anything more than gratitude, least of all political favors, if Pierce won the election. Still, he was realistic enough to perceive that he and his family did have need of material assistance. The Concord house that he and Sophia had bought and called "The Wayside" needed extensive repairs. Moreover, he needed somehow to provide for the education of his children. He had also told Sophia he would at some future time take her to Italy to see the paintings and statues about which he had read. In addition, he had long hoped to visit the home of his ancestors, in England.

When Pierce won, he appointed Hawthorne consul to Liverpool, presaging a highly significant period in Hawthorne's career as a writer. At that time, the consul would actually benefit financially from being in a busy port. Because there was a very brisk trade between England and the United States, transacted largely in Liverpool, the position would be extremely lucrative.

While waiting for the details regarding his post as consul to take shape, Hawthorne began once again turning classical myth into juvenile literature. He drew upon Charles Anthon's *Classical Dictionary,* as he had in the past. He had his narrator, Eustace, recast the tales of Theseus and the Minotaur, the Pygmies, Cadmus and the dragon's teeth, Ulysses's visit to Circe's palace, and Jason and the Golden Fleece. *Tanglewood Tales* was completed on March 9, 1853. He then wrote an introduction and sent the off manuscript, writing to his longtime friend Richard Henry Stoddard: "They are done up in excellent style, purified from all moral stains, recreated as good as new, or better, and fully equal, in their own way, to Mother Goose." In addition, he commented to Stoddard that he had never done anything else as well as these "old baby-stories." Unfortunately, Hawthorne's writings for children have not received the recognition they richly deserve. Children did figure in two uncompleted romances, both of which were posthumously published: *The Dolliver Romance and Other Pieces* (1876) and *Doctor Grimshaw's Secret: A Romance* (1883). Hawthorne's fiction for children has attracted little critical attention, however, and he did not publish other writings for juveniles. Still, his *Wonder-book* and *Tanglewood Tales* have both been republished many times. In addition, some individual tales, such as "The Golden Touch," have appeared separately, often with lavish illustrations.

The Hawthornes sailed to Liverpool, England, in July 1853 aboard the Cunard Line paddle wheeler NIAGARA. They were given places of honor at Captain Leitch's table and were accompanied by WILLIAM D. TICKNOR. At first, the family stayed at a hotel, Waterloo House, but they then moved to a boardinghouse, Mrs. Blodgett's, on Duke Street. On August 6, they moved to the Rock Ferry Hotel, across the river Mersey, and, somewhat later, they rented a substantial stone house in ROCK PARK, one of the first gated communities in England (Turner, *Nathaniel Hawthorne: A Biography,* 263–265). The Hawthornes would live in Europe, principally in England and Italy, until 1860.

Hawthorne took up his duties as consul on Monday, August 1, 1853. He kept extensive notebooks throughout his term, some of which were, unfortunately, revised by Sophia after his death. (The manuscripts are now in the Pierpont Morgan Library; they were edited by Randall Stewart and published by Oxford University Press in 1941.) Because Liverpool was the chief portal of trade in England, Hawthorne was responsible for dealing with both commercial and diplomatic matters. His duties included interviewing sailors who claimed to be American (Hawthorne calls them "rogues"); evaluating and assisting other people, including women, who purported to be destitute American citizens; attending formal dinners given

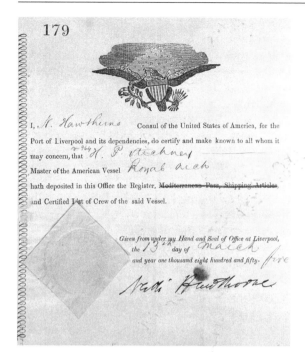

Inscription from a consular document signed by Hawthorne in 1855, when he was consul to Liverpool. *(Courtesy of the Peabody Essex Museum)*

in his honor by local officials, including the mayor; assisting with inventories of the personal effects of American citizens who had died in Liverpool; and attending inquests. Hawthorne retained many of the employees of his predecessors, including the vice-consul, James Pearce, and the chief clerk, Henry J. Wilding, who provided excellent guidance for him. He was also assisted by the outgoing consul, Thomas Crittenden. He wrote hundreds of letters, published in two volumes: those to friends, acquaintances, and family (*The Letters* 1853–1856) and *The Consular Letters*, related to the business of the consulate, problems caused by Americans abroad (deaths, crimes, breakdowns), and other matters. Some of these were drafted by his chief clerk, although Hawthorne approved them before they were sent.

By 1855, Hawthorne had become disillusioned with his office. He observed in his notebook that he was leading a "weary life" and was sick of "brutal captains and brutish sailors." He had to deal with "beggars, cheats, simpletons, unfortunates, so mixed up that it is impossible to distinguish one from another"; in self-defense he was forced to distrust them all (*The English Notebooks by Nathaniel Hawthorne*, ed. Stewart, 190). He also suffered much financial hardship during his tenure as consul. At first, he could retain consular fees and build up some savings, although he still had to draw salaries for his clerks and other employees from these fees. The fee-retention system was then abolished, and his salary was barely sufficient to support his family. On the plus side, however, he made many English friends while serving out his term in Liverpool. Among his first callers were HENRY BRIGHT, an English writer and university graduate who had met Hawthorne during a visit to America, and his father. According to Turner, their friendship was one of Hawthorne's "most satisfying relationships during his residence in England" (*Nathaniel Hawthorne: A Biography*, 268).

He was also very attentive to his family. Among the highlights of the Hawthornes' lives in England were visits to London, the Lake District, Leamington, Hammersmith, and many other places of interest. Before returning to America, the family toured Lincoln, Boston, Peterborough, Nottingham, Manchester, and Scotland. Throughout his time in England, Hawthorne kept an English notebook, later published, and wrote hundreds of letters, also published.

Hawthorne resigned the consulship in February 1857. One reason was that James Buchanan had become United States president. In 1863, Hawthorne published *Our Old Home*, a collection of 12 sketches based on his experiences as American consul in Liverpool. He was criticized in Britain for arguing that it was undeniable that an American "was continually thrown upon his national antagonism by some acrid quality in the moral atmosphere of England." He declared that the English thought "so loftily of themselves, and so contemptuously of everybody else" that it was difficult to "stay in a good humor with them." According to Turner, Hawthorne knew the sketches would "stir resentment" in England (*Nathaniel Hawthorne*, 161).

At the conclusion of his term as American consul in Liverpool, Hawthorne and his family went to the Continent. They traveled to France and Italy in January 1858 and then back to England. They were to spend a year and four months in Italy; they did not return to America until 1860. Hawthorne's knowledge of Italian history and love of the poetry of Dante, Petrarch, and Boccaccio made him particularly eager to visit Florence and Rome. Hoeltje remarks that the couple approached Italy "with the heightened sentiments of the time . . . vivified for them, as for many others, by their sympathetic and enthusiastic reading" of Lord Byron's *Childe Harold's Pilgrimage.*

The Hawthornes went by steamer to Boulogne and on by train to Amiens and Paris. After a few days, they continued by train to Marseille. The family was accompanied by Ada Shepard, a young college graduate who had been strongly recommended by Mary Mann, Sophia Hawthorne's sister. She acted as companion and tutor to the children. In Paris, they were joined by the astronomer Maria Mitchell, a professor at Vassar College who had discovered a new comet in 1847; she had asked to travel to Rome in their company.

They continued on by train to Dijon, Lyon, and Marseille. From there, they traveled aboard the Neapolitan steamer *Calabrese* to Genoa, a journey of a week. They toured some of the sights in Genoa, including the Balbi palace, "the stateliest and most magnificent residence" Hawthorne had ever seen (*The French and Italian Notebooks,* 49). The family continued to Leghorn and Civita Vecchia by steamer and went on by carriage to Rome, where they arrived in the latter part of January 1858.

Unprepared for the winter weather they encountered, the Hawthornes were cold and wretched. Along the way, Hawthorne had caught a cold and a fever, which marred their first two weeks in Rome. They stayed at Spillman's hotel while seeking lodgings and finally settled at 37, Via Porta Pinciana, where they had a suite of 10 rooms. Wearing all their winter clothes at once, the family shivered, but still went out sightseeing every day. They were disappointed by Saint Peter's, by the number of pickpockets and beggars, and by the sight of a "shabby population smoking bad cigars" (*French and Italian Notebooks,* 53–59). But it was carnival

time in Rome, and the children, at least, enjoyed themselves.

It was not until the Hawthornes felt better physically that they warmed up to the city and began their explorations in earnest. They wrote to and called on people whom they had met, or to whom they had introductions, such as the artists William Wetmore Story, C. G. Thompson, Joseph Mozier, George Loring Brown, and Maria Louisa Lander. They also established social contact with Harriet Hosmer, William Cullen Bryant, and Fredrika Bremer. By late May 1858, they had had many social invitations and visited all of the major churches, villas, palaces, and art galleries of Rome.

They left Rome on May 24 by carriage. By that time, Hawthorne had become very fond of the city,

Nathaniel Hawthorne, 1861. Photograph by Silsbee and Case. *(Courtesy of the Peabody Essex Museum)*

writing in his notebook, "It is very singular, the sad embrace with which Rome takes possession of the soul" (*French and Italian Notebooks*, 232). They were prevented by rain from viewing the famous Cascade of Terni but saw the town itself.

They continued on to Spoleto, Perugia, Foligno, Assisi, Pasignano, and Arrezzo, where they saw Petrarch's house. The family arrived in Florence in early June. They had been given a letter of introduction to the American sculptor Hiram Powers, who arranged for them to engage the lower floor of the Casa del Bello, for 50 dollars a month. It had many rooms around a courtyard, a terrace, a garden with a fountain, and luxurious furnishings. Hawthorne remarks in his notebook that it was like the "Paradise of cheapness which we were told of" but which they had "vainly sought" in Rome. They engaged a servant and arranged for the delivery of dinner every day from a cook shop. Powers and his family became good friends during the Hawthornes' stay in Florence.

They also saw ROBERT BROWNING and his wife, ELIZABETH BARRETT BROWNING, several times, at the home of Isabella Blagden, in her villa at Bellosguardo, outside Florence. She also introduced them to Thomas Trollope, elder brother of the British novelist Anthony Trollope, who wrote a number of books dealing with Italian life and history.

In Florence, they visited the Boboli Gardens, the Uffizzi Gallery, the Cathedral, and the Pitti Palace. After Hawthorne took Julian to the Uffizzi Gallery, he declared in his notebook that his son had passed a "sweeping condemnation upon everything he saw, except a fly, a snail-shell, a caterpillar, a lemon, a piece of bread, and a wine-glass, in some of the Dutch pictures." Hawthorne recalled that, when young, he himself used to experience a "weary lack of appreciation" in picture galleries (*French and Italian Notebooks*, 350).

From Florence, the family went on to Siena, Viterbo, and Sette Vene. They returned to Rome in October 1858 and remained there until May 1859. While in Rome, Una became seriously ill with "Roman fever," a dreaded illness similar to malaria, from which she suffered for six months. According to Turner, quinine was one of the few medicines available, but it was fatal if given too often.

Una finally seemed to have recovered by April 19, although she apparently suffered the aftereffects of the illness as long as she lived. Turner observes that Hawthorne "never recovered from the anguish her illness caused him" (*Nathaniel Hawthorne: A Biography*, 334–335).

Hawthorne's Bowdoin classmate and friend General Franklin Pierce (formerly President Pierce) and his wife had arrived in Rome on March 10 and frequently visited twice a day until April 19. They offered much support. Hawthorne commented in his notebook that Pierce had "undergone so great a sorrow of his own, and has so large and kindly a heart, and is so tender and so strong, that he really did us good, and I shall always love him the better for the recollection of these dark days" (*French and Italian Notebooks*, 518). The Pierces had seen their only child, an 11-year-old son, killed in a train wreck two months before Franklin Pierce took office as president in 1853.

In early April 1859, while the family was still in Rome, Hawthorne had begun work on a romance about an American journeying to England to claim an ancestral estate. His creative instincts, however, were actually impelling him toward a different theme, inspired by several works of art: Guido's portrait of Beatrice Cenci, the statue of the *Dying Gladiator* in the Capitoline Museums, and a dancing faun and a copy of the *Faun of Praxiteles* in the Villa Borghese (he saw another copy of the *Faun of Praxiteles* in the Capitoline Museums). Hawthorne took his family to Florence in the middle of May, for the summer, to avoid the health risks of staying in Rome. They lived in Rome and Florence until May 1859, when they returned to England.

Hawthorne had already drafted *The Marble Faun*, but the family spent another year in England while he rewrote the book and saw it through British publication. This step ensured that he would have a British copyright (Baym, *The Shape of Hawthorne's Career*, 251). In England, the novel was published in February 1860 as *Transformation*. It was published a week later in America as *The Marble Faun*. The subtitle, in both editions, was "The Romance of Monte Beni," a line suggested by JAMES T. FIELDS. Set in Italy, the novel concerns the adventures of three young American artists in

Rome—Kenyon, Hilda, and Miriam—and their friend Donatello, a young Italian nobleman.

Henry Fothergill Chorley, writing in the British *Athenaeum* in 1860, praised the "scenic power and beauty" of the work but questioned Hawthorne's reliance on the "elevating influences of remorse on certain natures." He considered Kenyon a "stone image" and believed Miriam to be a reincarnation of Zenobia, heroine of *The Blithedale Romance.* Hilda, he suggested, was very like Phoebe in *The House of the Seven Gables.* He found Donatello more original and powerful, with his transformation from semimythical creature to a "sad, conscience-stricken human being." However, Miriam's "agony and unrest" and the Faun's transformation were too vague to be satisfying.

James Russell Lowell, who reviewed the novel for the *Atlantic Monthly* in April 1860, wrote that the 19th century had produced "no more purely original writer than Mr. Hawthorne." The actors and incidents in the novel were "vistas" through which readers might see the moral from "different points of view," pointing skyward, but "inscribed" with suggestive hieroglyphs. Lowell praised the conception of Donatello, initially a creature of "mere instinct," who is awakened through sin to a conception of the necessity of atonement. He considered him the most original and imaginative character in the book. The novel was "steeped in Italian atmosphere," with landscapes "full of breadth and power." Hawthorne conceived characters, both "psychological and metaphysical," but did not "draw them." The characters were "acted upon by crime, passion, or circumstance, as if the element of Fate were as present to his imagination as to that of a Greek dramatist." The novel embodied "the most august truths of psychology," combined with "the most pregnant facts of modern history."

Grave of Nathaniel Hawthorne, Concord, Massachusetts. *(Courtesy of Concord Free Public Library)*

When it was published, upper-class Americans on the Grand Tour used it as a guide, as did families "recently risen to authority and wealth." In 1866, when Lucretia and George Frederic Jones took their four-year-old daughter Edith (later Edith Wharton) to Europe for six years, it was Hawthorne's Rome to which she was introduced by her nurse, and which she remembered all her life.

The family returned to The Wayside, in Concord, in 1860, but Hawthorne was not well. Although he grew less robust over the next three years, he made trips to New York and Maine. His work was not going well, and he was despondent. He became seriously ill in the spring of 1864. Pierce visited him and urged Hawthorne to accompany him in his private carriage to country places such as trout streams and old farmhouses. They would relive their youthful years and escape their present-day cares. They left on May 16, going north to Lake Winnipesaukee in New Hampshire. Then they continued on to Plymouth, New Hampshire, and stayed at the Pemigewasset House. On the night of May 18, Hawthorne died in his sleep. Pierce telegraphed Sophia and notified others. It is thought that he might have died of a brain tumor, because for weeks before embarking on the carriage trip with Pierce, he had suffered pain, weakness, and loss of control over his limbs.

Sophia Hawthorne was too devastated to manage any of the funeral arrangements, which she left to Una, Julian, and Judge Rockwood Hoar of Concord. Pierce accompanied the body to Boston, where Julian met him on May 20. They had the body embalmed without Sophia's knowledge. Louisa May Alcott and others decorated the Congregational Church in Concord for the service on the afternoon of May 23. The pallbearers included Ralph Waldo Emerson, Henry Wadsworth Longfellow, James Russell Lowell, James T. Fields, Charles Eliot Norton, and other prominent writers and poets of New England.

Hawthorne was buried in Sleepy Hollow Cemetery in Concord on a hilltop under the pines. Emerson, the Alcotts, Elizabeth Peabody, Henry David Thoreau, and many other literary figures would also be buried there. James Freeman Clark, who had married the Hawthornes, performed the ceremony (Miller, *Salem Is My Dwelling Place*, 499–522).

PART II

Works A–Z

"Alice Doane's Appeal"

This is the only story that survived from Hawthorne's first book, SEVEN TALES OF MY NATIVE LAND. He destroyed the others and later rewrote "Alice Doane's Appeal." It was published in *The TOKEN* (1835).

The story opens on a June afternoon with the narrator, a young man, leading two young ladies on a walk into the countryside. They arrive at Gallows Hill, which has been invaded by the "wood-wax" weed, a plant that destroys all other vegetation. The "dust of martyrs" lies beneath their feet, as this is the hill where the Salem witches were hanged in 1692.

The young man begins reading aloud from his manuscript, about the murder of a young man, Leonard Doane, that had taken place a century and a half earlier. Doane had lived in Salem for several months. He was devoted to his sister, Alice, and disapproved of her attachment to Walter Brome. The feeling is seemingly mutual: Doane senses that he and Brome share a "hateful sympathy" in their "secret souls." He kills Walter Brome, a shameful act that he later confesses to a fiendish and omniscient small wizard, who is already aware of the crime. Doane then has doubts about his sister's purity and feels remorseful over the murder of Brome.

As the tale closes, the "wretched" brother and sister visit a graveyard. The writer of the tale recounts leading them to a graveyard in which each family tomb has "given up" its inhabitants. They see the dead of many generations; even men who had been "venerable" while alive are now "contorted" by "intolerable pain or hellish passion" or, occasionally, by an "unearthly and derisive merriment." This "company of devils and condemned souls" has come to revel in the discovery of the crime. The crime is, in fact, that of the wizard, who has "cunningly" manipulated Walter Brome into tempting Alice to sin and then led Leonard Doane to murder him.

As the narrator finishes reading the manuscript, he realizes that he and the two young women are near the wizard's grave, and that the wood-wax plant has sprouted from "his unhallowed bones." The girls begin to laugh. The narrator is "piqued" that the story, based on the authority of "ancient superstitions," has not made them tremble. He keeps them on the hill longer and presents small vignettes of the lives of the people forming the procession: a mother accused by her son, a once proud but now broken man, a "frenzied multitude." At the rear he visualizes Cotton Mather on horseback, a friend of the devil and a "blood-thirsty man" marked by "vices of spirit" and "errors of opinion." He begins describing a scaffold, but the young ladies, who are now trembling, persuade him to descend the hill. They watch the twinkling lights of the distant village at twilight, regretting that the "barren" hill has no "relic of old" to commemorate the "errors of an earlier race."

The story has been a confusing one to many readers. The inner tale, in which a wizard is blamed for the tragedy, raises the question of whether the charges are justified, although the narrator seems to consider them unjustified. Frederick Crews sees both plots as "exercises in displacement" and argues that Hawthorne's "sense of history" arises from "guilt over family conflict" (Crews, Frederick C., *The Sins of the Fathers: Hawthorne's Psychological Themes* [New York: Oxford University Press, 1966], 44–60). Nina Baym believes the story reflects Hawthorne's predilection for writing gothic tales in which the inner story and the frame must conflict with each other (Baym, Nina, *The Shape of Hawthorne's Career* [Ithaca, N.Y.: Cornell University Press, 1976], 37–38). On the whole, readers have considered the story a frustrating one, and critics have regarded it as a failure. At the same time, it reveals what will be a continuing interest of Hawthorne's in using the past as material for fiction.

FOR FURTHER READING

Bell, Michael Davitt, *Hawthorne and the Historical Romance of New England* (Princeton, N.J.: Princeton University Press, 1971), 68–73; Fossum, Robert H., *Hawthorne's Inviolable Circle: The Problem of Time* (Deland, Fla.: Everett/Edwards, 1972), 13–22.

"Ambitious Guest, The"

Short story first published in *The New-England Magazine* in June 1835, when it was signed only "By the author of 'The Gray Champion.'" It was later reprinted in the *Essex Register*, the *Salem Advertiser*, and the *Ladies Cabinet of Fashion, Music, and Romance* (London). In 1842, it was collected in the second edition of *Twice-Told Tales*.

The story concerns a contented family residing in the Notch of the White Hills, a bleak location in New England on the stagecoach route between Maine, on one side, and the Green Mountains and the shores of the Saint Lawrence River, on the other. They are often startled by the sound of stones tumbling down from the mountain. Their home is but a "primitive tavern," where travelers might stop for a night's food and lodging and meet with "a homely kindness, beyond all price." Stage coaches and teamsters bound for local markets frequently draw up at the cottage door.

One evening, a melancholy young man appears and is made welcome by the entire family. After dinner, he reveals to them his ambition not to be forgotten after his death. A certain unease settles over the family, and the father wishes they were settled in a safer town. The grandmother informs them that she has already assembled her burial clothes, many years earlier, but makes one request now: that they hold up a mirror when she is in her coffin, so that she can make sure everything is perfectly arranged.

Suddenly the characters hear the sound of sliding stones, and the whole family rushes out directly into the "pathway of destruction." Although the cottage survives intact, "the Slide" kills the entire family and the young man; their bodies are never found. Hawthorne particularly mourns the "high-souled youth" who dreamed in vain of "Earthly Immortality."

Sharon Cameron believes the story's emphasis is on "the human desire to exchange life itself for an embodied meaning" (Cameron, Sharon, *The Corporeal Self: Allegories of the Body in Melville and Hawthorne* [Baltimore, Md.: Johns Hopkins University Press, 1981], 111–114, 128–131). The young stranger "could have borne to live an undistinguished life," but confesses, "I cannot die until I have achieved my destiny. Then, let Death come! I shall have built my monument!" Cameron points out that the character "focuses on the certainty of the monument rather than on what it is to represent or on how it is to be achieved." Similarly, the father dreams of a house at the base of the White Mountains and a "slate grave-stone . . . with just my name and age, and a verse of a hymn, and something to let people know, that I lived an honest man and died a Christian." The stranger exclaims in agreement that "it is our nature to desire a monument, be it slate, or marble, or a pillar of granite, or a glorious memory in the universal heart of man."

FOR FURTHER READING

Friedman, Thomas, "Strangers Kill: A Reading of Hawthorne's 'The Ambitious Guest,'" *Cuyahoga Review* 1, no. 2 (fall 1983), 129–140; Plambeck, Vernon L., "Hearth Imagery and the Element of Home in Hawthorne's 'The Ambitious Guest,'" *Platte Valley Review* 9, no. 1 (April 1981), 68–71; Sears, John F., "Hawthorne's 'The Ambitious Guest' and the Significance of the Willey Disaster," *American Literature: A Journal of Literary History, Criticism, and Bibliography* 54, no. 3 (October 1982), 354–357.

American Magazine of Useful and Entertaining Knowledge, The

A picture magazine founded by a group of engravers in September 1834 (Cantwell, *Nathaniel Hawthorne: The American Years*, 176).

The magazine was in a state of chaos when, in January 1836, Hawthorne was recruited by the poet Thomas Green Fessenden to take over the publication. Hawthorne boarded with Fessenden; his wife, Lydia; and Fessenden's niece, Catherine Ainsworth. He was expected to edit and produce the entire magazine while receiving little or no salary.

Hawthorne wrote much of the magazine until his resignation, in August 1836. His own contributions were impressive, ranging from biographical essays to articles on many subjects. These included pieces on the Boston Tea Party, the Chinese Pyramids, the Church of Saint Sophia, the Flathead Indians, and the Schenectady Lyceum (Cantwell, 174–189).

Ancestral Footstep, The

A group of 21 copybook entries for intended sketches that Hawthorne wrote in Rome between April 1 and May 19, 1858. They were published posthumously, first in the ATLANTIC MONTHLY (1882–83) and later in *The American Claimant Manuscripts*. According to his biographer Arlin Turner, Hawthorne had intended to depict a variety of legends and ceremonies. These included the tale of the Bloody Footstep at Smithell's Hall near Bolton, England; the story of a hospital with 12 ancient pensioners; and a description of the loving cup ceremony he had witnessed at the London mayor's dinner (Turner, 377–378).

"Antique Ring, The"

Short story first published in February 1843 in *Sargeant's New Monthly Magazine of Literature, Fashion, and the Fine Arts*. It is believed that Hawthorne wrote the story at the Old Manse in Concord, Massachusetts, after moving there with Sophia Hawthorne soon after their marriage.

The story is concerned with contemporary society, although its larger framework is based on the historic legend about a ring given to the earl of Essex by Queen Elizabeth I.

As the narrative begins, a young lawyer, Edward Caryl, has presented his fiancée, Clara Pemberton, with an antique engagement ring. She asks him to return to her with a story describing how many times in the past this ring has been the "pledge of faith" between two lovers, and whether their vows were kept or broken. The task is a congenial one for Edward, who has few clients, much time for leisure, and a strong interest in publishing poetry,

criticism, and essays in "fashionable periodicals." Hawthorne calls him a "carpet knight in literature." He goes away to write the legend of the ring, which he returns to tell Clara and her friends, who are "genial auditors" if not reliable critics.

Edward invents a legend about Lord Cecil, the condemned Earl of Essex, who, the evening before his execution, is visited by the Countess of Shrewsbury in the Tower of London. When she appears in the earl's prison chamber, she finds him toying with the ring. Wishing to take revenge on him for a previous slight, the countess offers to return the jewel to the lady connected with it in the earl's mind. He explains that the ring has magic powers and was once owned by the British wizard Merlin. He has been told by Queen Elizabeth to take the jewel to her in his hour of greatest need and to plead for mercy. He believes such an action will be of no use in light of the "artifices and intrigues" of courtiers plotting his downfall. Nevertheless, he is suddenly convinced that the ring may yet have the power to set him free.

The countess asks him to entrust her with the task of conveying the ring to the queen. He almost gives it to her, but, as she bends over to receive it, it casts a red glow on her face, giving it an "ominous expression." Regardless, she persuades the earl to give her the ring and then immediately betrays his trust. She keeps the ring, fails to present his case to the queen, and takes no action when the earl is hanged the next day.

Only when she is on her deathbed does the countess reveal her treachery and seek forgiveness from Elizabeth. The remorseful queen shakes the dying countess in spite. When the attendants prepare the countess's body for burial, they find that the ring has imprinted a dark red circle on her breast, which they believe is the "glow of infernal fire" from hell. The attendants are too frightened to remove the ring, which goes with the guilty countess into her tomb.

Years later, Lord Cromwell's soldiers desecrate the Shrewsbury family vault and take "Merlin's antique ring," which inflicts disaster and death on all of its subsequent owners in England.

The legend then crosses the Atlantic. In a local church, according to Edward, a "fervid preacher" solicits charitable contributions from his poor congregation. The self-approving Deacon Trott, whose mahogany collection box is filled with banknotes and silver half-eagles, criticizes the mountain of copper coinage in the box of the "simple and kindly" Deacon Tilton. Tilton's own box is filled with copper coins, shopkeeper's tokens, and a crisp new banknote, which, on inspection, turn out to be counterfeit. Deacon Trott taunts him, but Deacon Tilton, unfazed, contributes 10 dollars from his own pocket. Suddenly they discover, beneath the heap of copper, a brilliant antique diamond ring, identical to the one given the Earl of Essex by Queen Elizabeth. The two deacons take the ring to a fashionable jeweler, from whom the narrator of the legend, Edward Caryl, purchases it.

Clara Pemberton's friends praise the tale, but she is not yet satisfied. She asks Edward what thought he embodied in the ring. He replies that the gem is the human heart, while the "Evil Spirit" is falsehood—"which, in one guise or another, is the fiend that causes all the sorrow and trouble in the world." Clara responds that she prizes the story "far above the diamond which enkindled [his] imagination."

"The Antique Ring" has attracted little critical attention, possibly an indicator of Hawthorne's own evaluation of it. He chose not to include it in his collections.

FOR FURTHER READING

Fletcher, Angus, *Allegory: The Theory of a Symbolic Mode* (Ithaca, N.Y.: Cornell University Press, 1964), 214–219; Folsom, James F., *Man's Accidents and God's Purposes: Multiplicity in Hawthorne's Fiction* (New Haven, Conn.: College and University Press, 1963); Newlin, Paul A., "'Vague Shapes of the Borderland': The Place of the Uncanny in Hawthorne's Gothic Vision," *Emerson Society Quarterly*, 67 (1972), 83–96.

"Artist of the Beautiful, The"

Short story first published in June 1844 in *United States Magazine and Democratic Review* and collected in *Mosses from an Old Manse* (1846).

As the story begins, a retired watchmaker, Peter Hovenden, walks along a village street with his daughter Annie. They gaze through the window of a small watch shop and observe a young man, Owen Warland, Hovenden's former apprentice, hard at work inside, as he has been for months.

There is a complete lack of sympathy between Owen and the other townspeople. Hovenden, for one, is skeptical of Owen's ingenuity and doubts that, as Annie suggests, he may be inventing a new type of timekeeper. He scoffs that Owen is incapable of "invent[ing] any thing better than a Dutch toy."

Father and daughter then pass the shop of a blacksmith, Robert Danforth, a manly figure laboring mightily at his forge. Hovenden speaks highly of the blacksmith, saying he knows what it is to work in gold, but, when all is said and done, he ultimately admires the worker in iron, who "spends his labor upon a reality." Moreover, no blacksmith is such a fool as Owen Warland. Robert Danforth greets Annie warmly, but she continues on with her father without replying.

Owen, we learn, is adept at carving small objects. He has always possessed a "delicate ingenuity" but is viscerally horrified by monstrous machines. On being taken as a child to see a steam engine, he had recoiled and become ill when confronted with the "size and terrible energy of the iron laborer." Owen's mind, in contrast, tends "naturally to the minute," as befits the "marvellous smallness and delicate power of his fingers." Hawthorne observes that size is unrelated to beauty; a minute object has the capacity to be as beautiful as the "arc of the rainbow."

Owen's relatives had hoped his "strange ingenuity" and the "minuteness in his objects and accomplishments" would make him well suited to become a watchmaker's apprentice, but Hovenden is concerned by Owen's failure to appreciate the importance of measuring time. Instead, he would occupy himself by endowing watches with musical mechanisms and decorating venerable clocks with processions of figures measuring "mirthful or melancholy hours."

After Hovenden and Annie disappear down the street, Owen is seized with a "fluttering of the nerves" caused by the sight of the old watchmaker's "pretty daughter." Robert Danforth then enters the watch shop with an anvil Owen has ordered. He asks whether the watchmaker is trying to discover "the perpetual motion." Owen replies that it can never be discovered, but, if it were, it would only be twisted into machines driven by steam and water power. When the blacksmith leaves, Owen admits to himself that all of his ambitions and his "passion for the beautiful" look "vain and idle" to the likes of Robert Danforth, whose "hard, brute force darkens and confuses" him.

He returns to a piece of minute machinery he has been devising but discovers, under a magnifying glass, that he has fatally ruined it under the influence of Robert Danforth's "brute force." The loss of months of labor drives him into a "strange despair" and effects a "cold, dull, nameless change" in him. The transformed Owen now manages to return to the previously neglected, practical business of a watchmaker with "dogged industry." As a reward for his work, the townspeople invite him to regulate the clock in the church steeple. He succeeds, and the town shows its approval. This becomes a "heavy weight upon his spirits" that keeps his work accurate and orthodox.

Hovenden learns of Owen's transformation and goes to his shop to congratulate him, advising him to rid himself of his "nonsensical trash about the beautiful," which he has never understood. Owen is cast down again by Hovenden's "cold, unimaginative sagacity"; he reflects that nothing exists for his former employer except "the densest matter of the physical world." Suddenly, Hovenden spots Owen's mechanical invention, with its tiny chains, wheels, and paddles, and accuses him of "witchcraft." He infers that Owen is possessed by an evil spirit and offers to exorcise him. Owen declares that Hovenden is his evil spirit.

After Hovenden leaves, Owen lapses into sluggishness and lets his business founder. He returns at night to his shop, to work on his invention. One night, Annie enters to ask Owen to repair her thimble, if he can condescend to do so, now that he is "so taken up with the notion of putting spirit into machinery." Owen is amazed by her remark about the "spiritualization of matter" and realizes

that she alone may be capable of comprehending him and imparting strength to his "lonely toil." He agrees to explain his secret to her, but before he can do so, she reaches out with her needle to touch a small whirligig lightly. She intends no harm, but he seizes her wrist in rage and anguish. He is immediately contrite but explains that she has "undone the toil of months, and the thought of a lifetime." The distraught Owen realizes that Annie lacks the "deep intelligence of love" for him that might have enabled her to understand him.

Upon receipt of a small inheritance that frees him from "the necessity of toil," Owen spends the next winter in anguish, drinking wine and losing any sense of purpose in life. Suddenly, in the spring, a butterfly flies in the window and flutters near his head. Owen takes this as an omen that he must give up drinking, and he returns to his work during the nighttime. One evening, Hovenden invites him to a celebration of Annie's engagement to Robert Danforth. At this news, he destroys his "little system of machinery," the product of months of his labor.

In Owen's longtime devotion to Annie, he had constructed a vision of an angelic figure that had little factual basis. Hawthorne observes that, even if he had won her, he would have been disappointed in her inevitable transmutation into an "ordinary woman." To Owen, however, Robert Danforth has snatched away his angel.

Owen then becomes ill; it is as though his body has only a "soft vegetable existence." He speaks of mechanical marvels such as Albertus Magnus's Man of Brass and the French dauphin's automated miniature coach and horses but now regards them as fabulous. He tells people he had once thought it possible to "spiritualize machinery" but has abandoned such ideas. He has, sadly, "lost his faith in the invisible" and relies on "common sense."

His skepticism, however, is only slumbering. He eventually awakens and has a long space of "intense thought, yearning effort, minute toil, and wasting anxiety." Suddenly he decides to call on Robert Danforth; Annie is now a matron and mother, and her father is at their fireside. Owen discovers a strong young toddler boy tumbling on the carpet. He discerns, in the child, a resemblance to Peter Hovenden.

Hovenden asks, maliciously, whether Owen has succeeded in creating "the beautiful." Owen says he has and draws out a bridal gift for Annie, what appears to be a jewel box carved of ebony and inlaid with pearl. The design on the box depicts a boy pursuing a butterfly, and then the butterfly as a winged spirit, while the boy ascends from earth to cloud. Annie places her finger on the edge of the open box, and a gorgeous jeweled butterfly flies out, radiating a white gleam. It is so lifelike that, when it waves its wings, Annie is awe-stricken. "Is it alive?" she asks several times. Owen replies that it may be said to "possess life," because it has absorbed his own being "into itself."

Robert Danforth is delighted with the butterfly, calling it a "pretty plaything." The butterfly alights on his finger and then makes a wide circuit of the room. Robert declares it "beats all nature" but then remarks that there is more "real use" in one blow of his sledgehammer than in the butterfly, which represents five years of Owen's labor.

The child claps his hands and seems to demand that he be given the butterfly as a plaything. Owen perceives that Annie, too, lacks complete aesthetic appreciation of his creation. Owen knows, and could have told them, that the butterfly is such a "gem of art" that a monarch himself might have regarded it as the most unique and wondrous of his treasures.

Annie invites her father to inspect the butterfly, which still rests on Robert's finger. Hovenden presses his finger to Robert's, but his touch causes the physical decline of the butterfly. Its gold fades, its body's purplish hue grows dark, and its "starry lustre" vanishes. Annie, horrified, cries, "It is dying!" Owen calmly explains that the butterfly has "imbibed a spiritual essence" and, upon exposure to the doubt and mockery it senses from Hovenden, it has lost its beauty. Annie implores her father to take his hand away and let the butterfly rest on her son's "innocent hand" instead. The butterfly improves, but the little boy has "an odd expression of sagacity" that reminds Owen of Peter Hovenden. The child's father is proud, however: "'How wise the little monkey looks!'" he whispers. Owen is concerned, nevertheless; the butterfly alternately

sparkles and grows dim, as if it detects a flaw in the child's nature.

The butterfly rises upward as though it would soar into the sky were it not for the ceiling. It then flutters down toward Owen's hand. Owen turns it away, saying it has now gone "out of the master's heart." It flies toward the child, who grabs it out of the air and smashes it in his hand. Annie screams and Peter Hovenden laughs in a "cold and scornful" way. Owen gazes on the scene placidly. He has risen high enough to achieve the beautiful; thus he has caught "a far other butterfly than this." The butterfly was only the symbol by which he had been able to make the beautiful perceptible to the senses. Therefore, it now has little value in his eyes. His spirit now "possessed itself in the enjoyment of the reality."

RECEPTION AND CRITICAL ANALYSIS

It is clear in "The Artist of the Beautiful" that Hawthorne does not believe that true aesthetic sensitivity lies merely in an antipathy to practical concerns or fantasy. Annie Hovenden does not even, in fact, find much satisfaction in Owen's ingenuity, although she is sensitive to his feelings.

In Hawthorne's view, the artist must try to unite masculine strength with feminine ingenuity in order to produce viable art. He insists that "it is requisite for the ideal artist to possess a force of character that seems hardly compatible with its delicacy; he must keep his faith in himself while the incredulous world assails him with its utter disbelief" (Lathrop, George P. II, ed., *The Works of Nathaniel Hawthorne*, 512).

The crucial scene is thought to be, by many critics, the one in which Annie goes to Owen's workshop. She carries the symbols of her occupation, thimble and needle, and seems to understand Owen's aim of "putting spirit into machinery." Owen infers that she possesses the gift of comprehending him and hopes that, perhaps, if he can gain her sympathy, he might have permanent "help and strength" in his lonely toil. However, a touch of her needle on the delicate machinery of his whirligig destroys his project. He says bitterly that she has "undone the toil of months" and that her touch has ruined him. He does not mean to be cruel to

Annie, but it is clear from this encounter that she is not "enlightened by the deep intelligence of love" for him.

Hawthorne does not suggest, in this tale, that one who is hostile to everyday problems and practical concerns is therefore an artist. Peter Hovenden, early in the story, comments that all Owen Warland can hope to create is a "Dutch toy." Owen's "art" is in fact vacuous, only a toy, and he lacks depth. His happiest period is when he wanders through the countryside, searching for the beautiful, and when he seeks to embody it in his butterfly. The butterfly is destroyed, but Owen retains his fantasies about it and remains happy. Nancy Bunge observes that he is able to do so because he "loves illusion, not art."

In 1851, *Mosses from an Old Manse* was reviewed by the poet and critic Henry T. Tuckerman in the *Southern Literary Messenger*. He praised the "happy ideas" embodied in "The Artist of the Beautiful" (Crowley, ed., *Hawthorne: The Critical Heritage*, 211). In a perceptive unsigned review titled "Hawthorne: The New England Artist," in the *Southern Review* (April 1870), the author sees Owen Warland as someone whose pursuits, as Hawthorne says, are "insulated from the common business of life"; he experiences a frozen "moral cold." He argues that Robert Danforth and Peter Hovenden represent the "opposite poles" of the New England character; the first espouses a hard materialism and the other a groveling, sneering selfishness. Both are "crushing" to the lover of beauty, that is, Owen Warland (Crowley, ed., *Hawthorne: The Critical Heritage*, 462).

Writing over a century later, the contemporary critic Gloria Ehrlich suggests that the story reflects serious personal problems in Hawthorne's life at the time; he was struggling to support a growing family on meager literary earnings. Peter Hovenden is unimaginative and utilitarian, while Robert Danforth is manly and strong; both "diminish Owen's personal life," yet they also serve to "refine . . . his conception of art." She believes that Owen's alternating periods of creativity and depression reflect Hawthorne's own professional vacillations. When Owen descends into drunkenness and inertia, he is actually in "a sleep of the spirit," a "wormlike condition" like that of the butterfly. In producing the miraculous butterfly, he evolves into a different person, just as Hawthorne himself, according to Ehrlich, prepares for a "renewed assault on the citadel of fame" even as he fortifies himself in the case of failure. In this tale, achievement is the equivalent of the freeing of the soul of the artist. Owen Warland must live in his own world as though he is victorious, even though he has been rejected by society as a whole, represented by Annie, Peter Hovenden, Robert Danforth, and the townspeople.

Daniel Hoffman sees in "The Artist of the Beautiful" Hawthorne's use of "metaphors from mythic prototypes of action and image." As in the case of the wood carver in "DROWNE'S WOODEN IMAGE," Owen Warland's "passion brings to life the image he has made"; in both stories, the "origin of artistic creation" is the "artist's love of beauty." While "Drowne's Wooden Image" is based on the Pygmalion legend, "The Artist of the Beautiful" borrows from "a suggestion from the story of Psyche, that the soul is bodied forth as a butterfly." Hoffman points out that the "life cycle of the insect provides organic imagery in the descriptions of Owen's appearance," from "his sinking into a stuporous fatness after his setback" to his "bursting forth in the glory of his successful achievement." The story also dramatizes "still another myth, Diotima's account in *The Symposium* of the ladder of love." As the reader follows "the course of Owen's devotion from Annie Hovenden, his chosen muse, to love of all beautiful things, thence to love of the idea of beauty," he is "reconciled, as Owen is, to his losing the hand of the girl" to the simple blacksmith. By the time Owen realizes that Annie does not understand him, "he no longer needs her" ("Myth, Romance, and the Childhood of Man," *Hawthorne Centenary Essays,* edited by Roy Harvey Pearce, 197–219 [Columbus: Ohio State University Press, 1964]).

Richard Fogle compares the story to *Pilgrim's Progress*, in which the artist is forced to make his way toward salvation. Owen Warland travels a difficult road through his own Slough of Despond, combating his Giant Despair, finally reaching the Heavenly City. He must battle the mass of society as represented by his former master, Peter Hovenden; the master's daughter, Annie; and the blacksmith,

Robert Danforth. In executing his ideal conception of the butterfly, Warland finally represents the superiority of the artist. He is isolated from society but preserves a certain sensibility that remains intact. His nature remains "unfallen" in a "fallen" world ("The Artist of the Beautiful," *Hawthorne's Fiction: The Light and the Dark,* [Norman: University of Oklahoma Press, 1952]).

Nina Baym views Owen Warland as an "inadequate" figure for his aesthetic vocation. His ambition is derived from neither a powerful emotion nor "a desire to enrich life," but rather from "the need to escape it." His mechanical ideal is "lifeless and depthless: a fragile, cold bauble." Baym argues that Owen's "conception of art" is "timid and shrunken" (*The Shape of Hawthorne's Career,* 105–112).

CHARACTERS

Danforth, Robert Blacksmith in Hawthorne's short story "The Artist of the Beautiful." We first see Robert Danforth moving about in his forge, silhouetted against its "red glare and alternate dusk." His figure is "well worthy to be viewed in so picturesque an aspect of light and shade, where the bright blaze struggled with the black night, as if each would have snatched his comely strength from the other."

Peter Hovenden, a retired watchmaker who hopes that his daughter, Annie, will marry Danforth, encourages her by saying it is a "good and wholesome thing to depend upon main strength and reality, and to earn one's bread with the bare and brawny arm of a blacksmith."

Danforth ultimately marries Annie. They have a strong baby boy, who, by destroying the intricate butterfly created by Owen as a bridal gift, expresses Danforth's suppressed hostility stemming from Annie's admiration of Owen. The pragmatic Danforth is contemptuous of Owen for even making a mechanical butterfly when "any child may catch a score of them in a summer's afternoon." However, when he inspects Owen's creation up close, he concedes that it beats "all nature" in its flight, even though it is still not as useful as his sledgehammer.

Hovenden, Annie (Annie Danforth) Character in "The Artist of the Beautiful." At the opening of the tale, Annie is the dutiful daughter of a retired watchmaker, Peter Hovenden, and is beloved by the watchmaker's apprentice, Owen Warland. At the end of the story, she has become the wife of the blacksmith, Robert Danforth.

Annie is pretty, sensitive, and devoted to her father. She is sympathetic to Owen and supportive of his pursuits but ultimately receptive to her father's encouragement about Danforth as a suitor.

Although Owen is in love with Annie, she cannot possibly live up to his vision of her. He has connected "all his dreams of artistical success with Annie's image," but unfortunately the "real" Annie is "representative of the world."

In the final scene, she is transformed into a matronly mother, yet she still blushes when Owen calls to give her a bridal gift and protests that it is not like him to stay away for so long. In fact, Owen has not even realized that Annie and Robert now have a baby boy, who has enough of his father's personality and strength that he destroys Owen's magnificent butterfly.

To Owen, Annie has "much of her husband's plain and sturdy nature" but is also imbued with a "finer grace" that could enable her to be "the interpreter between strength and beauty." Still, Owen does not fail to realize that Danforth is a more suitable husband for Annie than he ever would have been.

Hovenden, Peter Watchmaker in "The Artist of the Beautiful," who must retire because of his failing vision. He hopes Owen Warland, his apprentice, will make a suitable substitute. Owen, however, has less interest in repair of ordinary timepieces than in his creative pursuits. He regards Hovenden as materialistic, unimaginative, and cold. He never meets him "without a shrinking of the heart." He believes that, of all the people he knows, Hovenden is the "most terrible, by reason of a keen understanding which saw so distinctly what it did see, and disbelieved so uncompromisingly in what it could not see."

The old watchmaker's beautiful daughter, Annie, is Owen's muse in many ways, but she marries a brawny young blacksmith who conforms more closely to Hovenden's concept of manhood.

Hovenden is marked by "cold, unimaginative sagacity, by contact with which everything was converted into a dream, except the densest matter of the physical world." Upon seeing Owen's mechanical butterfly in his shop, Hovenden declares that Owen's "evil spirit" lives within it. Owen replies that Hovenden is in fact his evil spirit, along with the "hard, coarse world."

When Owen takes his bridal gift, the ingeniously wrought mechanical butterfly, to Annie and Robert Danforth's home, Hovenden is at their fireside and mocks Owen, asking whether he has succeeded in creating "the beautiful." Owen triumphantly declares that he has arrived in order to disclose it. Unfortunately, the toddler son of Annie and Robert, aided by his mischievous grandfather, touches the butterfly and causes its destruction. Hovenden then bursts into a "cold and scornful laugh," but Owen is unfazed because, despite the loss of the butterfly itself, "his spirit possessed itself in the enjoyment of the reality."

Warland, Owen Character in "The Artist of the Beautiful" who represents the aesthetic principle. Owen Warland experiences numerous periods of creativity and depression, but, in his art, he joins the natural world and the creative artistic achievement to which he aspires. His butterfly represents a type of creative magnetism, a reconciliation of spirit and the material world. In a curious way, he actually needs his periods of "torpid slumber" as kindling for his periods of imaginative sensibility.

Hawthorne characterizes Warland's mind as "microscopic," in accordance with his "diminutive frame" as well as with the "marvellous smallness and delicate power of his fingers." Peter Hovenden can make "nothing" of Owen, whose indifference to the measurement of time disqualifies him as a watchmaker. Moreover, Owen cannot control his emotions. Although he hopes to put the "spirit of beauty into form," he is subject to the fluttering of his nerves and the throbbing of his heart when he sees Annie pass by his shop with her father. His condition quickly causes him to give up work on his secret "exquisite mechanism" for the evening.

The townspeople, also, are unable to appreciate Owen's artistry. His ingenious projects destroy his "credit" with them, even when the creations are basically rational, as when he connects a musical mechanism with the works of his watches, "so that all the harsh dissonances of life might be rendered tuneful." His clients are from a "steady and matter-of-fact class of people" who take "Time" seriously. They view it as either "the medium of advancement and prosperity in this world, or preparation for the next." Owen's pursuits, as Hawthorne describes them, are "insulated from the common business of life."

After he suffers a nervous breakdown and a period of continual drinking, he recovers and contrives to make a splendid mechanical butterfly for Annie as a wedding gift. Although it is "the bridal-gift of a poor watchmaker to a blacksmith's wife," Owen regards it as a "gem of art that a monarch would have purchased with honors and abundant wealth, and have treasured it among the jewels of his kingdom, as the most unique and wondrous of them all." Unfortunately, the "spiritual essence" of the butterfly dies when it is caught and crushed by the toddler son of Annie and Robert Danforth. Owen, surprisingly, is not unduly upset, because he realizes that the physical symbol of the beautiful is insignificant compared with the spiritual enjoyment of "the reality" of art and life.

Nancy Bunge observes that when Owen tries to make machinery appear to be natural, he is reshaping reminders of his "limits." His art is a plaything, and he lacks true depth. She argues that he "resembles a petulant child irritated by reality's demands." He is happiest not while he is working, but while he is wandering through the countryside, permitting various images to pass in and out of his mind: "Sweet, doubtless, were these days, and congenial to the artist's soul. They were full of bright conceptions, which gleamed through his intellectual world, as the butterflies gleamed through the outward atmosphere, and were real to him for the instant, without the toil, and perplexity, and many disappointments, of attempting to make them visible to the sensual eye." She suggests that Owen loves "illusion," not true art (Bunge, *Nathaniel Hawthorne: A Study of the Short Fiction,* 37).

FOR FURTHER READING

Baxter, Annette K., "Independence vs. Isolation: Hawthorne and James on the Problem of the Artist," *Nineteenth-Century Fiction* 10 (1955): 225–231;

Baym, Nina, *The Shape of Hawthorne's Career* (Ithaca, N.Y.: Cornell University Press, 1976); Berthea, Dean Wentworth, "Heat, Light, and the Darkening World: Hawthorne's 'The Artist of the Beautiful,'" *South Atlantic Review* 56 (November 1991): 23–35; Bunge, Nancy, *Nathaniel Hawthorne: A Study of the Short Fiction* (New York: Twayne, 1993); Crowley, J. Donald, ed., *Nathaniel Hawthorne: The Critical Heritage* (London and New York: Routledge, 1970); Ehrlich, Gloria, *Family Themes and Hawthorne's Fiction: The Tenacious Web* (New Brunswick, N.J.: Rutgers University Press, 1984); Fay, Stephanie, "Lights from Dark Corners: Works of Art in 'The Prophetic Pictures' and 'The Artist of the Beautiful,'" *Studies in American Fiction* 13 (spring 1985): 15–29; Fogle, Richard, "The Artist of the Beautiful," in *Hawthorne's Fiction: The Light and the Dark* (Norman: University of Oklahoma Press, 1952); Grant, William E., "Nathaniel Hawthorne," *Dictionary of Literary Biography*, edited by Bobby Ellen Kimbel, vol. 74, 143–163 (Detroit: Gale Research, 1988); Newberry, Frederick, "'The Artist of the Beautiful': Crossing the Transcendent Divide in Hawthorne's Fiction," *Nineteenth-Century Literature* 50, No. 1 (June 1995): (78–96); Prochazka, Martin, "Mechanic?—Organic? The Machines of Art in 'The Artist of the Beautiful,'" *Litteraria Pragensia: Studies in Literature & Culture* 10 (2000): 3–15; Schriber, Mary Sue, "Emerson, Hawthorne, and 'The Artist of the Beautiful,'" *Studies in Short Fiction*, 8 (1971): 607–616; Wohlpart, A. James, "The Status of the Artist in Hawthorne's 'The Artist of the Beautiful,'" *American Transcendental Quarterly* 3, no. 3 (September 1989): 245–256.

"Bell's Biography, A"

Sketch or tale first published in the KNICKERBOCKER, or *New-York Monthly Magazine*, in March 1837.

The tale is told from the point of view of a writer (Hawthorne), who is reminded by the bell's tolling "iron tongue" that it is time to begin his biography of the bell. The writer imagines that he (Hawthorne uses the third person for the bell) is of French manufacture, and that the metal of which he is made was supplied by a brass cannon captured when Louis XIV defeated the Spaniards. He was then given to the Jesuits who converted American Indians, and he reposed in Our Lady's Chapel, built of logs, on Lake Champlain.

The "hostile faith" of the Puritans, led by Good Deacon Lawson, defeated the Roman Catholic outposts and burned the chapel, but nearby Indians, who heard him tolling and saw the chapel burning, then attacked and killed the Puritans. At the close of the Old French War, log cutters discovered him in a swamp. He was auctioned in Boston, on King Street, and bestowed on a meetinghouse, the King Street Chapel. His tones pealed to celebrate the victories of Washington and Lafayette in the Revolutionary War and have, ever since, "tolled a requiem for all alike." He has announced mornings and the end of toil, marked births and deaths, and serves as "the voice of fleeting time" that still teaches men "no lessons for eternity."

FOR FURTHER READING

Jordan, Gretchen Graf, "Hawthorne's 'Bell': Historical Evolution through Symbol," *Nineteenth-Century Fiction* 19, no. 2 (September 1964): 123–139.

Biographical Stories for Children

A collection of biographies of interest to children, first published in Boston by Tappan and Dennet (1842). It includes biographies of Benjamin West, Sir Isaac Newton, Samuel Johnson, Oliver Cromwell, Benjamin Franklin, and Christina, queen of Sweden.

"Birth-Mark, The"

Short story published in *The Pioneer* in March 1843 and reprinted in *The Pathfinder* (New York) the same month. It was later collected in MOSSES FROM AN OLD MANSE (1846).

The story should be read in the context of science and technology at the end of the 18th century, which were assuming, as Melissa Pennell puts it, more "dominant roles" in American life than religion. Mary Shelley's 1818 novel *Frankenstein* had explored the consequences of a scientist's infusing an inanimate being with life—no small feat, but one that produced a destructive monster (Pennell, 48). Hawthorne's tale is based on the premise that science can reverse or eradicate natural flaws with impunity.

In "The Birth-Mark," a devoted scientist, Aylmer (his name is a variant of *Elmer,* meaning noble), attempts a misguided mission: to correct the one flaw with which his otherwise perfect wife, Georgiana, is afflicted—a birthmark on her left cheek in the shape of a small crimson hand. This "defect" assumes an increasing magnitude in his mind. Aylmer is neither insane nor evil but is convinced that science and reason are all-powerful to the point of supplanting common sense. He is convinced he can safely remove the birthmark. Georgiana presciently believes the stain may go "as deep as life itself" and is opposed to any such endeavor. She blushingly protests that it has often been called a "charm," and in the past she has been "simple enough to imagine it might be so."

Aylmer protests that it might be considered a merely charming flaw on another face, but Georgiana has come almost "perfect from the hand of Nature," and, therefore, the birthmark shocks him as "the visible mark of earthly imperfection." Hawthorne describes the mark as "interwoven . . . with the texture and substance of her face." It has a "delicate bloom" and a tint of crimson and thus disappears when she blushes, but if she turns pale, it assumes "an almost fearful distinctness." Some of Georgiana's suitors had declared her birthmark to be so delicate that a fairy might have left its impression there, "in token of the magic endowments that were to give her such sway over all hearts." More than one of them would have risked his life for the privilege of "pressing his lips to the mysterious hand."

Admittedly, however, certain people, principally jealous women, have termed it a "bloody hand" and declared that it destroyed the effect of her beauty. Male admirers often went no further than wishing it away, "that the world might possess one living specimen of ideal loveliness without the semblance of a flaw." Despite himself, Aylmer finds himself agreeing with critics of Georgiana's beauty. He becomes obsessed with the idea of removing the flaw altogether, the better to possess the very essence of perfection. The "crimson hand" has become the "symbol of his wife's liability to sin, sorrow, decay, and death," all of which he believes he can avert by such a procedure. Each morning, he gazes at her face and sees her imperfection; he assumes a peculiar expression that causes her to shudder. Each morning, she turns pale as he stares at her, and the crimson hand emerges more clearly, "like a bas-relief of ruby on the whitest marble."

Aylmer dreams that, aided by his servant Aminadab, he cuts into Georgiana's cheek, only to discover that the birthmark recedes even deeper, catching hold of her heart. Recalling the dream, he feels guilty. But Georgiana pleads with him to proceed with the surgery, even if there is only a remote chance of success. Aylmer says he is "fully competent" to remove it. She asks him not to spare her, even if the birthmark takes "refuge" in her heart.

The "pale philosopher" then leads the "cold and tremulous" Georgiana to his laboratory. The birthmark becomes highly visible, and Georgiana faints on the threshold of the laboratory. Aylmer summons his grotesque shaggy assistant, Aminadab, to revive her. They take her to a room that Aylmer has converted into her boudoir, where the scientist and his servant surround her with "optical phenomena" and try various experiments that both amaze and terrify Georgiana. While waiting for the surgery, she finds a large folio with detailed accounts of Aylmer's various past experiments but discovers that his "lofty" experiments still fall short of his ideal. She then sings to her husband to "quench the thirst of his spirit."

While Aylmer continues his preparations, Georgiana experiences a sensation in the birthmark that produces a systemic "restlessness." She realizes that Aylmer has concealed his anxiety over the experiment in order to reassure her, but still she insists on submitting to whatever draught he gives her, even if it is poisonous. He gives her a crystal goblet full of a colorless liquor, a few drops of which restore a blotchy geranium plant. She drinks the liquid and suddenly feels exhausted. She informs him her "earthly senses" are closing over her spirit. He is not alarmed but simply writes down all of her symptoms in his folio book. The birthmark begins to fade as Georgiana sleeps. He wakes her, only to find that she is convinced she is dying. As the last tint of the birthmark fades, she dies. Ultimately, Aylmer has failed to "look beyond the shadowy scope of time" and find the "perfect future in the present."

RECEPTION AND CRITICAL ANALYSIS

"The Birth-Mark," written in 1843, was Hawthorne's first work of fiction after his own marriage, to Sophia Peabody. Aylmer, the story's protagonist, is also a newlywed, as well as a scientist, artist, and aesthete. Hawthorne's marriage had forced him to become increasingly aware of his wife's vulnerability to death, just as Aylmer becomes aware of Georgiana's fragility. The birthmark on her cheek is "the spectral hand that wrote mortality, where he would fain have worshipped." Aylmer, however, desires to persist in his lifelong control over nature, which takes the form of correcting what he perceives as Georgiana's flawed complexion.

When "The Birth-Mark" was collected in MOSSES FROM AN OLD MANSE (1846), Margaret Fuller's review in the New-York Daily Tribune (June 22, 1846) heralded the story as embodying "truths of profound importance in shapes of aerial elegance." She believed "the loveliest ideal of love and the beauty of feminine purity" shone in this story. In contrast, the reviewer for Blackwood's Edinburgh Magazine (November 1847) wrote that, unlike Poe, whose work relied upon "close detail" and an "agglomeration of facts," Hawthorne "appears to have little skill and little taste for dealing with matter of fact or substantial incident." The critic objects to the general improbabilities of Hawthorne's stories; in "The Birth-Mark" in particular, he finds fault with the "preposterous motive" that prompts a "dearly loving" husband to an "operation of the most hazardous kind." He posits the question "Can any one recognise in this elaborate nonsense about ideal perfection, any approximation to the feeling which a man has for the wife he loves?"

A century and a half later, Liz Rosenberg observes that Hawthorne employs three systems of thought, popular at the time, in examining Aylmer's dilemma ("'The Best That Earth Could Offer': 'The Birth-Mark,' a Newlywed's Story"). All are applied to the problem of "union versus separation": alchemy, animism, and Emersonian transcendentalism.

Allusions to alchemy recur throughout the story: Aylmer has a large library of works related to alchemy, and he wishes to "ascend from one step of powerful intelligence to another, until the philosopher should lay his hand on the secret of creative force, and perhaps make new worlds for himself." He envisions this journey, however, as one of his own making; it is a distillation of his individual effort, and Georgiana has only a passive role. He interprets her "physical imperfection" as a "spiritual one" and kills her in the process of attempting to cure her. Shannon Burns observes that Aylmer is not even a good alchemist: "The old alchemists searched for an integrated, unified personality: Aylmer wants a perfect and pure distillation" ("Alchemy and 'The Birth-Mark,'" 154).

Another system of thought that was prevalent in the mid-19th century was animism, a philosophy that embraced and yet divorced spirit and matter. Animists believed that inanimate objects, such as stones and clods of earth, possessed spirits of their own, and that soul and spirit existed apart from physical matter. If Aylmer's assistant's name is reversed, then Aminadab stands for "bad anima." The scientist and his servant are opposites: Aylmer, with his pale, intellectual face, represents the highest form of humans' being, while Aminadab represents the lowest form of humans' physical nature. Aylmer is working in matter, but his spirit is actually burdened with clay. Georgiana stands between the two men. She is associated with blood, love, and marriage; she is highly sensitive and initially regards Aylmer's meddling with her health as unjustified—it is in fact a "tingling" at her heart. She seems to sense that it will ultimately be deadly to her, but because of her misguided devotion to her husband, she actually becomes a martyr to romantic love.

The story also explores the transcendentalism espoused by Hawthorne's friend Ralph Waldo

Emerson, in which there is, ideally, a reconciliation between spirit and matter. James Mellow argues that, to Hawthorne, Emerson was a victim of the obsession with mind and matter: "Mr. Emerson—the mystic, stretching his hand out of cloud-land, in vain search for something real" (Mellow, *Nathaniel Hawthorne in His Times*, 208). Hawthorne once described Emerson in his journal as "a great searcher for facts; but they seem to melt away and become unsubstantial in its grasp." E. Michael Jones observes, in *The Angel and the Machine*, that the age of Emerson was marked by the opposition of mind and matter. In Hawthorne's view, Emerson was the victim of both the mechanist and idealist philosophies (Jones, 18). Aylmer represents transcendentalism at its worst. In rejecting Georgiana because of her imperfection, Aylmer loses his chance for happiness (Rosenberg, "'The Best That Earth Could Offer': 'The Birth-Mark,' a Newlywed's Story," passim).

Nina Baym makes the point that in "The Birth-Mark" Hawthorne examines questions of sexuality that lie behind "the protagonist's social alienation"; she regards Aylmer's aversion to Georgiana's birthmark as a "rationalized distaste for sexuality" (*The Shape of Hawthorne's Career*, 110).

Hawthorne was fascinated by the idea of uncontrolled biological research and abhorred immoral experimentation, which he believed, in conjunction with undue reliance on science, could lead to tragic consequences. Georgiana is similar to many 19th-century heroines in her passivity: She sacrifices herself to her love for Aylmer. But if she had resisted his experiments, she would have regarded herself as disloyal.

William E. Grant observes that in stories such as "The Birth-Mark" and "RAPPACCINI'S DAUGHTER," Hawthorne treats scientists as "objects of suspicion." His recurring interest in "obsession, or what his generation called monomania," is evident in his stories' "treatments of monomaniacal characters who bring about their own downfalls and frequently those of people closest to them through their pursuits of ideals that lead them to try to improve nature" ("Nathaniel Hawthorne").

Robert B. Heilman theorizes that "The Birth-Mark" is a parable about humans' attempts to achieve perfection in nature. In the process, he may "destroy the organic life from which the imperfection is inseparable." In this story, "science itself has become religion," and thus Aylmer fails to "regard evil as real." For the scientist, evil becomes something "manageable, subject to human control, indeed removable," as opposed to its Christian sense: "a reality which can ultimately be dealt with only by divine grace." Georgiana's birthmark represents original sin—humans are born imperfect—but Aylmer's "tragic flaw is to fail to see the tragic flaw in humanity." His obsession with perfecting matter suggests that he is actually attempting to doctor the symbol of matter, not its substance, which he cannot perceive. Knowledge, for him, has the aim of achieving visible and physical goals, not spiritual ends, which, in fact, he is incapable of formulating or attaining (Heilman, "Hawthorne's 'The Birth-Mark': Science as Religion").

CHARACTERS

Aminadab Aylmer's laboratory assistant in Hawthorne's short story "The Birth-Mark." His name is a reverse anagram for *bad anima*. He represents the worst form of humans' physical nature: He is described as having "low stature, but bulky frame, with shaggy hair hanging about his visage." He executes all details of the scientific experiments conceived and imposed by his master on the beautiful young Georgiana, who embodies the "spiritual element" of human nature.

Nancy Bunge observes that because Aminadab possesses vast physical strength and "earthiness," he undertakes to perform unpleasant tasks in order to free Aylmer to "cultivate delusions of transcendence" (*Nathaniel Hawthorne: A Study of the Short Fiction*, 29).

Melissa Pennell points out that despite his intellectual and physical deficiencies, Aminadab has an appreciation of Georgiana's "sexual potency" and allure, insights that her husband increasingly lacks as he grows ever more obsessed with his experiments (*Student Companion to Nathaniel Hawthorne*, 50). Indeed, before the experiments begin, when Georgiana faints on the threshold of Aylmer's laboratory, Aminadab "mutter[s] to himself, 'If she were my wife, I'd never part with that birthmark.'"

Aylmer Scientist in "The Birth-Mark." At the opening of the story, Aylmer has persuaded a beautiful young woman, Georgiana, to become his wife. He has "devoted himself, however, too unreservedly to scientific studies, ever to be weaned from them by any second passion." His love for his wife thus takes second place to his love of science.

Soon after their marriage, he becomes obsessed with the birthmark on her cheek and asks whether she has ever considered having it removed. Aylmer is convinced he has the abilities to make her "perfect"; after taking her to his laboratory, he tries to assuage her fears by practicing his magic. He causes a plant to grow suddenly, bearing a perfect, lovely flower, but when Georgiana touches it, it turns black—an unfortunate omen for his scientific experiment. He makes a primitive photograph of her, but her features are blurred and blighted—except her cheek, where the hand is still visible. Despite her reservations, Georgiana promises that she will "quaff whatever draught" he gives her, even "a dose of poison," if offered by his hand. Although Aylmer is profoundly moved by her trust and devotion, he does not give up his experiment. She drinks the potion he has concocted, which succeeds in fading the birthmark but also kills her.

Aylmer is a scientist and an aesthete, but both his judgment and his alchemy are fallible. As Shannon Burns remarks, traditional alchemists searched for an "integrated, unified personality"; Aylmer, in contrast, wants a "perfect and pure distillation." He is the victim of his lifelong search for ultimate control over nature.

Georgiana Doomed heroine of "The Birth-Mark." The young and beautiful Georgiana helplessly submits to the scientific experiments of her husband, Aylmer, who is obsessed by her birthmark and wants to prove his omnipotence by making it disappear. Georgiana has a valid premonition that the stain goes "as deep as life itself" and is initially opposed to any such endeavor. She is highly sensitive, however, and when she sees that her husband is repulsed by the "spectral hand that wrote mortality, where he would fain have worshipped," she shudders at his gaze.

Georgiana naively begins to despise the mark as much as her husband does. She realizes he will never be content until he tries to remove it and urges him to proceed with his experiments, no matter what the cost. As Nancy Bunge observes, Georgiana even grows to "despise her own humanity" and to hope her blemish can be removed. Her relationship with him demands that she "mediate a formidable battle between self-esteem and self-hate" (*Nathaniel Hawthorne: A Study of the Short Fiction*, 29).

Giving her husband permission to excise the birthmark seems to ennoble Georgiana. She declares that despite the risks, "danger is nothing" to her, and that life with "this hateful mark" is "a burden which I would fling down with joy." Aylmer responds by referring to her as "noblest, dearest, tenderest wife." Georgiana tells him not to dream of sparing her, even if the birthmark extends as deep as her heart. Unfortunately, the poison in her cheek can be erased only by death.

As she dies, however, Georgiana is ambiguous about having permitted her husband to perfect her appearance. She tells Aylmer that he has "aimed loftily" and "done nobly." She urges him not to feel guilty, nor to repent that "with so high and pure a feeling, you have rejected the best the earth could offer." Millicent Bell interprets this final statement of Georgiana's as indicative of Hawthorne's struggle with romanticism: He yearns to depict life as found, which is in perpetual conflict with his romantic yearning for a "superior ideal of absolute beauty" (*Hawthorne's View of the Artist*, 134). Brenda Wineapple observes that the birthmark disappears because "the ideal cannot exist in disembodied form" (*Hawthorne: A Life*, 174–175).

FOR FURTHER READING

Baym, Nina, *The Shape of Hawthorne's Career* (Ithaca, N.Y.: Cornell University Press, 1976); Burns, Shannon, "Alchemy and 'The Birth-Mark,'" *American Transcendental Quarterly* 48 (1979): 147–158; Grant, William E., "Nathaniel Hawthorne," *Dictionary of Literary Biography*, Vol. 74, edited by Bobby Ellen Kimbel, (Detroit: Gale Research, 1988); 143–163; Heilman, Robert B., "Hawthorne's 'The Birth-Mark': Science as Religion," *South Atlan-*

tic *Quarterly* 48 (October 1949): 575–583; Jones, E. Michael, *The Angel and the Machine* (Peru, Ill.: Sherwood Sugden, 1991); Lammers, John, "Powers' Eve Tempted: Sculpture and 'The Birth-Mark,'" *Publications of the Arkansas Philological Association* 21, no. 2 (fall 1994): 41–58; Mellow, James, *Nathaniel Hawthorne in His Times* (Boston: Houghton Mifflin, 1980); Pennell, Melissa, *Student Companion to Nathaniel Hawthorne* (Westport, Conn.: Greenwood Press, 1999), 48–51; Rosenberg, Liz, "'The Best That Earth Could Offer': 'The Birth-Mark,' a Newlywed's Story," *Studies in Short Fiction* 30, no. 2 (spring 1993): 145–151; Rucker, Mary E., "Science and Art in Hawthorne's 'The Birth-Mark,'" *Nineteenth-Century Literature* 41, no. 4 (March 1987): 445–461; Weinstein, Cindy, "The Invisible Hand Made Visible: 'The Birth-Mark,'" *Nineteenth-Century Literature* 48, no. 1 (June 1993): 44–73.

Blithedale Romance, The

Hawthorne's third novel, which he began planning in Lenox, Massachusetts, was written largely in 1851, when he and his family lived in the home of the Horace Manns in West Newton, Massachusetts. It was published in 1852.

Sophia Hawthorne's mother, ELIZABETH PALMER PEABODY, had made it known that she thought more highly of HORACE MANN, Hawthorne's brother-in-law and husband of her daughter Mary, than of Hawthorne, and her preference irritated him. She also sent him copies of Mann's political speeches attacking Hawthorne's longtime friends and political allies, such as General FRANKLIN PIERCE. (Pierce, after being elected U.S. president in 1852 and taking office in 1853, would appoint Hawthorne United States consul at Liverpool, England.)

The Blithedale Romance is based on the period Hawthorne spent in 1841 at the transcendentalist Brook Farm Institute of Agriculture and Education, in West Roxbury, Massachusetts. BROOK FARM was founded by the American editor, reformer, and literary critic GEORGE RIPLEY, a Unitarian minister in Boston. His translations of the works of German theologians during his editorship of the *Christian Register* formed the basis of the American transcendentalist movement. In April of 1841, Ripley and 20 other members of the Transcendental Club moved to Brook Farm, a property of about 200 acres on the Charles River, about nine miles from Boston. Ripley, who became president of the community, hoped that it would embody "Christ's idea of society." The residents' time would be divided between manual and mental labor, and he hoped eventually to establish a boarding school on the property (Hoeltje, *Inward Sky: The Mind and Heart of Nathaniel Hawthorne*, 168). Among those associated with the institute were Albert Brisbane, WILLIAM ELLERY CHANNING, GEORGE W. CURTIS, CHARLES ANDERSON DANA, and Theodore Parker.

Hawthorne bought stock in Brook Farm but lived there only from April to November of 1841. Ultimately, he found communal living unappealing—not surprisingly, considering his own "introverted, intensely private, and skeptically conservative" nature. What drew him there in the first place? The "simplest and perhaps quite sufficient answer is economic: he could support himself there, he thought, and still find time to pursue his writing career" (Beauchamp, Gorman, "Hawthorne and the Universal Reformers," *Utopian Studies,* 13 [spring 2002]: 38).

RALPH WALDO EMERSON viewed the entire experiment with skepticism, calling Brook Farm "the Age of Reason in a patty-pan." The exercise in utopianism lasted for a few years but was abandoned by 1847. By 1852, the community had long since been disbanded.

The novel is essentially a "satire against social reformers," as Louise DeSalvo observes (*Nathaniel Hawthorne,* 97). Brenda Wineapple terms the work a "psychological roman à clef . . . a book about male friendship and mesmerism, utopian idealism and erotic women, women authors and passive men, none of them able to confront precisely what they want" (*Hawthorne: A Life,* 247).

SYNOPSIS

Chapter I: "Old Moodie"

The narrator, Miles Coverdale, a poet of independent means, is returning to his bachelor apartments in Boston after seeing an exhibition of the "Veiled Lady," a "phenomenon in the mesmeric line." This was a popular form of spiritualism at the time, with public entertainments based on magic performances, seances, and hypnotism. The identity of the "Veiled Lady" is an enigma at first.

An elderly man, Mr. Moodie, approaches the narrator and says he has heard that Coverdale is going to an experimental farm community at Blithedale the next day. Moodie asks whether Coverdale knows a lady named Zenobia. Coverdale replies that he has heard of such a person, but "Zenobia" is only her public name. Moodie says he will go to Coverdale's rooms in the morning to explain the favor he requests but the next day does not appear.

Chapter II: "Blithedale"
The next day, on a gusty April afternoon, Coverdale "plunged into the heart of the pitiless snowstorm, in quest of a better life." He makes his way to Blithedale with three companions; there is talk of a new paradise on Earth. A man named Hollingsworth had planned to travel with the group but is delayed and makes the journey later.

The travelers are warmly received at Blithedale by Mrs. Foster, wife of the farm manager, Silas Foster. As the newcomers exchange greetings, Zenobia ("not her real name") enters the parlor, her "figure and deportment" those of a queen.

Chapter III: "A Knot of Dreamers"
Zenobia welcomes them in a "fine, frank, mellow voice." She tells Coverdale she has read his poetry, and he is flattered. He describes her as having a "fine intellect," with "health and vigor." She is a strong presence at Blithedale, wearing a new hothouse flower in her hair each day; she is like a goddess of the Sun and bloom, a Flora or Ceres.

She will act as hostess to the newcomers for the evening, but the next day they will be "brethren and sisters." (There are a total of four women at Blithedale to take over domestic chores.) Coverdale feels an "influence breathing out of her, such as we might suppose to come from Eve." The women then take their leave to prepare supper while the men continue their discussion by the fire.

Silas Foster enters from the dreary storm, observing that in such bad weather, the newcomers will wish they were in town again. Coverdale believes, however, that they have left "the rusty iron framework of society" behind in order to lead exemplary lives, sharing the farm labor and offering up "earnest toil" as prayer.

Foster speaks little except for "practical purpose": He asks which of them is the best judge of swine, since one of them must go to the next Brighton fair to buy six pigs. Moreover, he calculates that it will take three "city folks" to do the work of a single field hand, and they will certainly fail at competitive market gardening. This appraisal is a shock to the newcomers.

Zenobia returns to call the men to supper. Her presence caused the men's "heroic enterprise to show like an illusion, a masquerade, a pastoral, a counterfeit Arcadia, in which we grown-up men and women were making a play-day of the years that were given us to live in."

There is further discussion of Hollingsworth, and why he has not appeared at Blithedale yet. Zenobia, who does not know Hollingsworth personally but declares herself "moved" by him, wishes he would focus, as a philanthropist, on people who are not "already past his help" rather than on "such a grimy, unbeautiful, and positively hopeless object as this reformation of criminals." Zenobia and Coverdale agree that philanthropists are difficult to tolerate.

Chapter IV: "The Supper-table"
The group sit down to supper together, drinking tea from earthen cups, experiencing their first "practical trial" of their theories of "equal brotherhood and sisterhood."

There is a knock at the door. Hollingsworth enters, wearing a shaggy greatcoat. A young girl is with him, but Hollingsworth seems not to know who she is except that she is a "young person who belongs here." The "depressed and sad" figure shivers "either with cold, or fear, or nervous excitement." She gazes worshipfully at Zenobia, who ignores her. Hollingsworth chastises Zenobia for her behavior, and she apologizes. The girl introduces herself as Priscilla (Zenobia's half sister, although this is not yet known to the reader). Hollingsworth explains that an old man took her to his lodgings and asked Hollingsworth to convey her to Blithedale. Foster suggests giving her hot tea and bacon and allowing her to stay at the farm and share the work.

Chapter V: "Until Bedtime"

After supper, Foster works at shoemaking, his wife knits, and the girls do needlework. Priscilla sits near Zenobia, looking at her with an expression of "humble delight." Coverdale wonders whether she has read some of Zenobia's stories. Zenobia suggests to him that Priscilla is most likely merely a "seamstress from the city," who has been stifled in a "small, close room," drinking coffee and eating a poor diet.

Priscilla gazes at them and begins crying. Coverdale wonders whether she has overheard them and been hurt by the "scornful estimate of her character and purposes." Zenobia soothes her by simply touching her hair. Priscilla, recovered, begins knitting a silk purse, and Coverdale realizes he owns one just like the one she is making. Despite the distraction of her work, Priscilla is upset by the storm outside.

Coverdale realizes that Hollingsworth is uninterested in their "socialist scheme," wishing only to reform criminals, and finds it difficult to tolerate the philanthropist's company.

The group discusses better names for their enterprise than "Blithedale" but cannot decide on one. Foster enters to remind them of early morning farm chores, and they retire. Coverdale goes "shivering" to bed and realizes he has caught a "tremendous cold."

Chapter VI: "Coverdale's Sick-Chamber"

The Blithedale inhabitants arise to begin "the reformation of the world," as Coverdale ironically describes it. Hollingsworth prays solemnly in his room, while Coverdale wonders why he has left his pleasant bachelor quarters and excellent meals at nearby hotels to go to Blithedale.

He has developed a terrible cold and is treated by a homeopathic doctor, who does him little good. Hollingsworth cheers him, although he insists to Coverdale that "severity of temper" is his most marked trait. The other members of the community are kind to him and nurse him as best they can.

Coverdale focuses on Zenobia, the "female reformer," who he decides should have been an actress. He finds her sensitive and beautiful but describes her as an "enchantress" and a "sister of the Veiled Lady." He wonders whether she has ever been married. Her deportment is "not exactly maidenlike." Zenobia is well aware of his interest and asks him what he seeks to discover in her. He tells himself he could never have fallen in love with Zenobia; she is, after all, a very bad cook.

Chapter VII: "The Convalescent"

As Coverdale improves, he wonders what has become of Priscilla. She gives him a nightcap she has made for him and a sealed letter that has arrived from Margaret Fuller. He realizes that Priscilla reminds him of Margaret Fuller and asks whether she knows her. (Fuller was the most famous woman transcendentalist, and a frequent visitor to Brook Farm.) Priscilla is puzzled and leaves the room.

Coverdale reads the works of Emerson and Charles Fourier and discusses them with Hollingsworth. He decides Hollingsworth was once benevolent but is no longer, as evident in his cold treatment of Priscilla. Hollingsworth's "philanthropic theory" is his pitfall; he wants to build an edifice to improve criminals. Coverdale finds his views impractical and suspects Hollingsworth has helped nurse him only to proselytize him. He even thinks Hollingsworth is becoming mad.

Chapter VIII: "A Modern Arcadia"

Miles Coverdale slowly recovers from his illness. On a balmy May morning, he leaves his room and goes into the barn, where he finds Zenobia and Priscilla. They have picked baskets full of flowers, some of which Zenobia uses to adorn Priscilla. She is clearly proud of Priscilla's improved health and happiness.

Priscilla bounds away to meet Hollingsworth, who is returning from the field. As they watch, she seems to listen to a voice calling her, but they see no one. Zenobia says she has seen this behavior in Priscilla before but does not know the cause. Priscilla suddenly loses her energy and is transformed back into the "wan and spiritless" girl of old.

Others have joined the Blithedale community during Coverdale's period of illness, giving it variety and interest. The residents have gradually grown accustomed to laboring in the fields, but neighboring farmers mock the commune, saying they raise weeds and know nothing about horticulture or farming. On the contrary, Coverdale suggests to Zenobia and Hollingsworth that they are in serious danger of forgetting their books and becoming merely "practical agriculturists." In their minds, they had spiritualized labor, but it turns out that their labor "symbolized nothing."

Zenobia believes Coverdale's intellect cannot help but be "strengthened and ennobled" by Hollingsworth's influence. Coverdale wonders what Hollingsworth plans to do with the "two proselytes" Zenobia and Priscilla, and "they with him."

Chapter IX: "Hollingsworth, Zenobia, Priscilla"

Coverdale pries into Hollingsworth's character and worries that the lifestyle at Blithedale will enable "any individual, of either sex, to fall in love with any other."

Priscilla is inept at all pursuits—she runs "falteringly," causes loads of hay to tumble down, and breaks crockery. Everybody senses "a pleasant weakness in the girl," which brings out their protectiveness of her. Coverdale says he does "not see much wisdom in being so very merry in this kind of a world," but Priscilla rejects his advice and continues to live in the moment, telling him that all her foolish actions are the "motions of [her] heart."

Zenobia thinks Priscilla needs a "duenna," an older governess or companion. She intends to fill this role, in order to teach Priscilla the "morals, manners, and proprieties of social life."

Hollingsworth and Zenobia become attached to each other, taking long walks together. The Blithedale community allows members to build their own cottages on the property, and the others assume Hollingsworth and Zenobia intend to do so.

Chapter X: "A Visitor from Town"

When Mr. Moodie visits the community, Coverdale recognizes him from his life in Boston but does not know his name. Hollingsworth greets him by name. Moodie turns out to be Priscilla's father. He asks about Zenobia, whom he has known since she was a child. He wants to know whether she is kind to Priscilla. When Hollingsworth replies that the

two women are "like an elder and younger sister" together, Moodie sighs with happiness.

As Old Moodie watches from behind the trunk of a tree, Priscilla appears at a window of the farmhouse, drawing along Zenobia, but Zenobia gives her a "haughty look, as from a mistress to a dependant." Moodie walks away, shaking his head, and then turns to shake his "uplifted staff."

Chapter XI: "The Wood-Path"

Coverdale decides to take a holiday and starts walking away from the farm. He is hailed by a rather disagreeable stranger, who asks about Zenobia. He wishes to see her in private and gives Coverdale his card. He calls himself "Professor Westervelt." He also makes inquiries about Priscilla. It will later be revealed that he has powers of mesmerism and exploits Priscilla—who turns out to be Zenobia's half sister, and Old Moodie's younger daughter—by displaying her as the "Veiled Lady." He makes his money from an audience eager to see "purity violated and modesty exhibited." Immature girls become sexual objects, as Zenobia later reveals.

Chapter XII: "Coverdale's Hermitage"

Coverdale has appropriated a woodland "hermitage." He sees Hollingsworth shouting harshly to the oxen and Priscilla sewing in Zenobia's window. Westervelt and Zenobia pass nearby in the woods, "earnestly" discussing Priscilla. Westervelt advises her to "fling the girl off" and "let her go." Coverdale cannot hear the next words whispered by Westervelt, but they inspire Zenobia with "horror and disgust."

Chapter XIII: "Zenobia's Legend"

As evening entertainment for those at Blithedale, Zenobia often presents *tableaux vivants* (static scenes from literature or drama, with costumes). She makes up a story, "The Silvery Veil," about the "Veiled Lady."

In Zenobia's story, a party of young men, including one called "Theodore," discuss the Veiled Lady. Some say she is beautiful; others, that she is ghastly. Theodore vows to solve the mystery of her identity. He sneaks into her private drawing room and hides himself during one of her performances. After the show, she suddenly materializes in the room and calls him by name. Theodore wants to know who and what she is.

She tells him to lift the veil, but as he attempts to do so she floats to the opposite side of the room. She then instructs him to go home and think of her no more, or else to lift the veil, whereupon he will find her in bondage. Before doing so, however, she wants him to kiss her while her breath "stirs the veil," with her face still hidden. If he chooses to lift the veil before kissing her, she will then be his "evil fate," cursing him to never draw another "breath of happiness."

Theodore is insulted by her suggestion that he pledge himself to someone whose face he has never seen. He almost laughs and says he will lift the veil first, then decide what he will do. He flings up the veil; sees a pale, lovely face; and then watches while the apparition vanishes. The veil rests on the floor and he is alone in the room. Where is the Veiled Lady? He does not know whether she was a spirit or not.

At the same time, a pale and shadowy maiden rises up among a "visionary people" who seek "the better life." She attaches herself to a lady there. One day, the lady is wandering in the woods and meets a figure with a dark beard, known to be a terrible magician. He tells the lady she is "in peril" because of a certain maiden who is her "deadliest enemy." The lady must take the veil he is offering, fling it over the maiden, and say, "Arise, Magician! Here is the Veiled Lady!" With the words of this spell, the magician will rise up from the Earth and seize the maiden, and thus will the lady then be safe.

The lady takes the veil, finds the girl, and throws the veil over her head. The girl gives her a look of terror and reproach, but at the words of the magic spell, the bearded man who had bartered away his soul appears. He flings his arms around the Veiled Lady, and she is his "bond-slave" from then on.

As Zenobia utters the "fatal words" of the magic spell in her tale, she flings a piece of gauze over the head of Priscilla, the "Veiled Lady." At the conclusion of the tableau, Priscilla nearly faints but is revived with a glass of water. As the novel continues, we discover that the veil is a symbol of the being of Priscilla: The veil both imprisons her and protects her.

Chapter XIV: "Eliot's Pulpit"

Coverdale, Hollingsworth, Zenobia, and Priscilla usually spend Sunday afternoons at a particular rock, known as "Eliot's pulpit." (John Eliot [1604–90], known as the "Apostle to the Indians," had once preached there to the Indians and had translated the Bible into their own language.) On these occasions, Hollingsworth would speak to any who were present. Coverdale states that his discourse was very moving, a "treasury of golden thoughts."

Zenobia has become increasingly difficult since her encounter with Westervelt. She promises to speak out "in behalf of woman's wider liberty." Coverdale tells her he would willingly be ruled by a woman endowed with "religious sentiment in its utmost depth and purity" and "refined from that gross, intellectual alloy" of every male theologian. Zenobia argues that man is only content when he can "degrade himself by stooping towards what he loves."

Hollingsworth disagrees with both Coverdale and Zenobia. He believes woman's "place is at man's side," as "sympathizer." Priscilla unquestioningly accepts all that Hollingsworth says. But surprisingly, Zenobia looks "humbled" and also agrees.

On the way home, Coverdale sees Zenobia take Hollingsworth's hand and press it to her bosom. The gesture is as clear as if she had "knelt before him" and "gasped out, 'I love you, Hollingsworth!'" Coverdale tells Priscilla it is a "delightful spectacle," but he knows she is upset. The chapter closes with Coverdale's spotting Zenobia and Hollingsworth standing on the site where the community thinks the couple intends to build their cottage.

Chapter XV: "A Crisis"

Coverdale and Hollingsworth discuss the future of the community. Coverdale says there must be children born there. They discuss future plans—namely, Hollingsworth's idea to adapt the community's land as the foundation for his project to reform criminals. Hollingsworth says Zenobia will be part of the scheme, but when Coverdale asks about Priscilla, he explodes, "'Why do you bring in the names of these women?'" He says Coverdale must "'sacrifice all to this great end, and be my friend of friends, forever.'" He is very rigid.

Coverdale tells him he doubts the wisdom of his scheme and will not join.

Chapter XVI: "Leave-takings"
Coverdale decides to leave the Blithedale community for a week or two. Foster objects to losing an efficient laborer, but Coverdale is, in fact, very discontented. His argument with Hollingsworth has affected the "moral atmosphere" of the community. He leaves so that he can talk with "the conservatives, the writers of the *North American Review*, the merchants, the politicians, the Cambridge men, and all the old 'blockheads'" who still kept a "death-grip" on some ideas that "had not come into vogue since yesterday-morning."

Priscilla gives him a little purse she has made as a keepsake. Coverdale takes leave of the pigs, who look dimly at him and utter a "gentle grunt." Silas Foster shakes his hand and invites him back to eat part of a spare rib when they are slaughtered.

Chapter XVII: "The Hotel"
Coverdale goes to a Boston hotel and is given a room in the back. Blithedale seems a vague and shadowy experience. He spends the first day smoking cigars and reading a novel. Then he looks out of the window. He can see into the rear of several fashionable residences. He orders a sherry cobbler and learns from the waiter that one of the buildings is a stylish boardinghouse. He looks at it and can see far into the interior. A dove sits on the peak of a dormer window, then flies across the intervening space toward Coverdale's building. At the last minute it swerves and flies up into the air.

Chapter XVIII: "The Boarding-House"
The next day, Coverdale wakens from a dream in which Hollingsworth and Zenobia stand on each side of his bed, "bent across it to exchange a kiss of passion." He gazes again at the opposite building. He sees a drawing room next to a small boudoir where a girl sits, apparently doing handiwork. Then Zenobia appears at the window, and he realizes the other figure is Priscilla. Westervelt is beside Zenobia. He senses that they repel each other.

Coverdale is heartsick about the coincidence, although he has known that Zenobia had retained an "establishment" in town. Westervelt gazes out of the window, recognizes Coverdale, and summons Zenobia. She acknowledges Coverdale with a gesture that is part salutation and part rejection: She lowers a curtain over the window.

Chapter XIX: "Zenobia's Drawing-Room"
Coverdale tries to account for the connections among Zenobia, Priscilla, Westervelt, and Hollingsworth but is mystified. He calls on Zenobia, who is playing the piano. She apologizes for lowering the curtain, but her manner is cold. Coverdale tests her by mocking Hollingsworth. Zenobia defends him, and Coverdale realizes Zenobia loves Hollingsworth. He asks about Priscilla, and Zenobia states that Priscilla is with her.

Chapter XX: "They Vanish"
Priscilla walks forward, and Coverdale says she is "as lovely as a flower." Zenobia accuses him of "interference" and continues to be hostile to him. He asks Priscilla when she will return to Blithedale and she says whenever "they" please to take her; she has no free will. Zenobia dismisses him, saying she and Priscilla have an engagement. Westervelt appears. The three descend the stairs and drive away in a carriage.

Chapter XXI: "An Old Acquaintance"
Coverdale is mystified and goes to a nearby saloon to seek Old Moodie, hoping to determine his relationship to Priscilla. Coverdale treats him to lunch and wine, and Moodie begins to talk.

Chapter XXII: "Fauntleroy"
Moodie describes a wealthy man he had known 25 years earlier, whom he calls "Fauntleroy." He lived in a home as richly appointed as a palace, with a lovely wife. Although his affection for her was "superficial," they had a beautiful daughter. Fauntleroy then committed a crime, which was discovered. He fled, his wife perished, and his estate was divided among his creditors. He moved to the city, changed his name to Moodie, and began living in a squalid street among the needy. He remarried and had another daughter, Priscilla, "pale and nervous." The second wife died. He told Priscilla stories of her elder sister, and her love for her sister grew, although she had never met her.

Priscilla is courted by a handsome, youthful man, but the neighbors are suspicious of him. Priscilla's elder sister, Zenobia, had been adopted by her uncle, who raised her in affluent surroundings. He died during her girlhood, and she inherited his wealth. She had hoped to promote a "better social state" and had thus gone to Blithedale; Priscilla follows her there. In response to a message, Zenobia calls on Moodie. He asks her to be kind to Priscilla. He tells Coverdale he loves Priscilla more.

Chapter XXIII: "A Village Hall"
Coverdale is stunned by Moodie's revelations, yet reluctant to "come again within their sphere." His "toil-hardened hands" become accustomed to gloves again. He attends a lecture in a village hall and sees a handbill advertising the Veiled Lady. Hollingsworth is in the audience. He tells Coverdale Zenobia is still at Blithedale. An exhibition of mysticism takes place, with "rapping spirits" and other wonders. Coverdale recognizes Westervelt on stage and asks Hollingsworth what he has done with Priscilla. He does not answer. Westervelt introduces the Veiled Lady, who is revealed as Priscilla. She flees to Hollingsworth.

Chapter XXIV: "The Masqueraders"
Coverdale returns to Blithedale. He is eager to see Hollingsworth, Zenobia, and Priscilla, but a sense of foreboding hangs over him. He arrives at the farm but sees no one he recognizes. He hears voices and laughter and finds a "fantastic rabble" made up of strange figures instead of the people he knows. There are Shakers, Negroes, Gypsies, and people dressed as mythological figures and Indians. Silas Foster, however, is leaning against a tree. The people begin dancing. Coverdale goes on to Eliot's pulpit and sees Hollingsworth sitting at its base, Priscilla at his feet, and Zenobia standing before them.

Chapter XXV: "The Three Together"
Zenobia is dressed as an Oriental princess. Suddenly she looks like marble. She laughingly tells Coverdale she has been on trial for her life. He looks at Hollingsworth, who now appears as grim as a Puritan magistrate. Priscilla seems to be a "pale victim." Coverdale has a strong sense that he has

just missed a battle of some sort. He perceives that Zenobia and Hollingsworth are no longer friends. Zenobia announces that for three days she has known a "strange fact" that threatens to impoverish her. She asks Hollingsworth whether he loves Priscilla and he admits that he does. Zenobia is furious, calling him a monster.

She catalogs his sins: He has developed a scheme for a "purer and higher" life but thrown Coverdale away since he would not be his slave. He was also ready to sacrifice Priscilla. Hollingsworth asks Priscilla to go with him, but she goes to Zenobia instead. Zenobia says she has been her own "evil fate" and has a melancholy future. Hollingsworth puts his arm about Priscilla and takes her into the forest.

Chapter XXVI: "Zenobia and Coverdale"
Coverdale stays with Zenobia, who looks about her, bewildered. She says Hollingsworth has kept Priscilla and flung away the sister who would have "served him better." She plans to leave Blithedale. She takes the jeweled flower from her hair and asks Coverdale to give it to Priscilla, who will make "as soft and gentle a wife as the veriest Bluebeard could desire," although she will "fade soon."

Zenobia admits she should have tried to win Coverdale's heart and not Hollingsworth's but says Hollingsworth has murdered her. She says she will leave the community because she is "sick to death of playing at philanthropy and progress." She calls Blithedale "the very emptiest mockery in our effort to establish the one true system." Coverdale takes her hand, which is cold. She says she is going to become a Catholic and enter a nunnery; the next time he hears of her she will be behind a black veil. She leaves. Coverdale falls asleep beneath Eliot's pulpit and awakes in moonlight.

Chapter XXVII: "Midnight"
Coverdale goes to the farm in search of Zenobia. Hollingsworth has not seen her; he asks Silas Foster to help them look for her. Silas deduces that Hollingsworth and Coverdale believe Zenobia has harmed herself but cannot understand why. "What on earth should the young woman do that for?" Silas exclaims. His eyes are "half out of his head" with surprise. He remarks that Zenobia "has more

means than she can use or waste, and lacks nothing to make her comfortable, but a husband." That, he continues drily, is "an article she could have, any day." He is sure their deduction is mistaken. Eventually, however, he agrees to organize a search party to ascertain the truth.

They take a long pole, with a hook, used to draw up the bucket from the well when a rope breaks, along with some long-handled hay rakes. They find Zenobia's shoe at the riverbank. Silas plies the rake and pulls up a "large mass of stuff," which turns out to be a tuft of water weeds. He pictures her at the breakfast table, laughing at them. He remarks that "life and death together make sad work for us all," but is still not convinced they will find her body.

Then Hollingsworth's pole strikes an object at the bottom of the river. Silas cries, "Hold on! . . . You have her!" They draw Zenobia out of the water and lay her on the ground beneath a tree. It is Silas who is the most touched. "Poor child!" he says, and his "dry old heart . . . vouchsafed a tear." He continues, "I'm sorry for her!" Zenobia's arms will not stay down. Foster realizes that Hollingsworth's pole has wounded her breast, but they believe she had not felt it. The men take her to the farmhouse on fence rails and boards from the boat. They hand over Zenobia's body to four "tire-women," who will dress it.

Chapter XXVIII: "Blithedale Pasture"
Coverdale thinks Zenobia should be buried at the base of Eliot's pulpit, but Hollingsworth believes the grave should be dug on the hillside where he and Zenobia had once planned to build a cottage. Old Moodie and Priscilla attend the funeral, along with Westervelt. Westervelt cannot forgive Zenobia for drowning herself and giving up all the future success she would have had as an actress and in other endeavors. Coverdale says none of it would have satisfied her heart. He despises Westervelt.

Years later, Coverdale seeks out Hollingsworth and finds him and Priscilla in a secluded lane. He asks where Hollingsworth's grand edifice is, and he replies that a small one answers his purposes. He also has not reformed any criminals. The grass grows beautifully on Zenobia's grave.

Chapter XXIX: "Miles Coverdale's Confession"
Coverdale had left Blithedale a week after Zenobia's death. He is a bachelor still but has one secret he believes he should reveal. He does so, in the final lines of the novel: "'I—I myself—was in love—with—Priscilla!'"

RECEPTION AND CRITICAL ANALYSIS

When the novel was published, it was attacked for not being up to the level of The SCARLET LETTER (published in 1850), which had been widely regarded by critics at the time as a masterpiece. Charles Creighton Hazewell, writing in the Boston Daily Times in July 1852, objected to setting a "deeply tragic tale" within the Brook Farm community and considered the plot completely unrealistic: "We find ourselves perpetually reflecting that what he tells us happened, could not have happened, which spoils the work as a romance." To Hazewell, the events of The Scarlet Letter, though "startling and terrible," were not at all improbable and, in fact, had much historic veracity (the punishment of Hester Prynne being a case in point). He found Zenobia completely disagreeable and unrefined, and Westervelt the only "sensible personage" in the story because he was "not a fool."

The anonymous Literary World reviewer would have preferred to see the Brook Farm experiment treated objectively. Edward Percy Whipple, writing in the influential GRAHAM'S MAGAZINE, on the other hand, praised the novel for its "searching observation of life, manners and character" and for the "humorous and descriptive scenes." The reviewer for the English Westminster Review, possibly George Eliot, predicted that the novel would never attain popularity but was, nevertheless, "a work of genius." Hawthorne, however, was handicapped by a "feebleness of moral purpose." Readers would have legitimately expected more about the practical operation of Brook Farm, a socialistic settlement, to illustrate the "good and evil" of the system. Hawthorne, however, "confines himself to the delineation of its picturesque phases, as a 'thing of beauty,' and either has no particular convictions respecting its deeper relations, or hesitates to express them." In theory, socialism could have been prominent enough to "fill the book" but in fact never grows into an "organic part of the story" and "contributes nothing whatever toward the final catastrophe" (*Nathaniel Hawthorne: The Contemporary Reviews,* 193–223, passim).

Whipple, in GRAHAM'S MAGAZINE, distinguished the task of the "romancer" from that of ordinary "novelists." The "romancer" does not need to pass the test of those who wish to analyze a text. Instead, the questions are "Has he novelty of nature? Is he an absolutely new power in literature?" Hawthorne passes these tests. Whipple considered the novel "the most perfect in execution of any of Hawthorne's works, and as a work of art, hardly equalled by anything else which the country has produced." He termed it an "organizing of the mind, with the strict unity of one of Nature's own creations." He held Zenobia's death to be the "great passage of the volume." Finally, he did not believe the novel yielded in "interest or value to any of Hawthorne's preceding works," but, rather, was their superior in "affluence and fineness of thought, and masterly perception of the first remote workings of great and absorbing passions (Crowley, J. Donald, ed., *The Critical Heritage: Nathaniel Hawthorne,* 253–256).

The novel has had, to many critics, a fatal flaw: the disjunction between its apparent polemical purpose, an exploration of the Brook Farm experiment, and its actual theatrical focus on performance, in the form of mesmerism, masquerades, dancing, and veils. Even if it is considered solely as a satire of social reform, the events are marked with a dualism that puzzles many readers. At the outset of their venture, the pilgrims believed that it would be easy to return to a "simple agrarian life and to simple Christian principles." They planned to become self-sufficient and to reject the "money-oriented, industrialized society" they saw developing around them. They would rely on "wisdom and purity" and bestow the "benefits of the highest, physical, intellectual and moral education in the present state of human knowledge" on the community (Miller, *Salem Is My Dwelling Place,* 187–188). Hawthorne writes in his diary of a few practical experiences at Brook Farm that figure in the novel. For instance, he drove to the Brighton Cattle Fair with the head farmer, William Allen, to buy baby pigs and sell a calf (Hoeltje, *Inward Sky: The Mind and Heart*

of Nathaniel Hawthorne, 176). In the novel itself, however, the baby pigs and the cattle fair seem as shrouded and shaded as the Veiled Lady. The reader who is expecting a sober account of the daily lives of the participants and the working out of problems inhibiting and promoting the experiment is frustrated by the paucity of detail that George Eliot, Thomas Hardy, Honoré de Balzac, or Charles Dickens might have supplied.

Instead, Hawthorne veers off into masked identities and the world of theater, several times shifting the scene back to Boston, from which the reformers have fled to establish their experimental community. He seems aware of this difficulty at the outset. In his preface to the novel, he states that he does not wish to deny that he had the community in mind but declares that he considers the institution "as not less fairly the subject of fictitious handling, than the imaginary personages whom he has introduced there." His "fictitious handling," however, is frequently meager. With more conviction, he emphasizes that he is not trying to "illustrate a theory, or elicit a conclusion, favourable or otherwise, in respect to Socialism," but rather to "establish a theatre . . . where the creatures of his brain may play their phantasmagorical antics, without exposing them to too close a comparison with the actual events of real lives." He insists that he has not sketched the "likenesses" of any persons at Brook Farm, such as the "self-concentrated Philanthropist," the "high-spirited Woman," the "weakly Maiden," or the "Minor Poet" (Preface, *The Blithedale Romance*). The "phantasmagorical antics" have impeded many readers since the novel was published.

Despite Hawthorne's disclaimer, both critics and readers have persisted in trying to identify the major characters as actual people. These attempts have not always been successful, however. For example, Hollingsworth, considered by many writers to be one of the most finely drawn of Hawthorne's male characters, is thought to be compounded of WILLIAM ELLERY CHANNING, who espoused prison reform for a time, and Samuel Gridley Howe, an abolitionist. Hollingsworth also reflects HORACE MANN (Brenda Wineapple, *Hawthorne: A Life,* 249). Readers and critics are on more solid ground when they recognize in Zenobia, an advocate of women's rights, a thinly veiled portrait of MARGARET FULLER, the American essayist, editor, teacher, and writer. In April 1841, when he was living at BROOK FARM, he wrote to Sophia that Margaret Fuller's cow was at the farm, and that she "hooks the other cows, and has made herself ruler of the herd, and behaves in a very tyrannical manner" (*Letters*, 15, 528). In 1850, after the Brook Farm community had disbanded, Fuller, her husband, and their infant son perished in a shipwreck off Fire Island, New York. Their bodies were never recovered, although that of the infant son washed ashore.

Miles Coverdale, the poet/narrator of *The Blithedale Romance*, is usually regarded as Hawthorne himself. It is only in this novel that Hawthorne uses a first-person narrator, although in stories and sketches such as "DR. HEIDEGGER'S EXPERIMENT" and "FOOT-PRINTS ON THE SEA-SHORE," he does make use of the first-person point of view. Coverdale presents special problems, however, in that he is himself ambivalent toward the concept of a utopian community. He is the first of Hawthorne's narrators who become characters within a novel. He is eager to join the experiment at Blithedale, but, as Terence Martin observes, that world has "no real need of him," as his narrative slowly reveals. Coverdale expects, unrealistically, to find an innocence and freshness in the country and assumes that human "falsehood and error" are confined to the city. On his journey to Blithedale he comments on how pleasant the snowy weather is and is rebuked by one of his companions, who tells him not to laugh "at what little enthusiasm" he has left (Martin, *Nathaniel Hawthorne*, 146). Moreover, as they travel, their "blithe tones of brotherhood" are ignored by travelers they meet, a reminder of the "difficult" task they are undertaking for the "reformation of the world." On arrival at the farm, Coverdale remarks ironically that the two serving girls employed by the resident farmer, Silas Foster, and his wife appear to be awkward, since they do not know what would be "their position in our new arrangement of the world." Few readers can visualize the reformed "world" Hawthorne has in mind, possibly because that world never really takes shape in his mind. The world

that is most real to him is multilayered, misty, symbolic, and transcendental, like the world of the carnival in *The MARBLE FAUN*.

Some critics, however, praise the symbolic patterns within the novel as a positive achievement and an index to Hawthorne's underlying intentions. Melissa Pennell points out that in *The Blithedale Romance*, as in a number of his works, Hawthorne develops specific image patterns that act as extended metaphors. She suggests that fires and hearths are a dominant symbol in the novel; some offer "real warmth," such as the one in the farmhouse on the evening of Coverdale's arrival. Others are false and unsubstantial, made with brush, and reveal "the superficial quality of the bonds among the participants." She also pinpoints "masks, veils, and pseudonyms" as image patterns that play an important role in the novel (Pennell, *Student Companion to Nathaniel Hawthorne*, 124).

Nina Baym relates the novel to Hawthorne's previous works, arguing that it should be regarded as an exploration of the sins of tyranny and repression. Hollingsworth is the "serpent" in the "Eden" of Blithedale because he is opposed to everything in which they believe. With Machiavellian aplomb, he joins the community for access to Zenobia's money; he is actually as "materialistic and ruthless" as the Pyncheons are in *The HOUSE OF THE SEVEN GABLES*. His real purpose in going to Blithedale is to acquire the property himself, as the site of his reform school. He would not encourage the "free relation between man and nature," but rather "shut people away from nature in an institution."

Baym suggests, further, that the "Maule-figure" in the novel is the narrator, Coverdale. He is not as radical as Holgrave, the artist figure in *The House of the Seven Gables*, who is descended from the Maule family, but is a passive dreamer who does not look beyond "comfort and pleasure." He looks back fondly on the "sweet, bewitching, enervating indolence" of his bachelor existence but believes, mistakenly, that by leaving that life behind he has strengthened himself. He wishes to become an esteemed poet, a writer of "true, strong, natural, and sweet" poetry, just as Holgrave hopes to perfect his skills as a daguerreotypist. His journey to Blithedale is an optimistic search for rejuvenation.

He believes he has found it in Zenobia and praises "the native glow of coloring in her cheeks . . . the flesh-warmth over her round arms, and what was visible of her full bust." The flower that she wears is an emblem of her sexuality.

Actually, however, Zenobia is playing a part. She is wealthy, but her true wealth lies in her "natural gifts." Her half sister, Priscilla, on the other hand, is poor but tries to earn money by making silk purses or by taking on the role of the "Veiled Lady." She is exploited and idealized in both enterprises and has become a symbol of "purity and innocence." Terence Martin observes that the "dark, sensual Zenobia" and the "light, ethereal Priscilla" are "two recurrent types of women" in Hawthorne's work. Some critics, however, have suggested that Priscilla has been a prostitute (Lefeowitz, Alan, and Barbara Lefeowitz, "Some Rents in the Veil: New Light on Priscilla and Zenobia in *The Blithedale Romance*"). Hawthorne's use of plays, tableaus, etc. suggests that he finds the whole enterprise of Brook Farm false and a pose, but he does not want to insult his peers openly.

CHARACTERS

Coverdale, Miles   A minor poet, he is the narrator of *The Blithedale Romance*. Coverdale is supposed by many critics to represent Hawthorne himself. Many of his observations originated in Hawthorne's journals.

Wineapple calls him the "first modern antihero . . . self-regarding, anxiety-ridden, paralyzed, and mistaken." She observes that the reason he joins the Blithedale community is an enigma, since he "prefers to stay insulated in his rooms, comforted with a good bottle of claret behind a thick curtain of cigar smoke." She points out, astutely, that he likes to conceal himself, watching others, unseen. He spies on Zenobia and Hollingsworth from the treetops; he is attracted to Zenobia, although he denies it. He seems to drift from Boston to Blithedale, suffering from boredom and having a mild curiosity about the experiment.

Coverdale admits to being confused about the other characters. Fairly late in the novel, he ponders "Zenobia's whole character and history: the true nature of her mysterious connection with Westervelt; her later purposes towards Hollings-

sworth, and, reciprocally, his in reference to her; . . . the degree in which Zenobia had been cognizant of the plot against Priscilla, and what, at last, had been the real object of that scheme."

Foster, Silas   In *The Blithedale Romance*, the farm manager at the transcendentalist community called "Blithedale," based on the real one of Brook Farm, West Roxbury, outside Boston. The most famous cooperative community of the 19th century, Brook Farm began as an attempt to enact various patterns and aspirations of transcendentalism.

In the novel, Foster is described as "stout," but very knowledgeable. He is to receive a "fair stipend" and be the "tutor in the art of husbandry" for the other participants in the utopian experiment. The first evening at Blithedale, Foster makes clear his view of the "city folks" who have arrived to take part in the experimental agricultural community; he figures that it will take three of them to do the work of only one field hand, and they will certainly fail at competitive market gardening. Moreover, none of them is likely to be a good judge of swine. Foster is never idle; he works at shoemaking in the evenings, while his wife knits.

Zenobia, one of the women who are members of the commune, perceives Foster as the sort of rustic celebrated by Robert Burns. She predicts to Coverdale that he will evolve into a combination of poet and unlettered farmer. Foster will be his prototype, "with his palm of sole-leather, and his joints of rusty iron." She unkindly describes his brain as made of a "Savoy cabbage" and predicts that Coverdale, should he model himself after Foster, will smoke "some very vile tobacco in the black stump of a pipe." His literature will be the "Farmer's Almanac," for, as with Foster, he will not "get as far as the newspaper." He will fall asleep when he finally sits down after supper, put on a blue coat on Sundays but think only of leaning over stone walls and considering corn growing. He will climb into pigsties and feel the hogs and guess how much they will weigh killed and dressed. It will, ironically, be Foster who directs the search party and makes practical decisions at the time of Zenobia's death, although he is not at first convinced that she has disappeared.

An anonymous contemporary reviewer, writing in the *North British Review* in November 1853, remarked that Foster was "the one point of reality in all the phantasmagoria of conceit, and its concomitant passions and imbecilities" (*The Blithedale Romance,* Norton Critical Edition, ed. Seymour Gross and Rosalie Murphy [New York: W. W. Norton, 1978], 277).

Hollingsworth   In *The Blithedale Romance,* he is a blacksmith by trade. It is he who takes Priscilla to Blithedale. Hawthorne describes him as brawny; he has "a great shaggy head" and "an abundant beard." He belongs, according to the author, "not in open sunlight" but by the fire of a cave. He is said to hammer "thought" out of iron after heating the iron in his heart. In the early days of the Blithedale community, he nurses Coverdale during his illness.

He considers the whole Blithedale scheme naive but is hoping, as Miller puts it, to "exploit the naiveté of the Blithedalers and further his own social-engineering scheme by taking over their property." Miller considers him a "monomaniac," but both Priscilla and Zenobia are drawn to him (Miller, *Salem Is My Dwelling Place,* 369–371).

Terence Martin calls Hollingsworth "one of the most firmly drawn" of Hawthorne's "men of Idea," a recurring element in Hawthorne's fiction. Brenda Wineapple terms him Hawthorne's "doppelgänger," or double. His "love" for Zenobia is tied to her wealth; she calls him a "cold, heartless, self-beginning and self-ending piece of mechanism."

Gorman Beauchamp sees Hollingsworth's personality as Hawthorne's conception of the ultimate "Universal Reformer": "radical, monomaniacal, ruthless." If Hollingsworth's character had been "the guiding spirit of Blithedale," then Hawthorne "could have merged the radical reformer and the utopian reform in a single encompassing experiment, demonstrating how personality and program re-enforced each other." Instead, Hollingsworth is depicted as a "subverter" of Blithedale's socialist experiment. He joins the community "only in hopes of using it as a means for furthering his own ends," his scheme to reform criminals. By pitting Hollingsworth against Blithedale and "his advocacy of a conflicting agenda of activism" against the utopian commune's ideals, Hawthorne "dissociates the reformer from the reform" and the "personality type that is drawn to utopia from the utopia to which, one would have thought, it would naturally be drawn" ("Hawthorne and the Universal Reformers," *Utopian Studies,* 13 [spring 2002]).

Old Moodie   In *The Blithedale Romance,* he is the father of two daughters, half sisters to each other: Priscilla and Zenobia. In a past life, he was Fauntleroy, a man of "wealth, and magnificent tastes, and prodigal expenditure." His life was focused on outward show and "external splendor." Zenobia, the daughter of his first wife, is the child of this splendor. Eventually, however, he lost his fortune and became liable to criminal prosecution. Although he escaped criminal trial, Fauntleroy was ruined and forced to hide himself away. He later remarried; his second wife was a "forlorn, meek-spirited, feeble young woman" and a "poor phantom." He had another daughter, Priscilla, by his second wife. She is described as "shadowy," having a "lack of human substance," a "ghost-child."

Priscilla   In *The Blithedale Romance,* she is the daughter of Old Moodie and the half sister of Zenobia. Sad and wan, she is so pale she appears to be in "habitual seclusion from the sun and free atmosphere, like a flower-shrub" that has "done its best to blossom in too scanty light." But when Zenobia caresses her, she has a "vivid look of joy." She occupies herself in part by freelancing as a medium, the Veiled Lady. This persona is in keeping with the vogue for spiritualism that had been popular in New York State a few years earlier. Her occupation puts her in the power of Westervelt, a shrewd charlatan.

Zenobia sounds a note of realism for Priscilla when she calls her half sister a "shadowy snow-maiden, who, precisely at the stroke of midnight, shall melt away at my feet in a pool of ice-cold water and give me my death with a pair of wet slippers." This is a prophecy of Zenobia's own death by drowning.

Hollingsworth marries Priscilla. At the end of the novel, Miles Coverdale confesses that he himself had always been in love with Priscilla.

Veiled Lady, The Character in Hawthorne's novel *The Blithedale Romance.* She is a "phenomenon in the mesmeric line" and is exploited by Professor Westervelt. Public entertainments based on magic performances, seances, and hypnotism were a popular form of spiritualism at the time. At first, the identity of the "Veiled Lady" is an enigma; she is later revealed to be Priscilla, half sister of Zenobia.

Westervelt Character in *The Blithedale Romance.* A rather disagreeable man who calls himself "Professor Westervelt," he is a showman; Priscilla, the half sister of Zenobia, has played a spiritualized lady in his act. He also has a past with Zenobia; when she drowns herself, he cannot forgive her for giving up the success she might have had under his control as an actress and in other endeavors.

Terence Martin observes that the "satanic figure" of Westervelt "bears a relation to the numerous characters in [Hawthorne's] tales and romances who seek to hold another in bondage."

Zenobia In *The Blithedale Romance,* she is the daughter of Old Moodie and older half sister of Priscilla. She is described as a "perfectly developed rose," with "no folded petal, no latent dew-drop" in it. Coverdale terms her name "a sort of mask in which she comes before the world, retaining all the privileges of privacy—a contrivance, in short, like the white drapery of the Veiled Lady, only a little more transparent."

Zenobia inherits great wealth from her father, Old Moodie, which is legally his, since he inherited it from his brother. Old Moodie remarks, "Zenobia has the splendor, and not the shame. Let the world admire her, and be dazzled by her, the brilliant child of my prosperity!" When Zenobia drowns herself, it is Silas Foster who, among the men, is the most touched. He remarks that "life and death together make sad work for us all."

Many critics have assumed that Zenobia is a portrait of Margaret Fuller, although she also has elements of other women Hawthorne knew, such as Mary Silsbee Sparks. Zenobia's interest in mesmerism may have originated in Elizabeth Peabody's attempt to have Una (Hawthorne's daughter) play the part of a medium (Miller, *Salem Is My Dwelling Place,* 366–367).

Gorman Beauchamp points out the contradictions in the "angry, frustrated" "proto-feminist" who fulminates "against the oppression of women and the narrowness of the meager opportunities afforded them." She has some of the "fanatical reformer's furious zeal," but there are "no alternative gender roles" at Blithedale—"nor is Zenobia ever shown trying to institute any." Like Coverdale, she does not belong, "intellectually or temperamentally," in a "utopian commune." Her "true motive," in fact, is the "quite unfeminist one" of "trying to catch a husband—Hollingsworth." Beauchamp proposes that her feminism is actually "an expression of purely personal frustration, a sublimation of unfulfilled sexual passion." As Coverdale says, women "are not natural reformers, but become such by the pressure of exceptional misfortune." Zenobia's "forcefully articulated feminism" serves as a "defense mechanism disguising her true feelings" ("Hawthorne and the Universal Reformers," *Utopian Studies* 13 [spring 2002]).

FOR FURTHER READING

Baym, Nina, "*The Blithedale Romance:* A Radical Reading," *Journal of English and Germanic Philology* 67 (1968): 545–569; Bell, Michael Davitt, *Hawthorne and the Historical Romance of New England* (Princeton, N.J.: Princeton University Press, 1971); DeSalvo, Louise, *Nathaniel Hawthorne* (Atlantic Highlands, N.J.: Humanities Press International, 1987), 97; FitzPatrick, Martin, "'To a Practised Touch': Miles Coverdale and Hawthorne's Irony," *American Transcendental Quarterly* 14, no. 1 (March 2000): 28–46; Grossberg, Benjamin, "'The Tender Passion Was Very Rife among Us': Coverdale's Queer Utopia and *The Blithedale Romance,*" *Studies in American Fiction* 28, no. 1 (spring 2000): 3–25; Kaul, A. N., "The Blithedale Romance," in *The American Vision: Actual and Ideal Society in Nineteenth-Century Fiction* (New Haven, Conn.: Yale University Press, 1963); Krieg, Joann Peck, "Justice and Mercy: The Virtues Unreconciled in America," in *Medievalism in American Culture,* edited by Bernard Rosenthal and Paul E. Szarmach (Binghamton, N.Y.: Center for Medieval & Early Renaissance

Studies, 1987); Lefeowitz, Alan, and Barbara Lefeowitz, "Some Rents in the Veil: New Light on Priscilla and Zenobia, *The Blithedale Romance*," *Nineteenth-Century Fiction* 21 (1966): 263–276; Mellow, James R., *Nathaniel Hawthorne in His Times* (Boston: Houghton Mifflin, 1980): 188–190; Miller, John N., "Eros and Ideology: At the Heart of Hawthorne's Blithedale," *Nineteenth-Century Literature* 55, no. 1 (June 2000): 1–21; Pennell, Melissa, *Student Companion to Nathaniel Hawthorne* (Westport, Conn.: Greenwood Press, 1999); Schriber, Mary Suzanne, "Justice to Zenobia," *New England Quarterly* 55 (1982): 61–68; Sprague, Claire, "Dream and Disguise in *The Blithedale Romance, PMLA*, 84 (1969): 596–597; Tanner, Laura E., "Speaking with 'Hands at Our Throats'": The Struggle for Artistic Voice in *The Blithedale Romance*," *Studies in American Fiction* 21, no. 1 (spring 1993): 1–19.

"Book of Autographs, A"

A sketch first published in *United States Magazine and Democratic Review* in November 1844. Turner states that it is "based on a volume of letters from the Revolutionary era," which Hawthorne uses to invent "character and incident" and thus evoke the "spirit of an earlier age" (Turner, *Nathaniel Hawthorne: A Biography*, 157).

FOR FURTHER READING

Taylor, John M. "Nathaniel Hawthorne Discovers Autographs," *Manuscripts* 51, no. 4 (fall 1999): 289–293.

"Buds and Bird-voices"

First published in the *United States Magazine and Democratic Review* in June 1843, this nature essay was signed by Hawthorne. The Hawthornes were living in the Old Manse, Concord, at the time he wrote it.

The essay is an account of the arrival of spring "weeks later than we expected, and months later than we longed for." He notes the many ways spring has "pressed" on the "footsteps of retreating winter"; the season is immanent in the fruit trees, riverbank vegetation, and shrubbery. He moves on to describe the birds, from crows, "sable harbingers of a brighter and livelier race," to songbirds such as swallows, blackbirds, and robins. He climbs a hill and views the river, in which the waters are subsiding and islands are emerging. The season represents a "periodical infusion of the primal spirit."

FOR FURTHER READING

Matthew J. Bruccoli, "A Lost Hawthorne Manuscript: 'Buds and Bird-Voices,'" *The Nathaniel Hawthorne Journal* 1971.

"Canal-boat, The"

First published in the *New-England Magazine* 9 (December 1835), this is one of Hawthorne's best American travel sketches. It was reprinted by James T. Fields in *Mosses from an Old Manse* (1854), along with several other sketches.

After his September 1832 tour of New England and upstate New York, Hawthorne recounts a journey along the Grand Canal aboard a horse-drawn passenger boat from Utica to Syracuse. He describes, with considerable irony, the accommodations, his fellow passengers, meals, and sights along the way.

He describes the boat as it appeared at Utica, his starting point, with "three horses harnessed to our vessel, like the steeds of Neptune to a huge scallop-shell, in mythological pictures." Along the way, there are locks with small grocery stores, thriving villages, and cities such as Utica. The passengers include a Virginia schoolmaster, who reads Virgil and who fails to duck before an impending bridge; a Detroit merchant; and a New England farmer. There are two sleeping compartments with 20 narrow bunks each, one for men and one for women, separated by a red curtain.

He imagines the surprise of the "sleepy Dutchmen" once De Witt Clinton's vision of a "watery highway" connecting the Hudson with Lake Erie was realized. The new river has carried "hard cash" and "foreign commodities" in exchange for their produce. It was, in fact, "the most fertilizing of all fluids," causing towns with theaters, churches, and other buildings to spring up. Alfred Weber observes that his travel sketches represent an attempt by the young Hawthorne to "gather materials for a national literature that celebrated the history, natural beauty, and future progress of the United States" (Preface to *Hawthorne's American Travel Sketches,* edited by Alfred Weber, Beth L. Lueck, and Dennis Berthold, x).

The bibliographic history of Hawthorne's travel sketches is complex. He apparently intended to collect the articles in a single book, which was never published, but, as he wrote to WILLIAM D. TICKNOR of Ticknor and Fields, it is "no bad stuff." This volume contains discussions of the three "Sketches from Memory" published in the *New-England Magazine* (*see* "The NOTCH OF THE WHITE MOUNTAINS" and "OUR EVENING PARTY AMONG THE MOUNTAINS"], in addition to four other sketches not published in Hawthorne's lifetime: "The INLAND PORT," "ROCHESTER," "A NIGHT SCENE," and "AN AFTERNOON SCENE."

FOR FURTHER READING

Alfred Weber, Beth L. Lueck, and Dennis Berthold, eds., *Hawthorne's American Travel Sketches* (Hanover, N.H.: University Press of New England, 1989).

"Canterbury Pilgrims, The"

Short story first published in *The SNOW-IMAGE, AND OTHER TWICE-TOLD TALES* (1852). The framework is loosely derived from Geoffrey Chaucer's *Canterbury Tales.* As the story opens, a young couple, Miriam and Josiah, dressed in old-fashioned clothes, are departing permanently from their native Shaker community. Near their former red-roofed Shaker village, they are greeted by a party of travelers consisting of three men, an aged woman, and a small girl and boy. When they question Miriam and Josiah, the two admit that they are leaving the Shakers and will henceforth be "of the world's people." Josiah says they are departing without

leave-taking because "father Job" is very aged and has "little charity for what he calls the iniquities of the flesh." The strangers promise not to betray them, but ask whether they might share their own stories with Josiah and Miriam.

They all seat themselves around a stone cistern. The chief spokesman, nearly 40 and stooped, states that he is a poet, a "verse maker," but his poetry has fallen on deaf ears. He is giving up his profession forever, having fallen "in a middle state between obscurity and infamy." Posterity, however, will regret having forced one of the "fathers of American song to end his days in a Shaker village." Hawthorne assures the reader that the poet is gentle and harmless despite his harangue.

The second man, about 50, states that he was once a merchant and owner of a fleet of ships that sailed to the East Indies, Liverpool, and other ports. He has had a spectacular failure, of which Josiah has never heard, to his astonishment. He hopes the Shakers will entrust the management of the village to him; in five years he will double their capital.

The third pilgrim is a countryman who labored in vain for many years to support himself and his young wife and children. His living has grown "poorer" and his heart "colder and heavier," until he has given up on the world and returned to the Shaker village. Miriam has not realized that the aged female pilgrim is his wife; she is just as disillusioned as her husband. She assures Miriam that they were "true lovers once." She predicts that if Miriam and Josiah marry, they will be kind to each other for two or three years, but Josiah will then grow gloomy and she will become peevish and eventually reenact the disillusioned lives of the older couple. Just then their children cry that they are tired and hungry. Josiah and Miriam look "mournfully" at each other, then embrace and declare that they are resolved never to return to the Shaker village. They will always love one another.

The young couple and the other group of travelers part, Josiah and Miriam to make their way in the outside world, and the Canterbury pilgrims to continue toward the Shaker village. They seek a home where "former ties of nature or society" will be sundered, and "old distinctions levelled," and where they will no longer be "weary outcasts."

CRITICAL ANALYSIS

As is his novel *The BLITHEDALE ROMANCE*, the short story "The Canterbury Pilgrims" is an example of Hawthorne's skepticism toward experiments in socialistic, communal group living.

Hawthorne became interested in Shaker communities while visiting Canterbury, New Hampshire, in the early 1830s. James Mellow notes that Hawthorne "conceded" that the Shakers had "a good and comfortable life, and if it were not for their ridiculous ceremonies, a man might not do a wiser thing than join them." After his visit, "he was apt to tease his sisters with his intention of adopting the celibate life of the Shaker community" (*Nathaniel Hawthorne in His Times,* 48–50).

Terence Martin observes that the young Shaker couple, Josiah and Miriam, "go into the world" despite hearing the travelers' "irresponsible and judicious advice to the contrary" (*Nathaniel Hawthorne* [Boston: Twayne, 1965]). Their "desire for life" and their "confidence in love" inspire them to reject what Hawthorne deems the "cold and passionless security" that characterizes the Shakers' extreme way of life. Martin sees "the direction of Miriam and Josiah, of the tale, and of Hawthorne's fiction" as "into life—into the imperfect, sin-burdened world where mortals grope for love and understanding."

FOR FURTHER READING

Arvin, Newton, *Hawthorne* (Boston: Little, Brown, 1929), 68–69; Baym, Nina, *The Shape of Hawthorne's Career* (Ithaca, N.Y.: Cornell University Press, 1976), 50–51; Johnston, Mark, "'The Canterbury Pilgrims': Hawthorne's Typical Story," *Essays in Arts and Sciences* 12, no. 1 (March 1983): 37–41; Lauber, John, "Hawthorne's Shaker Tales," *Nineteenth-Century Fiction,* 18, no. 1 (June 1963): 82–86; Martin, Terence, *Nathaniel Hawthorne* (Boston: Twayne, 1965); Mellow, James, *Nathaniel Hawthorne in His Times* (Boston: Houghton Mifflin, 1980), 48–50; Secor, Robert, "Hawthorne's Canterbury Pilgrims," *Explicator* 22 (1963): 8; Waggoner, Hyatt, "Hawthorne's 'Canterbury Pilgrims': Theme and Structure," *New England Quarterly* 22 (1949): 373–387.

"Celestial Rail-road, The"

An allegorical satire, based on John Bunyan's *Pilgrim's Progress,* issued in one volume by Wilder & Co., Boston, in 1843. It was published in 18 parts in *Voices of the True-hearted* between November 1844 and April 1846.

The narrator embarks on a pilgrimage to the region of the Earth containing the famous city of Destruction, a "populous and flourishing town." A railroad has recently been established between the city of Destruction and the Celestial City. The narrator leaves his hotel and goes to the Station House. En route there he enjoys the company of another gentleman, whose name is Mr. Smooth-it-away. He has not, himself, visited the Celestial City, yet seems to be very well acquainted with its laws, customs, policy, and statistics—in fact, just as well acquainted with them as with those of the city of Destruction, of which he is a native.

The coach rattles out of the city and passes across a bridge, which, although elegantly constructed, seems too slight to the traveler to sustain very much weight. A quagmire, the Slough of Despond, lies on each side, far below. Mr. Smooth-it-away remarks that the dismal quagmire could easily be converted to firm ground, but we learn that many fruitless efforts have been made in the past to carry out this arduous task. The narrator cites the efforts of John Bunyan, who had mentioned that "twenty thousand cart-loads of wholesome instructions had been thrown into it" without effecting any improvement. Mr. Smooth-it-away replies that "instructions" could not be expected to provide much material amelioration of conditions. In fact, to construct a foundation, they had thrown in "books of morality, volumes of French philosophy and German rationalism, tracts, sermons, and essays of modern clergymen, extracts from Plato, Confucius, and various Hindoo sages," as well as commentaries on Scripture. He advocates filling the entire bog with similar matter. The narrator, however, observes that the bridge is vibrating and heaving up and down, making him skeptical about its construction.

At the Station House, many passengers await the departure of the cars. There are eminent magistrates, politicians, and men of wealth. There is a ladies' waiting room, where the "flowers of fashionable society" converse pleasantly. Hawthorne remarks ironically that "even an infidel would have heard little or nothing to shock his sensibility." The narrator asks where Mr. Greatheart is, but Mr. Smooth-it-away says he has grown too stiff and narrow to lead the group; moreover, he has had a feud with Prince Beelzebub that might have led to quarrels.

The engine appears, looking like a "mechanical demon." The chief engineer is Apollyon, the enemy of Christian, the hero of *Pilgrim's Progress*. En route to the Celestial City, the train passes a tavern that was a well-known stopping place for pilgrims and mentioned by Bunyan as the Interpreter's House. The train rushes past the place where Christian's burden, in Bunyan's tale, had fallen from his shoulders at the sight of the cross. The passengers discuss their own burdens, which are supplemented by favorite Habits, which they have, however, left in the baggage car.

They reach Hill Difficulty, a rocky mountain through which a tunnel has been constructed. The materials removed have been used to fill up the Valley of Humiliation. The narrator expresses a wish to visit the Palace Beautiful and meet charming young ladies such as Miss Prudence, Miss Piety, and Miss Charity. Mr. Smooth-it-away laughs and answers that they are all old maids now and scarcely recognizable.

The travelers reach a cavernous stopping place, which is a forge for the manufacture of railroad iron. The inhabitants are "strange, half-shaped monsters" with grotesque faces; some are smoking cigars. The narrator sees several who had, he is sure, been passengers on the train in the beginning. One is Mr. Take-it-easy, who has left the train and met old acquaintances. He says the forge is "very warm" and suits him well.

The train continues and eventually reaches the city of Vanity Fair. This is the "capital of human business and pleasure." There the narrator finds an "unlimited range of society," including powerful, wise, and witty people. There are pretty young women, authors, statesmen, speculators, princes, poets, generals, artists, actors, and philanthropists, all dwelling in the city of Vanity. Mr. Smooth-it-away escorts the narrator through the Fair, and he describes all the wares for sale.

Every street in Vanity has its church, and there are many varieties of clergy. Among them are the Reverend Mr. Shallow-deep, the Reverend Mr. Stumble-at-truth, the Reverend Mr. This-to-day, and the Reverend Mr. That-to-morrow, the Reverend Mr. Clog-the-spirit, and the Reverend Dr. Wind-of-doctrine. These "eminent divines" are aided by "innumerable lecturers, who diffuse such a various profundity, in all subjects of human or celestial science, that any man may acquire an omnigenous erudition, without the trouble of even learning to read." One stock or scrip, called Conscience, is in great demand; it is the "only thing of permanent value."

The narrator is warned by Mr. Stick-to-the-right that he will never really reach the Celestial City. The lord of that city has refused to grant an act of incorporation for the railroad, and, without it, no passenger can ever hope to enter his dominions. Moreover, every man who buys a ticket loses the purchase money, which is the "value of his own soul." Mr. Smooth-it-away is scornful, saying that those who are warning the narrator should be indicted for libel. They continue on the railroad toward the Celestial City. They pass over the Enchanted Ground, with visions of fountains, foliage, and fruit.

They then pass through the land of Beulah and reach the Celestial gates. There they see a steam ferryboat, and the narrator hurries on board. His luggage is lost. The narrator is astonished to discover that Mr. Smooth-it-away has not accompanied him, but is standing on the shore waving farewell. To his horror, Mr. Smooth-it-away is then transformed into an apparition of the Devil or Fiend, with lurid flames darting from his eyes. He shouts that he has only traveled this far for the pleasure of the narrator's company. Then he utters a fiendish laugh. The ferry paddle wheels dash would-be passengers with frigid spray.

The narrator wakes "with a shiver and a heartquake" and is extremely grateful to realize it has all been just a dream.

CRITICAL ANALYSIS

"The Celestial Rail-road" is considered by many critics to be an excellent satire of John Bunyan's

Pilgrim's Progress. Hawthorne succeeds in ridiculing human nature without bitterness, adapting Bunyan's emblems to the age of steam with considerable success. Hawthorne is skeptical about efforts to substitute technological advances and tremendous industrial wealth for actual moral progress, as is clear in the story. As long as humans are contemptuous of the reality of "The Slough of Despond," they are not able to enact true reforms. The results will, instead, be only superficial.

Terence Martin terms "The Celestial Rail-road" the best of the "processional" tales, in which Hawthorne describes large groups of people who undertake a journey together, who "move through time or space and thereby illustrate some fundamental truth, or aberration, of human nature" (*Nathaniel Hawthorne,* 30). In this work, Hawthorne makes fun of the "optimistic, pastel religiosity of his day." Martin observes that Hawthorne substitutes a new monster, the German Giant Transcendentalist, for Bunyan's "Pope and Pagan." Although the processionals are not among Hawthorne's best work, their "expansive movement" and their "focus on the collective rather than on the individual" are of interest insofar as they reveal the author's willingness to experiment with form.

FOR FURTHER READING

Martin, Terence, *Nathaniel Hawthorne* (Boston: Twayne, 1983); Pattison, Joseph C., "'The Celestial Rail-road' as Dream-Tale," *American Quarterly* 20 (1968): 224–236; Roulston, C. Robert, "Hawthorne's Use of Bunyan's Symbols in 'The Celestial Rail-road,'" *Kentucky Philological Association Bulletin* (1975): 17–24.

"Chiefly about War-matters"

Satirical essay about the CIVIL WAR, first published in the ATLANTIC MONTHLY in July 1862. It was signed by "A Peaceable Man." Hawthorne had written a frank description of President Lincoln when he first submitted it, but the editor, JAMES T. FIELDS, thought it was in questionable taste and omitted it. The section was published after Hawthorne's death.

Wineapple terms the essay "Swiftian, corrosive and funny" (*Hawthorne: A Life,* 349). Hawthorne suggests sending old men to war rather than young ones and considers war itself a "savage feat of recidivism." At the same time, he makes clear many of his views on larger social issues. Turner observes that Hawthorne was dealing "with immediate and momentous questions" that had divided his relatives and friends (*Nathaniel Hawthorne: A Biography,* 365).

FOR FURTHER READING

Aaron, Daniel, *The Unwritten War: American Writers and the Civil War* (New York: Alfred A. Knopf, 1973); Yokozawa, Shiro, "Nathaniel Hawthorne's Mental Attitude toward the Civil War," *Journal of the English Institute* 11 (1980): 27–41.

"Chimaera, The"

Children's story published in A WONDER-BOOK FOR GIRLS AND BOYS (1852).

As the story opens, a "handsome young man" named Bellerophon approaches the Fountain of Pirene, on a hillside in Greece. He holds a bridle "studded with brilliant gems" and "adorned with a golden bit." He sees an old man, a middle-aged man, a little boy, and a maiden near the fountain. The middle-aged man asks why he carries a bridle but has no horse. Bellerophon replies that he is seeking the "winged horse Pegasus," who was said to drink from this fountain in their "forefathers' days." The middle-aged man mocks him for believing in a winged horse. The "old, gray man" says he "used to believe there was such a horse" when he was a youth but has forgotten the truth. The maiden thinks she has seen him and heard his "brisk and melodious neigh." The little boy "very readily" tells Bellerophon that he has seen Pegasus reflected in the water many times.

Bellerophon watches for the winged horse around the Fountain of Pirene for many days. The "rustic people" of the neighborhood laugh at him, and the "country boys" find him foolish. While he is waiting for Pegasus to appear, the narrator explains Bellerophon's motivation.

A "terrible monster," a Chimaera, is doing much mischief in a country called Lycia. The creature has a lion's head, a goat's head, a snake's head, and a tail like a boa constrictor's. The king, Iobates, asks Bellerophon to fight the Chimaera, for he is "one of the bravest youths in the world." Bellerophon, however, realizes the monster is too swift to fight on foot; he needs "the very best and fleetest horse that could anywhere be found." This is why he has traveled to Greece, with an "enchanted bridle" that will make Pegasus be "submissive" and recognize Bellerophon "for his master."

Finally, after many days of waiting, Bellerophon spots the winged horse. After Pegasus drinks from the fountain and frisks about, he lies down to rest. Bellerophon runs suddenly from his hiding place and leaps onto the horse's back. Pegasus rears and bounds into the air and even turns a somersault, but once the golden bit is in his jaw, he becomes "as manageable as if he had taken food, all his life, out of Bellerophon's hand."

Pegasus and Bellerophon journey to Lycia to find the three-headed Chimaera's cavern. Bellerophon successfully kills the Chimaera with the winged horse's help. After his victory, he returns to the Fountain of Pirene to set Pegasus free, but the horse rests his head on his master's shoulder and refuses to leave him.

"Chippings with a Chisel"

First published in the UNITED STATES MAGAZINE AND DEMOCRATIC REVIEW in September 1838, this sketch recalls Hawthorne's encounter with Mr. Wigglesworth, a dedicated carver of lettering and ornaments on tombstones.

Hawthorne met Wigglesworth at Edgartown, on the island of Martha's Vineyard, Massachusetts. Hawthorne tells him he has no desire for a stone over his own grave; the thoughts of those left behind should "soar upward with the butterfly— not linger with the exuviae that confined him." Mr. Wigglesworth calls him "heathenish" and asks whether he would advise forgetting his friends once they are buried. Hawthorne replies that to remem-

ber them properly, he would forget their cast-off remains. At the same time, he wonders whether life's "dark shadowing," the "sorrows and regrets," might have as much "real comfort" in them as what men call "life's joys."

FOR FURTHER READING

Franklin, Rosemary F., "The Seashore Sketches in *Twice-told Tales* and Melville," *English Language Notes* 21, no. 4 (June 1984): 57–63.

"Christmas Banquet, The"

Subtitled "From the Unpublished 'Allegories of the Heart,'" this story was noted in Hawthorne's journal as early as 1836. It was published in MOSSES FROM AN OLD MANSE in 1846. This is the second of his tales with this subtitle; the other is "EGOTISM; OR, THE BOSOM-SERPENT."

This tale is a recounting of a story that Roderick Elliston, the principal character in "Egotism," has composed. It is a result of his former sad experience of living with a serpent in his bosom, which manifested itself outwardly in his "glittering eyes," undulating walk, and "sickly white" complexion with a "greenish tinge." As told by Elliston, the tale is actually an attack on the lack of substantial existence of people who live in an "ideal" dream world. Hawthorne considers such a world to be warped and unsubstantial.

The story opens in the garden of Roderick Elliston and his wife, Rosina (whose cousin, George Herkimer, a young American sculptor, brought her back to her husband in "Egotism"). Elliston has composed a story as a result of his experience with the serpent. He discusses his story with Rosina and Herkimer. The tale supposedly deals with a definition of the "spiritual" nature of the artist but in fact represents Hawthorne's reaction against the transcendentalist idea of art and artists. This conception held that the artist must become absorbed in the "Over Soul" in order to create anything worthwhile; inspiration must arise from "the current of the invisible." Elliston's story will describe a character who is a "hopeless puzzle," a man who might as well be carved out of marble. He will be endowed with a mockery of intellect but lack the "inestimable touch of a divine Creator." He will be unable to respond to the demands of the spirit. He is seriously flawed because he is "unsubstantial."

Roderick then begins to read a tale about a bequest left by an eccentric old gentleman. It is for the purpose of establishing a substantial fund. The annual interest from this fund is to be expended in preparing a Christmas Banquet for "ten of the most miserable persons that could be found." In this way, the "stern or fierce expression of human discontent" will not be drowned. The purpose of the gathering is to perpetuate the eccentric old gentleman's "sad and sour dissent from those systems of religion or philosophy which either find sunshine in the world, or draw it down from heavens." This is a subtle attack by Hawthorne on the philosophy of transcendentalism, whose proponents are too occupied with fantastic schemes to deal with actual conditions.

The task of inviting the guests to attend the gathering falls to two trustees of the fund. The decorations for the banquet are ordered not to be festive; instead, there is to be a hall hung with deep purple curtains and adorned with branches of cypress and wreaths of artificial flowers. A sprig of parsley should be placed beside each plate. A "sepulchral" silver urn is to be filled with wine. Following an old Egyptian custom, a skeleton shrouded in a black mantle is to sit at the head of the table.

Wohlpart observes that the banquet attacks those who live in the "fantastic world" represented by the juxtaposition of actual human beings suffering misery and the imaginary, shown by the purple curtains. The guests are "blighted, fate-stricken," and "fancy-tortured." When the guests inquire as to the meaning of the wreath of cypress, held on high by a skeleton arm, one of the stewards replies that it is a crown for the "wofullest" of the guests.

Roderick then introduces Gervayse Hastings, the main character in the tale. When he first arrives at the banquet, he is described as a "young man of smooth brow, fair cheek, and fashionable mien." The other guests are mystified by his appearance as he scrutinizes the "ill-starred banqueters." The steward assures them that Hastings has been admitted to the banquet on the basis of a "full investigation and thoughtful balance of his claims." He insists that no other guest at the table is "better entitled to his seat." As the banquet proceeds, however, it is apparent that Hastings is not successful in his "attempts to catch its pervading spirit." He is cold and isolated from the group. He looks miserable and uncomprehending and reacts to utterances of "deep, strong thought" with bewilderment. His conversation lacks the "powerful characteristics of a nature" that has been "developed by suffering." He does not understand the various thoughts and emotions expressed by the guests—to him they are merely shadows of the actual world.

At the next year's Christmas Banquet, Hastings returns, apparently sneering at the other guests' "gloomy figures." One man, with a "blood-stain on his conscience," is sure that Hastings has never "passed through the dark valley." A lady asks him to depart, since his soul "has never been shaken." Another guest, Mr. Smith, says he knows the lad well, is sure he has fair prospects, and, therefore, he has no right to be among them. The stewards, however, beg the guests to receive Hastings, pleading that he does indeed have sorrows, and that no guests at the table would exchange his own heart "for the one that beats within that youthful bosom." A man dies of a heart attack at the banquet, and the other guests are horrified. They observe that Hastings is gazing at the man without emotion and ask him why he is not trembling. Hastings replies that he would welcome the experience of having more feelings. He complains that men pass before him "like shadows on the wall—their actions, passions, feelings, are flickerings of the light—and then they vanish!" No one is able to give him what he seeks.

Gervayse Hastings alone is invited to all of the subsequent banquets, but he remains cold and isolated. He attends the banquet every year, and every year he is more miserable. Those who know Hastings have little fondness for him. His children are cold toward him and his wife weeps openly. He becomes middle-aged and then old. He has never felt grief, though. By the time he becomes an old man, he has still been unaffected by time; he has no "life within a life."

At the final banquet, it becomes clear that the banqueters, with the exception of Hastings, have grown in character because of their suffering. The veiled skeleton of the founder of the banquet sits opposite Hastings, who is now a withered figure, "stately, calm, and cold." Hastings is asked what lessons he has learned from attending the banquets, but he answers that he knows only his own misfortune. He is asked what misfortunes he has suffered. Hastings replies that no one will understand, but he feels as though his heart is a "thing of vapor"; he has possessed neither "joys nor griefs" in his whole life. He is unable to establish relationships with other people. He then grows cold and seemingly dies, since his shadow ceases to flicker on the wall.

When the tale is finished, Roderick and Rosina discuss its meaning. Rosina says she has an "idea" of Gervayse Hastings, but it is only because of her own thought. He is an intellectual concept, an unsubstantial idea with little connection to "the human heart." Gervayse Hastings does not establish any relationships with other people and never becomes a "real" character to the reader.

Roderick Elliston, who has been writing this story, says that if Hastings could have "imbibed one human grief," he could have described his character better and depicted him as a more sympathetic human being. However, Hastings is a "moral monster" and has lived "on the outside of everything."

Wohlport remarks that the story "depicts that type of artistic creativity that is based solely on the imagination and has no connection to humanity." He observes that Hawthorne, in describing a central figure who is only a concept, an abstraction, ensures that the tale will remain known as a work of imagination only. It "remains unconnected in any way to the actual" ("Allegories of Art, Allegories of Heart: Hawthorne's 'Egotism' and 'The Christmas Banquet,'" *Studies in Short Fiction* [summer 1994]: 455).

RECEPTION AND CRITICAL ANALYSIS

The story belongs to a group of artist stories Hawthorne produced, including "The ARTIST OF THE BEAUTIFUL." It deals with the difficulties faced by the artist and the illusory nature of art as a whole. In placing a premium on the artist's use of the imagination, however, Hawthorne causes a rift between him and humanity at large; as a result the artist is afflicted with a frigid heart and a tendency toward diseased self-contemplation. This condition can only be corrected by the devotion and love of a wife. Gervayse Hastings, however, does not have this comfort. He is alienated from life and in fact represents the "moral monster" Hawthorne himself had feared he would become before he met and fell in love with Sophia.

Two literary sources have been proposed for the story: Voltaire's *Candide,* in which there is a banquet for miserable people (Davidson, "Voltaire and Hawthorne's 'Christmas Banquet'"), and Samuel Johnson's *Rambler,* nos. 82 and 105 (Davidson, "Hawthorne's Use of a Pattern from the *Rambler*"). "The Christmas Banquet" also focuses on the theme of the isolation of the artist, as do several of Hawthorne's other short stories, including "The BIRTH-MARK" and "RAPPACCINI'S DAUGHTER."

As an allegory, the story has attracted severe criticism. Edgar Allan Poe declared that Hawthorne was "infinitely too fond of allegory, and can never hope for popularity as long as he persists in it" ("Review of *Twice-told Tales,*" *Graham's Magazine* 20 [April–May 1842]: 254). Henry James concurred: "It has never seemed to me, as it were, a first-rate literary form . . . it is apt to spoil two good things—a story and a moral, a meaning and a form" (*Hawthorne* [New York: Harper, 1879]).

A more enthusiastic Herman Melville wrote anonymously in "Hawthorne and His Mosses" (*Literary World,* August 17 and 24, 1850). Responding to characterizations of Hawthorne as a merely "pleasant writer," he declared "The Christmas Banquet" a "fine" subject "for a curious and elaborate analysis," exhibiting the "hither side of Hawthorne's soul." Hawthorne "availed himself of this mystical blackness" to produce "wondrous effects" in his writing. Melville charged that "perhaps no writer has ever wielded this terrific thought with greater terror than this same harmless Hawthorne," whom he described as "immeasurably deeper than the plummet of the mere critic." The two writers met in the Berkshires in western Massachusetts.

FOR FURTHER READING

Davidson, Frank, "Hawthorne's Use of a Pattern from the *Rambler,*" *Modern Language Notes* 63

(1948): 545–558; Davidson, Frank, "Voltaire and Hawthorne's 'The Christmas Banquet,'" *Boston Public Library Quarterly* 3 (1951): 244–246; Shinn, Thelma J., "A Fearful Power: Hawthorne's Views on Art and the Artist as Expressed in His Sketches and Short Stories," *Nathaniel Hawthorne Journal* 8 (1978): 121–135; Wohlpart, A. James, "Allegories of Art, Allegories of Heart: Hawthorne's 'Egotism' and 'The Christmas Banquet,'" *Studies in Short Fiction* (summer 1994): 449–461.

"Circe's Palace"

Story published in TANGLEWOOD TALES FOR GIRLS AND BOYS in 1853.

The narrative opens with background on King Ulysses, who after the siege of Troy spends 10 years journeying back to Ithaca. During his voyage, he faces, among other things, a "terrible hurricane" and the "monstrous giants" of Laestrygonia. After such trials, he is happy to reach a pleasant green island.

Ulysses decides to explore the island to see whether he can find food for his hungry men. From a clifftop, he sees a distant palace of "snow-white marble" with "stately towers." He assumes it is the "residence of some great nobleman or prince," who may have a "plentiful banquet" of food.

As he sets off for the palace, he encounters a "pretty little bird" with a "circle of golden feathers round its neck, and on its head a golden tuft, which looked like a king's crown in miniature." After the bird tries to "drive him back," Ulysses thinks it knows of "some danger that awaited him." He decides to return to the ship, and on his way he is able to kill a stag for his hungry men.

The next day, Ulysses proposes that the men form two parties, one of which will go to the palace to ask for food. Then, if its inhabitants prove "inhospitable," the remainder of the men will be able to escape. It is decided that Eurylochus, a chief officer, will lead 22 men to the palace, while Ulysses and the others stay behind. Eurylochus meets the same purple bird and is inclined to turn back, but most of his men disagree.

They continue on their way, but as they approach the palace, they are met by a pack of lions, tigers, and wolves. Instead of devouring them, however, the beasts wag their tails and behave as "well-bred house dogs." Still, Eurylochus thinks he sees "something fierce and savage" in their eyes, for their "mildness seemed unreal." The men enter the palace and see a fountain that takes on various shapes, possibly by magic. They hear a woman's voice singing, the noise of a loom, and other voices talking and laughing. Although Eurylochus reminds his men that even a "young maiden" can cause harm, as did she who "beguiled three of our friends into the palace of the king of the Laestrygons," his companions cannot be dissuaded. While he waits behind a pillar in the outer hall, the others head into the next room.

The men are greeted by a beautiful woman and four others. The beautiful woman shows them the tapestry she has been weaving in her loom. They are astonished to see representations of "their own figures" on recent adventures. She invites the hungry men to dine in a "magnificent saloon," where they are encouraged to "eat their fill" and "quaff wine abundantly," but when the men are not looking, the women laugh and even the servants "grin and sneer." The hungry mariners swill their liquor and gobble their food "like pigs in a sty." Then the beautiful woman points at each man with a "slender rod," her face smiling in a "wicked and mischievous" manner. She tells them they have "abused a lady's hospitality" with behavior "suited to a hog-pen." Because they are "already swine in everything but the human form," they are turned into hogs by the enchantress, who then drives them out into the back yard.

Meanwhile, Eurylochus is waiting behind the pillar in the entrance hall. He hears first the sounds of a feast, and then a "tremendous grunting and squealing" and "sudden scampering." At the "swinish uproar" resounding through the palace, he flees back to the ship to tell Ulysses what has transpired.

Ulysses sets off to rescue his comrades, but, once again, meets the purple bird crying and "using all the art it could to persuade him to go no farther." As he continues on the path, he meets a young man wearing a cloak and winged cap, and carrying a staff carved with two serpents. Ulysses immediately recognizes him as Quicksilver.

Quicksilver tells him the island is enchanted by the wicked Circe, who "changes every human being into the brute, beast, or fowl whom he happens most to resemble." The purple bird was once King Picus, who was "rather too proud of his purple robe, and his crown, and the golden chain about his neck." The lions, wolves, and tigers were once "fierce and cruel men." Quicksilver gives Ulysses a "rare and precious" white flower, advising him to "smell of it frequently" while in the palace in order to defy Circe's magic.

When Ulysses reaches the palace, Circe welcomes him and leads him into the saloon. She gives him a goblet of enchanted wine, but Ulysses holds the white flower to his nose, and it protects him from her mischief. He then draws his sword and seizes Circe, who begs to be spared. After she gives a "solemn oath to change back his companions," he lets her go.

Circe transforms the swine back into men, and the purple bird back into a king. Ulysses lets the lions, tigers, and wolves remain as they are, however, and "thus give warning of their cruel dispositions, instead of going about under the guise of men." After he summons the rest of his men, they all rest and refresh themselves in Circe's enchanted palace.

"Civic Banquets"

Unsigned essay about speech making first published in the ATLANTIC MONTHLY in August 1863.

"Consular Experiences"

Sketch of English life first published in *Our Old Home* (1863).

"David Swan—A Fantasy"

An unsigned tale that first appeared in *The* TOKEN AND ATLANTIC SOUVENIR in 1837. It was reprinted several times, including in TWICE-TOLD TALES in 1837, sometimes with "A Fantasy" added. When first printed, it had no attribution. The editor, Samuel Goodrich, was guilty of printing several other pieces by Hawthorne without his name. Hawthorne's friend HORATIO BRIDGE warned him about the danger of this practice:

"The Token" is out, and I suppose you are getting your book ready for publication. . . . I hope to God that you will put your name upon the title-page, and come before the world at once and on your own responsibility. You could not fail to make a noise and an honorable name, and something besides.

"I've been thinking how singularly you stand among the writers of the day; known by name to very few, and yet your writings admired more than any others with which they are ushered forth. . . . Your articles in the last "Token" alone are enough to give you a respectable name, if you were known as their author." (Daniel G. Hoffman, "Myth, Romance, and the Childhood of Man," in *Hawthorne Centenary Essays*, edited by Roy Harvey Pearce, 197–219 [Columbus: Ohio State University Press, 1964].

The title character is a 20-year-old man from New Hampshire who is traveling to Boston to work for his uncle, owner of a grocery store. After half a day of walking, the young man falls asleep in the shade while waiting for the stagecoach. Various travelers, including a middle-aged widow, take admiring notice of him. A temperance lecturer sees him as "an awful instance of dead drunkenness by the road-side." David Swan sleeps through it all.

A wealthy couple whose son has died stop nearby so their servants can repair a faulty carriage wheel. They are drawn to David's "open countenance" and "innocent sleep," so much so that they almost waken him and make him their heir, but then feel foolish and drive on.

A "pretty young girl," daughter of a successful merchant, approaches and chases a monstrous bee away from the sleeping David. She admires him, blushes, and continues on her way.

Two men with dark faces, rascals "who got their living by whatever the devil sent them," pass by and almost rob him but are chased away by a dog that suddenly appears. Through it all, David sleeps quietly, "neither conscious of the shadow of death when it hung over him, nor of the glow of renewed life."

David eventually awakens and hails a commercial carriage. He continues his journey to Boston, unaware that he has been visited by phantoms of Wealth, Love, and Death. Hawthorne concludes that despite the intrusion of "viewless and unexpected events" in our paths through life, Providence provides enough regularity to render "foresight" at least "partially available." David's story ends, for most readers, with little insight into his character or motivation.

RECEPTION AND CRITICAL ANALYSIS

Since Hawthorne returned to the home of his mother after college, and lived there for 12 years, some biographers have interpreted the story as autobiographical. It has been called a "dream" story, in which what happens to a character while he is sleeping is related after he wakes. The 20th-century critic James Folsom suggests that the story projects a universe in which there is a relationship between the ultimate reality and the everyday world.

Hawthorne's contemporary Horatio Bridge, in a review in the April 5, 1837, issue of *Age*, observes that the story is "a conception which will impress some readers very strongly, while others will see little merit in it." He deems the "execution" of the story "admirable," along with the author's ability "ingeniously" to illustrate the "dreamlike flow" of events so that the "passing scenes" seem "rather like visions sweeping past the sleeping David than like realities."

Elizabeth Palmer Peabody, in the March 24, 1838, *New-Yorker*, delights in the story's "quietness," the "apparent leisure" with which Hawthorne "lingers around the smallest point of fact, and unfolds therefrom a world of thought, just as if nothing else existed in the outward universe but that of which he is speaking." She remarks that the "hurried manner that seems to have become the American habit—the spirit of the steam-engine and railroad, has never entered into him." For Peabody, the plot of "David Swan" is evidence of Hawthorne's belief that "every man's mind is the centre of the whole universe—the *primum mobile*—itself at rest, which wheels all phenomena, in lesser or greater circles, around it."

For Andrew Preston Peabody, the story is "a leaf out of the everyday book of life, illustrating the safe and narrow path by which a kind Providence guides us between hidden precipices and chasms, by unseen pitfalls both of sorrow and of deceptive joy" (*Christian Examiner and General Review*, November 1838).

FOR FURTHER READING

Folsom, James F., *Man's Accidents and God's Purposes: Multiplicity in Hawthorne's Fiction* (New Haven, Conn.: College and University Press, 1953), 22–24; Male, Roy R., *Hawthorne's Tragic Vision* (Austin: University of Texas Press, 1947), 6.

"Devil in Manuscript, The"

Tale first published in NEW-ENGLAND MAGAZINE in December 1835, signed "Ashley A. Royce." It was later collected in *The* SNOW-IMAGE, AND OTHER TWICE-TOLD TALES (1852).

Hawthorne and his Bowdoin friend HORATIO BRIDGE had chosen "new signatures" to use in their correspondence; Bridge was "Edward" and Hawthorne "Oberon," the king of fairies in *A Midsummer Night's Dream* (Miller, *Salem Is My Dwelling Place*, 96). Oberon is a writer and an intimate friend of the narrator in this tale.

The narrator assumes the role of Horatio Bridge, a friend of Hawthorne the writer and student at law, here known as "Oberon," in order to comment on his own work. The narrator finds the poet Oberon in a state of unrest. As Oberon looks at his writings, he declares that the devil is in them and he plans to burn them. They have drawn him away from the beaten path of the world, and no one will publish them (he has tried 17 publishers). He believes there is a demon in his manuscripts. The loyal friend is shocked and suggests various remedies, such as pulling the nose of the publisher or publishing his work himself. Secretly, he has concluded that Oberon's tales "would make a more brilliant appearance in the fire than anywhere else."

The narrator and Oberon share a bottle of champagne, which causes Oberon to draw the tales back toward himself, "like a father taking a deformed infant into his arms." He recalls the circumstances of composition of his various tales—the moods in which he wrote, his work polishing and brightening them, and his frustrations. As Oberon tosses more wood on the fire, the visitor recalls many excellent passages in his work showing "high imagination" and "deep pathos." He tries in vain to dissuade Oberon from burning his work.

Heedless, Oberon throws all of them into the fire and imagines them as standing "like martyrs amid the flames." The earth flares up with a "lurid brightness" and throws off a "broad sheet of fire." The extinguished embers stir to life and fly up the chimney, setting the entire building on fire. Oberon has lost all sense of reality and believes his tales have gone out and "startled thousands in fear and wonder from their beds." He thinks his brain has "set the town on fire" and is triumphant.

Oberon is similar to detached observers in Hawthorne's works, such as Kenyon in *The MARBLE FAUN* and Holgrave in *The HOUSE OF THE SEVEN GABLES*. All are spectators, commenting liberally on events but not, themselves centrally involved for the most part. Marius Bewley imagines Oberon as burning his manuscript to atone for his antisocial behavior, not unlike Ethan Brand, who commits suicide in the lime kiln (Bewley, Marius, *The Complex Fate: Hawthorne, Henry James, and Some Other American Writers* [New York: Gordian Press, 1967], 61). Another scholar, Jean Normand, suggests that the story reenacts Hawthorne's sense of isolation after his accident in 1818, when he became a semiinvalid after suffering an injury to his foot (*Nathaniel Hawthorne: An Approach to an Analysis of Artistic Creation*, translated by Derek Coltman [Cleveland: Case Western University Press, 1969], 8–15). Whether or not these identifications can be completely defended, there is no doubt that, in the early stages of his writing career Hawthorne was mistreated by some editors and ignored by others. He often felt frustrated, and his alienation is arguably reflected in "The Devil in Manuscript."

FOR FURTHER READING

Doubleday, Neal Frank, *Hawthorne's Early Tales: A Critical Study* (Durham, N.C.: Duke University Press, 1972); Williamson, James L. "'Young Goodman Brown': Hawthorne's 'Devil in Manuscript,'" *Studies in Short Fiction*, 18, no. 2 (spring 1981): 155–162.

Doctor Grimshaw's Secret

In 1860, Hawthorne began a romance based on the attempt of an American to reclaim his English inheritance. He abandoned the work after beginning two drafts. His son, JULIAN HAWTHORNE, used the two drafts to put together a work he published in 1882 as *Doctor Grimshawe's Secret,* and in 1883, he supplied the *Century Magazine* with Hawthorne's notes for *Doctor Grimshaw's Secret* (Turner, *Nathaniel Hawthorne: A Biography,* 378–379).

FOR FURTHER READING

Wineapple, Brenda, "The Biographical Imperative; or, Hawthorne Family Values," in *Biography and Source Studies* 6, edited by Frederick Karl (New York: AMS Press, 1998).

Dolliver Romance, The

Hawthorne planned a novel with this title that was never completed. He wanted to write a sketch of HENRY DAVID THOREAU, who died in 1862, as a preface to it. The sketch would have incorporated the legend of a man who believed he would not die; Hawthorne had heard this legend from Thoreau. The incomplete manuscript of the novel lay on Hawthorne's coffin at his funeral in 1864 (Leary, *Nathaniel Hawthorne,* 189–190).

In 1876, three fictional fragments were published posthumously under the title *The Dolliver Romance.*

"Dragon's Teeth, The"

A children's story published in *TANGLEWOOD TALES*, 1853.

As the story opens, Cadmus, Phoenix, and Cilix, the three sons of King Agenor, and their beautiful little sister, Europa, are playing in a meadow near the seashore in their father's kingdom of Phoenicia. The three boys gather flowers and make them into garlands "with which to adorn little Europa."

The boys run off to chase a "splendid butterfly," but Europa briefly falls asleep in the grass. She wakens to find a "snow-white bull" not far from her. Startled, she calls out to her brothers, but they do not hear her.

After she recovers from her initial fright, she sees that the bull is quite beautiful and gazes at her tenderly. He runs little races and eats clover out of her hand; she strokes his forehead and hangs her own flower garlands on him. When he realizes Europa is no longer afraid of him, he is "overjoyed" and can "hardly contain himself for delight." He frisks through the meadow, full of gratitude.

He kneels at her feet and indicates that he wishes to give her a ride. She climbs on his back and the bull races with her to the plain where her brothers are. She "scream[s] with delight," while her dumbfounded brothers stand "gaping at the spectacle of their sister mounted on a white bull, not knowing whether to be frightened or to wish the same good luck for themselves." The bull prances "round among the children as sportively as a kitten."

The girl then rides away on the bull but still feels "a little remnant of fear" in her heart. The bull races with her into the sea and Europa screams, but her brothers cannot save her. When the boys tell their father, King Agenor, what has happened, he orders them to bring her back, and not to enter his presence until they do. Queen Telephassa, their mother, weeps bitterly and insists on accompanying them on the search. Their playfellow Thasus arrives to help. All of the children and the queen leave to search for Europa. As they depart the palace, King Agenor calls after them, "Remember! Never ascend these steps again without the child!"

Year after year, the group searches for Europa, but they cannot find her. They ask every farmer if he has seen the bull, but none of them has. Their royal clothes are in tatters, so they exchange them for lowly attire. Soon they resemble a "gypsy family" more than a queen, three princes, and a young nobleman.

Phoenix grows "weary of rambling hither and thither to no purpose" and feels it is a "mere foolish waste of life." He gives up and, because his father has forbidden him to return to the palace, says he will build a "hut of branches" and dwell in it. The others help Phoenix build a "comfortable," "home-like" "sweet rural bower." Over the years, a city grows up around his hut, which eventually becomes "a stately palace of marble" from which Phoenix rules over his new subjects.

The others continue onward on their search, but they often, "at the close of a weary day's journey," recall the pleasant spot where they left Phoenix.

Cilix is the next to give up the search, as he believes there is "no substance" in the life they are leading. The others refuse to follow his example, but they first help him build his own habitation. As they say good-bye, Cilix cries out that "it seemed just as melancholy a dream to stay there, in solitude, as to go onward," but his mother bids him to stay behind "if his own heart would let him." Soon a city grows up around Cilix's hut, too, and he is proclaimed king.

One morning, Thasus sprains his ankle and is unable to continue the search. He stays behind and builds a bower; it, too, grows into a "thriving city" and he becomes a king.

Telephassa and Cadmus continue their search. Telephassa is very weary, finds a "solitary spot," and stays there for what she calls "a good long rest," bidding Cadmus to "wander no more on this hopeless search" but instead to go to Delphi and "inquire of the oracle" what to do next. She then dies and is buried there.

Cadmus continues to Delphi and asks the oracle where to look for his sister. The voice of the oracle says he must "seek her no more," but "follow the cow" and make his home where it lies down. He sees a brindled cow and follows her a great distance, despite his fatigue. It seems as if "there were something about the animal that bewitched people," since several other people join them.

The secret of the cow is that it is enchanted: The people "could not possibly help following her, though all the time they fancied themselves doing it of their own accord." The others grow "very fond" of Cadmus and resolve "to help him build a city wherever the cow might lie down." She finally lies down on "a fertile and lovely plain." Cadmus and his companions settle there. Suddenly an immense dragon appears, kills his companions, and devours them. Cadmus kills the dragon with his sword.

As he laments the "melancholy fate which had befallen those poor, friendly people" and wonders whether he is "doomed to lose everybody whom he loved," Cadmus hears a voice telling him to pluck out the dragon's teeth and plant them. He does so and sees the Sun shining over the field. Men with swords and spears spring up, along with trumpeters. He is told to throw a stone into the midst of the armed men. He does so, and they begin fighting one another.

Finally, only five warriors are left. They are "the boldest and strongest of the whole army." The voice says they will help him build a city. They do so and construct a home for each man but leave the building of the palace for last. When the men go to lay the foundation for the palace, they discover "the most magnificent palace that had ever been seen in the world," which "had grown up out of the earth in almost as short a time as it had taken the armed host to spring from the dragon's teeth."

The workmen call Cadmus king. He sees a beautiful stranger, who the voice says is Harmonia, a "daughter of the sky, who is given you instead of sister, and brothers, and friend, and mother." The voice tells him he "will find all those dear ones in her alone." As the years go by, they dwell happily in the palace with "a group of rosy little children," who are taught by the five old soldiers.

Cadmus teaches the children "their A B C— which he invented for their benefit," "lest there should be too much of the dragon's tooth in his children's disposition." Many little people, the narrator remarks, "are not half so grateful to him as they ought to be."

"Dr. Bullivant"

An unsigned historical portrait of a Puritan apothecary, written by Hawthorne, that appeared in the *Salem Gazette* on January 11, 1831. Turner remarks

that in carrying out research on New England history to look for possible subjects, Hawthorne had "an eye to the definition and growth of the national character and to broad human and moral problems as well" (Turner, *Nathaniel Hawthorne: A Biography*, 56).

"Dr. Heidegger's Experiment"

Tale first published as "The FOUNTAIN OF YOUTH" (unsigned) in KNICKERBOCKER, or *New-York Monthly Magazine*, in January 1837. The editor, LEWIS GAYLORD CLARK, who had solicited the story, wrote to Hawthorne after it was published, thanking him and offering laudatory comments. He declared that he had "rarely read anything which delighted" him more.

As the story opens, Dr. Heidegger has invited four venerable friends to meet him in his study. They are Mr. Medbourne, Colonel Killigrew, and Mr. Gascoigne, along with a "withered gentlewoman," the Widow Wycherly. All have been unfortunate in life and are now "melancholy old creatures . . . whose greatest misfortune it was that they were not long ago in their graves." Mr. Medbourne had been a prosperous merchant at one time, but unfortunate speculations have caused him to lose his wealth; he is now "little better than a mendicant." Colonel Killigrew had been addicted to the pursuit of "sinful pleasures" and had wasted his best years. He is now afflicted with gout and "divers other torments of soul and body." Mr. Gascoigne had once been a promising politician, but his reputation has declined and he is now a man of "evil fame," ruined in the political arena. Time has buried him from the "knowledge of the present generation, and made him obscure instead of infamous." The Widow Wycherly had been a great beauty in her day, but she has now lived for many years in deep seclusion, thanks to the "scandalous stories" that have circulated about her and "prejudiced the gentry of the town against her." Each of the three gentlemen had been an early lover of the Widow Wycherly.

Dr. Heidegger's study is a "very curious place, festooned with cobwebs and besprinkled with antique dust." It contains many strange possessions, including a bust of Hippocrates, a skeleton, and a full-length portrait of a young woman who had "died on the bridal evening" before marrying the doctor, as well as a large folio volume bound in black leather, reputed to be a book of magic. When touched, the book causes the skeleton to rattle and the young lady in the portrait to put one foot on the floor.

The doctor tells his friends he wants to perform an experiment in his study and he needs their assistance. The friends acquiesce, and he takes a large book, the "magic folio," to the table. He opens it and takes out a dried rose. He says it was given him by Sylvia Ward (the lady in the portrait) and he had in fact planned to wear it at their wedding. He says it can bloom again and throws the rose into a vase of water; a friend has sent him the water. It promptly blooms. The friends consider it a conjurer's trick.

The doctor asks whether they have heard of the "Fountain of Youth" for which Ponce De Leon searched in vain. He assures them that De Leon had not searched in the right place. He offers them some of his miraculous water, within which bubbles constantly rise. He warns them that if they drink it, they will pass again through the "perils of youth" but will become patterns of virtue for the young.

They drink the water, which makes them feel young and cheerful again. They demand more, and their appearance becomes youthful. They compliment one another on their youthful looks and verify them in the mirror. They begin singing youthful songs and become preoccupied with themes and projects dating from their youth. The more they drink of the water, the younger they become. The Widow Wycherly dances with each of the men.

They beg for more of the "wondrous water." They cry, "We are younger—but we are still too old! Quick—give us more!" The doctor fills their glasses and then refills them. With "philosophic coolness," he remarks, "You have been a long time growing old. Surely, you might be content to grow young in half an hour! But the water is at your service."

Colonel Killigrew compliments the Widow Wycherly on her increasing youth. When she rushes to see her appearance in a mirror, she finds that she has indeed grown younger looking. She stands before the mirror "courtesying and simpering to her own image, and greeting it as the friend whom she loved better than all the world beside."

The guests have another draught of the Fountain of Youth and then another. The men begin vying for the attentions of the Widow Wycherly. They struggle with one another. Their exertions are so violent that the table is overturned and the vase broken. The "Water of Youth" flows across the floor, moistening the wings of a butterfly that "had alighted there to die." The butterfly now flies through the room and settles on Dr. Heidegger's head. He gazes at Sylvia's rose, which appears to be fading. It shrivels up and becomes dry and fragile. "I love it as well thus as in its dewy freshness," he says. The butterfly flutters down from the doctor's head and falls upon the floor. All four friends shiver and soon grow old again. The doctor is reconciled to age, but the four friends have learned nothing from the experience and resolve to make a pilgrimage to Florida, where they can drink from the Fountain of Youth "at morning, noon, and night."

RECEPTION AND CRITICAL ANALYSIS

"Dr. Heidegger's Experiment" explores Hawthorne's intense fascination with the elixir of life. The four friends are not at all improved by momentarily regaining their youth, although the tale has a certain degree of vigor and much charm. The story has a few revealing biographical overtones, suggesting that it represents one of Hawthorne's conversations with himself. It is, moreover, one of the fullest expressions in the author's fiction of his fascination with the idea of an elixir that promises eternal life. In addition, the story "reveals the fascination with the moral implications of science" that Hawthorne develops in later work (Grant, William E., "Nathaniel Hawthorne," *Dictionary of Literary Biography,* Vol. 74, edited by Bobby Ellen Kimbel [Detroit: Gale Research, 1988]).

Edgar Allan Poe called the story "exceedingly well imagined" and "executed with surpassing ability" in *Graham's Magazine* (May 1842).

Park Benjamin, in the March 1838 *American Monthly Magazine,* remarked that some of Hawthorne's work, including "Dr. Heidegger's Experiment," "rivals Irving himself in occasional graphic thoughts and phrases, and partakes not a little of his picturesque mode of viewing a topic." The story of the four venerable friends "transformed into as many gay, frisking creatures in 'the happy prime of youth'" "struck" the critic as "a very apt companion-piece to Irving's 'Mutability of Literature.'"

In the March 10, 1837, issue of the Boston *Daily Advertiser,* the anonymous reviewer of TWICE-TOLD TALES wrote that "Mr. Hawthorne is endowed, in no inconsiderable degree," with "the mysterious essence called genius." But the critic continues by observing that the "contents of his volume are of unequal merit," and he prefers "the grace and sweetness of such papers as 'Little Annie's Ramble,' or 'A Rill from the Town-pump,' to those of a more ambitious cast, and in which the page glows with a wider and more fearful interest, like 'The Minister's Black Veil' and 'Dr. Heidegger's Experiment.'"

Twentieth-century critics received the story with mixed reactions. Some condemned it; others, such as Neal Doubleday, praised it. Doubleday terms it "a little masterpiece, without fault of taste or failure in tone." He admires Hawthorne's "controlled tension," which, in his opinion, swings between the comic surface and the deeper, highly somber implications of the tale. Laurence Scanlon, writing in *Nineteenth-Century Fiction,* sees the story as a caricature and a demonstration of Hawthorne's use of irony. He focuses on Hawthorne's use of the word *venerable* to describe friends who are not venerable. He sees Dr. Heidegger as a caricature of Hawthorne himself; he is mocking his own experiments with fiction.

Janice L. Willms observes that unlike Hawthorne's other stories about "wicked scientists" whose experiments "result in the death of one who is ignorant of the power of the science," this "little vignette" is "airy." Dr. Heidegger's "intent seems to be benign," in contrast to that of the scientists in "The BIRTH-MARK" and "RAPPACCINI'S DAUGHTER." No one in this story dies, and the "experimental effects are reversible." Still, there is "a hint of the sinister" in Hawthorne's description of the doctor's study, as well as in Heidegger's decision "not to partake of the magic liquid" with his guests.

FOR FURTHER READING

Doubleday, Neal Frank, *Hawthorne's Early Tales: A Critical Study* (Durham, N.C.: Duke University Press, 1972); Gibbens, Victor E., "Hawthorne's Note to 'Dr. Heidegger's Experiment,'" *Modern Language Notes* 60, no. 6 (June 1945): 408–409; Hastings, Louise, "An Origin for "Dr. Heidegger's Experiment," *American Literature: A Journal of Literary History, Criticism, and Bibiography* 9, no. 4 (January 1938): 403–410; Scanlon, Lawrence E., "That Very Singular Man, Dr. Heidegger," *Nineteenth-Century Fiction* 17, no. 3 (December 1962): 253–263.

"Drowne's Wooden Image"

Tale first published in *Godey's Magazine and Lady's Book* in July 1844. It was signed "By Nathaniel Hawthorne, Author of 'Twice Told Tales,' etc." and was the only one of Hawthorne's works to be published in *Godey's.* It was collected in MOSSES FROM AN OLD MANSE, vol. 2, in 1846.

It is uncertain when and where Hawthorne wrote the story. It was possibly composed in February or March 1844, when he and Sophia were living at the Old Manse. Some critics, however, have assigned the tale to an earlier period.

"Drowne's Wooden Image" is set in early Boston. Drowne, a young wood carver, is about to transform a large oak log into a ship's figurehead, but he has not decided upon the exact shape. The owner of the brig *Cynosure,* Captain Hunnewell, who has commissioned him to carve a figurehead for the ship, wants "such a figure head as old Neptune never saw in his life." The exact nature of Drowne's creation will be a strict secret; Drowne is sworn not to betray any details. Drowne suggests various designs, including a likeness of the king and a carving of Britannia with the trident. The captain then privately describes what he has in mind.

Hawthorne interrupts the narrative to explain that Drowne is the first American to have attempted to depict the human figure in nautical figureheads. Having carved ornamental pump heads, wooden urns for gate posts, and decorations "more grotesque than fanciful" for mantelpieces, he has gone on to create figureheads for vessels, "decked out in gorgeous colours" and "magnificently gilded."

The captain urges Drowne to get to work on his figurehead, and Drowne does so at odd hours and in strict secrecy. Eventually, however, his friends perceive that a female figure is taking shape.

The "celebrated painter" John Singleton Copley, then a young man, visits Drowne. He has "recognized so much of moderate ability in the carver, as to induce him, in the dearth of any professional sympathy, to cultivate his acquaintance." He looks about the workshop and sees Drowne's "inflexible images of king, commander, dame, and allegory." In Copley's opinion, Drowne's images lack spirit and do not resemble living people; in none of the figureheads "did it seem as if the wood were imbibing the ethereal essence of humanity." Copley calls Drowne a "remarkable person" and says he has seldom met with another man who "could do so much." He says Drowne's depiction of General Wolfe is nearly a "breathing and intelligent human creature." Though Copley tries to praise the work, Drowne sees through the guarded comments and acknowledges that they are true. But he assures the painter that "a light" has entered his mind since the previous works were created.

Copley then sees a remarkable "half-developed figure" in a corner of the workshop, carved by an "inspired hand." She is full of promise, although she remains incomplete. He admires it greatly and terms Drowne "a modern Pygmalion in the person of a Yankee mechanic."

The figurehead gradually takes shape. Copley visits every day to see it and perceives that it is a female in "foreign dress," wearing a "hat of singular gracefulness," a "chain about the neck," a "watch in the bosom," and other ornaments. Copley is astonished at its quality and terms it "as ideal as an antique statue, and yet as real as any lovely woman whom one meets at a fireside or in the street." He only wishes the figure were in marble and hopes Drowne will not "desecrate" the "exquisite creature" by painting her.

Captain Hunnewell, however, urges Drowne to paint the figure, as his ship will be ridiculed in foreign ports if it has an "unpainted oaken stick" over the prow. Drowne agrees that she should be painted, explaining that he is relying on a "well-spring of inward wisdom" gained as he works upon the figure. Copley realizes the "very spirit of genius" in Drowne, for "how otherwise should this carver feel himself entitled to transcend all rules, and make me ashamed of quoting them?" As he gazes at Drowne, Copley sees an "expression of human love," which is the "secret of the life that had been breathed into this block of wood."

Drowne does paint her, enhancing Copley's sense that she is actually a "creature" of his heart. He finishes the figure and throws opens his door to the townspeople so that they may see his work. They are stunned by her beauty and presence. Copley even fancies that the image is "secretly enjoying the perplexed admiration of himself and all other beholders."

Copley assumes that Drowne plans to make his fortune by selling her and encourages him to send the "fairy queen" to England, where she might earn him a thousand pounds. Drowne, however, insists he has not created the figure for money. There is a rumor that Drowne has been seen "kneeling at the feet" of the figure and "gazing with a lover's passionate ardor" into her face. The "bigots" in town hint that it would not be surprising if an "evil spirit" were to "enter this beautiful form, and seduce the carver to destruction."

As Drowne's creation becomes famous, people travel from far and wide to see her. One morning, the captain of the *Cynosure* emerges from his house with a "young lady in a foreign habit" on his arm. She is identical to Drowne's image in every respect, strolling along and fluttering her fan so rapidly that it breaks. An elderly Puritan man declares that Drowne has sold his soul to the devil. Others exclaim that the image has come to life.

The captain and the young woman go to Drowne's door and disappear inside. Copley follows the couple into the shop and sees the wooden image "in her usual corner," where Drowne is mending her beautiful fan. Captain Hunnewell is not in the studio, but his voice can be heard from "the other side of a door that opened upon the water." He is urging a lady to sit down in his ship. Copley, with "a smile of intelligence," proclaims Drowne a "truly fortunate man." He remarks that the beautiful young lady was the subject who inspired the wood carver's genius and "first created the artist who afterwards created her image."

The "light of imagination" has "departed" from Drowne's face, and he is now once again "the mechanical carver that he had been known to be all his lifetime." He explains that he had wrought the image in "a kind of dream," and now he finds himself "broad awake." From that point on, Drowne continues working "in his own mechanical style" for many years.

The narrator remarks that "in every human spirit there is imagination, sensibility, creative power, genius," which "may either be developed" or "shrouded in a mask of dulness until another state of being." He observes that for Drowne, there had been "a brief season of excitement, kindled by love," which "rendered him a genius" for one occasion only.

The story concludes with news that there is a rumor in Boston about a "young Portuguese lady of rank" who had fled from her home in Fayal and traveled to America on board Captain Hunnewell's ship. She had been sheltered in his residence until a "change of affairs."

CRITICAL ANALYSIS

The primary source of "Drowne's Wooden Image" is thought to be the Pygmalian myth. It is likely that Hawthorne read Ovid's *Metamorphoses*, book 10, in Latin during his school days and would have been familiar with the legend. Neal Frank Doubleday observes that in Hawthorne's tale Copley declares, "Who would have looked for a modern Pygmalion in the person of a Yankee mechanic!" In retelling the myth, Hawthorne substitutes an American setting and an American cast. Ovid's sculptor, who works in marble, is transformed at the outset of the tale into a wood carver of ships' figureheads. In carrying out this metamorphosis, Hawthorne may have followed examples set by two contemporary American writers, Washington Irving and William Austin.

The principal idea presented in the story is that Drowne, an ordinary carver of ship figureheads, can be ennobled and even lifted to the level of genius by his powers as a creative artist. Arlin Turner observes that this notion is compatible with

Sophia's and Hawthorne's emphasis on the effectiveness of dreaming, especially when accompanied by their deep spiritual love (*Nathaniel Hawthorne: A Biography,* 161).

A. James Wohlpart theorizes that Hawthorne's "conception of the artist" can be seen in the two "distinct" types found in his stories of the 1840s. Hawthorne "critiques soundly" the artist "who attempts to rise above humanity and create in a God-like manner an art unaffected by human desire or faith." In "The BIRTH-MARK" and "RAPPACCINI'S DAUGHTER," the "artist-figures" are "separated from humanity because of their cold intellect and desire to control others." In contrast, artists of the other type, "who love[s] humanity and use[s] this love to inspire art," such as the wood carver in "Drowne's Wooden Image" and Owen Warland in "The ARTIST OF THE BEAUTIFUL," are the only "successful artists"—"those figures who are able to create art even while remaining human, a status achieved through their love of others and their attachment to the real world." These artists retain "'warmth of heart,' that is . . . love for their fellow humans" ("Allegories of Art, Allegories of Heart: Hawthorne's 'Egotism' and 'The Christmas Banquet,'" *Studies in Short Fiction* (summer 1994): 449–461).

Nancy Bunge suggests that "Drowne's Wooden Image" focuses on the development of the protagonist's emotional strength. At the outset of the story, he is a craftsman, but when he succeeds in carving the beautiful female figurehead, a work of art with a rare vitality, his character shifts to that of an artist. Drowne's creative genius arises from love: Copley looks at him and sees an "expression of human love which . . . was the secret of the life that had been breathed into this block of wood." The appearance of the woman identical to Drowne's finished image enacts the story's moral. As the narrator remarks, "In every human spirit there is imagination, sensibility, creative power, genius, which, according to circumstances, may either be developed . . . or shrouded in a mask of dulness. . . . To our friend Drowne, there came a brief season of excitement, kindled by love. It rendered him a genius for that one occasion, but, quenched in disappointment, left him again the mechanical carver in wood, without the power even of appreciating the work that his own hand had wrought." Drowne realizes his artistic potential only briefly. Hawthorne suggests that even noble art is still subject to human restraints, but love has the power to elevate a man above himself, even if temporarily.

Frederick Crews argues that "Drowne's Wooden Image" is the only one of Hawthorne's tales in which art results from a "withdrawal from sexual reality." The sculptor is inspired by his genuine love of a work of art. Drowne bends over the "half-created shape" and stretches forth his arms "as if he would have embraced and drawn it into his heart." In his insistence on the power of love to inspire artistic creation, Hawthorne embraces transcendentalism. Drowne produces his one masterpiece when love enkindles his heart; he is thus able to generate a female figure who is delicate and beautiful, and who walks and breathes. He undergoes a metamorphosis. Formerly, he had been unable to find within himself the quality of soul needed to animate his creations. Working in "a kind of dream" kindled by love, he is empowered to produce a miraculous woman who walks "in mirth" and is able to flutter her fan. As he labors, a "well-spring of inward wisdom" gushes within the artist, endowing him with "strength, and soul, and faith."

CHARACTERS

Copley, John Singleton (1738–1815) Boston portrait painter, known for his attention to detail and uncompromising truth in depicting those who sat for him. He lived in England from 1774 until his death, except for a year spent in Italy studying the works of old masters. In England, he painted a number of important portraits and large historical canvases. In the opinion of many art historians, these works show a greater technical skill and more artistic grace than the New England portraits on which he built his reputation.

In "Drowne's Wooden Image," the character of Copley is still a young man but already a "celebrated painter" when he visits Drowne's workshop. Copley's function in the story is to provide the viewpoint of a connoisseur, which leads the reader not only to value Drowne's artistic ability, but also to appreciate his integrity. Copley confirms the remarkable character of the figure, exclaiming, "If she be other than a bubble of the elements . . . I must look upon her face again!"

Drowne The hero of "Drowne's Wooden Image," Drowne is a young wood carver in early Boston. In the course of the story, Drowne evolves from a craftsman into an artist, but, by the end, he is once again a merely mechanical carver. In his temporary transformation, he resembles the mythological figure of Pygmalion. As the narrator remarks, when Drowne is at the peak of his powers, his genius is "kindled by love," making him "a genius for that one occasion." Afterward, however, "quenched in disappointment," he reverts to being the "mechanical carver . . . without the power even of appreciating the work that his own hand had wrought."

FOR FURTHER READING

Baym, Nina, *The Shape of Hawthorne's Career* (Ithaca, N.Y.: Cornell University Press, 1976); Bell, Millicent, *Hawthorne's View of the Artist* (New York: New York State University Press, 1962); Bunge, Nancy, *Nathaniel Hawthorne: A Study of the Short Fiction* (New York: Twayne, 1993); Crews, Frederick C., *The Sins of the Fathers: Hawthorne's Psychological Themes* (New York: Oxford University Press, 1966); Doubleday, Neal Frank, *Hawthorne's Early Tales: A Critical Study* (Durham, N.C.: Duke University Press, 1972); Male, Roy R., "'From the Innermost Germ': The Organic Principle in Hawthorne's Fiction," *English Literary History* 20 (1953): 218–236; Turner, Arlin, *Nathaniel Hawthorne: A Biography* (New York: Oxford University Press, 1980).

"Duston Family, The"

See "HANNAH DUSTON."

"Earth's Holocaust"

A short story first published in *Graham's Lady's and Gentleman's Magazine* in May 1844. It was collected in 1846 in MOSSES FROM AN OLD MANSE, vol. 2 (1846).

The tale opens with an announcement that at some unspecified time, the world has been so much burdened with "worn-out trumpery" that its inhabitants have decided to dispose of it in a general bonfire on a broad prairie in the American West. The blaze attracts travelers on foot, women, men on horseback, wheelbarrows, baggage wagons, and other vehicles containing articles judged "fit for nothing but to be burnt."

The narrator explains to a bystander that the fire was at first kindled by using recent newspapers and magazines. Then family pedigrees were tossed in, along with such "earthly distinctions" as the French Legion of Honor and English orders of nobility.

Suddenly, a gray-haired man "of stately presence," a nobleman, rushes up and protests the burning of such signs marking the advance from "barbarism" to the "privileged orders" of patrons who kept literature and fine arts alive. He shrinks back before the contemptuous crowd.

A multitude arrives from "beyond the sea," bearing royal robes, crowns, globes, and the scepters of emperors and kings. Some have descended from Saxon princes. They have fallen into contempt, as have the theatrical robes and crowns from the Drury Lane Theatre. In addition, the trappings of titled Continental royalty—the emperor of Austria's mantle, the czar of Russia's scepter—are thrown in.

There follows a procession of Washingtonians, including the Irish disciples of Father Theobald Mathew (a Franciscan friar who transformed Ireland into a temperance stronghold in the 1830s and 1840s). As vintage liquors are tossed into the flames by the reformers, there are protests from "respectable gentlemen with red noses," who ask what the world is good for without jollity and the "solace" of alcohol. The reformers then toss "boxes of tea and bags of coffee" into the flames, as well as "crops of tobacco." Bank notes, fashionable clothes, and medicines disappear into the flames.

The assembled people continue to toss in their prized possessions, both literal and symbolic. The "playthings of war" melt in the flames, as well as a guillotine, marriage certificates, and paper money (because "universal benevolence" would now be the "golden currency" of the world).

Books and pamphlets are thrown into the blaze to rid the world of "dead men's thought." A "thin volume" of poems by WILLIAM ELLERY CHANNING (Channing was a friend of Hawthorne's) is particularly flammable, but Hawthorne notes that portions of it "hissed and spluttered in a very disagreeable fashion." The respectable works of certain writers melt away rather than burn; they turn out to be made of "ice." Hawthorne confesses that he has searched with a "fatherly interest" for his own works, which are not to be found. He hopes that "in their quiet way" they have contributed "a glimmering spark or two" to the "splendor of the evening." A bookseller mourns the burning of his bound volumes. A philosopher tosses in his theories, but the "combustion" is "by no means brilliant."

Ecclesiastical accoutrements are thrown into the flames, including miters, croziers, fonts, and sacramental vessels. The onlooker concludes that "wood-paths" will, from then on, be the "aisles" of their "cathedrals." Bibles, too, are tossed in.

As the conflagration blazes, a "grave bystander" assures the onlooker that the flames have not destroyed truth, which will be "raked up at last." A copy of the Bible has survived the flames with "dazzling whiteness," although marginal notes and commentaries are consumed by the flames.

The narrator/onlooker asks whether he is correct in assuming that the conflagration has performed a useful function in consuming what is evil. The observer refers him to the hangman, thief, and murderer who are clustered near the fire consuming the last of the brandy provided by the "toper." The hangman suggests that once his companions have finished the brandy he might help them to a "comfortable end upon the nearest tree" and then hang himself, since "this is no world for us, any longer."

But a "dark-complexioned personage" appears and objects that "there is one thing that these wiseacres have forgotten to throw into the fire, and without which all the rest of the conflagration is just nothing at all." Because they have not thrown "the human heart itself" into the flames, it cannot be purified and will thus "re-issue all the shapes of wrong and misery—the same old shapes, or worse ones—which they have taken such a vast deal of trouble" to burn. The "old world" will survive.

The narrator affirms the validity of this argument. Humans' "age-long endeavor" to attain perfection is doomed to failure, since only the intellect has been reformed—and not the human heart, which must undergo purgation in order to banish evil. The entire effort is doomed, since the intellect is but a "feeble instrument" to "discern and rectify" what is wrong. The narrator then observes that it matters little whether the bonfire has been a "real event" or only a "phosphoric radiance," a "parable" of his own brain.

RECEPTION AND CRITICAL ANALYSIS

Herman Melville found the moral of "EARTH'S HOLOCAUST" "profound, nay, appalling." He remarked that by the end of the story, "nothing is left but the all-engendering heart of man," which, "remaining still unconsumed," makes the "great conflagration" for "naught" ("Hawthorne and His Mosses," *Literary World*, August 17 and 24, 1850).

Gorman Beauchamp contrasts The BLITHEDALE ROMANCE, "Hawthorne's most ambitious attempt to depict the type of the Universal Reformer, to "Earth's Holocaust," "one of the most complex and successful of his allegorical satires," in which he presents "the spectacle of Universal Reform itself." In this story, universal reform is presented "quite literally"—in fact, "all the 'evils' that have plagued human history are consigned to the flames of a great bonfire of the vanities." The tone of "Earth's Holocaust" is "playful in manner" but "wholly serious in intent—and patently didactic." It may seem "old-fashioned and literal" to modern readers, but, as Hyatt Waggoner suggests, it may reveal "the meanings Hawthorne intended to express in his fiction," such as his views on the "theme of social reform in Blithedale." Beauchamp declares "Earth's Holocaust" to be Hawthorne's "clearest credo on the subject of utopian reform" ("Hawthorne and the Universal Reformers," *Utopian Studies*, 13 [spring 2002]).

Terence Martin observes that Hawthorne begins this story with "Once upon a time," and that by "adopting the convention of the fairy tale,"

the author "achieves at a stroke the imaginative freedom he requires." This type of opening line introduces the reader to a "modern fable," complete with "a moral regarding human wisdom or folly." In this case, the lesson learned is that "reform will fail if the human heart is not first purified." Hawthorne employs the form of the fairy tale in other stories as well, such as "The GREAT CARBUNCLE," "The LILY'S QUEST," and "THE HOLLOW OF THE THREE HILLS."

In Denis Donoghue's view, Hawthorne "had no trouble imagining universal evil, Original Sin, without the theology of it." He points out that in "EARTH'S HOLOCAUST," the narrator "attributes evil to a defect of 'the Heart . . . wherein existed the original wrong, of which the crime and misery of this outward world were merely types.'" Hawthorne as narrator believes that one only need "purify that inner sphere," and then the "many shapes of evil that haunt the outward" will turn from "realities" to "shadowy phantoms" ("Hawthorne and Sin," *Christianity and Literature* 52 [Winter 2003]).

FOR FURTHER READING

Donoghue, Denis, "Hawthorne and Sin," *Christianity and Literature* 52 (winter 2003): 215–234; Dunne, Michael, "Natural and Imposed Order in Two Sketches by Hawthorne," *Nathaniel Hawthorne Journal* 8 (1978): 197–202; Hostetler, Norman H., "'Earth's Holocaust': Hawthorne's Parable of the Imaginative Process," *Kansas Quarterly* 7, no. 4 (1975): 85–89; Martin, Terence, *Nathaniel Hawthorne* (Boston: Twayne, 1983).

"Edward Fane's Rosebud"

Short story first published in the KNICKERBOCKER, or *New-York Monthly Magazine*, in September 1837. It was not attributed to Hawthorne. Nina Baym suggests that Hawthorne conceived of the story to meet what he thought were the demands of the marketplace, "pathos with a moral" (Baym, Nina, *The Shape of Hawthorne's Career*, 53–93).

The story begins with an exploration of the physical effects of aging, especially on women.

Hawthorne directs the reader's attention to the Widow Toothaker, a nurse "of great repute" who has "breathed the atmosphere of sick-chambers and dying-breaths" for at least 40 years.

She sits beside her "lonesome hearth," reviving her "sad old heart" by sipping a beverage called "Geneva," a mixture of an alcoholic drink and hot water. She is "a picture of decay and desolation." Her maiden name had been Rose Grafton, and she was, in her youth, much loved by Edward Fane. Fane is now a "grand old gentleman" with powdered hair.

When young, they had wept for Edward's little sister, Mary, who died at the age of three. Edward's mother, a "rich and haughty dame," had disapproved of Rose and forced her son to break off their friendship.

Rose had then married Mr. Toothaker and "soon began to love him." However, he had a disease of the joints and become increasingly feeble. When the story opens, he is bedridden, devotedly attended by Rose. She never answers him peevishly and never fails "in a wife's duty to her poor sick husband." As he dies, he wonders what Rose might have done for her first love, since "she has been so true and kind to a sick old man like me."

Rose is an attractive widow, "still fair enough to captivate a bachelor," but Mr. Toothaker has "cast a spell" around her. She now feels "ill at ease with the healthy and the happy." Even her husband's disease has captivated her, and his death cannot "dissolve the nuptials." She evolves from wife to widow to Nurse Toothaker and is much in demand in the latter capacity. She becomes the "patron-saint of young physicians, and the bosom friend of old ones." Death himself is so familiar with her, he greets her at the bedsides of those who are ill.

As Nurse Toothaker dozes in a reverie by the fire, a knock at her door summons her to nurse old General Fane, ill on his deathbed. She hurries to him, crying out, "Edward Fane remembers his Rosebud!" There is still a "germ of bliss" within her because of her constancy. The memory of this bliss is a symbol that in "some happier clime, the Rosebud may revive again with all the dew-drops in its bosom."

As in several other of Hawthorne's tales, such as "The WEDDING-KNELL," "The WHITE OLD MAID," and "The SHAKER BURIAL," death and disappointed love are characteristic of "Edward Fane's Rosebud." Rosebud in her piety, equated as it is with death, will contrast with Hawthorne's most famous female character, Hester Prynne in The SCARLET LETTER.

FOR FURTHER READING

Levin, Harry, The Power of Blackness: Hawthorne, Poe, and Melville (New York: Alfred A. Knopf, 1958), 58; Walsh, Thomas F., Jr., "'Wakefield' and Hawthorne's Illustrated Ideas: A Study in Form," Emerson Society Quarterly 19 (1960): 32.

"Edward Randolph's Portrait"

Tale first published in the UNITED STATES MAGAZINE AND DEMOCRATIC REVIEW in July 1838, the second in a series with "HOWE'S MASQUERADE," "LADY ELEANOR'S MANTLE," and "OLD ESTHER DUDLEY." The series was later published in the 1842 edition of TWICE-TOLD TALES under the title LEGENDS OF THE PROVINCE-HOUSE.

On a chilly, windy night, the same narrator goes back to the Province-house, in search of the elderly gentleman whom he had met on his earlier visit. The narrator hopes to snatch "from oblivion some else unheard-of fact of history." The "old tradition-monger" is, as expected, sitting in the barroom by the fire. His name is Mr. Bela Tiffany.

Mr. Tiffany recounts a legend about an ancient, dark picture, which used to hang in one of the apartments above the bar during the rule of many successive governors. It is still in its place at the start of Lieutenant-Governor Hutchinson's term.

One afternoon, Hutchinson receives word that a British fleet is approaching from Halifax, carrying three regiments to counter the insubordination of the people. The troops want permission to occupy the fortress of Castle William and the town itself. Instead of signing the order, the Lieutenant-Governor sits and scrutinizes the painting. He attracts the notice of two young persons, his kinsman Francis Lincoln, the Provincial Captain of Castle William, and his niece, Alice Vane (cousin of Lincoln). Alice was a "pale, ethereal creature" who had lived in Italy until orphaned; there she had acquired a taste for art. Noticing her uncle's "steadfast gaze," she wonders whether the dark picture could be a famous masterpiece.

Hutchinson does not immediately reply, so the young Captain of Castle William tells her of the legends about the picture. One is that it depicted the Evil One, taken at a witch meeting near Salem, and that a demon lived "behind the blackness of the picture, and had shown himself, at seasons of public calamity, to more than one of the royal governors." Alice suggests cleaning the canvas, since "the original picture can hardly be so formidable as those which fancy paints instead of it." Her cousin asks whether it is possible to restore such a dark picture, to which Alice replies, "Such arts are known in Italy."

Hutchinson then declares it was a portrait of Edward Randolph, whom Captain Lincoln describes as the man "who obtained the repeal of the first provincial charter, under which our forefathers had enjoyed almost democratic privileges," and who was "styled the arch enemy of New England, and whose memory is still held in detestation, as the destroyer of our liberties!" Captain Lincoln says "the curse of the people followed this Randolph wherever he went, and wrought evil in all the subsequent events of his life." The curse was also outwardly visible, making the wretched Randolph's face "too horrible to be looked upon."

Hutchinson declares "these traditions are folly" to those who have proved "how little of historic truth lies at the bottom." Alice wonders, however, whether even "such fables have a moral," and whether this dreadful portrait has hung so long in this room because when "the rulers feel themselves irresponsible, it were well that they should be reminded of the awful weight of a People's curse." As she leaves the room, she smiles at the picture and cries, "Come forth, dark and evil Shape! It is thine hour!"

That evening, Lieutenant-Governor Hutchinson sits in the same room with the Selectmen of Boston, a couple of members of the Council, a major of the British army, and the Captain of Castle William. Alice Vane is "partly shrouded in the voluminous folds of one of the window-cur-

tains," and her presence is noticed by only a few. The chairman of the Selectmen argues against allowing the British troops—"mercenary sworders and musketeers"—into town, for "if one drop of blood be shed, that blood shall be an eternal stain upon your Honor's memory." Hutchinson responds that he cannot "wait till the mob shall sack the Province-House," as they did his private mansion. He utters, "The King is my master, and England is my country!" and is about to sign the order to allow occupation of Castle William by royal troops.

He is interrupted, however, when Captain Lincoln directs his attention to the dark picture, now covered by a black silk curtain. Assuming his niece has had something to do with this, he summons Alice. She snatches away the curtain and reveals a still dark, but now visible, portrait of a tortured Edward Randolph, cursed by the people for trampling on their rights. Everyone in the room is "astonished and awe-stricken," but Hutchinson's voice has a "tone of horror." Alice warns the Lieutenant-Governor to avoid such a crime as Randolph committed but to no avail. Hutchinson, though momentarily trembling, tries to "shake off the spell of Randolph's countenance" and tells Alice her "painter's art," "Italian spirit of intrigue," and "tricks of stage-effect" cannot "influence the councils of rulers and the affairs of nations." He snatches the pen once again, signs the name of Thomas Hutchinson, and shudders "as if that signature had granted away his salvation." Alice Vane asks that heaven forgive his deed.

When Hutchinson lies dying later, in England, he appears to be "choking with the blood of the Boston Massacre." Francis Lincoln, former Captain of Castle William, sees in his face a likeness to that of Edward Randolph and wonders whether he feels "the tremendous burthen of a People's curse."

Mr. Tiffany tells the narrator that the picture has since been removed from the Province-House and is supposedly in an "out-of-the-way corner of the New England Museum." As the narrator takes leave of the fireside in the Province-House, he hears whistling winds and "ghostly sounds" that remind him of the earlier events.

"Egotism; or, the Bosom-Serpent"

A short story first published in UNITED STATES MAGAZINE AND DEMOCRATIC REVIEW in March 1843 and reprinted in The Pathfinder the same month. The subtitle is "From the Unpublished 'Allegories of the Heart.'" This is the second of his tales with this subtitle; the other is "The CHRISTMAS BANQUET." The word Egotism in the title is followed by an asterisk. Hawthorne explains in a note that he attempts to give a "moral significance" to a "physical fact" that has been "known to occur in more than one instance."

The story begins when a young American sculptor, George Herkimer, returns after spending five years in Europe. He seeks out Roderick Elliston, the estranged husband of his cousin Rosina. As he approaches the Elliston mansion, he is horrified to hear several boys shouting, "'Here comes the man with a snake in his bosom!'" Herkimer realizes the boys must be referring to his cousin's husband. He waits at Elliston's gate for the "personage, so singularly announced," to appear. Soon he observes a "lean man" with "glittering eyes" and long black hair approaching. He undulates "in a curved line" along the pavement, rather than "walking straight forward with open front." He reminds Herkimer of a serpent; even his complexion is "sickly white" with a "greenish tinge."

Herkimer recognizes him as Elliston. The man exclaims, "It gnaws me! It gnaws me!" several times and assures George that having a snake in one's bosom is the "commonest thing in the world"— only the very "pure and wholesome" are exempt. Elliston scarcely listens when Herkimer tells him he is carrying a message from Rosina. Instead, he mutters, "It gnaws me! It gnaws me!" and disappears into the house.

Herkimer learns from a local physician that the condition had developed over the four years since Elliston's separation from his wife. The townspeople were perplexed, proposing myriad explanations: an "incipient stage of insanity," a "general blight," guilt, dyspepsia, and mysterious unknown causes. Elliston realized he had become the "subject of curiosity and conjecture" and "estranged himself from all companionship."

He had also consulted various quacks and learned from his servant, Scipio, that one of them is reputed to have prescribed a powder that caused a snake to leap from his bosom onto the floor. Upon hearing this rumor, Elliston had "ceased to shun the world, but rather solicited and forced himself upon the notice of acquaintances and strangers." This "craving for notoriety" was "a symptom of the intense morbidness which now pervaded his nature," for all persons who are "chronically diseased" are "egotists" who take pleasure in "displaying the wasted or ulcerated limb, or the cancer in the breast." Elliston had exhibited signs of insanity, taunting upright citizens with their misdeeds and accusing a clergyman of swallowing a snake in a cup of sacramental wine.

The tale evolves with an almost Jesuitical logic. The reader's natural skepticism gives way to a perception that the physical serpent is an emblem of moral affliction—what, in medieval literature, is called the "agenbite of inwit," or the "prick of conscience." Hawthorne suggests that each man makes his own "actual serpent," the result of his particular "fatal error, or hoarded sin, or unquiet conscience."

Roderick Elliston had become so obsessed with his own misdeeds and those of other "decent people" that his relatives confined him to a mental institution, where the physicians treated him with opium, alcohol, and tobacco smoke. He gazed into a mirror for days, with his mouth open, imagining he could see the serpent in his throat. The doctors realized they were unable to help him and that he was no danger to others and thus released him.

It is the day after his release that his first encounter with Herkimer takes place. After an interval, Herkimer returns with a companion to seek Elliston at his house, "a large, somber edifice of wood with pilasters and a balcony." Once it had been a magnificent historic residence, of which only vestiges remain. The two visitors are shown inside by Scipio, whose face is "almost sunny with intelligence and joy" as he greets one of them.

The companion remains in the arbor while Herkimer finds Elliston in the garden beside a fountain, reading a book on the "natural history of the serpent-tribe." Elliston explains that Scipio has heard that a serpent once lived in the fountain and tormented Elliston's great-grandfather and others, but he himself believes the serpent is his "own snake" and not an "heir-loom." When Herkimer asks its origins, Elliston says "there is poisonous stuff in any man's heart, sufficient to generate a brood of serpents," but declares that because Herkimer has none in his bosom, he "therefore cannot sympathize with the rest of the world."

Elliston then throws himself face down in the grass, writhing and hissing, insisting that he has engendered the serpent by his own "diseased self-contemplation." The only remedy is "an impossible one," for it would require him to forget himself.

Herkimer's companion, Elliston's estranged and gentle wife, Rosina, enters the garden and bends over him. "Then forget yourself, my husband," she advises, "in the idea of another." Her countenance is marked by "hope and unselfish love." She touches Elliston with her hand, and the sculptor senses a "waving motion" through the grass and a "tinkling sound" from the fountain, as though the fiend had plunged into the water.

Roderick Elliston begs Rosina to forgive him; she weeps with "happy tears." Herkimer observes that whether the serpent was a "physical reptile" or a "tremendous Egotism" that manifested itself in the form of jealousy, it had been "as fearful a fiend as ever stole into the human heart." Can a breast be purified, Herkimer wonders, "where it has dwelt so long?" Rosina answers with a "heavenly smile" that the serpent had only been a "dark fantasy." They will dwell no more on the "dismal" past, which shall "fling no gloom upon the future." Instead, they will think of the episode as "an anecdote in our Eternity."

RECEPTION AND CRITICAL ANALYSIS

Some critics have seen the story as influencing "The Jolly Corner," by HENRY JAMES. Herman Melville read the story four years after its publication and praised its "mystical blackness." He compared Hawthorne's "power of darkness" with that of Shakespeare ("Hawthorne and His Mosses," *Literary World,* August 17 and 24, 1850). Henry James, however, found something "stiff and mechanical,

slightly incongruous" in the story, as if "the kernel had not assimilated its envelope" (*Hawthorne,* 1879).

At the beginning of the story, Hawthorne inserts a disclaimer, stating, "The physical fact, to which is here attempted to give a moral significance, has been known to occur in more than one instance." Shortly afterward, Elliston's associates observe "a singular gloom spreading over his daily life, like those chill, grey mists that sometimes steal away the sunshine from a summer's morning." Rosina had attempted in vain to find a cure for her husband's suffering. After four years of estrangement, she asks Herkimer to make a journey to their home in order to attempt treatment for Elliston's ailment. Before he pays a visit to the residence, Herkimer believes Elliston's delusion is rooted in either a "diseased fancy" or a "horrible physical misfortune."

Herkimer then consults an "eminent medical gentleman" in order to gather information on Elliston's condition. According to the doctor, who speaks freely with Herkimer, Elliston has isolated himself from his wife and from all other human companions. James Wohlpart suggests that Hawthorne is here endorsing the transcendental aesthetic that "held that the artist must become lost in the ideal world . . . and thus separated from humanity."

Roderick Elliston has himself become the subject of morbid curiosity and conjecture, not only because of his delusion, but also because of his uninhibited manifestation of it in public. He has "estranged himself from all companionship," as Wohlpart observes. Elliston not only succumbs to the delusion that he has a serpent residing in his bosom, but also has no inhibitions about making his hallucination public. In this way, as Wohlpart points out, he embraces his own created world and becomes, "in effect, a godlike figure." He suggests that the serpent itself becomes a symbol of a "monstrous egotism." Several critics have associated this egotistical disease with transcendentalism, which focuses on isolation and on the delusion that humans might join the "Over Soul through passively submitting to its electrical currents" (Wohlpart, "Allegories of Art," 274).

Interestingly, Hawthorne, according to Edward Wagenknecht, refused to "commit himself irrevocably to the serpent as either actual or symbolic" (Wagenknecht, *Nathaniel Hawthorne: The Man, His Tales and Romances,* 197).

Throughout the story, Roderick Elliston is negatively associated with disease rather than human love or warmth. In the four years of estrangement from his wife, Rosina, he has attracted the attention of many physicians. After he begins stalking the city and speaking about the serpent in his bosom, he is removed from society and confined to an insane asylum. Some critics have suggested that the story may be read as an allegory focusing on the "weight of guilt on the spiritual and psychological consciousness of man" (Bush, "Bosom Serpents," 181).

Erich S. Rupprecht is among those critics who consider "Egotism" one of Hawthorne's lesser works. He observes that the "symbolic burden of the story clearly overwhelms the literal." The "meaning" of the story becomes everything, overshadowing the "narrative aspect of the tale." Rupprecht suggests that the story "never manages to achieve much power or emotional resonance" because Elliston never "comes alive as a character," and because the serpent, "which so obviously represents egotism," never "fully engages one's interest or belief." For him, the "supernatural element" in the story is limited to playing a "rather heavy-handed role as an expedient literary device," with the result being a story that approaches "outright allegory" and thus seems "too obvious and labored" to modern readers ("Nathaniel Hawthorne," *Supernatural Fiction Writers,* edited by E. F. Bleiler, vol. 2, 707–715).

Hawthorne himself may have thought little of these "outright" allegories. As Terence Martin points out, Hawthorne "was not a master allegorist" and in later years "looked with disfavor on what he called his 'blasted allegories.'" Martin adds that the "thinness" of such allegories "caused Melville to say that Hawthorne needed to frequent the butcher, that he ought to have 'roast beef done rare'" (*Nathaniel Hawthorne,* 67).

CHARACTERS

Elliston, Roderick   In "Egotism; or, the Bosom-Serpent," he is the estranged husband of Rosina Elliston, who is a cousin of the sculptor George Herkimer. Elliston has been afflicted with the delusion that he is harboring a serpent in his chest. He is introduced as a "wretched being" and reminds Herkimer of a serpent.

Elliston's condition mystifies the townspeople. He eventually withdraws from town life and exhibits signs of insanity as his suffering continues. The physical serpent is an emblem of moral affliction; Elliston feels diseased within himself.

When Herkimer pays a second visit to Elliston, he takes along "a companion," who remains in the arbor while Herkimer finds Elliston in the garden, reading a book on the natural history of serpents. Elliston has concluded that the serpent was engendered by his own psyche. Herkimer's companion, who turns out to be Elliston's estranged wife, Rosina, enters the garden and bends over him. "Forget yourself, my husband," she gently advises, "in the idea of another." When she touches Elliston, they are reconciled, and the serpent retreats with a "waving motion" through the grass.

Arlin Turner suggests that it is his love for Rosina that finally redeems Elliston from the "diseased self-contemplation" that has been responsible for producing and nourishing the serpent (*Nathaniel Hawthorne: A Biography,* 161).

Elliston, Rosina   In "Egotism; or, the Bosom-Serpent," Rosina is the estranged wife of Roderick Elliston. During their separation, which extends over several years, Elliston becomes possessed by the delusion that he harbors a snake in his bosom, and that such an affliction is very common—only the very "pure and wholesome" are exempt.

A "sad and tremulous" Rosina is taken to see her husband by her cousin, George Herkimer, who is also a friend of Elliston's. Herkimer advises her to remain in the arbor and to decide intuitively "whether, and when, to make [her] appearance." She tells him, "God will teach me. . . . May he support me too!" When Rosina emerges from the arbor and touches her estranged husband, the shadow of his anguish is reflected in her countenance, but it mingles there with "hope and unselfish love."

The reader is not told why the pair have been estranged and separated, but the decisive steps taken by her cousin, George Herkimer, and Rosina's love for Elliston are given credit for reuniting them.

Herkimer, George In "Egotism; or, the Bosom-Serpent," he is a sculptor and the cousin of Rosina Elliston, the estranged wife of Roderick Elliston. After five years in Europe, Herkimer returns in order to assist Rosina and her husband. He learns from a local physician that Elliston's condition has developed over the four years since his separation from Rosina and from all other human companions.

Herkimer first appears on the day after Elliston's release from a mental institution, to which his relatives have committed him for evaluation. The physicians there have determined that he poses no danger to himself or to others and therefore permit him to leave.

Elliston has withdrawn from society and scarcely listens when Herkimer tells him he has a message from Rosina; instead, he disappears into his large house. This severance from society reflects the Transcendental aesthetic that the true artist ought to be alienated from the community at large and only concerned with his own self-created inner world.

Herkimer returns with Rosina, whose touch and whose advice to forget himself "in the idea of another" drive the serpent away. The character of Herkimer acts as an intermediary between the couple, as well as a messenger of sanity.

FOR FURTHER READING

Arner, Robert D., "Of Snakes and Those Who Swallow Them: Some Folk Analogues for Hawthorne's 'Egotism; or, the Bosom Serpent,'" *Southern Folklore Quarterly* 35 (4); Barnes, Daniel R., "The Bosom Serpent: A Legend in American Literature and Culture," *Journal of American Folklore* 85 (1972); Schechter, Harold, *The Bosom Serpent*; Schechter, Harold, "The Bosom Serpent: Folklore and Popular Art," *Film Quarterly*, 43, no. 2 (Winter, 1989): 46–50; Wohlpart, A. James, "Allegories of Art, Allegories of Heart: Hawthorne's 'Egotism' and 'The Christmas Banquet,'" *Studies in Short Fiction* (summer 1994): 449–461.

"Endicott and the Red Cross"

Unsigned short story first printed in the *Salem Gazette* in 1837, then in *The* TOKEN (1838) and collected in the second edition of TWICE-TOLD TALES (1842).

The tale, or sketch, opens in Salem, Massachusetts, two centuries before Hawthorne's time. The "trainband," a militia company of all the men in the town between the ages of 16 and 60, is gathered for "martial exercise."

The English flag, displaying the "Red Cross," is flung out over the "company of Puritans." The townspeople oppose the tyrannical measures of the English king, Charles I, and the British parliament but are even more defiant in their resistance to Roman Catholicism. They are led by John Endicott, "a man of stern and resolute countenance." He has a "grizzled beard" sweeping over his "glittering steel" breastplate. The "highly polished" breastplate reflects "the whole surrounding scene," including the plain architecture of the town meetinghouse, which has "neither steeple nor bell to proclaim it" and a wolf's head nailed over the door, a token of the wilderness. The wolf has "just been slain within the precincts of the town," and its blood is still "plashing on the doorstep" of the meetinghouse. The critic Sacvan Bercovitch calls the breastplate the "dominant symbol" of the story, reflecting the community, the other soldiers, and the austere mien of Endicott.

Other emblems of "Puritanic authority" are nearby: the whipping post, around which the soil has been "well trodden by the feet of evil-doers, who had there been disciplined"; the pillory; and the stocks. Puritan wrongdoers are punished for their various crimes "for the space of one hour at noonday." For example, a suspected Roman Catholic is in the pillory, while a man who has dared toast the king (Charles I) is confined in the stocks. A man and a woman stand on the meetinghouse steps. The man is a "tall, lean, haggard personification of fanaticism," who bears on his breast the label "A WANTON GOSPELLER." This message indicates that he has dared to give his private interpretations of Scripture, opinions that have not been sanctioned "by the infallible judgment of the civil and religious orders." A woman who has complained of the church elders is punished by being forced to wear a cleft stick on her tongue, in "appropriate retribution" for having wagged her "unruly" tongue against those figures of authority. Her "countenance and gestures" suggest, however, that she would eagerly repeat this offense should the stick be removed.

Those colonists who are convicted of more serious crimes are physically maimed for life, with punishments including having their ears cropped or their cheeks branded. One man is required to submit to wearing a permanent neck halter, while a young woman "with no mean share of beauty" is doomed to wear a scarlet letter A to indicate "Adulteress," "in the eyes of all the world"; even her own children know what the initial signifies. The "lost and desperate" young woman has tried to disguise the meaning of the letter by embroidering the "fatal token" in "scarlet cloth, with golden thread and the nicest art of needle-work." This description presages The SCARLET LETTER, which many critics consider to be Hawthorne's finest novel.

The narrator observes that despite "these evidences of iniquity," the "times of the Puritans" are not necessarily "more vicious than our own." He explains that it was "the policy of our ancestors to search out even the most secret sins, and expose them to shame," unlike the custom nowadays.

While the militia await their orders, the captain, John Endicott, spots an "elderly gentleman, wearing a black cloak and band, and a high-crowned hat, beneath which was a velvet skull-cap." It is Roger Williams, the Puritan minister of Salem. He carries a staff and his shoes are "bemired," as though he has been "travelling on foot through the swamps of the wilderness." His aspect is that of "a pilgrim, heightened also by an apostolic dignity." Endicott greets him, and Williams reports that he has been entrusted with a sealed letter from the royal governor, Winthrop.

As Endicott reads the letter, "a wrathful change" occurs on his countenance. Blood glows through his face until it seems "to be kindling with an internal heat," and it almost seems that his breastplate will become red-hot with the "angry fire of the bosom which it covered." Endicott shakes the letter "fiercely in his hand" so that it rustles "as loud as the flag above his head." He announces that it contains "black tidings," which Roger Williams already knows. Williams tells Endicott that Governor Winthrop begs him that the "news be not suddenly noised abroad, lest the people be stirred up into some outbreak, and thereby give the King and the Archbishop a handle" against the colony.

Endicott says grimly that the governor is "a wise man, and a meek and moderate," but he must follow his "own best judgment." He gathers all the soldiers and townspeople in the square and delivers a stirring speech asking whether they have left the "green and fertile fields" and "cottages" and "old gray halls" of England behind for nothing. They have traveled to this "howling wilderness" because they desire to enjoy their own "civil rights" and the "liberty to worship God" as they please. The Wanton Gospeller interrupts, asking whether what he is saying signifies true "liberty of conscience," but Endicott shakes his sword at him and replies, "I said, liberty to worship God, not license to profane and ridicule him."

Endicott continues, calling Winthrop a "son of a Scotch tyrant" and "grandson of a papistical and adulterous Scotch woman," and is about to ask why they should listen to him. Roger Williams protests that his words are "not meet for a secret chamber, far less for a public street." Endicott silences Williams and turns to the most ominous matter at hand. He warns the colonists that King Charles I and Archbishop Laud want to establish "idolatrous forms of English Episcopacy."

He urges the crowd to protest and then orders the flag lowered. He thrusts his sword through the cloth and cuts the Red Cross "completely out of the banner." As he waves the "tattered ensign above his head," the royalist in the stocks objects and shouts "Treason, treason!" The people, however, cry out triumphantly in support of Endicott and give their sanction "to one of the boldest exploits" recorded in American history. Hawthorne comments that Endicott's "rending of the Red Cross from New England's banner" represents "the first omen of that deliverance which our fathers consummated, after the bones of the stern Puritan had lain more than a century in the dust."

CRITICAL ANALYSIS

This story, in which a suspected Roman Catholic is in the pillory, dramatizes the Puritan resistance to Roman Catholicism as well as the colonists' defiance of English authority.

Terence Martin views the tale as a "rehearsal for the American Revolution" and argues that Hawthorne employed the colonial past as a way of formulating a continuity in the "American revolutionary spirit." John Endicott embraces, in his speech and in his actions, a distinctive fanaticism even as he encourages the colonists to resist oppression by England. In this way, Hawthorne reveals the American past and sheds light on his reader's concept of national identity, solving in his own way the American writer's problem of "the constraints of a lack of tradition." Hawthorne's rendering of the past is by no means without ambivalence, however. The story demonstrates that the colonists, in their zealotry, were not cognizant of liberties other than their own. When an enraged Endicott is interrupted by the Wanton Gospeller on the subject of the "liberty to worship God according to our conscience," Martin observes that Endicott is able to "resist oppression in one breath" and yet "show himself a raging zealot in the next," but however "intolerant" and self-righteous, the captain still breathes "the spirit that would culminate in the American Revolution." Hawthorne paints Endicott's character with complexity and ambivalence: He presents in Endicott "a portrait of the hero as tyrant." Martin sees Hawthorne's "ambivalence toward the Puritans" as a consequence of "his ambivalence toward the institutions of the past and present. Democracy is both necessary and glorious; but to have it, one must eliminate the king" (*Nathaniel Hawthorne*).

William E. Grant reminds us that Hawthorne "makes use of an actual historical event" for "his own purposes." Historically, John Endicott's tearing of the "red cross of Saint George, the patron saint of England," from a British flag was "in all likelihood a religious gesture," because the cross symbolized the Church of England and, to the Puritans, suggested idolatry." In Hawthorne's story, however, the religious gesture is imbued with political meaning; he "links Puritan defiance of royal authority" to the "events of the American Revolution nearly a century and a half later." Grant explores "the extent to which Hawthorne's treatment of the Puritan leader is ironic." He acknowledges that Endicott's "passionate stand against Old World tyranny marks him as a legitimate American hero" but observes that the setting of the tale—the reflection in Endicott's breastplate, painting a "picture of Puritan intolerance unrivaled in Hawthorne's writings"— "suggests other possibilities." Hawthorne never resolves the "tension between Endicott as symbol of religious intolerance and as emblem of heroic resistance to foreign domination of New England." While he acknowledges "what is admirable" in the Puritan past, Hawthorne "nevertheless recognized that the little commonwealth was, in some respects, compromised from the beginning by evils which mimicked those of the Old World from which the Puritans fled" ("Nathaniel Hawthorne").

The tale is also instructive in the art of the writing of history. John Nickel observes that it was published during the "first boom period of U.S. historiography" and comments that Hawthorne himself was alert to the dangers of creating myth even as he dramatized historical events ("Hawthorne's Demystification of History in 'Endicott and the Red Cross'"). He realized the pitfalls inherent in producing "subjective interpretations of the past as revelations of natural, eternal laws." The historian George Bancroft had, in Hawthorne's opinion, fallen into the trap of creating "romantic historiography" with his immensely popular *Bancroft's History of the United States,* the first volume of which was published in 1834. It is known that Hawthorne borrowed this book from the Salem Athenaeum from April 13 to May 6, 1837. Hawthorne did not regard his historical account of the incident involving Endicott as absolutely objective, but, rather, as a subjective creation and interpretation. He considered himself at liberty to construct meaning for the past, and to shape his writing accordingly. His telling of history contains an "imaginative truth" but is not, and could not be, completely literal and objective. Nickel argues that Hawthorne actually constructs a "false myth," suggesting that Endicott's action was not political but religious. For Puritans, the Roman Catholic Church was an invidious institution, deserving of condemnation, whereas the question of whether Massachusetts was independent of England was of secondary importance.

Stephen Orton proposes a "de-centering of traditional significance" in Hawthorne's use of "a multitude of doubles and symbols to undermine any strict historical or moral reading" of "Endicott and the Red Cross." This decentering "point[s] ultimately to an absence of significance, questioning not only the morality of the characters in the story but the emptiness of literary and religious themes." Orton observes that Hawthorne introduces, "at a feverish pace," symbols that at first glace seem "explicit in their relations to the Church and faith." However, any attempt to "attribute significance" to such symbols only "reveals a lack of uniformity." The story constructs "a series of dualisms and doubles, but proceeds to conflate them, multiply them, and oppose them." Hawthorne confuses not only the "historical attributes and actions" of the two main characters, but also the chronology of historical events. He "raises questions about the ambiguous relationships between church and state in the New World, between colony and motherland, between liberty and repression." His "liberally modified" version of historical events leaves out the fact that in actuality, Roger Williams may have encouraged Endicott to deface the flag and not restrained him; that Williams would have been 30 or 31 at the time of this story and not an "elderly gentleman," as Hawthorne describes him; that Endicott was actually "censured for his action"; and that the king's letter was relayed by the governor and not Williams. As readers, we see the town only as a reflection in the captain's shield. Thus we see "not the actual town but a reflection of it, not the real Word of the King, but a re-statement by translation." As is often the case with Hawthorne, we see the "allegorical, narrated, mythologized nature" of his world ("De-centered Symbols in 'Endicott and the Red Cross'").

At the same time, the tale has an emotional component that is both moving and persuasive. The appearance of Roger Williams injects a rational and cautionary note. After Endicott has excised the red cross representing the tyranny of Charles I and Roman Catholic popery from New England's ban-

ner, the narrator puts his act in context. He calls it "the first omen of that deliverance which our fathers consummated, after the bones of the stern Puritan had lain more than a century in the dust."

Interestingly, in "The WHOLE HISTORY OF GRANDFATHER'S CHAIR," Hawthorne's collection of stories told by an elderly patriot to his grandchildren, Grandfather's account of "The Red Cross" (which was published in 1841) somewhat differs from "Endicott and the Red Cross." John W. Crowley observes that unlike Hawthorne's telling here, in which Roger Williams "counsels restraint," Grandfather's version "implicates Williams in Endicott's action"; the character of Roger Williams admonishes Endicott, "For mine own part, were it my business to draw a sword, I should reckon it sinful to fight under such a banner." In Grandfather's account, Endicott "takes Williams literally, translating his religious idealism into action." Crowley suggests that, "so far as seeking divine guidance is not Endicott's business and drawing a sword is not Williams', these men foreshadow a split in New England culture between secular and religious concerns, between adventurousness and idealism" ("Hawthorne's New England Epochs").

CHARACTERS

Endicott, John Main character in the 1837 tale "Endicott and the Red Cross." In this story, Hawthorne paints a picture of John Endicott, a deputy official in the colonial government and the future first governor of Massachusetts, that is far from consistently flattering. He depicts Endicott as representative of the "Puritanic" idea of a strict division between Protestantism and Roman Catholicism. Harold Bush suggests that Hawthorne presents Endicott in a negative way in order to challenge and correct "the prominent and pervasive romantic constructions of Puritanism" that were prevalent in his day ("Re-inventing the Puritan Fathers: George Bancroft, Nathaniel Hawthorne, and the Birth of Endicott's Ghost," 132). Hawthorne had clearly envisioned, and targeted his story toward, a reader who resisted formulaic constructions of popular history based on legend.

In his depiction, Hawthorne departs from the conventional portrait of Endicott as a simplistically true leader of the people in their united and heart-felt resistance against royal tyranny. Instead, he creates a much more complex and ambiguous character, portraying Endicott as an ill-tempered despot as well as political hero.

The captain is challenged by the "Wanton Gospeller," who dares to suggest that Endicott's definition of "liberty of conscience" is flawed. Endicott speaks "imperiously" to Roger Williams, telling him his own spirit is "wiser" than that of Williams because he is capable of perceiving that King Charles I of England and Archbishop Laud are bent on persecuting the colonists further. They wish to establish "idolatrous forms of English Episcopacy; so that, when Laud shall kiss the Pope's toe, as cardinal of Rome, he may deliver New England, bound hand and foot, into the power of his master." When he cuts the red cross out of the banner, the high churchman in the pillory accuses him of having rejected the symbol of Christianity.

Some critics believe that, in this tale, Hawthorne takes care to warn his readers against unilaterally endorsing Endicott's menacing and fanatical character and implicitly advises them to reexamine the way in which "heroic" figures are portrayed in conventional histories.

Roger Williams Character in "Endicott and the Red Cross." In Hawthorne's telling of the story, the Puritan minister of Salem is a mild-mannered "elderly gentleman." Historically, Williams would have been a young man at the time of the event and known for his own Protestant zealotry. John Nickel observes that if Endicott symbolizes the colonists' aversion to Roman Catholicism and the authority of the pope, then Roger Williams represents "the more radical separation of spiritual concerns from social and political powers" ("Hawthorne's Demystification of History in 'Endicott and the Red Cross,'" 347).

FOR FURTHER READING

Bercovitch, Sacvan, "Endicott's Breastplate: Symbolism and Typology in 'Endicott and the Red Cross,'" *Studies in Short Fiction* 4 (1967): 289–299; Bremer, Francis J., "Endicott and the Red Cross: Puritan Iconoclasm in the New World," *Journal of American Studies* 24 (1990): 5–22; Crowley, John W., "Hawthorne's New England Epochs," *ESQ* 25, no. 2 (second quarter 1979): 59–70; Grant, William E., "Nathaniel Hawthorne," in *Dictionary of Literary Biography*, Vol. 74, edited by Bobby Ellen Kimbel, 143–163 (Detroit: Gale Research, 1988); Martin, Terence, *Nathaniel Hawthorne* (Boston: Twayne, 1965); Nickel, John, "Hawthorne's Demystification of History in 'Endicott and the Red Cross,'" *Texas Studies in Literature and Language* 42 (winter 2000): 347–363; Orton, Stephen, "De-centered Symbols in 'Endicott and the Red Cross,'" *Studies in Short Fiction* 30 (1993): 565–573.

"Ethan Brand"

Short story signed "Nathaniel Hawthorne" and first published as "The Unpardonable Sin. From an Unpublished Work" in the *Boston Weekly Museum* on January 5, 1850. It was reprinted as "Ethan Brand" in the *Lowell Weekly Journal and Courier* in 1851 and appeared that year in *Holden's Dollar Magazine*. It was collected in *The Snow-image, and Other Twice-told Tales* in 1852. The subtitle of the story is "A Chapter from an Abortive Romance."

The tale opens at nightfall on an isolated hillside in the Berkshire mountains. A lime burner, Bartram, sits at his kiln (in which he burns marble, converting it into lime, which is used for fertilizer). Bartram is the successor to Ethan Brand, who used to be engaged in the lime-burning business.

Bartram and his small son, Joe, playing nearby, hear a slow and solemn roar of laughter, which Bartram attributes to a drunken man from the "bar-room in the village," at the foot of the mountain. The setting is the same place where the legendary Ethan Brand had begun his search for the "Unpardonable Sin" many years earlier. The kiln is a "round, tower-like structure, about twenty feet high, heavily built of rough stones," with an opening at the top where marble can be thrown in and converted to lime.

Ascending the hillside is a human form, a man with wild "grizzled hair" and "deeply-sunken eyes," who looks into the kiln and tells Bartram he is actually Ethan Brand, returned from his search for the "Unpardonable Sin." The father sends Joe to the tavern to summon the villagers and tell them the news that Ethan Brand has returned. In the 18 years that he has been gone, the villagers have told stories about "this strange man," who reputedly "had conversed with Satan himself." According to rumor, Ethan Brand "had been accustomed to evoke a fiend" from the kiln each night, "in order to confer with him about the Unpardonable Sin."

Brand explains to Bartram that the Unpardonable Sin is "a sin that grew within [his] own breast." It is, in fact, the "sin of an intellect that triumphed over the sense of brotherhood with man, and reverence for God, and sacrificed everything to its own mighty claims." Bartram believes Brand to be a madman.

The villagers who had been in the tavern now appear, including the stage agent, who had long kept a desk in a corner of the bar; Lawyer Giles, an "elderly ragamuffin" who had once been a respected attorney but is now a soap boiler; and the village doctor, ruined by alcohol. The three "worthies" urge Ethan Brand to drink from a black bottle, but he refuses.

The doctor tells Brand he is no better than an aged man nearby, old Humphrey, who has been seeking his daughter Esther for many years. Brand's eye "quailed beneath the old man's," for among his many crimes, he had made the girl "the subject of a psychological experiment," with "cold and remorseless purpose," and "perhaps annihilated her soul, in the process." He admits his action is another "Unpardonable Sin."

Meanwhile, an old German Jew, also called the Dutchman, passes by with a diorama on his back. Some of the younger villagers ask to look at the diorama photographs, but they are fraudulent and worn out. Little Joe peeps into the box containing the diorama but turns pale when he realizes "the eye of Ethan Brand was fixed upon him through the glass."

The villagers then depart, and Bartram and Joe retire to their hut. Ethan Brand sits under the stars contemplating the learning he has acquired and realizes it was gained at the cost of his hardened heart. He had become a "fiend" at the moment when his "moral nature had ceased to keep the pace of improvement with his intellect." His heart had "withered" and "hardened" and "perished," and he was "no longer a brother-man" but "now a cold observer, looking on mankind as the subject of his experiment, and, at length, converting man and woman to be his puppets, and pulling the wires that moved them to such degrees of crime as were demanded for his study."

Brand has "produced the Unpardonable Sin" and thus has attained "his highest effort and inevitable development" of life's labor. He finally yields to the "consuming fire of the kiln," crying out, "O Mother Earth, who art no more my Mother, and into whose bosom this frame shall never be resolved! O mankind, whose brotherhood I have cast off, and trampled thy great heart beneath my feet! . . . Farewell all, and forever. Come, deadly element of Fire,—henceforth my familiar friend! Embrace me as I do thee!" His demonic laughter is heard that night, even penetrating the dreams of the lime burner and his son.

The next morning, the sun is "pouring its gold upon the mountain-tops" and the valleys smile "cheerfully in the promise of the bright day that was hastening onward." Little Joe believes the sky and mountains are both rejoicing in Brand's disappearance. Bartram then finds Ethan Brand's skeleton in the lime kiln. Within the ribs of his skeleton is "the shape of a human heart." A perplexed Bartram wonders whether Brand's heart was "made of marble," for it has "burnt into what looks like special good lime." He stirs the bones with his pole and the "relics of Ethan Brand" are thus "crumbled into fragments." There is an implicit suggestion in the description of Brand's marblelike heart that this "withered" organ has been made cold and unfeeling. With Brand's death, however, the atmosphere of gloom that had prevailed the previous evening is dispersed.

CRITICAL ANALYSIS

Terence Martin believes that in this story, Hawthorne "articulates most explicitly the theme of a man of ideas that had run through his fiction for almost twenty years." Ethan Brand is, like many

Hawthorne characters, a man "whose obsession with a single idea has made him absolutely committed to its realization"; in fact, in this story, the head vanquishes the heart to such an extent that the latter turns to marble. Other Hawthorne characters—including Aylmer, Hollingsworth, Rappaccini, and Roger Chillingworth—commit the sin of victimizing other human beings "by a programmatic use of the intellect divorced from the heart." However, those characters are motivated by a "finite intention," with a goal that is "within the realm of human conception"; Aylmer, for instance, wants to make Georgiana flawless, while Hollingsworth has the ulterior motive of taking over Blithedale for his own penal reform scheme. What distinguishes Brand is that he consciously wishes to "conceive of a sin so vast that God could not forgive it." Martin argues that "a man who could commit a sin so great that God could not forgive it would, by that very fact, have outreached God." His sin "would demonstrate that 'Heaven's else infinite mercy' was indeed finite and limited." In sum, "whereas other Hawthorne characters would be godlike, Ethan Brand would be God." His efforts over 18 years to commit the Unpardonable Sin result in untold evil acts, such as making a young local girl "the subject of a psychological experiment"—a "deliberate act of destruction" in which Brand simply "uses the girl as a means to an end" (Martin, *Nathaniel Hawthorne*).

William E. Grant notes that stories such as "Ethan Brand," "The BIRTH-MARK," and "RAPPACCINI'S DAUGHTER" are all "important treatments of the scientist in Hawthorne's short fiction." Aylmer, Rappaccini, and Ethan Brand are "empiricists . . . whose science proceeds by experiment rather than authority." Their "tragic results" suggest that Hawthorne had "serious misgivings about the new scientific methods becoming prevalent during his lifetime." In Grant's opinion, "Ethan Brand" rivals "in imaginative power the best of Hawthorne's short fiction, but it lacks the formal distinction that characterizes his best stories." The main character of the story "explicitly dramatizes" the author's fear that "science might subordinate moral values to experimental curiosity." It is the "imbalance between the head and the heart that

characterizes his scholar-scientists and leads to their downfall." As the narrator of the story puts it, Brand has "lost his hold of the magnetic chain of humanity"; his search for the Unpardonable Sin has "disturbed the counterpoise between his mind and heart," and the subordination of his heart to his intellect has caused the former to wither within him. Hawthorne's earlier scientists "may have erred from misplaced and even monomaniacal worship of the ideal," but none of them can be considered "inherently evil." The "Faustian" Ethan Brand, however, conducts his search for the Unpardonable Sin "in total disregard of any moral consideration," and his character may in fact deserve punishment for committing that sin which "sacrificed everything to its own mighty claims" ("Nathaniel Hawthorne").

Many critics see the story as a cautionary tale about Hawthorne's "Unpardonable Sin." This sin may be described as "divorcing one's head from one's heart and oneself from humanity" (Harris, Mark, "A New Reading of 'Ethan Brand': The Failed Quest"). Several details in "Ethan Brand" have led readers to conclude that Brand succeeds in his search for the Unpardonable Sin: First, at the kiln, 18 years earlier, Brand meets with the Devil, who supposedly starts Brand on his search. Second, there is something special, even unique, within Brand, the "solitary" and "meditative" lime burner, that has led him to his search and is still evident in him when he returns to the town of Graylock. Third, the narrator emphasizes the magnitude and importance of the Unpardonable Sin and Brand's commission of it. Fourth, late in the story, the narrator states what the Unpardonable Sin is and that Brand has committed it. Finally, Brand kills himself because he has committed the Unpardonable Sin.

As noted by William B. Stein, a careful examination of the story reveals that all of these "facts" are false. One of the alleged proofs of Brand's finding the Sin is the supernatural help he gets from the Devil, with whom he has allegedly made a "compact" at the lime kiln, "the abode of the Devil." However, nothing supernatural takes place at the kiln; nor does the kiln have any causal function in Brand's search. What we are told about Brand's presearch musings at the kiln is that "he had thrown his dark thoughts into the intense glow of [the] furnace, and melted them, as it were, into the one thought that took possession of his life."

Building on this argument, Harris challenges the assumption made by many critics that Brand has in fact committed the Unpardonable Sin and argues that Hawthorne's story is "as ironic as it is serious." In his view, Brand's motive for chasing after the Unpardonable Sin is his desire to "render himself the object of public notice," and that explains why he has returned to his old town. Eighteen years earlier, he "begins his search as nothing but a common man," only to return from it a "common failure"—and it is this fact, rather than his successful commission of the Unpardonable Sin, that drives him to suicide. Harris notes that Hawthorne repeatedly uses the words *seem* and *apparently*, which suggest that neither Brand nor the lime kiln is meant to have any supernatural associations. When Brand feels slighted by the rejection and disbelief of the doctor and the other villagers, he reacts "bitterly." In fact, he "wants people to care," a paradoxical desire that "proves that he has not committed the Sin." As Harris points out, "why would a man who has divorced himself from human sympathy return to his fellows for their approval, unless he still desired that sympathy?" If Brand had been successful in his search, "he would not be upset by the rejection he receives," but would instead "revel in it"—"or, more likely still, he would never have come back to receive it." He may well have thought he had found the Unpardonable Sin until his return to Graylock, where the "unwelcoming reception" he is met with makes him recognize his desire for a greater one. Brand commits suicide not because he has successfully committed the sin, but because he has "devoted 18 years of his life to a search that has failed" and because he does not receive the "welcome, approval, and awe" of the villagers that motivated his return. He is "unable to accept that he is not a legend after all, that his very return has deromanticized him in everyone's eyes rather than having the opposite, intended effect." Because he has failed both to find the Unpardonable Sin and to convince anyone else of his success, he "ends his life still refusing to admit his failure."

Some critics consider the story a flawed work. Robert E. Morsberger calls "Ethan Brand" an "imperfect work of art about an extremely potent idea." In his view, the main character remains undeveloped, with his life described in mere synopsis. He argues that the story "strains credulity" and is "guilty of what Poe called 'the heresy of the didactic.'" Hawthorne shows the reader only the "consequences" of the Unpardonable Sin and not the act itself; this lack of an "adequate narrative" leaves "Ethan Brand" with the feel of a "legend or fairy tale." Because of this, Morsberger suggests, the reader approaches the tale as allegorical rather than as "plausible." Brand's experimentation on and ruin of the young girl Esther, for instance, are "too vague and . . . tossed off in a sentence." Because Hawthorne "fails to incarnate the Unpardonable Sin in a sufficiently sinister form," he is thus forced "to spell out for us what the sin is" ("Ethan Brand: Overview").

Hawthorne himself had doubts about the story. He remarked that he had "wrenched and torn" the idea from his "miserable brain, or rather, the fragment of an idea, like a tooth ill-drawn and leaving the roots to torture me" (Miller, *Salem Is My Dwelling Place*, 266).

CHARACTERS

Bartram   The lime burner in "Ethan Brand." He has taken over the lime-burning business from Ethan Brand, who left the area 18 years earlier in search of the "Unpardonable Sin." Bartram burns marble in his kiln, converting it into lime, which is used for fertilizer. He is assisted by his small son, Joe. The narrator describes Bartram as an "obtuse, middle-aged clown," a boor. He is a simple man who troubles himself "with no thoughts save the very few that were requisite to his business."

When Ethan Brand returns to the kiln after many years, Bartram at first threatens to throw lime at him. He feels uncomfortable around Brand, haunted by his own sins, which rise up within him and make his memory "riotous with a throng of evil shapes that asserted their kindred with the Master Sin, whatever it might be, which it was within the scope of man's corrupted nature to conceive and cherish." Bartram's little son, Joe, empathizes to a certain extent with Brand. He pities him and, of the characters in the story, is the most sympathetic.

Brand, Ethan   The antihero of Hawthorne's tale "Ethan Brand," a former lime burner who may have sold his soul to the devil and committed many "Unpardonable Sins." When he is an old man he returns to his native village, a legendary figure owing to his 18-year absence and sinister exploits. During his life away from the village, he has enveloped himself in a "bleak and terrible loneliness."

He had once been a "simple and loving man," watching his fire and feeling "tenderness," "love and sympathy for mankind," and "pity for human guilt and woe." But slowly he underwent a change, as he began to "contemplate those ideas which afterwards became the inspiration of his life." He lured away a village girl, Esther, and made her the subject of psychological experiments that "perhaps annihilated her soul." After 18 years away, Brand has acquired much learning, but, on his return, he realizes it was gained at the cost of his hardened heart. He has become a "fiend" at the moment when his "moral nature" ceased to "keep the pace of improvement with his intellect."

On his return to his former town, his expression resembles that of a "fiend on the verge of plunging into his gulf of intensest torment." He claims to the villagers that he has committed the "Unpardonable Sin," the divorcing of his head from his heart. However, some critics doubt that he actually succeeded in this effort; Mark Harris suggests that he is ultimately a "failure," although he cannot admit this to others or perhaps even to himself. He has been rejected by everyone and in turn rejects humanity by committing suicide in Bartram's kiln.

FOR FURTHER READING

Bell, Michael Davitt, *Hawthorne and the Historical Romance of New England* (Princeton, N.J.: Princeton University Press, 1971); Butts, Leonard, "Diorama, Spectroscope, or Peepshow: The Question of the Old German's Showbox in Nathaniel Hawthorne's 'Ethan Brand,'" *Studies in Short Fiction* 20, no. 4 (fall 1983): 320–332; Davison, Richard Allan, "The Villagers and 'Ethan Brand,'" *Studies in Short Fiction* 4 (1967): 260–262; Grant, William E., "Nathaniel Hawthorne," in *Dictionary of Literary Biography*, Vol. 74 edited by Bobby Ellen Kimbel, 143–163 (Detroit: Gale Research, 1988); Harris, Mark, "A New Reading of 'Ethan Brand': The Failed Quest," *Studies in Short Fiction* 31, no. 1 (winter 1994): 69–77; Klingel, Joan E., "'Ethan Brand' as Hawthorne's Faust," *Studies in Short Fiction* 19, no. 1 (winter 1982): 74–76; Martin, Terence, *Nathaniel Hawthorne* (Boston: Twayne, 1983); Marx, Leo, "Ethan Brand," in *The Machine in the Garden and the Pastoral Ideal in America* (New York: Oxford University Press, 1964), 265–277; McElroy, John, "The Brand Metaphor in 'Ethan Brand,'" *American Literature: A Journal of Literary History, Criticism, and Bibliography* 43, no. 4 (January 1972): 633–637; Miller, Edwin, *Salem Is My Dwelling Place* (Iowa City: University of Iowa Press, 1991); Morsberger, Robert E., "Ethan Brand: Overview," *Reference Guide to American Literature*, 3rd ed., edited by Jim Kamp (Detroit: St. James Press, 1994); Stein, William Bysshem, *A Study of the Devil Archetype* (Gainesville: University of Florida Press, 1953); Stock, Ely, "The Biblical Context of 'Ethan Brand,'" *American Literature: A Journal of Literary History, Criticism, and Bibliography* 37, no. 2 (May 1965): 115–134.

"Famous Old People"

Subtitled *Being the Second Epoch of Grandfather's Chair,* this volume was published by E. P. Peabody, 13 West Street, Boston, in 1841. Elizabeth PALMER PEABODY, sister of SOPHIA PEABODY HAWTHORNE, would become Hawthorne's sister-in-law in 1842. The Peabody family had moved from Salem to 13 West Street, Boston, in July 1840. Elizabeth opened a bookstore there specializing in foreign titles; she also published other books and the *Dial*, the transcendentalist journal.

This was the first edition and the only printing of the volume. It contained a "Preface," a section of biographies entitled "Famous Old People," and the stories "The OLD-FASHIONED SCHOOL," "The REJECTED BLESSING," "The PROVINCIAL MUSTER," and "The ACADIAN EXILES."

The biographies included in "Famous Old People" are of the American artist Benjamin West, the British scientist Sir Isaac Newton, the Yankee scientist and inventor Benjamin Franklin, the English biographer and man of letters Samuel Johnson, and Queen Christina of Sweden (known as the "warrior queen"). Cantwell suggests that Hawthorne chose these figures because each symbolizes an aspect of life "intelligible to children" or a virtue he wanted them to emulate. For example, West is depicted as a child of seven in 1745, an untaught artist studying a slumbering child in a cradle (Cantwell, *Nathaniel Hawthorne: The American Years*, 311).

This volume should not be confused with *Grandfather's Chair: A History for Youth.*

"Fancy's Show Box"

An unsigned tale that first appeared in *The* TOKEN in 1837, with "A Morality" added to the text title. It was reprinted in the *Salem Gazette* on March 14, 1837, under the signature "By N. Hawthorne."

Hawthorne begins by defining *guilt* as a "stain upon the soul." He asks the rhetorical question "Will guilty thoughts . . . draw down the full weight of a condemning sentence, in the supreme court of eternity?" He presents an imaginary figure, "Mr. Smith," an elderly moral gentleman sitting alone in his luxurious home, sipping a glass of old Madeira. His children are at work and his grandchildren are in school. His silver hair is the emblem of a "life unstained except by such spots as are inseparable from human nature."

His thoughts stray to the "misty past" and he imagines three figures entering the room: Fancy, in the garb of an itinerant showman with a box of pictures on her back; Memory, with a finger between the leaves of a huge manuscript volume she carries; and Conscience, her face shrouded in a "dusky mantle."

They gather near and show him living scenes, such as a young couple, the woman kneeling in "shame and anguish" before the young man, who displays "triumphant scorn." Mr. Smith recognizes her as Martha, an early "cottage-love" he had hurt deeply. He tries to take comfort in her marriage to someone else, but Memory reads of his "sinful thought" while Conscience tortures him with guilt.

Memory then shows another scene, in which mirth and revelry had ended with a quarrel with Edward Spencer, dearest friend of his youth. He had angrily flung a bottle at Spencer but had not hit him; the next morning, they shook hands with a "hearty laugh." Conscience smites him again. In other pictures, he is portrayed as "stripping the clothes from the backs of three half-starved children." Smith had mounted a lawsuit against the children, who had been joint heirs to a large estate; his claims had turned out to be legally invalid, but the events still torture him.

The three spirits proceed to portray the "ghosts of all the never perpetuated sins, that had glided through the life-time of Mr. Smith." At last the figures vanish. Hawthorne observes that a "scheme of guilt" may appear to be like truth. The writer may create a "villain of romance," fitting him with "evil deeds," who will almost meet the "villain of actual life." But, he concludes, there is "no such thing in man's nature, as a settled and full resolve, either for good or evil, except at the very moment of execution." Man must not "disclaim his brotherhood"; his heart will be polluted even though his "hand be clean." Finally, "Penitence must kneel, and Mercy come from the footstool of the throne," or the gate of heaven will never open. Hawthorne thus argues against severe moral judgment of others, even when it seems justified.

Fanshawe

Hawthorne's first novel, published anonymously in 1828, at his own expense. Hawthorne later tried to acquire all copies and destroy them. He succeeded to the extent that the volume is now an extremely rare collector's item. His dissatisfaction with the novel ran so deep that he never told Sophia that he had written FANSHAWE. The novel comprises 10 brief chapters.

Chapter I
The story is set at Harley College (assumed by critics to represent BOWDOIN COLLEGE). The heroine, Ellen Langton, has arrived to live with the college president and his wife, Dr. and Mrs. Melmoth, as their ward. Previously, Ellen had been living with her paternal aunt, who is now dead. Her father, a prosperous

overseas merchant, next entrusts her to his longtime friend Dr. Melmoth, who convinces his wife that the 18-year-old will profit by her instruction.

Ellen considerably brightens the lives of the Melmoths, who have no children of their own, and is also extremely attractive to the young men at Harley College. Her "loveliness" draws "numerous admirers," and around the time of her arrival at Harley, there is even a "general and very evident decline in the scholarship of the college."

Edward Walcott, an undergraduate, quickly becomes her "constant companion" in part through his personal connection to Dr. Melmoth. Edward is tall and handsome, with a "natural grace" enhanced by "early intercourse with polished society." He is a respectable scholar, though not too concerned about his future, as he also possesses a "considerable command of money."

Chapter II

Edward Walcott must compete with another undergraduate, known simply as Fanshawe, for Ellen's attention. Ellen first meets Fanshawe when she is out with Edward on an afternoon horseback ride. Fanshawe possesses "a face and form such as Nature bestows on none but her favorites. There was a nobleness on his high forehead, which time would have deepened into majesty," and his features are "formed with a strength and boldness, of which the paleness, produced by study and confinement, could not deprive them." But his "thin pale cheek" and the "brightness of his eye" betray his poor health.

While the threesome are out riding, they pause for refreshment at a small cottage where two elderly women, sisters, are attempting to cook. They are evidently waiting for the son of one of them. The house is "small and squalid," and its occupants wretched and mournful.

Upon their return home, Fanshawe attempts to study but is distracted by the "unaccustomed thoughts in his bosom now." He has already spent years in "solitary study" and "scorned to mingle with the living world" and now feels the thrill of connection and the "exulting tide of hope and joy."

Chapter III

A few months pass. Ellen deftly handles the two rivals, neither of whom she prefers to the other,

when a stranger enters the picture. The threesome are taking a walk by a stream when they see an angler fishing under an oak tree. He has "bold and rather coarse features," appears "strong and active," and is apparently little more than 30 years of age. He claims to be a stranger but knows enough to catch a fish where the stream has worn a hollow under an old oak tree. He asks Ellen whether she would like to try to cast for fish, as they would "love to be drawn out by such white hands as those." Ellen shrinks back, but the angler repeats his request and calls her by name, and she agrees to try. He says something to her in a low tone that causes her eyes to flash with anger and "an indignant blush" to rise high on her cheek. She takes her leave and asks Edward and Fanshawe to escort her home.

Edward returns to the oak tree to seek out the stranger, who has since disappeared. He has left behind one fish, however, to struggle and gasp on the bank, a metaphor for his later treatment of Ellen. Edward throws him back into the water.

Ellen sits at a parlor window overlooking the garden, going over "a thousand motives" for why "an entire stranger should venture to demand of her a private audience." The stranger then appears in the garden, hinting that he has a message from her father that he must deliver to her alone. He tells her that her father is a "ruined man" and gives her a letter in his writing.

Fanshawe, meanwhile, has been watching; he now approaches to inquire what Ellen is doing in the garden "at such an hour, and with such a companion." He offers his arm to take her back to the house, but the stranger objects and declares that Miss Langton is under his "protection." "Retire, sir," Fanshawe replies, fixing his eyes on the stranger, who slowly withdraws. Fanshawe asks Ellen's forgiveness and tells her there is evil in the stranger. Ellen recognizes that Fanshawe has the power of a "superior mind."

Chapter IV

The scene shifts to the village inn. The landlord, Hugh Crombie, has a history of mischief and truancy but is now married to a prosperous widow, Sarah Hutchins. He sees a traveler approaching the inn; he once knew this man, long ago, but now nei- ther is particularly pleased to see the other. Nev- ertheless, they begin drinking together and discuss embarking on a joint venture.

The traveler is the son of one of the women in the wretched cottage but has not stopped to see her on his return to the village. He asks Hugh to describe Ellen, reveals the news that Ellen's father has drowned, and declares his plans to marry her. Hugh says he will not aid in "her ruin," but the traveler's arguments are so "effectual" that eventu- ally Hugh is persuaded to assist him.

Chapter V

Edward Walcott is in the inn with another student, Glover, drinking wine. The student believes he has seen Ellen at the inn, but Hugh Crombie denies it. Fanshawe then enters and, though in troubled spirits himself, inspires jolly conversation and sing- ing by Edward and Glover. They joke with Hugh Crombie, calling him "Professor."

A cloaked figure enters; all four rush up to the intruder. They discover that it is Dr. Melmoth. In his capacity as clergyman, he has visited the widow Butler, one of the elderly women in the cottage (and mother of the traveler). He is shocked to see the three students at such an establishment, but Crombie pretends they have been searching for Dr. Melmoth. As they are leaving, Dr. Melmoth opens one of the inn doors by mistake and finds Ellen Langton inside.

Edward is overcome with agitated emotion upon the discovery of Ellen here. Fanshawe takes his arm and says to him, "She has been deceived. She is innocent: you are unworthy of her if you doubt it." Edward asks what right Fanshawe has to speak of her innocence. Dr. Melmoth then asks Ellen what the meaning of her presence is and leads her from the inn to take her home.

After Ellen's departure, an extremely upset Edward drinks "huge successive draughts" of wine and hurls chairs through the window and into a looking glass. Crombie speaks to a man in the pas- sageway, who turns out to be the traveler, But- ler, who threatens to throw an andiron at Edward. Edward recognizes the man as the angler. Hugh calms them by proposing a duel in the morning. He puts Edward to bed in one of the rooms in the inn.

Chapter VI

Dr. Melmoth escorts Ellen home, where she slips quietly to bed, unseen by his wife. The next morn- ing, the mail arrives, an event that occurs only every two weeks. The newspaper contains news that the ship on which Ellen's father had taken passage has been found floating bottom up and that John Langton is presumed drowned. Mrs. Melmoth goes upstairs to inform Ellen, but at the same time her husband discovers in his mail a message that her father was not aboard the ship. He is, in fact, on his way to their home and should arrive in a few days. Meanwhile, Ellen has disappeared, and her room is empty. Dr. Melmoth goes to the inn, but no one there knows where Ellen is. Although Hugh Crombie acknowledges that a stranger has been at the inn, he denies "all acquaintance with his char- acter, or privity to his purposes."

Chapter VII

Edward Walcott, feeling miserable the next morn- ing, learns that the widow Butler has died the pre- vious night. He recalls her as the sick woman in the cottage. The whereabouts of her son are unknown, but it is rumored that he left town with Hugh Crombie years ago, and that Ellen's father had met him in "foreign parts" and tried to make "a man of him," but he was too wicked. Edward also learns that Dr. Melmoth himself has gone to try to find Ellen, who was "run away with" the previous night.

Edward rushes to the tavern and asks for a horse to be saddled so that he may search for Ellen. Hugh Crombie advises him to forget the girl ever existed. After Crombie gives him cider laced with brandy, Edward rides away. He overtakes Fanshawe, who is also searching for Ellen, and then Dr. Mel- moth, who proposes that he and Edward continue together. Casting themselves in the role of squire and knight, they ride along until they meet three strangers on horseback riding toward them. One is Ellen's father, who is traveling with two servants. He inquires about his daughter. Dr. Melmoth says he has been a "careless shepherd" and the "lamb has strayed from the fold." Several villagers are attempting to listen to their conversation, so Mr. Langton and his servants turn around and continue up the hill with Dr. Melmoth. They reach a tavern, where they stop to discuss the situation in private. Edward would have mentioned the incident with the angler, Butler, but Mr. Langton has "honored him with no sort of notice."

As Edward gazes down at the townspeople from the tavern window, he sees an individual with a dark countenance, a seaman, who tells him, falsely, that Ellen and her companion have gone toward the seacoast. Edward does not believe him. Meanwhile, the villagers are gathered together and appear to be speculating on her whereabouts.

This community scene, according to Robert E. Gross, prefigures other important public gatherings in Hawthorne's later novels: Dimmesdale's confession at the end of *The Scarlet Letter*, the gathering of townspeople outside the Pyncheon mansion in *The House of the Seven Gables*, the masqued revel toward the conclusion of *The Blithedale Romance*, and the carnival scene in *The Marble Faun*. He observes that in each novel Hawthorne presents such scenes as an index of "busy curiosity," a "unifying activity." The "community background integrates the characters and their drives with . . . the world of hustle and bustle, where social status is the thing that counts" ("Hawthorne's First Novel").

Chapter VIII

Ellen, meanwhile, has been in a "state of insufferable doubt and dismay" since her encounter with the angler. She has read the letter from her father, which "seemed to her inexperience to prove beyond a doubt that the bearer was the friend of her father, and authorized by him, if her duty and affection were stronger than her fears, to guide her to his retreat." Butler, aware of Mr. Langton's wealth, has artfully induced her to elope with him, using the ruse that she would be assisting her father, who is in distress. She considers confiding in Fanshawe, whose judgment she trusts, but unfortunately has no opportunity to consult him.

Ellen leaves the Melmoths' home with the angler. As he guides her, she feels "completely in his power" and suddenly experiences a change of heart. "A thousand reasons forced themselves upon her mind, seeming to prove that she had been deceived," but Butler claims she has a "faithful guide" in him.

They reach the wretched little cottage where his mother is dying. He stands in the shadows, his face "muffled in his cloak," but finally speaks to her. His mother beams with joy and throws her arms around his neck before dying. Despite the "evil life" the angler has led, he still feels guilt for the neglect and "misery he had brought upon his parent." Still, it does not "produce in him a resolution to do wrong no more." He then insists to Ellen that they continue on their journey. Ellen now realizes he is a "lawless and guilty man" who will not even stay to attend his mother's funeral.

When they exit the cottage, they find their horses have disappeared. Butler leads Ellen on foot through the forest to a cave. For a time Ellen sits in the cave, but then she decides to escape. Butler, a "false guide," intercepts her and, in a dark mood, seems "fiend-like."

Chapter IX

Fanshawe, meanwhile, has gone to the cottage of Butler's deceased mother, where the surviving sister is being comforted by other women. Since he is dressed in black, they assume he is a lay clergyman. The sister whispers to him, "I know whom you come to seek—I can direct you to them." However, she would like to be "bettered" by her information, so Fanshawe puts his purse into her hand. She tells him to "follow the path behind the cottage, that leads to the river-side. Walk along the foot of the rock, and search for them near the water-spout." As he leaves, she mutters to herself that his steps may lead to his death.

Fanshawe becomes bewildered as he tries to make his way and soon finds himself on a precipice. Looking over, he sees Ellen far below, entreating Butler. When she falls upon her knees, he throws a small rock near the pair in order to draw their attention. Butler then tries to ascend the cliff in order to attack Fanshawe, but when he is within a few feet of the summit, he falls backward down the precipice and meets "the fate he intended for Fanshawe."

Fanshawe climbs down to the base of the precipice, where Ellen has fainted. He rests her motionless head against his shoulder and feels "a joy, a triumph, that rose almost to madness. It contained no mixture of hope; it had no reference to the future: it was the perfect bliss of a moment,—an insulated point of happiness." He kisses her for the first and last time, with no thoughts of the future or the past, but only of the moment. He sprinkles her with water from the fountain in order to awaken her. They return to the cottage, where news of Ellen's safe return spreads to the town and to Dr. Melmoth.

With the death of Butler, his aunt becomes the "sole inheritrix" of the cottage. The narrator gives a brief history of the "evil and unfortunate" Butler, whose "harsh father" and "untamable disposition" had driven him away from his hometown. While in a foreign country, he had "attracted the notice of Mr. Langton," who looked after him and "gradually trusted him in many affairs of importance." Butler's "youthful indiscretions," however, estrange him from Langton, and he becomes "irrecoverably ruined and irreclaimably depraved."

Chapter X
Ellen falls ill and is confined to her chamber for several weeks. Her father tries to share his "abundance" with Fanshawe, her rescuer, in gratitude "for the inestimable service he had rendered," but Fanshawe's "flushed brow and haughty eye" preclude his offering any sort of reward. Mr. Langton understands that his rescue was not prompted by any thought of money but by love for Ellen.

Edward Walcott, although anxious for news of Ellen, stays away from the Melmoths' mansion. Ellen sees that Edward, "feeling the superior, the irresistible strength of his rival's claim, had retired from the field."

Ellen encourages Fanshawe, but he believes a relationship with him would result in misery for her. He predicts she will have a "long and happy" life, whereas his is destined to be "short, but not altogether wretched." This is the last time they see each other. Fanshawe returns to his studies with vigor but dies at age 20.

Shortly after the last visit with Fanshawe, Ellen and Mr. Langton return to the seaport and live there for several years. Four years after Fanshawe's death, Edward Walcott and Ellen Langton marry and have "uncommonly happy" lives. Meanwhile, Hugh Crombie reforms and dies an "honest man."

RECEPTION AND CRITICAL ANALYSIS
Joseph T. Buckingham succinctly summarized *Fanshawe* in the *New-England Galaxy* issue of October 31, 1828, as a "love story" with, "like ten thousand others, a mystery, an elopement, a villain, a father, a tavern, almost a duel, a horrible death, and—Heaven save the mark!—an end."

The reviewer for the Boston *Daily Advertiser* termed the novel "the first effort of a Collegian" but conceded that the plot was "true to nature" and did not violate the laws of probability (November 12, 1828). He described Ellen as so satisfied with her rival lovers that she is "like the ass between two bundles of fragrant hay." The reviewer suggested that the flaws in the book were due to the "author's want of confidence in his own power"; Hawthorne was "fearful of going too far, and does not proceed far enough." Although he deemed the "nameless stranger" "excellently drawn" and frequently found an "elegance of language" in the book, he critiqued the characters as "not wholly original."

William Leggett, writing in the November 22, 1828, issue of *Critic: A Weekly Review of Literature, Fine Arts, and the Drama,* was more encouraging, noting that the novel was not the first attempt of the author and should not be his last. He declared that the "mind that produced this little, interesting volume, is capable of making great and rich additions to our native literature." He considered the plot improbable and believed Ellen's flight lacked motivation but praised the language as "simple, chaste and appropriate," and the author's heart as "alive to the beauties of nature, and the beauties of sentiment." The novel exhibited "sincerity, and ease, and urbanity" rather than a "parade of manners" or "mock sentiment," and its characters possessed an "irresistible attraction." Sarah Josepha Hale, the founder of *Godey's Lady's Magazine,* also recommended the book and declared it "worth buying and reading" (*Ladies Magazine* 1 [November 1828]).

More than 100 years later, Stanley Williams writes that the characters in *Fanshawe* are "thin and two-dimensional, the dialogue pretentious; but a contemporary was right in declaring that in *Fanshawe* we may detect the weak and timid presence of all of Hawthorne's peculiar powers" (*Literary History of the United States*, Vol. 1, edited by Robert E. Spiller et al., 421–422).

William E. Grant agrees that the "original, American quality Melville recognized in Hawthorne was there almost from the beginning, though he did need to labor to get out from under the European influences that are so apparent in his earliest work." In particular, the imitative *Fanshawe* suffers from a setting that "never emerges from a generalized Gothic vision that owes more to Scott than to experience." Hawthorne apparently recognized the novel's flaws and therefore made efforts to disown it ("Nathaniel Hawthorne").

John L. Idol observes that despite the failures of Hawthorne's first attempt at writing a novel in the style of Sir Walter Scott, *Fanshawe* "foreshadowed what was to come: stylistically, it revealed Hawthorne's reliance upon such authors as Addison, Steele, and Samuel Johnson as mentors in shaping his sentences; thematically, it announced his interest in the dark side of human nature; and psychologically, it established his penchant for reflective, retiring young men who face difficult struggles as they attempt to cope with the world beyond their studies or writing desks." He acknowledges the great distance between Fanshawe and Arthur Dimmesdale but suggests that Hawthorne "took the first steps toward the Puritan minister in describing Fanshawe" ("Nathaniel Hawthorne").

Robert Gross points out that many elements in the novel recur in Hawthorne's mature work, such as the diabolical laughter of Ethan Brand ("ETHAN BRAND"), an abduction (as in *The MARBLE FAUN*), drunkenness (as in "The ARTIST OF THE BEAUTIFUL"), and madness (as in "EGOTISM; OR, THE BOSOM-SERPENT"). Gross also observes that many images in the novel are paired: the "labyrinthine garden with the intricate forest path," as well as the pool with the fountain, the recess beneath the bank with the cave in the rock, the gasping fish with Ellen, and the "ascetic scholar with the rapist adventurer."

Gross suggests that Hawthorne's diction in the novel is stilted and the syntax "overly cadenced," but that the style presages his mature prose. For example, he compares the topography at Harley College to the "Happy Valley of Abyssinia." Hawthorne works into this novel, as he would in his later ones, "moral or psychological reflections" and categorizes events into "general classes of experience." His fiction, beginning with this novel, is "not only profound but also lurid." The events of his final novel, *The MARBLE FAUN*, certainly bear out this observation.

Evan Carton sees in Hawthorne's works the recurring character type of the "misfit male dreamer," someone of "highly developed intellectual, spiritual, or artistic sensitivity who seeks to evade conventional male responsibilities" or to "resist the dominant paradigm of manliness that he often finds embodied in a hypermasculine counterpart." These character pairs are found in examples such as Fanshawe and Butler in *Fanshawe,* as well as Owen Warland and Robert Danforth in "The Artist of the Beautiful," Coverdale and Hollingsworth in *The Blithedale Romance,* and Donatello and Kenyon in *The Marble Faun.* Carton observes that Hawthorne typically "treats his male romantics with a mixture of wistful affection and ironic condescension," perhaps seeing in these characters aspects of his own youthful self as an imaginative dreamer ("Nathaniel Hawthorne").

In Terence Martin's view, the distinction is between the "man of imagination" and the "man of affairs," or the inner man and the outer man. The intensely scholarly Fanshawe contrasts with the social Edward Walcott, who is only a "respectable" student yet possesses a "natural grace" enhanced by "early intercourse with polished society." The novel's attitude toward Fanshawe is ambivalent, however. He is portrayed sympathetically, but his character is limited and ultimately doomed to "solitude, study, and death" at the age of 20. Although he has a chance at happiness with Ellen Langton, he "ultimately relinquishes hope of winning her hand in order to resume his courtship of death." It is left to Edward Walcott, who lives the more "ordinary life," to marry Ellen and live an "uncommonly happy" life.

CHARACTERS

Butler The villain of Hawthorne's novel *Fanshawe*. He first appears as a mysterious angler, fishing under an oak tree, who claims to be a stranger but seems to have information about Ellen Langton and her father. Butler manipulates Ellen into eloping with him by convincing her that her father is still alive and in distress. A "lawless and guilty man," he is motivated by the Langton family wealth.

Fanshawe

The hero of the novel *Fanshawe*. His rival, Edward Walcott, describes him as "a deep scholar and a noble fellow," and Ellen sees in him the power of a "superior mind." He is pale and weak, however. As J. M. Tyree observes, the "cause of his sickness is books," and his symptoms are "something like literary consumption" ("Fanshawe's Ghost," *New England Review* [summer 2003]). Fanshawe's passion for Ellen seems to have a "beneficial effect upon his health," creating color in his pale cheeks and reducing the brightness in his eyes. Although he is the one who saves Ellen from Butler, it is ultimately Walcott who marries her.

Langton, Ellen   The heroine of *Fanshawe*, she has gone to Harley College to live with its president and his wife. Her beauty and sweetness brighten the lives of the Melmoths and soon earn "the love of everyone within the sphere of her influence." Among her many admirers are Walcott and Fanshawe.

Melmoth, Dr.   The president of Harley College and the guardian of Ellen Langton in *Fanshawe*. The narrator describes him as "diligent and successful in the arts of instruction." The students "regarded him with an affection that was strengthened by the little foibles which occasionally excited their ridicule."

Walcott, Edward   The rival to Fanshawe for Ellen Langton's affections in *Fanshawe*. He is tall and handsome and a member of a wealthy family. Thanks to his personal connection to Dr. Melmoth, he quickly becomes Ellen's "constant companion."

FOR FURTHER READING

Bode, Carl, "Hawthorne's *Fanshawe*: The Promising of Greatness," *New England Quarterly* 23 (1950): 235–242; Carton, Evan, "Nathaniel Hawthorne," in *American Writers* (New York: Scribner, 1998), 145–167; Goldstein, Jesse Sidney, "The Literary Source of Hawthorne's Fanshawe," *Modern Language Notes* 60, no. 1 (January 1945): 1–8; Grant, William E., "Nathaniel Hawthorne," *Dictionary of Literary Biography*, Vol. 74 edited by Bobby Ellen Kimbel (Detroit: Gale Research, 1988) 143–163; Gross, Robert Eugene, "Hawthorne's First Novel: The Future of a Style," *PMLA* 78, no. 1 (March 1963): 60–68; Idol, John L., Jr., "Nathaniel Hawthorne," *Dictionary of Literary Biography*. Vol. 223, edited by Wesley T. Mott: (Detroit: Gale Research, 2000) 183–218; Martin, Terence, *Nathaniel Hawthorne* (Boston: Twayne, 1983); Robinson, Danny, "Rufus Wilmot Griswold and Hawthorne's 'Early Unavowed Romance,'" *Resources for American Literary Study* 12, no. 1 (spring 1982): 43–49; Stallings, D. T., "*Fanshawe*: A Revised List of Extant First Editions," *Nathaniel Hawthorne Review* 27, no. 2 (fall 2001): 14–15.

"Feathertop"

Titled "Feathertop: A Moralized Legend," this story was first published in the *International Monthly Magazine of Literature, Art, and Science* 2 (February 1852) and 3 (March 1852). It was then collected in MOSSES FROM AN OLD MANSE (1852).

Hawthorne's notebook from 1840 contains a suggestion for a story about a scarecrow made by a modern magician, "the semblance of a human being," with legs in the form of laths and a pumpkin for a head. He planned to have a tailor transform it into "quite a fashionable figure" (Turner, *Nathaniel Hawthorne*, 237).

As the story opens, we see Mother Rigby, "one of the most cunning and potent witches in New England," smoking her pipe. She asks "Dickon" (an invisible spirit) to get more coals, as she is planning to make a scarecrow. It will be "fine, beautiful, and splendid," rather than "hideous and horrible," so as not to scare little children. She will create a "fine gentleman of the period, so far as the materials at hand would allow."

Mother Rigby fashions a backbone out of a broomstick on which she has taken many an "airy gallop" at night, uses pieces of furniture and household oddments for the limbs, and makes a body out of a "meal-bag stuffed with straw." The scarecrow's clothes include an embroidered plum-colored coat from London (rumored by neighbors to belong to the devil's wardrobe), a velvet waistcoat, and scarlet breeches "once worn by the French governor of Louisbourg." The figure wears silk stockings and a wig that had belonged to Mother Rigby's dead husband, topped off with a "rusty three-cornered hat, in which was stuck the longest tail-feather of a rooster."

When finished, the scarecrow is "wonderfully human," with a "strangely self-satisfied aspect" and an expression "betwixt scorn and merriment" suggesting that it understands itself to be a "jest at mankind."

Mother Rigby is so pleased with her handiwork that she decides to give it life. "I didn't mean to dabble in witchcraft to-day," she says, "but a witch I am, and a witch I'm likely to be, and there's no use trying to shirk it. I'll make a man of my scarecrow, were it only for the joke's sake!" She inserts her pipe into the scarecrow's mouth and orders it, "Puff, darling, puff!" A whiff of smoke issues from the scarecrow's mouth. The "bewitched" pipe seems to have a glowing coal in it, and the scarecrow keeps puffing.

The narrator admits that it may all be a "spectral illusion, and a cunning effect of light and shade," but Mother Rigby has a mesmerizing influence on her creation. She beckons to the scarecrow with such "magnetic potency" that "it seemed as if it must inevitably be obeyed." The scarecrow, although described by the narrator as only a "poor combination of rotten wood, and musty straw, and ragged garments," is "compelled to show itself a man, in spite of the reality of things."

It does not become human fast enough, angering Mother Rigby. We see "a glimpse of her diabolic nature (like a snake's head, peeping with a hiss out of her bosom)." She orders it, "Puff away," calling it a wretch. The scarecrow manages to send volleys of tobacco smoke into the cottage and seems to "take denser substance." She orders it to speak, and it does, in a "poor stifled voice," saying, "Mother . . . I would fain speak; but being without wits, what can I say?" She says it has brains enough to "babble."

The scarecrow replies it is at her service, and that pleases Mother Rigby.

She orders it to go into the world and play its part, since "not one man in a hundred" has more substance than it does. She imparts a secret word, a token it will use for introductions. It is to be known as "Feathertop," since it has a feather in its hat; she has also put feathers into the "hollow" of its head. Feathertop will win the heart of a particular young girl, Polly Gookin, daughter of Justice Gookin.

Feathertop goes off somewhat stiffly, but his bearing and attire make him a distinguished figure in town. He is thought to be a foreign nobleman, a "High German," a Dutchman, or even an ambassador from France. Only two individuals in town possess "insight enough to detect the illusive character of the stranger"—a little child who cries out "some unintelligible nonsense about a pumpkin" and a dog who sniffs at Feathertop's heels and then skulks away with a howl.

At Polly's home, her father introduces him as "the Chevalier Feathertop" and then calls him "Lord Feathertop." Master Gookin is "nervous, fidgetty, and very pale" while making the introduction. He notices the painted figures on the bowl of Feathertop's pipe are "in motion" and believes they are "a party of little demons." He fears that because of some past promise to "the Evil Principle," he must now sacrifice his daughter for those misdeeds.

Feathertop and Polly are left alone in the parlor, where Feathertop shows himself to be a "practised man of the world." Polly is oblivious of his "fantastical impression" and seems charmed by him until she sees his reflection in a mirror. The mirror is "one of the truest plates in the world" and "incapable of flattery," and she shrieks at the sight of it. When Feathertop looks at their reflection, he seems "not the glittering mockery of his outside show, but a picture of the sordid patchwork of his real composition, stript of all witchcraft."

A despairing Feathertop flees back to Mother Rigby, who threatens to torment Master Gookin or to make Polly hideous. Feathertop protests and explains that he has now "seen himself" for the "wretched, ragged, empty thing" that he is. Mother Rigby pities him, since there are, in the world, "thousands upon thousands of coxcombs and charlatans" made of no better material, and who "never see themselves for what they are." She could easily give him another chance and send him out again the next day but believes he has "too much heart to bustle for his own advantage" in what is "such an empty and heartless world." She turns him into a scarecrow after all and proclaims that it is an "innocent and useful vocation" that will suit Feathertop well.

FOR FURTHER READING

Durr, Robert Allen, "Feathertop's Unlikely Love Affair," *Modern Language Notes* 72, no. 7 (November 1957): 492–493; Elbert, Monika M., "Hawthorne's 'Hollow' Men: Fabricating Masculinity in 'Feathertop,'" *American Transcendental Quarterly* 5, no. 3 (September 1991): 169–182; Rucker, Mary E., "The Art of Witchcraft in Hawthorne's 'Feathertop': A Moralized Legend.'" *Studies in Short Fiction* 24, no. 1 (winter 1987): 31–39; Westbrook, Ellen E., "Exposing the Verisimilar: Hawthorne's 'Wakefield' and 'Feathertop,'" *Arizona Quarterly: A Journal of American Literature, Culture and Theory* 45, no. 4 (winter 1989): 1–23.

"Fire-worship"

Allegorical short story first published in the *United States Magazine and Democratic Review* in June 1843.

In it, Hawthorne mourns the replacement of the open fireplace by the "cheerless and ungenial stove" in the "old gray parsonage." (At the time, the Hawthornes were living in the Old Manse, in Concord, Massachusetts.) He misses the "brilliant guest," the "quick and subtle spirit" of the domestic fire, despite the fact that he can now read and write without numbness.

The narrator confesses that he himself has been guilty of putting up stoves in the kitchen, parlor, and bedchamber. One consequence will be the breakdown of "domestic life" into separate corners. Even worse, "furnace-heat" will spread into more homes, causing conversation to become restricted to debate and "moral intercourse" to be "chilled with a fatal frost."

FOR FURTHER READING

Bell, Millicent, "Hawthorne's 'Fire Worship': Interpretation and Source," *American Literature: A Journal of Literary History, Criticism, and Bibliography* 24, no. 1 (March 1952): 31–39.

"Foot-prints on the Sea-shore"

A vignette printed in 1892 on sepia paper, by Samuel E. Cassino, Boston, with etched illustrations by Louis K. Harlow. It was later published in the *United States Magazine and Democratic Review* and included in *Twice-told Tales*.

Hawthorne recounts the pleasure of being summoned by the ocean for a "last ramble" on the beach in September. He describes the extensive stretch of firm sand, the roar of the surf, a group of girls who vanish into the shadow of the rocks, and a flock of seabirds. Pleasant pastimes during his walk include writing verses in the sand with his staff (walking stick), exploring the ruin of a rampart, and climbing through rocks where, occasionally, seals and birds have come to grief. He makes a meal of a few biscuits he has and then flings himself down on the sand, basking in the sunshine, composing stories until a crowd of "gloomy fantasies" begins to haunt him in the darkening twilight.

Far below he sees a fishing party of men and women take their skiff to shore, land on the beach, and begin to heat a kettle of chowder and cook their "scaly prey" over a fire made of driftwood. They see Hawthorne, hail him as "Sir Solitary!" and invite him to share their meal of chowder and fried fish. He considers declining but immediately accepts, admitting that despite his "solitary joys," this is the "sweetest moment of a Day by the Sea-Shore."

FOR FURTHER READING

Franklin, Rosemary F., "The Seashore Sketches in *Twice-told Tales* and Melville," *English Language Notes* 21, no. 4 (June 1984): 57–63.

"Fountain of Youth, The"

An unsigned tale first published in KNICKERBOCKER, or NEW-YORK MONTHLY MAGAZINE, in January 1837. It was later collected as "Dr. Heidegger's Experiment" in TWICE-TOLD TALES. See "DR. HEIDEGGER'S EXPERIMENT."

"Fragments from the Journal of a Solitary Man"

A sketch first published in the AMERICAN MONTHLY MAGAZINE in July 1837 and later collected in The DOLLIVER ROMANCE AND OTHER PIECES (1876).

The narrator describes the death of his friend "Oberon" of a "pulmonary" condition (possibly tuberculosis). He has been requested to burn Oberon's papers, signifying that his writings have not been accepted by the world at large. He does so, with the exception of Oberon's journal.

Oberon had lived the life of a "solitary man" in a small village, "singularly averse to social intercourse." He had only traveled to the "metropolis" on occasional visits. His writings, however, had been much admired. The narrator calls him "unequivocally the most original I ever knew," with a "very charming" writing style. Arlin Turner observes that he is closely akin to the Oberon of "The DEVIL IN MANUSCRIPT" (Nathaniel Hawthorne: A Biography, 74).

The narrator examines the journal and quotes meaningful passages from it, including dreams Oberon had once had of visiting Broadway, only to awaken and find that he has been visiting it after his death.

He explains that Oberon had been orphaned and oppressed in his native village by his guardians. He had left and gone to Niagara Falls, the culmination of his travels. He had fallen ill there after four months but found the "kindest looks and tones of strangers" to be "unsoothing."

Returning to his native village later, disillusioned, to die, he watches the monthly practice of the fire engine company and observes small changes in the town. He concludes that it has been better to "compress" his enjoyments and sufferings "into a few wild years" and then rest in an "early grave." He sees that certain old men he remembered are still living in the village, "hale and hearty." Rolling about are happy little children, born since his departure.

Oberon wonders how the villagers will receive him. He determines to explain that "a man may go far and tarry long away, if his health be good and his hopes high; but that when flesh and spirit begin to fail, he remembers his birthplace and the old burial-ground, and hears a voice calling him to come home to his mother and father." He realizes that he loves his home and is content to die there.

Miller observes that Oberon is a "self-image" of Hawthorne, a picture of the "artist looking at himself as he depicts himself." He had, of course, traveled to Niagara Falls, but, like Oberon, he has had dreams of seeing "the Pyramids," "Persia and Arabia," and "all the gorgeous East" (Salem Is My Dwelling Place, 97, 107).

FOR FURTHER READING

Flibbert, Joseph, "Fragments from the Writings of a Solitary Man: Defeat and Death in Hawthorne's Shorter Works," Forum 3 (April 1995): 1–11.

"Gentle Boy, The"

Unsigned story first published in The TOKEN in 1831; it was dated 1832 and was published without attribution. It was collected in 1837 in TWICE-TOLD TALES after Hawthorne made extensive revisions. In 1839, the story was published separately; it was later reprinted a number of times in pirated editions of Hawthorne's tales.

The story was probably written in the fall of 1829, when Hawthorne borrowed William Sewel's History of the Rise, Increase, and Progress of . . . the Christian People Called Quakers from the Salem Athenaeum. He may have read other accounts of the Quakers as well. The characters of Tobias Pearson and Catharine, mother of the Quaker boy Ilbrahim, both have historical antecedents. Several conversions to Quakerism among Puritans are also known to have taken place.

"The Gentle Boy" was one of the most popular of Hawthorne's tales during his lifetime (Crews, *The Sins of the Fathers*, 61). In January 1839, SOPHIA PEABODY made a drawing of the principal character, Ilbrahim, for a separate edition published later that year. According to her sister, ELIZABETH PEABODY, when Sophia showed her sketch to Hawthorne and asked whether it resembled his mental picture of Ilbrahim, he replied, "He will never look otherwise to me" (Turner, *Nathaniel Hawthorne: A Biography*, 120). At that time, Hawthorne and Sophia Peabody were not yet married.

The story opens in 1656, when members of the Quaker sect begin appearing in New England and practicing their religion of peace. Guided by "the command of the spirit," their behavior sometimes seems irrational to the Puritans. In 1659, the governor of Massachusetts causes two Quakers to be hanged from a fir tree and, as a result, martyred. Their bodies are thrown into a grave off the side of a road.

A middle-aged Puritan man traveling along the road thinks he hears wailing, a "sound more mournful than even that of the wind." He finds a small boy of six, named Ilbrahim, crying beneath the fir tree and leaning upon a "hillock of fresh-turned and half-frozen earth." The boy is "pale" and "bright-eyed," with an expression of "sorrow, fear, and want." The Puritan offers to take him home and provide supper and a bed for him, but Ilbrahim says it is his father who lies in the grave below, and he must stay there. He also admits that he last tasted bread and water in prison two days ago, when his father was still alive. The Puritan tells himself he must not "leave this child to perish, though he comes of the accursed sect." Finally he persuades Ilbrahim to go with him.

The Puritan traveler, whose name is Tobias Pearson, takes him in his arms and carries him to the cottage he has built. They are received by his wife, Dorothy. Tobias introduces her to Ilbrahim and explains that "christian men" have "cast him out to die." He tells her that "his heart had prompted him, like the speaking of an inward voice," to take the boy home. Dorothy asks the

boy about his mother and learns that she has been taken from the prison into the wilderness, where she was "left to perish there by hunger or wild beasts." Dorothy immediately accepts Ilbrahim and tells him she wishes to be his mother. The adoption of the child of the "pernicious sect" alienates the other Puritans, however, and they begin to persecute the Pearsons and call them "backsliders."

They take Ilbrahim to public worship at the meetinghouse, where he keeps gazing at a woman wearing a cloak, whose face is "muffled in a hood." During the service, the Puritan minister speaks of the "danger of pity" and the evil of the Quakers. He says that "such was their devilish obstinacy in error, that even the little children . . . were hardened and desperate heretics." Then the mysterious woman rises from the front row and goes to the pulpit. She sheds her cloak and appears in a "shapeless robe of sackcloth," her "raven hair" strewn with "pale streaks of ashes." She has a "deathly white" face and is "wild with enthusiasm and strange sorrow" as she speaks passionately against the persecution of Quakers. She utters a lengthy imprecation against all who "shed the blood of saints," who have "slain the husband, and cast forth the child, the tender infant, to wander homeless, and hungry, and cold, till he die; and have saved the mother alive, in the cruelty of their tender mercies." She turns out to be Catharine, Ilbrahim's natural mother, and is about to be sent to prison for her actions.

When she gazes upon Ilbrahim and realizes he is still alive, she sobs and embraces him. It seems as though "the indulgence of natural love" has "given her mind a momentary sense of its errors, and made her know how far she had strayed from duty, in following the dictates of a wild fanaticism." She laments that she has "ill performed a mother's part" and will leave Ilbrahim "no inheritance but woe and shame." Dorothy stands and approaches the Quaker woman, offering to be the boy's mother. The Quaker woman says she is not of their people, and Dorothy admits that, but she argues that they are both Christians "looking upward to the same Heaven," and that, if she is allowed to care for him, he will meet his natural mother in heaven. The Quaker asks whether Dorothy will teach the boy "the enlightened faith which his father has died for," but Dorothy cannot promise this, explaining that she must "breed him up in the instruction which Heaven has imparted to us" and "pray for him the prayers of our own faith." The Quaker woman then asks about Dorothy's husband. Tobias walks forward, and Ilbrahim's mother notes a "hesitating air" in him and an inability to meet her eyes. She declares that she hears an inner voice addressing her: "Leave thy child, Catharine, for his place is here, and go hence, for I have other work for thee." She entrusts the boy to the Pearsons and leaves in order to preach the Quaker faith. The reader learns that her mission has already led her to "many lands of Christendom" as well as Turkey, and that she has previously endured persecution by Catholics.

Pearson and his wife acquire parental rights to Ilbrahim, who becomes "a piece of the immoveable furniture of their hearts." He becomes more "childlike" in their care, and his "airy gaiety" is "like a domesticated sunbeam" to them. He has a delicate spirit, however, and Dorothy nurtures him "with the gentle care of one who handles a butterfly." Ilbrahim remains the object of "scorn and bitterness" in the community and avoids calling attention to himself among the neighboring children. One day, the Pearsons take in a boy two years older, who is injured in a fall from a tree near their home. This boy is "sullen and reserved," but Ilbrahim, the "child of persecution," seems to feel a bond with the suffering convalescent. Ilbrahim amuses and entertains him in his sickbed, although the older boy retains his "dark and stubborn nature." Eventually he returns to his own home to continue his recovery. Once he is well, he joins his playmates behind the meetinghouse, leaning on a staff for support. Ilbrahim approaches, but the "brood of baby-fiends" attacks him with sticks and stones. The older boy calls out, "Fear not, Ilbrahim, come hither and take my hand." But when Ilbrahim reaches him, the "foulhearted little villain" strikes him with his staff. A few neighbors interrupt the attack and take Ilbrahim home. He has suffered not only bodily harm, but also—and even worse—injury to his "sensitive spirit."

Many months later, on a bitter winter evening, Tobias has received a Quaker visitor who reads Scripture to him. When he sees that his words have little effect on the sullen and bitter Tobias, he asks, "Art thou he that wouldst be content to give all, and endure all, for conscience' sake; desiring even peculiar trials, that thy faith might be purified, and thy heart weaned from worldly desires?" Ilbrahim's mother, Catharine, then arrives at the door. She says she is the "messenger of glad tidings," for the king has sent letters to stay any futher executions. She looks around the room for her son and shrieks with agony when told he is very ill. Though Ilbrahim is near death, he senses his mother's presence. Catharine kneels by his bedside and embraces him. As he dies, he says earnestly, "Mourn not, dearest mother. I am happy now."

The reader learns that despite the king's mandate, the "colonial authorities, trusting in the remoteness of their situation . . . shortly renewed their severities" in persecuting the Quakers. As Catharine ages, her "fanaticism" becomes ever "wilder by the sundering of all human ties." Over time, the Puritans begin to pity more than persecute the Quakers. At the end of her life Catharine returns to the home of the Pearsons, where her "fierce and vindictive nature" is "softened"; it is as though Ilbrahim's "gentle spirit came down from heaven to teach his parent a true religion." The others in the settlement now pity her and "do her the little kindnesses" that "are not costly." At her death, a "long train of her once bitter persecutors" follows her with "tears that were not painful" to her place "by Ilbrahim's green and sunken grave."

RECEPTION AND CRITICAL ANALYSIS

This story has a universal appeal thanks to its domestic setting and to the tragic circumstances of the killing of a fatherless child, only six years old, by negligence. There is also a scarcity of responsible adults here; all the inhabitants of Ilbrahim's "miserable world" withdraw from him and close up their "impure hearts" against him. They deliver an implicit message: They are holier than the child is. Frederick Crews states that the story is plausible and literal, compared with some of Hawthorne's other tales. Hawthorne himself admitted that "nature here led [me] deeper into the universal heart than art has been able to follow."

"The Gentle Boy" is one of Hawthorne's most noted Puritan tales. In the story, there is a psychological opposition between Puritans, represented as a rather sadistic sect, and Quakers. The narrator condemns Puritan intolerance and exposes the cruel punishments Puritans inflicted on women in the name of religious righteousness. Some critics consider the work an "imaginary atonement" by Hawthorne for the role his ancestor, William Hathorne, played in the persecution of Quakers.

The *Literary Gazette; and Journal of the Belles Lettres, Arts, Sciences* published a unique review on June 22, 1839: "We confess we cannot tell what to make of this sentimental rhapsody. There is a pretty outline illustration."

Horatio Bridge, however, in an April 5, 1837, review in *Age*, deemed the story "beautifully written" and declared that the author had "struck a vein of the deepest pathos." He found Ilbrahim a character of "tenderness and beauty, more fit for Heaven than for the world, and therefore inevitably crushed by human sufferings and wrongs."

Elizabeth Palmer Peabody's review of TWICE-TOLD TALES, in the March 24, 1838, *New-Yorker,* proclaimed "The Gentle Boy" "more of a story than any of the rest." She described Ilbrahim as an "angelic child" in whom "we see human nature in its most perfect holiness, its infinite tenderness, its martyr power, pleading, with all the eloquence of silent suffering, against the time-hallowed sins and ever renewed errors of men."

Park Benjamin concurred in a January 26, 1839, review in the *New-Yorker,* calling "The Gentle Boy" an "affecting and beautiful story." He singled out SOPHIA Peabody's accompanying original illustration for particular mention, pronouncing the "softly and delicately drawn" work as a "display of the most exquisite genius."

Washington Allston's review in the *Christian Register and Boston Observer* (January 19, 1839) also lavished praise, describing "The Gentle Boy" as an "exquisite little tale" with "an appropriateness to these times its author probably never dreamed of." He considered the story a "poem on toleration," and pointed out that the "persecuting sect" appeared the worst, but that "the persecuted sect also" is portrayed unsympathetically. Allston wrote that there was "not a stronger appeal for a rational and benignant religion" than the "silent sufferings of the little Ilbrahim." He suggested that the story would also provide a lesson for children, teaching them "to reverence the religious associations of others, however they may seem to be wild and fanatical," and to learn of death "as a deliverer from the sufferings of life."

Moving ahead to the current century, Gorman Beauchamp observes that Hawthorne's Puritan stories—among them "The Gentle Boy," "The MAYPOLE OF MERRY MOUNT," and "ENDICOTT AND THE RED CROSS"—all present the Puritans as "rigid, self-righteous, persecutorial in imposing their vision of truth upon the world." The Puritans' "purpose, of course, was the utopian goal of founding . . . a City on a Hill, a New Jerusalem." Beauchamp sees in the tales a "skepticism" toward the Puritans' "fanatical zeal to redeem the world, with the whipping-post and brand when necessary" ("Hawthorne and the Universal Reformers").

Although the narrator is critical of Puritans, he is also not sympathetic to Quakers. In fact, he regards both sects as fanatical. Crews points out that Hawthorne undercuts the Quaker "pretensions to divine guidance." Their supposed willingness to be martyred is actually, as Crews sees it, intense masochism. The child, Ilbrahim, is subjected to the "cruel delinquency of the Puritans and the negligent deliquency of the Quakers." Tobias, seemingly a kindly paternal figure, is in actuality not a good father for Ilbrahim. All of his own children have died, and his fellow Puritans interpret this as a judgment against him. He has, in their eyes, been perhaps too solicitous about his children's earthly happiness (Crews, *The Sins of the Fathers*, 65–69).

Terence Martin proposes that the story effectively illustrates "the dehumanizing effects of a religious idea." Hawthorne exposes the extremes of both Puritan severity and Quaker fanaticism, showing the effect of each on the other: "Persecution was at once the 'cause and effect' of Quaker extravagance." He particularly condemns the destructive band of Puritan children, the "baby-fiends" whose "instinct of destruction" is "far more loathsome than the blood-thirstiness of manhood." Throughout the story, Hawthorne maintains a "rigorous and unsentimental" portrayal of the Puritans. He also spares no sympathy for the fanatical Catharine, who has "embraced an idea which appears noble in the abstract but is so demanding that it urges her to 'break the bonds of natural affection' and martyr her love." In Hawthorne's view, Catherine neglects "the holiest trust which can be committed to a woman." As Martin observes, "a faith that can exist only at the expense of the heart is, for Hawthorne, no valid faith at all"; and in his portrayal, both Quakers and Puritans have a "narrow, twisted, egocentric, and abstract" view of the world that "lacks a sense of humanity at its center" (Crews, *Nathaniel Hawthorne*, 71–72).

CHARACTERS

Catharine   The mother of the Quaker boy Ilbrahim in "The Gentle Boy." After the encounter at the Puritan meetinghouse, she leaves her son with the Pearsons in order to preach the Quaker faith. She is sincere in her belief that she must "break the bonds of natural affection" and choose the life of a religious fanatic, relinquishing her role as a mother.

Ilbrahim   Principal character in "The Gentle Boy." The six-year-old Quaker boy has a "pale, spiritual face"; "eyes that seemed to mingle with the moonlight"; and a "sweet airy voice." The Pearsons, his adoptive Puritan parents, attempt to "convince him of the errors of his sect," but his Quaker roots are "strong as instinct," and he can "neither be enticed nor driven from the faith which his father had died for." Despite this "stubbornness," the boy maintains a "grave and decorous demeanor" when the Pearsons take him to a Puritan meetinghouse, "such as might befit a person of matured taste and understanding, who should find himself in a temple dedicated to some worship which he did not recognise, but felt himself bound to respect."

Pearson, Dorothy   The adoptive mother of the Quaker boy Ilbrahim in "The Gentle Boy." She accepts him immediately because she has an even "quicker tenderness than her husband." When she first listens to Ilbrahim's bedtime prayer, she marvels "how the parents that had taught it to him could have been judged worthy of death." The Pearsons, and Dorothy in particular, dote on Ilbrahim, lavishing him with the "gentle care of one who handles a butterfly." Dorothy turns out to be more of a mother to him than the wild and fanatical Catharine, his natural mother.

When the Pearsons take Ilbrahim to Sunday worship at the meetinghouse and are shunned by their neighbors, Tobias finds it "difficult to sustain their united and disapproving gaze," but Dorothy "merely drew the boy closer to her" and "faltered not in her approach." After Catharine discovers her son is alive and moans in anguish, Tobias feels "agitated and uneasy," with a "certain feeling like the consciousness of guilt" oppressing him. Dorothy, in contrast, remains "free from the influence that had begun to work on his," and she rises to tell Catharine she will be the boy's mother.

Terence Martin observes that Dorothy is the only person in the story who "has consistently ameliorated the harshness of [Ilbrahim's] existence"; her "rational piety" marks her as neither Puritan nor Quaker, and her "capacity for love, at once the cause and the effect of her belief in the sanctity of a human heart, stands opposed to the forces of abstraction in the tale" (*Nathaniel Hawthorne*).

Pearson, Tobias   The adoptive father of the Quaker boy Ilbrahim in "The Gentle Boy." Throughout the story, Tobias, although a Puritan, has much natural empathy for Quakers; he is just and kind to them as well as to his fellow Puritans. When the boy first tells him that his "father was of the people whom all men hate," Tobias lets go of his hand "as if he were touching a loathsome reptile," but immediately recovers his composure because he possesses a "compassionate heart, which not even religious prejudice could harden into stone." He convinces himself he cannot "leave this child to perish" even though he is from the "accursed sect"; after all, he reasons, "Do we not all spring from an evil root? Are we not all in darkness till the light doth shine upon us?" As he carries the boy home, his heart stirs "with shame and anger against the gratuitous cruelty" of the persecution of Quakers.

Tobias is prompted to rescue the boy by a feeling like the "speaking of an inward voice," a description that echoes the Quaker belief in a Holy Spirit that speaks to each person. The narrator describes Tobias as "in a state of religious dulness" at the opening of the story; he is "mentally disquieted, and longing for a more fervid faith than he possessed." His adoption of Ilbrahim leads to a "softened feeling, an incipient love for the child's whole sect," though he also retains a "contempt" of their "tenets and practical extravagances." Over time and much thought, however, the "foolishness of the doctrine" becomes less evident, and the "points which had particularly offended his reason assumed another aspect, or vanished entirely away."

FOR FURTHER READING

Beauchamp, Gorman, "Hawthorne and the Universal Reformers," *Utopian Studies* 13 (spring 2002): 38–52; Crews, Frederick, *The Sins of the Fathers: Hawthorne's Psychological Themes* (New York: Oxford University Press, 1966); Doubleday, Neal Frank, *Hawthorne's Early Tales: A Critical Study* (Durham, N.C.: Duke University Press, 1972); Gross, Seymour, "Hawthorne's Revisions of 'The Gentle Boy,'" *American Literature* 26 (1954): 196–208; Martin, Terence, *Nathaniel Hawthorne* (Boston: Twayne, 1965); Miller, Edwin Haviland, "'Wounded Love': Nathaniel Hawthorne's 'The Gentle Boy,'" *Nathaniel Hawthorne Journal* 8 (1978): 47–54; Newberry, Frederick, "Hawthorne's 'Gentle Boy': Lost Mediators in Puritan History," *Studies in Short Fiction* 21, no. 4 (fall 1984): 363–373.

"Ghost of Dr. Harris, The"

Short story written on August 12, 1856, but unpublished during Hawthorne's lifetime. It was printed in THE NINETEENTH CENTURY in January 1900 and reprinted in *The Living Age* in February 1900.

It is a humorous ghost story in which the narrator seemingly accepts supernatural events as a matter of course.

"Golden Fleece, The"

Story first published in TANGLEWOOD TALES FOR GIRLS AND BOYS: BEING A SECOND WONDER-BOOK

(London: Chapman and Hall, 1853). C. E. Fraser Clark Jr., editor of *Nathaniel Hawthorne: A Descriptive Bibliography*, states that Hawthorne's American publisher Ticknor and Fields allowed Chapman and Hall to publish the book before American publication, in order to protect the English copyright. It was published the same year in Boston by Ticknor, Reed, and Fields.

The story concerns the life of Jason, son of the dethroned King of Iolcos. As an infant, he was sent away to be reared and educated by Chiron, a Centaur (half-man and half-horse). Now a "tall and athletic youth," Jason resolves to "seek his fortune in the world." Wearing his father's golden sandals and carrying a spear in each hand, he sets out to punish Pelias for wronging his father and taking over his kingdom.

Faced with a swollen and turbulent river, he is asked by an old woman to carry her and her peacock across the water. She seems to know his name and tells him that if he is not strong enough to carry her across, then neither is he "strong enough to pull King Pelias off his throne." He agrees, though cold torrents rage and thunder down from the steep side of Olympus. Jason catches his foot between two rocks and loses one of his golden sandals. Once across, he looks sadly at his bare foot, but the old woman tells him King Pelias will turn "pale as ashes" when he sees it.

Jason then travels to a town at the foot of a mountain, where the subjects of King Pelias are enjoying a holiday. The king is about to sacrifice a black bull to Neptune, who is said to be his father. The people notice that Jason wears only one sandal and are "greatly struck with something in his aspect." The "murmur and hum of the multitude, in their surprise at the spectacle of Jason with his one bare foot," grows so loud that it disturbs the sacrificial ceremony and angers the king. The people shout that Jason fulfills a prophecy, made by the Talking Oak of Dodona, that a stranger with one sandal will cast Pelias down from his throne.

The "crafty and evil" King Pelias tries to entrap Jason with a question. He asks Jason what he would do "if there were a man in the world, by whom . . . you were doomed to be ruined and slain." Jason answers honestly, telling him that "if he had his worst enemy in his power," he would send him "in quest of the Golden Fleece," "the most difficult and dangerous" task in the world. Pelias then orders Jason to undertake the voyage and return home with the Golden Fleece. Jason agrees on the condition that, if he succeeds, the king will give Jason his crown and scepter.

Jason first goes to Dodona, where he asks the Talking Oak for counsel. He is told to ask Argus, the shipbuilder, to construct a galley with 50 oars. When the ship, the *Argo,* is built, Jason returns to the Talking Oak, who asks that Jason cut off one of its branches and have it carved into a figurehead for the galley. An invisible hand guides the carver into producing a figure of a beautiful woman with a "grave and majestic" face. The helmet on her head covers long ringlets, and her shield bears a representation of the head of Medusa with snaky locks. The figurehead tells him to summon all the heroes of Greece to man the oars of the galley. These include Hercules; the twin brothers Castor and Pollux; Theseus; Orpheus; "two sons of the North Wind . . . who had wings on their shoulders, and, in case of a calm, could puff out their cheeks" and blow a breeze; prophets and conjurers "who could foretell what would happen to-morrow"; and a beautiful young woman named Atalanta. They are known as the Argonauts and promise to row to "the remotest edge of the world," if need be. The boat is so heavy that the 50 heroes are unable to push it into the water; the *Argo* is launched only when Orpheus plays his harp.

The heroes discuss the Golden Fleece, which originally belonged to a Boeotian ram who took two endangered children on his back and fled with them to Colchis. One of the children, Helle, was drowned, but the other, Phrixus, was carried safely ashore by the ram, who then died. The fleece of the "faithful ram" was then "miraculously changed to gold," becoming "one of the most beautiful objects ever seen on earth." It now hangs "upon a tree in a sacred grove."

The tale continues with the Argonauts' many adventures and "marvelous incidents, any one of which would make a story by itself." At one island, they are received by King Cyzicus, who tells them of the "six-armed giants" who have killed some of

his people and ravaged his country. They are no braver than ordinary men, however, and the Argonauts successfully slay a large number and make "the rest take to their heels."

At Thrace, they find Phineus, a "poor blind king" who has been "deserted by his subjects" and is "terribly tormented by three great winged creatures, called Harpies." The Argonauts lure the Harpies, who have the faces of women and the bodies of vultures, with a feast spread on the shore. As the Harpies grab the food and fly away, the two winged sons of the North Wind give chase and frighten the Harpies away from King Phineus.

On one island, the Argonauts are "assailed by what seemed a shower of steel-headed arrows" but are actually feathers being shot down by a large "flock of troublesome birds." The oaken figurehead advises the men to "make a clatter" by banging their swords upon their shields, and they are able to drive the birds away.

On this same island, they meet the two sons of Phrixus in a small vessel, heading to Greece "in hopes of getting back a kingdom that had been wrongfully taken from their father." The princes had been "brought up at Colchis, and had spent their play-days in the outskirts of the grove" that contained the Golden Fleece. They offer to turn back and guide the Argonauts to Colchis but warn Jason that the Golden Fleece is "guarded by a terrible dragon, who never failed to devour, at one mouthful, every person who might venture within his reach."

The Argonauts sail to Colchis, where Jason asks the "stern and cruel looking" King Æetes for permission to take the Golden Fleece. The king frowns angrily at the thought of losing "his chief treasure," which he desires in his own possession. The king tries to scare Jason by warning that before meeting the dragon, he must tame his two fiery "brazen-footed and brazen-lunged bulls," made by the blacksmith Vulcan. He must then yoke the bulls to a plow, "plow the sacred earth in the Grove of Mars, and sow some of the same dragon's teeth from which Cadmus raised a crop of armed men."

The king's daughter, Medea, promises to help Jason with his tasks. She is a young enchantress who was taught by Circe, her father's sister, and she knows the secret of the old woman with the peacock and the oaken figurehead. She gives him a golden box that contains a "charmed ointment" that will help him against the "fiery breath" of the bulls, as well as a basket that contains the dragon's teeth.

The angry bulls charge Jason, but, protected from their scorching breath by the ointment, he "takes the bull by the horns" and breaks "the spell of their fiery fierceness by his bold way of handling them." He then yokes the bulls, harnesses them to the plow, and sows the dragon's teeth. The teeth turn into an army of fierce warriors, who rush to attack Jason. Medea tells him to throw a stone among them; it causes them to fight among themselves until the last man stretches "lifeless on the field."

Despite his successes, the king tells Jason that he would have failed were it not for the "enchantments" of his "undutiful daughter" and forbids him to attempt to take the Golden Fleece. Medea then warns him that unless he sails away before the next sunrise, the king plans to burn his galley and put the Argonauts "to the sword."

An hour before midnight, Medea leads Jason into the sacred grove, where the fleece hangs from a tree, gleaming like "the golden glory of the setting sun." The "terrible dragon" that guards it has "enormous jaws . . . nearly as wide as the gateway of the king's palace." But Medea has a gold box that contains a magic sleeping potion, which she pours down the dragon's throat. Jason takes the Golden Fleece from the tree and hurries away, passing the old woman with the peacock. As he nears the galley, the figurehead calls to him, "Make haste, Prince Jason! For your life, make haste!" He boards the galley, the Argonauts give a "mighty shout" at the "sight of the glorious radiance of the Golden Fleece," and they sail triumphantly homeward.

"Golden Touch, The"

A retelling of the legend of King Midas; it appeared in the first edition, first printing, of A WONDER-BOOK FOR GIRLS AND BOYS (1852).

King Midas is more fond of gold than of anything in the world except his small daughter, whom the narrator calls Marygold. He spends all day in a basement room in his palace, counting his wealth. He sometimes takes gold objects into the light of the one sunbeam from his window. He is not satisfied, however, and will not be "unless the whole world were to become his treasure-room, and be filled with yellow metal which should be all his own."

A young stranger goes to see him and asks what would make him completely satisfied. He answers that he would be happy if everything he touched turned to gold. He is granted the Golden Touch, and the next morning he discovers that everything he touches turns to gold. The linen covering on his bed turns into "a woven texture of the purest and brightest gold," a bedpost becomes a "fluted golden pillar," the tassel of a window curtain grows into a heavy "mass of gold," and his clothes turn into "a magnificent suit of gold cloth." But the book he touches becomes illegible, he cannot see through his gold spectacles, and he is rather disappointed to see a handkerchief hemmed by Marygold turn to gold.

At breakfast, Marygold goes to the table "crying bitterly" because all of the roses have turned to gold and no longer have any fragrance. Midas tries to comfort her but is "ashamed to confess that he himself had wrought the change which so greatly afflicted her." The king's food then turns to gold, and his coffee becomes molten gold "the instant his lips touched the liquid." His meal is now "literally the richest breakfast that could be set before a king, and its very richness made it absolutely good for nothing."

Midas begins to doubt "whether, after all, riches are the one desirable thing in the world." As he groans with hunger, Marygold tries to comfort him with a hug. Midas gives her a kiss, and the girl instantly turns into a "golden statue." The distraught king wrings his hands and wishes that "he were the poorest man in the wide world, if the loss of all his wealth might bring back the faintest rose-color to his dear child's face."

The stranger then reappears and Midas asks to be rid of the Golden Touch. The stranger tells him that "the commonest things, such as lie within everybody's grasp, are more valuable than the riches which so many mortals sigh and struggle over." He tells Midas to sprinkle water from his river over the objects he wants to turn back into their former shape and texture, including Marygold, and to do so with "earnestness and sincerity."

After restoring Marygold to life, Midas decides it is not necessary "to tell his beloved child how very foolish he had been, but contented himself with showing how much wiser he had now grown." Years later, King Midas tells his "marvellous story" to Marygold's children. He assures them that, ever since that morning, he has hated the sight of anything gold except their "glossy ringlets" in a "rich shade of gold, which they had inherited from their mother."

"Good Man's Miracle, A"

Uncollected tale published in *The SNOW-IMAGE AND UNCOLLECTED TALES* (Columbus: Ohio State University Press, 1974).

The narrator informs the reader that "in every good action there is a divine quality, which does not end with the completion of that particular deed, but goes on to bring forth good works in an infinite series."

As the story opens, Mr. Robert Raikes, who happens to be in London, passes through a street "inhabited chiefly by poor and ignorant people." He reflects that there is "much evil to be remedied within a morning's walk of his own home." Children are splashing in dirty water; others are idle or quarreling. They are growing up "with none but bad examples before their eyes, and without the opportunity of learning anything but evil." He wishes he could save them. Nearby, a poor but "neater and more respectable woman" is gazing at the inhabitants of the street. She tells Mr. Raikes that Sundays are "a thousand times worse," since some of the children find employment on weekdays.

Mr. Raikes is not a rich man, but it occurs to him to establish little schools on the Sabbath for the children. He will hire "respectable and intelligent women" to teach them. The narrator states that this was the origin of Sunday schools, which spread from England to America and "to countries at a world-wide distance, where the humble name of Robert Raikes had never been pronounced." Every Sunday, children go to Sunday school and receive instruction that has been "more profitable to them than all the gold on earth."

"Gorgon's Head, The"

Children's story first published in *A WONDER-BOOK FOR GIRLS AND BOYS* (1852).

The story is a retelling of the tale of Perseus and his mother, Danaë, the daughter of a king. They are put into a chest by wicked people, who set them adrift on the sea. They end up safely on the island of Seriphus, where a kind fisherman befriends them.

The fisherman's wicked brother, the "bad-hearted" King Polydectes, decides to send Perseus, who has grown up to become a "handsome youth," on a dangerous and fatal mission. He sends Perseus to get the head of the Gorgon Medusa as a bridal gift for Princess Hippodamia. The Gorgons are three sisters who are "strange and terrible monsters," with locks of snakes rather than hair, long tusks instead of teeth, brass hands, bodies covered with scales, and wings of golden feathers. If a mortal gazed at one, he would be instantly changed into "cold and lifeless stone."

The rogue Quicksilver, a "brisk, intelligent, and remarkably shrewd-looking young man," offers to aid Perseus. He promises his wise sister's assistance as well. Quicksilver first exhorts Perseus to polish his shield "till you can see your face in it as distinctly as in a mirror." He then takes him to the Three Gray Women—the sisters Nightmare, Shakejoint, and Scarecrow—who share one eye and one tooth, and who will lead him to the Nymphs. Though the Three Gray Women have just a single eye, it is "as sharp-sighted as half a dozen common eyes." Perseus snatches the eye and tells them he will return it if they guide him to the Nymphs with the "flying slippers, the magic wallet, and the helmet of darkness." They appear at first to know nothing of the Nymphs but finally tell Perseus what he wants to know.

Following the women's directions, Perseus finds the "young and beautiful" Nymphs. They give him a magic embroidered purse, winged shoes, and a magic helmet that conceals Perseus from view.

Quicksilver and Perseus, accompanied now by Quicksilver's sister, fly over the island inhabited by the Gorgons. Quicksilver's sister cautions Perseus to look only at the Gorgons' reflections in his shield, not directly at them. He kills the sleeping Medusa and places her head in the magic wallet, which grows large enough to contain it. Perseus flies away from the other Gorgons, who cannot see him because he wears the helmet of invisibility.

When Perseus reaches home, he cannot find his mother, who has been treated so poorly by the wicked king that she has "taken refuge in a temple." Perseus goes straight to the king, who is not pleased to see him return safely from what was meant to be a fatal mission. But when Polydectes, his evil counselors, and his "ill-behaved" subjects insist on gazing at the head of the Medusa, they turn into white marble. At the story's close, Perseus goes off to find his mother and tell her "she need no longer be afraid of the wicked King Polydectes."

Grandfather's Chair: A History for Youth

A volume of stories from New England published in 1841 in Boston by E. P. Peabody (ELIZABETH PALMER PEABODY, sister of Hawthorne's fiancée, SOPHIA PEABODY; the Peabody family had moved to 13 West Street, Boston, in July 1840). It was published in New York by Wiley and Putnam. The book actually appeared in December 1840. The contents included a "Preface," "Grandfather's Chair," "The Lady Arbella," "The Red Cross," "The Pine-tree Shillings," "The Indian Bible," and "The Sunken Treasure." This was the first of three small books for children published by Elizabeth Peabody; the others were FAMOUS OLD PEOPLE and LIBERTY TREE, both of which appeared in 1841.

"Graves and Goblins"

Unsigned story first published in the *New-England Magazine*, 8 (June 1835): 438–444.

In this story the narrator is a ghost; he states that all "true and noble thoughts," all earthly wisdom and inspiration, derive from the spirits of past intellects. A phantom must haunt the grave until "purified" and until "the passions of the living world" are forgotten.

He recalls that in early childhood he had selected a spot in the country for his grave. However, he had died unexpectedly early, in his youth, and was buried in the crowded town cemetery. He meditates on the other ghosts who haunt the cemetery. One has the "guilt of blood" on him; another is a lofty patriot. One is sorry for his earthly mistress but is admonished to forget his dead mistress: "She has forgotten you!" A maiden has died, her lineage extinct. She was "hurried" away by angels. The ghost steals into the sleep of a writer and tells him "dreamy truths" he writes down as his own.

The speaker longs for the maiden he once loved to summon him; his visits may "hallow the well-springs" of her heart. She may eventually "seek the upper stars" and meet him there.

FOR FURTHER READING

Bezanson, Walter E. "The Hawthorne Game: 'Graves and Goblins,'" *ESQ: A Journal of the American Renaissance* 54 (1969): 73–77.

"Gray Champion, The"

Short story probably written in 1828; it was first published in the *NEW-ENGLAND MAGAZINE*, January 1835, and reprinted in the *Essex Register* the same month. It was then collected in *TWICE-TOLD TALES* in 1837.

The story concerns the historic struggle in April 1689 between the government of Sir Edmund Andros and the Puritans of Boston. It may also have been based on the participation of a judge in an Indian skirmish at Hadley, Massachusetts, during King Phillip's War in 1675. Both events are recorded in a book Hawthorne checked out from the Salem Athenaeum in 1826, Thomas Huchinson's *History of Massachusetts*, published in 1765.

The opening paragraphs of the story present the background for the conflict between the colonists and King James II. Andros, a "harsh and unprincipled soldier," had arrived in Boston in 1686 as royal governor but had become extremely unpopular for his oppressive treatment of the clergy, the press, and the people, with arbitrary fines, seizure of private land, and other serious offenses.

In 1688, William of Orange, ruler of the Netherlands, landed in England and drove James II from the English throne, securing the restoration of civil and religious rights in New England. News of this event did not, however, reach Boston until 1689.

Hawthorne describes a riveting confrontation on King Street, on an April afternoon near sunset, between the colonists and a group led by Governor Andros, the Episcopal clergyman of King's Chapel, and other representatives of the British Crown. The colonists, descendants of the original Pilgrims, still bear their ancestors' "strong and sombre features," "sober garb," "general severity of mien," "gloomy but undismayed expression," and "the confidence in Heaven's blessing on a righteous cause." As they gather in the street, the previous governor, "good old Governor Bradstreet," nearly 90 years of age, appears in order to ask the people to pray for the welfare of New England.

The soldiers approach the "religious multitude" of Puritans, marching "like the progress of a machine" and leading the group of "despotic rulers." These include the much-detested Sir Edmund Andros and his "favorite councillors," who are the "bitterest foes of New England." The rulers are "flushed with wine" and "proud of unjust authority." The figure who stirs up the "deepest feeling" in the crowd is the Episcopal clergyman of King's Chapel, the "fitting representative of prelacy and persecution." Andros is attempting to frighten the Puritans into submission. The narrator terms the scene a picture of "the deformity of any government that does not grow out of the nature of things and the character of the people."

A voice in the crowd cries out, "O Lord of Hosts . . . provide a Champion for thy people!" The crowd draws back, and suddenly there is a "twilight shadow" cast over King Street. An "ancient man" appears and confronts the armed band. This "gray patriarch" wears the old-fashioned dress of a Puritan "of at least fifty years before," including "a dark cloak and a steeple-crowned hat." He has a sword on his thigh and a staff in his hand. When he turns, his face has an aspect of "antique majesty." No one recognizes him. He marches down the street with a "warrior's step." He mesmerizes the crowd, speaking in "accents long disused, like one unaccustomed to converse, except with the dead of many years ago"; they look to him for the "deliverance of New England." His "stately form, combining the leader and the saint," "could only belong to some old champion of the righteous cause, whom the oppressor's drum had summoned from his grave."

The Gray Champion tells Andros, "I am here, Sir Governor, because the cry of an oppressed people hath disturbed me in my secret place; and beseeching this favor earnestly of the Lord, it was vouchsafed me to appear once again on earth, in the good old cause of the Saints." He then declares ominously to Andros that James, the "popish tyrant," is no longer in power, and that by the next day, the governor's power will have ended and he will be imprisoned. His voice stirs the souls of the colonists, eclipsing Governor Andros and inspiring the crowd to confront the soldiers.

At that point, Governor Andros fixes his gaze on the crowd. He sees that they are "burning with that lurid wrath, so difficult to kindle or to quench," and orders his soldiers to retreat. Before the end of the next day, Andros and his supporters are imprisoned. Word that King James has abdicated arrives, and King William is "proclaimed throughout New England."

Some people report that after Andros's retreat, Bradstreet is "seen to embrace a form more aged than his own." Others claim to have seen the Gray Champion fade away, "melting slowly into the hues of twilight, till, where he stood, there was an empty space." No one knows his identity, but the narrator says he has heard that "whenever the descendants of the Puritans are to show the spirit of their sires, the old man appears again," in times of "darkness, and adversity, and peril." He is "the type of New England's hereditary spirit," and his "shadowy march" pledges that "New England's sons will vindicate their ancestry."

RECEPTION AND CRITICAL ANALYSIS

In this tale, Hawthorne dramatizes the riveting power of the past. He sees colonial history, moreover, as prefiguring the spirit of the American Revolution. When the Gray Champion, in Puritan dress, answers the cry of an oppressed people, he anticipates later American history and becomes a popular hero.

Hawthorne's contemporary Horatio Bridge, writing in the April 5, 1837, issue of *Age*, felt that the story showed "a massive simplicity of conception," with a somber tone "as befitted the people and times." He wrote that Hawthorne's story showed "an original and a fortunate idea, that of making the old man the type of the hereditary spirit of New England, and connecting his reappearance with the great occasions on which that spirit is, and shall be manifested."

William E. Grant observes that this story about the Gray Champion, who looks like a "resurrected spirit from the first generation of Puritans" and speaks in a "voice of prophecy," introduces themes and techniques found throughout Hawthorne's later works. In this early story, the author takes "poetic license" with facts, creating a "regional, or even national, myth by realizing the symbolic possibilities inherent in his historical source." The "uncertainties surrounding the appearance, disappearance, and identity" of the Gray Champion provide "just the degree of the mysterious that Hawthorne described as the meeting between reality and fantasy." Grant notes that as his Puritan ancestors did, "Hawthorne saw the events of history as symbols for deeper truths, but while they sought religious truths he sought to create the 'truth of fiction'" ("Nathaniel Hawthorne").

Hawthorne follows the paradigm of a lively scene ending in a tableau. Before the procession appears, there is an air of excitement and anticipation. Then the atmosphere shifts when the procession is arrested and thrown back by the venerable old Puritan, who resembles an Old Testament prophet. The scene has a dramatic presentation, as pointed out by George E. Woodberry, who terms Hawthorne's technique "partly pictorial, partly theatrical, always dramatic" (*Nathaniel Hawthorne*, 135). Mark Van Doren observes that here Hawthorne stops short of the graphic depiction of violence and focuses instead on the "painting of august and awful crowds." His pictures "yield sounds as well as sights." The Gray Champion has a "stately form, combining the leader and the saint, so gray, so dimly seen, in such an ancient garb" that it immediately identifies him as a champion of the "righteous cause, whom the oppressor's drum had summoned from his grave." He becomes an apocryphal figure emanating authority that is almost supernatural.

The tale has generated several diverse interpretations. Nina Baym offers a pro-Puritan reading, arguing that the story is "unambiguously patriotic and its attitude toward Puritanism entirely affirmative." Frederick Crews, however, interprets the story as delivering a subversive message from Hawthorne. He suggests that Hawthorne views Puritans as hypocritical, for while they publicly espouse justice and freedom, the subtext is that the colonists do not meet "tyranny with freedom" but, instead, establish a "rival system of ancestor-worship."

Michael Davitt Bell (*Hawthorne and the Historical Romance of New England*) interprets the story as a "sincere expression" of the conservative ideal of the revolution. This ideal eventually manifested itself in widespread public attachment to the figure of George Washington as the "Father of our Country." Kenneth Dauber suggests that in this tale New England's "hereditary spirit" is celebrated in order that, simultaneously, "it may be demythologized" (*Rediscovering Hawthorne*). Royal tyranny is presented in terms of its effect on the revolutionary settlers.

The identity of the Gray Champion is not revealed, but this apocryphal figure is said to walk in King Street or in Lexington or on Bunker Hill—he is "the type of New England's hereditary spirit," and his "shadowy march" pledges that "New England's sons will vindicate their ancestry." Hawthorne seizes on known facts in order to enlarge them into legend in a compelling way.

FOR FURTHER READING

Baym, Nina, *The Shape of Hawthorne's Career* (Ithaca, N.Y.: Cornell University Press, 1976); Bell, Michael Davitt, *Hawthorne and the Historical*

Romance of New England (Princeton, N.J.: Princeton University Press, 1971); Crews, Frederick, *The Sins of the Fathers: Hawthorne's Psychological Themes* (New York: Oxford University Press, 1966); Dauber, Kenneth, *Rediscovering Hawthorne* (Princeton, N.J.: Princeton University Press, 1977); Grant, William E., "Nathaniel Hawthorne," *Dictionary of Literary Biography.* Vol. 74, edited by Bobby Ellen Kimbel, 143–163 (Detroit: Gale Research, 1988); Kruse, Horst, "Hawthorne and the Matrix of History: The Andros Matter and 'The Gray Champion,'" *Forms and Functions of History in American Literature*, edited by Willi Paul Adams, 103–119 (Berlin: Schmidt, 1981); Royer, Diana, "Puritan Constructs and Nineteenth-Century Politics: Allegory, Rhetoric, and Law in Three Hawthorne Tales." In *Worldmaking.* Vol. 6, edited by William Pencak, 211–240 (New York: Peter Lang, 1996); Van Doren, Mark, *Nathaniel Hawthorne* (New York: William Sloane, 1949); Woodberry, George E., *Nathaniel Hawthorne* (London: Chelsea House, 1980).

"Great Carbuncle, The: A Mystery of the White Mountains"

Unsigned short story first published in *The* TOKEN in 1837 and attributed to "The Author of the Wedding Knell." It was then collected in TWICE-TOLD TALES, of which 1,000 copies were published by the American Stationers' Company in March 1837. There were many pirated editions of the book after the first edition.

Based on an Indian tradition, this tale is founded on a legend that has been questioned, but never entirely discredited. The story concerns a "wondrous gem" sought by a "party of adventurers," seven men and one young woman, in the rugged and remote Crystal Hills of New Hampshire near the Amonoosuck River. They build a "rude hut of branches" and spread out their food supplies on a rock.

The adventurers are neither friends nor partners; each, "save one youthful pair," has traveled there "impelled by his own selfish and solitary longings."

The eldest of the party, a "tall, lean weather-beaten man" of 60, known as the Seeker, is dressed in animal skins. Another in the group is Doctor Cacaphodel, a "little elderly personage" who has "wilted and dried himself into a mummy by continually stooping over charcoal furnaces, and inhaling unwholesome fumes, during his researches in chemistry and alchemy." He is said to have drained all his blood in a failed experiment; he has never been a well man since. The other members of the group are Ichabod Pigsnort, a "weighty merchant" who, according to his enemies, wallows "naked among an immense quantity of pine-tree shillings" twice a day; a man referred to as the Cynic, who is "chiefly distinguished by a sneer" and a pair of "prodigious spectacles"; a poet whose diet seems to be "fog, morning mist, and a slice of the densest cloud within his reach, sauced with moonshine"; Lord de Vere, a haughty young man who wears a "plumed hat" and clothing with "rich embroidery"; and a handsome rustic youth, Matthew, with his "blooming" young wife, Hannah.

The group members tell stories of the "circumstances that brought them thither" and of the "innumerable attempts" that have been made to seek the gem. The man with a sneer asks what each individual "proposes to do with the Great Carbuncle, provided he have the good hap to clutch it."

The Seeker says it is his fate to "keep up the search for this accursed stone," that it is the "pursuit alone" that keeps him alive; if he finds it, he will take it to a cavern, grasp it in his arms, "lie down and die, and keep it buried with me for ever." The doctor plans to analyze the stone—he will grind part of it into powder, dissolve part in acid, and melt or set fire to the rest—and then publish the results. Ichabod Pigsnort says he will sell the gem to the "best bidder among the potentates of the earth, that he may place it among his crown jewels." The poet wishes to hide the gem under his cloak, take it home, and "gaze upon it" until "it shall be diffused throughout my intellectual powers, and gleam brightly in every line of poesy that I indite." Lord de Vere declares that there is "no fitter ornament for the great hall" of his castle than the Great Carbuncle. The young couple, Matthew and Hannah, will keep it in their cottage for "light in the long winter evenings."

The sneering Cynic, however, refuses to admit there is such a jewel. He has "come three thousand miles . . . for the sole purpose of demonstrating to the satisfaction of any man, one whit less an ass than thyself, that the Great Carbuncle is all a humbug!" The narrator describes him as "one of those wretched and evil men, whose yearnings are downward to the darkness, instead of Heavenward, and who, could they but extinguish the lights which God hath kindled for us, would count the midnight gloom their chiefest glory."

Suddenly, a "gleam of red splendor" illuminates the mountain. Matthew and Hannah awaken to find that all the others have abandoned the hut. They climb the mountain through the mist into the "bleak realm of upper air," where "nothing breathed, nothing grew." They follow a radiant light to the edge of a "deep, bright, clear, and calmly beautiful" mountain lake, which turns out to be an enchanted "lake of mystery" and the "long sought shrine of the Great Carbuncle." At the base of the cliff below the stone, they find the body of the Seeker. Matthew wonders whether the "joy of success has killed him," or "perhaps the very light of the Great Carbuncle was death." The Cynic gazes at the Great Carbuncle but, owing to the "wilful blindness of his former life," is metaphorically and physically blinded. Matthew and Hannah decide to abandon the Great Carbuncle and be content in their cottage and never again "desire more light than all the world may share with us." They descend the mountain, guiding the blinded Cynic.

From this hour, "when two mortals had shown themselves so simply wise, as to reject a jewel which would have dimmed all earthly things, its splendor waned." When other pilgrims reach the cliff, they find only "an opaque stone, with particles of mica glittering on its surface." Another legend persists that "as the youthful pair departed, the gem was loosened from the forehead of the cliff, and fell into the enchanted lake, and that, at noontide, the Seeker's form may still be seen to bend over its quenchless gleam."

RECEPTION AND CRITICAL ANALYSIS
ELIZABETH PALMER PEABODY's review in the *New-Yorker* (March 24, 1838) praised the story for com-

bining "the wild imagination of Germany, and its allegoric spirit, with the common sense that the English claim as their characteristic," as well as the "reliance on the natural sentiment which we love to believe will prove in the end to be the true American character." She wrote that the story awakened "that feeling and thought which is too fine in its essence for words to describe."

Terence Martin observes that throughout Hawthorne's work, "heart and hearth are intimately related." This point is abundantly clear in a story such as "The AMBITIOUS GUEST," whose characters are "ironically killed by a rockslide when they rush out of their house in search of shelter; their home stands untouched" (*Nathaniel Hawthorne*, 65). Martin suggests that for Hawthorne, "home, clearly, is of the heart; to be heartless is to be homeless; for home is the institution to which man may safely entrust his humanity."

Martin further proposes that "The GREAT CARBUNCLE"—as well as stories such as "The GREAT STONE FACE"—draws a moral "concerning the values inherent in domesticity and the futility of searching abroad for something to be found more surely at home." The young couple, Matthew and Hannah, reject the "awful blaze of the Great Carbuncle" to return to their "humble cottage." There, Matthew declares, "The blessed sunshine, and the quiet moonlight, shall come through our window. We will kindle the cheerful glow of our hearth, at eventide, and be happy in its light. But never again will we desire more light than all the world may share with us" (*Nathaniel Hawthorne*, 65).

FOR FURTHER READING
Benjamin, Park, "Hawthorne Unveiled." In *Nathaniel Hawthorne's Tales* (New York: W. W. Norton, 1987), 327–328; Martin, Terence, *Nathaniel Hawthorne* (Boston: Twayne Publishers, 1983).

"Great Stone Face, The"

Short story first published in the *National Era*, January 24, 1850, and reprinted in the *Essex County Mercury and Danvers Courier* (Salem) on

February 6, 1950. It was later collected in *Tales of the White Hills* (Boston: James R. Osgood and Company, 1877).

As the story opens, a mother and her little son, Ernest, are sitting at the door of their cottage, discussing the Great Stone Face, which they can plainly see even though it is miles away. According to the narrator, it is a "work of Nature in her mood of majestic playfulness." It is a rock formation that resembles a giant profile or face, with "noble" features and a "grand and sweet" expression. Many people believe the "valley owed much of its fertility to this benign aspect that was continually beaming over it."

The child imagines that if the Great Stone Face could speak, it would have a pleasant voice. He says that if he could see a man with such a face, he would love him dearly. The mother tells him of an Indian legend that a child would be born at some future time who was "destined to become the greatest and noblest personage of his time," and "whose countenance, in manhood, should bear an exact resemblance to the Great Stone Face." Such a man had not yet appeared, so some people have concluded that this legend is "nothing but an idle tale." The boy hopes he will live to see him, and the mother, not wanting to discourage him, says, "Perhaps you may."

Ernest grows up to become a "happy yet often pensive child," and then a "mild, quiet, unobtrusive boy" who possesses "more intelligence . . . than is seen in many lads who have been taught at famous schools." But Ernest's teacher is none other than the Great Stone Face, which he gazes at for hours each day.

A rumor spreads throughout the valley that a man resembling the Great Stone Face has appeared at last; he is called "Gathergold." He had left the valley years before and become an "exceedingly rich merchant" and the owner of a fleet of ships. Now a wealthy man, he resolves to return to his native valley "and end his days where he was born." He orders a splendid marble palace built on the site of his father's old farm and then hires upholsterers "with magnificent furniture" and a "whole troop of black and white servants." When he finally arrives, he is drawn by a four-horse carriage. He passes by a crowd of assembled people and drops some copper coins on the ground for some beggars.

Ernest is "deeply stirred by the idea that the great man, the noble man, the man of prophecy" is finally to appear. He sees no likeness, however, between the Great Stone Face and Mr. Gathergold, who has a "low forehead, small, sharp eyes . . . and very thin lips." Ernest is perplexed that the people see in Mr. Gathergold "the very image of the Great Stone Face."

As the years pass, Ernest grows up to be an "industrious, kind, and neighborly" young man. Mr. Gathergold dies, having lost his wealth before his death—and the people concede "that there was no such striking resemblance, after all, betwixt the ignoble features of the ruined merchant and that majestic face upon the mountain-side."

An "illustrious" general, called Old Blood-and-Thunder, returns to his native valley to retire. The throng of people are giddy with recognition. One bystander declares that the Great Stone Face is "Old Blood-and-Thunder himself, in a monstrous looking-glass! And why not! He's the greatest man of this or any other age, beyond a doubt." Ernest, however, sees no "such a resemblance as the crowd had testified."

Years pass and Ernest is now a middle-aged preacher. He has "become known among the people" as "more than an ordinary man"; the world is a better place because of the "good deeds that dropped silently from his hand." The people now admit "their mistake in imagining a similarity between General Blood-and-Thunder" and the Great Stone Face. They are now excited by reports of a "certain eminent statesman" called Old Stony Phiz, who has arrived to visit his native valley. He is an eloquent, "wondrous man," well received by the admiring people, but, again, Ernest sees "little or no likeness."

Ernest becomes an "aged man" who is "known in the great world" beyond the valley; professors and other men travel to speak with him. When his guests pass the Great Stone Face on their way out of the valley, they look up and imagine they have "seen its likeness in a human countenance" but cannot recall where.

After reading the works of a new poet, a native who has been away, Ernest is so thrilled by the words that he addresses the Great Stone Face, "O, majestic friend, is not this man worthy to resemble thee?" The poet returns home to the valley and seeks out Ernest, of whom he has heard. The poet has known "the wittiest and the wisest" of men in his travels, but has never met anyone like Ernest, whose "thoughts and feelings gushed up with such a natural freedom, and who made great truths so familiar by his simple utterance of them." Ernest, on the other hand, values the poet's living images. The "sympathies of these two men instructed them with a profounder sense than either could have attained alone"; they lead one another "into a high pavilion of their thoughts."

Ernest hopes, after reading the poems, that the poet has fulfilled the prophecy, but he does not resemble the Great Stone Face. The poet sadly tells Ernest that his own name must be added to those of Mr. Gathergold, Old Blood-and-Thunder, and Old Stony Phiz as "another failure" of his hopes. He says he is "not worthy to be typified by yonder benign and majestic image," for his poems have only "a strain of the Divinity" in them.

The poet and Ernest attend a gathering of local neighbors in the open air. Ernest ascends into a small stone niche, a "natural pulpit," and gazes at his audience with kindness. He speaks his thoughts, which are the "words of life" because "a life of good deeds and holy love was melted into them." The poet feels that "the being and character of Ernest were a nobler strain of poetry than he had ever written." Ernest's face assumes a "grandeur of expression," one "imbued with benevolence," which compels the poet to throw his arms aloft and shout, "Behold! Behold! Ernest is himself the likeness of the Great Stone Face!"

The people look at Ernest and believe that what the poet says is true. The prophecy has been fulfilled. Ernest himself, however, takes the poet's arm and walks slowly homeward, still hoping that "some wiser and better man than himself" will appear, "bearing a resemblance to the Great Stone Face."

(The Great Stone Face, also known as the "Old Man of the Mountain," near Franconia, New Hampshire, collapsed in 2003.)

CRITICAL ANALYSIS

Earl Rovit writes that he often introduces his students "to Transcendentalism by having them read 'The Great Stone Face,' which is almost a textbook illustration of Emersonianism" ("Contexts for Hawthorne: The Marble Faun and the Politics of Openness and Closure in American Literature," *Journal of English and Germanic Philology* 92, no. 1 [January 1993]: 145).

Terence Martin suggests that, like "The Great Carbuncle," this story draws a moral "concerning the values inherent in domesticity and the futility of searching abroad for something to be found more surely at home" (*Nathaniel Hawthorne*).

FOR FURTHER READING

Lynch, James J., "Structure and Allegory in 'The Great Stone Face,'" *Nineteenth-Century Fiction* 15, no. 2 (September 1960): 137–146.

"Hall of Fantasy, The"

Short story first published in the *Pioneer*, February 1843, signed by Hawthorne and reprinted the same month in the *New York World*. It was later collected in MOSSES FROM AN OLD MANSE.

The narrator describes the Hall of Fantasy, which has white marble floors; a "lofty dome, supported by long rows of pillars"; and grand windows with an "elaborateness of workmanship, that have nowhere been equalled, except in the Gothic cathedrals of the old world." The combination of "Grecian, Gothic, Oriental, and nondescript" architectural styles gives the edifice "the impression of a dream"; it is likely to "endure longer than the most substantial structure that ever cumbered the earth."

Not everyone enters the "noble hall," but most persons visit at some point in life. On the narrator's most recent visit, he finds himself surrounded by a crowd of people. A friend explains that those "who have affairs in that mystic region, which lies above, below, or beyond the Actual, may here meet, and talk over the business of their dreams." The hall contains numerous statues of great men and, in its center, an enchanted fountain.

The "water-drinkers" are men of "grave and lofty musings" and a "liveliness of expression"; they include some familiar names. Although the narrator feels an "inward attraction towards these men," he is glad to leave behind the "shy, proud, unreasonable set of laurel-gatherers." He loves their works but has "little desire to meet them elsewhere." The friend, "himself a student of poetry," points out the narrator's prejudice and says these "men of genius are fairly gifted with the social qualities"; this brotherhood of authors asks "nothing better than to be on equal terms with their fellow-men." The narrator replies that the world disagrees, for society receives authors as if they do not belong and questions whether they are fit for other pursuits.

Next they see a group of "shrewd, calculating" men of business, whose "sagacity gave them the command of fortune." Their talk is "matter-of-fact," so that even the "wildest schemes," such as building cities in the hearts of forests, or redirecting mighty rivers to run cotton mills, "had the aspect of everyday realities." The friend says these men "mistake the Hall of Fantasy for actual brick and mortar," whereas "the poet knows his whereabout, and therefore is less likely to make a fool of himself in real life."

The narrator and his friend continue on to see another group of dreamers, the "inventors of fantastic machines." With them are models of their inventions, such as a "railroad through the air, and a tunnel under the sea."

Looking around, the narrator takes in all of the inhabitants of the hall. He says that "even the actual" can become "ideal, whether in hope or memory," thus beguiling the "dreamer into the Hall of Fantasy." Some "unfortunates" conduct their life and business here and "contract habits which unfit them for all the real employments of life." But a few men are able to discover "a purer truth than the world can impart" on their visits here.

Despite the "dangerous influences" of the hall, the narrator is thankful that such a "refuge from the gloom and chillness of actual life" exists, whether for the prisoner to escape his cell, the sick man to leave his bed, the exile to "revisit his native soil," or the mourner to let go his "heavy sorrows." The friend comments that the "fantasies of one day are the deepest realities of a future one." The narrator finds it "difficult to distinguish them apart," for, as his friend points out, his "faith in the ideal"

is deeper than he realizes. Looking around at the "noted reformers of the day, whether in physics, politics, morals, or religion," the narrator sees there is "no surer method of arriving at the Hall of Fantasy, than to throw oneself into the current of a theory." Those who "rejoice in the progress of mankind" will see their leaders here.

In a far corner of the hall, a crowd has assembled around Father Miller, who has announced that the "destruction of the world was close at hand." As the narrator and his friend leave the Hall of Fantasy, he looks back and almost wishes that "the whole of life might be spent in that visionary scene, where the actual world, with its hard angles, should never rub against me." But he realizes that "for those who waste all their days" here, the prophecy of Father Miller is "already accomplished, and the solid earth has come to an untimely end." We should be content, then, with "merely an occasional visit, for the sake of spiritualizing the grossness of this actual life, and prefiguring to ourselves a state, in which the Idea shall be all in all."

CRITICAL ANALYSIS

Terence Martin observes that although Hawthorne's Hall of Fantasy has dangers—for those who live there permanently and "contract bad habits which unfit them for all the real employments of life"—a "place of refuge" like this still fulfills a need. Martin notes that people who "never find their way into the Hall possess 'but half a life—the meaner and earthlier half,' just as those who never find their way out of the Hall 'waste all their days' among unrealities." For Hawthorne, the role of the imagination is "to serve as a unique and judicious critic of reality"; one must withdraw "into the realm of imagination" in order to view "the rigorous confinement of life" before returning to the world with a "fuller understanding of the human condition" (*Nathaniel Hawthorne*).

"Hannah Duston"

This is the story of the capture of Hannah Duston of Haverhill, Massachusetts, by Indians in the 17th century, and her heroic escape. It was published in the *American Magazine of Useful and Entertaining Knowledge,* May 1836. It is sometimes titled "The Duston Family." The captivity narrative was a popular genre, and others who wrote the story of Hannah Duston included Cotton Mather, John Greenleaf Whittier, and Henry David Thoreau.

Hannah Duston was born in Haverhill, Massachusetts, in 1659; her maiden name may have been Emerson. She was married to Thomas Duston (also spelled *Dustin* or *Durston*).

Hawthorne tells the sad story of Hannah Duston's capture in March 1698. The Dustons lived in the frontier settlement of Haverhill. In the absence of her husband, after she had just borne her eighth child, an Indian war party broke in upon their "remote and defenceless town." Her husband, Goodman Duston, heard the war whoop and alarm and quickly rode home. He saw "dark wreaths of smoke eddying from the roofs of several dwellings near the road side; while the groans of dying men,— the shrieks of affrighted women, and the screams of children, pierced his ear, all mingled with the horrid yell of the raging savages." Trembling, he rode on faster. As he neared the house, he saw his seven elder children, all between two and 17 years of age, "issuing out together, and running down the road to meet him." He asked them to move quickly along the road to the nearest garrison.

He rushed into his wife's bedchamber; she lay in bed with her newborn infant, attended by her nurse, the widow Mary Neff. He asked her to flee for her life. Then "the Indian yell was heard: and staring wildly out of the window, Goodman Duston saw that the blood-thirsty foe was close at hand." He apparently then thought of the other seven children and was confident his wife could hold her own. He seized his gun and rushed out of doors again, "meaning to gallop after his seven children, and snatch up one of them in his flight, lest his whole race and generation should be blotted from the earth, in that fatal hour." Unfortunately, all of the children stopped suddenly and "resigned their charge into his hands," seeming to say, "'Here is our father! Now we are safe!'"

The father managed to escape with the children to the Garrison of Onesiphorous Marsh on Pecker's Hill. Hannah Duston and Mary Neff were captured, along with Samuel Lennardson. Hannah Duston returned home after killing and scalping her captors as they slept. She was considered a heroine and was the first woman in the United States to have a monument erected in her honor. It may be seen in Haverhill, Massachusetts.

"Haunted Mind, The"

Sketch first published in Twice-told Tales, 1837.

The piece is a reflection on being startled into a dreamlike state after being suddenly awakened from slumber, yet realizing that one's dream has not receded. The person finds himself awake in a world of dreams, in an "intermediate space where the business of life does not intrude." It is too cold for thoughts to "venture abroad," and it is tempting to desire a "whole existence in bed, like an oyster in its shell."

Then the haunted mind remembers the living world. The awakened sleeper becomes troubled, and memories of early sorrow crowd in, along with remorse. Reminders of the living world appear: visions of loved ones, scenes of travel, rainbows, sheets of snow, the twittering of birds, the bounding of a ship, rosy girls in a ballroom, and the theater. The clock sounds "the knell of a temporary death," portending the final journey of the soul to its eternal home, in death.

CRITICAL ANALYSIS

Hawthorne's sketch describes "the nature of the neutral ground" and "suggests its relation to disencumbered experience." Terence Martin finds in this piece the "essential features of Hawthorne's fiction," such as the "horror of inner guilt" and the "comforting domestic associations of the heart." The sketch also serves as a "paradigm of the creative process." The setting of the sketch is "neutral ground"—which is the "stage for creation, out of time, between yesterday and tomorrow"; the meeting of this neutral ground and the "haunted mind, in which the imagination floats free," provides the "potential instant of imaginative creation." (*Nathaniel Hawthorne*).

"Haunted Quack, The: A Tale of a Canal Boat—by Joseph Nicholson"

Sketch that first appeared in *The Token* in 1831; it was later included in *Tales and Sketches*. It was attributed to Hawthorne by F. B. Sanborn.

The piece opens with an account of the author's journey to Niagara. The roads had became impassable at Schenectady, forcing him to continue to Utica by canal boat. The weather is "dull and lowering," and none of the few passengers on board is of sufficient interest to motivate him to make a friendly overture. It is rainy, and the tow path is slippery. The boat is pulled by "lazy beasts."

The narrator has neglected to take along any books and soon feels "the foul fiend Ennui" overcoming him. The boat moves along at only four miles an hour. It has berths, however, and passengers can order food and drink. When the last passenger leaves the cabin, the narrator begins reading the book he has left behind; it is called *The History of Witches, or the Wonders of the Invisible World Displayed,* by Glanville. By midnight, he has fallen asleep over the pages of the book.

Suddenly the narrator is awakened by a muttering voice, "broken by groans and sounds of distress." He sees a tall, thin, "shabbily dressed" young man with a "pallid and cadaverous" face, sleeping on one of the cabin benches. He has been "restless and unquiet, keeping away from the table at meal times, and seeming averse from entering into conversation with the passengers." Hawthorne believes he might be a fugitive "or else a little disordered in mind." He is about to rouse him, when the man says, ominously, "Go away, go away. . . . Why do you continue to torment me? If I did poison you, I didn't mean to do it, and they can't make that out more than manslaughter. Besides, what's the use of haunting me now? Ain't I going to give myself up, and tell all? Begone! I say, you bloody old hag, begone!" With a wild expression, the man starts up and stands trembling before the narrator.

The man wants to confess his "horrid crime." He tells the narrator his name is Hippocrates Jenkins,

and he grew up in a canalside village. After his parents died, he was apprenticed to a shoemaker but grew tired of what he "foolishly deemed" a "particularly mean occupation." He had always been interested in medicine and was invited to become an apprentice to Doctor Ephraim Ramshorne. It was unclear whether the doctor had graduated from college, but he was successful because he had somehow managed to force all competitors "to quit the field." The young man spent his time "compounding certain quack medicines of Ramshorne's own invention," which yield "no inconsiderable profit." He longed for the day when he could dispense his own medicines but vowed to try them on dogs or cats first.

Doctor Ramshorne then died of apoplexy, although Hippocrates had given him a great deal of his own medicine. He tells the narrator, "I . . . resolved to commence quacking—I mean practising—on my own account." He became Ramshorne's successor and decided that where Ramshorne had given one dose, he would give six. He built a good practice in the village and was well liked.

Hippocrates invented new medicines, "mostly of an innocent nature," but he satisfied his conscience "with the reflection, that if they did no good, they could at least do no harm." In an "evil hour," however, he created a "curious mixture, composed of forty-nine different articles," which he called "The Antidote to Death, or the Eternal Elixir of Longevity" (realizing that his drugs would not find as good a market under a more humble title).

The drug turned out to be the catalyst for all his troubles. Granny Gordon, the wife of the blacksmith, was known as "the rib of the village Vulcan." She was a woman who sought stimulating scenes of distress and took a morbid pleasure in "beholding the varieties of human suffering and misery." The "din of her eternal tongue" was as bad as the sound of her husband's anvil. She was like a witch, slipping into patients' homes and muttering threats and abusive remarks.

The young doctor had befriended Granny Gordon, who was willing to take his treatments, "the more disgusting, the greater . . . its virtue." One day he sent her the new potion, telling her to take it cautiously. The drug made her much worse; she appeared to be dying. Hippocrates hurried to her bedside and found her in convulsions. Her bed was surrounded by accusatory village women. Her husband accused him of poisoning his wife (although he had regularly abused her himself). The patient held up the empty bottle and exclaimed, "This is your doing, you villainous quack you . . . you have poisoned me, you have . . . but I'll be revenged; day and night my ghost shall haunt—" And then Granny Gordon fell back and apparently died.

Hippocrates had then rushed out of the room with the "dying curse" ringing in his ears; seeing no future for himself in the village, he immediately went by stagecoach to New York. He had been haunted, however, by the ghost of Granny Gordon and decided to give himself up, for "hanging itself is better than this state of torment."

The narrator tries to comfort the young doctor, who seems "more at his ease" after unburdening himself. When the boat nears the wharf, Hippocrates accidentally loses his balance and slips into the water. The village men pull him out and tell him they have been looking for him. Granny Gordon has survived his treatment and is flourishing. One of the village women, Betsy Wilkins, has confirmed in an affidavit that she heard Bill Gordon, the blacksmith, swear that he would kill the doctor. Gordon is about to go on trial. The sheriff asks Hippocrates to jump into the wagon and go to the tavern to dry his clothes.

At that point, Gordon, a "brawny fellow with a smutty face," walks up and shakes Hippocrates's hand, saying, "By goles, doctor, I am glad to see you. If you hadn't come back, I believe it would have gone hard with me. Come, man, you must forgive the hard words I gave you. My old woman soon got well of her fit, after you went away, and says she thinks the stuff did her a mortal sight o' good."

In the tavern, the young doctor is told by one of the farmers that they all believe Granny will "now last forever." Hippocrates has gained a reputation as a "nation smart doctor, who had a power of larning, but gave severe doses."

The story ends with Hippocrates's thanking the narrator for his sympathy and "gaily" taking his leave. He intends to return to his practice; the nar-

rator admonishes him to be more careful with his medicines in the future.

Historical Tales for Youth

A two-volume collection of tales published in 1842. It contained GRANDFATHER'S CHAIR, FAMOUS OLD PEOPLE, LIBERTY TREE, and BIOGRAPHICAL STORIES.

"Hollow of the Three Hills, The"

Hawthorne's first published story, which appeared in the *Salem Gazette* on November 12, 1830; it was later collected in TWICE-TOLD TALES (1837).

As the tale opens on an autumn day near sunset, two women are meeting in a hollow among three hills; a putrid pool is nearby. One lady is young and graceful, "though pale and troubled"; the other is elderly and "meanly dressed," withered and shrunken. The "aged crone" asks why the younger woman has requested this meeting.

The younger woman, a stranger, explains that she has left loved ones behind and wishes to know their fate. The elderly woman bids her kneel down and put her head on the old woman's knees. As she does so, the edge of her garment is dipped into the pool. She hears a prayer and what seem like other voices. They belong to an aged, despondent man and a broken, decayed woman, who sit by a "melancholy hearth" and speak of their wandering daughter, who bears "dishonor along with her" and leaves "shame and affliction" on them. The young woman looks up but finds herself still "kneeling in the hollow between three hills."

The old hag tells her to cover her face again. She begins "the monotonous words of a prayer that was not meant to be acceptable in heaven." Strange murmurings "thicken" about them, and there are sounds of shrieks, groans, sobs, and rattling chains. The young woman hears a "manly and melodious" voice speak of a woman who has broken her wifely vows, of "a home and heart made desolate." She looks up and sees the withered woman smiling at her.

She asks to listen to one more voice. The "evil woman" weaves her spell again, and the sounds turn into the tone of a death knell. The younger woman hears mourners passing along with a coffin, and before them a "priest reading the burial service." There are "whispered but distinct" words "breathed against the daughter who had wrung the aged hearts of her parents—the wife who had betrayed the trusting fondness of her husband—the mother who had sinned against natural affection, and left her child to die."

After the sounds of the funeral procession fade away, the elderly woman nudges the kneeling lady, who does not lift her head. The withered crone chuckles over her "sweet hour's sport."

CRITICAL ANALYSIS

Though this story is a "short, compact narrative presenting but one scene," Arlin Turner observes that it "embodies many of the materials and the qualities of style, method, and outlook that have come to be recognized as Hawthornesque." The witch conjures up sounds that remind the young woman of the suffering she has caused others. The story functions as "a tale of guilt, or rather, a tale of the effects of guilt on a young woman" ("Nathaniel Hawthorne").

Erich Rupprecht also recognizes in this early work the exploration of themes that recur throughout Hawthorne's career: "guilt, isolation, the complicated chain of consequences arising from human actions, and the impingement of the past upon the present" ("Nathaniel Hawthorne").

Terence Martin observes that the younger woman is only able to "look back into her life to see the tragic consequences of her actions" by submitting to the "crone's powers, with their suggestion of Satanic darkness." She experiences her "visions of society" through witchcraft and evil. Because she has committed sins "against the heart and against natural affection"—for Hawthorne, "heinous offenses"—she can only get a "glimpse of society" and "measure the extent of her isolation" by consorting with evil, by turning to "powers antithetical to love and trust" (*Nathaniel Hawthorne*, 44).

FOR FURTHER READING

Johnston, Paul K., "Playing at Work: Nathaniel Hawthorne's Triple Thinking in 'The Hollow of the Three Hills,'" *Nathaniel Hawthorne Review* 23, no. 2 (fall 1997): 1–16; Jurjiaka, Susah K., "Rage Turned Inward: Woman against Herself in Hawthorne's Fiction," *Mount Olive Review* 7 (winter–spring 1993–94): 33–40; Rupprecht, Erich, "Nathaniel Hawthorne," in *Supernatural Fiction Writers*, Vol. 2 (New York: Scribner, 1985), 707–15; Turner, Arlin, "Nathaniel Hawthorne," in *Dictionary of Literary Biography*, Vol. 1, edited by Joel Myerson, 80–101 (Detroit: Gale Research, 1978).

House of the Seven Gables, The

Ticknor, Reed, and Fields of Boston published 1,690 copies of the first edition, first printing, of the novel on April 9, 1851. By September 1851, there had been four printings. The original manuscript that served as the printer's copy is located in the Houghton Library at Harvard University (Clark, Jr., C. E. Frazer, *Nathaniel Hawthorne: A Descriptive Bibliography*, 168–169).

Hawthorne wrote the novel at a time when he had established his reputation as a notable writer. He and his family were living in the "red house" at Lenox, Massachusetts, in an agreeable and stimulating literary atmosphere. Their stay in Lenox had been prompted by Hawthorne's dismissal from the Salem Custom House in June 1849. At the time, Sophia's wealthy friend Caroline Sturgis Tappan and her husband were staying at the estate of Anna and Samuel Ward in Lenox; they offered the family the handyman's small red house at no cost, and the Hawthornes accepted. Hawthorne insisted, however, on paying $50.00 for rent (Wineapple, *Hawthorne: A Life*, 191–231; Turner, *Nathaniel Hawthorne: A Biography*, 213). There was a noted literary colony in Lenox and in nearby towns such as Pittsfield, Stockbridge, and Great Barrington, including the editor and writer EVERT DUYCKINCK,

This Salem mansion is considered by some to be the original "House of the Seven Gables." It was once owned by Susan Ingersoll, a distant cousin of Hawthorne's whom he visited on occasion. *(Courtesy of the Library of Congress)*

HERMAN MELVILLE, OLIVER WENDELL HOLMES, the actress FANNY KEMBLE, and Catharine Maria Sedgwick.

When he finished the novel in January 1851, Hawthorne stated that he preferred it to his previous novel, *The SCARLET LETTER*. He assumed it would find greater favor with the public and with critics, but that has not been the case.

The House of the Seven Gables is, as Hawthorne explains in his preface, a romance, which he defines as "a legend prolonging itself" and connecting a bygone time with the present. The writer of a novel must aim at "a very minute fidelity, not merely to the possible, but to the probable and ordinary course of man's experience." A romance, however, implies a certain sensibility, a conviction that events and personalities recur throughout time and even throughout the generations of a family. In *The House of the Seven Gables,* therefore, the task of the first chapter is to establish the origins

of this legend. The tale of Colonel Pyncheon and Matthew Maule proves the central event of the novel, although it occurs more than a century before the majority of the book takes place. The events leading to the origin of the House of the Seven Gables include a number of patterns and character traits that future characters will exhibit in very similar ways. This romantic sensibility that Hawthorne employs is therefore very deterministic; the sins of Colonel Pyncheon will be revisited upon his descendants, while Matthew Maule's progeny will bear similar burdens. The history of the Maule family is intimately connected to the history of the Pyncheons. The death of Matthew Maule is not merely an isolated event that connects the two families. The connection between the Maules and the Pyncheons will recur and become clearer as the novel progresses. The author also indicates that the Maules possess strange powers passed down from the wizard Matthew Maule. Hawthorne leaves it unclear as to whether Matthew Maule himself possessed mystical powers—the reason for his execution—but does assume that the Maules have some strange power.

The "House of the Seven Gables" itself is a physical representation of the Pyncheon and Maule family histories. The house essentially contains the old Maule hut, inextricably linking the two families. When it was first built, it spoiled Maule's Well, a metaphor for the Pyncheons' destruction of the Maule family legacy as well as an indication that the Pyncheons have disrupted the natural order. As the story begins, the house, much as have the Pyncheons themselves, has fallen into a state of decay. Hawthorne advises against connecting the "imaginary events" in the story with a particular locality. This admonition has, of course, been ignored for a century and a half, as visitors flock to Salem, Massachusetts, and tour the house reputed to be the original "House of the Seven Gables."

SYNOPSIS

Chapter I: "The Old Pyncheon Family"

The House of the Seven Gables is a "venerable" though "weather-beaten" mansion on Pyncheon Street, in a town in New England. It was built 160 years ago.

It is actually on the site of a hut originally owned by Matthew Maule, on a street that was once called Maule's Lane. The site was chosen because of its proximity to a natural spring. As the town grew, the property became "exceedingly desirable" to its claimant, Colonel Pyncheon. The colonel was instrumental in convicting Matthew Maule of witchcraft and having him hanged, with the result that a curse became associated with the house. With the noose tied around his neck, Maule uttered a prophecy as he pointed at Pyncheon: "God will give him blood to drink!"

After Maule's death, Colonel Pyncheon planned to build a mansion over what the village people considered "an unquiet grave." Matthew Maule's son, THOMAS Maule, a builder, superintended construction of the house and became its architect. Soon after construction on the new house began, the spring became polluted and the water of "Maule's Well" grew "hard and brackish."

When the house was completed, a "ceremony of consecration" was held and all the townspeople were invited to the festivities. It was on this day that Pyncheon's grandson found the colonel dead in his study, with blood "on his ruff" and saturating his "hoary beard." The doctors disagreed on the cause of death; one proclaimed it a "case of apoplexy," while others "adopted various hypotheses, more or less plausible."

Pyncheon's son inherited his "rich estate," and he and the following generations of Pyncheons were all characterized by "an absurd delusion of family importance." Nevertheless, each generation contained "one descendant of the family gifted with a portion of the hard, keen sense, and practical energy, that had so remarkably distinguished the original founder."

The narrator "cherishes the belief" that many of the Pyncheon descendants "were troubled with doubts as to their moral right" to the mansion, though "of their legal tenure there could be no question." He wonders whether "each inheritor of the property—conscious of wrong, and failing to rectify it—did not commit anew the great guilt of his ancestor."

Thirty years before the events of the novel, an "old bachelor" member of the Pyncheon family (Jaffrey Pyncheon) began "rummaging old records" and concluded that Matthew Maule, the wizard, had been "foully wronged out of his homestead, if not out of his life." This man suffers a "violent death," a crime for which his nephew, Clifford Pyncheon; is tried and convicted.

Another nephew of this man, Judge Jaffrey PYNCHEON, inherits his uncle's fortune and makes himself an "exceedingly respectable member of society." He now lives in a country house a few miles away.

The only Pyncheon in residence at the House of the Seven Gables is Miss Hepzibah Pyncheon, aged 60, who has inherited the right to live there during her lifetime.

Chapter II: "The Little Shopwindow"

Miss Hepzibah Pyncheon is regarded as pathetic by the town, but also as ludicrous. After she dresses in the morning, she looks at a miniature kept in a secret drawer of an escritoire; it is a "likeness of a young man." She has never had a lover, however.

She puts away the miniature and wipes away tears. She then goes into her parlor and gazes with reverence at a map of the original Pyncheon territory and a portrait of old Colonel Pyncheon.

Hepzibah worries constantly about her expenses. In order to augment her income, she forces herself to reopen the cent shop that had once been in the house. Despite her misgivings, the "patrician lady is to be transformed into the plebeian woman" by the threat of poverty.

The narrator remarks that the fortunes of humankind often exhibit the entanglement of "something mean and trivial with whatever is noblest in joy and sorrow." Poetic insight consists of the ability to discern "the beauty and the majesty" within "sordid" garb.

Chapter III: "The First Customer"
Holgrave, a daguerreotypist (or photographer), and a tenant in Miss Hepzibah Pyncheon's house, is her first customer. (The daguerreotype was first in vogue when Hawthorne was writing the novel.) Holgrave is a "slender young man," 21 or 22 years of age, who is "grave and thoughtful." He offers Miss Pyncheon his best wishes in her new venture. She begins crying, saying she is too old, feeble, and helpless to succeed; she wishes she were in the family tomb. He tells her she will now have the sense of "healthy and natural effort for a purpose"; working is considered a privilege in present society. He tries to buy some biscuits, but she gives them to him without charge.

The reader learns in a later chapter that Holgrave is a descendant of Matthew Maule; he is described here as having "a dark, high-featured countenance," and he says he misuses "Heaven's blessed sunshine" by tracing out human features through its "agency."

Miss Hepzibah overhears two laborers making fun of her appearance and predicting she will not do well with the shop. A small boy, Ned Higgins, tries to buy a gingerbread man; she gives it to him. He returns for another one; this time she asks for his cent.

Chapter IV: "A Day behind the Counter"
Hepzibah's wealthy, detestable cousin, Judge Jaffrey Pyncheon, walks past and gazes at the shop with a frown and then a smile. When he glimpses Hepzibah, his "acrid and disagreeable" smile changes into one of "complacency and benevolence." She feels nothing but "bitter emotion" at the sight of him, however.

Uncle Venner, a kindly man locally regarded as somewhat mentally deficient, enters and asks when "he" (Clifford) is expected home. He advises Hepzibah to smile at her customers, for a "stale article" delivered with a smile "will go off better than a fresh one that you've scowled upon."

An omnibus pulls up in front of the house and a pretty girl steps out carrying a trunk. Hepzibah realizes she is Phoebe Pyncheon, a kinswoman from the country. She had written she was coming, but her letter was not delivered. Hepzibah says she can only stay one night, as her presence might disturb Clifford.

Chapter V: "May and November"
Phoebe awakens the next day and peeps out of the window at the garden. She sees a luxuriant white rosebush. Many of the blooms are blighted or mildewed, but, from a distance, it is beautiful. The bush was planted by Alice Pyncheon, Phoebe's great-great-grand-aunt, two centuries earlier. Phoebe wanders into the garden and picks some flowers.

When she returns to the house, Hepzibah tells her she cannot afford to keep her, and she must return to her own home. Phoebe says Hepzibah will find her a "cheerful little body" and she will earn her own bread. Hepzibah says the master of the house is returning home, and shows her the miniature of Clifford Pyncheon. Phoebe is greatly surprised, as she thought Clifford had been "a long while dead."

Phoebe offers to tend the shop for the day and proves to be an adept shopkeeper. She represents "the stern old stuff of Puritanism with a gold thread in the web," in contrast to the arrogant early colonel and his descendants. The girl's optimism and cheer draw out Hepzibah in spite of herself. Hepzibah shows her Alice Pyncheon's harpsichord and tells her about the lodger, Mr. Holgrave. Phoebe concludes that he sounds as if he is a radical, with his strange companions, who include "reformers, temperance lecturers, and all manner of cross-looking philanthropists."

Chapter VI: "Maule's Well"

Phoebe enters the Pyncheon garden and sees that there has been careful labor bestowed on it. There are a fountain and a hen coop, although the hens are hardly larger than pigeons. Phoebe finds scraps and feeds them.

She sees a young man, Holgrave, in the garden; he explains that he lodges in one of the gables. He shows her a daguerreotype of someone whom Phoebe takes to be a Puritan ancestor. She associates it with the miniature Hepzibah has shown her, which Holgrave wishes to see for himself. Phoebe does not really like Holgrave, but she agrees to take over the flowerbed while he tends to the vegetables. As he leaves the garden, he tells her not to drink from "Maule's well," for its water is "bewitched."

Upon returning to the house, Phoebe is sure someone is in the room with Hepzibah and thinks she hears someone speak to her. Hepzibah denies it. Phoebe climbs to her chamber but believes she hears a footstep mounting the stairs.

Chapter VII: "The Guest"

Phoebe helps Hepzibah prepare breakfast. She hears the sound of the same footsteps from the night before. It is Clifford, who has been in jail for 30 years after being falsely accused of murdering his uncle.

Clifford is now thin and gray; his years in prison have made him terrified of light. He is wearing an "old-fashioned dressing-gown of faded damask." Phoebe realizes he is the original of the beautiful miniature; the dressing gown is the same as the one in the picture. He is pleased with the food and flowers Phoebe offers him. The narrator describes Clifford's nature as that of "a Sybarite."

When he glimpses the portrait of their ancestor, he impatiently asks Hepzibah to remove the "odious picture." She says it cannot be taken down, so Clifford asks that it at least be covered with a curtain.

The shop bell rings, upsetting Clifford further. Hepzibah explains that she has to earn a living now, for they are "very poor."

Chapter VIII: "The Pyncheon of Today"

Phoebe begins to tend the shop. Ned Higgins enters and reveals that Clifford is Hepzibah's brother. Phoebe wonders where he has been all these years.

Judge Pyncheon enters next, carrying a gold-headed cane. He realizes who Phoebe is and tries to kiss her as a cousin. She draws back. She has been kissed by other cousins but perceives his face as "cold, hard, immitigable, like a day-long brooding cloud." Phoebe then realizes that Judge Pyncheon is the original sitter for Holgrave's miniature. She suddenly feels herself overpowered by a quality of "benevolence" in him, which the narrator compares with the "peculiar odor" a serpent emits prior to "fascination."

Judge Pyncheon perceives that his cousin Clifford has arrived home and tries to see him. He asks whether Phoebe has heard of "his history," but she insists there is "no frightful guest in the house, but only a poor, gentle, childlike man." Judge Pyncheon tries to step through the doorway, but Phoebe and Hepzibah bar the way.

Clifford cries to Hepzibah to spare him from seeing Judge Pyncheon, who eventually retreats. Hepzibah explains that he is a horrible person, and Phoebe realizes that evil can roost in high places.

Chapter IX: "Clifford and Phoebe"

According to the narrator, there is something "high, generous, and noble" in the composition of Hepzibah. She is devoted to her somewhat demented brother and endeavors to "wrap Clifford up in her great, warm love." She provides books he used to enjoy, but he is not interested. He does not like her appearance now, as her features are "harsh with age and grief." He cannot help his attitude, however, as he is a "lover of the beautiful." Moreover, she realizes she is a "grief" to him. She turns to Phoebe, who becomes essential to the comfort, if not the "daily life," of both Clifford and Hepzibah.

Clifford begins to yearn for the presence of Phoebe; he likes to hear her sing. He has never "quaffed the cup of passionate love" and knows it is too late. To him, Phoebe is a "simple story," "a verse of household poetry." Phoebe regards him with "native kindliness."

The three fall into a routine. Clifford sleeps most of each morning; Hepzibah tends him then, while Phoebe manages the shop. After their midday meal, Hepzibah runs the shop while Phoebe acts as Clifford's nurse, guardian, and playmate.

Chapter X: "The Pyncheon Garden"

Every afternoon, Phoebe takes Clifford to the garden and reads aloud to him. He is not interested in the works of fiction, though he tries to feign emotions matching her reactions. He responds better to poetry in whose rhythm and rhyme he delights. He also enjoys watching the hummingbirds and seeing the flowers. He amuses himself with the chickens, which now roam free because it "troubled him to see them in confinement."

He is disturbed, however, by what he sees in Maule's Well. He hangs over the water, in which he seems to see "beautiful faces" but also sometimes a "dark face" gazing at him.

On Sundays, after Phoebe attends church, she joins Hepzibah, Clifford, Holgrave, and Uncle Venner in the garden. Phoebe carries out bread, currants, and water. One Sunday afternoon, Clifford murmurs sadly, "I want my happiness! It is late!" The narrator suggests, however, that there is no happiness in store for Clifford, unless a "quiet home in the old family residence, with the faithful Hepzibah," and "long summer afternoons with Phoebe, and these Sabbath festivals with Uncle Venner and the Daguerreotypist, deserve to be called happiness."

Chapter XI: "The Arched Window"

Phoebe occasionally encourages Clifford to look out on the life of the street from an arched window. The energy of the street interests him, but he is unable to deal with "unaccustomed things" and to "keep up with the swiftness of the passing moment." He takes "childish delight" in the organ grinder's music but is upset by the countenance and "deviltry of nature" of his monkey.

One day, a "political procession," with "hundreds of flaunting banners, and drums, fifes, clarions, and cymbals," marches through town and passes the house. Clifford almost climbs from the window onto the balcony and jumps but is pulled back by Hepzibah and Phoebe. They believe he may be "merely disturbed by the unaccustomed tumult," but the narrator observes that perhaps he

needs to take a "deep, deep plunge into the ocean of human life," or perhaps "he required nothing less than the great final remedy—death!"

One Sunday, Clifford asks Hepzibah whether she ever goes to church and says he would like to go. They dress and go downstairs, but once they cross the threshold, Clifford says they have "no right among human beings." They are ghosts who are doomed to stay inside their old house. Also, children might be afraid of the sight of him.

Clifford blows soap bubbles from the window, a favorite amusement of his as a child. One hits the nose of Judge Pyncheon, who is passing by. He asks, with a touch of sarcasm, whether his cousin is still blowing soap bubbles. Clifford has an attack of anxiety.

Chapter XII: "The Daguerreotypist"

Clifford rests each day after a bit of exercise. Phoebe is then free for the remainder of the day. She grows less cheerful, however, and "less girlish, but more a woman."

Phoebe turns to Holgrave for company. Although he is only 22, he has held many positions: country schoolmaster, salesman, and political editor of a country newspaper. He is self-educated and self-sufficient. Phoebe senses, however, that his "law" differs from her own. He has a "lack of reverence" for what she considers "fixed."

Holgrave inquires frequently about Clifford. Phoebe says she does not think it right to pry into his moods, but Holgrave disagrees. He has read little but has a "deep consciousness of inward strength." He wishes to discard the "moss-grown and rotten Past" and hates the House of the Seven Gables.

He asks Phoebe whether she has heard the story of Matthew Maule and Colonel Pyncheon; she has. He then tells her he has written for such magazines as *Graham* and *Godey* and has now written up an "incident of the Pyncheon family history" as a legend he hopes to publish. Holgrave reads Phoebe the story he has written about Alice Pyncheon.

Chapter XIII: "Alice Pyncheon"

Holgrave's tale concerns the intermingled fates of and recurrent hostility between the Maules and Pyncheons.

Thirty-seven years after the house was built, the grandson of old Colonel Pyncheon, Gervayse Pyncheon, asks Scipio, his black servant, to summon the carpenter Matthew Maule (the only son of Thomas Maule, and grandson of the wizard Matthew Maule). Matthew feels a bitter sense of "hereditary wrong," believing that the Pyncheon house is standing on "soil which should have been his own." As he enters the house, he hears Alice Pyncheon's harpsichord.

Mr. Gervayse Pyncheon's apartment is decorated in a costly style, with furniture from Paris and Venice. One object that appears out of place is a large map, or surveyor's plan, of a tract of land. The other is a portrait of the stern old Colonel Pyncheon.

Gervayse Pyncheon is a "middle-aged and really handsome man." When Scipio ushers in Maule, Gervayse deliberately finishes his coffee. He then inquires about missing documents to the "lands eastward." They discuss the matter at length. It is believed that the wizard Matthew Maule gained possession of the "great eastern claim, in exchange for an acre or two of garden ground." Though Gervayse was just a child at the time of his grandfather's death, he remembers that Thomas Maule had had "some job to perform, on the day before, or possibly the very morning of the Colonel's decease." Matthew Maule resents the "insinuated suspicion" that his father had something to do with the missing papers.

Gervayse then tries to make "great pecuniary offers" to Matthew Maule, who at first turns a "cold ear to these propositions," before asking for the House of the Seven Gables in exchange for the papers. They agree to this bargain, but before Matthew will help Gervayse with the lost documents, he insists that Gervayse's beautiful daughter, Alice, be summoned.

Alice Pyncheon agrees to help her father and is convinced that a lady, "while true to herself," can have nothing to fear from anyone. Matthew Maule hypnotizes Alice, in part to use her as a "kind of telescopic medium" through which he might get a "glimpse into the spiritual world," and in part to seek revenge against the Pyncheon family. Matthew lifts up his arms as though he is directing a "slow, ponderous, and invisible weight" upon her. He hypnotizes Alice and seems to possess her. While in a trance, she describes her vision of the old wizard Maule and his son, Thomas, as they try to prevent Colonel Pyncheon from releasing a parchment document to his heirs.

Even after Alice awakens from her trance, she becomes Matthew Maule's "mesmerized slave." It turns out that her father has "martyred his poor child to an inordinate desire for measuring his land by miles instead of acres." From then on, no matter where she finds herself, she must obey Matthew Maule's commandments, whether to laugh or cry or dance a jig. When Matthew weds a laborer's daughter, he commands Alice to wait on his bride. She does so and finally awakens from her "enchanted sleep." But she heads outside into "an inclement night," catches cold, and dies prematurely. There was a "great funeral" for her, but Matthew Maule is very upset, as he had not meant for Alice to be destroyed—only played with and humbled.

Chapter XIV: "Phoebe's Good-bye"

Holgrave tells Phoebe how happy he is now in the House of the Seven Gables, and Phoebe answers that she also is happy, since she has been able to help Hepzibah and Clifford. She says she must return to her home in the country but will come back after "a little while." He observes that both Hepzibah and Clifford now "exist by" her, and she says frankly that she is not sure whether he wishes her cousins "well or ill."

Holgrave explains that he does not wish "to help or to hinder," but rather to look on and "analyze," to explain matters to himself. He is equivocal, pointing out that the drama related to the house has gone on for nearly 200 years. Phoebe is alarmed, thinking Holgrave is holding something back.

Holgrave notes that Judge Pyncheon "still keeps his eye on Clifford, in whose ruin he had so large a share." He says Judge Pyncheon is an enigma and does not trust him. Phoebe is puzzled. They say good night.

Phoebe takes the train home two mornings later. Uncle Venner begs her to return quickly, before he goes to the poorhouse. To him she is an angel, essential to the well-being of her cousins.

Chapter XV: "The Scowl and the Smile"
A period of rain ensues, confining Clifford inside. There are fewer customers in the shop, for a rumor has circulated that Hepzibah sours the small beer and other commodities by scowling on them. She has a woebegone aspect. On the fifth morning, Clifford does not go to breakfast. Hepzibah later hears him playing Alice Pyncheon's harpsichord.

The shop bell rings; it is Judge Pyncheon. He claims he wishes to help Clifford and Hepzibah, but she says there is nothing he can do. He continues to probe and offer help, provoking her to an indignant outburst. The narrator analyzes Judge Pyncheon, finally estimating him as a "hard, cold man." The judge becomes even sterner after witnessing "Hepzibah's wrath." He tells her he plans to see Clifford. He was, in fact, responsible for freeing him from prison. Hepzibah does not believe it.

The judge explains that their late uncle Jaffrey had concealed his property by making foreign investments, but had left it all to him except Hepzibah's life interest in the house. Judge Pyncheon believes Clifford has the clue to a hidden portion of Jaffrey's estate. Hepzibah is incredulous. He insists that Clifford had told him about it before their uncle's death. He now threatens Hepzibah, saying he has had Clifford watched since his return and is prepared to confine him to an asylum because of actions such as nearly flinging himself into the street from the arched window. He insists on questioning Clifford about his secret.

Hepzibah is horrified. She says Clifford is not insane, but such interrogation would make him so. She will call Clifford, though, but begs Judge Pyncheon to be "merciful." The judge waits in the parlor in the "great ancestral chair" said to be the same one in which Colonel Pyncheon died.

Chapter XVI: "Clifford's Chamber"
Hepzibah goes to Clifford's room but does not find him there. She calls for help from Judge Pyncheon as she runs down the stairs. Judge Pyncheon does not stir from his chair, though Hepzibah runs to search other rooms and continues to scream about her missing brother. Clifford then appears on the threshold of the parlor. Judge Pyncheon remains there, slumped over and unresponsive.

Clifford points into the room and says that they can live without such weight anymore and be "as light-hearted as little Phoebe herself." He wears an ancient cloak and bids her take her purse and go with him. The two depart together, leaving Judge Pyncheon still sitting in the parlor.

This chapter adds yet another mysterious and tragic death to the House of the Seven Gables. The narrator presents Judge Pyncheon's sudden demise as an ambiguous event. All of the apparent evidence points to Clifford as a murderer. Hepzibah finds him in the room alone with the dead body, and he immediately suggests that they escape from the house. This fulfills the narrator's prophecy earlier in the story, that it would require death to cure Clifford of his sensitivity. However, it is the death of Judge Pyncheon rather than of Clifford, as might have been expected. The reader may infer that Clifford has murdered Judge Pyncheon, yet his death is also a replica of the mysterious death of Colonel Pyncheon. Moreover, the frail Clifford seems an unlikely murderer.

Chapter XVII: "The Flight of Two Owls"
Hepzibah and Clifford leave the House of the Seven Gables and go to the train station, where they board a train. Hepzibah asks Clifford whether it is all a dream. Clifford says, "On the contrary, I have never been so awake before!" The train is a novelty to the two travelers, as are the other passengers. Clifford, however, senses that Hepzibah is preoccupied with thoughts of Judge Pyncheon. He urges her to be happy with him. She cannot adjust to everything, for her mind is "too unmalleable to take new impressions so readily as Clifford's"; he, in contrast, has a "winged nature." Clifford now assumes the role of guardian of Hepzibah, reversing their previous functions.

He tells the conductor they are "riding for pleasure" and chats with an old gentleman in their car, saying that the railroad is destined to "do away with those stale ideas of home and fireside, and substitute something better." He remarks that railroads free men from being prisoners in "brick, and stone, and old worm-eaten timber"; they are better off living "nowhere." Houses are stumbling blocks to human happiness. He recalls a certain house he knows, with seven gables and a little shop on the side. He envisions an elderly man sitting in an "oaken elbow-chair," dead, with a flow of blood on his shirt and open eyes, who taints the house. He would like to see the house torn down or burned. He feels himself in the "heyday" of his youth, "with the world" and his "best days" before him.

Hepzibah tries to silence Clifford, but he continues talking and arguing with the old gentleman. The man becomes vexed by Clifford's musings on such topics as the telegraph. When the old man concedes that telegraphs may be useful for detecting bank robbers and murderers, Clifford defends these criminals as possibly enlightened and still having their rights. He posits that there might be a dead man with a bloodstain on his shirt in the house of another man who has fled on a railroad, and asks the old man whether the fleeing man's rights should not be infringed.

When the train stops at a solitary way station, Clifford and Hepzibah disembark, finding themselves in a desolate little town. They are physically and metaphorically isolated, alone in an empty, abandoned place. Clifford begins to shiver and sink and turns himself over to Hepzibah to take the lead now.

Chapter XVIII: "Governor Pyncheon"
Judge Pyncheon remains in the House of the Seven Gables, dead but with his eyes open. He still holds his watch, which continues to move without him. It was supposed to be a busy day for him. He had planned to make more investments, buy a horse, and take measures for the renewal of his late wife's tombstone. He was also scheduled to visit his family physician, to whom he would have described his symptoms of "dimness of sight and dizziness of brain," along with a "disagreeable choking, or stifling, or gurgling, or bubbling in the region of the thorax," and a "throbbing and kicking of the heart." That night, instead of sitting dead in the House of the Seven Gables, Judge Jaffrey Pyncheon was to meet with members of his party and announce his candidacy for governor.

Chapter XIX: "Alice's Posies"
Uncle Venner is the first person to stir the day after the storm. He goes down Pyncheon Street, where "one mystic branch" hangs down before the main entrance of the House of the Seven Gables. This golden branch is like the branch that gained Aeneas and the Sibyl admittance into Hades. Uncle Venner observes the posies that remain in the angle between the two front gables, traditionally known as Alice's Posies. Tradition holds that Alice carried the seeds for these flowers from Italy.

Uncle Venner makes rounds to collect food scraps for his pig, but this morning there is no pan on the back doorstep of the House of the Seven Gables. Hepzibah usually sets it out, but Uncle Venner decides it is too early to knock on the door to inquire. Holgrave, however, calls out to him from the window. The two of them wonder where Clifford and Hepzibah are, and Uncle Venner says he saw Judge Pyncheon go into the shop the day before; perhaps Jaffrey has taken them into the country.

Mrs. Gubbins goes to the closed shop for breakfast supplies and brims over "with hot wrath against the absent Hepzibah." The lady across the street says she saw Hepzibah and Clifford leave the day before and thinks they are probably at Judge Pyncheon's country house. Ned Higgins screams that he wants a gingerbread elephant, and a passing neighbor remarks that Smith, the livery-stable keeper, wonders why Judge Pyncheon has not asked for the horse he left at the stable the day before. One of the judge's hired men has already made inquiries about his absence.

Several suppliers attempt to deliver goods to the closed shop. The butcher peers through the shop curtain and sees a man's legs; he assumes they are Clifford's. The Italian organ grinder arrives with his monkey and plays under the Pyncheon elm. Near the doorstep, he finds an engraved card of Judge Pyncheon's with his schedule written on it; it was probably dropped there the day before. Two passing men decide to take the card to the city marshal.

Not more than a half-hour later, Phoebe returns from her country visit to the House of the Seven Gables. Ned Higgins screams that there is something sinister in the house, but she goes inside, with some apprehension.

Chapter XX: "The Flower of Eden"
Holgrave, looking "paler than ordinary" and smiling at Phoebe with "genuine warmth," grasps her hand

as she enters. He tells her that they are alone in the house; a terrible event has occurred. He shows her a daguerreotype of Judge Pyncheon, which was made within the last half-hour. He tells her that the judge is dead and the others have vanished. He admits that there are hereditary reasons that connect him strangely with that man's fate and tells her that he has not opened the doors to call in witnesses because it is better for Clifford and Hepzibah. Their flight will throw "the worst coloring" over the event.

Holgrave believes that Judge Pyncheon "could not have come unfairly to his end," for there is a physical predisposition among the Pyncheons to die in this way. However, because Clifford's uncle died in the same manner 30 years ago, then Clifford would automatically fall under suspicion again. His escape further distorts the matter.

Despite the events, Holgrave feels some joy at that moment, for he realizes that he loves Phoebe and declares his feelings for her. He says she is his "only possibility of happiness." She reciprocates his love.

They hear footsteps at the door; Clifford and Hepzibah have returned home. Clifford appears to be the stronger of the two. He says that he thought immediately of Phoebe and Holgrave when he saw Alice's Posies in bloom. He says that the flower of Eden has bloomed likewise in the old house.

Chapter XXI: "The Departure"

The sudden death of Judge Pyncheon creates "a sensation." Among the talk of how excellent the judge was, there lingers a "hidden stream of private talk." Judge Pyncheon was in his youth a wild and brutish man.

Thirty or 40 years ago, he had been searching through the apartment of his uncle, old Jaffrey Pyncheon, at or near the moment of his death. While he was ransacking the desk and private drawers, his uncle found him and was startled. He "seemed to choke with blood," fell upon the floor, and died. The younger Jaffrey had found his uncle's recent will, which favored Clifford, and destroyed it, leaving intact an older will in his favor. At that time, the murder had been falsely fixed on Clifford, who was then living with his uncle.

Because the death of Judge Pyncheon was caused by the same physical affliction responsible for the death of Clifford's uncle, people were now ready to believe Clifford innocent of the judge's death. Clifford returns to the house with Hepzibah, vindicated and now a free man.

Meanwhile, Judge Pyncheon had died childless, although he did not realize it. A week after his death, a Cunard steamer carried news that his son had died of cholera just as he was returning home. Clifford and Hepzibah, along with Phoebe, are now wealthy, since they are Judge Pyncheon's only heirs.

The shock of Judge Pyncheon's death has a "permanently invigorating" effect on Clifford; the judge had weighed heavily on his psyche. Soon after receiving their inheritance, Clifford, Hepzibah, and Phoebe plan to move into Judge Pyncheon's mansion. Holgrave wonders why the judge built a house of wood instead of stone, for then he could have passed this house down among the generations—a reversal of his previous beliefs, as Phoebe laughingly points out.

Before they depart, the group sits in the parlor of the House of the Seven Gables. Clifford has a vague recollection of some "rich secret" associated with Colonel Pyncheon's portrait, but he cannot remember the details. Holgrave, however, finds a recess in the wall behind the portrait, in which the map and deed to the eastern land had been hidden. Phoebe asks how he learned the secret, and Holgrave admits that it was his "only inheritance" from his ancestors: he is actually a Maule, a descendant of the old wizard. The claim, however, is now worthless.

Holgrave proposes to Phoebe. She assures Uncle Venner that he shall never go to his "farm," or the poorhouse, but live in a cottage in their new garden. Clifford also invites Uncle Venner to join them at the judge's country estate. As the Pyncheons leave, two men remark on how Hepzibah opened a cent shop and seemingly became rich from it. The novel closes with Uncle Venner's thinking he hears a "strain of music" and imagining that Alice Pyncheon, "after witnessing these deeds, this by-gone woe and this present happiness, of her kindred mortals," was giving "one farewell touch of a spirit's joy upon her harpsichord, as she floated heavenward" from the House of the Seven Gables.

RECEPTION AND CRITICAL ANALYSIS

Herman Melville wrote a letter to Hawthorne on publication of the novel (*see* Part IV, Melville and Hawthorne), stating that the contents of the book did not "belie its rich, clustering, romantic title." He and his family had spent "almost an hour in each separate gable." He compared the book to a "fine old chamber, abundantly, but still judiciously, furnished with precisely that sort of furniture best fitted to furnish it. There are rich hangings, wherein are braided scenes from tragedies! There is old china with rare devices, set out on the carved buffet; there are long and indolent lounges to throw yourself upon; there is an admirable sideboard, plentifully stored with good viands; there is a smell as of old wine in the pantry; and finally, in one corner, there is a dark little black-letter volume in golden clasps, entitled 'Hawthorne: A Problem.'" He praised the marriage of Phoebe and Holgrave as a "fine stroke, because of his turning out to be a Maule." He concluded by asking Hawthorne, "If you pass by Hepzibah's cent-shop, buy me a Jim Crow (fresh) and send it to me by Ned Higgins" (Rosenthal, Bernard, ed., *Critical Essays on Hawthorne's* The House of the Seven Gables, 23–25).

Henry Fothergill Chorley, writing in the *Athenaeum* (England) in May 1851, remarked, "We rarely find so much strength of grasp and so much self-restraint united as in the entire tale." He objected, however, to Hawthorne's "playing with an idea and placing it in every chameleon light of the prism," as his digressions interrupt the narrative (*Nathaniel Hawthorne: The Contemporary Reviews*, edited by John L. Idol Jr. and Buford Jones, 164–166).

George Ripley, reviewer for *Harper's New Monthly Magazine* (May 1851), praised the characters as having "the air of old acquaintance," one "managed with admirable artistic skill." He declared the novel "unsurpassed" by Hawthorne's other writings (Idol and Jones, 167–168).

The novel was favorably reviewed by Henry T. Tuckerman in the June 1851 *Southern Literary Messenger*. He remarked that the "scenery, tone and personages of the story" were "imbued with a local authenticity . . . we seem to breathe, as we read, the air of and be surrounded by the familiar objects of a New England town." He was delighted that Hawthorne opened a vista "into that beautiful and unexplored world of love and thought that exists in every human being, though overshadowed by material circumstance and technical duty." He found that Phoebe so embodied the "healthy spring of life" that she was able to "magnetize the feelings as well as engage the perceptions of the reader." Clifford, "when relieved of the nightmare that oppressed his sensitive temperament," had justly experienced an "Indian-summer of the soul." He thought that the reformer Holgrave and the "genially practical Phoebe" were perfectly matched, and that she would "win him to conservatism" (Rosenthal, ed., *Critical Essays on Hawthorne's* The House of the Seven Gables, 41–43).

Hawthorne's friend JAMES RUSSELL LOWELL wrote an enthusiastic letter. He remarked, "I have been so delighted with 'The House of the Seven Gables' that I cannot help sitting down to tell you so. I thought I could not forgive you if you wrote anything better than 'The Scarlet Letter;' but I cannot help believing it a great triumph that you should have been able to deepen and widen the impression made by such a book as that." He called the novel "the most valuable contribution to New England history that has been made." He even predicted that Salem would build Hawthorne a monument for having shown that "she did not hang her witches for nothing" (Crowley, ed., *The Critical Heritage: Nathaniel Hawthorne*, 191).

EVERT AUGUSTUS DUYCKINCK, writing in *Literary World*, characterized the actual house of the seven gables as possessing one gable for each deadly sin. He found it a "ghostly, mouldy abode, built in some eclipse of the sun . . . founded on a grave" and inviting "wrath supernal." Inside, he found every "darker shadow of human life," with "passions allied to crime." Within the house, wealth "withers" and "the human heart grows cold." Sunshine cast its rays in, but "only to show us the darkness." Despite this melancholy view of the book, he found the scenes and vivid descriptions "dramatic and truthful." He saw, in Hawthorne, clear "streaks" of his "Puritan ancestry."

Duyckinck particularly praised Hawthorne's depiction of Hepzibah Pyncheon. He sympathized with the effort it cost her to sacrifice family pride by opening a shop in one of the gables of the building and considered Hawthorne's depiction of her painful first day to be "not only a view of family pride in its shifts and reluctance," but also a picture of "all the doubts and irresolutions which beset a sensitive mind on the entrance upon any new sphere of duty in the great world." He concluded by remarking, "This is Hawthorne's province of the world. In it his life is original, fanciful, creative" (Crowley, ed., *The Critical Heritage: Nathaniel Hawthorne,* 192–194).

Twentieth-century critics saw the novel in myriad ways. Peter Buitenhuis, writing in *The House of the Seven Gables: Severing Family and Colonial Ties,* makes the point that any reading must take into account "all the forces working on Hawthorne's imagination—personal, social, political, religious, historical, psychological, formal, and traditional—as well as the needs of the market and the audience" (25). Nina Baym has argued, however, that the happy ending was not mandated by the marketplace, but rather by an "inner censor" of Hawthorne that "directed him to be a writer of happy stories."

In her article "Hawthorne's Holgrave: The Failure of the Artist-Hero," Baym observes that, although Holgrave is the "best" Maule, he lacks "intellectuality." The death of Judge Pyncheon causes him to become less creative, not more so. He declares his love for Phoebe, she believes, as a way of repossessing the Pyncheon property. He is no longer a social radical but prepares to lead the life of a country squire. Holgrave's conversion may be "morally desirable" but leads to his "absorption into the system." That is, he subscribes to the Pyncheon wish for possessions instead of the Maule wish for freedom (Rosenthal, *Critical Essays on Nathaniel Hawthorne's* The House of the Seven Gables, 63–73).

Bruce Michelson, in "Hawthorne's House of Three Stories," suggests that the novel is about the "loss of the self." There is danger in an overabundance of tradition and of change, as well as in an excess of "reality." He cites Clifford's remark "'We are ghosts! We have no right among living beings—no right anywhere but in this old house,

which has a curse on it, and which, therefore, we are doomed to haunt!'" He and Hepzibah are too old to change, and they are ultimately confined to their own natures. Their world is one of "enduring reverie." Holgrave, however, is allowed to escape from both the Maule past and the Pyncheon past. Living high up under the roof, he exercises his intellect, dabbling in art, magic, and science. Phoebe is not really a part of Holgrave's world. In the cent shop, however, she invites "commerce with everyday life."

It is significant that the Maules and the Pyncheons leave the house together, as they have lived together. As Michelson puts it, this ending represents a "modest chance to start over," though not to escape evil completely. The novel ends on a note of "cautious, plausible human hope."

The House of the Seven Gables is a complex exploration of multigenerational conflict over property and human values. The social levels and codes of behavior of the Pyncheon and Maule families and their descendants fluctuate. Each generation has villains (such as Matthew Maule the wizard, Matthew Maule the carpenter, and Colonel Pyncheon), victims (such as Alice Pyncheon and Clifford Pyncheon), and figures whose conciliatory actions reconcile the two families (such as Holgrave and Phoebe).

Richard Fogle observes that the novel "holds unflinchingly to its dark theme of the American original sin and its gradual expiation in centuries of anguish." The house itself is an important symbol; its huge chimney is its heart, while Maule's Well and its gardens represent the tainted Eden of its past (Introduction, *The House of the Seven Gables* [New York: Collier Books, 1962]).

Weather is an important motif, tied to the emotions, hopes, and anxieties of the characters at every turn. After Hepzibah opens the cent shop and realizes it may not prosper, she tells Uncle Venner that she may, someday, need to retire with him to his farm. He assures her there is nothing more pleasant than spending a "whole day on the sunny side of a barn or a woodpile, chatting with somebody as old as one's self." His encouragement causes Hepzibah to entertain notions of "festal glory" and she determines to greet her customers with a "sunny smile." The arrival of her young cousin Phoebe introduces sunlight to the dark house. Phoebe, as Fogle observes, is a "golden mean between extremes." Hepzibah warns her that the house "lets in the wind and rain" but never sunshine. Phoebe insists, however, that she is a "cheerful little body" and will busy herself in the garden. She begins cooking breakfast; she is "bright, cheerful, and efficient."

The twin motifs of darkness and light pervade the flashback to the tragic death of Alice Pyncheon, an ancestor of the present-day Pyncheons. Gervayse Pyncheon's landscape by Claude, acquired in Europe, represents an effort to restore "sunny recollections." The painting has "a shadowy and sun-streaked vista," yet it is in conflict with the dark Matthew Maule, the carpenter who hypnotizes Alice.

Fogle argues that Clifford cannot face the "broad sunshine of reason" (quoted in Rosenthal, "Introduction," *Critical Essays on Hawthorne's The House of the Seven Gables,* 11). Sunlight represents "reality" to Hawthorne, on both the literal and imaginative levels. He states that the "literal" sunlight signifies the "broad noon of common day"; it is used in his work to signify God, as in traditional Christian symbolism. On an imaginative level, however, sunlight is more congruent with softer, less direct light, the "slanting ray" of early morning or late afternoon.

The symbolism of rain and storm, however, signifies "the long lapse of mortal life, and accompanying vicissitudes that have passed within" (chapter I). At the consecration of the house, for example, an event that the townspeople in full force attend in their best clothes, the owner, Colonel Pyncheon, fails to appear. The high sheriff of the county demands that he welcome the lieutenant-governor, who is the representative of King William. The guests crowd in to the colonel's study, only to find him in an oaken elbow chair, pen in hand. His little grandson runs in and shrieks with terror. An early guest, Death, has crossed the threshold. Pyncheon's ruff and beard are saturated with blood. Since that time, many generations of Pyncheons have come and gone. The house, built by the son of Matthew Maule, has been marked by a well with sour water, a garden full of weeds, and windows over which moss encroaches.

Phoebe's departure later in the novel for a visit to her family home has a logistical necessity, as she would not have otherwise abandoned Clifford and Hepzibah, but it also paves the way for a time of rain and storm. As Hepzibah frantically searches for her brother, she looks through a "dense gray pavement of clouds" that have gathered, "as if to symbolize a great, brooding mass of human trouble, doubt, confusion, and chill indifference, between earth and the better regions." The town is "water-girdled" and each wharf is a "solitude." The effect is to obscure the interior scene as well as the exterior setting. In the interior gloom, Hepzibah is unable to see the figure of Judge Jaffrey Pyncheon clearly enough to determine that he has died. When Clifford enters, his face is pale and wild; he points to the judge's corpse with a look of joy and an invitation to Hepzibah to join him in dancing, singing, and playing. He is wearing a cloak from "long ago," dating back to before his false imprisonment. They hurry away, leaving the body of the judge as a "defunct nightmare."

When Holgrave and Phoebe return to the house and search for Hepzibah and Clifford, they have fallen in love: The "bliss which makes all things true, beautiful, and holy shone around this youth and maiden." The daguerreotype, another example of the intersection between light and shadow, is an extremely important symbol within the novel. In the chapter called "The Daguerreotypist," we learn that Holgrave's work as a daguerreotypist is the latest of many occupations he has had—he has been, among other things, a lecturer on mesmerism, an amateur but competent dentist, and a traveling peddler. Despite these varying occupations, he has never "lost his identity" but rather carried the "innermost man" with him. He seeks "mental food" from Phoebe, Hepzibah, and Clifford, not "heart sustenance." He has, nevertheless, an inward strength that imparts warmth to all his endeavors.

After Hepzibah and Clifford return to the house, where they find Holgrave and Phoebe together, it is Clifford who says, "the flower of Eden has bloomed" in the "darksome house." Hepzibah and Clifford, however, are not emblems of this renaissance. Nina Baym suggests that Hepzibah is the "symbol of the Pynchon strength become withered and impotent," whereas Clifford is not truly an artist but "a travesty of one" who has been castrated by his imprisonment (*The Shape of Hawthorne's Career*, 158–159).

The Maule/Pynchon dynasty must depend on rejuvenation by Holgrave and Phoebe in order to survive. Hawthorne implies that their union will dispel the bitter resentment displayed by earlier Maules and redirect that hostility into positive, creative channels for Holgrave, even as it neutralizes the Pynchon capacity for retribution and transforms it into the benign competence and energy characteristic of Phoebe.

CHARACTERS

Gubbins, Mrs. "Irascible housewife" in *The House of the Seven Gables*. After the death of Judge Jaffrey Pynchon (whose body is still in the House of the Seven Gables) and the flight of Clifford Pyncheon and Hepzibah Pynchon, Mrs. Gubbins goes to the House of the Seven Gables to make some purchases from Hepzibah's cent shop. She is a fat woman but makes "prodigious speed" up the steps to the shop door. She is indignant that no one answers her ring, for she requires a half-pound of pork in which to fry some "first-rate flounders" for her husband's breakfast.

Demanding and greedy, Mrs. Gubbins is a foil to the gentle, shy Hepzibah. The reader is doubly glad when Hepzibah shares in the inheritance of the late Judge Pynchon and gives up her duties as shopkeeper; she will no longer have to endure the abuse of such townspeople.

Higgins, Ned A small boy in *The House of the Seven Gables*, Ned Higgins is the first customer in Miss Hepzibah Pynchon's cent shop. She has opened it out of necessity and feels ashamed that she has been forced to do so. Ned buys a gingerbread man, for which the urchin has an all-devouring appetite. He is, according to the narrator, "the very emblem of Old Father Time" in his "all-devouring appetite for men and things . . . and because he, as well as Time, after ingulfing this much of creation, looked almost as youthful as he had been just that moment made" (ch. VIII).

Ned serves as messenger, intermediary between adults, and newsagent. His reactions to various events are frank and uninhibited. As soon as Clifford is established in the home of his sister, Ned walks over to ask Phoebe, "Mother wants to know . . . how Old Maid Pynchon's brother does? Folks say he has got home" (ch. VIII). His news is always accurate, although his interpretation of it is simplistic.

After Judge Jaffrey Pynchon's death in the House of the Seven Gables, and the flight of Hepzibah and Clifford, Phoebe returns to the house from her visit to the country. She discovers Ned outside, some distance down the street. He is "stamping, shaking his head violently, making deprecatory gestures with both hands, and shouting to her at mouth-wide screech." He begs her not to enter: "Don't you go in! There's something wicked there! Don't—don't—don't go in!" He himself refuses to approach "near enough to explain himself" (ch. 19). The judge's corpse is, of course, "wicked" to Ned, although it is a blessing to Phoebe, Holgrave, Hepzibah, and, most of all, Clifford.

Holgrave A young daguerreotypist who is a lodger in the House of the Seven Gables. Holgrave is a descendant of the Maule family, ancient enemies of the Pyncheons, though the reader and other characters are unaware of this until late in the novel. Despite inheriting the characteristic Maule "darkness," he resists the temptation to control Phoebe Pynchon. He knows he cannot save the house or its occupants.

When we meet him, he is a slender young man in his early 20s; despite his physical vigor, he has a grave expression. He encourages Hepzibah when she establishes a cent shop in order to earn money to support herself.

In conversation with Phoebe, Holgrave explicitly brings out the narrator's theory concerning representation. He believes that his daguerreotypes draw out the hidden characteristics of their subjects.

Holgrave has been termed a "disciple of progress." As he points out, there has been "strife amongst kindred," especially among the Pyncheons and the Maules. He has a thorough knowledge of the Pynchon family but believes in progress; he does not believe that houses should outlast the life of the builder. However, he is unrealistic in his hope and expectation that tremendous change can be effected within one generation (Martin, *Nathaniel Hawthorne*, 125).

Flibbert points out that Holgrave studies the world of the Pyncheons with a certain detachment, but, at the same time, wants to ferret out Pyncheon secrets. He terms Holgrave's occupation as a daguerreotypist the equivalent of his being "an artist of the ugly," that is, arriving at a literal depiction of his subjects. The painter, on the other hand, colors his renditions with his own emotions and subjective sentiments ("'That Look Beneath,' Hawthorne's Portrait of Benevolence in *The House of the Seven Gables*," *Critical Essays on Hawthorne's* The House of the Seven Gables).

Richard Fogle suggests that Holgrave "hovers as it were between audience and stage." Holgrave remarks of a portrait of Judge Pyncheon that he has taken, "the original wears, to the world's eye . . . an exceedingly pleasant countenance, indicative of benevolence." He admits, however, that most of his depictions are "unamiable." Judge Pyncheon, in fact, is later described as thoroughly evil; his countenance is false and he himself is the most sinister figure in the novel (*Hawthorne's Imagery*, 52–57).

During his time of residence in the House of the Seven Gables, Holgrave has startled Hepzibah Pyncheon by his strange companions, "men with long beards, and dressed in linen blouses, and other such new-fangled and ill-fitting garments; reformers, temperance lectures, and all manner of cross-looking philanthropists; community-men, and come-outers . . . who acknowledged no law, and ate no solid food." After Phoebe returns from her visit to her family, he startles her with his "lack of reverence for what was fixed." Holgrave has managed to travel in Europe and has worked as a country schoolmaster, salesman, and political editor of a country newspaper. He has also lectured on mesmerism. The narrator implies that his career as a daguerreotypist will probably not be a permanent one.

Holgrave enthusiastically espouses liberal values that clash with Hepzibah's reliance on heredity. He finds heroism in Hepzibah and restriction in her status as a Pyncheon. Despite his varied occupations, however, he does not violate his integrity of conscience.

Maule, Matthew, I ("the wizard") In *The House of the Seven Gables*, Maule was the original owner of a small hut on Maule's Lane (later Pyncheon Street), in Salem, Massachusetts. The hut was built in this location because of its close proximity to a natural spring. A prominent citizen of the town, Colonel Pyncheon, claimed the property when it became desirable in view of the spring.

Maule continued to cling to what he considered his property. The dispute between the two men continued for many years. The issue was only resolved when Maule was tried for the crime of witchcraft and executed as one of the obscure "martyrs to that terrible delusion, which should teach us . . . that the influential classes . . . are fully liable to all the passionate error that has ever characterized the maddest mob." Colonel Pyncheon then devised a claim to Maule's lot, and to a large tract of land that was adjacent, on the strength of a prior claim. He built a family mansion, the House of the Seven Gables, atop Maule's original hut. Upon completion of its construction, the natural spring became polluted.

At Maule's execution, with Colonel Pyncheon watching on horseback, Maule "had addressed him from the scaffold, and uttered a prophecy, of which history as well as fireside tradition, has preserved the very words. 'God,' said the condemned man, pointing his finger, with a ghastly look at the undismayed countenance of his enemy, 'God will give him blood to drink!'"

Matthew Maule was supposed to have haunted the House of the Seven Gables, as he claimed to be the rightful owner of the site on which the house stood. His ghost would have a hand in all the affairs of the Pyncheons "and make everything wrong with them, though it should be a thousand years after his death."

During the long history of the Maules and the Pyncheons, the Pyncheons continued to draw the famous curse on themselves, as seen in the ultimate death of Judge Jaffrey Pyncheon, who tried, but failed, to seize the property of his more feeble cousins, Hepzibah Pyncheon and Clifford Pyncheon.

Maule, Matthew, II ("the carpenter") Grandson of Matthew Maule ("the wizard") in *The House of the Seven Gables.*

Holgrave reads Phoebe the story he has written about the Pyncheon family history. In his reconstruction of events, 37 years after the House of the Seven Gables was built, the carpenter Matthew Maule, son of Thomas Maule, is summoned by Gervayse Pyncheon, grandson of Colonel Pyncheon. Matthew is bitter at his sense of "hereditary wrong," believing that the Pyncheon family mansion is standing on land that should belong to him.

Gervayse asks him for information about missing deeds to the "lands eastward," a matter they discuss at length. Matthew Maule, very proud, resents Gervayse's suspicions and detests his European manners. Matthew takes revenge on him by hypnotizing his daughter, Alice Pyncheon.

In effect, Matthew seduces Alice. He mesmerizes her and gives her commands. He lifts up his arms as though he is directing a "slow, ponderous, and invisible weight" upon her; he seems to possess her. After she waits on his bride, she catches cold and then dies—although Maule had meant only to humble Alice, not kill her. His anger is driven not only by Gervayse's arrogance, but also by his wish to display his strength and energy. When Alice is hypnotized, she feels like "a power that she little dreamed of had laid its grasp upon her maiden soul. A will, most unlike her own, constrained her to do its grotesque and fantastic bidding."

Maule, Thomas In *The House of the Seven Gables,* Thomas Maule is the architect and builder of the House of the Seven Gables. He is the son of Matthew Maule I ("the wizard"), original owner of a small hut on Maule's Lane (later Pyncheon Street), which later becomes the site of the House of the Seven Gables. He is the father of Matthew Maule II ("the carpenter").

Hawthorne anticipates readers who might find it incredible that the son of Matthew Maule I would build a house for one of the Pyncheons. He takes pains to explain that Thomas Maule was regarded as "the best workman of his time." Also, it was considered in keeping with what the narrator terms "the general coarseness and matter-of-fact character of the age" that the wizard's son should be willing "to earn an honest penny, or, rather, a weighty amount of sterling pounds, from the purse of his father's deadly enemy."

He describes the house as seen by those who attended its "consecration," or opening reception: "On every side the seven gables pointed sharply towards the sky, and presented the aspect of a whole sisterhood of edifices," with "many lattices" with "small, diamond-shaped panes." The second story projected over the base, and the third over the second. Among those visiting the house for the ceremony were clergymen, elders, magistrates, deacons, and members of the plebeian classes.

Pyncheon, Alice Historic character in *The House of the Seven Gables* whose death is caused by Matthew Maule II ("the carpenter").

Alice Pyncheon's harpsichord is still in the house. She is the one who originally planted a luxuriant white rosebush in the garden of the house; although many of the blooms are blighted or mildewed, the bush is still beautiful from a distance.

We do not meet her, but hear the sad story of her life from Holgrave, Hepzibah Pyncheon's lodger. Holgrave has written about an "incident of the Pyncheon family history" as a legend he hopes to publish; he reads it aloud to Phoebe Pyncheon.

The novel takes place 37 years after the House of the Seven Gables was built. In it, Gervayse Pyncheon, grandson of Colonel Pyncheon, summons Matthew Maule II to the house and inquires about the missing documents to the "lands eastward." It is believed that Matthew's grandfather, the wizard, gained possession of the great eastern claim in exchange for an acre or two of garden ground.

Matthew seeks revenge against the Pyncheon family by hynotizing Gervayse's beautiful young daughter, Alice. She agrees to cooperate with Matthew in order to help her father; she also convinces herself that a lady, "while true to herself," can have nothing to fear from anyone. Matthew successfully puts her in a trance and seems to possess her. While under his influence, she describes her vision of the old wizard Maule and his son as they tried to prevent Colonel Pyncheon from releasing a parchment document to his heirs.

Even after Alice awakens, she remains Matthew Maule's "mesmerized slave." From then on, no matter where she finds herself, she must obey his commandments to laugh or cry or even dance a jig. When Matthew weds a laborer's daughter, he forces Alice to wait on his bride. She then finally wakes from her trance, heads out into the rain, catches cold, and eventually dies. There is a great funeral for her, but Matthew is very upset; he had not meant for Alice to be destroyed, only trifled with and humbled.

Pyncheon, Clifford The brother of Hepzibah Pyncheon. He has spent the greater part of his life in prison, having been wrongfully convicted of a murder. Upon Clifford's impending arrival, his devoted sister becomes agitated, for she has waited for this moment for years and now fears that Clifford will be repulsed by her aged scowl and the state of disarray within the House of the Seven Gables.

Hawthorne portrays Clifford as a man who barely exists. He has no possessions—he still wears the same ancient cloak he had as a young man—and is no longer part of society. He returns to the House of the Seven Gables, which was to be his inheritance, as a guest. When he approaches the door, it seems he lacks the strength to walk, and his speech is perfunctory and ill defined, as if he were merely going through the motions of interaction with Hepzibah and his cousin Phoebe Pyncheon. Just as poverty has taken its toll on Hepzibah, decades in prison have reduced Clifford to a fragile state, which he demonstrates through extremes of emotion. He is able to experience great pain and simple pleasures; he responds intensely to beauty, although he is melancholy and ineffectual. Childlike, he is locked into his own illusions. He is represented, at the beginning of the novel, as a thin gray cloud, dim and indeterminate. As he sits at the breakfast table, his facial expression "seemed to waver, and glimmer, and nearly to die away."

When Clifford first glimpses the portrait of his ancestor Colonel Pyncheon, he has an intense emotional reaction; it induces a feeling of panic and near-physical pain, and he begs to have it covered. This aversion to the portrait serves as a reminder of the inescapable Pyncheon past and the curse of the wizard Matthew Maule on the Pyncheon family. In an attempt to escape the gloom of the dismal House of the Seven Gables, Clifford suggests to Hepzibah that they not live there, but go to Europe instead. When Clifford learns that Hepzibah has been forced to open a shop, he bursts into tears.

In most respects, Clifford is like a child who responds only to simple pleasures and pain. As his life goes on within the safety of his sister's household, he finds the company of his cousin Phoebe very tranquil and soothing. She serves as nurse, guardian, and playmate simultaneously.

Pyncheon, Colonel In *The House of the Seven Gables,* the ancestor of Miss Hepzibah Pyncheon and Clifford Pyncheon. He had coveted the land of Matthew Maule I ("the wizard") and had been instrumental in convicting him of witchcraft and having him hanged. At the execution, Maule, "with the halter about his neck," had addressed Pyncheon from the scaffold and "uttered a prophecy": "'God,' said the dying man, pointing his finger, with a ghastly look, at the undismayed countenance of his enemy, 'God will give him blood to drink!'" Ever since, there has been a curse associated with the House of the Seven Gables, which was built on top of Maule's original hut.

During the long history of the Maules and the Pyncheons, the latter family continue to draw the famous curse on themselves, as illustrated by the death of Colonel Pyncheon's descendant Judge Jaffrey Pyncheon, who tries, but fails, to seize the property of his more feeble cousins, Hepzibah Pyncheon and Clifford Pyncheon.

Pyncheon, Gervayse Historic character in *The House of the Seven Gables,* the grandson of the old Colonel Pyncheon and father of Alice Pyncheon.

According to Holgrave's written account of the Pyncheon family history, 37 years after the House of the Seven Gables was built, Gervayse had summoned the carpenter Matthew Maule (only son of Thomas Maule). At that time, Matthew was bitter at his sense of "hereditary wrong" and believed that the Pyncheon house was standing on land that rightfully belonged to him.

Gervayse Pyncheon's apartment is decorated in a costly style, with furniture imported from Paris and Venice. He is a middle-aged, handsome man with European manners and aspirations. He questions Matthew about missing documents to the "lands eastward," and his eagerness for further riches results in his sacrifice of his beautiful young daughter, Alice. He encourages her to cooperate with Matthew, who proceeds to hypnotize her as revenge against the Pyncheon family.

When, years later, Phoebe Pyncheon is given a tour of the House of the Seven Gables, she is shown a painting originally owned by Gervayse Pyncheon. It is a landscape by the French painter Claude, acquired in Europe as part of an effort to bring back "sunny recollections." The painting has "a shadowy and sun-streaked vista," yet it is in conflict with the dark Matthew Maule, the carpenter who had hypnotized Alice Pyncheon.

Pyncheon, Hepzibah Miss Hepzibah Pyncheon is an elderly spinster living alone in the House of the Seven Gables. Hawthorne's portrait of her—nervous, sensitive, inept, but well-meaning—immediately enlists the reader's sympathy. The only other occupant of the house is her lodger, Holgrave, a respectable and orderly young artist who lives in a remote gable.

Hepzibah has dwelled in strict seclusion for decades. She sheds tears at the sight of a certain miniature that represents the face of her brother, Clifford Pyncheon, as a young man. As she nervously busies herself with the arrangement of some wares in her cent shop, it is clear that she has been reduced to poverty, despite her familial legacy and possession of the House of the Seven Gables.

As a descendant of the once-distinguished Pyncheon family, she is clearly a lady with pedigree and tradition. She is a direct representation of her ancestors, embodying gentility and grace. In opening the shop, she is making a democratic gesture, but a painful one. We learn that she is only taking this step as part of her commitment to caring for her childlike brother, Clifford, released after being unjustly imprisoned for 30 years. At the same time, Hepzibah is about to emerge as an individual separate from a long and distinguished family tradition.

Pyncheon, Judge Jaffrey The most evil character in *The House of the Seven Gables,* the wealthy, detestable cousin of Miss Hepzibah Pyncheon and her brother, Clifford Pyncheon. He was responsible for sending Clifford to prison for many years for a murder he did not commit. The judge assumes an attitude of kindly benevolence toward all the Pyncheons, but it is artificial. He disapproves of Hepzibah's courageous effort to earn her way by opening a little cent shop in her home.

Judge Pyncheon is proud of his wealth, real estate, and clothing; he is always seen carrying a gold-headed cane. He continually grasps for power, hoping to become governor of Massachusetts. He is a churchgoer and proud of his civic responsibilities, but, underneath, he is devious and immoral. As a young man, he was wild and brutish and stole from his old bachelor uncle; he is an emblem of the Pyncheon family greed.

At the end of the novel, Judge Pyncheon is found slumped over and unresponsive in the parlor of the House of the Seven Gables. Initially, Hawthorne presents his sudden demise as an ambiguous event. Many circumstances point to Clifford Pyncheon as the murderer, since, after Hepzibah finds him in the room alone with the dead body, he immediately suggests that they flee the house. They go into the street, leaving the corpse sitting in the parlor.

Judge Pyncheon's death recalls the mysterious death of his ancestor Colonel Pyncheon as well as that of his uncle, also named Jaffrey. The frail Clifford, however, seems an unlikely murderer. Moreover, the judge had planned, the day of his death, to visit his family physician; he had been experiencing dimness of sight and dizziness, along with the "throbbing and kicking" of his heart.

Pyncheon, Phoebe A country kinswoman of Miss Hepzibah Pyncheon, owner of the House of the Seven Gables. Phoebe arrives unexpectedly one day for a visit. She had written in advance to say she was arriving, but her letter was not delivered on time. Hepzibah tells her she cannot afford to keep her, and she must return to her home. Phoebe says Hepzibah will find her a "cheerful little body" and she will earn her own bread. She offers to tend the cent shop, established by the destitute Hepzibah as a way of earning money, and proves to be an adept shopkeeper. She represents "the stern old stuff of Puritanism with a gold thread in the web."

As time goes on, Phoebe becomes an indispensable part of the household. She makes a success of the cent shop; her optimism and cheer draw out Hepzibah and soften her bitter attitude; and she is a great favorite of Clifford's, who regards her as "a verse of household poetry." She serves as his nurse, guardian, and sympathetic friend. Holgrave, too, is attracted to Phoebe. When he realizes that he loves her, he announces that she is his "only possibility of happiness."

Venner, Uncle Local villager in *The House of the Seven Gables.* He is a "humble resident of Pyncheon Street," known to the whole neighborhood as Uncle Venner and regarded as somewhat mentally deficient.

Still, there is at times "a vein of something like poetry" in the old gardener, and he encourages Miss Hepzibah Pyncheon by offering many "golden maxims." For example, he advises her to smile at customers in order to make a success of the cent shop she is attempting to establish.

He is extremely kind to Hepzibah and plays a vital role as he watches over her and the House of the Seven Gables. Early in the novel, we meet him when he asks Hepzibah when "he" (her brother, Clifford) is expected home, and after the storm and the flight from the house by Hepzibah and Clifford, it is Uncle Venner who is the first person to make inquiries.

FOR FURTHER READING

Abel, Darrel, "Hawthorne's House of Tradition," *South Atlantic Quarterly* 52 (October 1953): 561–578; Andola, John, "Nathaniel Hawthorne's Use of Mesmerism in Four Major Works," *Dissertation Abstracts International* 42, no. 4 (October 1981): 1631A–1632A; Baym, Nina, *The Shape of Hawthorne's Career* (Ithaca, N.Y.: Cornell University Press, 1976); Beebe, Maurice, "The Fall of the House of Pyncheon," *Nineteenth-Century Fiction* 11 (1956): 1–17; Dabundo, Laura, "The Fall of the House of the Seven Gables and Other Ambiguities of the American Gothic," in *Approaches to Teaching Gothic Fiction: The British and American Traditions* (New York: Modern Language Association of America, 2003); Dillingham, William B., "Structure and Theme in *The House of the Seven Gables,*" *Nineteenth-Century Fiction* 14 (June 1959): 59–70; Doubleday, Neal Frank, "Hawthorne's Use of Three Gothic Patterns," *College English* 7 (January 1946): 258–259; Kaul, A. N., *Hawthorne: A Collection of Critical Essays* (Englewood Cliffs, N.J.: Prentice-Hall, 1966); Levin, David, "A Historical Reconsideration of Maule's Curse," *Southern Review* 17, no. 4 (October 1981): 803–813; Loges, Max, "Hawthorne's *The House of the Seven Gables,*" *The Explicator* 60, no. 2 (winter 2002): 64–66; Madsen, Deborah, "Hawthorne's Puritans: From Fact to Fiction," *Journal of American Studies* 33 (December 1999), 509–517; Matthiessen, F. O., "The House of the Seven Gables," in *American Renaissance: Art and Expression in the Age of Emerson and Whitman* (New York: Oxford University Press, 1941); Michelson, Bruce, "Hawthorne's House of Three Stories," *New England Quarterly* (June 1984): 163–183; Ragan, James F., "Social Criticism in *The House of the Seven Gables,*" in *Literature and Society,* edited by Bernice Slote, 112–120 (Lincoln: University of Nebraska Press, 1964); Rosenthal, Bernard, ed., *Critical Essays on Hawthorne's* The House of the Seven Gables (New York: G. K. Hall, 1995); Winters, Yvor, *Maule's Curse* (New York: New Directions, 1938).

"Howe's Masquerade"

Tale first published in the UNITED STATES MAGAZINE AND DEMOCRATIC REVIEW in May 1838, the first in a series with "EDWARD RANDOLPH'S PORTRAIT," "LADY ELEANORE'S MANTLE," and "OLD ESTHER DUDLEY." The series was later published in the 1842 edition of TWICE-TOLD TALES under the title LEGENDS OF THE PROVINCE-HOUSE.

The narrator begins by recalling walking along Washington Street in Boston and seeing a "stately edifice" opposite the Old South Church designated "Old Province-House, kept by Thomas Waite." He has often intended to visit the mansion of the former royal governors of Massachusetts and steps through the courtyard into the barroom. An elderly gentleman sits in the bar, "smacking his lips" with zest. The narrator sips a drink prepared by Mr. Waite and then asks him for a tour of the mansion.

He must "draw strenuously" upon his imagination to find anything of interest in the house, which, "without its historic associations," now seems like a mere tavern. The floors are decayed, and the formerly spacious chambers have been subdivided into small rooms for single lodgers, but the staircase is still magnificent and the brick walls "as sound as ever."

Back in the bar, the elderly gentleman still lounges in his chair. He is either a lodger there or a "familiar visitor of the house," and he knows interesting stories about the history of Province-House. He recounts a legend about a masked ball given by Sir William Howe, "during the latter part of the siege of Boston," in order to "hide the distress and danger of the period" behind the "ostentation of festivity." The guests include "officers of the British army" and the "loyal gentry of the province"; they are attired as ladies and gentlemen of the British royal court of various periods, as well as figures of comedy such as Falstaff and Don Quixote. One group dresses in ragged regimental clothes, representing such personages as General George Washington and other officers of the American army; they present a mock interview between American rebels and the British commander in chief, which excites laughter for the most part.

Colonel Joliffe, however, expresses displeasure. The stern old man is a Whig (antecedent of the Republican Party) and a Puritan. He was once a famous soldier, "formerly of high station and great repute in the province"; some guests are surprised that a man of his Whig principles would stay in Boston during the siege and show up, with his granddaughter, at the party of Sir William Howe.

At nearly midnight, rumors circulate that a new spectacle is about to be exhibited, though Sir William Howe says he knows nothing about "this new foolery." Muffled drums are heard from the street, as though a funeral procession has halted outside the house. Howe calls to the leader of his musicians to stop playing "that dead march," but the drum major, whose face has gone pale, says his musicians are not responsible, and that he has never heard that march except "at the funeral of his late Majesty, King George the Second."

The ghostly figures of Puritan governors, wearing garb of "antique fashion," appear at the top of the stairs and wave triumphantly as they go outside. Colonel Joliffe identifies them as the "rulers of the old, original Democracy of Massachusetts": Endicott, Winthrop, and others. Another group of specters descend the stairs; they are the past "rulers of this land," including Governor Bradstreet ("the last of the Puritans"), the tyrant Sir Edmund Andros, Sir William Phips, and the Earl of Bellamont. Miss Joliffe says, "Now, were I a rebel, I might fancy that the ghosts of these ancient governors had been summoned to form the funeral procession of royal authority in New England."

The next group of figures includes Governor Beicher, Governor Dudley, Governor Shute, and Governor Burnet. Miss Joliffe thinks "they were miserable men, these royal governors of Massachusetts." Sir William Howe and his guests watch the "progress of this singular pageant" with "anger, contempt, or half-acknowledged fear, but still with an anxious curiosity." The next shadowy figures resemble "the successive rulers of the province," including "the well-remembered Hutchinson" and a "military figure" named Gage, who had "recently been master of the Province-House, and chief of all the land."

The peal of trumpets accompanies the final, shrouded figure, whose "stately and martial" gait, military cloak, and gilded sword resemble those of Sir William Howe. Howe recoils from the figure with a "look of wild amazement, if not horror." At the threshold, the figure shakes "his clenched hands in the air," a gesture of "rage and sorrow" that Sir William Howe himself later repeated, when, "for the last time, and as the last royal governor, he passed through the portal of the Province-House."

Colonel Joliffe smiles sternly at the British general and says, "Would your Excellency inquire further into the mystery of the pageant?" Howe warns him to "take care" of his head, which has "stood too long on a traitor's shoulders." The colonel, accompanied by his granddaughter, departs, announcing that the empire of Britain is at its "last gasp" and the "shadows of the old governors" are attending its funeral.

This was the "last festival that a British ruler ever held in the old province of Massachusetts Bay." Some believe that Colonel Joliffe and his granddaughter "possessed some secret intelligence in regard to the mysterious pageant of that night."

When the elderly gentleman finishes his story, the narrator draws a breath and looks around the room, trying to imagine the "romance and historic grandeur" in the setting. He thinks to himself that it is "desperately hard work, when we attempt to throw the spell of hoar antiquity over localities with which the living world, and the day that is passing over us, have aught to do." Still, as he glances at the "stately staircase" and emerges through the "venerable portal," he experiences a "thrill of awe" as he returns to the throng of people on Washington Street.

CRITICAL ANALYSIS

William E. Grant observes that the "procession of figures from the American past" that appears to Sir William Howe not only forms "the funeral procession of royal authority in New England," as Miss Joliffe puts it, but also serves to "underline the connections Hawthorne clearly sees between the Puritan past and the political history of American independence." The narrator's acknowledgment that it is "desperately hard work, when we attempt to throw the spell of hoar antiquity over localities with which the living world, and the day that is passing over us, have aught to do" reflects Hawthorne's own frustration with the "lack of a lengthy American past." As he wrote years later in the preface to *The MARBLE FAUN*, it was difficult for an American writer to craft "a romance about a country where there is no shadow, no antiquity, no mystery, no picturesque and gloomy wrong." Grant suggests that it "may have been this lack of historical distance" that made Hawthorne "less

comfortable with the events of the American Revolutionary period than with those of the Puritan years" and comments that Hawthorne was "rarely as successful in imaginatively dramatizing this history as that of the seventeenth century." Although the "Legends of the Province-House" reflect "the most momentous change in American history," Grant states that they never approach the quality of "The GRAY CHAMPION" and "ENDICOTT AND THE RED CROSS," which exhibit the "symbolic power and mythic dimensions characteristic of his best work in a story with a Revolutionary War setting" ("Nathaniel Hawthorne").

FOR FURTHER READING

Grant, William E., "Nathaniel Hawthorne," in *Dictionary of Literary Biography*. Vol. 74, edited by Bobby Ellen Kimbel, 143–163 (Detroit: Gale Research, 1988).

"Intelligence Office, The"

Short story first published in the *UNITED STATES MAGAZINE AND DEMOCRATIC REVIEW*, March 1844, and reprinted in *The Rover, The New World*, and the *Salem Gazette* the same year. It was collected in the first edition of *MOSSES FROM AN OLD MANSE* in 1846.

As the story opens, a grave figure is seated at a desk in a corner of a metropolitan office. He is continually approached by people who have specific requests. A mechanic is looking for an affordable tenement; a single gentleman seeks "economical board"; a "faded beauty" inquires after "her lost bloom."

The next to enter is a stranger wearing "ill-suited" clothes and the "characteristic expression of a man out of his right place." He asks whether this is the Central Intelligence Office. The figure at the desk asks the stranger's business. He replies that he wants his "true place in the world," that "which nature intended me to perform when she fashioned me awry, and which I have vainly sought, all my lifetime!" The Intelligencer takes the stranger's application but warns him that most people "are, more or less, in your predicament." The stranger leaves in a despondent state.

A youth appears, his heart yearning for something—he knows not what. It burns "with an intolerable fire" and "tortures" him all day long, so he wishes to dispose of it. The officer shows him a young woman, but it is not revealed whether the youth gives up his heart "into her custody."

The "agency of the passions and affections" is not always successful in its work. Sometimes a heart is taken in, one "of such exquisite material, so delicately attempered, and so curiously wrought," that no match can be found for it.

Still, anyone who "has missed anything valuable, whether out of his heart, mind, or pocket, would do well to make inquiry" here. A man approaches who has searched all over the world for a "precious jewel" he has lost. The officer opens a drawer in his oaken cabinet and displays the many jewels and other articles that "had been picked up in the streets, until the right owners should claim them." The young man claims the "Pearl of Great Price," but the officer refuses to give it to him and he runs madly into the street.

A "fashionable young gentleman" asks for a damask rosebud, a "gift of his lady-love," that he has lost from his buttonhole. A variety of errands lead people to visit the office, "where all human wishes seemed to be made known" and "negotiated to their fulfilment."

Next enters an older man who wishes to dispose of his estate, which he has assembled through business enterprises all over the world. In the process, he has acquired "an incumbrance of a certain nature," a burden that he wishes the purchaser of the estate to assume. But the officer says the next possessor of his estate will have a "similar incumbrance, but it will be of his own contracting, and will not lighten your burthen in the least." The "man of deplorable success" leaves, "laden with the weight" of his "accursed acres" and "infernal mansion" crushing his soul and "compressed into an evil conscience."

Many more applicants for positions appear. A "small, smoke-dried figure" says he was one of the "bad spirits" who waited upon Dr. Faustus in his laboratory. A "Man in Red," who "had aided Napoleon Buonaparte in his ascent to imperial power," seeks service but is rejected because he lacks "familiarity with the cunning tactics of the present day."

Each person has a different issue, all recorded in a "great folio" by the Man of Intelligence. The folio is the record of human nature though human wishes. Some seek positions; some wish to sell their goods or possessions. A soldier desires a new leg, a "weary wretch" desires a "creditable method of laying down his life," many wish to "exchange their youthful vices for others better suited to the gravity of advancing age," and a few hope to "exchange vice for virtue." People are least willing to give up "the habits, the oddities, the characteristic traits . . . somewhere between faults and follies, of which nobody but themselves could understand the fascination."

The "strangest wishes," from some men of science, are "to contend with Nature, and wrest from her some secret, or some power." The "most ordinary wish" is, of course, for "wealth, wealth, wealth." Others, depending on their circumstances, wish for power, youth, a fashionable coat, a new novel, a kingdom, a neighbor's wife, a crust of bread.

This folio is "probably truer, as a representation of the human heart," than reality, for it contains a more complex view of the world: "more of good and more of evil," "more redeeming points of the bad, and more errors of the virtuous."

Then a "grandfatherly personage" enters the office in search of "To-morrow," for he has pursued it all his life with the assurance that "To-morrow has some vast benefit or other in store for me."

Finally there appears a man with a face full of "sturdy vigor," a "large, warm heart," and a "powerful intellect." He says he seeks Truth. The Man of Intelligence tells him he must "achieve the miracle" for himself. The Intelligencer explains that his "agency in worldly action" is "merely delusive." He is only a "Recording Spirit," not a "minister of action," because the desire of each man's heart in fact "does for him whatever I seem to do."

The tale ends with the bustle and roar of the city, the "rush and tumult of man's life, in its noisy and brief career," drowning out the words of the two speakers.

FOR FURTHER READING

Cohen, B. Bernard, "Emerson's 'The Young American' and Hawthorne's 'The Intelligence Office,'"

American Literature: A Journal of Literary History, Criticism, and Bibliography 26, no. 1 (March 1954): 32–43.

"John Inglefield's Thanksgiving"

Story first published in the UNITED STATES MAG-AZINE AND DEMOCRATIC REVIEW in March 1840. It was signed "By Rev. A. A. Royce." The next month, it was reprinted in the *Boston Nation* under the same signature. It was collected in *The* SNOW-IMAGE, AND OTHER TWICE-TOLD TALES, with Hawthorne's name on the title page, in 1852.

The nucleus of the story appeared in Hawthorne's notebook sometime in late 1836 or early 1837: "To picture a virtuous family, the different members examples of virtuous dispositions in their way; then introduce a vicious person, and trace out the relations that arise between him and then, and the manner in which all are affected" (*Centenary Edition of the Works of Nathaniel Hawthorne*, 8, 251.22–25).

As the tale opens, the blacksmith John Inglefield and his family are sitting around the hearth after Thanksgiving dinner. His son, a student of theology at Andover, and his daughter, Mary, 16, are there, along with a former apprentice, Robert Moore, now a journeyman. Mrs. Inglefield had died four months earlier, but a vacant chair is kept at John Inglefield's right hand in her memory. He cherishes "the grief that was dear to him."

A second family member has gone away since the previous Thanksgiving, Mary's sister, Prudence. No chair has been kept for her. She enters, having spent many months away in "guilt and infamy." She takes the vacant seat, "as if it had been reserved on purpose for her." She looks the same, as if she had "merely stepped away from her father's fireside for half an hour." To John Inglefield, she is "the very image of his buried wife." He cannot "speak unkindly to his sinful child," but he cannot "take her to his bosom," either. He tells her how much her mother would have rejoiced to see her. Prudence says that when she first entered, she was "so dazzled by the firelight, that she seemed to be sitting in this very chair."

The rest of the family greets her. Her brother is about to go to the South Pacific as a missionary but holds out his hand with affection—like a brother, but also like a clergyman "speaking to a child of sin." Prudence pulls back "somewhat hastily from his grasp." Mary tries to hug her but is rebuffed when Prudence cries, "Do not you touch me. Your bosom must not be pressed to mine!" Mary shudders as she feels "something darker than the grave was between Prudence and herself." Prudence calls to Robert Moore to greet her, and he overcomes his "pride and resentment" to press her hand to his bosom. She smiles sadly and tells him he must not give her too warm a welcome.

It has been said of Prudence that she "had a faculty, even from childhood, of throwing her own feelings, like a spell, over her companions." The others are thankful she has returned. John Inglefield's heart grows "warm and merry within him." Prudence's brother is "frolicksome as a school-boy," while Robert Moore gazes at her "with the bashful earnestness of love new-born."

At eight o'clock Prudence pours herb tea for her father. He says she has made her old father happy again, but they miss her mother. Just as the family is preparing for domestic worship, Prudence puts on her cloak and hood and begins to leave. The family is shocked. She turns toward them to bid farewell, but her face has changed so that "sin and evil passions glowed through its comeliness, and wrought a horrible deformity." The gleam in her eyes is like "triumphant mockery, at their surprise and grief." Inglefield cries out, "Stay and be your father's blessing—or take his curse with you!" She lingers for a moment, but the family can see by her expression that she is "struggling with a fiend." She opens the door and vanishes into the darkness.

The reader learns that Prudence has a secret trangression about which she feels guilty. She is one of the "painted beauties" at the theater of a neighboring city. Her visit to her family has only been "one of those waking dreams in which the guilty soul will sometimes stray back to its innocence." Sin is "careful of her bond-slaves," and that "dark power" would snatch Prudence "from her father's hearth" and "from the gate of heaven." Her sin and its punishment are "alike eternal."

CRITICAL ANALYSIS

The tale has not been well received by critics. Mark Van Doren calls it "moral melodrama without moral meaning" (*Nathaniel Hawthorne*, 108).

Terence Martin observes the intimate connection between heart and hearth in Hawthorne's work. In this story, home is a "stable and secure institution of the heart which beckons even to the errant daughter, whose fall is measured in terms of her moral distance from home" (*Nathaniel Hawthorne*, 65).

FOR FURTHER READING

Baym, Nina, *The Shape of Hawthorne's Career* (Ithica, N.Y.: Cornell University Press, 1976), 57; Chandler, Elizabeth Lathrop, *A Study of the Sources of the Tales and Romances Written by Nathaniel Hawthorne before 1853* (Darby, Penn,.: Arden Library, 1978), 28–29; Stein, William Bysshe, *Hawthorne's Faust: A Study of the Devil Archetype* (Hamden, Conn.: Archon Books, 1968), 79–80; Van Doren, Mark, *Nathaniel Hawthorne: A Critical Biography* (New York: Viking, 1966), 108.

"Lady Eleanore's Mantle"

Tale first published in the UNITED STATES MAGAZINE AND DEMOCRATIC REVIEW in December 1838, the third in a series with "HOWE'S MASQUERADE," "EDWARD RANDOLPH'S PORTRAIT," and "OLD ESTHER DUDLEY." The series was later published in the 1842 edition of TWICE-TOLD TALES under the title LEGENDS OF THE PROVINCE-HOUSE.

The landlord of the Province-House, Mr. Thomas Waite, has invited the narrator (the "humble notetaker") and his friend, Mr. Tiffany (the "ingenious tale-teller"), to an oyster dinner. Another guest present is a "venerable personage, whose own actual reminiscences went back to the epoch of Gage and Howe"; he is an "aged loyalist" whose "attachment to royalty, and to the colonial institutions and customs that were connected with it, had never yielded to the democratic heresies of after times." After dinner, the host uncorks a fine bottle of Madeira. Mr. Tiffany drinks the "precious liquor" with "peculiar zest," and after his third glass he recounts a tale that takes place nearly 120 years ago.

During the time when Colonel Shute is governor of Massachusetts Bay, his distant relative, a "young lady of rank and fortune" named Lady Eleanore Rochcliffe, arrives from England to "claim his protection as her guardian." The governor's wife had been "as a mother to her childhood" and hopes her life in New England will save her from the "artifices and corruptions of a court." Unfortunately, Lady Eleanore has a "harsh, unyielding pride" and a "haughty consciousness of her hereditary and personal advantages, which made her almost incapable of control."

Her ship lands at Newport, Rhode Island, where the governor's coach, drawn by four black horses with an escort of gentlemen on horseback, meets her to convey her to Boston. She has an "almost queenly stateliness" combined with "the grace and beauty of a maiden in her teens." Among the women, a rumor circulates that Lady Eleanore's "embroidered mantle," which possesses "magical properties of adornment," is responsible for the charm of her appearance.

As she arrives at the Province-House in Boston, the bell of the Old South Church is tolling for a funeral, an unfortunate sign. An English officer, Captain Langford, thinks the funeral should have been postponed, but a popular physician, Doctor Clarke, tells him that in America, "a dead beggar must have precedence of a living queen. King Death confers high privileges."

When the carriage arrives, a pale young man prostrates himself before the coach, "offering his person as a footstool" for Lady Eleanore. Governor Shute inquires as to the meaning of his action, but Lady Eleanore steps on his form and extends her hand, saying playfully but scornfully, "When men seek only to be trampled upon, it were a pity to deny them a favor so easily granted—and so well deserved!" The moment is symbolic: an "emblem of aristocracy and hereditary pride, trampling on human sympathies and the kindred of nature." The young man, whose name is Jervase Helwyse, is a "youth of no birth or fortune," but he had met Lady Eleanore before and fallen in love with her.

Governor Shute, although he is shocked at Lady Eleanore's behavior, gives a splendid ball for her. She wears the embroidered mantle that is rumored to have "magic properties, so as to lend a new and untried grace to her figure each time that she put it on." Lady Eleanore stands within a "small and distinguished circle," apart from the "general throng" of guests. Sometimes her expression looks weary or scornful. Most of the whispering is about her "exceeding beauty," but it is marked tonight by something "wild and unnatural." Some observers detect in her a "feverish flush and alternate paleness of countenance."

At first she is surrounded by admirers, but her sarcastic comments repel and perplex them, and they all withdraw except Captain Langford (the English officer), a Virginia planter, an Episcopal clergyman, and Governor Shute's private secretary. She wearily refuses even the Champagne and sinks into a damask chair. Jervase Helwyse kneels at her feet and gives her wine in a silver goblet. He asks her to take a sip of the "holy wine" and pass the goblet among the guests as a sign that she has not sought to withdraw from the "chain of human sympathies." The Episcopal clergyman asks where Jervase has obtained the sacramental vessel, which is recognized as belonging to the Old South Church. The governor's secretary believes it is poisoned. When Captain Langford seizes Jervase Helwyse, the cup overturns onto Lady Eleanore's mantle.

Bystanders try to lead Jervase away, but he begs Lady Eleanore, with a "wild, impassioned earnestness," to throw off the mantle, crying, "Cast it from you! It may not yet be too late! Give the accursed garment to the flames!" She laughs scornfully and tells him farewell. As he is dragged away by the other men, he says with sadness that they will meet shortly, when her face wears "another aspect."

From across the room, Doctor Clarke has been watching Lady Eleanore with "keen sagacity." He speaks privately with Governor Shute, who then announces to the guests that the festivities must end because of an "unforeseen circumstance."

After the ball, a "dreadful epidemic" ensues, ravaging the upper classes first and then the lower ones with "pit-marks." It is the "Small-Pox," a form of "Asiatic cholera, striding from shore to shore of the Atlantic, and marching like destiny upon cities far remote." Its origin is traced to Lady Eleanore's mantle, within which the contagion had lurked. The mantle had been made by a "woman on her death-bed, and was the last toil of her stiffening fingers, which had interwoven fate and misery with its golden threads." There is widespread hatred of Lady Eleanore, and the people cry that her "pride and scorn had evoked a fiend."

One day a "wild figure," Jervase Helwyse, approaches the Province-House, climbs a pillar, takes down the blood-red flag that marks "every dwelling into which the Small-Pox had entered," and goes inside the mansion. Governor Shute confronts him, asking what he seeks and exclaiming, "There is nothing here but Death." Jervase declares, "Death will not touch me, the banner-wearer of the pestilence! Death, and the Pestilence, who wears the aspect of the Lady Eleanor, will walk through the streets tonight, and I must march before them with this banner!"

Governor Shute permits the "mad youth" to climb the steps, but Jervase is confronted at the top by the physician, Doctor Clarke, who tells him that Lady Eleanore's nurse has died, and that the lady has carried a "curse" to the shores of America. Jervase still wants to see her. He enters her chamber and finds her inside a canopied bed, complaining of thirst. She struggles to hide her face and says the "curse of Heaven" has struck her because she would not call man her brother, nor woman her sister. She wrapped herself in "PRIDE as in a MANTLE" and "scorned the sympathies of nature," and therefore has "nature made this wretched body the medium of a dreadful sympathy." She cries, "You are avenged—they are all avenged—Nature is avenged."

The "malice of his mental disease" and the "bitterness lurking at the bottom of his heart" awake within Jervase. He shakes his finger at her with an "outburst of insane merriment," snatches her "fatal mantle," and rushes from the house, impelled by his "crazed intellect." That night, bearing the red flag of pestilence, he leads a torchlight procession with an effigy of Lady Eleanore in the middle, enveloped in her mantle. They arrive opposite the Province-House, where the mob burns the effigy.

From that time on, the pestilence abates. Supposedly, however, a "female form" still haunts a "certain chamber" of the Province-House.

Mr. Tiffany's story is applauded by the narrator, Mr. Thomas Waite, and the "old loyalist."

"Legends of the Province-house"

A group of four previously published tales collected under this title in TWICE-TOLD TALES (1842 edition): "HOWE'S MASQUERADE," "EDWARD RANDOLPH'S PORTRAIT," "LADY ELEANORE'S MANTLE," and "OLD ESTHER DUDLEY."

Liberty Tree

A volume of previously published stories for children published in March 1841 by "E. P. Peabody, 13 West Street." ELIZABETH PEABODY, one of the sisters of SOPHIA HAWTHORNE, ran a small publishing company from her home at 13 West Street, on Boston's Beacon Hill. The printer was S. N. Dickinson, 52 Washington Street. The full title of the book was Liberty Tree with the Last Words of Grandfather's Chair.

"Lily's Quest, The: An Apologue"

Story published in The Southern Rose, 7 (January 19, 1839), and in several other magazines before being collected in the second edition of TWICE-TOLD TALES (1842).

As the story opens, two lovers, Adam Forrester and Lilias Fay, set out to find a site on which to build "a little summer-house, in the form of an antique Temple." It will be a "Temple of Happiness," consecrated to "all manner of refined and innocent enjoyments."

They are followed by a relative of Lilias Fay, an old and melancholy man named Walter Gascoigne. He disparages each site they find; each one has been "blighted by Sorrow" in one way or another. The "old lunatic" has legends of suffering for every spot they consider; he has "a gift to know whatever evil and lamentable thing had stained the bosom of Mother Earth," and his voice appears "like a prophecy of future woe."

They finally find a spot that seems ideal. It stands within a group of trees, with an ancestral mansion on one side and an "ivied church" on another. A pale lily is growing there. The old man gives "no word of dissent," though there is an "inscrutable smile" on his face.

The "fairy structure" of the temple rises, built of white marble with a vaulted dome. However, the local people imagine that the edifice is planned after an "ancient mausoleum" and is "intended for a tomb." They also notice Lilias Fay's delicate form "growing every day more fragile, so that she looked as if the summer breze should snatch her up, and waft her heavenward." Lilias Fay and Walter Gascoigne observe the progress of the temple every day. As it nears completion, a day is appointed for a "rite of dedication."

On the evening before the dedication, Adam Forrester looks toward the portal of her dwelling and Lilias seems to become invisible. The next morning, she is found lifeless in the temple. Adam wants to bury her there, converting this Temple of Happiness into a tomb. As the sexton digs a grave beneath the temple's marble floor, he finds an "ancient sepulchre," which contains the forgotten "bones of generations that had died long ago." Walter Gascoigne tells Adam that he has found "no better foundation for your happiness, than on a Grave."

Adam then has a "vision of Hope and Joy" and understands the "mystery of Life and Death." He opens his arms toward heaven and cries, "Joy! Joy! On a Grave be the site of our Temple; and now our happiness is for Eternity!" A ray of sunshine breaks through the sky and glimmers down into the sepulchre. Walter Gascoigne stalks away; his gloom, "symbolic of all earthly sorrow," can no longer abide there now that the "darkest riddle of humanity was read."

FOR FURTHER READING

Levy, Leo B., "The Temple and the Tomb: Hawthorne's 'The Lily's Quest,'" *Studies in Short Fiction* 3 (1966): 334–342.

"Little Annie's Ramble"

Story published in YOUTH'S KEEPSAKE: A CHRISTMAS AND NEW YEAR'S GIFT FOR YOUNG PEOPLE (1835) before being collected in the first edition of TWICE-TOLD TALES (1837).

The story opens with the town crier ringing his bell and shouting news of the arrival of the circus. Little Annie stands on her father's doorstep, feeling an "impulse to go strolling away—that longing after the mystery of the great world—which many children feel." The narrator impulsively invites Annie, whom he knows, to go with him. They walk through a throng of people and a "tumult" of horses and trucks and carts, but Annie "passes on with fearless confidence." Her eyes "brighten with pleasure" at the sight of an organ grinder playing on the street, the "silks of sunny hue" glowing in shop windows, her reflection in the mirrors at the hardware store, the pies and cakes at the confectioner's, and the doll at the toy shop.

They enter the circus. Annie is interested in looking at the exotic animals such as the elephant and tiger. Meanwhile, the narrator imagines the animals' thoughts: The polar bear, for instance, is "absorbed in contemplation" and misses his iceberg and cubs. The monkeys, however, are "unsentimental" and "ill-natured." Annie does not love them, for their "ugliness shocks her pure, instinctive delicacy of taste" and bears a "wild and dark resemblance to humanity."

As they move through the noisy crowd, the town crier rings his bell again, this time shouting that a little girl of five is missing, "in a blue frock and white pantalettes, with brown curling hair and hazel eyes." The narrator realizes he had forgotten to tell her mother he was taking her along on a ramble. As they hasten home, he reflects that the "charm of childhood" has revived his spirits. He praises the "free and simple thoughts" and "native

feeling" of children. He would like to be a child again himself. Since that is impossible, it has been "good to steal away from the society of bearded men, and even of gentler woman, and spend an hour or two with children." Their "moral nature" is a tonic for aged men.

FOR FURTHER READING

Van Tassel, Mary M., "Hawthorne, His Narrator, and His Readers in 'Little Annie's Ramble,'" *ESQ: A Journal of the American Renaissance* 33, no. 3 (1987): 168–179.

"Little Daffydowndilly"

Children's story published in *Boys' and Girls' Magazine* in August 1843. It was collected in *The SNOW-IMAGE, AND OTHER TWICE-TOLD TALES* in 1852.

The subject of the story, a little boy named Daffydowndilly, resembles a flower in his nature. He only likes to do what is "beautiful and agreeable" and dislikes work of any kind. He is put under the care of Mr. Toil, a strict schoolmaster with a "severe and ugly countenance." He misses his indulgent mother and runs away from school to find her.

He meets a stranger, a man of "grave and sedate appearance," who inquires where he is going. Daffydowndilly has never told a lie in his life, so he confesses the truth. The stranger says he also knows Mr. Toil and will go with him to a place where no one has ever heard of him. They see a haymaker, a carpenter, an army captain, and a fiddler, all busily working and directing those they are supervising. Everyone they pass, even a scarecrow, is busy with a job. They rest under some trees, only to see Signor Far Niente, reclining in the shade; he is idle but miserable. The stranger identifies all of them as brothers of Mr. Toil.

Little Daffydowndilly begs to be taken back to school, since there is "nothing but Toil all the world over." The school is nearby, as he and his companion have traveled "in a circle instead of a straight line." Daffydowndilly looks up and realizes that his companion also bears a likeness to Mr. Toil.

From then on, the boy is more diligent, for he has discovered that "diligence is not a whit more toilsome than sport or idleness." As he becomes better acquainted with Mr. Toil, he realizes that his "smile of approbation" makes his face as pleasant as even that of his mother.

"Main-street"

Sketch published in *The Snow-Image, and Other Twice-Told Tales* (1852). The title was sometimes "Main Street" or "Main-Street" when later published.

The theme of the story is a panoramic overview of the transformation of a small segment of New England by immigrants from England. The narrator, or showman, takes daily walks along the principal street of his native town. He imagines a sequence of "characteristic scenes" that have taken place on the street during the period of its existence, more than two centuries. He devises an imaginary pictorial exhibition, in the form of a puppet show, by means of which he proposes to call up the ghosts of the past.

He first takes the spectator back to the original tract of forest, an "ancient and primitive wood" that is now Main Street. A "majestic and queenly" Indian woman, the "great Squaw Sachem," moves through the leaves. Her second husband, the Indian chief Wappacowet, stalks beside her. Both are unaware of the "stately hall" the white man will build on the very spot where they walk, or of the "noble Museum" which will someday contain Indian arrowheads as "memorials of a vanished race."

At this point an "acidulous-looking gentleman" takes exception to the exhibition, criticizing it as stiff and graceless. The showman replies that "human art has its limits" and asks the spectator to use his imagination.

The earliest white settler, Roger Conant, strides through the scene; he is a "man of thoughtful strength" who has "planted the germ of a city" here. Inside his cottage, his English wife sings a psalm and laughs at her children's antics. Nearby are their neighbors' dwellings; soon the "forest-track" will

be a street. The white settlement is viewed from afar by Indians, traveling from their wigwams to watch and feeling, perhaps, "saddened by a flitting presentiment that this heavy tread will find its way over all the land."

A ship arrives, bearing merchandise from England and a governor, Endicott, for the new settlement. His wife, Anna Gower, a "rose of beauty from an English garden," leans on his arm. A "gentlemanly person" in the audience predicts that since Anna, Endicott's first wife, will have no children, other women with her hereditary beauty will appear.

The "Anglo-Saxon energy" goes to work: A house of worship appears, carpenters build a large house of English oak sent over by ship, and the blacksmith and wheelwright fashion new objects. The wildlife that used to live on the site withdraw. Indians enter the settlement with the skins of beaver, otter, bear, and elk, which they sell to Endicott. The firstborn of Naumkeag, John Massey, plays near his father's threshold. More and more people throng to New England, including Emanuel Downing, Nathaniel Ward (the minister of Ipswich), and Ann Hutchinson. More houses are built. A Thursday lecture series is inaugurated.

Strict Puritan laws are implemented; people are punished in public for minor transgressions. An "idle fellow" is bound to the whipping post; another man wears a halter about his neck; and a woman is chained to a post for "no other offense than lifting her hand against her husband." Hawthorne's ambivalence toward Puritanism is evident when he writes, "Let us thank God for having given us such ancestors; and let each successive generation thank him, not less fervently, for being one step further from them in the march of ages."

Then Quakers begin to enter, trampling on Puritan laws. Cassandra Southwick is led to prison; Ann Coleman is dragged through the street, naked from the waist up. The Indians launch King Philip's War. Prisoners are executed on Gallows Hill. There are witch trials. The Great Snow of 1717 buries the countryside and villages.

Suddenly a wire is broken in the machinery and the scene will not move; the street remains buried beneath the snow, and "the fate of Herculaneum and Pompeii has its parallel in this catastrophe." The showman is unable to move forward to the deeds of the present and the sights of the future. He offers a refund to any spectator who "may feel dissatisfied with the evening's entertainment"; the critic stretches out his hand and demands his quarter back.

"Man of Adamant, The: An Apologue"

Tale first printed in *The* TOKEN, unsigned, in 1837, and then collected in the first edition of *The* SNOW-IMAGE, AND OTHER TWICE-TOLD TALES (1852).

Richard Digby considers himself the sole custodian of the "treasure of a true faith," although Hawthorne describes him as "the gloomiest and most intolerant of a stern brotherhood." He builds himself a "tabernacle in the wilderness," in the "dreariest depths of the forest," and curses the village meetinghouse, regarding it as a "temple of heathen idolatry." He exults in turning away from the cottages and fields and sitting alone beneath a tree and reading his Bible. After three days of journeying, he discovers a gloomy cave, enters, and congratulates himself for finding a place where his "soul will be at peace" and where the wicked cannot find him. He considers his own prayers to be more acceptable than those of others, and here his voice will not be "mingled with the sinful supplications of the multitude."

The cave is hung with what appear to be icicles, but they have become "as hard as adamant." Richard Digby is supposed to suffer from deposits of "calculous particles within his heart, caused by an obstructed circulation of the blood," which might someday "change his fleshly heart to stone." He is not convinced of his malady, however.

On the third day of his sojourn in the cave, he sees Mary Goffe standing before him. She is a young woman he had converted to his beliefs back in England. She says she has arrived to check on his condition, for a great physician has given her "the skill to cure it." Richard Digby casts her away, telling her that he is "sanctified" and she is "sinful." She begs him to return to the village with her, saying he and his "fellow-men" need each other. Ignoring her, Richard opens his Bible and reads.

The "heavenly and ethereal" Mary leans against a tree beside the cave. She takes him "hallowed water" from a nearby fountain and asks him to drink and then let them read together one page of the "blessed volume." Richard Digby eyes her with a "fixed and evil frown," looking like "a marble statue, wrought by some dark-imagined sculptor to express the most repulsive mood that human features could assume." The "more heavenly" Mary looks, the more distasteful she is to Richard. He strikes down the cup of water, orders her to tempt him no more, and then dies. The form of Mary Goffe melts into the sunbeams; she had actually died months before and been buried in an English churchyard. The narrator says, "Either it was her ghost that haunted the wild forest, or else a dream-like spirit, typifying pure Religion."

A century later, children are playing at the foot of a hill. They hide in the thick foliage and then shriek and run home. Their father, a farmer, trying to discover the source of their fright, peers through the foliage and discovers the entrance to a cave. He sees the figure of a man sitting in the sepulchre; his corpse has been petrified so he looks like a sculpture "carved in the same gray stone that formed the walls and portal of the cave." The farmer and his wife, assisted by the children, throw pebbles and stones into the cave, followed by earth. They obliterate all traces of the discovery, leaving only the legend, which is transmitted to their children and their grandchildren. Today there is only a grassy patch on the hillside, and few believe there had ever been a cave or a statue, but "grown people avoid the spot," as do children. The shape of Richard Digby sits within, repelling "the whole race of mortals," but not from heaven. He is repelling them from the "horrible loneliness of his dark, cold sepulchre."

CRITICAL ANALYSIS

Terence Martin observes that Richard Digby is just one of Hawthorne's characters who "insist on a religious idea to the detriment or exclusion of humanity." Digby's religion is "unique," as it consists of "the one idea that of all the people in the world only he has the key to salvation." Martin notes that for Hawthorne, the Shakers "champion a view hardly less extreme: the basic tenet of their religion amounts to a communal renunciation of 'the magnetic chain of humanity' out of a deluded concern for salvation" (*Nathaniel Hawthorne*, 56).

Hawthorne also deals with the theme of persons who become inanimate in "ETHAN BRAND" and "DROWNE'S WOODEN IMAGE."

FOR FURTHER READING

Bland, R. Lamar, "William Austin's 'The Man with the Cloaks: A Vermont Legend': An American Influence on Hawthorne's 'The Man of Adamant,'" *Nathaniel Hawthorne Journal* (1977): 139–145; Gallagher, Edward J., "Sir Kenelm Digby in Hawthorne's 'The Man of Adamant,'" *Notes and Queries* 17 (1970): 15–16; Gautreau, Henry W. Jr., "A Note on Hawthorne's 'The Man of Adamant,'" *Philological Quarterly* 52 (1973): 315–317; Jones, Buford, "'The Man of Adamant' and the Moral Picturesque," *American Transcendental Quarterly: A Journal of New England Writers* 14 (1972): 33–41.

Marble Faun, The

Hawthorne's last novel, published in February 1860. In May 1859, the Hawthorne family returned to England from Italy. Hawthorne had drafted the novel already, but they spent another year in England while he rewrote it and then saw it through British publication. This step ensured that he would have a British copyright (Baym, *The Shape of Hawthorne's Career*, 251).

The Marble Faun is set in Italy, a country Hawthorne had come to know and appreciate during his residence in Florence and Rome from the spring of 1858 through the spring of 1859. In his preface to the novel, he states that Italy was chiefly valuable to him as the setting because it afforded him "a sort of poetic or fairy precinct, where actualities would

Nathaniel Hawthorne in 1860, the same year he would publish his final work, *The Marble Faun*. From a copy of the photograph by Mayall taken in London in that year. *(Courtesy of the Peabody Essex Museum)*

not be so terribly insisted upon as they are, and must needs be, in America." He laments that in his "dear native land," it was difficult for an American writer to write "about a country where there is no shadow, no antiquity, no mystery, no picturesque and gloomy wrong."

Hawthorne wrote to JAMES T. FIELDS that "no place ever took so strong a hold" of his being as Rome. He had, however, been "miserable" there (perhaps a reference to his daughter Una's brush with death when she contracted "Roman fever," a dreaded illness, similar to malaria, from which she suffered for six months).

While there, he had been much impressed by two statues in the Villa Borghese in Rome, a dancing faun and a copy of the *Faun* of Praxiteles (he saw another copy of it in the Capitoline Museums). In his notebook, he recorded a visit to the basement floor of the Casino of the Villa, filled with statuary. His impression may have been the genesis of the novel:

... a Faun, copied from that of Praxiteles, and another, who seems to be dancing, are exceedingly pleasant to look at. I like these strange, sweet, playful, rustic creatures, almost entirely human as they are, yet linked so prettily, without monstrosity, to the lower tribes by the long, furry ears, or by a modest tail; indicating a strain of honest wildness in them. Their character has never, that I know of, been wrought out in literature; and something very good, funny, and philosophical, as well as poetic, might very likely be educed from them. (Rome, April 18, 1858; *The French and Italian Notebooks,* edited by Thomas Woodson, 173)

In February 1860, the novel was published in England as *Transformation.* It was published a week later in the United States as *The Marble Faun.* The subtitle, in both editions, was "The Romance of Monte Beni," a title suggested by James T. Fields.

SYNOPSIS

Chapter I: "Miriam, Hilda, Kenyon, Donatello"
The novel opens in the sculpture gallery in Rome's Capitoline Museums, which are located in two buildings, the Palazzo Nuovo and the Palazzo dei Conservatori, on a square, the Piazza del Campidoglio, designed by Michelangelo.

Hawthorne introduces the four principal characters: Miriam, a dark-eyed young painter; Hilda, a slender, brown-haired New England young woman, also a painter; Kenyon, a young American sculptor; and Donatello, a young Italian nobleman. The three foreigners agree that their friend Donatello bears a strong resemblance to the *Faun of Praxiteles.*

Chapter II: "The Faun"
Miriam playfully teases Donatello, asking him to "shake aside those brown curls ... and let us see whether this marvellous resemblance extends to the very tips of the ears." Donatello, speaking in Italian with a Tuscan accent, pulls away and warns them not to touch his ears. He is full of "animal life," but his friends make allowances for him, as they might for a child. Kenyon observes that he has the "gift of eternal youth."

As the four friends go downstairs and leave the palace, they see lurking behind one of the nearby pillars a man who is "dark, bushy, bearded, wild of aspect and attire." They recognize him as Miriam's "Model."

Chapter III: "Subterranean Reminiscences"
Miriam is described as an enigmatic figure, warm and passionate but with a mysterious background. Nobody knows anything about her, "either for good or evil." People have speculated that she may be the daughter of a great Jewish banker, a German princess, or the lady of an English nobleman.

There is a flashback to a time, several months earlier, when the group of friends had visited the vast Catacomb of Saint Calixtus with a guide. Miriam had become separated from the group.

Chapter IV: "The Spectre of the Catacomb"
Kenyon, Hilda, and Donatello had all shouted for Miriam. She had emerged from the shadows, looking pale and nervous in the flickering flame of her torch. She had reported that she had been led back by an "old messenger," who was now standing in the shadows. He had been wearing a cloak, apparently made of buffalo hide, and looked like an antique Satyr with a conical hat and a "wild visage." They had seen similar figures on the Spanish Steps, however, waiting to serve as models for artists.

The guide had referred to the stranger as the old "pagan Phantom" who had sought to betray the "blessed saints." The guide had explained the legend of Memmius, or "Man-Demon," a spy during the persecutions of Christians under Emperor Diocletian. He had been offered absolution and a Christian blessing but had refused; now he was seeking someone to guide him into the daylight. Supposedly, however, he would not accept guidance; he would teach the modern world an antique sort of crime and then return to the catacomb.

Other explanations for the spectre's identity are suggested: He might have been a Roman beggar, a thief, a political offender, an outlaw assassin, or a lunatic "fleeing instinctively from man." Miriam laughingly suggests that the spectre, "who had been an artist in his mortal lifetime," had promised to teach her the long-lost secret of fresco painting.

In the ensuing months, the stranger "never long allowed her to lose sight of him," haunting her footsteps and often appearing at her studio. Miriam becomes despondent, melancholy, and moody. Donatello remains apprehensive about the "dusky, death-scented apparition."

Chapter V: "Miriam's Studio"
Donatello visits Miriam's studio, at the top of a palace built 300 years earlier. He finds Miriam sewing, not painting, and realizes she is sad. He sees, in a corner of her studio, a mannequin, a "jointed figure." He cannot understand Miriam's teasing; he is gentle, naive, and playful, though she considers him a "mere boy," and a simple one at that.

Miriam shows him some of her startling sketches depicting women acting vengefully and mischievously toward men. Donatello detests them. Miriam remembers that he is like a Faun; therefore he "cannot suffer deeply" and "can but half enjoy." She asks him to sit for her someday; he demonstrates a jolly dance she would like to capture on canvas.

She then shows him a picture of a beautiful woman; it is her self-portrait. He remarks that the picture "gazes sadly . . . as if some evil had befallen it." She sees that he can have dark moods.

Chapter VI: "The Virgin's Shrine"
Miriam wanders outside and walks to Hilda's neighborhood. She sees a flock of white doves near the old medieval tower in which Hilda resides. There is a shrine of the Virgin up in one of the angles of the battlements; a lamp has been burning before the Virgin's image for centuries, and now Hilda is responsible for keeping it lit.

Miriam climbs up the tower staircase to visit Hilda, the daughter of Puritan forebears. An orphan, she enjoys her freedom in Rome but has lost the "impulse of original design." She is now a copyist, spending her days in galleries and palaces. She often copies the details of a picture, "some high, noble, and delicate portion" of them.

Chapter VII: "Beatrice"
Hilda is well known in Rome and is watched over by "Custodes," elderly women who believe she is vulnerable and naive. She shows Miriam her copy of Guido's Beatrice Cenci; the portrait is "the very saddest picture ever painted or conceived," with an "unfathomable depth of sorrow" that makes the viewer "shiver as at a spectre."

Miriam, the "dearest friend whom she had ever known," tells Hilda she is going away and entrusts her with a "pacquet" for safekeeping. If she has not returned to Rome in four months, Hilda is to deliver the pacquet to Signor Luca Barboni at the Palazzo Cenci.

As Miriam leaves the tower, she looks up to see Hilda, who is concerned about "something very sad and troubled" in her friend's manner. Kenyon sees the light kiss Hilda throws down to Miriam and wishes it had been meant for him.

Chapter VIII: "The Suburban Villa"
Donatello visits the Villa Borghese and prances among the artificial ruins. They are known to be rather dangerous in summer because of the risk of malaria. Donatello runs races with himself, embraces a tree as a Faun might have embraced a Nymph, and throws himself down, kissing violets and daisies. He climbs a tree to watch for Miriam then drops down beside her.

Chapter IX: "The Faun and Nymph"
Miriam jokes with Donatello, urging him to make her known to his "kindred" of the woods—water nymphs, a Satyr, or Bacchus. Donatello tells her he loves her. She calls him a "foolish boy" and points out that there are not "two creatures more unlike, in this wide world, than you and I." She says she is a "dangerous person"; following her footsteps will lead to "no good." She says it was a "sad mischance" that has sent him from his village home among the Apennines—"some rusty old castle," she imagines—to her side. He remembers his happy upbringing, reminiscing about the village celebrations and the woods, but claims he is happier now, with Miriam. The two laugh together, chase each other in the forest, and gather flowers to make into garlands. They hear music in the grove and decide to go look for Donatello's "kinsman Pan."

Chapter X: "The Sylvan Dance"
Miriam and Donatello dance in the grassy glade by the fountain, where they have come across a small band of musicians. They and a number of others,

drawn to the music, join hands and dance with "childlike gaiety."

Then Miriam sees the strange figure she has seen before. She tells Donatello he must leave her. Donatello's expression has a look of "animal rage"; he is ready to clutch the stranger by his throat, but Miriam urges him to leave her to her "doom."

Chapter XI: "Fragmentary Sentences"
Miriam and her "strange follower" talk in the woods. She says he follows her too closely. He replies that she "must vanish out of the scene, quit Rome with me, and leave no trace whereby to follow you." He reminds her that he has considerable power over her. Their past lives have some "strange and dreadful history."

She says he is her "evil genius" and she is his. Suddenly she is struck by the notion that he might be a lunatic. She begs him to go his way and leave her free, but he says they are "bound together, and can never part again."

Chapter XII: "A Stroll on the Pincian"
After putting the finishing touches on her portrait of Beatrice Cenci, Hilda goes to the Pincian Hill, hoping to hear some music. There she meets Kenyon. They hear the "faint sound of music, laughter, and mingling voices" and see Donatello on one of the paths, moving sadly along.

Looking down toward the Piazza del Popolo, Hilda and Kenyon see Miriam enter the Porta del Popolo and stand by the fountain. She appears to be intimating to a figure attending her that she wishes to be left alone. The Model, however, remains "immoveable." To Kenyon's horror, she seems to kneel to her "dark follower." He imagines the "nameless vagrant . . . dragging the beautiful Miriam through the streets of Rome, fettered and shackled more cruelly than any captive queen of yore."

Kenyon views Miriam as a mystery and is uncertain even about her nationality—whether German, English, or American. He asks Hilda whether she is "sure of her" and argues that "Rome is not like one of our New England villages, where we need the permission of each individual neighbor for every act that we do, every word that we utter, and every friend that we make or keep."

As Hilda and Kenyon make their way down the street, they see the Model walking up the Via Sestina, "drawing his tattered cloak about his face." At the foot of the Spanish Steps, Miriam stands alone, seemingly bewildered, with her hand pressed upon her brow. Hilda goes down to see about Miriam, and Kenyon tries to follow the Model.

Chapter XIII: "A Sculptor's Studio"
Miriam goes to Kenyon's studio, near a house with a tablet announcing that Canova had worked there. As she looks around at the marble busts, she thinks to herself, "As these busts in the block of marble, so does our individual fate exist in the limestone of Time. We fancy that we carve it out; but its ultimate shape is prior to all our action."

The narrator sees the "endless endurance" and "indestructibility" of a marble bust as disadvantages. The subject's descendants will only recall a "dusty-white ghost," and the busts remind us how "little, little time" anyone's features will "be of interest to any human being."

Kenyon shows Miriam a marble carving of Hilda's hand; he fears he will never win her love, however.

Chapter XIV: "Cleopatra"
Miriam suggests that the art of sculpture has "wrought itself out, and come fairly to an end." New sculptors only imitate earlier subjects. She teases Kenyon to admit that "sculptors are, of necessity, the greatest plagiarists in the world."

Kenyon shows her his clay model for a sculpture of Cleopatra. Its face is a "miraculous success." Miriam proclaims it a "great work" and recognizes its "truth."

Her voice suddenly sounds "unnatural," and she tells Kenyon she is tortured by a secret and wishes to confide in him. He is willing to listen to her, but he also doubts whether confession will do her good, as it will most likely change their relationship forever. She decides not to tell him the secret, which she thinks of as a "dark-red carbuncle" that is "too rich a gem to put into a stranger's casket." As she leaves the studio, she finds the Model waiting for her on the street.

Chapter XV: "An Aesthetic Company"
The American and English colony of artists and sculptors living in Rome gather in the apartment

of an "eminent member of the aesthetic body" for a reception. The host displays a collection of artifacts, such as carvings, sketches, seals, and bronze figures. Hilda believes some are by Guido. Kenyon asks about another one, and Donatello identifies him as Miriam's Model. The picture dates back more than two centuries, however. The four friends decide to meet at the Church of the Cappuccini the next morning in order to look more closely at Guido's Archangel.

Chapter XVI: "A Moonlight Ramble"

The young people set off for a moonlight ramble to the Fountain of Trevi. Miriam plans to sip the waters, as tradition states that "a parting draught at the Fountain of Trevi ensures the traveller's return, whatever obstacles and improbabilities may seem to beset him." As she leans over the fountain, the Model appears beside her and mutters something. He seems to be inviting her to bathe her hands and does so himself "with the utmost vehemence." Miriam takes up some water in her hand and practices an "old form of exorcism by flinging it in her persecutor's face" and crying out, "Vanish, Demon, and let me be free of you, now and forever!" The "strangely repulsive and hideous" man continues washing his hands, however, and still motions to Miriam to "follow his example."

Donatello takes offense and is ready to drown the Model. There is a "tiger-like fury gleaming from his wild eyes," and he shudders with "rage and horrible disgust." Miriam tries to soothe him, saying the Model is merely "mad; and we are as mad as he, if we suffer ourselves to be disquieted by his antics." Donatello sighs and says he has a "burning pain" in his heart because of her.

The group leaves the Fountain of Trevi and walks to the Coliseum.

Chapter XVII: "Miriam's Trouble"

At the Coliseum, they see "much pastime and gaiety": young people running races, playing hide-and-seek, talking and singing. Hilda points out, with a "thrill of uneasiness," a "spectre," going around the circle of shrines on his knees and praying. She and Kenyon recognize him as the Model. They notice that Miriam has left the others and disappeared. Donatello has followed her and sees her gesticulat-

ing wildly within an obscure arch. She begs him to flee from her for his own good; there is a "great evil" hanging about her. Kenyon, not far away, observes the Model praying and sees his face distinctly; he believes the "kneeling pilgrim" is merely performing a penance, without actual penitence.

The group leaves the Colosseum and arrive at the Forum.

Chapter XVIII: "On the Edge of a Precipice"

In the Forum, they discuss the chasm that reportedly opened and swallowed Curtius and the Palace of the Caesars. They climb from the Forum and make their way to the Piazza of the Campidoglio, on the summit of the Capitoline Hill. Miriam wishes she had Hilda's ability to trust in God.

They follow a path to a small courtyard bordered by a parapet on the edge of a steep precipice. The friends take in the view of the city from this vantage point. Around midnight, Hilda and Kenyon begin to head home. When Hilda realizes that Miriam has remained behind, however, she heads back alone because she is worried about her.

Donatello and Miriam are still looking over the edge of the precipice, discussing the men who had "been flung over here, in days gone by." A figure walks forth from a niche and approaches Miriam, who is overcome with a "cold, sick despair." As the others descend the Capitoline Hill on the city side, Hilda is returning through the door of the courtyard when she is startled by the "noise of a struggle" and a "loud, fearful cry." She witnesses "the whole quick passage of a deed, which took but that little time to grave itself in the eternal adamant."

Chapter XIX: "The Faun's Transformation"

Miriam is horrified and asks Donatello what he has done; he replies that he only did what her eyes bade him do. Over the parapet, the Model lies in a heap on the pavement below. Miriam turns to her "fellow-criminal" and embraces him, so that the "horrour and agony of each was combined into one emotion, and that, a kind of rapture." The deed knots them together "for time and eternity, like the coil of a serpent." It draws them "closer than a marriage-bond."

As they walk arm in arm back into the city, Miriam says, "One wretched and worthless life has been sacrificed, to cement two other lives forever-more." Donatello agrees that they are "cemented with his blood." She murmurs that there shall be no remorse, that night at least. They wander through the city together and pass Hilda's window, where they see her praying. Miriam calls out, "Pray for us, Hilda! We need it!" But the window closes immediately and Hilda's figure disappears. Miriam believes this is a sign that "the cry of her condemned spirit" has been "shut out of heaven."

Chapter XX: "The Burial Chaunt"
The next morning, Miriam, Donatello, and Kenyon meet at the Church of the Capuchins. They discuss Hilda's absence, and Kenyon says the last time he saw her was when she turned back to rejoin Miriam and Donatello in the courtyard. Miriam is startled to learn this fact, but she is not worried about Hilda because she saw her later, leaning from her window. She says the Virgin is "bound to watch over the good child."

Kenyon asks Donatello why he is "out of spirits." He notices the absence of Donatello's usual "youthful gaiety" and "fresh glow of animal spirits."

The three friends enter the church and find the corpse of a monk on an elevated bier. The sacristan shows them Guido's painting of the Archangel, but they still miss Hilda and her perspective on art. Meanwhile, Donatello is very upset by the sound of a burial chant from beneath the church. He feels as if the dead monk "were lying right across [his] heart."

Chapter XXI: "The Dead Capuchin"
Miriam and Donatello, to their horror, recognize the monk as the same man Donatello had flung over the precipice the previous night, believing he was following Miriam's wishes. The dead monk is clad in the "brown woollen frock of the Capuchins"; a stream of blood flows from his nostrils. Kenyon says it may be because his blood has not yet congealed, but Miriam recalls an old superstition about blood flowing from a murdered person's body when the murderer enters the church.

Miriam looks more closely at the corpse and recognizes the face "that she remembered from a far longer date than the most intimate of her friends suspected." In his features, she sees the "evil spirit

which blasted her sweet youth" and "compelled her . . . to stain her womanhood with crime." She touches the body and identifies him by the scar on his brow.

She stops trembling and asks where the monk will be buried. The sacristan shows her the grave in the cemetery beneath the church, which is now ready for him. After a time, perhaps 30 years, the monks' skeletons are removed and placed in niches in the walls to make room for new arrivals. Miriam gives the sacristan a large gift so that masses may be said for the monk.

Chapter XXII: "The Medici Gardens"
Miriam takes Donatello, who is trembling, to the gardens of the Villa Medici. Donatello says he can never be comforted. Miriam tells Donatello she loves him, but he says he will never be happy again. He may never think of Miriam apart from the "frightful visage" of the monk staring over her shoulder. Miriam asks that he fling her away and try to forget her. Although she yearns to embrace him, she walks away, leaving Donatello lying in a stupor on a stone bench. Eventually he leaves the garden, "bewildered with the novelty of sin and grief." He no longer resembles the Faun of Praxiteles.

Chapter XXIII: "Miriam and Hilda"
Miriam feels "astray in the world" after leaving Donatello. She decides to call on Hilda to ask why she had not appeared at the Church of the Capuchins that morning and to discuss the previous night's events. Her heart quakes as she remembers what Kenyon had said about Hilda's retracing her steps toward the courtyard. She realizes that she would choose "infamy in the eyes of the whole world" rather than in those of Hilda alone. There are ominous signs as she nears Hilda's tower: The doves outside her window are not cooing and the window curtain is closed. She resolves to have "one parting kiss" from Hilda, if their friendship is indeed over.

Hilda sits in her painting room. She considers herself stained with guilt. Miriam climbs the staircase and enters, opening her arms to her friend. Hilda makes an "involuntary repellent gesture" and says she cannot forgive Miriam. She says she witnessed the murder and saw the look that passed from Miriam's eyes to Donatello's; it was a "look of hatred, triumph, vengeance" that commanded Donatello to commit murder.

She asks Miriam what she should do with the burden of this "terrible secret." Miriam says it will not help her to "bear testimony" against her and advises her to talk to Kenyon. Hilda replies that she cannot because Kenyon seems to want to be something more to her than a friend. Miriam assures her that such a secret will "frighten his new-born love out of its little life."

Hilda says Miriam's deed has "darkened the whole sky," but she will keep it a secret. She now understands "how the sins of generations past have created an atmosphere of sin for those that follow," for while there is a "single guilty person in the universe, each innocent one must feel his innocence tortured by that guilt."

Chapter XXIV: "The Tower among the Apennines"

In June, Kenyon leaves Rome and travels to Monte Beni, Donatello's country house, a small castle in Tuscany. Donatello, now referred to as a count (one of the Counts of Monte Beni), lives near the top of a square tower connected to a spacious residence.

Upon Kenyon's arrival, he sees Donatello leaning from one of the battlements; the young count invites him in and says he has looked for Kenyon for a long time. Donatello now lives alone in his ancestral home with a few elderly servants. Stella, the old housekeeper, is the only woman.

Kenyon senses that his friend has changed; he is no longer a "sylvan and untutored youth," nor the Faun of Praxiteles. He is pale and thin, and a "certain gravity" in his gait has replaced his former "irregular buoyancy."

Chapter XXV: "Sunshine"

Donatello tells him of the large family who once inhabited the castle; he is the last of his line. They are attended by the old retainers Stella, Tomaso, and Girolamo. Donatello introduces Kenyon to the last remaining of the "pleasant customs" of his forefathers—a precious golden wine called Sunshine.

Kenyon asks whether he might model Donatello; he says that now that he is more familiar with

Donatello's face, he no longer sees such a resemblance to the Faun of Praxiteles. Donatello says yes, but he will not uncover his ears.

When Kenyon mentions Miriam, Donatello trembles—it is unclear whether from anger or terror—but then asks his guest to tell him what he knows about her. Kenyon reports that she left Rome just a day or two after their visit to the Church of the Capuchins.

Kenyon believes his friend has changed, losing the "simple grace that was the best of Donatello's peculiarities." The next morning, Kenyon is awakened by the clamor of a tribe of beggars, who apparently receive alms and depart. He believes, however, that he is the only visitor.

Chapter XXVI: "The Pedigree of Monte Beni"

Kenyon learns much about the history of the Counts of Monte Beni from the butler, Tomaso. They are one of the oldest families in Italy, originating from the Pelasgic race in prehistoric times. They trace their lineage to a progenitor "not altogether human," a "sylvan creature" or Faun who marries a "mortal maiden." At least once a century, a descendant of this union reveals a "wild paternity." Although "kindly and pleasant," the family is "capable of savage fierceness." Its hereditary "peculiarity" is often manifested in furry ears shaped like pointed leaves, which become more visible with age.

Kenyon inspects many old family portraits, reads "musty documents," and talks with Tomaso and the peasantry on neighboring estates. He learns that Donatello had grown up as a playmate of ordinary children and of woodland creatures. He had been considered a delightful "sylvan Faun." He has now changed, however; he no longer has a "merry smile." The world has grown too evil for him, it is said.

Kenyon suggests to Tomaso that love and marriage might cure Donatello, but Tomaso is equivocal, saying they might, but they might make him worse. Kenyon believes Tomaso is concealing something from him.

The two young men are diverted by the golden Sunshine wine and by wandering musicians and traveling jugglers, dancers, and actors. A cloud, however, still hangs over the "once Arcadian precincts," and Donatello continues to "sit and brood" in his tower.

Chapter XXVII: "Myths"

On occasion, Donatello descends from his tower to accompany Kenyon on his rambles. They visit a dell with a little fountain. Donatello says it is where his "eldest forefather," a Faun, took home a human maiden and married her. Another tale is connected with the fountain, that of a long-lived woman who dwelled there and loved one of his ancestors, a knight with furry ears. One day he goes to the fountain and calls the nymph in a frightful tone, but she does not appear. The knight has tried to wash off a bloodstain left by his guilt over a crime. The nymph "might have comforted him in sorrow, but could not cleanse his conscience of a crime." He mourns for her his whole life and has a sculptor carve her statue, but, despite the artist's efforts, he cannot help but make her "forlorn, and forever weeping."

Donatello himself used to call her, but she has never answered. He tells Kenyon he once had the gift of uttering "a murmur, a kind of chaunt," to summon the "furry people and the feathered people" of the woods. He utters the call for Kenyon, who is concealed in the shrubbery. To Kenyon, it sounds like prelinguistic utterances. Finally there are a whir of wings and a scamper of little feet, although he cannot see any creatures. Donatello cries out and flings himself to the ground. Kenyon emerges from hiding but sees only a brown lizard. Donatello says it is a sign of death; all nature shrinks from him and shudders at him, and "no innocent thing can come near."

Rising from the ground, Donatello then assumes a "mask of dull composure." Kenyon sees that he has much to hide and that he hides it well, but neither he nor Tomaso knows how to help him. Tomaso comments that, unlike women, "men are but rough nurses for a sick body or a sick spirit."

Chapter XXVIII: "The Owl-Tower"

One day Kenyon asks Donatello to show him his tower. He would like to understand the history and traditions associated with it, but Donatello is indifferent to them. He does note that an Englishman reported to be a magician traveled from Florence just to see the tower. Kenyon knows the person, a "necromancer," who lives in an old mansion near the Ponte Vecchio. Donatello says the man has a white beard and has known "mighty poets."

Kenyon still wants to climb the stairs and view an approaching thunderstorm. Donatello sighs that the tower has a "weary staircase" and "dismal chambers" and is "very lonesome at the summit." Kenyon replies that the tower "resembles the spiritual experience of many a sinful soul," which struggles "upward into the pure air and light of Heaven, at last."

Donatello leads the way and they ascend the tower. They reach a large chamber, once a prisoner's cell. The necromancer discovered that a monk was once confined there, 500 years ago, and was later burned at the stake. Tomaso has told him legends about a hooded monk creeping up and down the stairs, the ghost of the ancient prisoner. In another room, even higher, they find a pair of owls, who presumably recognize Donatello. The two young men continue to the top room, just below the roof, which is Donatello's "own abode," his "own owl's nest." The room is simply furnished, but there are many Catholic artifacts along with a "hideous" carved human skull.

They continue up to the top of the tower. Kenyon praises the scenery, the villages and church spires, the "majestic landscape" in the midst of many mountains, some with cities standing on their summits. He thanks Donatello for letting him "behold this scene" and tells him it "strengthens the poor human spirit." However, he is unable to preach with "a page of heaven and a page of earth" spread before him; he says it is a "mistake to try to put our best thoughts into human language," for the "higher regions of emotion and spiritual enjoyment" are only "expressible by such grand hieroglyphics as these around us."

Kenyon notices a small green shrub growing out of the pavement; it is "the only green thing there." Donatello says it has always grown there. Kenyon declares it must have a moral or it would have perished. Donatello responds that it teaches him nothing, but he throws an ugly worm that might have destroyed the plant over the battlements.

Chapter XXIX: "On the Battlements"

As they stand on the battlements, Kenyon admits that he is tempted to throw himself down to the ground and die quickly. Donatello is horrified and says such a death would occur only after a long period of suffering. The two friends move on to more pleasant subjects, although Kenyon perceives that Donatello is now subject to a "misty bewilderment of grievous thoughts." A "soul" has been "inspired into the young Count's simplicity." He evinces more intelligence and an individuality that have resulted from grief and pain.

Kenyon suddenly feels a "strong love" for Hilda, although she has not encouraged him. He asks whether Donatello will return to Rome in the autumn. Donatello answers no—he hates Rome, and with good cause.

When Kenyon turns to descend from the tower, Donatello refuses to accompany him; he says he must keep a vigil there. He thinks of becoming a monk, but Kenyon objects to the idea. Donatello calls him a heretic. As it darkens, they hear a woman's voice singing sadly in German. It brings tears to Kenyon's eyes and makes Donatello sob. It fades away, but Donatello tells Kenyon the voice had no message for him; it is better for him not to hear it. Kenyon leaves the "poor penitent" on the tower.

Chapter XXX: "Donatello's Bust"

Kenyon has been modeling Donatello's portrait bust, trying to draw out his "personal characteristics." It seems to him that Donatello evinces different traits at each sitting. Feeling "hopeless of a good result," the sculptor lets his hands work "uncontrolled," yielding to a "skill and insight, beyond his consciousness." Donatello does not recognize himself in the bust until he catches a glimpse of a "distorted and violent look" that Kenyon has accidentally created in the clay. Donatello believes it reflects his dreadful crime and asks that it remain and serve as a permanent reminder. Kenyon, however, remolds the bust and changes its face to a "higher and sweeter expression than it had hitherto worn." The result retains the "features of the antique Faun, but now illuminated with a higher meaning."

Alone for the rest of the day, Kenyon wanders around the grounds of Monte Beni, eating clusters of ripe grapes. He yearns for Hilda. When he returns to the residence, Tomaso summons him to speak with the "Signorina."

Chapter XXXI: "The Marble Saloon"

Earlier, Kenyon had already discovered the chapel of Monte Beni, a solemn room that has been "left to itself, in dusty sanctity." At that time, he had also discovered another guest in the castle, whose presence is still unknown to Donatello. They had spoken on this previous occasion, and now Kenyon is summoned to another meeting.

He passes through the chapel into a magnificent saloon, whose walls and floors are encased in "polished and richly coloured marble." Miriam appears, pale and dressed in mourning. Her steps are so feeble that it appears she "might sink down on the marble floor." Kenyon is "shocked at her appearance." She has been brooding all night about her crime and wishes to sacrifice herself. Her voice is cold and indifferent. She laments that she will always be "an object of horrour in Donatello's sight." She knows this because his hand had touched hers one morning, and a "cold shiver" ran through him.

Kenyon assures her that Donatello loves her still and may be aware, because of her singing, of her presence in the castle. Miriam wonders why Donatello has not welcomed her, but Kenyon explains that their friend is possessed by the idea of a "lifelong penance," a "method of sharp self-torture." Miriam asks whether he is too much changed to accept her. Kenyon is sure Donatello is developing a capacity to perceive "deep truths." A "soul and intellect" have formed out of his "bitter agony," and his "former simplicity" is now intermixed with a "new intelligence," but he is "bewildered" by the new revelations. Miriam cries that she could help him, by instructing and elevating him, but if he shuddered at her touch she would die.

Kenyon offers to take Donatello away from the castle on a "ramble among these hills and valleys." If Miriam were on the same route, there might be a reunion with Donatello. Miriam is skeptical of the plan but agrees to try. They decide to meet in two weeks' time, at the statue of Pope Julius on the square of Perugia.

As Kenyon is about to leave the saloon, Miriam asks whether she has shocked him by her "betrayal of woman's cause" and "lack of feminine modesty." She declares she lives "only in the life of one [Hilda] who perhaps scorns and shudders" at her. Kenyon tells her that, although he knows she has shocked Hilda, she is still capable of "many high and heroic virtues." Miriam hopes he will win Hilda's "high and virgin heart."

Chapter XXXII: *"Scenes by the Way"*
Kenyon and Donatello set out on their journey through the nearby broad valley and a "small, ancient town." Donatello has ridden ahead but stops at small shrines and "great black Crosses" on the waysides. He seems to have converted the "otherwise aimless journey" into a "penitential pilgrimage," stopping at each shrine and cross to kneel and say a prayer.

More than once, Kenyon thinks he sees Miriam kneeling near a shrine, but Donatello says he was absorbed in prayer and did not see her.

Chapter XXXIII: *"Pictured Windows"*
The travelers reach ancient towns perched on hillsides. Kenyon tells Donatello about his "native country," a "fortunate land" where "each generation has only its own sins and sorrows to bear," unlike these old towns, where "it seems as if all the weary and dreary Past were piled upon the back of the Present."

Kenyon and Donatello often visit cathedrals and Gothic churches. Kenyon calls the stained-glass windows symbols of "the glories of the better world." He notices "a figure in a dark robe" lurking near them. Kenyon speculates that Milton never saw such windows as these, but only "the dusty windows of English cathedrals, imperfectly shown by the gray English daylight." Here, in contrast, "God Himself is shining through them." But Donatello does not share Kenyon's emotions; he trembles at the sight of the "awful Saints" and the "figure above them," who "glows with divine wrath."

As the two friends travel from village to village, they are besieged by crippled and maimed people, beggars, and ragged children. These people are poor but still live in houses, raise vegetables, have pigs and chickens to kill, and drink wine. Donatello,

however, is always "exceedingly charitable," as a coin may ward off a "vindictive curse."

Kenyon says they will reach the pope's statue in Perugia in one more day.

Chapter XXXIV: *"Market-Day in Perugia"*
The travelers reach the hilltop town of Perugia, where Kenyon expresses interest in viewing frescoes by Perugino and paintings by Fra Angelico in the Church of San Domenico. Donatello objects that Fra Angelico's paintings depict angels who look as though they have "never taken a flight out of heaven" and "Saints [who] seem to have been born Saints, and always to have lived so." Instead, they stroll through the town, where it is market day.

Kenyon admires the bronze statue of Pope Julius III, occupying a pedestal in the piazza. He and Donatello go closer to see the statue "bestowing a benediction." Kenyon hopes that travel has benefited Donatello and made him less morose; indeed, he seems to have a "healthier spirit" now, and his eyes shine with a "serene and hopeful expression" as he gazes at the statue. Donatello describes the "wound" that is still "rankling" in his soul and "filling it with poison."

Chapter XXXV: *"The Bronze Pontiff's Benediction"*
After the clock strikes noon, Kenyon sees Miriam near the bronze statue and tries to take her to Donatello. She insists, however, that Donatello must take the initiative and speak her name "of his own accord." As she gazes up at the statue of the pontiff, her beauty attracts the attention of many Italians. She dares not glance at Donatello, who is still leaning against the balustrade surrounding the statue.

Miriam tells Kenyon that she has news of Hilda. She worries that Hilda is depressed, for she lives "quite alone, in her dove-cote," in "such solitude, with despondency praying on her mind." Kenyon plans at once to go to Rome.

Donatello walks over and speaks to Miriam. She deduces that he still loves her; he asks her forgiveness. She asks him to "fling" her away, for "no good" can follow "such mighty evil." He insists that their "lot lies together," but his conscience is "perplexed with doubt." Kenyon hesitantly states that he would like to speak to both of them but does not wish to be intrusive. They plead with him to speak. He tells Miriam that Donatello has begun to be educated by his "terrible misfortune" and she is responsible; he tells Donatello that Miriam has "rich gifts of heart and mind" and is what he needs. They have a bond that should not be "rent asunder." Both agree that Kenyon has "spoken the truth."

Kenyon continues, however, saying that their bonds are entwined with "black threads." Therefore, their relationship should be for "mutual support," not "earthly happiness." They should take each other's hands for "mutual elevation and encouragement" only. He says that if the "highest duty" of either one requires the sacrifice of the other, they should not hesitate. Meanwhile, the crowd looks on, assuming they are betrothed.

Kenyon takes leave of his friends, saying he is going to Rome. The three imagine they are receiving a blessing from the bronze statue.

Chapter XXXVI: "Hilda's Tower"
Hilda had planned to spend the summer in Rome, unafraid of the "pestilential" summer atmosphere. (Here Hawthorne refers obliquely to "Roman fever," a form of malaria that was very virulent at the time and had afflicted his daughter Una for six months. People frequently died of it, since there was little treatment at the time except quinine.)

She finds herself very depressed, however; her knowledge of Miriam's crime weighs on her. A young Italian artist, Signor Panini, makes a quick sketch of her gazing at a spot of blood on her white robe and later develops it into a portrait. When queried by a picture dealer, he denies that it depicts a crime committed by Hilda. He explains that a man has been slain in her presence and has stained her life. The dealer insists, however, that she has stabbed her lover and is repenting it; he will call the picture "The Signorina's Vengeance." The narrator comments, "Thus coarsely does the world translate all finer griefs that meet its eye!"

Chapter XXXVII: "The Emptiness of Picture-Galleries"
Hilda forces herself to visit the galleries of the old palaces but is still depressed. An old German artist she often meets advises her to return to America and avoid the unwholesome Roman air. She tells him she is afflicted by torpor. Moreover, she detects in many later Italian pictures a "deficiency of earnestness and absolute truth." This is not true, however, of the works of Fra Angelico.

Hilda continues wandering through galleries, growing more and more despondent. She suffers the "exile's pain" and dreams of her native village, with its elms and "neat, comfortable houses." She leans over the battlements of her tower, longing to see Kenyon, at the very moment he is at Monte Beni looking toward Rome.

Chapter XXXVIII: "Altars and Incense"
The narrator declares that if the Jesuits had known of Hilda's situation, they would have managed to convert her to Catholicism. The melancholy young woman wanders from church to church and shrine to shrine, but her "appreciation of Art" prevents her from being vulnerable to conversion. On a visit to Saint Peter's, she is particularly taken with a mosaic of Guido's Archangel treading on the Devil. She kneels, prays, and cries. Adjacent to the shrine is a picture by Guercino, depicting a maiden's body in the "jaws of the sepulchre" while her lover weeps over it and her spirit looks down from heaven on it. It makes Hilda realize the possibility of rising "above her present despondency that she might look down upon what she was." She has a presentiment of relief, and a hopefulness flutters in her heart.

Chapter XXXIX: "The World's Cathedral"
While still in Saint Peter's, she sees shafts of light through the Dome, illuminating mosaic figures of two Evangelists. She approaches a confessional, sees a woman leaving in "peace and joy," and asks whether it is "so sweet" to go to the confessional. The woman answers with an "affectionate smile" that her heart is "at rest now." Hilda walks among the confessionals, noting that each is marked as receiving confessions in a different language.

She discovers one marked "Pro Anglica Lingua." She makes her confession, revealing her knowledge of the murder but withholding all names. The relief of telling her "terrible secret" makes her sob; she finally feels like "a girl again." The priest steps out of the confessional and asks her to stand up; he says he is sure this is her first confession. She admits she is from New England and was reared as what he calls a "heretic." He exclaims that he was also born in New England and asks whether she has thought of asking for absolution. Hilda says she could not ask for absolution from "mortal man." The priest says the "sacred seal of the Confessional" does not apply to her; thus it is his duty to make the crime known to the authorities. Hilda is horrified and says she believes she entered to the confessional "by the direct impulse of Heaven." The priest then says he believes he need not reveal the matter, as it is "already known in the quarter which it most concerns."

He then asks whether, as a reward for him, she will allow him to bring her as a "stray lamb" into the "true fold." Hilda says she will only go so far as Providence guides her. She is a daughter of the Puritans and may never return to the confessional. However, he may someday see her thank him for it in "the better land." She kneels and receives his blessing "with as devout a simplicity as any Catholic of them all."

Chapter XL: "Hilda and a Friend"

As Hilda kneels to receive the priest's benediction, Kenyon watches; he has been leaning against the balustrade before the high altar. She is delighted to see him. As she approaches, she seems "imbued with sunshine" or with a "glow of happiness." She seems transfigured and tells Kenyon she is a "new creature" because a burden has been lifted from her heart. Kenyon almost asks whether she has flung her "angelic purity into that mass of unspeakable corruption, the Roman Church" but restrains himself.

Hilda and Kenyon debate whether Saint Peter's should have stained-glass windows. She notices his "disturbed gaze" and asks why he looks "so sorrowfully" at her. He admits that he was shocked to see her at the confessional. She says she will never go to one again; it was the "sin of others" that had driven her there. Kenyon interrogates her as to whether she is a Catholic but satisfies himself that she is not.

They go out, through the Piazza of Saint Peter's and toward the bridge of Sant' Angelo; Hilda's spir-

its have lifted and she is almost in a childlike state of exaltation. She tells him she thinks of going home to America. He escorts her to her tower, where doves fly out to greet her with "joyful flutterings and airy little flights." Peace has "descended upon her like a dove." After she climbs to the top, she waves down to Kenyon, who looks "sad and dim." He looks up and thinks she looks "like a spirit"; he believes her to be "unattainable."

Chapter XLI: "Snow-drops and Maidenly Delights"

Kenyon, according to the narrator, is in love with Hilda, but he doubts that Hilda loves him. She seems content with a "calm intimacy" that keeps him "a stranger in her heart." Months pass and English visitors arrive in the city. Native Romans resign themselves to winter misery.

Kenyon's artisans have been at work carving his Cleopatra, which Hilda greatly admires. Kenyon, however, believes it lacks the "spiritual part" of his idea. He has now begun a carving of Donatello's face. Hilda does not find it a striking likeness but perceives that "a soul is being breathed into him." She says it is the Faun, "but advancing towards a state of higher development." Kenyon marvels at Hilda's insight though she wonders whether this "striking effect" is a result of the bust's "unfinished state." He agrees that she is right and decides to leave Donatello's bust untouched.

Chapter XLII: "Reminiscences of Miriam"

Hilda and Kenyon discuss Donatello. Kenyon tells her he is sadly changed. She answers, "No wonder!" and he realizes she knows the truth about the crime. Kenyon does not understand how she found out the facts but tells her that Miriam has confessed to him. He argues that there can be "a mixture of good" in "things evil," and that even the "greatest criminal" may seem "not so unquestionably guilty." Kenyon believes both Miriam and Donatello are partners in guilt, but they are also heroic.

Hilda believes both are in the wrong; Kenyon calls her a "terribly severe judge." At the same time, after she bids him farewell, she thinks about Miriam and believes she has failed her friend. She suddenly remembers the sealed pacquet Miriam had given her, to be delivered to a certain destination if her friend were absent from Rome after four months.

She immediately sets off to the "foulest and ugliest part of Rome" and begins to climb the steps of the Cenci palace. An old woman warns her the palace is a "spot of ill omen for young maidens." Nevertheless, Hilda enters and begins climbing three flights of stairs.

Chapter XLIII: "The Extinction of a Lamp"
Kenyon and Hilda had informally decided to meet in the Vatican galleries. He goes, but she does not appear. He returns home and tries to work with a large lump of clay but finds it impossible. He goes out again and walks along the Corso. He sees a person in a white robe and a mask; such figures are said to be persons of rank who assume penitential garb to expiate a crime. The penitent asks him whether all is well and disappears. Kenyon is sure it is Donatello; his gloom deepens.

After dining in a cafe and seeing a comedy at the Teatro Argentino, he makes his way through a narrow street, where he sees Miriam beckoning from a carriage. She asks whether all is well, using "identical words" to those of the penitent earlier that evening. Kenyon is startled to see her dressed in clothing "richer than the simple garb" she usually wore and remembers hearing rumors from the past that she was actually very wealthy. He notices a man with a "sallow Italian face," whom he does not recognize, sitting beside her in the carriage. Miriam whispers that she can tell Kenyon nothing, but "when the lamp goes out, do not despair!" He hurries to Hilda's tower, but the lamp that has always burned there quivers and sinks, leaving the battlements in darkness.

Chapter XLIV: "The Deserted Shrine"
Kenyon asks a passerby to verify that the lamp burning at the Virgin's shrine has been extinguished. They agree that it has, and the passerby is horrified. He has heard from a priest that if the Virgin withdraws her blessing and the light goes out, the Palazzo del Torre will "sink into the earth, with all that dwell in it." Kenyon searches within, in vain, for Hilda.

He leaves and returns several times the next day. He sees the doves at her tower, but Hilda is not there. Others who live on the lower floors seem attached to her, and they offer many plausible suggestions, but they do not offer to join Kenyon in actively searching for her. The narrator reflects that a French concierge would have been cognizant of all comings and goings, but the general entrance and main staircase of such a residence in Rome are not monitored. The wife of the person who sublets Hilda her apartment lets him in, but he still cannot find her. He does notice, however, that her small tabletop writing desk has disappeared.

Chapter XLV: "The Flight of Hilda's Doves"
Kenyon feels that a light has gone out; the idea of Hilda had been "like a taper of virgin wax, burning with a pure and steady flame." He now finds Rome dreary and feels crushed by the "ponderous gloom of the Roman Past." He feels guilty that he did not warn her against the risks she continually encountered. He distrusts the sensual, pampered priesthood and the many localities for crime in Rome. Hilda has had no protector or guide. He tries to convince himself that her "sanctity" has been a safeguard.

Kenyon stops working and spends all his time searching for Hilda. Even her doves have lost hope that she will appear and have taken flight. One day, however, he meets the very priest Hilda had encountered in the confessional. He wants to publish a narrative about her testimony to the "efficacy of the Divine ordinances of the Church" in her finding immediate relief after her confession. Kenyon wonders whether Hilda is a prisoner of a religious order.

He does not begin searching within the various convents in Rome for Hilda, though, because he receives a "communication" from an "unknown hand" that causes him to leave Rome immediately.

Chapter XLVI: "A Walk on the Campagna"
He leaves the city through the gate of San Sebastiano and walks along the Appian Way. It is lined with massive tombs long ago stripped of their bas-reliefs and other adornments to decorate palaces and churches. He crosses the Campagna, accompanied by a prancing and frolicsome buffalo calf. He reaches a partial excavation where he discovers a sculpted torso; he finds a head and places it on the body. It is either the prototype or a repetition of the Venus of the Tribune. He wonders whether it is a

good or bad omen that he looks for Hilda but finds a "marble woman."

He hears small hoofs approaching, accompanied by a man's and a woman's voices speaking in Italian. A peasant and a contadina salute him.

Chapter XLVII: "The Peasant and Contadina"

The two figures are Donatello and Miriam, dressed for Carnival time. They wanted Kenyon to see their newly discovered statue. They also have news Donatello wants to share, but Miriam holds back. She wants them to enjoy "a little longer" the life they once led, without past or future. She calls it a "sweet, irresponsible life" that he has inherited from his "mythic ancestry, the Fauns of Monte Beni."

At last Miriam tells Kenyon that Hilda is safe. She then reveals much about her own life that had perplexed Kenyon, speaking of her part-English, part-Jewish parentage on her mother's side, and of her paternal Italian heritage. Through him she is descended from a princely southern Italian family of "great wealth and influence." She reveals a name that startles Kenyon, "for it was one, that, only a few years before, had been familiar with the world, in connection with a mysterious and terrible event."

Her family had arranged her betrothal to a wealthy but evil and treacherous marchese. When of age, Miriam had "utterly repudiated" the marriage contract. She had fled her home and was thought to have committed suicide. She created a "new sphere" for herself and felt "almost her first experience of happiness," until the adventure of the catacomb. The "spectral figure" she encountered there was the "Evil Fate" that had haunted her throughout her life. He had entered the catacomb for penance but had actually begun persecuting Miriam.

Miriam says Hilda will join them in two days. She thinks the crime in which she and Donatello took part was a blessing in disguise, for it changed "a simple and imperfect nature to a point of feeling and intelligence." The three friends plan to gather the day after the next one, on the Corso, in front of the fifth house on the left, beyond the Antonine Column. Kenyon reflects that today Donatello is once again "the sylvan Faun," and Miriam "his fit companion."

Chapter XLVIII: "A Scene in the Corso"

It is Carnival time on the Corso, a "narrow stream of merriment." To Kenyon, it is all a mockery compared with the "frolic spirit" of the previous year. The populace look on and the nobility and priesthood take little part. Only hordes of Anglo-Saxons take up the "flagging mirth."

Still, most people would have enjoyed the gaiety. There are baskets brimming with bouquets, gorgeous carpets hanging from windows, decorated palace fronts, windows alive with the faces of women and "rosy girls," and carriages with festal figures—all making up a "sympathy of nonsense."

As Kenyon watches, two figures pass before him. Both wear black masks, but one seems to be a peasant of the Campagna, and the other a *contadina* in her holiday costume.

Chapter XLIX: "A Frolic of the Carnival"

Kenyon loses sight of Miriam and Donatello in the crowd but is besieged on all sides by merrymakers and "gay persecutors." It is all a "feverish dream" to him. Miriam and Donatello return, in the garb of peasant and *contadina*. There is a "profound sadness" in her voice; she appears to have been crying. The three friends join hands and say farewell.

Alone again, Kenyon waits for developments in the portico of a palace on the Corso, as instructed. An Abbate is sitting in the rear of the balcony with the English owner and his two daughters. Looking up, he sees the Abbate "lean forward and give a courteous sign of recognition"—it is the same priest who had seen Hilda in the confessional.

There is a "bustle" on the other side of the street, involving a "small party of soldiers" who are "perhaps arresting some disorderly character." Kenyon overhears people in the crowd talking of "a peasant and a contadina." Suddenly, a single rosebud flies from the balcony and hits Kenyon "gently on his lips"; he looks up and sees Hilda, pale and bewildered, in the private balcony of the amazed Englishman and his daughters. The Abbate whispers an explanation to the gentleman—she has been summoned forth from a "secret place" to the balcony. They do not speak, but Hilda returns to her living quarters and the Virgin's shrine and her doves.

Chapter L: "Miriam, Hilda, Kenyon, Donatello"

The narrator does not account for the "mystery of Hilda's disappearance" or her release. There is speculation that a "pledge of secrecy had been exacted," or she had been warned not to "reveal the strategems of a religious body, or the secret acts of a despotic government." The narrator suggests that a woman may have arranged the mode of Hilda's release and "made it the condition of a step which her conscience . . . required her to take."

A few days later, Hilda and Kenyon are walking through the streets of Rome, deep in conversation. They go into the Pantheon, Hilda to pay respects to the tomb of Raphael and Kenyon to admire the building. They discover a "female penitent" kneeling below the open dome, or "Eye," of the Pantheon; though she is veiled, Hilda believes she is Miriam and trembles with emotion.

Suddenly, Hilda asks whether Donatello was ever really a Faun. Kenyon answers that he had a "genial nature," Faun or not. He observes that Donatello had perpetuated a "great crime," and his remorse, "gnawing into his soul," had awakened his high "capabilities moral and intellectual." They argue whether sin is ever uplifting; Kenyon states that "sin has educated Donatello, and elevated him." He asks whether sin, then, is like sorrow, "merely an element of human education, through which we struggle to a higher and purer state than we could otherwise have attained."

Meanwhile, the kneeling penitent extends her hands "with a gesture of benediction," and they know certainly that she is Miriam. They do not greet her, for her hands, "even while they blessed, seemed to repel." Hilda and Kenyon become engaged and plan to return to America. Before they leave, Hilda receives a bridal gift, a bracelet made of "seven ancient Etruscan gems" that had each belonged to a prince. She recognizes the bracelet as Miriam's and her eyes fill with tears. She still cannot imagine what Miriam's and Donatello's lives are to be.

Postscript

The postscript is an explanation by Hawthorne, as "the Author," in answer to readers' demands for "further elucidations respecting the mysteries of the story." He cannot answer the question as to whether Donatello actually had "furry ears."

The Author does confess that he, Hilda, and Kenyon had climbed to the top of Saint Peter's, where he had asked Hilda about the contents of Miriam's "mysterious pacquet," addressed to Signor Luca Barboni. Hilda has no knowledge of the contents, but Kenyon says that Luca Barboni may have been the assumed name of a "personage" very high up in the Papal Government. Miriam would have needed the "support of some influential person" in order to maintain her privacy and live an "isolated life," for her "every movement" was most likely watched by the "priestly rulers." If she had planned to leave Italy and seek "real obscurity in another land," then the pacquet might have contained "certain family documents, which were to be imparted to her relative as from one dead and gone."

Kenyon points out that with Miriam's disappearance and the murder of the monk, the authorities "must have been led to see an obvious connection between herself and that tragical event." So when Hilda delivered the pacquet, she became implicated in the plot because she was known to be a friend of Miriam's. Hilda herself reveals that during her disappearance, she was a prisoner in the Convent of the Sacré Coeur in the Trinità de' Monti, in the "kindly custody of pious maidens" and watched over by a "dear old priest."

The Author wants to know Miriam's "real name and rank," which Kenyon does not provide. He is surprised by the question and tells the Author to "think awhile," and he will "assuredly remember it." Donatello, he says sadly, is in prison. Miriam remains "at large," for "her crime lay merely in a glance." And to answer the Author's final question, Kenyon replies, "smiling mysteriously," that he knows whether Donatello's ears resembled those of the Faun of Praxiteles, but "may not tell."

RECEPTION AND CRITICAL ANALYSIS

Henry Fothergill Chorley, writing in the British *Athenaeum* in 1860, praised the "scenic power and beauty" of the novel but questioned Hawthorne's reliance on the "elevating influences of remorse on certain natures." He considered Kenyon a "stone image" and believed Miriam to be a reincarnation of Zenobia, from *The BLITHEDALE ROMANCE*. Hilda, he suggested, was very like Phoebe in *The HOUSE OF THE SEVEN GABLES*. He found Donatello more original and powerful, with his transformation from semimythical creature to a "sad, conscience-stricken human being." However, Miriam's "agony and unrest" and the Faun's transformation were too vague to be satisfying.

JAMES RUSSELL LOWELL, who reviewed the novel for the *Atlantic Monthly* in April 1860, wrote that the 19th century had produced "no more purely original writer than Mr. Hawthorne." The actors and incidents in the novel were "vistas" through which readers might see the moral from "different points of view," pointing skyward, but "inscribed" with suggestive hieroglyphs. Lowell praised the conception of Donatello, who, initially a creature of "mere instinct," awakened through sin to a conception of the necessity of atonement. He was the most original and imaginative character in the book. The novel was "steeped in Italian atmosphere," with landscapes "full of breadth and power" both "psychological and metaphysical." Hawthorne conceived his characters, but did not "draw them." The characters were "acted upon by crime, passion, or circumstance, as if the element of Fate were as present to his imagination as to that of a Greek dramatist." The novel embodied "the most august truths of psychology," combined with "the most pregnant facts of modern history."

Hawthorne's English friend HENRY BRIGHT reviewed the novel in the British *Examiner* in 1860. He found that the novel lacked the narrative perfection of *The SCARLET LETTER* but contained a profound moral lesson, that "evil may enlarge a character for good." He considered the descriptions of Italian scenery and Roman ruins the finest part of the novel and praised Hawthorne's "grace of style" (*Nathaniel Hawthorne: The Contemporary Reviews*, 247–252, passim).

When it was published, upper-class Americans on the Grand Tour used it as a guide, as did families "recently risen to authority and wealth." In 1866, when Lucretia and George Frederic Jones took their four-year-old daughter Edith (later Edith Wharton) to Europe for six years, it was Hawthorne's Rome to which she was introduced by her nurse and that she remembered all her life. In her autobiography, *A Backward Glance*, she recalled "the lost Rome" of her "infancy," the "warm scent of the box hedges on the Pincian, and the texture of weather-worn sun-gilt stone." She remembered playing in the ruins of the Imperial Forum, driving in a carriage out to the Campagna and the Appian Way, seeing the "Piazza di Spagna throned with Thackerayan artists' models," visiting Saint Peter's, which had a "million-tapered blaze," and walking on the grounds of the Villa Doria-Pamphili (*A Backward Glance*, 29–34).

The novel was censured by 20th-century critics for having too many picturesque touristic details. Udo Nattermann, however, argued that *The Marble Faun* "successfully defines the foreign experience" by using "Gothic elements" to portray the development of character. Hyatt Waggoner observes that Hawthorne was more interested in the general idea of guilt as a common human emotion than in a particular sinful act. Therefore, the central action in the novel, the murder committed by Donatello, is ambiguous. We are not sure he is really responsible for the murder, just as we are not absolutely sure that in "Roger Malvin's Burial," Reuben Bourne committed an evil act when he left Roger Malvin to die. Waggoner argues, "All Rome, all history, made the crime inevitable, and its spreading effects leave no one untouched, not even the spotless Hilda" ("The Marble Faun," 165).

Many critics believe that *The Marble Faun* should have been Hawthorne's finest novel because of its setting—the underground world of Rome and the catacombs—and the archetypal initiation of Donatello and Hilda. Compared with *The SCARLET LETTER*, however, it is loosely focused. The character of Hilda is too much a stereotype, despite her innocence. Hawthorne attempts to develop the theme of Rome as representing culture and corruption, in contrast to America, embodying innocence and morality, but fails—unlike Henry James, who later developed the theme of Europe versus America with great success. Waggoner believes that "thematic considerations alone cannot save the novel" ("The Marble Faun," 174).

In *The Marble Faun: Hawthorne's Transformations*, Evan Carton observes that the publication of the novel in America in 1860 coincided with the tumultuous events that would culminate in the Civil War. He sees the novel as a "valuable index to this transitional moment in American cultural consciousness." He interprets it as a study of disorientation, based as it is on the experience of Americans on unfamiliar ground. It prefigures later novelists' exploration of the "international theme," especially Henry James's, and of the debate about romance versus realism in American fiction. It is of special significance because it helped "mold the imaginations and purposes" of William Dean Howells, Mark Twain, and Henry James (12–16).

Millicent Bell recounts her experience attending a Hawthorne conference in Rome in 1998 and finding copies of the novel in the hands of many "belated passionate pilgrims" who retraced Hawthorne's steps between sessions. She finds that, in the novel, the "scenic is so prominent that it preempts character and plot." She notes that visitors to Italy reenacted Hawthorne's itineraries in Rome, Siena, and other places for many years after 1860. She suggests that a "Victorian air of moralism" marks the novel and argues that Hawthorne's "aesthetic observations" and "descriptive digressions" impede the narrative. At the same time, Bell observes that it was as close to a best-seller as Hawthorne achieved. As does Carton, she sees it as a precursor to the "international novel" later beloved of Henry James. At the time of its publication, booksellers sometimes sold special copies with photographs of noted sights tipped in, and some publishers produced editions with "interleaved reproductions of such pictures" ("The Marble Faun and The Waste of History").

Terence Martin pinpoints the principal problem that has impeded the appreciation of many critics and readers for the novel. The very setting that seems one of the novel's most appealing aspects is in fact one of its major problems. He points out that the "fairy precinct" is actually "corroded with history," the history of the catacombs, Donatello's castle, and the very historic landscape of Rome and Italy. References to Etruscan, Roman, and Christian history crowd the fabric of the novel. Hawthorne, in fact, states that he had hoped to inspire in the reader "a vague sense of ponderous remembrances; a perception of such weight and density . . . that the present moment is pressed down or crowded out, and our individual affairs and interests" would therefore become less real. The novel is, however, weighted down by history, unlike *The Scarlet Letter,* which has few references to the past other than Hawthorne's statement that the founders of a new colony allot a portion of their land to a cemetery and another section to a prison. That earlier novel unquestionably has a brilliant economy that is lacking in *The Marble Faun.* However, as Martin points out, this novel represents "Hawthorne's final attempt to win through to a redemptive vision." He succeeded in acknowledging "the marble complexity of the world of men," but, in his finest creation within the novel, Hilda, he pays tribute to her "innocence," "simplicity," and her "unerring sense of moral direction" (Martin, *Nathaniel Hawthorne,* 176).

CHARACTERS

Donatello In *The Marble Faun,* a young Italian nobleman who resembles the statue of the *Faun of Praxiteles.* Hawthorne had seen a copy of the statue in the Villa Borghese in Rome and thought it "a natural and delightful link betwixt human and brute life, with something of a divine character intermingled." When he saw the original statue in the Capitoline, he began to think of a romance built around the character.

Donatello seems to have "nothing to do with time" and to have a "look of eternal youth in his face." He appears almost part animal rather than altogether human, but an animal "in a high and beautiful sense." The resemblance between Donatello and the Faun is one of the central themes of the novel. The Faun is a link between human and animal, "neither man nor animal, and yet no monster, but a being in whom both races meet on friendly ground." Donatello is immature and simple; he must be educated by Miriam, whom he loves. During the process, he also educates Miriam.

Donatello is of ancient noble ancestry, but at the same time he is a child of nature. After he murders Miriam's Model, he says he was only doing what her eyes had commanded him to do—but he later perceives that he has lost his innocence.

At the same time, he has become more perceptive about the human condition. A new maturity and intelligence replace the sensuality and selfishness of his youth.

Hilda   A slender, brown-haired New England woman, a painter. After arriving in Rome, she has lost "the impulse of original design" and ceases to "aim at original achievement." She is humble and modest; she devotes herself to copying old Italian masters rather than attempting original paintings of her own. She tries "to catch and reflect some of the glory which had been shed upon canvas from the immortal pencils of old."

She is described in *The Marble Faun* as having a "pretty and girlish face" and "a hopeful soul"; she sees "sunlight on the mountaintops." Her freedom and independence characterize her as a forerunner of such heroines as Henry James's Daisy Miller and William Dean Howells's Lydia Blood. She is described as enjoying many wanderings about Rome but always returning "as securely as she had been accustomed to tread the familiar street of her New England village. . . . Thus it is, that, bad as the world is said to have grown, Innocence continues to make a Paradise around itself, and keep it still unfallen." Hilda is sometimes called "Dove," which was Hawthorne's private name for his wife, Sophia.

Hilda tends a shrine to the Virgin Mary, which is located in the tower where she lives. The shrine consists of a lamp burning before an image of the Virgin. Although she is not a Catholic, Hilda worships the purity of the shrine. Of the four characters, she is, in many ways, the most sensitive to the history and aura of Rome. She remarks of the reliefs of Trajan's monument: "There are sermons in stones . . . and especially in the stones of Rome."

Kenyon   A young American sculptor, a friend of Donatello, Hilda, and Miriam. He is an intellectual, although many readers have found him stuffy. Miriam tells him he is "as cold and pitiless" as the marble in which he works. He is supposed to have suffered through a tragic emotional experience in his youth. He represents the detached observer of life.

His masterpiece is his statue of Cleopatra, in which Cleopatra is caught during a respite between "two pulse-throbs." Kenyon is able, according to the narrator of *The Marble Faun,* to depict Cleopatra's "latent energy and fierceness" to the extent that she "might spring upon you like a tigress, and stop the very breath that you were now drawing, midway in your throat." The statue thus conveys Kenyon's intuitive comprehension of human passion. He has also sculpted Hilda's hand in marble; it is a symbol of her purity, which he worships.

Kenyon's character has been assumed to be modeled on William Wetmore Story, an American sculptor whom Hawthorne and his family had known in Rome. Story was the son of the founder of the Harvard Law School, Joseph Story; Hawthorne had met him through the Boston lawyer George Hillard. He was the acknowledged leader of the American artists' colony in Rome. Brenda Wineapple calls him a "man of marble, cold and stiff," and considers him an "artist without style, locked into a moral code and afraid to take a risk" (*Hawthorne: A Life*, 321). In his Italian notebook, however, Hawthorne describes a day with Story and his family at the Villa Belvedere in Siena; he calls him "the most vicariously accomplished and brilliant person—the fullest of social life and fire—whom I have ever met; and without seeming to make an effort, he kept us amused and entertained, the whole day long; not wearisomely entertained neither, as we should have been if he had not let his fountain play naturally." At the same time, Hawthorne perceived a "morbid sensibility" within Story (*Hawthorne, French and Italian Notebooks*, 446–447, 737).

Miriam   A dark-eyed young painter of mysterious background, depicted as having a Jewish aspect. Her family was wealthy, and a marriage to her cousin had been arranged with a view to increasing the family fortune. But the character of the cousin, according to the narrator of *The Marble Faun,* was marked by "traits so evil, so treacherous, so vile, and yet so strangely subtle, as could only be accounted for by the insanity which often develops itself in old, close-kept races of men, when long unmixed with newer blood." Miriam rebelled against her father and refused to marry her cousin. Kenyon says of her, "Young as she is, the morning light seems already to have faded out of her life."

Her studio is supposed to have been modeled on the studio of Harriet Hosmer.

Todd Onderdonk deems Miriam "an incarnation of Hester Prynne," in both her "artistic and penitential aspects." As does Hester's needlework on her scarlet letter, Miriam's art "can only dramatize or embellish her guilt," for "all other themes are closed to her." The paintings in her studio, which Donatello finds so abhorrent, are all "marred with the figure of the distant and isolated onlooker, unable to participate in the distaff joy." Finally, as Hester is, she is "ultimately set aside," in a "state both marginalized and irredeemable." She serves no purpose in life other than that of "self-abasement."

"Model, the" This unnamed fifth character in *The Marble Faun,* also referred to in the novel as a Capuchin monk, played a mysterious role in Miriam's past. He is described as "dark, bushy, bearded, wild of aspect and attire." Miriam regards him as the "evil spirit which blasted her sweet youth" and "compelled her . . . to stain her womanhood with crime."

John L. Idol Jr. observes that Hawthorne avoids giving this character a "distinctive personality" in order to "sustain the mystery that he deemed proper to a romance." Instead, the Model is an "allegorical figure" representing, variously, "evil, Miriam's conscience, the taint in man since Adam's fall, and a burden of guilt that cannot be wished or washed away." He is also the "catalyst" for Donatello, transforming him "from the state of innocence to the state of experience, from thoughtless gaiety to reflective self-examination, and from Arcadian simplicity to contemporary complicity in the affairs of mankind"—in short, from faun to man. Idol also compares the Model to CHILLINGWORTH, IN *The SCARLET LETTER*, a character whose "efforts to do evil have the ironic effect of bringing Dimmesdale back to the path of salvation."

FOR FURTHER READING

Bell, Millicent, "*The Marble Faun* and the Waste of History," *Southern Review* 35, no. 2 (spring 1999): 354–370; Carton, Evan, *The Marble Faun: Hawthorne's Transformations* (New York: Twayne, 1992); Hawthorne, Nathaniel, *The French and Italian Notebooks,* edited by Thomas Woodson, Centenary Edition of the Works of Hawthorne, 14, (Columbus: Ohio State University Press, 1980); Idol, John L. Jr., "Nathaniel Hawthorne," in *Dictionary of Literary Biography.* Vol. 223, edited by Wesley T. Mott, 183–218 (Detroit: Gale Research, 2000); Idol, John L. Jr.; and Jones, Buford, eds., *Nathaniel Hawthorne: The Contemporary Reviews* (Cambridge: Cambridge University Press, 1994): 247–253; Kaul, A. N., *Hawthorne: A Collection of Critical Essays* (Englewood Cliffs, N.J.: Prentice-Hall, 1966); Levine, Robert S., "'Antebellum Rome' in *The Marble Faun,*" *American Literary History* 2 (1990): 19–38; Marks, Patricia, "Virgin Saint, Mother Saint: Hilda and Dorothea." In *Hawthorne and Women: Engendering and Expanding the Hawthorne Tradition,* edited by John L. Idol Jr. and Melinda M. Ponder (University of Massachusetts Press, 1999) 151–158; Martin, Terence, *Nathaniel Hawthorne* (Boston: Twayne, 1983, 163–180); Natterman, Udo, "Dread and Desire: 'Europe' in Hawthorne's *The Marble Faun,*" *Essays in Literature* 21, no. 1 (spring 1994): 54–68; Onderdonk, Todd, "The Marble Mother: Hawthorne's Iconographies of the Feminine," *Studies in American Fiction* 31 (2003): 73; Pages, Christina M., "Innocence and Violence: Two Sides of a Face: A Study of Miriam and Hilda in Relation to Beatrice Cenci in Nathaniel Hawthorne's *The Marble Faun,*" in *The Image of Violence in Literature, the Media, and Society,* edited by Will Wright and Steven Kaplan, 453–457 (Pueblo: Society for the Interdisciplinary Study of Social Imagery, University of Southern Colorado, 1995); Schiller, Emily, "The Choice of Innocence: Hilda in *The Marble Faun,*" *Studies in the Novel* 26, no. 4 (winter 1994): 372–391; Tellefsen, Blythe Ann, "'The Case with My Dear Native Land': Nathaniel Hawthorne's Vision of America in *The Marble Faun,*" *Nineteenth-Century Literature* 54, no. 4 (March 2000): 455–479; Waggoner, Hyatt H., "The *Marble Faun,*" in *Hawthorne: A Collection of Critical Essays,* edited by A. N. Kaul (Englewood Cliffs, N.J.: Prentice-Hall, 1966); Wegner, John, "Contemporary Inspiration for Kenyon in *The Marble Faun,*" *Nathaniel Hawthorne Review* 23, no. 1 (spring 1997): 26–38.

"May-pole of Merry Mount, The"

Short story first published in *The* TOKEN in 1836 and collected in TWICE-TOLD TALES in 1837. It was also published in *Legends of New England* by James Osgood & Co. in 1877.

Hawthorne prefaces the story with a note on the "curious history" of the early settlement of Mount Wollaston, or Merry Mount, a "gay colony" given to festive celebrations and nostalgic for the folk celebrations of England.

At sunset on Midsummer Eve, the colonists have decorated a pine tree "reared from English seed," dressing it with boughs, flowers, ribbons, and a silken banner. The May-Pole is surrounded by a "wild throng" garbed as animals (a bear, a goat, a wolf, etc.). Their faces are distorted and they wear "fools-caps" and "little bells appended to their garments."

A band of Puritans stand watching, believing those taking part are "devils and ruined souls." Two airy forms then appear: a youth in "glistening apparel" and a "fair maiden." An English priest stands behind them, "canonically dressed" but decked with flowers in the "heathen fashion."

The priest enjoins the crowd to sing a chorus "rich with the old mirth of Merry England" and lend their voices to the "nuptial song of the Lord and Lady of the May." The narrator explains that the couple were actually to be married, although their titles had to be "laid down at sunset."

The May Lord looks into the eyes of the Lady of the May, whose name is Edith, and sees that she is pensive. She tells her intended, Edgar, that she fears it is all "a dream," that the shapes of their friends are "visionary," and their "mirth unreal." She wonders what is the "mystery" in her heart.

A shower of "withering rose leaves" drifts down from the May-Pole, and the young lovers feel a "dreary presentiment of inevitable change," as though they no longer belong at Merry Mount. The narrator says that "no sooner had their hearts glowed with real passion, than they were sensible of something vague and unsubstantial in their former pleasures." Once they "truly loved," they "subjected themselves to earth's doom of care, and sorrow, and troubled joy." This is "Edith's mystery."

The narrator then steps out of the narrative to explain the history of the colonists of Merry Mount. They were "mirth-makers of every sort," but Puritans viewed these early English settlers as indulging in too much pleasure, gathering "wandering players," "mummers," "rope-dancers," and "mountebanks." These colonists imported the "hereditary pastimes of Old England" and danced at least monthly around "their altar," the May-Pole. Unfortunately, nearby was a Puritan settlement, "most dismal wretches," who disapproved of the customs of "English mirth." They were grim and determined to reform the merry colonists.

Returning to the events of the narrative, the Puritans have appeared at the settlement of Merry Mount. Their "darksome figures" intermix with the "wild shapes of their foes" around the May-Pole. The leader of the Puritans is Governor John Endicott himself, the "Puritan of Puritans," who condemns the festivities and assaults the "hallowed May-Pole." He orders the May-Pole cut down and some of the revelers put in the stocks. He demands no mercy to "the wretch that troubleth our religion."

The "iron man" softens, though, to the Lord and Lady of the May, for Edith and Edgar love each other and are legitimately married. Their "youthful beauty" appears "pure and high," especially "when its glow was chastened by adversity." Their people's "foes" are triumphant, "their friends captive and abased, their home desolate, the benighted wilderness around them, and a rigorous destiny, in the shape of the Puritan leader, their only guide." Endicott orders only that Edgar's hair be cut and that they dress in more decent attire. He says they have "qualities" that may make them fit to toil and pray as Puritans.

Endicott then throws a wreath of roses from the May-Pole over their heads—a "deed of prophecy," according to the narrator. In the equivocal ending of the tale, they continue heavenward, "supporting each other" along the stern Puritan path, and not regretting the "vanities of Merry Mount."

CRITICAL ANALYSIS

In introducing the parties in this story, the narrator explains, "Jollity and gloom were contending for an empire." At the outset of the story, the Merry Mounters are gaily dressed for a mirthful frolic, masquerading as monsters, Indians, and beasts of the forest. The narrator remarks, "Had a wanderer, bewildered in the melancholy forest, heard their mirth, and stolen a half-affrighted glance, he might have fancied them the crew of Comus, some already transferred to brutes, some midway between man and beast, and the others rioting in the flow of tipsy jollity that foreran the change." But the only spectators are a band of Puritans hidden in the forest. To the Puritans, the Merry Mounters are the equivalent of "those devils and ruined souls with whom their superstition peopled the black wilderness."

In this tale, the Merry Mounters are pitted against the dour Puritans, whose "festivals were fast-days, and their chief pastime the singing of psalms." Nancy Bunge suggests that the two newlyweds from Merry Mount, Edith and Edgar, know about mirth, since they have spent their lives at Merry Mount. However, once they have declared their love, they become vulnerable to care and sorrow. They have subjected themselves to "earth's doom of care and sorrow, and troubled joy, and had no more a home at Merry Mount." As they take life seriously, they begin to suffer pain. Governor Endicott threatens the Merry Mounters with brandings, stripes, and imprisonment. When Edith and Edgar ask for each other's punishment, Endicott realizes they can become valuable Puritans. They evince sensitivity and loyalty. In time the Puritans, subject to tremendous pessimism, conquer the Merry Mount world. This story, "The GENTLE BOY," "ROGER MALVIN'S BURIAL," and "MY KINSMAN, MAJOR MOLINEUX" are all concerned with the request for a home and the search for a parent.

Michael Davitt Bell suggests that, with its opposition between light and darkness, the story may be read as a "psychological fable—as an allegory of the opposition of heart and head, of unbridled sensuality and iron repression." The Puritans are impervious to impulse and have "cut themselves off from life." However, the "hedonism" of the "revelers" fails to achieve a happy mean. There must be a balance between the "claims of the heart and head" (*Hawthorne and the Historical Romance of New England,* 120).

As Terence Martin observes, Hawthorne attacks both the frivolous Merry Mounters and the stern Puritans. The "moral gloom of the world" supersedes the former "systematic gayety." Once Edith and Edgar graduate from folly, they arrive in an austere adult world with which they must contend. Martin concludes that the resolution of the tale "leaves no room for sentimentality or empty wishes. . . . The Lord and Lady of the May must walk the stern path of the Puritans, wasting no regrets on a life from which their doubts and love had alienated them" (*Nathaniel Hawthorne,* 77–80, 88–89).

CHARACTERS

Edgar In "The May-Pole of Merry Mount," Edgar is the bridegroom of Edith. Both reside in the settlement at Merry Mount. The pair love each other deeply. Their wedding is a magical affair, steeped in Elizabethan traditions such as a wreath of roses, hanging from the lowest bow of the tree that serves as the May-Pole. The wreath is thrown over their heads as a symbol of their "flowery union."

During the ceremony, the "pensive glance" on Edith's face makes Edgar feel apprehensive. He asks whether the "wreath of roses" is later intended to hang above their graves. He begs her not to tarnish their "golden time" by "any pensive shadow of the mind," because it is possible that nothing in their future will be brighter "than the mere remembrance of what is now passing."

Edith In "The May-Pole of Merry Mount," Edith is the bride of her beloved Edgar. They are married by a "flower-decked priest" with such Elizabethan revelries as "morrice-dancers, green-men, and glee-maidens, bears and wolves, and horned gentlemen" in attendance at the wedding, which takes place in a rustic setting. There is a "venerated May-Pole." They are to be partners for the "dance of life."

However, from the moment that they love each other, Edith and Edgar find that they are subject to worldly cares and sorrows. They no longer belong at Merry Mount.

FOR FURTHER READING

Bell, Michael Davitt, *Hawthorne and the Historical Romance of New England* (Princeton, N.J.: Princeton University Press, 1971); Bunge, Nancy, *Nathaniel Hawthorne: A Study of the Short Fiction* (New York: Twayne, 1993); Crowley, J. Donald, ed., *Nathaniel Hawthorne: The Critical Heritage* (London and New York: Routledge, 1970); Ehrlich, Gloria, "Family Themes and Hawthorne's Fiction: The Tenacious Web," in *Family Themes and Hawthorne's Fiction* (New Brunswick, N.J.: Rutgers University Press, 1984); Joplin, David D., "'May-Pole of Merry Mount': Hawthorne's 'L'Allegro' and 'Il Penseroso,'" *Studies in Short Fiction* 30, no. 2 (spring 1993): 185–192; Martin, Terence, *Nathaniel Hawthorne* (Boston, Mass.: Twayne, 1983); Smith, Gayle L., "Transcending the Myth of the Fall in Hawthorne's 'The May-Pole of Merry Mount,'" *Journal of the American Renaissance* 29, no. 2 (1983): 73–80; Weltzien, Alan O., "The Picture of History in 'The May-Pole of Merry Mount,'" *Arizona Quarterly: A Journal of American Literature, Culture, and Theory* 45, no. 1 (spring 1989): 29–48.

"Minister's Black Veil, The: A Parable"

Tale published in *The Token* in 1836 and collected in the first edition of *Twice-Told Tales* in 1837.

As the story opens, the sexton of the Milford meetinghouse is ringing the bell for services. Parson Hooper, a bachelor of about 30, is walking toward the meetinghouse wearing a black crape (Hawthorne's spelling of *crepe*) veil. He is reputed to be a good, though not energetic, preacher. The congregation is all "astir" over the "mysterious emblem" on his face. After the service, the people hurry out in confusion. Mr. Hooper greets them without explaining the veil. Some people believe it makes him "ghost-like."

Mr. Hooper wears the veil for the afternoon service as well. He later conducts a funeral for a young woman, which is followed by a procession in which he still wears the veil. One mourner imagines "that the minister and the maiden's spirit were walking in hand and hand."

An evening wedding is scheduled for the "handsomest couple" in Milford. Mr. Hooper wears the veil to perform the ceremony, introducing gloom to the occasion. The bride has a "death-like paleness" that makes some people whisper "that the maiden who had been buried a few hours before, was come from her grave to be married." After the ceremony, Mr. Hooper raises a glass of wine to his lips and catches a glimpse of his reflection; he shudders at the sight and spills the wine.

The next day, the villagers speculate further on the veil, but no one dares ask Mr. Hooper. His fiancée, Elizabeth, is the one person in the village who dares ask him directly to remove the veil. She says there is nothing terrible in the veil except that it hides his face, which she is "always glad to look upon." He replies that the veil is "a type and a symbol," and he is "bound to wear it ever, both in light and darkness, in solitude and before the gaze of multitudes." He remarks that "no mortal eye will see it withdrawn" and it will separate him "from the world." He says it is a "sign of mourning." Elizabeth worries that people may believe he hides his face "under the consciousness of secret sin."

Elizabeth begins to cry, finally feeling the "dreadful gloom that had so overawed the multitude." She rises and stands trembling before him and turns to leave the room. He begs her not to desert him over what is "but a mortal veil." "You know not how lonely I am," he says, "and how frightened, to be alone behind my black veil." She says he must lift the veil but once and look at her. He refuses, and she says good-bye.

From them on, no one attempts to remove the veil or ask what it hides. But the people of the village either avoid him or stare at him, and children flee from him. Mr. Hooper himself avoids his own reflection. Rumors abound that his "conscience tortured him for some great crime, too horrible to be entirely concealed." The veil hangs "between him and the world," separating him from "cheerful brotherhood and woman's love" and keeping him "in that saddest of all prisons, his own heart."

The only benefit of the veil is that it makes Mr. Hooper a "very efficient clergyman." He becomes a man of "awful power," leading an "irreproachable" life yet one "shrouded in dismal suspicions." As he grows older, he is called "Father Hooper."

After many years, he becomes mortally ill and is nursed by Elizabeth. He becomes confused and is near death. The minister of Westbury approaches him and leans over to lift the veil, but Father Hooper presses his hands against his face and says it must never be lifted while he is on Earth. The minister asks "with what horrible crime upon your soul are you now passing to the judgment?"

Father Hooper asks why they tremble at him alone; they should be trembling also at each other. He cries that men have avoided him, women "shown no pity," and children fled—only because of his black veil. He says it is the "mystery" of the crepe that has made it so awful. He dies, but they keep him veiled as they put him into his coffin and bury him.

CRITICAL ANALYSIS

The veil has been used as a symbol in works by other authors, including *Mysteries of Udolpho,* by Ann Radcliffe, and in stories by Charles Dickens. In this story, the character of Mr. Hooper is based, according to a footnote by Hawthorne, on another clergyman, Mr. Joseph Moody of York, Maine. In Moody's case, the veil was a handkerchief rather than a veil, but it was emblematic of the profound guilt he suffered over accidentally killing a beloved friend in his youth.

This story, written in 1836, has been termed the first of Hawthorne's short stories built around a central symbol. The important issue raised by the veil is not why Hooper donned it so much as to pinpoint its influence on the course of his life. The veil isolates him from humanity and is an emblem of his martyrdom to spiritual truth. His emotional life has been curtailed and he has cut himself off from others on the basis of an abstract religious conviction (Martin, 74–75).

Since the character himself never reveals the mystery of the black veil, readers have been forced to propose their own theories. EDGAR ALLAN POE, as well as other critics, have suggested that Hooper wears the veil as penance for a "specific sin," perhaps connected with the young woman whose funeral he conducts. Other theories are that the veil symbolizes the sins of his congregation, but that in the end it has made him a monster, severing his link with humanity.

It also has been argued that Mr. Hooper withdraws from society as a result of misguided religious zeal. He is a spiritual extremist, similar to Catharine in "The GENTLE BOY" and Father Ephraim of "The SHAKER BRIDAL." Frederick C. Crews suggests that Hooper, as are Young Goodman Brown, Aylmer of "The BIRTHMARK," and Giovanni of "RAPPACCINI's daughter," is a "sexual escapist." Elizabeth offers "spiritual" help but is rejected. Mr. Hooper is separated from his community and lives out his life in a state of pessimism, severed from human love and companionship.

Other people in the village respond to the veil, often by recognizing and confronting their own sins. However, they also shun Mr. Hooper. They cease inviting him to weddings or Sunday dinner. They regard him as a "living parable of evil" (Bunge, *Nathaniel Hawthorne: A Study of the Short Fiction,* 19). He is an emblem of depravity and a bitter corrosive unhappiness. His fiancée, Elizabeth, in contrast, does not abandon him. She continues to accept the veil and even protects it on his deathbed because she realizes it means a good deal to him. She loves him also: "There was the nurse, no hired handmaiden of death, but one whose calm affection had endured thus long . . . in solitude, amid the chill of age, and would not perish, even at the dying hour." She cannot embrace his philosophy, though, so the marriage is cancelled.

It may be said that the one aspect of the minister that separates him from other people is also an emblem of his humanity. Crews points out that Hooper is neither a "mild-mannered bachelor in clerical garb" nor an "Antichrist in his pride and despair." Rather, he is a "self-deluded idealist."

Another conflict in the story is the disparity between unconscious and conscious thoughts within individuals. However, even at the end of the story, Hooper continues to repress his thoughts; he cannot admit their "hold upon his own imagination" (Crews, 107–111). The veil not only intensifies the minister's influence, but also becomes an emblem of the passion for concealment that afflicts all human beings to a greater or lesser degree.

FOR FURTHER READING

Bell, Millicent, *Hawthorne's View of the Artist* (New York: New York State University Press, 1962); Bunge, Nancy, *Nathaniel Hawthorne: A Study of the Short Fiction* (New York: Twayne, 1993); Carnochan, W. B., "'The Minister's Black Veil': Symbol, Meaning, and the Context of Hawthorne's Art," *Nineteenth-Century Fiction* 24, no. 2 (September 1969): 182–192; Coale, Samuel, "Hawthorne's Black Veil: From Image to Icon," *CEA Critic: An Official Journal of the College English Association* 55, no. 3 (spring–summer 1993): 79–87; Crews, Frederick C., *The Sins of the Fathers: Hawthorne's Psychological Themes* (New York: Oxford University Press, 1966); Dauber, Kenneth, *Rediscovering Hawthorne* (Princeton, N.J.: Princeton University Press, 1977); Davis, William V., "'The Minister's Black Veil': A Note on the Significance of the Subtitle," *Studies in Short Fiction* 23, no. 4 (fall 1986): 453–454; Martin, Terence, *Nathaniel Hawthorne* (Boston: Twayne, 1965); McCarthy, Judy, "'The Minister's Black Veil': Concealing Moses and the Holy of Holies," *Studies in Short Fiction* 24, no. 2 (spring 1987): 131–138; Newman, Lea Bertani Vozar, "One-Hundred-and-Fifty Years of Looking At, Into, Through, Behind, Beyond, and Around 'The Minister's Black Veil,'" *Nathaniel Hawthorne Review* 13, no. 2 (fall 1987): 5–12; Timmerman, John H., "Hawthorne's 'The Minister's Black Veil,'" *Explicator* 41. no. 3 (spring 1983): 29–30; Voigt, Gilbert P., "The Meaning of 'The Minister's Black Veil,'" *College English* 13, no. 6 (March 1952): 337–338.

"Minotaur, The"

Tale first published in the English edition of *Tanglewood Tales, for Girls and Boys, Being a Second Wonder-Book*, in 1853.

The tale is a retelling of the Greek legend of Theseus. As a child, Theseus lives in the city of Troezene, ruled by his grandfather, King Pittheus. He has never seen his father, King Aegeus of Athens, and longs to do so. His mother, Aethra, says he must be strong enough to lift a certain rock and tell her what is hidden beneath it before he can set out to see him.

In time, he is strong enough to stir the rock. It has been placed over a cavity, within which are a sword with a golden hilt and a pair of sandals. Aethra says these belonged to his father, who placed them beneath the stone for his son. Theseus immediately wants to go to Athens and seek his father. His grandfather advises him to go by sea, in order to avoid the "robbers and monsters" he would encounter by road. But Theseus is eager to meet with such excitement and thus goes by land. He takes the sword and has many adventures on his way to Athens, clearing the land of robbers such as the "wicked villain" Procrustes and the "great scoundrel" Scinis. He also kills an enormous sow that has been terrorizing farmers.

By the time he reaches Athens, he has performed many "valiant feats" that earn him fame as "one of the bravest young men of the day." However, the "bad-hearted nephews" of the old King Aegeus, Theseus's cousins, are jealous of him, as is Medea, the "wicked enchantress" who is now his father's wife and wants the kingdom to pass to her own son, Medus. The cousins pretend to be glad he has arrived and plan for him to enter the king's presence as a stranger, to see whether he is recognized or not. While he waits at the door, they tell the king a young man has arrived who wishes to kill him and take his royal crown. Medea prepares a goblet of poisonous wine. A fly tumbles into it and dies; she smiles.

When Theseus sees the "stately and majestic" king, he is choked by "tears both of joy and sorrow" and is unable to make the speech he has planned. Medea tells the king it is because the young man feels guilty. The king believes he has seen the youth before and prepares to embrace him, but Medea casts a spell over him so that he cannot recognize the truth. He invites Theseus to drink some of the poisoned wine, but he feels guilty and his hand trembles. Before Theseus can drink, Aegeus sees the gold-hilted sword and asks how he acquired it. Theseus explains that it belonged to his father and he has just become strong enough to lift the stone, take the sword and sandals, and travel to Athens to find him. The king embraces him.

When Medea realizes what is happening, she hurries away in her "fiery chariot," drawn by hissing serpents. She leaves with her son, the king's best robes, and the stolen crown jewels. However, as she shakes her hands to curse the cheering crowd below, she accidentally drops many of the jewels. The people of Athens gather them up and take them back to the palace, but the king is so happy that he allows them to keep the gems.

Prince Theseus is taken into "great favor" by the king. Both the king and his subjects admire Theseus for his "heroic deeds," which include catching a mad bull. One morning, the king tells him it is the day when the youths and maids of Athens draw lots to see which seven youths and seven maids will be devoured by the Minotaur. He retells the legend of King Minos of Crete and the Minotaur.

Theseus begs to be the seventh young man this year; he will fight the Minotaur himself. The king objects, but Theseus is adamant. As he is about to depart for the island of Crete, the king says he will watch for the return of Theseus's ship, which has black sails, from the top of the cliff. If Theseus defeats the Minotaur, he should raise bright sails. As the ship nears Crete, Theseus sees a giant human figure striding from cliff to cliff. The shipmaster says it is Talus, the Man of Brass. When the ship nears the harbor, Talus asks why they have arrived and then allows them to pass.

King Minos of Crete examines them to see whether they are plump enough for the monster. Theseus asks the "stern and pitiless king" whether he is "appalled" at his own monstrous actions, whether he trembles at offering them to be devoured. The cruel king then decides Theseus will be the Minotaur's first morsel. King Minos's "beautiful and tender-hearted" daughter, Ariadne, stands near the throne. She weeps at the fate of the maidens and youths and begs her father to set them free, especially Theseus. The king refuses and they are jailed.

Just before midnight, Ariadne opens the jail door and leads Theseus out to the ship, but he will not leave his companions. She gives him his sword and takes him to a gate into the marble labyrinth built by Daedalus. The Minotaur is in the center; Theseus is to seek him. Ariadne gives him one end of a silken string so he can find his way back out again.

He reaches the ugly monster, who is emitting a hoarse roar. Theseus is fearless. A dreadful fight ensues. The monster misses Theseus and breaks off one of his horns against the wall. He rushes at Theseus again and grazes his left side, but Theseus hits his neck with his sword and slices off his head. He feels the twitch of the silken cord and returns to Ariadne.

They awaken the captives and prepare to flee before the king awakens and avenges the Minotaur. Theseus begs Ariadne to join them, but she refuses, as her father is old and has no one else to love him.

When the ship sails, Talus tries to strike a blow at the vessel but misses and tumbles into the sea. The 14 youths and maidens are in "excellent spirits" on the voyage home. The ship nears the coast of Attica, but in all of the merriment, Theseus forgets to hoist the sunny sails instead of the black ones. King Aegeus assumes his son has been eaten by the Minotaur and, miserably depressed, falls over the cliff and is drowned.

Theseus is "out of spirits" at the "melancholy news." He goes on to become king, summons his mother to Athens, takes her advice in "matters of state," and becomes a "very excellent monarch . . . greatly beloved by his people."

"Miraculous Pitcher, The"

Story printed in A WONDER BOOK for Girls and Boys.

The tale is a retelling of the legend of Philemon and Baucis. The old couple, very poor, sit at their cottage door, talking about their garden, their cow, their bees, and their grapevine. They hear the shouts of children and the barks of dogs growing louder and assume a traveler is approaching. They wish their neighbors would show "a little more kindness to their fellow-creatures" rather than setting their dogs upon them. As little as they have, Philemon and Baucis always welcome strangers and treat them kindly. In fact, they "would cheerfully have gone without their dinners, any day, rather than refuse a slice of their brown loaf, a cup of new milk, and a spoonful of honey" to a weary traveler.

The "selfish and hard-hearted" villagers teach their children to shout at strangers and pelt them with stones, and they keep large dogs to bark at and even bite them. At the same time, they are obsequious to rich travelers. They care only about money and "nothing whatever for the human soul, which lives equally in the beggar and the prince."

Two strangers, humbly clad, are pursued by a crowd of shrill children and fierce dogs. Philemon welcomes them while Baucis goes into their cottage to prepare bread and milk. The younger of the two strangers, a "slender and very active figure," asks why they live in such a bad neighborhood. The children have spattered their clothes with mud, and one of the dogs has torn his cloak. Still, he is in "good spirits." He is dressed in an odd cap with a cloak, even though it is summer, along with a "singular pair of shoes." He carries a strange-looking staff with a small pair of wings near the top and two snakes carved on it. When they reach the cottage door, Philemon invites them to rest.

The elder of the two strangers, a tall and grave-looking man, asks whether there was not once a lake covering the spot where the present village is. Philemon says not in his day, or even in his grandfather's. The stranger remarks that it would be better if a lake were rippling over the villagers' dwellings again, since they are so unfriendly. Philemon senses that the stranger is extraordinary in some way and is a little frightened of him, but then the stranger's face becomes "kindly and mild."

While Baucis prepares food, the two travelers talk with Philemon. The younger man, who is "shrewd and witty," says his name is Quicksilver. The elder stranger converses gravely and wisely and seems to be the "grandest figure" ever to visit the cottage. Philemon tells him that he and Baucis have lived in the cottage from their youth upward and hope to die, as they have lived, together. The stranger replies that it is "fit" that their wish be granted. It seems to Philemon that the sunset clouds throw up a "bright flash from the west" and kindle "a sudden light in the sky."

Baucis invites them to supper, apologizing for the simple fare. She says they would have gone without eating themselves in order to offer them something better. The elder stranger says an "honest, hearty welcome" can turn "the coarsest food to nectar and ambrosia." As they go inside, the odd-looking staff spreads its wings and hops with "gravity and decorum" to Quicksilver's chair. Quicksilver praises the feast and says he never felt hungrier in his life. He asks for more milk, but Baucis is embarrassed, for all the milk has been given to him and to the elder stranger. Quicksilver takes up the pitcher of milk and says there is more inside. To Baucis's astonishment, he refills their bowls and the pitcher keeps miraculously refilling. Moreover, the "dry and crusty" bread becomes "light and moist," the honey is the color "of the purest and most transparent gold," and the grapes grow larger and juicier.

When Philemon goes to pour more milk for his guest, he finds a "little white fountain" forming at the bottom of the pitcher. He questions Quicksilver, who says his miraculous staff is always playing such tricks. That night, Philemon and Baucis sleep on the floor and give up their bed to the travelers.

The next morning, the guests decline to wait for Baucis to cook breakfast but propose to set out early instead. They ask Philemon and Baucis to show them the road. As they walk together, Philemon remarks that if only the neighbors realized what a "blessed thing" it is to offer hospitality to strangers, they would tie up their dogs and not allow their children to fling another stone. Baucis says she plans to go that very day and tell the neighbors "what naughty people they are." Quicksilver says, "slyly smiling," that he fears she will find none of them at home.

The older traveler's brow assumes a "grave, stern, and awful grandeur" yet is serene. Philemon and Baucis gaze reverently into his face. He says that when men do not have brotherly feelings toward the humblest stranger, they are "unworthy to exist on earth." Quicksilver then asks the "dear old people," with "mischief in his eyes," where the village is that they had mentioned.

Philemon and Baucis turn toward the valley in order to point out the meadows, houses, gardens, street, children, and businesses. Instead, there is only a broad lake, the waters of which "dance, glitter, and sparkle in the early sunbeams." They ask what has become of their neighbors.

The elder traveler says they no longer exist as men and women, since there was "neither use nor beauty" in their lives. They never exercised "kindly affections" between man and man. Quicksilver adds that they have all been transformed into fishes; this "needed but little change, for they were already a scaly set of rascals, and the coldest-blooded beings in existence." He tells Philemon and Baucis that if they want to eat a nice broiled trout, they can throw in a line and pull out their old neighbors. Baucis shudders and says she could never put one of them on her gridiron.

The elder traveler assures them they will have ample milk, honey, bread, and other provisions. Philemon and Baucis ask only to live their lives together and "leave the world at the same instant." The stranger says their wish will be granted. He also transforms their cottage into a "tall edifice of white marble." The elderly couple fall on their knees to thank them, but the two travelers suddenly vanish.

Philemon and Baucis continue to live in the "marble palace" and offer all travelers their hospitality. The milk pitcher is always full of sweet milk, unless a "cross and disagreeable curmudgeon" sips it, when it turns sour. The old couple live a long time in their palace. Finally, one morning, they fail to appear. Their overnight guests search everywhere. The guests then see two "venerable trees" that not been there the day before. Their boughs are intertwined together, as though they are embracing each other. A deep breeze springs up. "I am old Philemon!" murmurs the oak. "I am old Baucis!" murmurs the linden tree. The two trees begin talking together and fling a hospitable shade around them; whenever a traveler passes by, the trees seem to murmur, "Welcome, welcome!" A kind, perceptive person builds a circular seat around both their trunks, where travelers can "repose themselves, and quaff milk abundantly out of the miraculous pitcher."

In this essay, Hawthorne addresses his reflection in the mirror. He observes that there is no one in the whole circle of his acquaintance he has studied more actively, yet of whom he has "less real knowledge." He speaks as if the image is another person, with access to the most profound of life's mysteries.

The image bears a strong resemblance to him, although his name suggests a French descent. Hawthorne would prefer, however, that his blood flow from a "bold British and pure Puritan source." Some genealogists have traced his origins to Spain, but he has never spoken about his paternal lineage; he "lacks the faculty of speech" to expound upon the subject.

There is great sympathy between the two "persons," and M. du Miroir has "duplicates of all his waistcoats and cravats" and other clothes. The serious events of their two lives remind the speaker of the "legends of lovers, or twin-children, twins of fate, who have lived, enjoyed, suffered, and died, in unison."

M. du Miroir has a faculty of conveying himself from place to place very rapidly. Even in the speaker's bedroom, M. du Miroir appears to meet him. Their fates are "blended." The speaker cannot escape him.

The speaker yearns for some "master-thought" to guide him through the labyrinth of life. The longing of humans to understand the mysteries of human experience is not likely to be fulfilled, but "divine Intelligence" has provided them with what they need to know. In this way, mortals "deify, as it were, a mere shadow of themselves, a spectre of human reason." He bids farewell to Monsieur du Miroir, saying that it may be doubted whether the image is "the wiser," even though his "whole business is REFLECTION."

FOR FURTHER READING

Richards, Sylvie L. F., "Nathaniel Hawthorne's 'Monsieur du Miroir' through Jacques Lacan's Looking Glass," *Nathaniel Hawthorne Review* 18, no. 1 (spring 1992): 15–20.

"Monsieur du Miroir"

Sketch first published in *The TOKEN* in 1837, signed by "the author of Sights from a Steeple." It was collected in *MOSSES FROM AN OLD MANSE*, 1846.

Mosses from an Old Manse

A collection of tales and sketches first published in 1846, in two parts, by Wiley and Putnam, New York.

The Hawthornes' Old Manse home. *(Courtesy of the Library of Congress)*

Part I contained "The OLD MANSE," "The BIRTH-MARK," "A SELECT PARTY," "YOUNG GOODMAN BROWN," "RAPPACCINI'S DAUGHTER," "MRS. BULL-FROG," "FIRE-WORSHIP," "BUDS AND BIRD-VOICES," "MONSIEUR DU MIROIR," "THE HALL OF FANTASY," "THE CELESTIAL RAILROAD," and "THE NEW ADAM AND EVE."

Part II contained "THE NEW ADAM AND EVE," "EGOTISM, OR THE BOSOM-FIEND [SERPENT]," "THE CHRISTMAS BANQUET," "DROWNE'S WOODEN IMAGE," "THE INTELLIGENCE OFFICE," "ROGER MALVIN'S BURIAL," "P.'S CORRESPONDENCE," "EARTH'S HOLO-CAUST," "THE OLD APPLE DEALER," "THE ARTIST OF THE BEAUTIFUL," and "A VIRTUOSO'S COLLECTION."

The reviewer for GRAHAM'S MAGAZINE called the two volumes an "exquisite collection of essays, allegories, and stories, replete with fancy, humor and sentiment." He worried that the work as a whole was "almost too fine for popularity" and termed Hawthorne a "finer and deeper humorist . . . than Addison or Goldsmith, or Irving, though not so obvious and striking in his mirth." He suggested that the tales were "certain of a life far beyond the present generation of readers."

Henry Fothergill Chorley, writing in the British *Athenaeum*, praised Hawthorne's "tone" and stated that few prose writers possessed "so rich a treasury in the chambers of their imagination." He singled out "The Birth-Mark," "The Celestial Rail-road," and "Young Goodman Brown" for special approval.

The reviewer for the *American Whig Review*, Charles Wilkins Webber, declared that Hawthorne "covers the broadest and the highest field yet occu-pied by the Imaginative Literature of the country."

He remarked on the "universality of Hawthorne's mind, and his honestly philosophical readiness to recognize all truths." He observed that Hawthorne "constantly writes Poems while he only pretends to be writing Tales" and declared that his "Life" had deepened since the publication of TWICE-TOLD TALES (*Nathaniel Hawthorne: The Contemporary Reviews*, edited by John L. Idol Jr. and Buford Jones 79–93, passim).

PREFACE TO *MOSSES FROM AN OLD MANSE*

In this preface, subtitled "The Author Makes the Reader Acquainted with His Abode," Hawthorne first describes the Old Manse. Brenda Wineapple observes that it is an "elegiac evocation of time past and passing" (*Hawthorne: A Life*, 192).

Hawthorne remarks that there is a certain melancholy to the time when "we stand in the perfected vigor of our life, and feel that Time has now given us all his flowers, and that the next work of his never idle fingers must be—to steal them, one by one, away!" Writing a year after the death of the previous occupant, Dr. Samuel Ripley, minister of the First Church in Concord, he describes the overgrown wheel track leading to the door. The "edifice" was protected by vegetation and "had not quite the aspect of belonging to the material world." Dr. Ripley had apparently lived in the house for 60 years without painting it. The Hawthornes had moved into the Old Manse soon after their marriage; they painted, papered, and carpeted the house, and Sophia provided fresh flowers for Hawthorne's study, in addition to pictures, engravings, and new furniture (Hoeltje, *Inward Sky: The Mind and Heart of Nathaniel Hawthorne*, 197).

RALPH WALDO EMERSON had written his essay "Nature" in the study. Hawthorne describes the room, with its three windows overlooking the river. He imagines Dr. Ripley standing at the window, witnessing the conflict between his parishioners and the "glittering line of the British on the hither bank" during the Battle of Concord. Outside, he has discovered the grave of two British soldiers who had been slain in the skirmish. He mentions the many strangers who travel during the summer to view the battlefield, as well as the pleasure of picking up centuries-old Indian arrowheads.

The orchard, planted by Dr. Ripley, has yielded cherries, currants, and apples. He describes the garden, with its summer squashes, and the beauty of the riverscape during rain. Many of Dr. Ripley's books have been left in the house. Hawthorne takes little interest in the theological volumes but appreciates the old newspapers and almanacs, which reproduce to his eye "the epochs when they had issued from the press with a distinctness that was altogether unaccountable." To Hawthorne, they are like "bits of magic looking-glass . . . with the images of a vanished century in them."

Sometimes WILLIAM ELLERY CHANNING joins Hawthorne for a fishing excursion on the river. When they have houseguests, they are likely to feel a "slumberous influence" upon them, falling asleep in chairs or in the orchard. Hawthorne is delighted by this, for it makes the precincts seem like "the Enchanted Ground through which the pilgrim travelled on his way to the Celestial City." He could offer them rest—others could give them "pleasure and amusement of instruction." Many of their visitors have been drawn to Concord by Emerson, who now lives at the opposite end of the village. Hawthorne states that "young visionaries" and "grayheaded theorists" traveled to Emerson's door "to invite the free spirit into their own thraldom." He himself has long admired Emerson as a poet "of deep beauty and austere tenderness" but "sought nothing from him as a philosopher."

By autumn, however, the manse seems "lonely as a hermitage." He concludes with many regrets about the "improvements" the owner of the house is now making, clearing away the "veil of woodbine" and the "aged mosses." He remarks that "the hand that renovates is always more sacrilegious than that which destroys." At the conclusion of the essay, he discloses that they will soon be moving to the custom house. He offers his collection of tales, *Mosses from an Old Manse*, to the reader, hoping he or she will imagine being ushered into the study while Hawthorne calls his attention to the tales themselves.

"Mr. Higginbotham's Catastrophe"

Story published, unsigned, as one segment of "The Story Teller No. II" in NEW-ENGLAND MAGAZINE, 7 (December 1834). It was then collected in TWICE-TOLD TALES in 1837. In a review in GRAHAM'S MAGAZINE, EDGAR ALLAN POE proclaimed the story "vividly original and managed most dexterously" (May 1842).

As the story opens, Dominicus Pike, a tobacco peddler, is making his way from Morristown to Parker's Falls. He is a "young man of excellent character," well liked by his customers and especially "beloved by the pretty girls along the Connecticut." He is also something of a gossip. He asks an "ill looking" traveler the latest news and learns that old Mr. Higginbotham, of Kimballton, had been murdered in his orchard the night before by an Irishman and a black man. They had hanged the body from a Saint Michael's pear tree, where no would find him until that morning.

Horrified, Dominicus continues on his way, pondering the "doleful fate" of Mr. Higginbotham, whom he had known, having sold him various tobacco products. He cannot understand how the traveler knows about the tragedy so early in the morning, especially when Kimballton is even further than Parker's Falls, but assumes he must have mistaken the day of the catastrophe. Dominicus tells the story "at every tavern and country store along the road," elaborating "till it became quite a respectable narrative." One listener is a former clerk of Mr. Higginbotham's, who describes him as a "crusty old fellow" who was in the habit of carrying "money and valuable papers" on his person.

That evening, Dominicus stays at a tavern near Parker's Falls; in the bar after dinner, he repeats the story of the murder. All but one of his 20 listeners are shocked at the news. The last, an elderly farmer, says the story cannot be true, or else he had enjoyed a glass of bitters with his ghost that very morning.

The next morning, Dominicus continues on his route to Parker's Falls. As he crosses the Salmon River, he meets a man with a bundle over his shoulder. Dominicus asks him to verify the story, since he is traveling from the direction of Kimballton. Then he notices that the man himself seems to have African blood; he is Ethiopian. The stranger turns a "ghastly white" and begins "shaking and stammering." He tells Dominicus it was not a colored man but an Irishman who hanged Higginbotham the previous night at eight o'clock. Dominicus is bewildered but decides that if he relates the story of the murder to others, he should be vague about the date of its occurrence, since Mr. Higginbotham's family might not have discovered the corpse yet.

Once in Parker's Falls, Dominicus tells the story of the murder but is vague about the date and whether it was committed by an Irishman or a black man. The news spreads quickly through town. The Parker's Falls Gazette publishes a story about it entitled "Horrid Murder of Mr. Higginbotham!" The reporter declares that the victim had been robbed of thousands of dollars. The town's selectmen decide to offer a reward of $500 "for the apprehension of his murderers, and the recovery of the stolen property."

Dominicus mounts the town pump and begins retelling the narrative. The mail stage then arrives in Parker's Falls; it had changed horses at Kimballton at three o'clock that morning. A mob meets it, demanding particulars of the murder. A lawyer inside produces a large red pocketbook, while Dominicus helps a young woman out of the coach. The lawyer tells the crowd that the story must be a falsehood contrived by Mr. Higginbotham's enemies, for he has a document given him at ten o'clock the previous evening by Higginbotham himself. The young lady introduces herself as Mr. Higginbotham's niece and declares she is en route to a visit with a friend near Parker's Falls. Her uncle had given her two dollars and fifty cents to pay her stage fare that very morning.

The townspeople are furious, not relieved, at learning their mistake. They begin to turn on Dominicus, deciding whether to "tar and feather him, ride him on a rail," or prosecute him. The young woman makes a successful appeal on his behalf. Dominicus thanks her and continues on his journey. He wonders how the second traveler was aware of the murder, if the story of the first traveler was merely a hoax. He also learns, during his travels, that Mr. Higginbotham employs an Irishman "of doubtful character."

Around dusk, Dominicus reaches the tollhouse at Kimballton turnpike. He nearly overtakes a man on horseback, who goes ahead of him through the gate. He inquires whether the toll gatherer has seen Mr. Higginbotham recently. The toll gatherer says Mr. Higginbotham has just passed through the gate ahead of Dominicus; he had been to Woodfield that afternoon, attending a sheriff's sale, and looked quite "yellow and thin," "more like a ghost or an old mummy than good flesh and blood."

Just before eight o'clock, Dominicus reaches Mr. Higginbotham's home and goes straight to his orchard and the pear tree. Someone is struggling beneath the tree. He rushes up and finds a sturdy Irishman trying to hang Mr. Higginbotham. It turns out that three men had plotted his robbery and murder, but two had "lost courage and fled, each delaying the crime one night by their disappearance."

Mr. Higginbotham takes Dominicus—his "champion . . . like the heroes of old romance"—into "high favor." He permits him to marry his pretty niece and settles his property on their children. After his death, much later, Dominicus Pike moves from Kimballton and establishes a large tobacco manufactory in the native village of the narrator.

FOR FURTHER READING

Duban, James, "The Sceptical Context of Hawthorne's 'Mr. Higginbotham's Catastrophe,'" *American Literature: A Journal of Literary History Criticism, and Bibliography* 48, no. 3 (November 1976): 292–301.

"Mrs. Bullfrog"

Short story first published in *The TOKEN* in 1837, signed "by the author of Wives of the Dead," and collected in *MOSSES FROM AN OLD MANSE* in 1846.

The story is narrated by Thomas Bullfrog, the "accomplished graduate of a dry-goods store." He has ministered to the "whims of fine ladies," supplying silk hose, satins, ribbons, chintzes, calicoes, tapes, gauze, and cambric needles, until, he says, he has grown up "a very lady-like sort of a gentleman." He has also become so sensitive to "female imperfection" that he is in danger of remaining unmarried or of "being driven to perpetrate matrimony" with his own image in the mirror.

He desires, in a wife, "the first bloom of youth, pearly teeth, glossy ringlets," as well as "delicacy of habits and sentiments," "a silken texture of mind," and "a virgin heart." He is afraid of becoming a "miserable old bachelor." Therefore, he journeys into another state and woos, wins, and marries a young woman named Laura within two weeks. At that point, he begins to estimate Mrs. Bullfrog's "deficiencies and superfluities."

They take two seats in a stagecoach and begin traveling to his home state and place of business; there are no other passengers with them. Mrs. Bullfrog is "charmingly" dressed, but when he tries to kiss her, she objects that he will "disarrange" her curls. She is traveling with a small basket, in which he assumes she has provided food for their journey. He reaches into the basket and touches the neck of a bottle, which his wife declares is Kalydor (used to treat complexions). He is familiar with Kalydor himself, but this bottle smells like cherry brandy.

The coach suddenly hits a pile of gravel and capsizes. Mrs. Bullfrog steps on her husband in order to climb out. Suddenly he hears a "strange, hoarse voice" shouting at the driver, "You have ruined me, you blackguard! I shall never be the woman I have been!" The person gives a "smart thwack" on the coachman's ear, misses it, and hits his nose, which begins bleeding. Thomas Bullfrog is startled to realize that the blows are being delivered by a "person of grisly aspect, with a head almost bald, and sunken cheeks, apparently of the feminine gender." There are "no teeth to modulate the voice." Yet this "phantom" wears a riding habit like Mrs. Bullfrog's.

He thinks at first that his wife has been annihilated in the accident, since he cannot see her body anywhere. The apparition, or "hobgoblin," shouts to him, urging that he help the "rascal" set up the coach and screeching to three countrymen in the distance to help as well. The countrymen come "running at full speed" to assist. The coachman, who is still bleeding, glances at Thomas Bullfrog with an "eye of pity." Together, they succeed in righting the coach.

Then a "sweet voice" from behind them thanks all of the men. The coachman declares, "Why, the woman's a witch!" Mrs. Bullfrog stands before them, with her "glossy ringlets" and a "most angelic smile." Thomas Bullfrog hears the coachman say to the other men, as he closes the door, "How do you suppose a fellow feels, shut up in a cage with a she-tiger?"

Thomas Bullfrog confesses that his feelings are now less ecstatic. He recalls a tale about a fairy who was a beautiful woman half the time and a hideous monster the other half. Has he married such a fairy? To distract himself, he takes up the old newspaper that had lined the basket. There is a "deep-red stain" in the basket from the broken bottle of "Kalydor," as well as a "potent spirituous fume." He discovers in the paper, which is two or three years old, a report of a trial "for breach of promise of marriage." A certain damsel had sued her husband for "perfidy." Thomas Bullfrog asks his wife whether she had been the plaintiff in this case. She says yes, but she assumed "all the world knew that."

Mr. Bullfrog covers his face and emits a "deep and deathlike" groan. His wife fixes her eyes on his face and urges him to "overcome this foolish weakness" and overlook the "little imperfections" in his bride. She reminds him that "women are not angels." He asks why she concealed the imperfections, and why she had sued the other man for breach of promise. She says he should be proud because she "triumphantly defended" herself and "punished the villain who trifled with her affections." Moreover, if she had not sued him, she would not have the $500 she now has with which to stock his own dry-goods store.

A newly ecstatic Mr. Bullfrog says, "Let me fold thee to my heart!" The basis of their "matrimonial bliss" is now "secure," and he rejoices at the "wrongs" that drove her to the "blessed law-suit." He proclaims himself a "Happy Bullfrog."

FOR FURTHER READING

Solensten, John M., "Hawthorne's Ribald Classic: 'Mrs. Bullfrog' and the Folktale," *Journal of Popular Culture* 7 (1973): 582–588.

"My Kinsman, Major Molineux"

Tale published in *The TOKEN*, 1832, and collected in *The TWICE-TOLD TALES*, 1889. Twenty years later, in 1851, the story was collected in *The SNOW-IMAGE*.

The tale begins with an account of the dislike of prerevolutionary colonists for royal governors sent from England, without choice on the part of the colonists.

On a moonlit evening, Robin, a youth of 18, takes a ferry to a small New England port to search for a kinsman, Major Molineux. Robin is a "country-bred" youth with "vigorous shoulders," "well-shaped features," and "bright, cheerful eyes"; he appears to be making "his first visit to town." He believes his kinsman is famous and wealthy and will be able to assist him in launching a career but does not realize that this is the evening the provincial citizens have chosen to tar and feather Major Molineux, who is despised as the representative of royal authority.

He first overtakes an elderly man who wears a "wide-skirted coat" and carries a "polished cane." When Robin asks whether he knows where Major Molineux's dwelling might be, the ill-tempered man becomes angry and says he knows "not the man you speak of." Robin decides the man must be a "country representative" who has never been invited to visit his kinsman's home and "lacks the breeding to answer a stranger civilly."

Robin continues to the center of business, a "succession of crooked and narrow streets," where he notices the "smell of tar." He finds an inn with a sign portraying a British soldier; within, there is a jovial supper party. Once inside, he notices a man near the door whispering with a group of "ill-dressed associates"; he has "deep and shaggy" eyebrows and nearly grotesque features. The innkeeper greets Robin, who says he will patronize the inn when he can better afford it, but he is looking for the dwelling of his kinsman, Major Molineux. He is met with a hostile reception and, mystified, goes back outside.

Growing tired and hungry, he finds a "street of mean appearance," with hovels leading toward the harbor. He passes a half-opened door and asks a pretty young woman whether she knows the address of his relative. She says Major Molineux dwells there but is asleep. She invites him inside, but when another door opens in the neighborhood, she retreats "speedily into her own domicile." A watchman approaches, calls Robin a "vagabond," and advises him to go home. A girl with a "saucy eye" tries to entice Robin upstairs, but he is from the "household of a New England clergyman" and resists the temptation.

He roams through the streets at random and then decides to knock at the door of every mansion. Near a church, determined to get an answer to his question, he blocks the way of a "bulky stranger, muffled in a cloak," who also rebuffs him. Robin persists, and the stranger then unmuffles his face and advises him to "watch here an hour, and Major Molineux will pass by." Robin recognizes the man from the inn, with his "forehead with its double prominence, the broad hooked nose, the shaggy eyebrows, and fiery eyes." However, the man's complexion has changed: "One side of the face blazed an intense red, while the other was black as midnight." The overall effect is that of "two individual devils" combined in one person, "a fiend of fire and a fiend of darkness." The hideous stranger is either Hawthorne's Satan or the evening's master of ceremonies. Robin waits on the church steps, homesick for his father's household. He hears a "murmur" sweeping "continually along the street," broken occasionally by "a distant shout." Fighting off sleep, he calls out to a passersby on the opposite side of the street, asking whether he must wait all night for Major Molineux. The gentleman feels sorry for Robin and responds by asking the nature of his business with Major Molineux. The youth explains that the well-off major had visited Robin's family in "great pomp" a year or two earlier and expressed

interest in helping establish Robin's future. He then describes the "ill-favored fellow" who had told him to wait for the major. The gentleman tells Robin he will wait with him.

They begin to converse but hear shouting in the nearby streets and the sounds of a trumpet. There is a great commotion. A stream of people begin moving toward the church amid a rattling of wheels and more shouting. An uncovered cart appears, illuminated by torchlight. Major Molineux sits in the cart, in "tar-and-feathery dignity." The "large and majestic" man is being driven out of town; his face is "pale as death" and his eyes are "red and wild." Foam hangs "white upon his quivering lip." His pride tries to hide his "overwhelming humiliation." He recognizes Robin, who is horrified to see his kinsman "reviled by that great multitude." The lantern bearer is behind him, "enjoying the lad's amazement." Opposite Robin, on a balcony, stands the old citizen he had first met, "in a fit of convulsive merriment." The whole crowd is laughing. The tumultuous throng presses on, leaving "a silent street behind."

Robin asks the gentleman to show him the way to the ferry, but his companion says he will do so only "some few days hence, if you continue to wish it." He says that, since Robin is a "shrewd youth," he may decide to remain in the town and "rise in the world" without the help of his "kinsman, Major Molineux."

CRITICAL ANALYSIS

Lionel Trilling has observed that, whereas Ilbrahim's quest in "THE GENTLE BOY" is for a mother, Robin's quest is for an authentic father figure. The young man of provincial birth and education, son of a rural clergyman, goes to the city at the age of 18 on his quest to become acquainted with the world. His kinsman, Major Molineux, has promised to assist him in his start in life. Wearing a three-cornered hat and rustic garments, with a heavy cudgel made of an oak sapling, Robin sets out at night on an archetypal journey of initiation.

To him the provincial city seems as awesome as the "London city" of his imagination (Male, 48–49). On his pilgrimage through the town, he is exposed to a hierarchy of temptations. He resists defying the mob on his kinsman's behalf, and he is not tempted by a woman leaning from an open window with a "saucy eye" and a "round arm." His experiences have been termed a "condensation of a lifetime journey with each incident reflective of society's institutions" (Doubleday, *Hawthorne's Early Tales*, 235).

Although he does not find his "cultured kinsman," his negative experiences prompt him to appreciate life in his father's household. He reflects on the way the evening would have been spent at home at a sunset worship service, his father "holding the Scriptures in the golden light that fell from the western clouds." There would have been thanksgiving for "daily mercies" and "supplications for their continuance." He had once listened to them wearily, but they were now among his "dear remembrances."

Terence Martin argues that the tale blends the themes of initiation into manhood with the colonial movement defying royal authority. Although Hawthorne characterizes Robin as a "shrewd youth," and Robin considers himself a good judge of human nature, he is inept at handling himself and does not realize that to the townspeople he is little more than a country lad. He is naively proud when he claims kinship with Major Molineux but evokes only laughter in the town. He also believes "physical retaliation" is the proper way of extracting guidance from the townspeople. The town gradually takes on "the aspects of a nightmare" to Robin. As he slowly learns to evaluate the grotesque, he is eventually moved to "a sort of mental inebriety." He finally realizes that he must establish his own identity within society (Martin, *Nathaniel Hawthorne*, 103–107).

The details Hawthorne employs in the story give it an almost photographic reality: Robin himself as the country boy just arrived in town, the barbershop, the tavern advertisements, and the pale, grizzled countenance of the major are all vivid. The major's frame is "agitated by a quick and continual tremor, which his pride strove to quell, even in these circumstances of overwhelming humiliation."

Nancy Bunge observes that Hawthorne is highly suspicious of convention. He contrasts Robin's country background with the cosmopolitan world he hopes to enter, but the latter is actually false and artificial. Robin is natural and naive and strives in vain to comprehend the hostility he encounters. He has a profound need, however, to believe the world is "rational." At times, this leads him to construct logical explanations for the absurd and the cruel. For example, when he meets the man with the red and black face he indulges in "philosophical speculations" that, somehow, satisfy him. Bunge points out that Robin needs to perceive people as reasonable. If society "does not function sensibly, how can he endure it, let alone rise in it?" (*Nathaniel Hawthorne*, 8).

In Robin's quest for a relative who will help him rise in the world, followed by his emancipation from his kinsman, some critics have detected a parallel with the American Revolution (Waggoner, Hyatt, *Hawthorne: A Critical Study*, 56–64). America has "come of age" by deposing colonial authority.

FOR FURTHER READING

Allison, Alexander W., "The Literary Contexts of 'My Kinsman, Major Molineux,'" *Nineteenth-Century Fiction* 23, no. 3 (December 1968): 304–311; Broes, Arthur T., "Journey into Moral Darkness: 'My Kinsman, Major Molineux' as Allegory," *Nineteenth-Century Fiction* 19, no. 2 (September 1964): 171–184; Bunge, Nancy, *Nathaniel Hawthorne: A Study of the Short Fiction* (New York: Twayne, 1993); Crews, Frederick C., *The Sins of the Fathers: Hawthorne's Psychological Themes* (New York: Oxford University Press, 1966); Doubleday, Neal Frank, *Hawthorne's Early Tales: A Critical Study* (Durham, N.C.: Duke University Press, 1972); Gross, Seymour, "Hawthorne's 'My Kinsman, Major Molineux': History as Moral Adventure," *Nineteenth-Century Fiction* 12, no. 2 (September 1957): 97–109; Male, Roy R., *Hawthorne's Tragic Vision* (Austin: University of Texas Press, 1957); Martin, Terence, *Nathaniel Hawthorne* (Boston: Twayne, 1965); Waggoner, Hyatt, *Hawthorne: A Critical Study* (Cambridge, Mass.: Harvard University Press, 1955).

"My Visit to Niagara"

Travel sketch published anonymously, "by the author of 'The Gray Champion,'" in the *New-Eng-*

land *Magazine* 8 (February 1835): 91–96. It did not appear during Hawthorne's lifetime but was later identified and collected by GEORGE PARSONS LATHROP. It has been reprinted in *Hawthorne's American Travel Sketches* (Alfred Weber, Beth L. Lueck, and Dennis Berthold, eds.).

Hawthorne's journey takes place in September 1832. As the sketch begins, he recounts taking the stagecoach from Lewiston, New York, to Manchester, New York. The only passengers are a Frenchman and he. When they reach the town of Manchester, bordering on the falls, Hawthorne does not rush to see them. Lighting a cigar, he walks toward Goat Island and signs the register in the tollhouse. He selects a walking stick and crosses the bridge to Goat Island. He goes along the path to the Horseshoe and stands on a "tremulous" bridge. Then he descends by a winding staircase to the base of the precipice.

He wishes he had never heard of Niagara until he had fully seen the falls, since the reality does not, at first, measure up to his idea of "foam and fury." He begins to realize, however, that Niagara qualifies as "a wonder of the world," because comprehending it takes him a long time. He later sits on Table Rock. When the time arrives to depart, he walks along a causeway down to the ferry. From that point of view, "the solitude of the old wilderness" is all his own. He terms it "Heaven's own beauty crowning earth's sublimity."

Weber observes that an exact reconstruction of Hawthorne's entire trip is impossible, but that it was his first extensive journey beyond New England. With this journey, he "became a member of the first group of American artists and writers who, like Irving, Bryant, Cole, Pratt, and Durand, traveled in the United States in order to explore the American landscape" ("Hawthorne's Tour of 1832," *Hawthorne's American Travel Sketches*, 21).

"New Adam and Eve, The"

Story first published in the UNITED STATES MAGAZINE AND DEMOCRATIC REVIEW in February 1843.

It is unclear how much compensation Hawthorne received for the story, although the editor of the magazine, JOHN L. O'SULLIVAN, was a close friend. He was a guest of Hawthorne and his wife, Sophia, for a few days in January 1843 at the OLD MANSE, Concord. This was the home built by William Emerson, grandfather of RALPH WALDO EMERSON, in 1769. Hawthorne and his wife rented the house for three years after their wedding in 1842. It is possible Hawthorne wrote the story between mid-December 1842 and mid-January 1843, but he was not paid for it until December 1843. Possibly the payment of $100 recorded by Sophia at that time covered several other contributions to the magazine as well.

As the story opens, Hawthorne addresses readers who are fettered in "truth and reality" and entreats them to imagine that the "Day of Doom" has "burst upon the globe, and swept away the whole race of men." Every living thing is gone from cities, fields, seashore, continents, and islands. There are no people and no footprints; there is no evidence of human accomplishments or "intellectual cultivation" or "moral progress." However, a new Adam and Eve have been created; they are capable of making a distinction between art and nature.

The narrator imagines the second day dawning after the Day of Doom. The natural beauty of the earth, sea, and sky still exists. Adam and Eve become disoriented; they do not recognize their surroundings. Eve wants only to gaze at Adam, but he wants to look about and take stock of the situation. They find decaying towns and cities without bustle or activity. They see only "squareness and ugliness, and regular or irregular deformity." Solitude is "death" in the city; in the country it would be life. Eve sees one small tuft of grass, which she grasps. Adam spots some clouds and tries to climb into them, but fails.

They ramble through the uncongenial city (Boston). Eve touches some fashionable Parisian fabric but cannot remember what it is for. Everything puts her in "a perfect maze." Then she takes a remnant of "exquisite silver gauze" and throws it around herself, giving Adam his "first idea of the witchery of dress." He dons a mantle of blue velvet, enhancing his appearance, and they go in search of "new discoveries." They ramble on and pass through a church but do not sense its purpose.

They enter a Court of Justice but have no idea of the purpose of the edifice; nor do they understand the Hall of Legislature they enter, or the prison or the stately mansion on Beacon Street. In the latter building, they are moved by what seems to be a strain of music from an Aeolian harp. The family portraits, however, have little appeal. In one apartment, they discover themselves in a tall mirror and then see a statue of a child. Adam perceives that they are following the footsteps of beings that once bore a likeness to them, but are no longer there.

They find that the house is in readiness for a grand dinner party, but the whole family and guests were apparently "summoned to the unknown regions of illimitable space." There is food on the table, such as turtle soup, but they are bewildered until they discover, on a side table, an apple. Eve eats it "without sin." They find some claret, hock, and Madeira; Eve rejects it, but Adam discovers some champagne. The cork explodes, however. They finally find some water in a glass pitcher and refresh themselves.

They pass down State Street, but nothing is happening in the "Sabbath of eternity." They toss about coins and packages of banknotes from a bank but cannot decipher their purpose. In a jeweler's shop, they don some gems, but Eve throws them away in favor of a bouquet of fresh roses. The narrator remarks that the "Creator" has caused them to "pass unconscious judgment upon the works and ways of the vanished race." Adam and Eve perceive that some of the edifices they see were erected by "beings similar to themselves" but fail to realize that even as "one portion of earth's lost inhabitants" enjoyed luxury, the other half was "toiling for scanty food."

In the suburbs, they encounter a granite obelisk (the Bunker Hill monument commemorating the first major battle of the American Revolution), which they take to be a "visible prayer." They fail to appreciate it, not understanding oppression. They then cross the Charles River and enter the library of Harvard University, where they pore over shelves of books. Adam tries in vain to penetrate the mystery of the written word, while Eve scans a

volume of "fashionable poetry," but she persuades him to leave the library in order that they may talk with each other. She "rescues him from the mysterious perils of the library." Eve thus prevents Adam from eating from the "Tree of Knowledge," saving him from his downfall. As it is, he can "enjoy a new world in our worn-out race." He can make his own errors.

The pair finally reach the cemetery of Mount Auburn in Cambridge. They tread the "winding paths, among marble pillars, mimic temples, urns, obelisks, and sarcophagi." They find a white marble sleeping child and decide to fall asleep near its figure. Adam suggests that even if their earthly life leaves them, God has imparted "the boon of existence, never to be resumed." Eve responds that no matter where they exist, they will always be together.

CRITICAL ANALYSIS

The primordial couple reenact, within the framework of a day's journey within Boston and its environs, the subject Hawthorne mentions in his notebooks: "the predicament of worldly people, if admitted to paradise" [*CE, 8, 18*]. Arlin Turner observes that they follow Milton's *Paradise Lost* in condemning humans' perversion of nature ("Hawthorne's Literary Borrowings," *PMLA* 51 [1936]: 543–562). Other sources are the Bible and Shakespeare's *King Lear*, particularly Lear's attack on hypocrites of the day (4. 6. 165–72).

Turner suggests that the nucleus of the subject may have been present in Hawthorne's journal entry made in September 1836. Here he imagined that the race of humankind and its cities might be swept away. A human pair, Adam and Eve, might then be put into the world without knowledge of their predecessors and then admitted to paradise. Hawthorne had also written to Sophia, during their engagement, of the story of Adam and Eve. "How happy were Adam and Eve! We love one another as well as they; but there is no silent and lovely garden of Eden for us." He speculated, however, that God might have reserved one for them since "the beginning of the world" (Daniel G. Hoffman, "Myth, Romance, and the Childhood of Man," *Hawthorne Centenary Essays*, edited by Roy

Harvey Pearce (Ohio State University Press, 1964), 197–219).

FOR FURTHER READING

Davidson, Frank, "Hawthorne's Hive of Honey," *Modern Language Notes* 61 (1946): 14–21; Dunne, Michael, "Natural and Imposed Order in Two Sketches by Hawthorne," *Nathaniel Hawthorne Journal* 8 (1978): 197–202.

"Night Sketches, beneath an Umbrella"

Unsigned sketch when first printed in *The New-Yorker* magazine, November 25, 1837. In 1839, the piece appeared in the *Salem Gazette* as "Night Sketches under an Umbrella. By N. Hawthorne."

The article begins as a meditation on a rainy day. Hawthorne recommends a book of travels as the best amusement for inclement weather, as it lends "distinct shapes and vivid colors to the objects which the author has spread upon his page. He can envision strange landscapes and outlandish figures." Such a book will conjure, for someone who cannot afford to travel, the mountains of Central Asia or an Oriental bazaar.

Unfortunately, with nightfall such visions vanish, and the reader may decide to take a walk. Outside he will find the remnant of a huge snowbank encumbering the sidewalk, or a wintry waste of mud and liquid filth, a veritable "Slough of Despond." In the town, rows of shops cast a glow beneath the canopy of the black night. He may meet a young couple en route to a cotillion, she in overshoes but he in dancing pumps.

The walker feels sorry for himself, without wife and children. He passes a stately mansion and hears sounds of music. At the edge of town, the mail coach, outward bound, splashes through the mud and water. A fearless man with a lantern made of pierced tin passes him, returning by the light of the lantern to his own fireside. He supplies the obligatory "moral" with which Hawthorne winds up his sketch, since he lacks a "more appropriate"

one. If he and his fellow night wanderers who pass through a stormy and dismal world "bear the lamp of Faith, enkindled at a celestial fire, it will surely lead us home to that Heaven whence its radiance was borrowed."

"Old Apple Dealer, The"

Sketch first published in *Sargent's New Monthly Magazine of Literature, Fashion, and the Fine Arts* in January 1843. It was reprinted in the *Salem Mercury* in December 1843 and collected in MOSSES FROM AN OLD MANSE.

The story opens with a description of an old man who sells gingerbread and apples at a railroad station. The narrator has studied him until he has become "a naturalized citizen" of his inner world, although the apple dealer would consider him a total stranger. He describes him as a "small man with gray hair and gray stubble beard," always wearing snuff-colored and gray clothes. He invariably looks cold, long-suffering, and pitiable.

He sits on a bench in the waiting room before two baskets. Between them stretches a board, on which are displayed cakes, gingerbread, apples, hard candy, and cracked walnuts. The apple dealer constantly rearranges his small stock of wares but has few customers. After a rare purchase is made, he rearranges his wares completely. The narrator speculates that in the past, he might have been a mechanic or tradesman. To his credit, he has never solicited charitable gifts or been driven to the almshouse.

When the train arrives, the customers spill from the railway cars, "full of the momentum which they have caught from their mode of conveyance." The narrator imagines the old dealer spending the "scanty coppers" he makes from his wares on more apples and more supplies to make more cakes and gingerbread. He speculates that he lacks enough individuality to be the object of his "own self-love," let alone that of the strangers about him. At the same time, he deduces that enough is written in his heart to form a deep and comprehensive volume. The "soundless depths of the human soul, and of eternity" have an "opening" through his breast, and he has a "spiritual essence" in his "gray and lean old shape."

RECEPTION AND CRITICAL ANALYSIS

In "Hawthorne and His Mosses" (1850; see Part IV), HERMAN MELVILLE quotes a sentence from the sketch that singles out those traits of the apple dealer that are enlarged in the version of the story published three years later. He praises Hawthorne's conception of the old apple dealer, observing that the character "is conceived in the subtlest spirit of sadness." He deduces that the apple dealer's "subdued and nerveless boyhood" points forward to his "abortive prime," which, in turn, contains a "prophecy and image of his lean and torpid age." He praises Hawthorne's insight, saying that the piece argues "such a depth of tenderness, such a boundless sympathy with all forms of being, such an omnipresent love, that we must needs say that this Hawthorne is here almost alone in his generation. . . . Such touches as these . . . furnish clues whereby we enter a little way into the intricate, profound heart where they originated."

Leo B. Levy speculates that Melville's first published story, "Bartleby the Scrivener," was inspired by Hawthorne's sketch. He argues that both works represent the "social and psychological consequences of a deprived and uncommunicative relationship to society." Both the sketch and the story depict a "microcosm of industrial-commercial America, with the central figure depicted against a background of profit and progress."

FOR FURTHER READING

Leo B. Levy, "Hawthorne and the Idea of Bartleby," *ESQ: A Journal of the American Renaissance* 47 (1967): 66–69.

"Old Esther Dudley"

Tale first published in the *UNITED STATES MAGAZINE AND DEMOCRATIC REVIEW* in January 1839, the fourth in a series with "HOWE'S MASQUERADE," "EDWARD RANDOLPH'S PORTRAIT," and "LADY ELEANORE'S MANTLE." The series was later published in the 1842 edition of *TWICE-TOLD TALES* under the title *LEGENDS OF THE PROVINCE-HOUSE*.

The narrator of the earlier legends recounts another tale, about Sir William Howe. Mr. Tiffany and Mr. Waite are all eager to hear the story of the "old loyalist." After another glass of wine, he looks into the fire and begins his narrative.

It opens at the "hour of defeat and humiliation" for Sir William Howe, who is leaving the Province-House and Massachusetts to return to England. He perceives that "the sway of Britain was passing forever from New England" and feels ashamed to be leaving a "dismembered empire"; he would have preferred to meet a "warrior's death" instead.

An aged woman, old Esther Dudley, sorrowfully bids him farewell. She is the descendant of an ancient family who had fallen into poverty, and she now has nominal duties at the Province-House, supervising the servants. There is a fable that she had entered the Province-House "in the train of the first Royal Governor, and that it was her fate to dwell there till the last should have departed."

Esther Dudley tells Howe that "Heaven's cause and the King's are one," and to "trust in Heaven to bring back a Royal Governor in triumph." Howe rebukes her, saying he is glad to be "the last in this mansion of the King." She has no other shelter, however, and Howe realizes that he cannot leave the "wretched old creature to starve or beg," so he gives her a purse full of golden guineas. She says she looks forward to his triumphant return. An emotional Howe asks whether she will leave and bid "farewell to a land that has shaken off its allegiance," but she obstinately refuses and says she will remain King George's "one true subject in his disloyal Province." Howe then leaves the Province-House in her care and gives her the key, to keep until he or some other royal governor should demand it.

Despite the departure of the British troops, the "venerable lady" is not driven from Province-House. The magistrates and subsequent governors do not object to her residence, since she assists with the care of the house. She lives on, year after year, remaining faithful to the king. This "undisturbed mistress of the old historic edifice" is thought, however, to have strange powers. There is a rumor that Esther Dudley is able to make the "governors of the overthrown dynasty," past "Indian chiefs," "grim Provincial warriors," and "severe clergymen" all reappear in an antique mirror in the mansion. Another rumor circulates that whenever she is lonely, she sends a black slave of Governor Shirley's to tombs and burial grounds, where he summons ghosts of long-ago guests to join her in the mansion at midnight. She also entertains the children of the town with gingerbread and games.

Living "continually in her own circle of ideas," she grows "partially crazed," however. She has "no right sense of the progress" of the Revolutionary War, holding a "constant faith that the armies of Britain were victorious" and "destined to be ultimately triumphant." Sometimes she believes the colonies are already "prostrate at the foot-stool of the King"; she would climb to the balcony, wearing her "mildewed velvets and brocades," to rejoice.

One day, she imagines a royal governor is arriving to receive the key to the Province-House given her by Sir William Howe. She goes into the countyard and meets a person of "gentle blood, high rank, and long-accustomed authority." Esther sinks down on her knees, offering the key, and says her "task in the Province-House, and on earth, is done," adding, "God save King George!" When the stranger replies that hers "is a strange prayer to be offered up at such a moment," Esther gazes at him with "fearful earnestness" and seems to recognize his face. It is actually the popularly elected governor Hancock of Massachusetts. The "heart-broken" old woman wonders whether she has "bidden a traitor welcome" and bids death to "come quickly."

Governor Hancock comforts her "with all the reverence that a courtier would have shown a queen," telling her that the world has changed around her, and that she is now a "symbol of the past." But although he represents a "new race of men" who project their lives "forward into the future," he tells his attendants that they should "reverence, for the last time, the stately and gorgeous prejudices of the tottering Past!"

Esther Dudley then sinks down to the ground, drops the key to the Province-House, says she has always been faithful to the king, and dies. Governor Hancock proclaims that they will "follow her reverently to the tomb of her ancestors" and then go "onward—onward! We are no longer children of the Past!"

The "old loyalist" finishes his narrative as the lamp fades and the fire dies down. The narrator compares the "lingering fire" to the way in which the "glory of the ancient system vanished from the Province-House, when the spirit of old Esther Dudley took its flight." As the Old South clock tolls the "hourly knell of the Past," they reflect on the "volume of history" told within the chambers of the Province-House.

"Old-Fashioned School, The"

This was the first edition and only printing of the volume. It contained a "Preface," a section of biographies entitled "Famous Old People," and the stories "The Old-fashioned School," "The Rejected Blessing," "The Provincial Muster," and "The Acadian Exiles."

"Old Maid in the Winding Sheet, The"

See "White Old Maid, The."

"Old News, No. I"

Unsigned sketch that appeared in the New-England Magazine, 8, in February 1835.

The narrator praises a small volume of what were once newspapers, "each on a small half-sheet, yellow and time-stained" and printed in a "rude old type." Instead of being ephemeral, as the original printer expected, they have acquired historical interest. The narrator conjures an image of the typical colonial reader, perhaps a prosperous merchant, earnestly poring over a speech by the king and looking carefully at the shipping news. Much of the paper is dull, written by an erudite clergyman or Cambridge professor.

He imagines New England in the time of King George II, a picturesque settlement on the edge of a vast forest. Unfortunately, it is subject to such afflictions as a smallpox epidemic and rigid Puritanism. Moreover, there is a brisk trade in "human commodities," or African slaves. The merchant wanders through the crooked streets of Boston, ordering gifts for his family and making arrangements to dispose of his cargo of wine and tobacco. He gives no thought to ordering a gravestone for himself. As the narrator turns over the volume, however, he seems to be wandering among the stones of a burial ground.

"Old News, No. II: The Old French War"

Unsigned sketch published in the NEW-ENGLAND MAGAZINE, 8, in March 1835.

A sequel to "OLD NEWS, NO. I," which was published in February 1835, this article continues Hawthorne's commentary on the characteristics of life and manners of colonial New England as deduced from a file of antique newspapers. The period under consideration is 20 years later than that in "OLD NEWS, NO. I."

The papers are now printed on whole sheets and contained in a larger folio. They are "stylish" and obviously issued in a metropolis known for its fashion and gaiety. The narrator assumes that the papers were spread out in British-style coffeehouses, perhaps on King Street, for "the perusal of the throng of officers" who might have been drinking wine in the establishment.

The content of the papers includes bulletins about the Prussian/Austrian war and the battles between England and France in the East Indies. Hawthorne satirizes the "travelled American . . . the ape of London foppery," who might have been wearing an embroidered coat, lace ruffles, and silk stockings. The articles, comprising "light literature," might have been by Fielding or Smollett. Significantly, they depict "newer manners and customs" that had superseded those of the Puritans, "even in their own city of refuge."

These imaginary readers appear to be pretending that New England itself is not their present home, but "merely a lodge in the wilderness, until the trouble of the times should be passed." Ironically, the old Puritans they despised would have subscribed to the same tenet. Even as the colonies gathered the strength that would "render them an independent republic," the wealthier classes were aspiring to form an "aristocracy, and ripening for hereditary rank."

The New England readers had been strongly affected by the conquest of Louisburg, on Cape Breton Island in Canada. Captured by New England in 1745, it was returned to France in 1748 but recaptured by the British in 1758. This victory was significant, confirming that New Englanders had "done a deed of history." The narrator applauds the details of their battles against the French but deplores the accounts of Indian atrocities directed at women and infants.

He is amazed to discover, in estate sale notices, mention of silk bed hangings, damask tablecloths, Turkish carpets, and "all things proper for a noble mansion." People dressed in silks, satins, gold brocade, and gold and silver lace, and they wore satin hats above their powdered hair. There were numerous carriages.

Sadly, a fire broke out on March 20, 1760, at the Brazen-Head in Cornhill, consuming nearly 400 buildings and essentially ending the opulent era of nostalgic attachment to England.

"Old News, No. III: The Old Tory"

Unsigned sketch first published in the NEW-ENGLAND, MAGAZINE 8, in May 1835.

The events take place 20 years after the period of intense fealty to Britain of loyal colonists, as depicted in "OLD NEWS, NO. II: The OLD FRENCH WAR." This was a period when "monarchical and aristocratic sentiments were at their highest."

The time is now in the middle of the American Revolution. The reader of the old newspapers is an "old, gray, withered, sour-visaged, threadbare sort of gentleman." He has grown too rigid mentally to change his opinions; he is Episcopalian, and he loves the king. When the British army was evacuated from Boston, sweeping away "the aristocracy of the colonies, the hereditary Englishmen," the writer remained to record his hostile impressions of the new era. He still secretly idolizes King George.

He is gazing at the "rebel newspaper" of the day. Even the sight of it provotees a "groan of spiteful lamentation." The emblem of joined heart and crown has been replaced by the depiction of a continental army officer holding the Declaration of Independence in one hand and a sword in the other. The actual paper used for the newspaper distresses him; it is of "rebel manufacture," thick and coarse, of a dingy blue color that is very difficult to read. He must wear gloves to handle it, for it is not fit for aristocratic fingers.

The paper is full of advertisements for land sales: Faithful loyalists have lost their patrimony. Virtual pirates are seizing and outfitting private ships. "Everything is French"—soldiers, sailors, milliners, dancing masters. Even coffeehouses, once considered British, must be "styled" American with an eagle above the door rather than the royal coat of arms. There are antiroyalist verses and advertisements for stolen cloaks and horses.

The writer laments the absence of the heart of the king, which had kept the people virtuous. He praises the active Tories who "clung to the losing side" in the Revolution and yielded their patrimonies for a pittance from the British. He cries, "Peace to the good old Tory!" These men were "greatly to be pitied, and often worthy of our sympathy." On the whole, his impressions of the revolutionary age are unpleasant, including the state of civil society and the war itself, "waged with the deadly hatred of fraternal enemies." In vain he searches for any "antique fashions" that actually lingered into the war of the Revolution.

"Old Ticonderoga"

First published in the *American Monthly Magazine* in February 1836 as "Old Ticonderoga: A Picture of the Past," this unsigned sketch was attributed to

Hawthorne when published in *The SNOW-IMAGE, AND OTHER TWICE-TOLD TALES* in 1852.

It is believed to be based on a journey Hawthorne made in either 1832 or 1833, although he only identifies himself as "The Story-Teller." Arlin Turner observes that Hawthorne himself recognized the symbolic value of his travels, which formed an archive he could use in creating imaginative literary materials. When using the materials later, however, he does not reveal himself as a traveler but veils his reactions, pretending to be, at various times, a disinterested observer (*Nathaniel Hawthorne*, 77).

In "Old Ticonderoga," however, so little is left of the ruins that he fuses layers of history, imagining scenes of war and peace and peopling the terrain with famous military figures. We see Arthur St. Clair, the Scottish-born major general who evacuated the fort before Burgoyne's advance, along with the British general John Burgoyne, who commanded the expedition from Canada against the American colonies, and others: Sir Robert Abercrombie, Lord William Howe, Baron Jeffrey Amherst, and the American Revolutionary soldier Ethan Allen.

"Old Woman's Tale, An"

Unsigned short story first published in the *Salem Gazette* in December 1830.

The anonymous narrator recollects an old woman, nearly a 100 years old, whom he had known in his childhood. She had lived in "the house where I was born" and was, perhaps, a servant. She spent each day crouched over the kitchen fire, "with her elbows on her knees and her feet in the ashes," telling him stories set in a village in the valley of the Connecticut River. Her narratives "possessed an excellence attributed neither to herself, nor to any single individual."

"Ontario Steamboat, An"

Sketch published in the *American Magazine of Useful and Entertaining Knowledge*, which Hawthorne edited from March to September 1836. The piece was collected in *Hawthorne as Editor* (Louisiana State University Press, 1941).

"Paradise of Children, The"

Story in A WONDER-BOOK FOR GIRLS AND BOYS, published in 1852, after Hawthorne's death. It is a retelling of the legend of Pandora.

Thousands of years ago, Pandora had been sent to be the "playfellow and helpmate" of another "father-less and motherless" child, Epimetheus. Upon entering Epimetheus's cottage, she sees a "great box" and asks what is in it. Epimetheus tells her its contents are a secret, to which he himself is not privy, and that she must ask no further questions.

At the time, the world was a different place. Everybody was a child, with no need for fathers or mothers, for "there was no danger, nor trouble of any kind." In this "pleasant life," there were "no labor to be done, no tasks to be studied," and the children never quarreled.

Every day, Pandora asks about the box, despite Epimetheus's efforts to distract her with "play with the other children" and with "ripe figs" and juicy grapes. One day, the increasingly peevish Pandora suggests he open the box, but his face shows "so much horror at the idea" that she becomes quiet.

She does ask how the box ended up in the cottage, to which Epimetheus replies that it was "left at the door . . . by a person who looked very smiling and intelligent," who wore an "odd kind of a cloak" and a cap with wings. His "curious staff" was carved with "two serpents twisting around" in a lifelike manner. Pandora recognizes the description of Quicksilver, who also brought her to the cottage. She speculates that he intended the box for her, and perhaps it holds dresses or toys or treats. Epimetheus insists, however, that they have no right to open the box until Quicksilver gives them permission to do so.

Epimetheus, tired of hearing about the box, goes out alone to amuse himself. Pandora is left by herself, admiring the beautiful box. One of the faces carved on its surface looks as though it might say,

"Do not be afraid, Pandora! What harm can there by in opening the box?"

Pandora decides to examine the "intricate knot of gold cord" that fastens the box, telling herself that she "need not open the box . . . even if the knot were untied." The narrator comments that it "might have been better for Pandora if she had had a little work to do, or anything to employ her mind upon, so as not to be so constantly thinking of this one subject." But back then, "children led so easy a life, before any Troubles came into the world, that they had really a great deal too much leisure."

Finally, her curiosity gets the better of her. She tries to lift the box, then unties the gold cord. Just as Epimetheus returns to the cottage, Pandora lifts the lid. He fails to stop her, for he, too, is curious. The cottage grows "dark and dismal," and a "sudden swarm of winged creatures" brushes past her. Epimetheus cries out in a "lamentable tone" that he has been stung by one of "a crowd of ugly little shapes, with bats' wings."

These creatures were "the whole family of earthly Troubles," including "evil Passions," "more than a hundred and fifty Sorrows," "Diseases, in a vast number," and "more kinds of Naughtiness than it would be of any use to talk about." They had been locked in the mysterious box "in order that the happy children of the world might never be molested by them," but Pandora and Epimetheus have failed to keep them safely locked away.

The children "fling open the doors and windows" to get rid of the Troubles, which quickly spread "all abroad." All the flowers now "droop and shed their leaves," and children who once seemed immortal grow older day by day.

The naughty Pandora and the sullen Epimetheus are still in their cottage when they hear a "gentle little tap" on the inside of the box lid. A "sweet little voice" asks to be let out. When the two children lift the lid, a "sunny and smiling little personage" emerges, "throwing a light wherever she went." The "fairy-like stranger" kisses Epimetheus where he has been stung, and Pandora on the forehead, and both children feel better immediately. She identifies herself as "Hope," whose destiny is "to make amends to the human race for that swarm of ugly Troubles." She says she will never desert them, even when they think she has "utterly vanished." The children promise to trust her, and since then everybody has trusted Hope.

The narrator confides that he "cannot help being glad" that Pandora opened the box, for despite the Troubles "flying about the world," that "lovely and lightsome little figure of Hope . . . spiritualizes the earth" and "makes it always new; and, even in the earth's best and brightest aspect, Hope shows it to be only the shadow of an infinite bliss hereafter!"

"Passages from a Relinquished Work"

Title of an unsigned story collected in NEW-ENG-LAND MAGAZINE in November 1834.

The speaker is the ward of a village parson, named "Parson Thumpcushion" because of the "very forcible gestures" with which he illustrates his doctrines. The narrator describes these gestures as marked by "pounding and expounding," "slapping with his open palm," and "banging with the whole weight of the great Bible."

The narrator refers to himself as a "gay and happy" youth, "wayward and fanciful," admitting that he does not have a suitable nature to become the ward of his guardian, possessed of the "stern old Pilgrim spirit." He values idleness, and that sets him apart from other men in New England. He makes matters worse by not studying medicine, law, or religion or opening a store or embracing farming. He exercises his "narrative faculty" by becoming a wandering storyteller.

He begins by traveling about almost at random, until one day he sees, near a spring, a young man about his own age who offers to share his loaf of bread and cheese. They continue walking on together. The narrator has yet to appear before an audience but continues to think of stories, storing their plots and characters in his memory.

After several months, the two arrive at a country town where a company is giving a series of "dramatic exhibitions." The narrator makes up bills announcing "the celebrated Story Teller" and rambles through the town. The storyteller then finds Eliakim, his fellow traveler, leading a prayer group in a schoolhouse. After this, he gathers an audience and begins the story of "MR. HIGGINBOTHAM'S CATASTROPHE," which follows "Passages from a Relinquished Work."

Peter Parley's Universal History on the Basis of Geography

A dictionary of geography written with SAMUEL GOODRICH, edited by Hawthorne with his sister Elizabeth. It was published in 1837 in two volumes by the American Stationers' Company, Boston. Both title pages had illustrations, and there were maps and engravings throughout. The *Universal History* would appear in many editions in the ensuing years (Turner, *Nathaniel Hawthorne: A Biography,* passim).

Hoeltje points out that the Peter Parley books pioneered a revision in writing for children. Whereas the Mother Goose rhymes were frequently "coarse and vulgar," presenting children with a distorted idea of the meaning of books, the Peter Parley books aimed to teach "the lessons of charity, piety, and virtue"; such works would displace the violence of stories like "Jack the Giant-Killer" and "Puss in Boots."

This was Hawthorne's first book for children. In these volumes as well as in A WONDER-BOOK FOR GIRLS AND BOYS, he wished to "purge out all the old heathen wickedness and put in a moral wherever practical" (Turner, *Nathaniel Hawthorne: A Biography,* 233). Hawthorne wrote to his sister Elizabeth, after he began the Universal History, that "it need not be superior in profundity and polish." He went so far as to envision a new type of literature for the young and even considered the prospect of devoting himself to writing for children (Hoeltje, *Inward Sky: The Mind and Heart of Nathaniel Hawthorne,* 106–107).

"Pomegranate-seeds, The"

A retelling of the myth of Proserpina and Ceres, the story was first included in TANGLEWOOD TALES FOR GIRLS AND BOYS, published in Boston by Ticknor, Reed, and Fields in 1853. It was advertised in the Athenaeum. The volume also included "The Wayside: Introductory," "The MINOTAUR," "The PYGMIES," "The DRAGON'S TEETH," "CIRCE'S PALACE," and "The GOLDEN FLEECE."

In the story, Mother Ceres is very busy with her crops. Her daughter Proserpina asks whether she may play with the sea nymphs while Ceres is away. Her mother gives permission but warns her not to stray or wander about the fields alone. The sea nymphs give Proserpina beautiful shells and make them into a necklace for her. To show her gratitude, she wishes to gather flowers in the fields to make into wreaths for her playmates. The sea nymphs are afraid to go upon dry land, however, for they must keep themselves "comfortably moist." Proserpina decides to run and gather flowers by herself while the sea nymphs wait by the water.

She strays farther and farther into the fields in search of the "freshest and loveliest blossoms," until she sees a large shrub "covered with the most magnificent flowers in the world." She plans to pull up the shrub and plant it in her mother's garden. After pulling and pulling "with all her might," she finally loosens the plant from the soil. The hole that is left spreads wider and wider, however, and grows deeper and deeper. Proserpina hears "the tramp of horses' hoofs and the rattling of wheels," and soon a "team of four sable horses" drawing a "splendid golden chariot" leap from the "bottomless hole." In the chariot is a noble man wearing rich clothing and a crown but looking "sullen and discontented."

He beckons Proserpina to go for a ride, but she is frightened by his "deep and stern" voice, which sounds like the "rumbling of an earthquake." The stranger grabs her and takes her into the chariot. He tells her his name is Pluto, "king of diamonds and all other precious stones." Proserpina cries to go home, but Pluto says he needs a "merry little maid" to cheer up his palace rooms.

They pass Pluto's "faithful mastiff," Cerberus, the three-headed dog, and enter his kingdom, where there are "rich veins of gold" among the rocks and "sparkling gems" along the road. The palace is "splendidly illuminated" with precious stones, but still there is a "kind of gloom" pervading it. The narrator suggests that Pluto has stolen away Proserpina because he has never been happy in the "tiresome magnificence" of his palace and desires "something to love."

Meanwhile, Ceres discovers Proserpina is missing. On her search, she comes upon one of the flowers from the shrub Proserpina had pulled up. Ceres recognizes "mischief in this flower," for it is the "work of enchantment." She meets Hecate, a melancholy dog-headed woman, who tells her she heard the shrieks of a young girl being carried away. Ceres seeks assistance from Phoebus, a "beautiful young man" who plays a lyre and seems to always sit in the sunshine. He says Proserpina was "snatched up by King Pluto, and carried off to his dominions."

Six months pass as Ceres searches for the entrance to Pluto's kingdom. In her despair, she decides that nothing shall grow until she has Proserpina back. The farmers and cattle and sheep are all suffering, but Ceres cannot be dissuaded.

In the meantime, Proserpina has been kept prisoner in Pluto's kingdom, where she has vowed she will "not taste a mouthful of food as long as she should be compelled to remain." Pluto tempts her with fancy treats, but she remembers her mother's warnings about the "hurtfulness of these things." Although she is a captive, Proserpina is "not quite so unhappy as you may have supposed." She plays with the many beautiful objects in the palace and seems to carry "nature and sunshine along with her." In her presence, the palace is not so dismal and gloomy.

Pluto wishes she would like him "a little better," and when she senses how lonesome he is, she is "smitten with a kind of pity." He asks again whether she is hungry, but he has a "cunning purpose"—for if she tastes "a morsel of food in his dominions, she would never afterwards be at liberty to quit them." Proserpina replies that she misses only her mother's bread and the fruit from her garden, so Pluto decides to send an attendant to fetch some fruit from the upper world. However, because Ceres has "forbidden any fruits or vegetables to grow," the servant finds just a single, dried-up pomegranate, which he presents to Proserpina on a golden tray.

When she sees the promegranate, she vows not to eat it but cannot resist taking a bite of the first fruit she has seen in Pluto's palace. Just then, Pluto and Quicksilver enter the room; the latter has been sent to Pluto to persuade him to "undo the mischief he had done." Proserpina immediately removes the fruit from her mouth, but Quicksilver notices that she has taken "a sly nibble of something or other." Pluto tells her that "a great many misfortunes have befallen innocent people" because of his actions, and he has decided to free her.

As Proserpina leaves Pluto, she feels "some regrets, and a good deal of compunction for not telling him about the pomegranate." But Quicksilver hurries her away, advising her not to say anything of what she has eaten. As she makes her way, the path grows "verdant behind and on either side of her," and the grass and grain begin to "sprout with tenfold vigor and luxuriance." She flings herself "upon her mother's bosom" with joy.

Ceres asks her daughter whether she tasted any food in Pluto's palace. Proserpina confesses that after six months of resisting, that very day she had bitten into a pomegranate. She did not swallow any, but six of the seeds remained in her mouth. Ceres exclaims in misery that for each seed, she must spend one month of every year in Pluto's kingdom. Proserpina assures her mother that "poor King Pluto" has "some very good qualities," and that although he did wrong in carrying her off, she "can bear to spend six months in his palace" and take "comfort in making him so happy."

"Procession on Life, The"

Essay published in the *UNITED STATES MAGAZINE AND DEMOCRATIC REVIEW*, 12, no. 59 (April 1843), signed "By Nathaniel Hawthorne." It was reprinted in the *SALEM GAZETTE* the same month, signed "By Nathaniel Hawthorne. From the *Democratic Review*."

This is an allegorical essay, in which the narrator sorts people into such categories as disease, sorrow, and crime, rather than into divisions based on occupations, achievements, or social or civic rank.

Brenda Wineapple observes that the essay reflects Hawthorne's "deep, pervasive pessimism originating . . . in his perception of himself as an outsider." His world was, as she puts it, one of "hard angles" (*Hawthorne: A Life,* 172).

"Prophetic Pictures, The"

Story first published in *The TOKEN AND ATLANTIC SOUVENIR* for 1837, unsigned. It was included in the first collection of *TWICE-TOLD TALES,* in 1837, and in later editions of Hawthorne's works. The story is considered to be a forerunner of "The ARTIST OF THE BEAUTIFUL."

Hawthorne provides a note about the story's source and composition date. The story was suggested by "an anecdote of Stuart, related in Dunlap's History of the Arts of Design—a most entertaining book to the general reader, and a deeply interesting one, we should think, to the artist." The painter Gilbert Stuart was a prototype for the nameless artist. William Dunlap, in his *History of the Rise and Progress of the Arts of Design in the United States,* includes an anecdote about Stuart's painting of General Phipps, brother of Lord Mulgrave. When it was finished, Lord Mulgrave exclaimed, "I see insanity in that face." General Phipps went to India and committed suicide as a result of insanity. Stuart, thus, was an able portrait painter, diving into the recesses of his subject's mind.

As the story opens, a woman named Elinor and her lover, Walter Ludlow, are discussing an artist who "not only excels in his peculiar art, but possesses vast acquirements in all other learning and science." He is a "polished gentleman" and a "true cosmopolite." Even more worthy of admiration, he is able to adapt himself to various characters so that all men and all women are mirrored in the painter's depictions of people. He paints his subject's mind and heart, and not just his or her features; he "catches the secret sentiments and passions, and throws them upon the canvas." Elinor displays great distress, as she will be sitting for the artist.

The artist "had been born and educated in Europe." In America, he searched for faces that were "the index of any thing uncommon, in thought, sentiment, or experience." His subjects had to be interesting to him for him to paint them. Some people believed him to be a magician.

The next day, Walter and Elinor visit this particular artist to have their portrait painted on the eve of their marriage. In his apartment, they see portraits of many prominent men, including Governor Burnett, Mr. Cooke, John Winslow, and various religious figures. They gaze at "three old pictures," including one of their own minister, the Reverend Dr. Colman.

The painter agrees to paint the couple, who are like "living pictures of youth and beauty, gladdened by bright fortune." He wishes to do both portraits in one picture, but because that would require a large piece of canvas, he decides to paint "two half-length portraits" instead. After they leave the apartment, Walter warns Elinor that the old women of Boston believe that the painter is known to produce prophetic pictures, no matter what the act or situation in which he paints his subject.

When the painter finishes, he looks at them with a "penetrative eye" and says "these two pictures will be my very best performances." At the "appointed hour," Walter and Elinor hurry to view the completed works. They enter the studio and at first glance utter a "simultaneous exclamation of delight," as Walter enthuses that they are "fixed in sunshine forever." After a closer look, however, both are alarmed. Walter, "doubtful and meditative," believes that Elinor's portrait has been altered since the day before, and that she now has a "strangely sad and anxious expression" of "grief and terror." When he looks at Elinor, he sees that she has changed and looks exactly like her portrait. Elinor suggests that Walter's portrait has also changed; it now has a "livelier expression," as if "some bright thought were flashing from the eyes." The painter declares that he is a "true artist," who "must look beneath the exterior." He quietly shows Elinor a "crayon sketch" he has made of two figures, which makes a "thrill" run through her.

After their marriage, Walter and Elinor hang their pictures side by side in their home. Some guests see a "look of earnest import" in Walter's portrait, and a "gloom" in Elinor's. One person suggests that the "melancholy strength" in Elinor's bears reference to the "wild passion" in Walter's.

Months later, the painter visits the couple. He thinks his portraits reveal a "fearful secret." When he enters their home, he sees that Elinor wears a look of "quiet anguish," whereas Walter is under a "spell of evil influence." Suddenly, Walter cries, "Our fate is upon us! Die!" and aims a knife at her bosom. The artist intervenes, saying, "Hold, madman!" He asks Elinor whether he had not warned her. Elinor admits that he did but says she loved Walter.

The narrator asks whether the "deep moral" of the tale is that if "all our deeds" were "shadowed forth and set before us, some would call it Fate," while others would be "swept along by their passionate desires." None would be turned aside by the "Prophetic Pictures."

FOR FURTHER READING

Bell, Millicent, *Hawthorne's View of the Artist* (New York: New York State University Press, 1962), 68–69; Dichmann, Mary E., "Hawthorne's Prophetic Pictures," *American Literature* 23 (1951): 188–202; Doubleday, Neal Frank, *Hawthorne's Early Tales: A Critical Study* (Durham, N.C.: Duke University Press, 1972), 109; Lundblad, Jane, *Nathaniel Hawthorne and the European Literary Tradition* (Cambridge, Mass.: Harvard University Press, 1947), 100; Valenti, Patricia D., "Viewing 'The Prophetic Pictures' during Its First One Hundred and Fifty Years," *National Hawthorne Review* 13, no. 2 (fall 1987): 13–15.

"Provincial Muster, The"

Short story collected in *FAMOUS OLD PEOPLE*, 1841. This volume was published by E. P. Peabody, 13 West Street, Boston, in 1841. ELIZABETH PALMER PEABODY, sister of SOPHIA PEABODY HAWTHORNE, would become Hawthorne's sister-in-law in 1842.

This was the first edition and only printing of the volume. It contained a "Preface," a section of biographies entitled "Famous Old People," and several other stories, including "The OLD-FASHIONED SCHOOL," "The REJECTED BLESSING," and "The ACADIAN EXILES."

The first volume in the trilogy was GRANDFATHER'S CHAIR: A HISTORY FOR YOUTH, published December 3, 1840. The second, FAMOUS OLD PEOPLE, was probably published on January 18, 1941; the final one, LIBERTY TREE, completed the trilogy in March 1841.

"Provincial Tales"

Unpublished collection of tales. In the 1820s and 1830s, Hawthorne tried to call the attention of the public to his stories. The publication of "Provincial Tales" would have been his third attempt, although they were never published in a single volume.

Elizabeth Chandler and Nelson F. Adkins suggest that at least six titles would have been included: "The GENTLE BOY," "ROGER MALVIN'S BURIAL," "MY KINSMAN, MAJOR MOLINEUX," "The GRAY CHAMPION," "The MAY-POLE OF MERRY MOUNT," and "YOUNG GOODMAN BROWN" (quoted by Adams, Richard P., "Hawthorne's *Provincial Tales*, 39–40). The six tales, according to Adams, all deal with "the transition from childishness to adolescence to maturity." It was in these tales, even though they were published separately in various periodicals, that Hawthorne began "to establish himself . . . as a romantic artist of the highest rank" (Adams, 57).

"P.'s Correspondence"

A sketch published in the UNITED STATES MAGAZINE AND DEMOCRATIC REVIEW in April 1845. In 1846, it was collected in MOSSES FROM AN OLD MANSE. The reviewer of *Mosses* in GRAHAM'S MAGAZINE termed the sketch "one of the most ingenious and striking of all Hawthorne's works" (unsigned

review in *Graham's Magazine*, November 1854; reprinted in *Nathaniel Hawthorne: The Critical Heritage*, 305). It takes the form of a description, supposedly by a half-madman, of many celebrated 19th-century figures, conjured as a mixture of the dead and the living.

The narrator begins by stating that his "unfortunate friend P." has lost the thread of his life by having long intervals of "partially disordered reason." In his mind the past and present are mixed, and he imagines that he is traveling, although he never leaves his "little whitewashed, iron-grated room." "P." does not see this affliction as a "delusion," but as an "involuntary sport of the imagination."

The narrator presents a letter from "P." dated February 29, 1845, purportedly from London. "P." admits that he is writing from his little room, though he claims to travel. He is, in fact, a "prisoner of Memory." He pretends to have met Lord Byron, not as a young poet (Byron died of malaria at the age of 36), but as a man of nearly 60, obese and wearing a wig. His "morals have been improving while his outward man has swollen to . . . unconscionable circumference." He also meets Robert Burns, who is 87; Burns tells him that Sir Walter Scott is still alive but is a "hopeless paralytic" who vegetates from "day to day."

"P." goes on to claim that he has encountered Napoléon Bonaparte, who is only skin and bones, attended by two policeman to guard against the theft of his star of the Legion of Honor (a supreme French decoration). Other famous figures who rise up in his imagination are the poets Percy Bysshe Shelley, Samuel Coleridge, William Wordsworth, and John Keats, as well as a number of famous actors. He mentions knowing the American poets James Greenleaf Whittier, a "fiery Quaker youth"; Henry Wadsworth Longfellow; and others. He concludes by pleading with his friend to answer him when he can and tells him to expect him home soon in the company of the poet Campbell, who wishes to visit Wyoming.

The reader may be frustrated by the fact that Hawthorne focuses very little on the narrator, except to say, in the beginning, that he takes a "pious pleasure" in editing the letters "for the public eye." The essay reveals Hawthorne's extensive knowledge of English literature, and his powers of invention in "aging" the literary figures he conjures in accordance with their known traits and youthful physical lineaments.

"Pygmies, The"

Story first published in TANGLEWOOD TALES FOR GIRLS AND BOYS: BEING A SECOND WONDER-BOOK (London: Chapman and Hall, 1853). C. E. Fraser Clark Jr., editor of Nathaniel Hawthorne: A Descriptive Bibliography, states that Ticknor and Fields allowed Chapman and Hall to publish the book before they did, in order to protect the English copyright. It was published the same year in Boston by Ticknor, Reed, and Fields.

In the story, an "earth-born Giant," named Antaeus, and a million "little earth-born people," called Pygmies, dwell together in a friendly manner in the middle of Africa. The narrator describes the many ways that Antaeus and the Pygmies help each other; for instance, Antaeus has gone to the Pygmies' assistance in their constant battles against the cranes, who sometimes swallow the little people alive.

One day, another Giant appears. Antaeus demands to know his name and what he wants. The stranger quietly and politely introduces himself as Hercules, on his way to the garden of the Hesperides "to get three of the golden apples for King Eurystheus." Antaeus blocks his way, for he hates Hercules because he is "said to be so strong." He strikes Hercules with a "monstrous blow" of his pine tree, but Hercules, "being more skilful than Antaeus," strikes back and makes him fall "flat upon the ground." Although the Giant is incredibly strong, Hercules is wiser and has already given thought to how to conquer him.

Meanwhile, the Pygmies have been shrieking and wailing as their city is destroyed by the fighting and as their friend, Antaeus, is defeated by Hercules. Hercules pays them no mind, however, and soon falls asleep, "weary with his exertions in the fight." Once he is asleep, the Pygmies plot to destroy him. The troops gather "sticks, straws, dry weeds, and whatever combustible stuff they could

find," piling it around Hercules's head. As soon as the "inflammatory matter" bursts into flames, Hercules sits up in bewilderment. At that moment, 20,000 archers let fly their arrows directly into Hercules's face, but no more than half a dozen are able to puncture his tough skin. After Hercules puts out the fire, he picks up a Pygmy and asks what the "little fellow" is. The "valiant Pygmy" declares they are his enemy, avenging their brother Antaeus.

Hercules bursts into laughter and declares the Pygmy "a wonder that outdoes them all." He is "touched with the little man's dauntless courage" and cannot help but acknowledge "such a brotherhood with him as one hero feels for another." He explains that he does not intend "intentional injury to such brave fellows" and promises to leave their kingdom at once. Laughing, he says, "For once, Hercules acknowledges himself vanquished."

The narrator suggests that today, in the Pygmies' "little histories of ancient times," it may be recorded that "a great many centuries ago, the valiant Pygmies avenged the death of the Giant Antaeus by scaring away the mighty Hercules."

"Rappaccini's Daughter"

Short story first published in the UNITED STATES MAGAZINE AND DEMOCRATIC REVIEW in December 1844 and collected in MOSSES FROM AN OLD MANSE in 1846, when it lacked the preface to the tale. The preface was inserted again in the 1854 edition for Ticknor, Reed, and Fields. It is thought that the preface might have been deleted because it alluded to JOHN O'SULLIVAN, a friend, and the DEMOCRATIC REVIEW. At that time, Hawthorne needed a political appointment to relieve his serious financial situation. In 1849, he lost his much-needed job at the Custom-House on the grounds of certain literary reviews for the Salem Democratic newspaper.

The tale concerns Giovanni Guasconti, a young man who has traveled from the south of Italy to study at the University of Padua. He takes lodgings in a "high and gloomy chamber of an old edifice," which looks down on a neighboring garden. The old housekeeper, Dame Lisabetta, explains that the garden belongs to Signor Giacomo Rappaccini, a "famous doctor" who is said to transform the plants into potent medicines.

Giovanni later watches from the window as Dr. Rappaccini examines the flowers and shrubbery with detached curiosity. The doctor is a "tall, emaciated, sallow, and sickly-looking man" with a face "marked with intellect and cultivation," but lacking "warmth of heart." His demeanor is "that of one walking among malignant influences, such as savage beasts, or deadly snakes, or evil spirits" that might injure him. He places a mask over his mouth and nostrils when he approaches one magnificent plant with purple blooms. Rappaccini then calls his beautiful daughter, Beatrice, out of the house to help him. To Giovanni, she is like a rare, but unapproachable flower. She is "redundant with life, health, and energy." Her father asks her to care for a plant that, as Giovanni has perceived, he himself has carefully avoided. There are other poisonous flowers in the garden, which the narrator describes as creeping "serpent-like along the ground."

The next morning, as he gazes down, the garden looks normal and bright to him. He calls on a professor of medicine at the university, Signor Pietro Baglioni, an old friend of his father, to whom he has a letter of introduction. Giovanni mentions Dr. Rappaccini, but Signor Baglioni tells him that Rappaccini prefers science to human life. His patients are interesting to him only as "subjects for some new experiment," and he would "sacrifice human life" or "whatever else was dearest to him" for the sake of knowledge. Rappaccini is thought to be developing new varieties of harmful "vegetable poisons." When Giovanni asks about his beautiful daughter, he learns that she is considered her father's intellectual and scientific equal and is greatly respected and admired in Padua.

After Giovanni returns to his lodgings, with a stop at the florist for a bouquet of flowers, he conceals himself near the window and sees Beatrice walking in the garden. She not only is beautiful and intelligent but also wears an expression of "simplicity and sweetness." She seems to resemble the magnificent shrub he has seen her father inspecting. She embraces the shrub and breathes its aroma, then plucks one of its purple "gemlike flowers" to

place beside her heart. Suddenly, a drop of moisture from the flower falls on the head of a small lizard on the garden path; it dies immediately. Beatrice sees this, sadly makes the sign of the cross, and arranges the flower on her bosom. As Giovanni watches in horror, a beautiful insect flies near her and then falls to the ground and dies.

Beatrice looks up at the window and sees Giovanni. He throws down his bouquet and asks her to wear the flowers "for the sake of Giovanni Guasconti." She thanks him, gathers the bouquet he has thrown down, and disappears into the house. He imagines that his bouquet has already begun to "wither in her grasp." Over the following days, Giovanni realizes he has fallen under the influence of Beatrice and should leave Padua but cannot bring himself to do so. She has installed "a fierce and subtle poison into his system," which is neither "love" nor "horror," but a "wild offspring" of both.

He walks through Padua as in a dream, trying to calm himself, and encounters Professor Baglioni, who insists on speaking to him. As they talk, a stooping man in black, his face looking "sickly and sallow," approaches along the street. It is Dr. Rappaccini, who inspects Giovanni as he passes. Professor Baglioni realizes that he is looking at Giovanni with the same cold gaze of study with which he has examined a bird, a mouse, or a butterfly he has killed. He believes Giovanni is now the subject of one of Rappaccini's experiments. He resolves to rescue him.

With Lisabetta's help, Giovanni gains admission to Dr. Rappaccini's garden through a "private entrance." He examines the shrubs and finds them all "fierce, passionate, and even unnatural"; several have an "appearance of artificialness" indicating they are "no longer of God's making, but the monstrous offspring of man's depraved fancy, glowing with only an evil mockery of beauty." Beatrice enters but claims she knows little about the plants. Giovanni is unsure whether the "fragrance in the atmosphere around her" is the poisonous odor of the flowers or the essence of her heart. He seems to gaze through her eyes into "her transparent soul" and ceases doubting her.

Beatrice then becomes gay and cheerful. She asks many questions and confides that she knows nothing of life beyond the garden. Giovanni realizes she is almost like an infant in her experience of the world. They stroll through the garden and walk near the powerful fragrant plant he has noticed before. She apologizes to the plant for having momentarily forgotten it. He asks whether he may pluck a blossom from it, but as he moves to do so, she shrieks and draws his hand back, screaming that "it is fatal." She hides her face and flees inside the house. Giovanni sees Dr. Rappaccini, who has apparently been watching them, in "the shadow of the entrance."

Back in his lodgings, Giovanni passionately visualizes Beatrice. He wakes in the morning with a burning, agonizing sensation in his right hand, "the very hand which Beatrice had grasped in her own when he was on the point of plucking one of the gemlike flowers." On the back of his hand, there is a purple print of her hand. He wraps a handkerchief about it and continues to think of her. They continue meeting in the garden, Giovanni descending from his quarters into "that Eden of poisonous flowers." They look at each other with love, but Beatrice is still reserved. When he imagines touching her, "horrible suspicions" rise, "monster-like," from his heart, that she is not the "beautiful and unsophisticated girl" he feels he knows.

Professor Baglioni calls on him one morning, but Giovanni does not confide in him, lest he be criticized. Baglioni tells him of the legend of an Indian prince who sent a beautiful woman as a present to Alexander the Great. She has a rich perfume in her breath, and Alexander falls in love with her. A physician then discovers a dreadful secret: her breath is poisonous. Giovanni calls this a "childish fable," but Baglioni detects a faint disagreeable fragrance emanating from Giovanni's hand. Baglioni warns him that "the fair and learned Signora Beatrice" might administer medicines to her patients, but "'woe to him that sips them!'" He then discloses that she is "as poisonous as she is beautiful." Her father has experimented with her and has obviously chosen Giovanni as another subject.

Baglioni then lays a silver vase on the table, made by the famous artist Benvenuto Cellini. He says it contains an antidote to the poison, and, if he gives it to Beatrice, she will be cured. Giovanni decides to test Beatrice and buys a bouquet from a florist. To his alarm, they begin to droop from his touch. He realizes he has poisoned breath when he breathes on a spider and it dies. Beatrice calls him from the garden and tells him her father created the shrub with the gemlike blossoms. She grew up with the plant, the "offspring of his science," and it is her sister. But she has been subjected to an "awful doom"—her father's passion for science has alienated her from all social interactions. She is "estranged" from "all society" and has no friends. He accuses her of drawing him into her "region of unspeakable horror," of filling his "veins with poison" and turning him into "as hateful, as ugly, as loathesome and deadly a creature" as she—a "world's wonder of hideous monstrosity." She moans and begins to pray to the Holy Virgin. He mocks her piety and shows that he has gained her power; he breathes on a swarm of insects and many of them die.

When she realizes the truth, she shrieks that it is her "father's fatal science," and that she "dreamed only to love" him. "Not for a world of bliss would I have done it," she says. Giovanni now believes he and Beatrice share a bitter solitude. He hopes to save her by means of the potion in the silver vial, and she begins to drink just as Rappaccini draws near. He has a "triumphant expression" like that of an "artist who should spend his life in achieving a picture or a group of statuary and finally be satisfied." He spreads his hands out in a blessing and tells them they need not fear her "sister shrub." Giovanni now "stands apart from common men," while Beatrice should be grateful for the "marvellous gifts" he has given her. She is as "terrible" as she is "beautiful," unlike a "weak woman, exposed to all evil and capable of none."

Beatrice replies that she would rather have been "loved, not feared." Her father's experiment has been a "miserable doom." For her, "poison had been life, so the powerful antidote was death." She dies "at the feet of her father and Giovanni." Professor Baglioni witnesses the scene from the window and shouts, in "a tone of triumph mixed with horror," "'Rappaccini! Rappaccini! and is *this* the upshot of your experiment!'"

CRITICAL ANALYSIS

Hawthorne recorded the germ of the story in his notebook between October 27, 1841, and January 23, 1842: "To symbolize moral or spiritual disease of the body:—thus, when a person committed any sin, it might cause a sore to appear on the body;—this to be wrought out." He also noted a legend about persons who inoculated themselves with snake venom and were then immune to snakebites. Beatrice follows this pattern of inoculation, immunization, and contagion. She is externally beautiful but is, in fact, poisonous.

It is thought that the story may have had its origin in a book by Madame Calderon de la Barca, *Life in Mexico.* In his notebook, Hawthorne observed that she speaks of persons who have been inoculated with the venom of rattlesnakes, which protects them from the power of venomous reptiles. Their own bite, however, becomes poisonous to persons not inoculated.

There is much ambiguity in the story, particularly in the representation of science. The two scientists are admirable to some degree. Rappaccini is devoted to science, and his experiments are intended to protect his daughter. Baglioni is concerned about the welfare of his old friend's son, Giovanni. Both fail, however, in their mission. Rappaccini misjudges what will give Beatrice happiness, and Baglioni's interference brings about her death.

The story was written, apparently, between mid-October and mid-November of 1844. According to Hawthorne's son Julian, when he read the unfinished manuscript to Sophia, she asked, "But how is it to end? Is Beatrice to be a demon or an angel?" Hawthorne confessed to his wife that he had no idea. Some critics are convinced that Beatrice's dilemma reflects the sheltered years Sophia endured at the hands of her overly solicitous mother; she was regarded as a semiinvalid and treated as one by her mother.

Randall Stewart suggests that Beatrice belongs to a group of women depicted by Hawthorne "whose nature is marked by a certain exotic richness." Others in this group include Hester Prynne in *The* SCARLET LETTER, Miriam in *The* MARBLE FAUN, and Zenobia in *The* BLITHEDALE ROMANCE. These women have a rare intellectual ability. Beatrice, for example, is described as "already qualified to fill a professor's chair." Dr. Rappaccini himself is characteristic of Hawthorne's devils and wizards. He is past middle age and has gray hair and a thin gray beard. He moves feebly, often in a "stooping" position. His face is "sickly and sallow," yet, at the same time, is "pervaded with an expression of piercing and active intellect." His eyes have a "strange, penetrating power" ("The Development of Character Types in Hawthorne's Fiction," *The American Notebooks* [1932], li–lix).

The story has echoes of Spenser's *Faerie Queene:* Beatrice and her unnatural garden parallel the dangerous Acrasis and the luxuriant Bower of Bliss. Other echoes are found in the sculptured doorway, the central fountain of pure water, and the erotic plants. Other literary influences on Hawthorne's tale may have been Keats's *Lania,* Shelley's *The Cenci,* and Mary Shelley's *Frankenstein.* In addition, Erasmus Darwin's account of the Upas tree in *The Botanical Garden* is a possible source.

Among Hawthorne's own works, the story has with some frequency been linked to "The BIRTH-MARK," which was published a year earlier; there are structural and thematic similarities in these two stories. For example, in both tales, a beautiful young woman is portrayed as the victim of a misguided scientist who purports to love her (Newman, *Hawthorne's Short Stories,* 258–259). In the case of "Rappaccini's Daughter," Beatrice's flaw is her poison; in the case of "The BIRTH-MARK," Georgiana's birthmark is her flaw. Both flaws are integral to the heroines and indeed turn out to be essential for life. In the case of Beatrice, her touch is the manifestation of her flaw. Here there is a symbol of sexuality, as there is in the case of Georgiana, whose hand-shaped birthmark is the external emblem of her flaw.

William E. Grant notes that monomania, or obsession, was an "enduring interest" of Hawthorne's. Three stories from MOSSES FROM AN OLD MANSE present "some of his best treatments of monomaniacal characters who bring about their own downfalls and frequently those of people closest to them" by pursuing "ideals that lead them to try to improve nature." Science is the "instrument through which such alterations of nature are undertaken" in this story as well as in "The Birth-Mark," while art serves a similar role in "The ARTIST OF THE BEAUTIFUL." Because both the scientist and the artist are "objects of suspicion" for Hawthorne, they share similar characteristics.

Richard Fogle calls the story the most difficult of Hawthorne's tales. Many critics have commented on it, and few would disagree as to its complexities, with varying estimates of the main characters as either reprehensible or heroic, ideal or grotesque.

Arlin Turner observes that Hawthorne later claimed he had written no important works during his years at the Manse in Concord, but only "a few tales and essays, which had blossomed out like flowers in the calm summer" of his heart and mind. Among them, however, were "The Birth-Mark" and "RAPPACCINI'S DAUGHTER," which were "among his best, and forecast the full-scale romances to come from his pen later" (*Nathaniel Hawthorne: A Biography*, 164).

This tale points up the variation in perspective between that of the detached scientist, Dr. Rappaccini, his beautiful daughter, Beatrice, and her naive would-be lover, Giovanni Guasconti. Rappaccini calls on Beatrice to touch the plants in the garden, if needed; she has an enviable intimacy with them. One reason is that she has been vaccinated against them, in a sense. She can handle them without harm and calls the most exotic and poisonous plant in the garden her "sister." She is both beautiful and terrible and has qualities of goodness and toxicity about her that Giovanni does not comprehend. Nancy Bunge argues that the tale turns on the human tragedy created by intellectual arrogance (*Nathaniel Hawthorne*, 70–71).

CHARACTERS

Guasconti, Giovanni Hero of "Rappaccini's Daughter." He is a "beautiful young man" from the south of Italy. He has gone to the city to study at the University of Padua and promptly falls under the spell of Beatrice Rappaccini.

Some critics believe that Hawthorne consulted Sophia about the names in the tale, since she had studied Italian as a girl. These names are significant: The word *guastaconti* means "a meddler into affairs." It is an appropriate choice for Giovanni, whose attempt to cure Beatrice results in her death.

Terence Martin observes that Hawthorne deliberately makes use of Dante in his tale. Giovanni recalls that one of the ancestors in his landlord's family was pictured by Dante as "a partaker of the immortal agonies of his Inferno." This association leads to his emphasis on the contrast between Dante's Beatrice, the "activating agent of grace," and Hawthorne's "poisonous" Beatrice, who "stands in need of love for spiritual sustenance and liberation." Giovanni is supposedly a "bringer of love" but, in fact, is shallow and affected. The bouquet he buys for Beatrice withers; he buys a second one but then gazes at himself in the mirror, a gesture both vain and indicative of his insincere character (*Nathaniel Hawthorne*, 94–97).

Roy Male points out parallels between this story and Dante's *Divine Comedy*. As is Dante, Giovanni is being instructed and tested. If he succeeds, he will win a "high and holy faith" through Beatrice. He may fail, however, because he lacks the ability to "attain and hold a religious faith or heavenly love against the challenge of materialistic skepticism." At the same time, he has the potential to transform his ardent passion into something "much nobler" (*Hawthorne's Tragic Vision*, 61).

Rappaccini, Beatrice In "Rappaccini's Daughter," she is the helpless victim of her sinister father, Signor Giacomo Rappaccini, a famous doctor who is said to transform plants into highly potent medicines. At the beginning of the story, Giovanni sees her as "redundant with life, health, and energy."

Not only is Beatrice beautiful, but she is also considered her father's intellectual and scientific equal. She is already well known for her youth and beauty, and although the townspeople are evidently aware of Rappaccini's malevolent experiments, they are powerless to protect Beatrice. As Giovanni learns from their meetings in the garden, she is like an infant in her limited experiences and leads a life of "such seclusion" that she knows nothing of the world beyond the garden walls. Her father's "fatal love of science" has "estranged" her from "all society." She has no friends or companions—only a poisonous shrub that she calls "sister."

Beatrice's role is played out on three levels. Her external beauty represents the entrance to her heart, but then her poisonousness parallels the hellish monsters who dwell a short distance within. Finally, her pure goodness represents the perfection and light in the depths of her being.

Rappaccini, Giacomo   Character in "Rappaccini's Daughter," the father of Beatrice. He has been called a "twisted genius." The narrator describes him as "a tall, emaciated, sallow, and sickly-looking man, dressed in a scholar's garb of black." His face, although "marked with intellect and cultivation," could never have "expressed much warmth of heart." An inhuman scientist, he has cultivated his intellect at the expense of his heart. He relishes scientific experimentation; his most sinister experiment is the transformation of his daughter Beatrice from an innocent young girl into a sorceress who is an instrument of death.

FOR FURTHER READING

Askew, Melvin W., "Hawthorne, the Fall, and the Psychology of Maturity," *American Literature* 34 (1962): 335–343; Ayo, Nicholas, "The Labyrinthine Ways of 'Rappaccini's Daughter,'" *Research Studies* (Washington State University) 42 (1974): 56–69; Baris, Sharon Deykin, "Giovanni's Garden: Hawthorne's Hope for America," *Modern Language Studies* 12, no. 4 (fall 1982): 75–90; Bunge, Nancy, *Nathaniel Hawthorne: A Study of the Short Fiction* (New York: Twayne, 1993); Cuddy, Lois A., "The Purgatorial Gardens of Hawthorne and Dante: Irony and Redefinition in 'Rappaccini's Daughter,'" *Modern Language Studies* 17 (winter 1987): 39–53; Grant, William E., "Nathaniel Hawthorne," in *Dictionary of Literary Biography.* Vol. 74, 143–163 (Detroit: Gale Research, 1988); Haviland, Beverly, "The Sin of Synecdoche: Hawthorne's Allegory against Symbolism in 'Rappaccini's Daughter,'" *Texas Studies in Literature & Language* 29 (fall 1987): 278–301; Hazlett, John Downton, "Re-Reading 'Rappaccini's Daughter': Giovanni and the Seduction of the Transcendental Reader," *ESQ: A Journal of the American Renaissance* 35 (1989): 43–68; Hovey, Richard B., "Love and Hate in 'Rappaccini's Daughter,'" *University of Kansas City Review* 29 (1962): 137–145; Jones, Deborah L., "Hawthorne's Post-Platonic Paradise: The Inversion of Allegory in 'Rappaccini's Daughter,'" *Journal of Narrative Technique* 18 (spring 1988): 153–169; Male, Roy R., "'From the Innermost Germ: The Organic Principle in Hawthorne's Fiction," *English Literary History* 20 (1953): 218–236; Martin, Terence, *Nathaniel Hawthorne,* (Boston: Twayne Publishers, 1983): 87–92; Rahv, Phillip, "The Dark Lady of Salem," *Partisan Review* 8 (1941), 362–381.

"Rejected Blessing, The"

Short story or anecdote published in FAMOUS OLD PEOPLE (1841). It was chapter V, part II, of GRANDFATHER'S CHAIR.

The story, as purportedly told by Grandfather to several of his small grandchildren, recalls the time of Governor Shute, who succeeded the "crafty politician" Governor Dudley of the province of Massachusetts Bay in 1716. Colonial governors, appointed by the king, had a difficult time because they needed to serve both the king and the people on whom they depended for their pay. Although King George had ordered colonial governors to "lay claim" to a fixed salary, very often the people they governed paid them much less. In 1722, Colonel Shute departed for England and complained to King George about the unruly colonists.

In 1721, Dr. Cotton Mather sat in his library reading a book published by the Royal Society of London. There had been a recent outbreak of smallpox in Boston, an "awful pestilence" that killed many inhabitants. Cotton Mather was extremely worried, not only for the population of Boston but also for his own son, Samuel. He read a letter written by an Italian physician about a cure for smallpox through inoculation that had succeeded in Greece, Turkey, and Africa. He vowed to consult other physicians and try to use it in the colony.

Mather called on many physicians in Boston, but these "grave and sagacious personages" refused to listen to him. Such a procedure as inoculation was not, they said, mentioned by the famous physicians Galen and Hippocrates; therefore, it could not be effective. The only physician who would listen was Dr. Zabdiel Boylston. When he and Mather walked the streets, "hisses were heard, and shouts of derision, and scornful and bitter laughter."

The smallpox epidemic spread. Throughout Boston there were red flags fluttering from dwellings, a signal that smallpox had entered the house and attacked family members. People refused to greet one another lest they be contaminated. Nevertheless, Cotton Mather inoculated his son, Samuel. Dr. Boylston tried the experiment also, saving many people except those who died of contamination caused by contact with garments of infected people.

After Mather's death, inoculation was universally practiced and saved thousands of people. Finally it was acknowledged that "the very thing for which they had so reviled and persecuted him was the best and wisest thing he ever did."

Hawthorne concludes by recommending that the children listening to the tale read a biography of Mather written by Mr. Peabody of Springfield.

"Rill from the Town-Pump, A"

Essentially a sketch rather than a story, this piece was first published in NEW-ENGLAND MAGAZINE in June 1835 (unsigned) and collected in TWICE-TOLD TALES (1837).

It is purportedly an utterance by the town pump in Salem, located at Essex and Washington streets. The pump sees itself as the personification and guardian of "the best treasure, that the town has," providing for the pauper, the fire department, and the public at large. It is "steady, upright," and "downright," stretching out its arms to rich and poor alike. It is "cup-bearer to the parched populace," with an iron goblet chained to its waist.

The pump suggests that human beings would do well to mimic the calm model found in nature itself, which is ever adaptable: "In the moral welfare, which you are to wage—and, indeed, in the whole conduct of your lives—you cannot choose a better example than myself, who have never permitted the dust, and sultry atmosphere, the turbulence and manifold disquietudes of the world around me to reach that deep, calm well of purity, which may be called my soul. And whenever I pour out that soul, it is to cool earth's fever or cleanse its stains."

It delivers a lecture on morality to the habitual tippler who has spent money intended for food for his children on drink and is now sober for the first time in 10 years. It then offers historical reminiscences. It depicts his origins in antiquity, when water presumably bubbled out of a spring within the "leaf-strewn earth." Sagamore Indians drank of it, until they discovered liquor ("fire-water"). It imagines Governor Endicott and Governor Winthrop drinking its pure water. Baptismal basins were filled at the pump, which also provided water for washing clothes.

In the final section, the pump depicts itself as a partner of the Cow. Together they will "tear down the distilleries and brew-houses, uproot the vineyards, shatter the cider-presses, ruin the tea and coffee trade, and, finally, monopolize the whole business of quenching thirst." In conclusion, the pump beseeches a young girl, who has filled her stone pitcher with water, to offer a toast: "Success to the Town-Pump!"

When "A RILL FROM THE TOWN-PUMP" was published in TWICE-TOLD TALES, the reviewer of the volume for the Salem Gazette singled it out for praise as "exceedingly well done." The reviewer for the Boston Daily Advertiser also expressed a preference for its "grace and sweetness." Hawthorne's old BOWDOIN COLLEGE friend HORATIO BRIDGE reviewed the volume for the publication Age. He declared that of all the tales, "the beautiful fiction entitled 'The Rill of the Town Pump' is likely to be the most popular, because it embodies the prevailing public sentiment upon a topic of universal interest'" (Nathaniel Hawthorne: The Contemporary Reviews, edited by John Idol, Jr. and Buford Jones, 19–22).

"Roger Malvin's Burial"

Story first published in 1838 in the TOKEN, dated 1832, but with no attribution. SAMUEL GOODRICH, the editor, persuaded Hawthorne to let him use it after Hawthorne had been unable to find a publisher for "PROVINCIAL TALES," a collection of which it would have been a part. The story was reprinted in the UNITED STATES MAGAZINE AND DEMOCRATIC REVIEW in August 1843, but it is thought that Hawthorne was paid little, if anything, for it, since the editor, JOHN O'SULLIVAN, was a close friend of his. The story was collected in MOSSES FROM AN OLD MANSE in 1846 (Newman, *Hawthorne's Short Stories*, 271).

The story is based on "Lovell's Fight" (or "Lovewell's Fight"), a raid in the spring of 1725 on the Pequawket Indian tribe in defense of the colonial frontiers. At that time, Captain John Lovewell commanded a small company of colonists from Dunstable, Massachusetts. They were ambushed and defeated by Indians at Fryeburg, Maine, a town near RAYMOND, MAINE, where Hawthorne spent several months as a boy.

Roger's surname is probably drawn from Thomas Symmes's *Historical Memoirs of the Late Fight at Piggwacket*, which was written in 1725. It describes several instances in which wounded men were left in the forest. A second source may be a ballad, later attributed to Thomas C. Upham, and a third may be an article titled "Indian Troubles at Dunstable," by Joseph Bancroft Hill.

As the story opens, two wounded survivors of the fight are making their escape through the woods. Roger Malvin, an aged and severely wounded soldier, and his young companion, Reuben Bourne, also wounded, are resting on a bed of "withered oak leaves" at the foot of a massive granite rock that is "not unlike a gigantic gravestone." Roger urges his youthful companion to desert him and try to find his way to safety. He says he is dying of his wounds, and Reuben must leave him there to preserve himself. Reuben protests that he cannot leave Roger "to perish and to lie unburied in the wilderness." He could never tell Dorcas, Roger's daughter, he had done such a thing. Roger answers that Reu-

ben must assure her he had assisted him for many miles and that, with his "earnest entreaty" and his blessing, he was forced to leave. The two men also entertain the "unfounded hope" that Roger's life "might be preserved" if Reuben is able to procure "human aid" for him.

Reuben gathers roots and herbs, "which had been their only food during the last two days," and places them "within reach of the dying man." He fastens his handkerchief to the top of an oak sapling as a signal to a search party. The handkerchief had previously bandaged a wound on Reuben's arm, and he vows "by the blood that stained it" that he will return, either to save Roger's life or to bury his body. Then he reluctantly leaves, carrying Roger's blessing to Dorcas and solemnly promising to return. Roger calls him back and asks Reuben to help him lean against the granite rock so that he can see his figure departing among the trees. Reuben leaves again and then creeps back; he hears Roger's fervent prayer for Reuben's own happiness and that of Dorcas.

He makes his way home but cannot bring himself to tell Dorcas of the circumstances in which he actually left her father in the forest. He tells her about Roger's severe wounds and their travels together but does not admit that he left Roger still alive. When she asks whether he "dug a grave . . . in the wilderness," he says he did what he could, and that a "noble tombstone" stands above his head. Dorcas takes comfort in her assumption that Reuben had provided "such funeral rites as it was possible to bestow," although this was not the case.

Dorcas repeats the story of "Reuben's courage and fidelity" to her friends, he is hailed as a hero, and soon the two are married. But Reuben is plagued with guilt over his "moral cowardice." He does not regret leaving Roger Malvin, but he is haunted by "mental horrors" over concealing the truth. He is also conscious of his "deep vow unredeemed" and senses Roger's "unburied corpse . . . calling to him out of the wilderness." He believes it is too late to take friends to search for Roger's bones but, year after year, suffers corrosive guilt. The "voice audible only to himself, commanding him to go forth and redeem his vow," becomes "like a chain binding down his spirit and like a serpent gnawing into his heart." Reuben turns into a "sad and downcast yet irritable man." He neglects the large farm Dorcas has inherited, quarrels frequently with his neighbors, is involved in "innumerable lawsuits," and finally becomes a "ruined man." His only recourse is to return to the wilderness and seek subsistence.

Meanwhile, Cyrus Bourne, their only child, grows up and is considered extremely promising. He is strong, gifted, and highly intelligent. Roger loves him more than he does Dorcas, for he recognizes, in Cyrus, what he himself had once been and at times seems to "partake of the boy's spirit." Cyrus is considered a "future leader," especially if the Indian wars recur. Reuben, however, grows increasingly selfish and moody. One autumn, he takes Cyrus with him to select a tract of land in the wilderness on which the family can settle. They work together for two months to clear it.

Early the following May, Reuben, Dorcas, and Cyrus bid farewell to their friends and take their belongings by horseback into the wilderness. Cyrus notices, however, that they are not following the course Reuben had laid out on their autumn expedition. He points this out, and Reuben momentarily alters their course, but he then reverts to their former direction. They set up an encampment on the fifth day.

While Cyrus wanders out "in search of game," Dorcas begins to prepare a meal. She notes that it is the 12th of May—the anniversary of Roger's death. Reuben is deeply wounded by her reminder and hastens away into the forest. He is, in the narrator's words, "unable to penetrate to the secret place of his soul, where his motives lay hidden." He believes a "supernatural voice" calls him onward; he hopes he will find Roger's bones and bury them, believing it is "Heaven's intent to afford him an opportunity of expiating his sin."

Thinking he hears a deer in the undergrowth, he fires into a thicket, only to discover it is the very thicket that has grown up about the remains of Roger Malvin. The upper part of the oak sapling to which he had tied his handkerchief has been blighted, however. The topmost bough is "withered, sapless, and utterly dead," though it had been "green and lovely, eighteen years

before." He thinks his own guilt has blighted the sapling.

Dorcas hears a gun in the distance and is sure her boy has shot a deer. She calls him but he does not appear. She goes in search of him, and finds Reuben looking at an object at his feet. His face is "ghastly pale" and his expression is one of "strong despair." He points out the body of Cyrus, lying near the broad granite rock where he had left Roger Malvin behind. He tells her that the rock is the gravestone of her "near kindred." Her tears will "fall at once over her father and her son." She does not hear him but shrieks and sinks "insensible by the side of her dead boy."

Suddenly, the top bough of the oak loosens itself and falls on Reuben, Dorcas, and Cyrus, and on Roger Malvin's bones. Reuben believes his sin is "expiated." The "curse was gone from him; and, in the hour, when he had shed blood dearer to him than his own, a prayer, the first for years, went up to Heaven from the lips of Reuben Bourne."

CRITICAL ANALYSIS

"Roger Malvin's Burial" has always had a deep appeal for readers because it treats the theme of irrational guilt. Henry James terms the story one of the "most original" of Hawthorne's tales (*Hawthorne*, 51).

The central question at the core of the story, debated by readers ever since it was published, is this: Why does Reuben kill his son? Neal Frank Doubleday argues that Reuben's motivation is the expiation of his guilt over leaving Roger Malvin to die in the wilderness (*Hawthorne's Early Tales: A Critical Study*, 197). Frederick C. Crews, in *The Sons of the Fathers: Hawthorne's Psychological Themes*, concludes that the killing is unconsciously motivated by remorse Reuben has harbored over the years (80–95).

Nancy Bunge proposes that Reuben's guilt destroys his life. He loves Dorcas and Cyrus, but when they leave town and begin traveling to seek a new life, his remorse impels him, unconsciously, to the place where he left Roger Malvin. As she puts it, "Reuben's peace costs too much." He kills not only his child, but also his relationship with Dorcas: "Even Dorcas, though loving and beloved, was far less dear to him; for Reuben's secret thoughts and insulated emotions had gradually made him a selfish man; and he could no longer love deeply, except where he saw, or imagined, some reflection or likeness of his own mind." There is a shift in the story from unconscious to conscious awareness. He must perform an expiation of his sins that is both necessary and inevitable.

The oak tree and the large granite rock are the two major symbols in "Roger Malvin's Burial." Both are introduced at the outset of the story, and they reappear in the final paragraph. Many critics have identified Reuben with the oak tree, since it is introduced as a "young and vigorous sapling" at the point when, as a young man, he abandons Roger Malvin. The tree is, therefore, introducing him to a new life. Mark Van Doren observes that the movement of the withered topmost bough of the tree, marked by Reuben's blood-stained handkerchief, is equivalent to the movement of Faith's ribbon in "YOUNG GOODMAN BROWN." It conveys "the force of Reuben's terrible secret . . . his incommunicable thought . . . that became 'like a chain binding down his spirit and like a serpent gnawing into his heart'" (*Nathaniel Hawthorne*, 81). The rock has often been assumed to represent the stone tablets of the Old Testament; it serves as both a gravestone and an altar. It would also be appropriate as the site of a blood offering in the pagan tradition. Reuben prays beneath the tree, hoping his crime is expiated and the curse lifted.

The story may have a biblical analogue in the story of Reuben, son of Jacob and brother of Joseph, in Genesis 27–50. He is compelled to leave a loved one in a situation of danger and live a lie; he also suffers from prolonged guilt. Reuben himself is "green and lovely" (native, young, and simple) before his act of sacrifice. Ely Stock argues that there are parallels between the story of Saul in I Samuel 18 and the Abraham-Isaac legend recounted in Genesis 12–24 ("History and the Bible in Hawthorne's 'Roger Malvin's Burial,'" 279–296).

However, many readers have simply deduced that Reuben is insane. Hyatt Waggoner suggests that in killing Cyrus, Reuben is actually killing "the symbolic extension of himself" (*Hawthorne: A Critical Study*, 97).

The frontier is another important metaphor within the story, with several parallels based on the frontier image. First, it functions as a geographical region, where civilization meets wilderness. It also becomes a psychological setting, where the past encounters the present. In addition, Reuben's journey into the depths of the wilderness to seek the body of Roger Malvin becomes an emblem of his excursion into his own heart. Reuben is, in fact, searching for his own cowardly deception and falseness, which have been hidden from him by his tendency toward self-deception.

FOR FURTHER READING

Bunge, Nancy, *Nathaniel Hawthorne: A Study of the Short Fiction* (New York: Twayne, 1993); Crews, Frederick C., *The Sons of the Fathers: Hawthorne's Psychological Themes* (New York: Oxford University Press, 1966); Doubleday, Neal Frank, *Hawthorne's Early Tales: A Critical Study* (Durham, N.C.: Duke University Press, 1972); Erlich, Gloria, "Guilt and Expiation in 'Roger Malvin's Burial,'" *Nineteenth-Century Fiction* 26, no. 4 (March 1972): 377–389; James, Henry, *Hawthorne* (New York: Harper, 1879); Mackenzie, Manfred, "Hawthorne's 'Roger Malvin's Burial:' A Postcolonial Reading," *New Literary History: A Journal of Theory and Interpretation* 27, no. 3 (summer 1996): 459–472; Martin, Terence, *Nathaniel Hawthorne* (Boston: Twayne, 1965); Milder, Robert, "Hawthorne's Winter Dreams," *Nineteenth-Century Literature* 54, no. 2: 165–201; Ortolano, Guy, "The Role of Dorcas in 'Roger Malvin's Burial,'" *Nathaniel Hawthorne Review* (fall 1999): 8–16; Stock, Ely, "History and the Bible in Hawthorne's 'Roger Malvin's Burial,'" *Essex Institute Historical Collections* 100 (1964): 279–296; Van Doren, Mark, *Nathaniel Hawthorne* (New York: William Sloan Associates, 1949); Waggoner, Hyatt, *Hawthorne: A Critical Study* (Cambridge, Mass.: Harvard University Press, 1955).

Scarlet Letter, The

The first edition, of 2,500 copies, was published in March 1850 by Ticknor and Fields, Boston. The second edition, also of 2,500 copies, was published in April 1850, and a third edition of 1,000 copies was published in September 1850 (Clark Jr., C. E. Frazer, *Nathaniel Hawthorne: A Descriptive Bibliography*, 140–148). Little remains of the original manuscript—just a single leaf with the title and the table of contents.

Hawthorne was employed in the Salem Custom House from 1846 to 1849, in a position he desperately needed. *The Scarlet Letter* was inspired, to a certain extent, by his experiences in that capacity. In the introduction to the novel, Hawthorne imagines his descendants' deploring his profession: "A writer of story-books! What kind of a business in life,—what mode of glorifying God, or being serviceable to mankind in his day and generation,—may that be? Why, the degenerate fellow might as well have been a fiddler!" He goes on to defend his writing: "Let them scorn me as they will, strong traits of their nature have intertwined themselves with mine." He explains that he was impelled to write the story of Hester Prynne in part because of his own Puritan ancestry, which he needed both to affirm and to resist.

In his preface to the second edition, Hawthorne remarks that the introduction to the first edition, called "The Custom-House," which he had termed a "sketch of official life," had "created an unprecedented excitement in the respectable community immediately around him." He observes that it could not have been more violent had he "burned down the Custom-House, and quenched its last smoking ember in the blood of a certain venerable personage, against whom he is supposed to cherish a peculiar malevolence." According to his description of the experience, the sketch has a "certain propriety," and he wishes to put himself in his "true position as editor."

He continues by describing the Custom-House and the men he supervises as surveyor of the revenue. He considered some of the men to be "in their strength and prime, of marked ability and energy." Others had white hair, which was "the thatch of an intellectual tenement in good repair." On the whole, however, they were "a set of wearisome old souls, who had gathered nothing worth preservation from their varied experience of life."

While he is employed in this capacity, one day he discovers a mysterious package containing a manuscript and a piece of red cloth with traces of gold embroidery that have lost their glitter. It is in the shape of a capital letter A. When he holds it near his chest it seems to burn him. He reads the manuscript and finds that it purports to have been written 100 years earlier by Jonathan Pue, a customs surveyor of the mid-17th century. This discovery provides the framework of the novel. Hawthorne undertakes the writing with some trepidation, aware that his Puritan ancestors would regard him as frivolous and "degenerate." He finds himself unable to focus on his tale while he is working in the Custom-House amid uninspiring men, but when a new American president is elected, and he must give up his post, he takes up the writing of his "romance" at home before his parlor fireside. The manuscript is about the experiences of a Puritan woman, Hester Prynne.

SYNOPSIS

The Custom-House: Introductory

The first section of the novel introduces the reader to Hawthorne's experience working in the Custom-House, which was germane to his fundamental concept of the entire work. The narrator, who is nameless, takes a post in the Salem Custom House, where taxes on imports entering the country are paid. The office is on a wharf that is in a deplorable state of repair, and it is in a building badly neglected and barely finished. He describes his fellow workers in the depressing office. Most of them are quite elderly and uninterested in their jobs; they are merely holding on because they have lifetime appointments. Their jobs were obtained, for the most part, through family connections of one kind or another. To Hawthorne, a young, energetic newcomer to his position, they are incompetent and even corrupt.

To make matters worse and more boring, few ships sail to Salem as they once did. On the second floor, which is unoccupied, he discovers some musty documents as he browses through the papers stored there. One manuscript that catches his eye is wrapped up together with a scarlet gold-embroidered cloth in the shape of an A. When he holds it close to his chest it seems to cause a burning sensation, so he lets it drop. He then begins to read the manuscript.

It was written, supposedly, by a long-ago customs surveyor, Jonathan Pue, who was employed there a century earlier. Pue had had an interest in local history and left an account of certain events that had occurred locally in the middle of the 17th century. They took place an entire century before Pue's lifetime and two centuries before the lifetime of the narrator himself.

We know that the narrator has had doubts about trying to make a living writing, because his highly regarded ancestors, who were Puritans, would have considered such an enterprise "frivolous." However, he does decide to write about the experiences of Hester Prynne. His account will not be precisely factual, but he will be loyal to the outline and the overall spirit of the original manuscript.

Hawthorne lost his post in the Custom House in June 1849 but continued to write—first an essay called "The Custom-house," and then the novel called *The Scarlet Letter.*

Chapter I, The Prison-Door

The novel opens outside a Boston prison during the 17th century. A crowd of dreary, somber people has assembled. The exterior of the edifice is forbidding, with a heavy oak door studded with iron spikes. Apparently it contains dangerous and unpredictable criminals. When new colonies are founded in Massachusetts, the reader is told, a prison and a cemetery are the first structures built.

One ray of hope is visible, however, a rosebush growing beside the prison door. Its blooms offer their "fragrance and fragile beauty" as well as a "sweet moral blossom" to the entering prisoner. It also provides some measure of relief to the condemned criminal as he goes to his doom, signifying that "the deep heart of Nature" will "pity and be kind to him."

Hawthorne's former office in the Salem Custom-House, where he worked as a surveyor from 1846–1849, and where the unnamed narrator of *The Scarlet Letter* comes upon the mysterious manuscript. *(Courtesy of the Peabody Essex Museum)*

The narrator of *The Scarlet Letter* was so impressed by Hester Prynne's story that he felt as if Surveyor Pue's ghost was insisting he publish the forgotten manuscript, as Pue had neglected to do. *(Illustration by Hugh Thomson)*

Chapter II, The Market-Place

As the crowd stares at the prison door, one woman in the crowd remarks that it would be "greatly for the public behoof" if all "malefactresses" were handed over to the mature women in the group, all church members. The door opens and the town beadle, an official who carries a sword by his side, emerges. He draws forth a beautiful young woman, whose name, we learn, is Hester Prynne. She is tall and elegant with glossy, dark, abundant hair; she is also ladylike. She emerges from the door and goes to a scaffold, that is, a raised platform. She is holding an infant, whose name, we will be told, is Pearl. She is to be publicly condemned. The women in the crowd jeer at her.

Hester Prynne wears an ornate embroidered badge on her chest; it consists of the letter A carefully stitched in gold and scarlet. One of the women concedes that she has "good skill at her needle."

We deduce, from the conversations reported here and there by the crowd, that she has been branded an adulteress because she has produced an illegitimate child, the infant she is holding in her arms. The A stands for *Adultery*. The town beadle calls to Hester. The adults begin staring at her and children begin taunting her.

As Hester faces the crowd, she reflects on her life in her native England. She recalls her village, her paternal home, and her parents. She remembers the countenance of a "misshapen" older man, "pale, thin, and scholar-like," whom she married in England and followed to Amsterdam. We deduce that she was probably not in love with him. She squeezes the baby, who begins crying.

Chapter III, The Recognition

Hester sees her husband (who, we will later learn, calls himself Roger Chillingworth) in the crowd; he had promised to follow her to America two years

Hester Prynne emerges from the prison, bearing the scarlet A and carrying baby Pearl. *(Illustration by Hugh Thomson)*

ago but had failed to arrive. His attire is a mixture of Native American and European styles of dress. He signals to Hester not to expose his identity.

He pretends to be a stranger and tells someone in the crowd that he has been "met with grievous mishaps by sea and land" and was recently kept captive by Indians. He asks for an explanation of Hester's crime and punishment and is told that Hester's husband had not followed her to America and she now has a three-month-old baby with another man. Chillingworth asks the identity of the child's father. He is informed that Hester has refused to reveal this information. Her punishment is to spend three hours on the scaffold and a lifetime of wearing the scarlet letter on her chest.

We meet the town fathers responsible for judging Hester: Governor Bellingham, Reverend Wilson, and a young minister, the Reverend Arthur Dimmesdale. The latter exhorts Hester to reveal the name of the baby's father, but she refuses. She responds that the baby will seek a heavenly father and not know an earthly one. Wilson delivers a sermon on sin and Hester is led back into prison. (The reader later learns that Dimmesdale is actually the father of the baby, but Hester keeps this fact secret.)

Chapter IV, The Interview
After returning to prison, Hester suffers from a "state of nervous excitement," and the infant is screaming because of their ordeal outside. The jailer leads in Roger Chillingworth, who has identified himself as a physician. Chillingworth tells her he is now well versed in alchemy and has also been taught medicine by the Native Americans with whom he lived. He gives the baby medicine and then offers Hester a cup of the potion, intended to make her more amenable to "authority." She refuses at first to drink it, suspicious that he wishes to poison her. She tells him she has thought of death and even prayed for it. She then drinks the potion.

He urges her to reveal the name of the child's father, but she refuses. Hester declares he may be the Devil in disguise; in that role he will lure her into a pact and damn her soul. He tells her he will "sooner or later" be able to seek out her unknown lover. Hester is sure he wants to take revenge on him.

Chillingworth visits Hester and offers her a potion she suspects is poison. *(Illustration by Hugh Thomson)*

Chillingworth enjoins Hester to keep his identity a secret, as she does the name of her lover. He does not want her to tell anyone, lest he be dishonored as the "husband of a faithless woman" or, he says, for "other reasons." He asks her to represent her husband as "one already dead" and not to give any sign of recognizing him. Hester says, "I will keep thy secret, as I have his."

As he departs, Chillingworth asks with a smile whether she wears the scarlet *A* in her sleep, and whether she has nightmares. She asks, in return, whether he is like "the Black Man that haunts the forest," and whether he has enticed her into a bond "that will prove the ruin" of her soul.

Chapter V, Hester at Her Needle
Within a few months Hester is released from prison but does not leave Boston. An outcast, she settles in an abandoned cabin on the edge of town. She supports herself by sewing. Her needlework is in

demand for officials' garments for public ceremonies, for "apparel of the dead body" for funerals, and for baby linens. Brides, however, do not commission her work, as it is considered unlucky to do so. She does some charity work but is often insulted.

She hides her secret even from herself, although from time to time it struggles out of her heart "like a serpent from its hole." Clergymen pause in the street when they see her and address words of exhortation. Children pursue her and call her names. Hester struggles to believe that "no fellow-mortal" is as guilty as she.

She considers fleeing back to England but finally believes that the torture of her daily shame will "purge her soul" and lead to a higher purity "than that which she had lost," because it would be a form of martyrdom. Her expert needlework becomes fashionable in the town, although she herself only dresses in the "coarsest" materials and dull colors. Her only ornament is the scarlet letter.

Chapter VI, Pearl

Her daughter, Pearl, is Hester's great consolation. She was purchased with Hester's "greatest treasure," her virginity. Hester worries about the effect of her origin on Pearl. Her daughter is beautiful and brilliant but has a strong will and is capricious; at times, she seems remote and not entirely human.

Hester dresses the child in the "richest tissues" that can be procured. At that time, there was strong discipline within the family, and parents applied the rod and enjoined scriptural authority to back up their rules. Hester, however, realizes she cannot always discipline Pearl; the child has a "strange remoteness and intangibility" and often wears a "mocking smile." Hester is sometimes brought to tears by her "sole treasure."

As she grows older, Pearl becomes an outcast among other children, who are intolerant of and mystified by her. Pearl, in turn, despises the other children. She practices "witchcraft" and makes up her own dramas in the forest. She tells her mother she has "no Heavenly Father."

Chapter VII, The Governor's Hall

Hester calls at Governor Bellingham's mansion to deliver a pair of ornate gloves she has made for him and to see whether it is true that Pearl might be taken from her because she is regarded as a "demon-child." She takes Pearl, dressed in crimson velvet with a design embroidered by her mother. On the way, they pass "somber" little Puritan children who decide to fling mud at Pearl and Hester, but Pearl rushes at them and puts them all to flight.

Once inside the mansion, the child is intrigued by the governor's suit of armor, which he has worn in battles with Native Americans. Hester is dismayed to see her own reflection, dominated by the scarlet letter, in the armor. Pearl begs for a rose from the bush outside the window but Hester hushes her as some men enter the room.

Chapter VIII, The Elf-Child and the Minister

Governor Bellingham, accompanied by Wilson, Chillingworth, and Dimmesdale, enters. The Governor is amazed by Pearl's appearance, comparing it with the dress prevalent in court masques during the time of King James.

Pastor John Wilson and Governor Bellingham walk ahead of Chillingworth and Dimmesdale, while the four men discuss whether Pearl should remain in Hester's custody. *(Illustration by Hugh Thomson)*

The men call Pearl a "bird of scarlet plumage" and a "demon-child." The Governor tells Hester they have discussed little Pearl and believe she ought to be taken away from her mother, dressed "soberly," and strictly disciplined. Hester responds that she can teach Pearl what she has learned from wearing the scarlet letter. They ask why Hester should be entitled to keep the child and raise her. Wilson tests Pearl's knowledge of religious subjects, but she capriciously refuses to answer and claims she was not made at all, but was plucked "off the bush of wild roses, that grew by the prison-door." Hester cries that God gave her the child; she is her "happiness" as well as her "torture." She asks Dimmesdale to speak for her, and he argues that the child is both a blessing and a curse. The Governor and Wilson are persuaded that they should not attempt to separate Pearl and her mother. Pearl has clearly taken to Dimmesdale.

Chillingworth tries to persuade the men to interrogate Hester further as to the identity of Pearl's father, but they refuse. Dimmesdale observes that the Heavenly Father made Pearl, but "made of no account" the distinction between "unhallowed lust and holy love." Pearl has come from "the hand of God" to work on Hester's heart. Hester is, moreover, forcibly reminded of her agony by the red symbol she wears.

Mistress Hibbins, Governor Bellingham's sister, invites Hester to a witches' gathering. She responds that she would have gone willingly if Pearl had been taken away from her.

Chapter IX, The Leech

Chillingworth has sworn Hester to secrecy about his past. The town welcomes and values him as a physician, especially since he has had some European training and has knowledge of Native American remedies because of his captivity. His character is evil, however. His deformed body parallels his deformed character, and he gradually becomes bent over toward the ground.

Dimmesdale has been having health problems. Since he refuses to marry any of the young women in town, Chillingworth recommends that he himself be allowed to live with him. They both take rooms in a widow's home next to a graveyard; Dimmesdale's room has tapestries depicting scriptural scenes of adultery, while Chillingworth's is outfitted with a small but sophisticated laboratory.

Chillingworth's face, once "calm, meditative" and "scholar-like," takes on an evil aspect after he moves in with Dimmesdale. Some townspeople believe that he is the incarnation of the Devil and that, haunted by Satan, he is battling for Dimmesdale's soul. He grows more like a snake than a human being.

The narrator states that "a man burdened with a secret should especially avoid the intimacy of his physician." Moreover, if the physician possesses "native sagacity and a nameless something more,—let us call it intuition," then the "soul of the sufferer" will be dissolved "and flow forth in a dark, but transparent stream."

Chapter X, The Leech and His Patient

Dimmesdale is a puzzle to Chillingworth, who tries to detect the cause of his condition. Chillingworth continues to act as Dimmesdale's "kind, watchful, sympathizing, but never intrusive friend." He does his best to discover the private details of Dimmesdale's life, since he is "strongly moved to look into the character and qualities of the patient." Dimmesdale, however, is suspicious of Chillingsworth's motives and refuses to confide in him. Chillingworth gathers herbs and weeds for making medicines. Dimmesdale asks one day about a particular plant. Chillingworth says he discovered it growing on an unmarked grave and is sure it represents the buried person's sin.

Outside, they see Pearl dancing in the graveyard and tossing burrs onto the scarlet letter on Hester's chest. Pearl sees them looking and drags Hester away, saying that the "Black Man" has taken possession of Dimmesdale.

Chillingworth tries to inquire into Dimmesdale's spiritual condition. Dimmesdale says that is a matter of concern to God and leaves the room. This response makes Chillingworth suspicious. A few days later, however, Chillingworth manages to look at Dimmesdale's chest while he is asleep. He rejoices at what he finds there, but the reader is not told what it is.

Chapter XI, The Interior of a Heart

Chillingworth continues to try to take revenge on Dimmesdale. Dimmesdale is suspicious of him and loathes him but the only revenge he can take is preaching sermons on sin. He longs to confess the truth of what he perceives as his disastrous sin to his parishioners, but he is unable to do so. At night he sees visions of Hester and Pearl. They are delusions, but he assigns meaning to them.

Meanwhile, Chillingworth's diabolical intellect sees a clear path before it. He has a "quiet depth of malice" that is emerging. He wants to make himself the trusted recipient of the clergyman's agonized confessions. In time he manages to become not a spectator, but an actor, in the poor minister's interior world. He is the "spring" that controls the "engine" of Dimmesdale's misery, but he acts with a "subtlety so perfect" that the minister, though he has a dim perception of some evil influence watching over him, can "never gain a knowledge of its actual nature."

Dimmesdale himself achieves a real popularity in the town through his intellectual gifts, his "moral perceptions," and his ability to experience and communicate emotion. He resolves to confess his problems from the pulpit but never manages to do so. He finally decides to hold a vigil on the scaffold where Hester once suffered.

Chapter XII, The Minister's Vigil

Dimmesdale mounts the scaffold one "obscure night" in early May. It is the same scaffold where Hester Prynne, several years earlier, had lived through "her first hour of public ignominy." He screams from his psychic pain, and his voice peals through the night and reverberates from the surrounding hills. His voice is not as loud as he believes, however. Mistress Hibbins hears the outcry and believes it to be "the clamor of fiends and night-hags." The Reverend Mr. Wilson, Dimmesdale's friend, has been praying in the death chamber of Governor Winthrop, who has just died. When Wilson passes by the scaffold, Dimmesdale imagines he has spoken to him, but he has not. He is almost delusional and laughs aloud. Pearl hears him and responds with her "light, airy, childish laugh." She and Hester have

been at Governor Winthrop's deathbed; Hester is making the burial robe. A meteor illuminates the sky and the minister sees a dull red A etched in the heavens. Chillingworth watches from a distance. He coaxes Dimmesdale down from the scaffold.

The next day, Dimmesdale delivers a powerful sermon. It is the "richest and most powerful" he has ever given. Afterward, however, the sexton gives him his black glove, which was found on the scaffold, and tells Dimmesdale the townspeople take the meteor to stand for "Angel," a sign that Governor Winthrop is now in heaven.

Chapter XIII, Another View of Hester

Pearl is now seven years old. Hester is active in charitable work in the village. She takes food to the doors of the poor, nurses the sick, and assists in times of trouble. She does not interfere with public or individual interests, and people have begun to regard her in a new light. They begin to consider that her scarlet A stands for *Able* and not *Adultery*. Her new life has a "blameless purity." Also, Hester does not demand any special privileges beyond her own work in order to secure food for her daughter and herself. She has "a woman's strength," and her life has turned, to a large degree, from "passion and feeling" to "thought."

Had it not been for the existence of Pearl, the narrator speculates that Hester might have had a historical identity similar to that of Ann Hutchinson, noted founder of a religious sect. Instead, Hester worries about her daughter and about whether she is harming Dimmesdale by keeping Chillingworth's identity secret.

After seeing Dimmesdale's vigil on the scaffold, Hester finds herself shocked by his condition. His nerve seems "destroyed" and his "moral force" has been weakened, although, intellectually, his faculties have retained their original strength. She resolves to meet Roger Chillingworth, her former husband, and try to rescue Dimmesdale from his grasp.

Chapter XIV, Hester and the Physician

She encounters Chillingworth while he is out collecting roots and herbs for his medicinal potions. Hester is shocked at the changes that have occurred

Hester encounters Chillingworth in the forest and deems him "striking evidence of man's faculty of transforming himself into a devil . . ." *(Illustration by Hugh Thomson)*

in him over the past seven years; he now seems to have a "fierce, yet carefully guarded look" and "a glare of red light out of his eyes." It is as if his soul is on fire and smolders darkly within his breast, bursting momentarily into flame. He has transformed himself into a "devil."

Hester decides to ask Chillingworth to stop tormenting Dimmesdale. He tries to flatter her by saying he hears good tidings of her in the village. He says the town council has actually debated whether the scarlet letter might, with safety, be taken away from her bosom. He declares he has made an entreaty that it be done immediately. Hester distrusts him and dislikes his false friendliness. She replies that if she were worthy of its removal, it would "fall away of its own nature, or be transformed into something that should speak a different purport." He replies that it actually shows "right bravely" on her bosom. Hester realizes that Chillingworth embodies the power to

transform himself into a devil. In order to do so, he has only to undertake a devil's office. For seven years, he has analyzed "a heart full of torture" with enjoyment.

She tells Chillingworth it is time to tell Dimmesdale the truth about his real identity. "You are beside him, sleeping and waking. You search his thoughts," she says, and he causes Dimmesdale to "die daily a living death"; yet he does not really perceive Chillingworth's evil nature. Chillingworth then realizes that Dimmesdale was Hester's lover. He insists that he has taken good care of Dimmesdale, as his physician. Hester replies that it would have been better if he had died at once.

Chillingworth insists that Dimmesdale has not repaid his debt to him—that is, Chillingworth has been devoted to him constantly, yet he has, himself, been transformed into a "fiend" by his hatred. Hester replies that Dimmesdale must be told the truth and learn Chillingworth's "true character." Chillingworth replies that he has "no such power" to pardon Dimmesdale.

Chapter XV, Hester and Pearl

Hester bitterly confesses to herself that she hates Chillingworth. She recalls long-ago evenings in a "distant land," Europe, when he would bask in her smile. Those scenes had once appeared happy to Hester, but now they are "among her ugliest remembrances." She cannot imagine how she ever married him. He has now betrayed her and thus treated her worse than she had once treated him. The narrator remarks that Dimmesdale has awakened "all her sensibilities," whereas what she had previously known was only a "marble image of happiness."

Meanwhile, by the seashore, Pearl pretends to be a mermaid and puts eel-grass on her chest in the shape of an A. Pearl tells her mother the A is related to Dimmesdale's habit of clutching his hand over his heart. Hester considers Pearl too young to know the truth, however.

Chapter XVI, A Forest Walk

Hester resolves to tell Dimmesdale the truth about Chillingworth's identity and waits for him in the forest and along the shores of the peninsula, where he often takes "meditative walks." He does not appear for several days, but Hester then learns that he is out of town visiting the Apostle Eliot. She plans to take Pearl to meet him on his route back. As they make their way along the footpath, Pearl states that the sunshine does not love her mother and hides itself because it is afraid of the scarlet letter on her bosom. She assumes that a scarlet letter will be on her own chest when she is a grown woman.

Hester and Pearl sit down in the forest. Pearl asks whether Dimmesdale, who is approaching, is the "Black Man" she has heard about in the village. Pearl wonders whether the "Black Man" has left a mark on Dimmesdale. He looks haggard and feeble and despondent but has no visible symptom of "positive and vivacious suffering" except that he keeps his hand over his heart.

Chapter XVII, The Pastor and His Parishioner
Hester and Dimmesdale encounter each other in the forest, where they can escape the public eye as well as Chillingworth. The narrator states that they meet "so strangely" in the dark wood that each questions the other's actual existence. "Hester! Hester Prynne!" Dimmesdale cries. "Is it though? Art thou in life?" She asks him, "Dost thou yet live?" Each appears to be almost a ghost, "awe-stricken at the other ghost" and also at himself and herself. Dimmesdale puts forth a cold hand and touches her "chill hand." They then feel they are, at least, "inhabitants of the same sphere." They join hands and sit on a mossy spot near a brook.

He asks whether Hester has found peace, and she asks him the same question. He says he has found nothing but despair; she observes that the people revere him and he has done much good. He says this has only caused him misery, not comfort. She says he has deeply repented and left his sin behind. She then confesses that Chillingworth was her husband. She holds Dimmesdale, burying his face against the scarlet letter on her chest. He forgives her, finally realizing that Chillingworth is a far worse sinner than either of them.

Hester declares that Dimmesdale has been "crushed" by "seven years' weight of misery." She urges Dimmesdale to liberate himself from the power of Chillingworth. The two plan to take a

ship to Europe, with Pearl, and live together as a family.

Chapter XVIII, A Flood of Sunshine
Dimmesdale gazes at Hester with hope and joy, but also with fear. Hester, with a "mind of native courage and activity," is at this point stronger and more powerful morally than Dimmesdale. The scarlet letter has been her "passport into regions where other women dared not tread," and the emblem has made her strong.

Dimmesdale, however, has always lived within the "scope of generally received laws," except in his affair with Hester. He has been hemmed in by the framework of his life as a priest. For seven years, Hester Prynne's life of "outlaw and ignominy" has prepared her for this hour. It has left Dimmesdale, in contrast, without hope and with the conviction that he is doomed.

Hester throws the scarlet letter away from her chest, lets down her abundant dark hair, and smiles. She delights in the belief that Pearl will know her father. She calls to her daughter, who approaches warily from the forest, where she has been adorning herself with violets, anemones, columbines, and twigs. Dimmesdale does not believe Pearl will love him. The girl slowly approaches, for she sees the clergyman.

Chapter XIX, The Child at the Brook-Side
Dimmesdale wonders whether Pearl has his "own features" in her face. She is beautiful but is not yet the "living hieroglyphic" that embodies the dark secret they want to hide—no one can deduce, at this point, her parentage.

Hester calls to Pearl to cross the brook and go to them, but she is suspicious and refuses. She begins shrieking and stamping her foot, pointing at the empty place on Hester's chest. Hester realizes that the girl misses the emblem she has always seen her mother wear. She puts it back on her bosom and gathers up her hair, confining it beneath her cap.

Pearl then goes to her, says she recognizes her mother, and kisses the scarlet letter. She refuses to embrace the minister, however, and wants to know why he is sitting with them. Hester answers that he loves little Pearl, though she does not reveal that he is her father. Pearl inquires whether he will return with them to the town "hand in hand, we three together." Dimmesdale kisses her on the brow, but Pearl runs to the brook and washes away his "unwelcome kiss."

Chapter XX, The Minister in a Maze

As Dimmesdale walks out of the forest, he looks back at Hester and Pearl, wondering whether his encounter with them had been real or he had dreamed it. He sees Pearl taking "her old place by her mother's side" and realizes he has not been dreaming. He thinks back upon their plans to leave the New World and find shelter and concealment in the Old World, with its "crowds and cities." There is a ship in the harbor that will sail for Bristol in four days; Hester will book passage for two individuals and a child.

Their meeting has left him in a strange state of mind, however, and the town takes on a new aspect for Dimmesdale in the light of their plans. He feels an "unaccustomed physical energy" and is seized with an urge to utter blasphemous words. Within a single day, his will undergoes a transformation. He is no longer melancholy but rather experiences a "revolution in the sphere of thought and feeling." He is incited to do something wild and wicked and is unsure he can control his impulse. He talks with one of his deacons and almost turns pale lest he involuntarily reveal his secret. He cannot recall texts of Scripture with which to comfort the eldest member of his church, a pious and exemplary old woman. He stops in the road and teaches wicked words to small Puritan children.

He returns home a different man: "a wiser one," with a "bitter kind of knowledge" of "hidden mysteries" that his former self could never have understood. Chillingworth offers him some medicine, for he appears "white and speechless," but he refuses to take it. He tells Chillingworth he does not need his drugs anymore; the physician becomes suspicious and aware that he is now "no longer a trusted friend," but Dimmesdale's "bitterest enemy."

Dimmesdale then throws his energy into writing his sermon for Election Day, a civil and religious holiday. The sermon is to be delivered "on the third day from the present," on the governor's inauguration day and the opening of the legislature.

Chapter XXI, The New England Holiday

Another public gathering takes place on the occasion of the installation of a new governor. The crowd includes townspeople, Native Americans, and sailors from the ship that Hester and Dimmesdale plan to take to Europe. Many of the spectators are dressed in their best, with an Elizabethan love of splendor. Hester, however, is wearing a "garment of coarse gray cloth." The scarlet letter reveals her "under the moral aspect of its own illumination." Her public face is like a mask, with the "frozen calmness of a dead woman's features."

The commander of the Bristol ship confides to Hester, to her horror, that Chillingworth will be joining them on the voyage as ship's doctor. He has told the captain that he is a member of Hester's party, and, as it happens, the ship needs a physician. Chillingworth smiles ominously at Hester from across the marketplace, a smile that conveys "secret and fearful meaning."

Hester stands beneath the scaffold in a "magic circle of ignominy," while townspeople, sailors, and Indians stare at her in the market-place. *(Illustration by Hugh Thomson)*

Chapter XXII, The Procession

The procession begins, with military men clad in burnished steel, followed by white-haired venerable men of "civil eminence." Dimmesdale follows, with a strong gait and air. Pearl asks her mother whether the minister is the same person who kissed her by the brook. Her mother cautions her: "We must not always talk in the marketplace of what happens to us in the forest." In the procession through the marketplace, Dimmesdale looks healthy and energetic.

Mistress Hibbins talks with Hester about Dimmesdale; she suggests that the Devil is Pearl's real father. She asks whether Dimmesdale and Hester have met in the forest; she has intuitively guessed this. Pearl wants to know whether Mistress Hibbins has seen what Dimmesdale wishes to hide by putting his hand over his heart. She tells Pearl she will ride with her, "some fine night," to see her father and she will then know "wherefore the minister keeps his hand over his heart."

Hester listens to Dimmesdale's sermon. Chillingworth sends a message to Hester via the shipmaster, that he will take Dimmesdale on board. Many people stare at Hester; she is in a "magic circle of ignominy."

Chapter XXIII, The Revelation of the Scarlet Letter

In his Election Day sermon, Dimmesdale emphasizes the relationship between God and the communities of humankind that are being established in the wilderness. The sermon is well received; his audience later testifies that "never had man spoken in so wise, so high, and so holy a spirit" as he had that day.

Afterwards the crowd looks at Dimmesdale with "awe and wonder." The minister turns toward the scaffold and holds out his arms. He summons Hester and Pearl and gazes at them with a "ghastly look," but one that has both tenderness and triumph in it. He has a foreboding of untimely death. He says God has led him there, and he then confesses his sin to the townspeople. He tears away his clothes from his chest and reveals a mark. After his confession, he collapses and Hester supports his head against her bosom. Chillingworth cries out that Dimmesdale has escaped him.

Pearl gives Dimmesdale the kiss she has previously refused to bestow on him. Her tears, falling on her father's cheek, pledge that she will "grow up amid human joy and sorrow, nor forever do battle with the world, but be a woman in it." Hester asks whether they will spend their afterlives together. Dimmesdale answers that it will be God's decision; he then dies.

Chapter XXIV: Conclusion

After Dimmesdale's death, there is much discussion of the mark on his breast that appeared when he was in the marketplace. Some people claim it was a scarlet letter like Hester's. Others say there was no mark: that Dimmesdale was simply revealing his own remorse and demonstrating that any man can be guilty of sin.

Chillingworth dies within a year of Dimmesdale and leaves Pearl a substantial legacy. She is the "richest heiress of her day" in the New World. Hester and Pearl disappear, and a legend grows around the scarlet letter. Hester returns years later to live in the same cottage by the seashore. Letters arrive with "armorial seals" upon them, presumably from Pearl; she has found a home in an "unknown region." Hester is seen, one day, embroidering a baby garment, thought by villagers to be for a grandchild.

Hester continues to be a source of support to those, especially women, who were "in the continually recurring trials of wounded, wasted, wronged, misplaced, or erring and sinful passion." After many years she dies and is buried in the King's Chapel graveyard beside Dimmesdale; they share a headstone. On the headstone is a scarlet A on a black background.

RECEPTION AND CRITICAL ANALYSIS

Writing in GRAHAM'S MAGAZINE, Edwin Percy Whipple declared that Hawthorne had produced something "really worthy of the fine and deep genius" which lay within him. He declared that the autobiographical section on the Custom House represented the "fountain of mirth" Hawthorne had at his command. The four principal characters showed a grasp of "individualities" ("Review of New Books," *Graham's Magazine* 36, no. 5 [May 1850]: 345–346).

Lewis Gaylord Clark, who reviewed the novel for the KNICKERBOCKER, declared it a "psychological romance" in which the human heart was "anatomized, carefully, elaborately, and with striking poetic and dramatic power." He described the scarlet letter itself as a character, "the hero of the volume" (*The Scarlet Letter,*" *Knickerbocker,* 35, no. 5 [May 1850]: 451–452).

The author of a piece published in the *North American Review,* unsigned but identified by the editor as Anne W. Abbott, pronounced the delineations of wharf scenery and the figures and personages of the Custom House "worthy of the pen of Dickens." She called Pearl, despite her naughty screams and wild laughter, "the only genuine and consistent mortal in the book." Overall, Hawthorne's "flow of expression" was delightful, but the subject itself was "revolting: with its 'pollution and vice'" (*North American Review* 71, no. 148 [July 1850]: 135–148).

Charles Creighton Hazewell, critic for the *Boston Daily Times,* praised the accurate depiction of the Puritans and declared Governor Bellingham and other characters to be drawn with "eminent fidelity" to history, even though Hawthorne did not claim his writings were "historical tales" (*Boston Daily Times,* 27, no. 4914 [May 16, 1851]: 2).

The critic for the *Portland Transcript* found the novel a "romance of singular merit and originality." He viewed Hester Prynne as an "erring but heroic woman," Chillingworth as a "wronged but malicious and horribly revengeful husband," and Dimmesdale as a man of "timidity and weakness." Hester's character is praised for her "fortitude" and her "uncomplaining, yet almost proud submission to the indignities inflicted upon her by the stern Puritans" (*Portland Transcript,* 13, no. 50 [March 30, 1850]: 3).

Henry James detected a certain charm about the novel that he found "very hard to express," stating that it only existed when an artist "touched his highest mark—a sort of straightness and naturalness of execution, an unconsciousness of his public, and freshness of interest in his theme" (Van Doren, *Nathaniel Hawthorne,* 145). He was one of the earliest critics to observe that the novel is not so much about adultery as about the ensuing moral situation and its resolution or lack of resolution.

Orestes Brownson, who reviewed the novel for *Brownson's Quarterly Review* (n.s. 4, no. 4 [October 1850]: 528–532), declared that the story was told with "great naturalness, ease, grace, and delicacy" but insisted that it was one that should not have been told, dealing as it did with "crime, an adulteress and her accomplice" and a "meek and gifted and highly popular Puritan minister in our early colonial days." His principal objection was that Hawthorne, while making the guilty parties suffer, did not manage to "excite the horror of his readers for their crime." He blamed him for seeking to excuse Hester Prynne, whose guilt, according to the reviewer, was compounded by the fact that neither of the guilty parties (Arthur Dimmesdale and Hester Prynne) is really repentant. Only their pride is wounded, not their respective consciences. Both continue to be complacent and self-satisfied and are free of self-reproach. They show no remorse for having "offended God" (*Nathaniel Hawthorne: The Critical Heritage,* edited by J. Donald Crowley, 177–178).

The Episcopal bishop Arthur Cleveland Cox attacked the novel in the *Church Review and Ecclesiastical Register* ("The Writings of Hawthorne," 3, no. 4 [January 1851]: 489–511), on the grounds that Hawthorne chose as the material for his romance the "nauseous amour of a Puritan pastor" and Hester Prynne, a "frail creature of his charge, whose mind is represented as far more debauched than her body." He suggested that it was a book "made for the market" and that it degraded American literature (*Nathaniel Hawthorne: The Critical Heritage,* edited by J. Donald Crowley, 182).

Among contemporary critics, this novel has long been considered a classic. Its themes have been analyzed, its characters dissected and described from an anthropological standpoint, its topography carefully identified. Few critics, however, have been able to provide insight into the genealogical framework of the novel.

An independent scholar, archaeologist, and historian, Peter A. Hutchinson, who lives in Phippsburg, Maine, and is a descendant of Stephen Bachiler and Thomas Chillingsworth, has carried out research on possible prototypes for Hawthorne's characters. In an unpublished article,

"Something about Mary . . . The Real and Adventurous Life of 'Hester Prynne,'" he suggests that Hawthorne may have based his tale on the story of the seaman Robert Beedle's widow, Mary. Beedle was a native of Kittery, Maine. After his death, his widow became housekeeper to the elderly minister Stephen Bachiler of Hampton, New Hampshire, in June 1832. When Bachiler was in his 80s, Mary became his fourth wife in order to silence rumors about their living together; they were married in Strawberry (or Strawbery) Bank, Portsmouth, New Hampshire. Mary had a documented affair with George Rogers, a neighbor, fisherman, and widower who had children. In 1650, the two were taken into York Court in Maine and accused of keeping company together; they were warned to stay apart. Mary became pregnant, and the two were taken into court again in 1651. She gave birth to a daughter. Both Mary and Rogers were sentenced to be whipped; Mary was also to be branded with the letter *A.* Stephen Bachiler filed for divorce, but he and Mary were ordered by a court to continue living together. Bachiler returned to England in 1654; Mary then became known as "the grass widow Bachiler." George Rogers lived out his life in Kittery and died in 1684. Mary Bachiler's daughter Mary lived near her mother throughout their lives. Hutchinson has pinpointed a number of similarities between these events and Hawthorne's novel. He believes Hawthorne was familiar with Mary's story because his ancestor Captain William Hawthorne had settled on the Piscataqua River in Kittery, Maine (now South Berwick, Maine), site of Mary Bachiler's property. (Hutchinson may be contacted at phutchinson@clinic.net for further discussion and information.)

The critic F. O. Matthiessen argues that Hawthorne was very close to achieving "wholeness" in *The Scarlet Letter.* In a chapter called "Allegory and Symbolism," in *The American Renaissance* (in *Twentieth Century Interpretations of* The Scarlet Letter [Englewood Cliffs, N.J.: Prentice-Hall, 1968]), he suggests that in this novel the elements are "inseparable" in the sense that, in the words of Henry James, "character, in any sense . . . is action, and action is plot." The novel grows "organically" out of the interactions of the characters, and little

in the novel depends on scenery (as much of *The Marble Faun* does). He singles out Pearl's "terrifying precocity" for praise, as in the scene when she refuses to go to Hester and Dimmesdale because she is outraged at Hester's removal of the scarlet letter.

Matthiessen focuses on the novel as an essentially theatrical work, built symmetrically around the three scenes on the scaffold. In chapter II, Hester Prynne emerges from the prison door and goes to the scaffold, where she is to be publicly condemned. She wears an ornate embroidered badge on her chest, the letter A carefully stitched in gold and red. The town beadle leads Hester through the crowd, every footstep agony for her. She ascends the wooden steps of the pillory and stands on the platform, holding Pearl. The crowd is "sombre and grave." Hester recalls her native English village, her paternal home, and her parents. She remembers the countenance of an older man, who is "pale, thin, and scholar-like," but misshapen physically; he is, we will learn, Roger Chillingworth, her husband, who sent her to America but failed to follow her as he had promised. She refuses to name the father of her child.

In chapter XII, Arthur Dimmesdale, father of Pearl, mounts the scaffold. He screams from his psychic pain, but the townspeople believe they are hearing a witch's voice. He is almost delusional and laughs aloud. In chapter XXIII Dimmesdale summons Hester and Pearl and mounts the scaffold that has been erected in the marketplace. He says God has led him there, and then he confesses his sin and dies. Chillingworth cries out that Dimmesdale has escaped him.

Terence Martin highlights the "essential duality or ambivalence" of Hawthorne's fictional world in *The Scarlet Letter.* The "ambivalent nature of reality" is evident in the characters of Hester, Dimmesdale and Chillingworth, and the scarlet letter itself: "all signify more than one thing; All must be considered in more than one way." Hester Prynne can be viewed as either a "virtual saint, a woman who walks in humility and patience," or an "unbending woman of pride, who glories in her sin." The scarlet letter, the symbol of her sin, is embroidered "fancifully"; she both "glories in her letter and suffers in her glory." Similarly, Pearl, the consequence of Hester's sin, "brings both pain and pleasure," both blessing and retribution. As a result, Hester "cannot hate her sin"; instead she "can only embrace all that the letter brings to her—suffering and joy, solitude, challenge, and a resulting independence of spirit." The community that brands her sees a "single signification" in the scarlet letter, but it grows to represent more. The *A* for *Adulterer* might also mean *Able* or even *Angel.* It could also stand for *Arthur,* which would "double its meaning of adultery and the ambivalence of Hester's attitude toward it" (*Nathaniel Hawthorne,* 105–127).

Frederick C. Crews discusses the novel in a chapter called "The Ruined Wall" in *The Sins of the Fathers* (in *Twentieth Century Interpretations of* The Scarlet Letter). He sees deep flaws in Hester's optimistic expectation that, once Dimmesdale has forgiven her for her secrecy and his desire for her has been revived, they can escape from New England and make a new beginning. Hester does not realize that it is not Chillingworth who is standing in the way of Dimmesdale's true rehabilitation, but rather his "own remorse." Therefore, the characters are prevented from achieving true happiness by their own "inner world of frustrated desires."

Richard Harter Fogle, in a chapter called "Irony" in *Hawthorne's Fiction: The Light and the Dark* (in *Twentieth Century Interpretations of* The Scarlet Letter), suggests that much of the force of the novel results from the theme of "secret sin." The dramatic irony of situation arises from concealment by Dimmesdale (his sin in having a child with Hester), Chillingworth (his identity as her husband), and Hester (her refusal to name the father of her child). All three characters are living lies; Pearl is the living emblem of their sin. Pearl's questions are "fiendishly apt" and her appearance is related to the scarlet letter worn by her mother. At the same time, her physical characteristics, actions, and utterances are always entirely appropriate to her age. She is never inconsistent or unchildlike.

In "Arthur Dimmesdale as Tragic Hero," Bruce Ingham Granger argues that the novel is the story not of Hester, but of Dimmesdale. Although he is the "familiar figure of Every-Christian," he is the only major character who "never functions symboli-

cally." Granger sees the novel as centering on "a good man's struggle with and eventual victory over the guilt he experiences after committing lechery." After his second meeting in the forest with Hester, who has been "wandering morally" over the past seven years, she becomes "more his enemy than the diabolical Chillingworth." Her love leads him to agree to a plan to flee the New World together, a "course of action more unorthodox than that which Chillingworth long ago imposed." Here Dimmesdale "has his Calvinist faith put to the supreme test." But, as Granger points out, no Christian "can deny his past, indeed his very birthright, and live at peace with himself." Following the impulses of Pearl, who desires public acknowledgment ("Go back with us, hand in hand, we three together, into the town," she says), Dimmesdale "finds the strength to face his responsibility and confess before he dies." He knows all along that "nothing short of confession can bring to an end the hypocrisy he has been making of his life"; he realizes that "fallen man in his search for redemption must have his faith tested by undergoing a lonely, dark, spiritual journey before he can discover the way to responsible action." Granger compares Dimmesdale to Job and Bunyan's Christian; each must judge himself and make his way alone. Upon the scaffold, where Dimmesdale confesses his sin and acknowledges his daughter, Pearl finally bestows a kiss upon him. Granger views Dimmesdale's confession as tragic, whereas Hester's "dynamic but lawless behavior in the forest is at best heroically pathetic" and not "ethically meaningful." She may be strong, but she is not tragic. Dimmesdale, in contrast, "knows himself to be a sinner" and never "mistakes penance done on earth for penitence." He sees with "unflinching honesty the distance separating his ideal from his actual self" and attempts to bridge this gap with his confession.

Edward H. Davidson discusses the novel in the light of the Christian doctrine to which New England Puritans subscribed. He states that Dimmesdale conforms to the historic principles of Christian thought. The character has a "fall" from apparent grace to damnation, and, because he does not expiate his sin, he has corrupted himself. He begins by deluding himself that his "body and soul are separate." Therefore, the "sufferings and privations" of one are not necessarily those of the other. Body and spirit need not agree with each other. When Chillingworth tells Dimmesdale that he has a "sickness" in his spirit that is manifested in his body, he is really stating that a bodily disease is an emblem of a spiritual sickness. Dimmesdale grows to believe that his fleshly existence is an emblem of his soul. His spirit is, therefore, evident every instant in his daily experience and in the conduct of his life. When he privately indulges in fasts, vigils, flagellations, and scourgings, even to the point of abusing his body, he has visions of "diabolic shapes." He is tormented by the idea that his appearance and behavior will reveal his inner secret. The torture inflicted by the anguish in his "inmost soul" is unrelenting. Dimmesdale ultimately ordains his own "corruption" by convincing himself that he deserves "moral freedom" in a "morally predestined world."

Sacvan Bercovitch, in "*The Scarlet Letter: A Twice-told Tale*," explores Hawthorne's adaptation of Puritanism as a "cultural legacy," and of the New England Puritans as a "symbol of national origins." The Puritans are the "imagined entry into official U.S. history," as well as the "official entry into an imagined U.S. history." In this society, the "key to democratic values lies in the conspicuous absence of sexuality." As other critics have pointed out, Hawthorne "bans not only the adulterous act, but the very word 'adultery.'" All of the main characters in the story itself "remain celibate forever, except possibly for Pearl, somewhere across the Atlantic." These characters are "born into a sinful world they never wanted and can't escape." Hester, Dimmesdale, and Chillingworth are all guilty of the sin of concealment and hypocrisy; Pearl herself is the "child of hypocrisy." The novel is also based on a "familiar dichotomy": The "heroism of the individual is directly proportionate to the evil of society." Therefore, the "more sinister they are, the more compelling is the argument for autonomy." Chillingworth's "sheer unloveableness" and the town's "unnatural moralism" help make the case for Hester and Dimmesdale. Still, for all the faults of the Puritan community, for Hawthorne it "provided exactly the sort of moral foundation he considered crucial for the mid-nineteenth-century republic." The author made the Puritan model the framework for the psychology of the novel. *The Scarlet Letter* is both a love story "narrated in the context of historical continuity, and vice-versa." It presents the "story of America" in multiple narrative variations: "civic versus individualist heroism, the self-governing community versus Emersonian self-reliance, good versus bad Puritans."

CHARACTERS

Bellingham, Governor　Character in *The Scarlet Letter*. The elderly governor of Massachusetts, who resembles an English aristocrat and who spends a great deal of time consulting the other town fathers. His elaborately furnished mansion is like that of an English nobleman, containing portraits of his ancestors. It is an attempt to replicate the Old World in the New World of the colonies, although the Puritans had rejected lavish displays along with intolerance.

The governor's garden is a parable of his failure: The ornamental plants fail to thrive, a symbol of the Old World principles that cannot be transplanted to the New World. Cabbages and pumpkins do flourish, however, providing necessary food. As he walks through his estate, he wears an elaborate ruff "in the fashion of King James's reign." The narrator remarks ironically that this attire causes his head to "look not a little like that of John the Baptist in a charger [platter]."

Governor Bellingham's widowed sister, Mistress Hibbins, is known to be a witch, but he is oblivious of her true nature and her nightly forest rides. He maintains her protected status in the community.

Chillingworth, Roger　"Roger Chillingworth" is a character in *The Scarlet Letter;* he is actually Roger Prynne, the husband of Hester Prynne, in disguise. He is an elderly scholar, who uses his knowledge to assume the identity of a doctor. He had sent her to Boston, Massachusetts, ahead of him, saying he needed to settle his affairs in Europe. He had eventually followed but had been captured by Native Americans and been delayed; people assumed he had been lost at sea. By the time he arrives, Hester has had an affair with Arthur Dimmesdale, a Puritan minister, and given birth to Pearl, her daughter.

Most critics concur that Chillingworth is the most evil character in the novel. He is introduced in chapter III, "The Recognition." When his wife, Hester Prynne, emerges from prison, wearing the scarlet letter and carrying her three-month-old baby, he is standing in the crowd, clad in a "strange disarray of civilized and savage costume." He is described as "small in stature, with a furrowed visage." Just as his mental faculties are skewed, his physical appearance is misshapen. One of his shoulders is higher than the other, and, when he looks at Hester with a "keen and penetrative" look, it is as though a "writhing horror" twists itself across his features, like a "snake gliding swiftly over them, and making one little pause, with all its wreathed intervolutions in open sight."

He now calls himself "Roger Chillingworth" and gestures to Hester that she should not reveal his identity. He becomes Dimmesdale's medical adviser and manages to lodge in the same house, the better to keep watch over his life. He discerns that Dimmesdale is the father of Pearl and devotes himself for the remainder of the novel to gaining revenge against Hester and Dimmesdale. She calls Chillingworth a "Black Man," because he tempts others to sin and mentally tortures them both.

The narrator states that Chillingworth had once been a "pure and upright man," but he becomes subject to a "terrible fascination" with Dimmesdale. He cannot rest until he has dug into his heart "like a miner searching for gold," or "like a sexton delving into a grave." Chillingworth sees Dimmesdale as "pure" but cannot stop probing his psyche. Dimmesdale is vaguely aware that "something inimical to his peace had thurst itself into relation with him," but is too naive to blame Chillingworth, who tells Dimmesdale he is a sick man and will become even sicker unless he confesses the "wound" or "trouble" eating away at his soul. When he finds Dimmesdale asleep one day, pulls aside his clothes, and finds out why the minister always clutches his heart, his ecstasy at the discovery is like that of "Satan . . . when a precious human soul is lost to heaven, and won into his kingdom." Chillingworth eventually appears to be

Chillingworth examines Dimmesdale's chest while the preacher sleeps. *(Illustration by Hugh Thomson)*

destroyed; his "moral force" has been "abased into more than childish weakness."

Dimmesdale, Arthur The Reverend Arthur Dimmesdale is a pivotal figure in Hawthorne's novel *The Scarlet Letter.* He is a young clergyman who becomes the lover of Hester Prynne and fathers her daughter, Pearl, born out of wedlock. He will not confess his paternity publicly but torments himself because of his culpability.

Dimmesdale had achieved fame in England as a theologian before emigrating to America. His sermons are eloquent and cogently argued, but he suffers continuous conflict about his need to confess his wrongdoing. As Pennell observes, he needs the "affirmation he gains through his congregation's approval" (*Student Companion to Nathaniel Hawthorne*).

An extremely hypocritical character, Dimmesdale cannot confess his relationship to Hester or his fathering of Pearl. When Hester Prynne is discussed in the marketplace by other women, before she first emerges from the prison, they describe her as a "malefactress" and a "hussy." One of the women says piously that the Reverend Dimmesdale "takes it very grieviously to heart that such a scandal should have come upon his congregation." Dimmesdale is described as full of religious fervor, a person "of very striking aspect, with a white, lofty, and impending brow, large, brown, melancholy eyes, and a mouth which, unless when he forcibly compressed it, was apt to be tremuous, expressing both nervous excitability and a vast power of self-restraint." Because Dimmesdale contrives to keep himself "simple and childlike," the people believe him possessed of a "freshness" and "dewy purity of thought" that affect them "like the speech of an angel." He hypocritically joins John Wilson in exhorting Hester to confess the truth about Pearl's paternity.

Eventually Dimmesdale's health begins to fail. The townspeople attribute this to his energetic application to his parochial duties, his continual studies, and his continual fasts and vigils. He grows emaciated; his once strong voice develops a "mel-

While beloved and revered by the townspeople for his piety, Dimmesdale is secretly consumed by guilt. *(Illustration by Hugh Thomson)*

ancholy prophecy of decay." He lies awake meditating on his sin. One night he climbs up on the scaffold, screaming with pain, although the townspeople assume they hear the voice of a witch.

On Election Day, there is a procession through the marketplace, along with loud music, costumes, and a holiday air. In a way, the crowds and festivities reenact the scene from years before, when Hester emerges from prison. Dimmesdale looks uncommonly healthy and energetic, though his sermon will emanate from an interior condition of sin. After he delivers his powerful sermon, he mounts the scaffold with Hester and Pearl and begins to confess the truth; he calls himself "the one sinner of the world." Dimmesdale announces that he, as Hester, has a red stigma (never described precisely by the narrator). Chillingworth cries, "Thou hast escaped me!" Dimmesdale then bids Hester farewell and dies.

Hibbins, Mistress Character in *The Scarlet Letter*. She is Governor Bellingham's "bitter-tempered sister." A few years after the events of the novel, she is executed as a witch.

Inspector, Custom-House Character in "The Custom-house," the introductory chapter of *The Scarlet Letter*. Hawthorne held the post of surveyor in the Salem Custom-House from March 1846 to June 1849. It was while he held this position that he began writing the novel. Brenda Wineapple argues that the legend that Hawthorne wrote the novel in a "white heat" after losing his post at the Custom-House is erroneous. Sophia Hawthorne herself stated that he was writing it in 1848 and would "rest by observing the sports and characteristics of the babies and record them" (Wineapple, *Hawthorne: A Life,* 202).

Hawthorne gives a satiric portrait of the Inspector of the Custom-House in the first section of the novel. The son of a revolutionary colonel, the Inspector was the patriarch of the Custom-House. His father, in fact, had created the office and appointed his son to fill it when he was still a young man.

When Hawthorne knew the Inspector, he was about 80, with a "florid cheek," "compact figure," and "brisk and vigorous step." His post at the Custom-House was secure. He possessed no "power of thought" or "depth of feeling" and had only a few "commonplace instincts," which served him well "in lieu of a heart." He had survived three wives and had fathered 20 children, many of whom had already died, but he did not mourn them deeply: "One brief sigh sufficed to carry off the entire burden" of his reminiscences of his family.

He was a "patriarchal personage" possessed of lively curiosity, but without a soul, heart, or mind. He had only "instincts." He could recollect all the good dinners he had ever eaten; certain flavors had lingered on his palate 60 or 70 years and were still fresh. He had "no higher moral responsibilities than the beasts of the field," but his "scope of enjoyment" was larger than theirs.

Of all the people Hawthorne has known, this man was "fittest" to be a Custom-House officer. He was incapable of suffering "moral detriment" from his mode of life, and, if he were to continue in office "to the end of time," he would be "just as good" and "sit down to dinner with just as good an appetite."

Miller, General Character in *The Scarlet Letter*. He is the Collector of the Salem Custom-House and its oldest inhabitant, a man who, after a long career in the military, had "retired" in order to spend the remainder of his life in the Custom-House. Hawthorne describes him in The section of the novel "The Custom-house," which is a prelude to the story.

Hawthorne remarks that the "independent position of the Collector" had kept the Salem Custom-House "out of the whirlpool of political vicissitude." It was this "whirlpool" that caused Hawthorne to consider political offices fragile. General Miller was one of the aged men he found in the Custom-House. He was "radically conservative" and only with difficulty "moved to change."

He regards the "old warrior" with affection and states that he had "noble and heroic qualities" that had enabled him to win a "distinguished name." He had "weight, solidity, firmness"—and, though he was in a state of physical decay to some extent, Hawthorne could imagine that if sufficiently stimulated he was capable of "flinging off his infirmities like a sick man's gown, dropping the staff of age to seize a battle-sword, and starting up once more a warrior."

At the same time, he was, somewhat improbably, fond of the sight and fragrance of flowers. He seemed to live "a more real life within his thoughts" than within the environment of the Collector's office. In fact, Hawthorne terms him "as much out of place as an old sword—now rusty, but which had flashed once in the battle's front, and showed still a bright gleam along its blade—would have been, among the inkstands, paper-folders, and mahogany rulers, on the Deputy Collector's desk" (Preface to *The Scarlet Letter*, subtitled "The Custom House").

Pearl Daughter of Hester Prynne in *The Scarlet Letter*. We first see Pearl as a baby in the arms of her mother. Hester, carrying her infant daughter, emerges from the prison and goes to a scaffold (that is, a raised platform). She is to be publicly condemned for adultery because she has produced an illegitimate child.

Pearl is Hester's chief consolation, purchased with her mother's "greatest treasure"—her virginity. Hester worries, however, about the effect of her origin on Pearl. Although she is undeniably beautiful, she is considered by some people in the community to be a child of Satan. Her connection with the scarlet letter puts the reader closer to the meaning of the book and to Hester Prynne's original downfall. Pearl is uncontrollable and hyperactive; she often exhibits a bad temper. At the same time, she is repeatedly presented as a child of nature. She does not attend prayer meetings; nor does she join the other children in the community in their wicked games, such as scourging Quakers. Instead, she plays alone in the forest and by the seashore with flora and fauna. When she makes a letter A for herself out of eelgrass, it is green, the color of nature, rather than red. For Pearl, green also signifies truth.

Pearl perceptively recognizes Chillingworth as the "Black Man," or devil in the community, telling Hester, "Come away, Mother! Come away or yonder old Black Man will catch you! He hath got hold of the minister already." She instinctively perceives Dimmesdale's true character. She also knows intuitively that Hester's explanation of the scarlet letter is not altogether frank: "Two or three times, as her mother and she went homeward, and as

Pearl is presented as a child of nature, who often plays by herself in the forest. In the scene depicted here, Hawthorne has likened Pearl to a brook, "inasmuch as the current of her life gushed from a well-spring as mysterious, and had flowed through scenes shadowed as heavily with gloom." *(Illustration by Hugh Thomson)*

often at suppertime, and while Hester was putting her to bed, and once after she seemed to be fairly asleep, Pearl looked up, with mischief gleaming in her black eyes. 'Mother,' said she, 'What does the scarlet letter mean?'"

In addition to her inquiries as to why Hester wears the scarlet letter on her chest, Pearl repeatedly asks why Dimmesdale keeps his hand over his heart. Pearl, in assessing the vital implications of the scarlet letter, clearly perceives that, in New England, human creativity, passion, and joy will not be acknowledged for many years. At the end of the novel, she leaves America, never to return, signifying this insight.

Prynne, Hester The protagonist of *The Scarlet Letter*, Hester Prynne wears the scarlet letter from which the title of the book is derived. It is a patch of fabric in the shape of an A, a significant emblem within the Puritan community signi-

fying that Hester is an "adulteress." While still a young woman, she married Roger Chillingworth, an elderly scholar, who dispatched her to America from Europe but who failed to follow her there. While waiting for her husband in Massachusetts, she had an affair with Arthur Dimmesdale and later gave birth to a daughter, Pearl. Neither of the guilty parties (Arthur Dimmesdale and Hester Prynne) is repentant about their love.

Hester's passion is equaled by her interior strength, thoughtfulness, and intelligence, which are equal to those of her husband and her lover. She spends the remainder of her life alienated from the Puritan citizenry, even though she does good works and is careful in raising Pearl, continually watching over her and instructing her. The community's

Though ostracized and condemned as sinful by the townpeople, Hester finds strength in her love for Pearl. In this scene, the "witchlady" Mistress Hibbins invites Hester to an evil gathering in the forest, but Hester refuses, insisting that she must stay home to take care of her daughter. *(Illustration by Hugh Thomson)*

treatment of "fallen" women is extremely unpleasant; they are continually examined and evaluated, and the least infringement of the moral strictures or laws of the town is punished. The Episcopal bishop Arthur Cleveland Cox termed Hester Prynne a "frail creature . . . whose mind is represented as far more debauched than her body" (*Nathaniel Hawthorne: The Critical Heritage,* edited by J. Donald Crowley, 182).

The late-19th-century novelist and critic W. D. Howells felt that in all fiction, "one could hardly find a character more boldly, more simply, more quietly imagined" than Hester Prynne. She "remains exterior and superior" to her transgression, and her sin is ultimately a "question between her and her Maker, who apparently does not deal with it like a Puritan." Howells observed, in the "contrasted fates" of Hester and Dimmesdale, the lesson that "to own sin is to disown it." He pointed out, however, that although Hester endured her punishment publicly, there was never confession—so perhaps "ceasing to do evil is . . . the most that can be asked of human nature" (*Heroines of Fiction,* Vol. 1, Harper & Brothers Publishers, 1901, 161–174).

Hawthorne once stated that he felt motivated to write the story of Hester Prynne in part because of his own Puritan ancestry. It should be noted that at the time the community was marked by a certain moral rigidity and harshness. Even the children were encouraged to reenact scourging Quakers (a particularly hated sect) or pretending to fight Indians and taking their scalps (Johnson, Claudia, *Understanding the Scarlet Letter,* 7). They have no sympathy for Hester, who was actually fortunate to have escaped some inhumane punishments advocated by the Puritan community for women carried away by their passionate feelings. Such punishments included public beatings, physical mutilation, and branding.

Darrel Abel suggests that Hester evinces a "moral inadequacy" throughout the novel. Some critics have argued that Hester is the exponent of a "new morality" and an advocate of sexual freedom for women. Abel, however, suggests that even though Hester may excite sympathy and compassion in readers, she still deserves "moral censure." This is true despite Chillingworth's marrying her when she was still naive about the needs of her nature and his failure to take into account the result of

Though a strict puritan clergyman, Reverend John Wilson is, as portrayed in this scene, "usually a vast favourite with children." Hester and Pearl are watching in the background. *(Illustration by Hugh Thomson)*

her "awakening passion." Dimmesdale sins against Hester in not accepting moral responsibility for his actions and in failing to carry out his pastoral duty toward her. At the same time, Hester depends on him for "moral erudition" that he does not give her. Ultimately, both men wrong Hester, as does society itself in ostracizing her and causing her injurious emotional isolation (Abel, Darrel, "Hawthorne's Hester," *College English,* 13 March 1952, 303–309).

Wilson, the Reverend Mr. John   Character in *The Scarlet Letter.* He is an elderly and distinguished Boston clergyman, a strict Puritan. Wilson sometimes finds Dimmesdale's eloquence highly persuasive, although he is a clergyman of the old school, preaching about hellfire and damnation and urging that sinners be harshly punished.

FOR FURTHER READING

Abel, Darrel, "Hawthorne's Hester," *College English* 13 (March 1952): 303–309; Bell, Michael Davitt, "Old and New Worlds in *The Scarlet Letter,*" *Readings on Nathaniel Hawthorne,* edited by Clarice Swisher

(San Diego: Greenburg Press, 1996); Bensick, Carol M., "Dimmesdale and His Bachelorhood: 'Priestly Celibacy' in *The Scarlet Letter*," *Studies in American Fiction* 21 (1993): 103–110; Bercovitch, Sacvan, "The A-Politics of Ambiguity in *The Scarlet Letter*," *New Literary History* 19 (spring 1988): 629–654; Bercovitch, Sacvan, "*The Scarlet Letter*: A Twice-told Tale," *Nathaniel Hawthorne Review* 22, no. 2 (fall 1996): 1–20; Chase, Richard, "The Ambiguity of *The Scarlet Letter*," *Readings on Nathaniel Hawthorne*, edited by Clarice Swisher (San Diego: Greenhaven Press, 1996); Clark, Michael, "Another Look at the Scaffold Scenes in Hawthorne's *The Scarlet Letter*," *American Transcendental Quarterly* n.s., 1 (1987): 135–144; Crews, Frederick C., *Sins of the Fathers: Hawthorne's Psychological Themes* (Berkeley: University of California Press, 1989); Donoghue, Denis, "Hawthorne and Sin," *Christianity and Literature* 52 (winter 2003): 215–234; Elbert, Monika, "Hester on the Scaffold, Dimmesdale in the Closet: Hawthorne's Seven Year Itch," *Essays in Literature* 16 (1989): 234–255; Fogle, Richard, *Hawthorne's Fiction: The Light and the Dark* (Norman, Okla.: University of Oklahoma Press, 1964); Gerber, John C, ed., *Twentieth-Century Interpretations of* The Scarlet Letter (Englewood Cliffs, N.J.: Prentice-Hall, 1968); Granger, Bruce Ingham, "Arthur Dimmesdale as Tragic Hero," *Nineteenth-Century Fiction* 19, no. 2 (September 1964): 197–203; Gross, Seymour, *A "Scarlet Letter" Handbook* (San Francisco: Wadsworth, 1960); Hutchinson, Peter, "Something about Mary . . . The Real and Adventurous Life of 'Hester Prynne'" (manuscript); Johnson, Claudia, *Understanding the Scarlet Letter* (Westport, Conn.: Greenwood Press, 1995); Jones, Buford, "What the Permanent Inspector Thought of His Portrait," *Nathaniel Hawthorne Review* 16, no. 1 (spring 1990): 16–17; Kesterson, David B., ed., *Critical Essays on Hawthorne's* The Scarlet Letter (Boston: G. K. Hall, 1988); Martin, Terence, *Nathaniel Hawthorne* (Boston Mass.: Twayne Publishers, 1983), Pennell, Melissa McFarland, *Student Companion to Nathaniel Hawthorne* (Westport, Conn.: Greenwood Press, 1999); Reid, Bethany, "Narrative of the Captivity and Redemption of Roger Prynne: Rereading *The Scarlet Letter*," *Studies in the Novel* 33 (fall 2001): 247–268; Tuckerman, Henry J., "Nathaniel Hawthorne," *Southern Literary Messenger* 17 (June 1851): 347–348; Van Doren, Mark, *Nathaniel Hawthorne* (New York: William Sloane Associates, 1949).

"Seven Vagabonds, The"

Short story first published in THE TOKEN AND ATLANTIC SOUVENIR in 1833 and collected in TWICE-TOLD TALES in 1837. Along with the two other Hawthorne pieces in this edition, "The CANTERBURY PILGRIMS" and the biographical sketch "SIR WILLIAM PEPPERELL," this story may well have been intended, from the beginning, for publication in the annual. Hawthorne was only paid an average of one dollar per page for the 27 contributions he made to the *Token*; his earnings from "The Seven Vagabonds" were, therefore, only about $23.

The tale was probably written in the fall of 1830 upon Hawthorne's return from his summer trip to Connecticut with Samuel Manning, one of his uncles. He wrote an enthusiastic account of his journey. Austin Warren, in *Nathaniel Hawthorne: Representative Selections*, suggests that Hawthorne's "shrewd, but by no means unkindly observations of his fellows" provides a link among the story, his travel sketches, and his account of the journey in his *American Notebooks*. The 1830 trip may well have provided the background of the story and served as its basis.

The narrator of the story begins by recalling one afternoon when he was rambling on foot and arrived at a point giving him a choice of three directions: the road to Boston, a branch leading to the sea, and a third, going over hills and lakes to Canada by way of Stamford, Connecticut. While he is deliberating, he sees a huge covered wagon, almost a small house on wheels. He calls out, primarily from curiosity, and a "respectable old personage" appears. The narrator gives him a small piece of silver and is invited to enter. The old gentleman says he is refreshing his cattle en route to the camp meeting at Stamford.

Inside the wagon, there are seats for 15 or 20 spectators, in addition to a miniature stage. The speaker shows him three-inch figures in the form of ladies, gentlemen, soldiers, and others, including dancers, blacksmiths, and tailors. When he turns the handle of a barrel organ, the statues come to life. There is even a troop of horses who prance in, along with a "Merry Andrew" (clown), a magician, and others. The narrator is intrigued and appreciative. He believes the proprietor of the show must have a very happy life.

A third person is present, a young man in his early 20s. He shows the narrator some books in a corner, praising them lavishly. The speaker already owns a number of them. The owner explains that he has converted a corner of the wagon into a bookstore, a true "Circulating Library." He hopes, in the course of the travels, to have the opportunity of meeting an elderly clergyman who might urge him to seek a college education. He also hopes to meet a "fair country school mistress." At night, his stock of books is transferred to a crowded bar room. He shows off his books to the assembled company. The narrator is charmed and vows that if he should ever "meddle with literature," it will be as a traveling bookseller.

At that point, there is the sound of pleasant voices, and a young damsel begins climbing the ladder into the wagon. She is assisted by a young man who seems out of place in "Yankee-land." He has a "mass of black shining curls clustering round a dark and vivacious countenance." The girl is wearing "gay attire combining the rainbow hues of crimson, green, and a deep orange." She is holding a fiddle, which her companion begins tuning. The "man of literature" welcomes them. The newcomer seems ill at ease speaking English.

They have a mahogany box, which the narrator later calls a "show box." It has a magnifying window that shows views of European scenes such as Venice, Mount Aetna, and Barcelona. The girl, when questioned, says they are en route to the Stamford camp meeting. The narrator wishes aloud that she were traveling alone. Another wayfarer enters the van bearing a circular testifying to his misfortune and asking for a contribution. He gives the narrator change for a five-dollar bill and offers to tell his fortune for 25 cents.

Another visitor enters, a refugee from the raging storm outside. He is an Indian, armed with a bow and arrow. The pretty girl questions him,

and he answers that he is going to shoot at the camp meeting at Stamford. She says they will all travel together with "merry thoughts." The narrator assumes the Indian prefers his own "solitary musings," but he accepts the girl's invitation and appears to anticipate the journey with enjoyment. The narrator reflects that Indians are a virtual "parliament" of "free spirits." They are vagrants with a long history extending over thousands of years. They have chased deer and demolished wooded areas and now rove along dusty roads.

The old showman now inquires about the destination of the narrator. He is startled, but confesses that he, too, is going to the camp meeting at Stamford. The showman asks him in what capacity he might be going. Each of those in the van is capable of earning a living, but he appears to be merely a "strolling gentleman." Quoting Milton's "L'Allegro," he addresses the fortune teller: "Mirth, admit me of thy crew!" "Mirth" declares he shall travel with them to the camp meeting.

They continue their "pilgrimage" on foot. They then meet a horseman riding toward them; he is a famous Methodist preacher and missionary. They rush forward and ask him for news from the camp meeting. He gazes at them in surprise: The speaker, the showman, the beggar, the fiddling foreigner and his "merry damsel," the bibliopolist, and the Indian. "Good people," he announces, the "camp meeting is broke up." The little group is "sundered at once to the four winds of Heaven." They all go their separate ways. The narrator continues toward the "distant city" with the Penobscot Indian.

The story captures much of one phase of Hawthorne's youth and offers an in-depth look at him at that time. He is both a sensitive observer and a young man eager for experience. Henry James singled this tale out in 1879 as one of the "delicate dusky flowers in the bottomless garden of American journalism." He stated that it possessed "something essential fresh and new" (*Hawthorne*, 44).

FOR FURTHER READING

James, Henry, *Hawthorne* (New York: Harper, 1879); Janssen, James G., "Hawthorne's Seventh Vagabond: 'The Outsetting Bard,'" *Emerson Society Quarterly* 62 (1971): 22–28; Lathrop, George

Parsons, *A Study of Hawthorne* (Boston: Osgood, 1876), 143–144.

Snow-Image, and Other Twice-told Tales, The

This collection of previously published stories, the last to be published during Hawthorne's lifetime, appeared in 1851.

See also "The CANTERBURY PILGRIMS," "The DEVIL IN MANUSCRIPT," "ETHAN BRAND," "JOHN INGLEFIELD'S THANKSGIVING," "LITTLE DAFFYDOWN-DILLY," "MAIN-STREET," "The MAN OF ADAMANT," "MY KINSMAN, MAJOR MOLINEUX," "OLD TICOND-EROGA," and "PREFACE TO *THE SNOW-IMAGE, AND OTHER TWICE-TOLD TALES.*"

PREFACE TO *THE SNOW-IMAGE, AND OTHER TWICE-TOLD TALES*

The preface takes the form of a letter to HORATIO BRIDGE, Hawthorne's longtime friend from BOW-DOIN COLLEGE. It was written at Lenox, Massachusetts, and is dated November 1, 1851.

Hawthorne admits that many of his critics have pronounced him "egotistical, indiscreet, and even impertinent" on the basis of his prefaces. He does not concur with such criticism, though, since the public as a whole has evinced more interest in his introductions than in the stories themselves. He is, in fact, only addressing a "very limited circle of friendly readers."

However, he states that he is addressing Bridge "as friend speaks to friend." He recalls their time at college, gathering blueberries in "study-hours," watching the great logs tumble along the current of the Androscoggin River, or catching trout. Even though he has become a "fiction-monger," he recognizes the "weary delay" he experienced in obtaining any recognition from the public.

Clearly discouraged about his writing career, Hawthorne states that he is now publishing a few pieces omitted from his earlier collections. Some of the sketches were among the earliest he wrote; others were written recently. He declares that the "public need not dread my again trespassing on its kindness, with any more of these musty and mouse-nibbled leaves of old periodicals, transformed by the magic arts of my friendly publishers, into a new book."

Tanglewood Tales for Girls and Boys, Being a Second Wonder-book

Story collection published in America by Ticknor, Reed, and Fields, in September 1853. This volume was initially planned as the second *Wonder-book* Hawthorne would write. In it, he retells six Greek myths dealing with revenge, transformation, and the long-term effects brought about in the course of time: "The MINOTAUR," "The PYG-MIES," "The DRAGON'S TEETH," "CIRCE'S PALACE," "The POMEGRANATE-SEEDS," and "The GOLDEN FLEECE" (Wineapple, Brenda, *Hawthorne: A Life*, 444).

The anonymous reviewer for GRAHAM'S MAG-AZINE termed the volume representative of Hawthorne's genius in "its most attractive form." He or she found the style of the narration "faultless" and observed that the "obedient words seem to melt softly into the mould of the author's fine conceptions." The book was "a work of art for children." The stories "evince the felicity and transforming power of genius, and are to be rigidly distinguished from ordinary books for children." The volume, "like all true children's books," affords "delightful reading to the old" (Crowley, J. Donald, ed., *The Critical Heritage: Nathaniel Hawthorne*, 282–284).

"Thomas Green Fessenden"

Sketch published in *The AMERICAN MONTHLY MAGAZINE* in January 1838 and reprinted in the *Essex Register* for January 25, 1838, and January 29, 1838. The newspaper noted that it was collected in *Fanshawe and Other Pieces* (Boston: James R. Osgood and Company, 1876).

Fessenden, as Hawthorne explains, was the eldest of nine children of the Reverend Thomas Fessenden. He was a native of Walpole, New Hampshire, the son and grandson of ministers. He attended Dartmouth College, graduating in 1796. He became a poet and an attorney, and he edited various newspapers. In 1822, he established the *New England Farmer*, which he edited until his death. He wrote agricultural handbooks such as the *Complete Farmer and Rural Economist* (1834). He was elected to the Massachusetts General Court in 1836.

He was also an inventor. In 1801, he went to England, where he was involved in several unprofitable ventures. He wrote a poem in opposition to the use of metallic tractors called "Terrible Tractoration"; it was published anonymously. Hawthorne called it "a work of strange, grotesque ideas, aptly expressed."

Hawthorne regretted not drawing from Fessenden "many details that would have been well worth remembering" but added that Fessenden was not "copious in personal reminiscences" and seldom spoke of the noted writers and politicians he had known. He stated that there was a movement to erect a monument to him in Mount Auburn Cemetery, in Cambridge. He concludes, "Let the laurel be carved on his memorial-stone—for it will cover the ashes of a man of genius."

"Threefold Destiny: A Faëry Legend, The"

Tale published in *The American Monthly Magazine* in March 1888 and collected in *Twice-Told Tales*, second edition (1842). It was signed "By Ashley Allen Royce."

The story opens with the premise that Hawthorne is presenting an allegory, combining the form of the fairy legend with the "characters and manners of familiar life."

A tall, dark figure, who has traveled widely, returns to New England. His arm casually touches that of a young woman on her way to an evening lecture. "Ralph Cranfield!" she cries. He recognizes her as his old playmate, Faith Egerton.

Cranfield has begun to believe that only one maiden will make him happy by her love. He will roam the world until he finds a beautiful woman wearing a jewel in the shape of a heart. He will say to her, "'Maiden, I have brought you a heavy heart. May I rest its weight on you?'" If she is his kindred soul, she will reply, touching the jewel, "'This token, which I have worn so long, is the assurance that you may!'"

He also thinks that a hidden treasure will be revealed only to him. He will have a sign—a hand pointing downward, and beneath it the Latin word "EFFODE—Dig!" When he does so, he will be rewarded by the treasure.

A third miraculous event will be the attainment of extensive influence over his fellow creatures. Three venerable men will claim an audience with him. One will be an ancient sage bearing a "heaven-instructed message" that will lead to "glorious results."

Cranfield sets forth to seek the maid, the treasure, and the venerable sage. As he walks through the village, no one recognizes him. He seems to arrive at the gate of his mother's small house. He sees an inscription, the Latin word *effode*, with a hand pointing downward. The door opens and an elderly woman appears; she is his mother. Morning breaks and news spreads of his return.

The villagers are glad for his mother's sake. The widow Cranfield looks out and sees three visitors from the village, Squire Hawkwood and two other men. They have arrived to see Ralph and to ask him to be the instructor of the village school. Ralph reflects on his travels. As he walks the village streets, his shadow lingers among "distant objects." Something tells him the village children are to be his charge.

He is then welcomed by Faith Egerton, who is wearing a heart-shaped ornament on her bosom. He is very pleased to see the brooch, his parting gift to her, and tells her he has nothing for her but a heavy heart. He rests the weight of his heart on her and clasps her to his bosom.

The reality of his new life sets in. He must till the earth around his mother's cottage to find the "mysterious treasure." He will not hold "warlike command, or regal or religious sway" over people but will rule over the village children. And finally, instead of the "visionary maid" for whom he was searching, he has found the playmate of his childhood. The narrator concludes, "Happy they who read the riddle without a weary world-search, or a lifetime spent in vain!"

Buford Jones, in "The *Faery Land* of Hawthorne's Romances," suggests that Spenser's *The Faerie Queene* is a possible source for the tale. He finds that Hawthorne's announced intention of following "the spirit and mechanism of the faery legend" points to Spenser's poem as such an analogue.

FOR FURTHER READING

Folsom, James F., *Man's Accidents and God's Purposes: Multiplicity in Hawthorne's Fiction* (New Haven, Conn.: College and University Press, 1963); Jones, Buford, "The *Faery Land* of Hawthorne's Romances," *Emerson Society Quarterly* 48 (1967): 106–124.

"Three Golden Apples, The"

Story in *A Wonder-Book for Girls and Boys*, published in 1852, after Hawthorne's death.

The narrator begins by giving background on the "golden apples" that grew "in the garden of the Hesperides." Many adventurous men have "set out in quest of this fruit" but failed because the tree is guarded by a dragon with 100 heads.

One day, a young hero wanders through Italy, wearing a lion skin and carrying a "mighty club." He meets some beautiful maidens "twining wreaths of flowers" beside a river and asks them the way to the garden of the Hesperides. They ask what he wants there, and he explains that "a certain king," his "severe and cruel" cousin, has ordered him to get three of the apples. The maidens try to convince him to turn back. He tells them "the story of his life," and of his many adventures fighting beasts and giants and monsters of all kinds. When he finishes his narrative, he tells the maidens his name is Hercules. They instruct him to find the Old One, or the

Old Man of the Sea, and to "hold him fast" until he provides further directions to the golden apples.

Hercules journeys onward toward the sea. At the end of a beach, he sees the sleeping figure of the Old One, a "web-footed and web-fingered" creature with scales on his arms and legs. He grabs the Old One's arm and leg, but is astonished to see the creature turn into a stag, a sea bird, a three-headed dog, a six-legged man-monster, and then a snake. The Old One has the "power of assuming any shape he pleased" but finally gives up and reappears as himself. He realizes he will not be freed until he tells Hercules "everything that he wanted to know," so he gives directions and warnings of the "many difficulties which must be overcome." These adventures include fighting a giant named Antaeus, being taken prisoner in Egypt, and passing through the "deserts of Africa."

When Hercules finally reaches the ocean, he spots an "immense cup or bowl" floating in the distance. The "lustrous" cup washes ashore near him, and he realizes it must have been "set adrift by some unseen power" and guided to this spot in order to take him to the garden of the Hesperides. He climbs inside the cup, which floats across the sea to an island. Here he meets Atlas, an "intolerably big giant" who is "as tall as a mountain" and supports the sky upon his head. Atlas tells him he is the only one who can go to the garden and take the golden apples. They agree that Hercules will hold up the sky temporarily, while the weary giant stretches his legs and gets the apples for him.

Hercules worries about what he will do if the giant fails to return, but eventually he sees Atlas approaching, carrying "three magnificent golden apples, as big as pumpkins, all hanging from one branch." The giant suggests he take the apples to the king himself and leave Hercules supporting the sky for "the next hundred years, or perhaps the next thousand." The impatient Hercules asks Atlas to take the sky back for just "one instant" while he makes a "cushion . . . for the weight to rest upon." The giant says he will take it back "only for five minutes," but Hercules promptly picks up the apples and sets off for home.

To this day, the giant—or "a mountain as tall as he"—still stands in that spot, and "when the thunder rumbles about its summit, we may imagine it to be the voice of Giant Atlas, bellowing after Hercules!"

"Time's Portraiture"

This sketch was published in The DOLLIVER ROMANCE, a collection of tales and sketches produced by Ticknor & Fields and James R. Osgood, first edition, first printing, in 1876. It takes the form of an oration titled "The Carrier's Address to the Patrons of the Salem Gazette, for the First of January 1838."

As a newspaper carrier, the speaker assumes the role of one of "Time's errand-boys." Time, the "old gentleman," sends the carriers about the town to let people know what they are thinking about and what they are doing. He tells the "Kind Patrons" of the newspaper that he has been forgotten by the "Muse" and cannot write verse for them. He must address them in prose.

He goes on to point out many erroneous stereotypes related to "Time." He is not the symbolic "Father Time" depicted on the Farmer's Almanac wearing a pair of wings and carrying an hourglass. Instead, he may appear as a fashionably dressed man with a gold watch. Time does not wander among ruins and sit on moldering walls and tombs. He may be found, rather, in the Essex Street promenade, walking with young men, inviting friends to drink champagne, and talking with merchants. Time can, however, be mischievous. He may cause a middle-aged man to age, for example.

Time is also eager to talk of modern novelties and does not dwell in the past. He may relate rumors or comment on boundary questions or scandals. He may criticize a sermon or a lecture. His literary tastes do not run to dusty tomes at the Athenaeum; he keeps up with the latest novels and works to correct such problems as railroad strikes. He attends weddings, pretending to be merry but secretly sighing. He hastens from the birth chamber to the bedsides of the dying. Time is not immortal but must himself die, as history has told us. He stirs up strife throughout the world.

The petition from the newspaper carrier concludes with a plea for any extra change newspaper readers may have in their pockets: "Be generous kind Patrons, to Time's errand boy." He may bear ships home safe from the Indies, new suits to lawyers, new patients to doctors, and golden crops and good markets to farmers. In another year, Time may again give to the newspaper patron his "loving little friend, The Carrier."

"Toll-Gatherer's Day, The: A Sketch of Transitory Life"

Sketch first published in UNITED STATES MAGAZINE AND DEMOCRATIC REVIEW, October 1837, and collected in TWICE-TOLD TALES, second edition (1842). EDGAR ALLAN POE, reviewing Twice-told Tales for GRAHAM'S MAGAZINE, termed it a "pure essay" rather than a tale.

The narrator reflects on the occupation of a toll-gatherer, one of the people whose natures are "too indolent, or too sensitive" to endure the weather and the "turmoil of moral and physical elements" to which the "wayfarers of the world" expose themselves. He imagines what a toll-gatherer's day might be like. The toll-gatherer is aroused from his slumbers by the "distant roll of ponderous wheels" and throws open the gates for the passage of a load of hay drawn by oxen. Then horses arrive drawing the mail coach, which may also have some sleepy passengers.

The toll-gatherer's hermitage is situated on a bridge above some murmuring waters. Inside, he has walls with advertisements nailed on them. As more vehicles arrive, he can estimate the weight of each one, the number of wheels, and the number of horses crossing the bridge. There may be a family chaise, occupied by a couple with a "rosy-cheeked little girl sitting gladsomely between them." Next is a four-wheeled "carryall," occupied by six "frolicksome maidens" and a single gentleman.

A country preacher arrives, en route to a "protracted meeting." A milk cart rattles along briskly, carrying milk in large tin canisters. Then a stylish barouche appears, containing a young man and a young woman beneath a snowy veil; another young white-robed woman sits in front. They are a married couple with one of their bridesmaids. Another carriage arrives with a "fragile figure" leaning against a "manly form"; she is apparently dying. As the day goes on, and the Sun grows hotter, the horses are increasingly sluggish.

At noon, the bridge is lifted to permit a schooner to pass through, but it sticks in the middle of the stream while various travelers wait impatiently. They are going both ways: a Frenchman with a hand organ, an itinerant Swiss jeweler, a train of wagons carrying various animals, a company of summer soldiers. Finally the schooner eases through, the bridge descends, and the toll-gatherer faces the westward sunset. He looks "seaward" and sees the lighthouse on a far island. He has witnessed, during such a typical day, "the whole procession of mortal travellers," but they seem a "flitting show of phantoms for his thoughtful soul to muse upon."

True Stories from History and Biography

A collection published in 1851, which was a prolific year for Hawthorne. The volume contained GRANDFATHER'S CHAIR and BIOGRAPHICAL STORIES.

GRANDFATHER'S CHAIR narrates the principal events in the history of New England in "exciting incidents, characteristic portraiture, and just reflections." The reviewer for GRAHAM'S MAGAZINE described Hawthorne's purpose as enlightening and for amusing young readers.

BIOGRAPHICAL STORIES depicts historical characters: Benjamin West, Sir Isaac Newton, Samuel Johnson, Oliver Cromwell, Benjamin Franklin, and Queen Christina. The *Graham's Magazine* reviewer declared that Hawthorne's genius was visible throughout the book, as particularly evident in "the ease with which it is accommodated to the comprehension of young readers." The historic characters have "the reality of actual men and women." The

stories give "living and distinct ideas of persons, who were before mere names and shadowy abstractions" (*Hawthorne: The Critical Heritage*, edited by J. Donald Crowley, 185).

Other works making an appearance that year were *The HOUSE OF THE SEVEN GABLES* and *The SNOW-IMAGE AND OTHER TWICE-TOLD TALES*.

Twenty Days with Julian and Little Bunny

The journal Hawthorne kept in Lenox, Massachusetts, in July 1851. (Hawthorne and his family lived in a house called The Red Shanty from May 1850 to November 1851.) Sophia, Una, and Rosebud, the baby, were out of town. Julian was at first delighted to have Rosebud gone; he told his father he could "shout and squeal just as loud as I please." He missed his mother greatly, though. Hawthorne noted that it was impossible to write, read, think, or even to sleep, "so constant" were Julian's appeals to him "in one way or another." At the same time, the child was "such a genial and good-humored little man" that he found an enjoyment intermixed with the annoyance.

They had a rabbit, Bunny, but Hawthorne felt there should really be two rabbits, "in order to bring out each other's remarkable qualities—if any there be." Julian became tired of Bunny and it was up to Hawthorne to collect leaves and feed him. He confided, in his notebook, that he was strongly tempted to "murder him privately," although he did not (*American Notebooks* [New Haven, Conn.: Yale University Press, 1932]: 213–217).

The journal was printed in an edition of 30 copies by Stephen H. Wakeman in 1904 and later reprinted (*American Notebooks*, 324).

Twice-told Tales

Collection of previously published tales, the first that appeared under Hawthorne's name. The first edition of 1,000 copies was published in 1837 and enjoyed immediate successs. HENRY WADSWORTH LONGFELLOW wrote a highly favorable review of it for the *North American Review* (July 1937; *see* Appendix), helping establish Hawthorne's literary reputation. The second edition appeared in 1842, and a third edition in 1851.

See also "DAVID SWAN," "DR. HEIDEGGER'S EXPERIMENT," "THE GENTLE BOY," "THE GRAY CHAMPION," "THE GREAT CARBUNCLE," "THE HAUNTED MIND," "THE HOLLOW OF THE THREE HILLS," "LEGENDS OF THE PROVINCED-HOUSE," "THE LILY'S QUEST," "LITTLE ANNIE'S RAMBLE," "THE MAY-POLE OF MERRY MOUNT." "THE MINISTER'S BLACK VIEL," "MR. HIGGINBOTHAM'S CATASTROPE," "PREFACE TO THE 1851 EDITION OF *TWICE-TOLD TALES*," "THE PROPHETIC PICTURES," "A RILL FROM THE TOWN-PUMP," "THE SEVEN VAGABONDS," "THE TOLL-GATHERER'S DAY," "THE VILLAGE UNCLE," "WAKEFIELD," and "THE WEDDING-KNELL."

PREFACE TO THE 1851 EDITION OF *TWICE-TOLD TALES*

In the 1851 preface, Hawthorne claims the distinction of having been, for many years, "the obscurest man of letters in America." He explains that the stories were first published in various magazines and annuals over a period of 10 or 12 years. During this time, he had no expectation of profit, only the pleasure of composition. Even after the first collected edition of 1,000 copies was published in 1837, Hawthorne recalls, any literary ambition the "Author" might have felt perished "beyond resuscitation, in the dearth of nutriment." He did not regard himself as addressing the "American public, or, indeed, any public at all." He was merely writing to his "known or unknown" friends. Even so, the *Twice-told Tales* gained a certain vogue; they had "the pale tint of flowers that blossomed in too retired a shade."

The volumes represent an opportunity "to open an intercourse with the world." He has written the preface only as an opportunity to express how much enjoyment he has owed the volumes both before and since their publication. The author, he believes, would have been judged on the "internal evidence" of the sketches to be a "mild, shy, gentle, melancholic, exceedingly sensitive, and not very forcible man, hiding his blushes under an assumed name, the quaintness of which was supposed, somehow or other, to symbolize his personal and literary traits."

He is convinced now, however, that the volumes have opened the way to "agreeable associations, and to the formation of imperishable friendships." Therefore, he is "satisfied with what the Twice-told Tales have done for him, and feels it to be far better than fame" (Crowley, J. Donald, ed., *The Critical Heritage: Nathaniel Hawthorne*, 228–229).

"Village Uncle, The: An Imaginary Retrospect"

Sketch published in *TWICE-TOLD TALES*, second edition, 1842, and later included in *LITTLE ANNIE'S RAMBLE AND OTHER TALES*, 1853.

The sketch depicts the recollections of an old man sitting before his fire on Thanksgiving night. As he looks about the room, memories of the past crowd into his mind. He recalls another room, more than a half-century ago, which lacked the ship's model, chest of drawers, books, and pictures now surrounding him. He has no regrets about the intervening years, however. If he were once again a solitary hermit, he would not have known the happiness he had with his wife, Susan.

He summons memories of her, asking her to stand before him once more in her cap and gown. He recalls seeing her standing on a bridge over a brook. This memory leads to many others, of the village where they once lived and of their children. He calls up recollections of the small grocery stores, the fleet of boats in the harbor, and their small dwelling. He then wanders, in his mind, to nearby rocky ledges overlooking the sea and visualizes the old fishermen he has known, some of whom had sailed on Marblehead schooners as far as Newfoundland.

Once he and Susan were married, he built a small cottage for them. It had a gateway made of a whale's jawbones, and a sitting room with a Bible, which he would read aloud in the evenings. When children arrived, he would lead them along the beach "and point to nature in the vast and the minute, the sky, the sea, the green earth, the pebbles and the shells."

His mind wanders on to his many friends and relatives, now deceased. Lest the reader believe his reminiscences to be melancholy, he insists that his "calm old age" is the happiest portion of his life. His pleasures are simple—the play of village children, the swoop of gulls, and the white sails of ships in the distance. Amid his reminiscences, however, he is aware that he may yet be subject to the "stern reality" of misfortune. For the present, however, he has "the prospect of a happy life, and the fairest hope of Heaven."

"Virtuoso's Collection, A"

Sketch published in the first edition of MOSSES FROM AN OLD MANSE (1846). As in "EARTH'S HOLOCAUST" and several other tales, Hawthorne depicts groups of people or things that move through space or time. They illustrate, as Terence Martin puts it, "some fundamental truth, or aberration, of human nature" (*Nathaniel Hawthorne*, 19).

In this tale or sketch, the writer recalls stepping into an imaginary museum with a notice: "To Be Seen Here: A Virtuoso's Collection." He encounters a rather enigmatic guide, a "middle-aged person," who escorts him through the museum. The guide points out a collection of stuffed animals; one, he declares, is "the wolf that devoured Little Red Riding-Hood." A lamb is purportedly the one in Spenser's *Faerie Queene*. Other animals appear with literary associations: Ulysses's faithful dog, Argus; Dr. Samuel Johnson's cat, Hodge; and a stag purportedly killed by Shakespeare.

There are Minerva's owl, Coleridge's albatross, Robinson Crusoe's parrot, the emperor Nero's fiddle, Claude's palette, Charles Lamb's pipe, Aladdin's lamp, the shield of Achilles, the golden thigh of Pythagoras, Peter Stuyvesant's wooden leg, and King Arthur's sword, Excalibur. He then stumbles over a large bundle, which is Christian's burden of sin, mentioned in Bunyan's *Pilgrim's Progress*. Other artifacts include the Philosopher's Stone and many famous missing books, including Joseph Smith's autographed Mormon Bible. The "Virtuoso" is finally revealed as "the Wandering Jew."

In such writings, in which Hawthorne tries to evoke the past from significant scenes in the present, there is a certain contrast between the tenuous vision of the past and the clear material concept of the present. The historical imagination is vague and can vary from person to person, writer to writer. Objects of perception are, however, substantial, even though there may be variations in people's recollections and mental reforming of them.

Charles Wilkins Webber, writing in an unsigned essay titled "Hawthorne," which appeared in the *American Whig Review*, stated that in this sketch Hawthorne gives "a real substance and entity to everything our childhood ever knew" (Crowley, J. Donald, ed., *Nathaniel Hawthorne: The Critical Heritage*, 133). Arlin Turner observes that Hawthorne had an "omnivorous curiosity," and that the sketch is not a mere catalog of famous artifacts. Instead, he adds a "figurative or an ironic touch" to each item from literature, mythology, geography, or history (*Nathaniel Hawthorne: A Biography*, 82–83).

This was the only tale Hawthorne wrote before his wedding. Brenda Wineapple suggests that the virtuoso may represent the "solitary, unmarried" Hawthorne. He is the "pitiless museum-keeper of the human heart."

"Vision of the Fountain, The"

Sketch published in NEW-ENGLAND MAGAZINE in August 1835, signed "By the Author of 'The Gray Champion,'" and reprinted in the *Salem Gazette* in March 1837. It was collected in TWICE-TOLD TALES (1837) and signed "By N. Hawthorne" in the *New-York Mirror* on April 28, 1838.

The sketch recalls Hawthorne's stay at the boarding school run by the Reverend Caleb Bradley (1772–1861) at Stroudwater, a suburb of Portland, Maine, from December 1818 to February 1819 (Turner, *Nathaniel Hawthorne: A Biography*,

20). HENRY WADSWORTH LONGFELLOW chose this sketch to illustrate Hawthorne's "bright, poetic style" (Crowley, J. Donald, ed., *Nathaniel Hawthorne: The Critical Heritage,* 16).

"Wakefield"

Short story probably written between 1832 and 1834. It was first published in the NEW-ENGLAND MAGAZINE in May 1835; it was signed "By the author of 'The Gray Champion.'" It was collected in TWICE-TOLD TALES, first edition, 1837.

The story is set in London. The source is announced at the outset of the narrative: "In some old magazine or newspaper, I recollect a story." It follows an account in William King's *Political and Literary Anecdotes of His Own Times* (1818) of a man named Howe. After seven or eight years of marriage, Howe left his wife one morning, supposedly to take a business trip, and did not return for 17 years. According to King, "After he returned home he never would confess, even to his most intimate friends, what was the real cause of such a singular conduct; apparently there was none."

Hawthorne's hero is named Wakefield. He is "intellectual, but not actively so"; his heart is "cold, but not depraved nor wandering." His acquaintances would be likely to select him as the man "surest to perform nothing today which should be remembered on the morrow." Only his wife sees in him a "quiet selfishness," a "peculiar sort of vanity," and a tendency to keep "petty secrets."

In the "dusk of an October evening," Wakefield leaves home and tells his wife he will be back within a week. He says he is going "into the country," but instead he finds an apartment "in the next street to his own." This enables him to see how she "will endure her widowhood" and how his absence affects the "little sphere of creatures and circumstances, in which he was a central object." He buys a red wig and old clothes in order to disguise himself. His proximity to home allows him to ascertain his wife's subsequent illness and recovery; he sees her growing "paler" and more "anxious" and in the third week notices a doctor

visiting the house. She "gradually recovers" in the space of a few weeks.

Over the next 10 years, the "self-banished" Wakefield haunts his house and remains "faithful to his wife." In the 10th year of separation, he has an anonymous face-to-face encounter with Mrs. Wakefield in a crowded street. He is now a "meagre" man with "small and lustreless" eyes; she is a "portly female" with a prayer book in one hand and the "placid mien of settled widowhood" on her face. Wakefield hurries back to his lodgings and wonders whether he is mad. Now that he leads the "life of a hermit," he has given up "his place and privileges with living men, without being admitted among the dead."

Hawthorne does not allow Wakefield to return to his wife until 20 years has passed (following the pattern set by Washington Irving in "Rip Van Winkle"). When he does return home, it is in an "unpremeditated moment." Wakefield is standing near the house, "wet and shivering," when he decides to go inside, where there is "a good fire to warm him," and "his own wife . . . to fetch the gray coat and small-clothes" for him.

The narrator closes with a statement on the horror of isolation from one's fellow men: "Amid the seeming confusion of our mysterious world, individuals are so nicely adjusted to a system, and systems to one another, and to a whole, that, by stepping aside for a moment, a man exposes himself to a fearful risk of losing his place for ever. Like Wakefield, he may become, as it were, the Outcast of the Universe."

CRITICAL ANALYSIS

In William King's account, Howe changes his name, dons a black wig, and takes a room in another part of London. Although Hawthorne changes some details of the story in his version, he retains King's emphasis on the central character's lack of motivation. Wakefield does not attend church services, however, unlike Howe, who managed to sit where he had a view of his wife (but was not visible himself).

In Hawthorne's tale, the narrator is flawed, in that his imaginings have no actual basis in reality. He makes up the story, basing it on a newspaper article about a man called Wakefield who leaves his wife, moves into an apartment near her residence, and lets her assume he has completely disappeared. For 20 years he is away, and then, without notice, he returns home. He imagines different constructions that might be attached to his story, including a moral: "There will be a pervading spirit and a moral, even should we fail to find them, done up neatly, and condensed into the final sentence." He is contemptuous of the implication that the story should even have a moral.

The narrator considers Wakefield's character to be weak from the outset. As is evident to only his wife, Wakefield is marked by a "quiet selfishness" and a "peculiar sort of vanity." She thinks that after he leaves, he opens the door and leans back in to smirk at her. She does not permit herself, therefore, to be identified as a widow during the ensuing 20 years. In this way, she establishes herself as a more reliable narrator so far as the reader is concerned.

Wakefield himself has been called a sadist, since he gains pleasure from hurting others. He becomes paranoid, since he does recognize his cruelty; this causes him to walk down the street sideways, to wander about apprehensively, and to look inward as he walks. He is, moreover, pleased when he anticipates the possibility of his wife's death. The narrator has been identified with Wakefield, but the journey and the narrative itself both lack coherence. Robert Chibka notes that the first paragraph, although it evokes a world devoid of moral or psychological cause and effect, "instills a desire for the golden world" where everything has a clear meaning ("Hawthorne's Tale Told Twice: A Reading of 'Wakefield,'" *ESQ* 28 [1982]: 230).

Terence Martin suggests that Wakefield is an "apostate from home." He leaves home out of whimsy and stays away because of a stubborn quality and also because of "a creeping paralysis of will." He eventually loses his place in the world (Martin, Nathaniel *Hawthorne*, 79).

Evan Carton ("Nathaniel Hawthorne") observes that many of Hawthorne's early works raise the question "whether one can know oneself at all." "Wakefield" suggests "the fragility, the inexplicability, and—anticipating a twentieth-century literary development—even the Kafkaesque absurdity of

the self." With a setting of London, the "prototype of the disorienting modern city," the story is one of the "earliest narratives of urban anonymity and alienation." But that alienation is, of course, "more psychological than environmental." Wakefield, an unremarkable man living an unremarkable life, vanishes from his life on a "perverse whim"—which turns into 20 years of alienation before his return home, a decision based on hardly more thought than his departure.

The closing lines of the story are the source for Hawthorne's principal statement on the horror of isolating oneself from humanity. Wakefield himself has been called a "stick figure" because of his emotional emptiness; his feelings and motivation are shallow and arid (Bunge, Nancy, *Nathaniel Hawthorne: A Study of the Short Fiction*, 38–39).

CHARACTERS

Wakefield Protagonist of "Wakefield," Hawthorne's tale built on the theme of isolation. The reader shares in the character's alienation. Hawthorne addresses the reader: "If the reader choose, let him do his own meditation; or, if he prefer to ramble with me through the twenty years of Wakefield's vagary, I bid him welcome." He asks, "What sort of a man was Wakefield? We are free to shape out our own idea, and call it by his name. . . . Let us now imagine Wakefield bidding adieu to his wife." Hawthorne thus establishes a certain intimacy with the reader.

Some readers, however, find it extremely difficult to relate to the enigmatic Wakefield. He becomes more human when he accidentally meets his wife, rushes home, throws himself on his bed, and "cries out passionately" his awareness of himself: "Wakefield! Wakefield! You are mad!" Hawthorne eventually assures the reader that he or she lives in a regulated, orderly world. Wakefield is an anomaly, an emblem of alienation.

FOR FURTHER READING

Carton, Evan, "Nathaniel Hawthorne," *American Writers* (New York: Scribner, 1998), 145–167; Chibka, Robert, "Hawthorne's Tale Told Twice: A Reading of 'Wakefield,'" *ESQ* 28 (1982); Doubleday, Neal, *Hawthorne's Early Tales: A Critical Study*

(Durham, N.C.: Duke University Press, 1972); Drake, Samuel Adams, *A Book of New England Legends and Folk Lore in Prose and Poetry* (Boston: Little, Brown, 1906); Martin, Terence, *Nathaniel Hawthorne* (Chapel Hill, N.C.: Twayne, 1983).

"Wedding-knell, The"

Story first published in THE TOKEN AND ATLANTIC SOUVENIR in 1836 and collected in TWICE-TOLD TALES (1837).

Mr. Ellenwood, 65, is an unworldly scholar and bachelor who has led an "aimless and abortive life." He is about to marry a wealthy widow, an early love who has had two previous marriages. The ceremony is to take place in an Episcopal church in New York. The wedding party is "made up of youth and gaiety" with the exception of the principal figures. Just as the bride reaches the threshold, the church bell in the tower peals a deep funereal knell.

As the wedding party advances up the aisle, the bell peals again, and seems "to fill the church with a visible gloom, dimming and obscuring the bright pageant, till it shone forth again as from a mist." The wedding party continues up the aisle. The rector speaks to them, recalling a marriage sermon given by the well-known Bishop Taylor, tinged with thoughts of mortality. He sends an attendant to silence the bell, but it continues to peal.

The widow seems apprehensive and confesses that she expects her two first husbands to accompany her bridegroom into the church. They will act as groomsmen. A "dark procession" makes its way up the aisle; it consists of the widow's former friends from her youth. They are now old and withered. The bridegroom enters in his shroud, or burial garment. He is referred to as a corpse. He invites his bride to be married to him, and then to go with him to their coffins.

The widow is horrified. She speaks to him, saying he is not well. He stands beside her, saying with a "wild bitterness" that she took away his youth and now he will not release her. Her other husbands enjoyed her youth and beauty; he must endure her decay and death. This is why he has summoned her "funeral friends." She begs him to marry her,

saying he is her true love and she wants to wed him for "Eternity." The ceremony proceeds, and at the end of the "awful rite" the organ's "peal of solemn triumph" drowns the "Wedding-Knell." The story ends with the union of "two immortal souls."

The story has a number of literary analogues, such as the German ballad "Lenore" (Lundblad, Jane, *Nathaniel Hawthorne and the European Literary Tradition* [Cambridge, Mass.: Harvard University Press, 1947]).

"White Old Maid, The"

Tale first published in the NEW-ENGLAND MAGAZINE in May 1835 and collected in TWICE-TOLD TALES, second edition, in 1842.

Nina Baym has termed the story an example of a "standard melodramatic gothic exercise" (*The Shape of Hawthorne's Career*, 48). The principal characters in the tale are two women. Edith, known in town as the "Old Maid in the Winding-sheet," is a "quiet, sad, and gentle" woman, now very elderly. She is entirely nonviolent and pursues her "harmless fantasies" without disturbing people. She lives alone and only emerges into daylight when she follows funeral processions.

The other woman, more sinister, arrives in the village in an elegant coach one day. A coachman is seated high in front and there is a footman behind. An ancient lady thrusts her head from the coach, preparing to descend. She has a look about her of something evil, unlike the White Old Maid. She is called the Old Maid. With a hideous grin, she enters the deserted mansion of old Colonel Fenwicke, now deceased. The mansion has been vacant for 15 years. Suddenly a shriek is heard emanating from the mansion; it is "too fearfully distinct for doubt."

An old clergyman and his attendant ascend the steps of the mansion. They arrive before a closed door, on their left, and an open door of a chamber, on their right. The clergyman points to the carved oak door on the left and says he recalls, "a whole lifetime" earlier, sitting within the chamber by the deathbed of a "goodly young man." He throws it open and discovers the corpse of the Old Maid in the Winding-Sheet on her knees before the corpse of the Old Maid. In her hand is a lock of hair, once sable but now covered with greenish mold. The story has been proposed as a source for William Faulkner's "A Rose for Emily."

FOR FURTHER READING

Barnes, Daniel R., "Faulkner's Miss Emily and Hawthorne's Old Maid"; Baym, Nina, *The Shape of Hawthorne's Career* (Ithaca: Cornell University Press, 1976); Van Doren, Mark, *Hawthorne* (New York: W. Sloane Associates, 1949).

Whole History of Grandfather's Chair, The

See GRANDFATHER'S CHAIR: A HISTORY FOR YOUTH.

"Wives of the Dead, The"

Tale first published in THE TOKEN in 1831, dated 1832, with no attribution. Hawthorne had sent it, along with several other tales, to SAMUEL GRISWOLD GOODRICH in 1829, hoping to find a publisher. Hawthorne did not include it in a collection until 1851. It was later collected in *The Gray Champion and Other Stories and Sketches by Nathaniel Hawthorne* (Cambridge, Mass.: Houghton Mifflin/Riverside Press, 1889).

Two young women, Margaret and Mary, both recent brides of brothers, have received bad news; their husbands are both reported to have died. Mary's husband was a sailor drowned in the Atlantic; Margaret's was a landsman, killed in warfare with Canada. Many callers have arrived in their home, including their minister, who whispers "comfortable passages of Scripture." Now the two young women, finally left alone, are sleeping restlessly. They find consolation in each other's experiences and weep together.

Later that night, Margaret suddenly hears a slow, steady knock on the door. She rises, seizes a lamp, opens the window, and sees Goodman Parker, a local innkeeper. He says he was afraid Mary might answer the door. He reports that Margaret's husband is "well and sound" and was not slain. Margaret's mind is "thronged with delightful thoughts" until she falls asleep.

Some hours later, Mary wakes. She cannot remember her vivid dream but hears a rapid knocking at the door. She opens it and sees a former suitor she has rejected, Stephen. He tells her he bears good news about her husband, who survived when their ship turned upside down. Mary feels much sympathy for Margaret, until she looks at her and finds she is asleep, with an expression of sublime joy. She sets down her lamp and rearranges Margaret's bedclothes.

RECEPTION AND CRITICAL ANALYSIS

James Hall's "The Annuals," a review of THE TOKEN for 1832, mentioned "The Wives of the Dead" as having "a touch of nature about it which goes to the heart, and a spirit which awakens interest."

The story has sometimes been compared with the sketch "Footprints on the SeaShore," both dealing with the motif of the sea. It has also been connected with *Seven Tales of My Native Land.* Hawthorne employs the American past in the story as a motif and an emblem. According to Nina Baym in "Hawthorne's Gothic Discards: *Fanshawe* and "Alice Doane's Appeal" (*Nathaniel Hawthorne Journal*, 4) the story is one of several Hawthorne wrote that are "antithetical to historical facts." Although he presents the actual facts objectively, he depicts American history as "a remote and shadowy meeting ground for the merger of the actual with the imaginary."

There are many structural parallels within the tale: Each wife is sleeping restlessly, each is awakened by someone outside, each stops herself from waking the other when good news arrives. The story has long been considered ambiguous, if not frustrating to readers. Some people believe the events of the night are only a dream, and that the reports that Margaret's and Mary's husbands are alive are only an illusion. The lamp is the lamp of human sympathy, suggesting that the men have indeed died. Other readers believe the experiences of the characters are actual events. One critic has stated that the two women both suffer from "estranged vision and confused perception" (Baym, *The Shape of Hawthorne's Career* New York: W. Sloan Associates, 1949), 32.

FOR FURTHER READING

Baym, Nina, "Hawthorne's Gothic Discards: *Fanshawe* and "Alice Doane's Appeal," *Nathaniel Hawthorne Journal* 4 (1974): 105–115; Baym, Nina, *The Shape of Hawthorne's Career* (New York: W. Sloan Associates, 1949), 32; Harris, Mark, "The Wives of the Living? Absence of Dreams in Hawthorne's 'The Wives of the Dead,'" *Studies in Short Fiction* 29, no. 3 (summer 1992): 323–329; Levin, Harry, *The Power of Blackness: Hawthorne, Poe, and Melville* (New York: Alfred A. Knopf, 1958); Schubert, Leland, *Hawthorne, the Artist: Fine Art Devices in Fiction* (Chapel Hill: North Carolina University Press, 1944).

Wonder-Book for Girls and Boys, A

Volume of classical myths, adapted for children, published in November 1851. It contained the retelling of six tales, about Medusa ("The GORGON'S HEAD"), Midas ("The GOLDEN TOUCH"), Pandora ("The PARADISE OF CHILDREN"), the Golden Apples ("The THREE GOLDEN APPLES"), Philemon and Baucis ("The MIRACULOUS PITCHER"), and Pegasus ("The CHIMAERA").

A notice in the *Boston Transcript* on October 9, 1851, announced the forthcoming publication of *A Wonder-Book for Girls and Boys*. The notice reprinted the preface, and the writer commented, "We have seen the sheets of this charming volume … Hawthorne touches nothing that he does not adorn" (Scharnhorst, Gary, *Nathaniel Hawthorne: An Annotated Bibliography of Comment and Criticism before 1900* [Metuchen, N.J.: Scarecrow Press, 1988], 92).

Evert A. Duyckinck, writing in *Literary World* on November 29, 1851, praised Hawthorne's ability to communicate with children, stating that he is "one of the best of all possible writers for children." Edwin Percy Whipple, reviewing the volume for GRAHAM'S MAGAZINE, pronounced the volume "the best of its kind in English literature. It is a child's story-book informed with the finest genius." Henry Fothergill Chorley, writing in the British magazine *Athenaeum*, declared that, although the *Wonder-Book* was meant for children, adults would be "glad to devour its wonders themselves" (*Nathaniel Hawthorne: The Contemporary Reviews*, edited by John L. Idol Jr. and Buford Jones [New York: Cambridge University Press: 1994], 181–183).

"Young Goodman Brown"

Story first published in April 1835 in the NEW-ENGLAND MAGAZINE as the work of the author of "The GRAY CHAMPION." Both stories are presumed to have been intended for publication in *The Story Teller*, a collection that never materialized. It is thought that had Hawthorne's projected "Provincial Tales" been published, it would have been included (Adams, Richard P., "Hawthorne's *Provincial Tales*," 39–40). The story was collected in the first part of MOSSES FROM AN OLD MANSE in 1846.

As the story opens, it is sunset in Salem village. Young Goodman Brown is taking leave of his bride of three months, Faith. She begs him not to go, the "pink ribbons of her cap" rustling in the wind, but he says he must complete his journey between nightfall and sunrise. He goes down a dreary road, expecting to see a "devilish Indian" behind every tree. He soon joins an older man of about 50, who bears a "considerable resemblance to him"; he carries a staff that has the likeness of a great black snake, "so curiously wrought that it might almost be seen to twist and wriggle itself."

The older traveler proudly recounts his own past to Young Goodman Brown. He helped Goodman Brown's grandfather lash a Quaker woman through the streets of Salem, and he fetched for his father a "pitch-pine knot" with which to set fire to an Indian village. Goodman Brown is amazed his father and grandfather never mentioned these crimes. He says that if he continued with his companion, he would be unable to "meet the eye of that good old man," the minister in Salem. His older companion shakes with "irrepressible mirth." Goodman Brown says that it would also break the "dear little heart" of his wife, Faith. The older man replies sardonically that he would certainly not have Faith come to any harm.

They see an old woman on the path, hobbling ahead of Goodman Brown and his companion. She is Goody Cloyse, whom Brown recognizes as a "very pious and exemplary dame"; she taught him his catechism when he was a child. Goodman Brown stays behind her, watching her proceed with "singular speed for so aged a woman." He sees the old man touch her neck with his serpentlike staff. "The devil!" she screams. Goody Cloyse and the old man converse about the "nice young man" to be taken into communion that night (i.e., Young Goodman Brown). Goodman Brown looks up in astonishment; when he looks down again, the older man has given her his staff and she has vanished. The older man then plucks a branch of maple to use as a walking stick; the twigs and little boughs shrivel at his touch.

Goodman Brown sits down suddenly and says he will not abandon his dear Faith and follow Goody Cloyse "to the devil." His companion says cynically he will think better of it by and by and offers his staff to help him along. He then vanishes, leaving Goodman Brown by the roadside. Two other figures approach; Brown recognizes the voices of the minister and Deacon Gookin. They are discussing the "deviltry" that is afoot for the night. Goodman Brown wonders why these "holy men" are "journeying so deep into the heathen wilderness"; he feels "faint and overburdened with the heavy sickness of his heart." He vows to "stand firm against the devil," with "Heaven above and Faith below."

Suddenly, a cloud crosses the sky and hides the stars. He seems to hear "a confused and doubtful sound of voices" from the depths of the crowd. The voices from above include one of a "young woman, uttering lamentations, yet with an uncertain sorrow." She is asking for a favor that it would grieve her to obtain. The multitude is encouraging her. Brown calls, "Faith! Faith!" He hears a scream, and

a pink ribbon floats through the air. He calls out that "Faith is gone."

"Maddened with despair," he seizes his staff and fairly flies along the forest path. He makes a frightful figure, "brandishing his staff with frenzied gestures" and shouting out "horrid blasphemy." The narrator observes that the "fiend in his own shape is less hideous than when he rages in the breast of man." Goodman Brown sees a red light before him; the "felled trunks and branches of a clearing" are burning and throwing up their "lurid blaze against the sky, at the hour of midnight." The forest is filled with "frightful sounds," including the "creaking of the trees, the howling of wild beasts, and the yell of Indians."

Then he hears what seems to be a hymn, a familiar one to him; when the voices of the singers die away, they are replaced by a chorus "of all the sounds of the benighted wilderness, pealing in awful harmony together." He then enters an open space, containing a large rock that appears to be an altar or a pulpit. It is surrounded by four pines that are burning, like candles. The surrounding foliage is in flames also. There is a congregation in the woods; they shine, then disappear in shadow. He recognizes the faces of leaders in the village; he has seen them on many Sundays looking "devoutly heavenward, and benignantly over the crowded pews." He sees Deacon Gookin, surrounded by "men of dissolute lives" and women of "spotted fame." The good people do not shrink from the sinners. They sing a mournful hymn. Goodman Brown wonders where Faith is. He is hearing what is, either in his dream or in reality, a witches' sabbath. He resists the ceremony, which he considers evil, and sees only the sinfulness of the townspeople.

Finally someone shouts, "Bring forth the converts!" Goodman Brown believes he sees his dead parents, yet he feels a "loathful brotherhood" with all of the people. Deacon Gookin seizes his arms and leads him to the blazing rock. A slender, veiled female figure is led between Goody Cloyse and Martha Carrier. A "dark figure" welcomes them to the company of "fiend-worshippers" and welcomes them to their "nature" and their "destiny." They are told that they will know the secret deeds of those present, such as the poisoning of husbands, the secret burials of children by "fair damsels," and the murders of their fathers by youths eager to inherit their wealth. They will understand the "deep mystery of sin, the fountain of all wicked arts."

The veiled figure is revealed as Faith, who is also in the conclave of wicked revelers. Goodman Brown beholds her, and they tremble "before that unhallowed altar" as the dark figure tells them that "evil is the nature of mankind." A basin in the rock contains a red liquid, possibly blood, to be used to "lay the mark of baptism upon their foreheads." Goodman Brown calls to Faith to "look up to heaven, and resist the wicked one." He staggers against the rock and finds it "chill and damp."

The next morning, he slowly enters the street of Salem village and sees the minister walking and meditating his sermon, Deacon Gookin praying, and Goody Cloyse catechizing a small girl. Faith bursts into joy "at sight of him." The narrator asks whether Goodman Brown had "fallen asleep in the forest and only dreamed a wild dream of a witch meeting." Regardless, after that night's "dream of evil omen," he is transformed into a "stern, a sad, a darkly meditative, a distrustful, if not a desperate, man." Instead of hearing a "holy psalm" on Sundays, he hears an "anthem of sin." The eloquent sermons of the minister, that "gray blasphemer," are tainted for him with dread. He shrinks from Faith. Years later, when he dies, his family carves "no hopeful verse upon his tombstone; for his dying hour was gloom."

RECEPTION AND CRITICAL ANALYSIS

It is clear that Hawthorne was indebted to the Salem WITCHCRAFT DELUSION of 1692–93. At that time, 141 people were arrested, 19 were hanged, and one was crushed to death during the Salem witch trials. Witchcraft was thus associated with nightmarish dreams, and with sin covered up by hypocrisy.

This tale is one of Hawthorne's most celebrated, dealing with the initiation of Young Goodman Brown into the true nature of the villagers he has assumed he knows, and into the cosmos of evil. Charles Wilkins Webber, writing in the *American Whig Review*, observed that the art of Hawthorne in the story is not "*idealizing* the real" but "humanizing

the unreal" ("Hawthorne," *American Whig Review* (September 1846), *Nathaniel Hawthorne: Contemporary Reviews*, edited by Idol and Jones, 88–92). HERMAN MELVILLE termed the story "a strong positive illustration of [the] blackness in Hawthorne" and called it "deep as Dante."

Mark Van Doren suggests that the story is remarkable in that "the storm of the tale" passes through Young Goodman Brown, "leaving no portion of his soul unblasted." When he leaves Faith to walk alone in the New England forest, he enters the devil's territory. Here the "shadow of sin" falls not only on Brown, but also on Faith, as symbolized by the fluttering pink ribbon. The ribbon suggests that Faith has become one of the devil's converts.

Despite his resistance to the ceremony in the woods, Young Goodman Brown is ultimately initiated into the evil that lurks within the villagers he has assumed he knows, as it does within the universe itself. Although he resists evil to a certain extent, in the tale sinfulness and nature are linked: "Verse after verse was sung, and still the chorus of the desert swelled between, like the deepest tone of mighty organ. And, with the final peal of that dreadful anthem, there came a sound, as if the roaring wind, the rushing streams, the howling beasts, and every other voice of the unconverted wilderness, were mingling and according with the voice of guilty man, in homage to the prince of all."

Frederick Crews terms the story a "patently symbolic" one. He suggests that Goodman Brown's case offers a "psychological paradigm" that is puzzling, in that Brown loses his "faith" in humankind by fleeing from a normal, loving wife named "Faith." Faith's sensual pleas to Brown to sleep "in your own bed to-night " are answered by his insistence that he must carry out his mysterious journey before sunrise. When he races toward the witches' sabbath, his own subjective thoughts are the equivalent of actual devils. At the assembly, Brown encounters likenesses of all the figures of authority and holiness in Salem village, as the devil points out: "There . . . are all whom you have reverenced from youth. Ye deemed them holier than yourselves, and shrank from your own sin, contrasting it with their lives of righteousness and prayerful aspiration." Yet, the devil continues, "here they are in all my worshipping assembly. This night it shall be granted you to know their secret deeds: how hoary-bearded elders of the church have whispered wanton words to the young maids of their households; how many a woman, eager for widows' weeds, has given her husband a drink at bedtime and let him sleep his last sleep in her bosom."

He tells Goodman Brown that he can "penetrate, in every bosom, the deep mystery of sin, the fountain of all wicked arts, and which inexhaustibly supplies more evil impulses than human power—than my power at its utmost—can make manifest in deeds." Goodman Brown is free to barter his soul for sexual sin. He can make his own pact with the devil. Crews terms Brown a "curiously preoccupied bridegroom" who "escapes from his wife's embraces to a vision of general nastiness" (101–102).

After Goodman Brown's night of "evil omen," he is transformed into a different man. The devil, whether actual or imaginary, has seized his imagination and cast a pall over the remainder of his life. He becomes disillusioned with humankind, losing his religious and moral "faith." In this process, he enters a dream world. Young Goodman Brown and Faith eventually live out their lives in what Terence Martin terms "a gloom" resulting from Young Goodman Brown's "inverted sense of moral reality" (*Nathaniel Hawthorne*).

CHARACTERS

Brown, Faith   Wife of Young Goodman Brown in Hawthorne's tale "Young Goodman Brown." As Young Goodman Brown takes leave of his bride of three months, Faith, she entreats him not to leave her. She argues that a "lone woman" is "troubled with such dreams and such thoughts that she's afeard of herself sometimes." He answers that he must carry out his mysterious journey before sunrise. After he departs, he thinks the look on her face was "as if a dream had warned her what work is to be done to-night." He intuitively realizes that he is leaving a "blessed angel on earth" and resolves that, from then on, he will "cling to her skirts and follow her to heaven."

While on his journey, Goodman Brown declares he will not abandon his dear Faith and follow those whom he meets in the woods. But when he hears the voice of a "young woman, uttering lamentations, yet with an uncertain sorrow," and being encouraged by the multitudes, he cries out, "Faith! Faith!" in a "voice of agony and desperation." He hears a scream, and a pink ribbon floats through the air. The ribbon is a symbol that Faith is becoming one of the devil's converts. He calls out "'Faith! Faith! . . . look up to heaven and resist the wicked one,'" but does not know whether his plea is in vain. The pink ribbon floating through the air may indicate that Faith actually subscribes to the evil that permeates the entire village.

Brown, Young Goodman   Hero of one of Hawthorne's most highly praised stories, "Young Goodman Brown," he represents the state of mind of Salem village during the witchcraft delusion of 1692.

His journey into the woods is one of initiation. Along the way, he encounters an older traveler who carries a serpentlike staff. This man proceeds thrugh "deep dusk" and "deepening gloom" to darkest night; he is taken to be the devil himself by most critics. Goodman Brown experiences inexplicable evil impulses and wonders whether he has made a contract with the devil. He becomes involved in a witches' sabbath in the forest. He returns to town with a new and bitter kind of knowledge and faces a lifetime of gloom.

His eyes are opened to the true nature of the other villagers. All of them, even ministers and elders, worship at the devil's altar. Goodman Brown and Faith are the latest members of the community to be received into this sinister fellowship. Some readers believe Goodman Brown rejects the insight he has been offered and thus continues his life in terms of social codes. Terence Martin notes that he has been given "such a monstrous perception of the scope, depth, and universality of evil that he is forever blind to the world as it normally presents itself" (*Nathaniel Hawthorne*, 89). However, Hawthorne himself has evoked in him a psychological state of awareness: Young Goodman Brown has not lost his religious faith so much as his belief in other human beings. When he dies, "they carved no hopeful verse upon his tombstone; for his dying hour was gloom."

Nancy Bunge argues that he despises the townspeople because he has witnessed their participation in the evil ceremony he himself had resisted. She suggests that Brown has a "classic case of projection." Because he is "unable to deal with his own frailty, he sees and hates it in everyone else"; the tale "seems to celebrate humility" (*Nathaniel Hawthorne: A Study of the Short Fiction,* 11).

FOR FURTHER READING

Abcarian, Richard, "The Ending of 'Young Goodman Brown,'" *Studies in Short Fiction* 3 (1966): 343–345; Bunge, Nancy, *Nathaniel Hawthorne: A Study of the Short Fiction* (New York: Twayne, 1993); Crews, Frederick C., *The Sins of the Fathers: Hawthorne's Psychological Themes* (New York: Oxford University Press, 1966); Humma, John B., "'Young Goodman Brown' and the Failure of Hawthorne's Ambiguity," *Colby Library Quarterly* 9 (1971): 425–431; Hurley, Paul, "Young Goodman Brown's 'Heart of Darkness,'" *American Literature* 37 (1966): 410–419; Johnson, Claudia D., "'Young Goodman Brown' and Puritan Justification," *Studies in Short Fiction* 11 (1974): 200–203; Kesterson, David B., "Nature and Theme in 'Young Goodman Brown,'" *Dickinson Review* 2 (1970): 42–46; Martin, Terence, *Nathaniel Hawthorne* (Boston: Twayne, 1965): Paulis, Walter J., "Ambivalence in 'Young Goodman Brown,'" *American Literature* 41 (1970): 577–584; St. Armand, Barton Levi, "'Young Goodman Brown' as Historical Allegory," *Nathaniel Hawthorne Journal* 3 (1973): 183–197; Williamson, James L., "'Young Goodman Brown': Hawthorne's 'Devil in Manuscript,'" *Studies in Short Fiction* 18, no. 2 (spring 1981): 155–162; Woodberry, George E., *Nathaniel Hawthorne* (New York, London: Chelsea House, 1980).

PART III

Related People, Places, and Topics

Academies of Fine Arts (Italy)
In March 1858, the Hawthorne family arrived in Rome. They stayed until the end of May 1858, when they departed for Florence. While in Rome, they visited the French Academy at the Villa Medici several times. It had been founded in 1666 by King Louis XIV and was established in the Villa Medici by Napoléon in 1803 (*French and Italian Notebooks*, 765). In addition, they visited the Academy of Saint Luke, also known as the Fine Arts Academy of Rome, near the Forum. Hawthorne noted that he particularly admired a Virgin and Child by Sir Anthony Van Dyke, in which two angels were singing and playing (*French and Italian Notebooks*, 169).

In Florence, the Hawthornes went several times to the Accademia delle Belle Arti, or the Academy of Fine Arts. There Hawthorne cared little for the paintings of Giotto or Cimabue but greatly admired Fabrizio Gentile's *Adoration of the Magi*, in which the "jewelled crowns . . . and all the magnificence of the Three Kings" were represented with "all the vividness of the real thing" (*French and Italian Notebooks*, 169).

In October 1858, the Hawthornes traveled to Siena, where they visited the Institute of Fine Arts. Hawthorne greatly admired a well-preserved fresco of the Crucifixion by the high Renaissance artist Sodoma (Giovanni Antonio Bazzi). He declared that Christ was "redeemed by a divine majesty and beauty . . . as much our Redeemer as if he sat on his throne in heaven" (*French and Italian Notebooks*, 452).

Agassiz, Jean Louis Rodolphe (1807–1873)
A native of Switzerland, Agassiz immigrated to the United States in 1846 as a lecturer. He became a professor at Harvard University and was curator of the Agassiz Museum in Cambridge. He also founded the Marine Biological Laboratory at Woods Hole, Massachusetts.

Agassiz exchanged letters and ideas with the leading men of his day. In 1848, Hawthorne arranged for him to lecture at the Salem Lyceum. He and Hawthorne were both members of the Saturday Club, a literary society to which Hawthorne had been elected. At Hawthorne's funeral, Agassiz and other members of the club picked violets and dropped them into his grave (Turner, *Nathaniel Hawthorne, passim*).

Akers, Benjamin Paul (1825–1861)
An American sculptor and a native of Maine, among whose works are *Una and the Lion and The Dead Pearl-Diver*.

When the Hawthornes visited Rome in April 1858, they met Akers, who escorted them to Monte Cavallo, from which they saw several twilight illuminations of Saint Peter's. SOPHIA HAWTHORNE remarked that it was like "the glorified spirit of the church made visible" (*French and Italian Notebooks*, 161).

Akers also took them to a number of artists' studios, including those of Hamilton Wilde and GEORGE LORING BROWN. Hawthorne's 1858 pocket diary notes that Akers escorted the family to the Coliseum (*French and Italian Notebooks*, 588) and often called on them in the evening. The

Hawthornes also knew Akers's brother Charles, who was in Rome part of the time they were there.

Alcott, Amos Bronson (1799–1888)   American transcendentalist philosopher, poet, and teacher. He founded the Temple School in Boston in 1834, and, in 1843, established the Fruitlands community.

In February 1852, Hawthorne purchased the Alcott house in Concord, Massachusetts, along with nine acres of land, for $1,500. The house had been built before the American Revolution. (Turner, *Nathaniel Hawthorne: A Biography,* 241–242). In June 1852, he wrote to EVERT AUGUSTUS DUYCKINCK to report the acquisition, stating that it was "no very splendid mansion" and had been neglected, so that it was "the raggedest in the world," but he was convinced it would eventually make "a comfortable and sufficiently pleasant home." Alcott had called it "Hillside," but Hawthorne rebaptized it The WAYSIDE, a name possessing a "moral as well as descriptive propriety" (*The Letters,* 16, 548).

Alcott, Louisa May (1832–1888)   The daughter of BRONSON ALCOTT, she was a writer of juvenile literature. Her *Little Women* (1868–69) is a classic. She was also the author of *Little Men, Eight Cousins, Rose in Bloom, Under the Lilacs,* and other works. Many of her books are still in print.

Her father, to whom his wife and children were devoted, had reduced his family to poverty by supporting various philanthropic and financial schemes. In order to aid the family, Louisa began writing when she was only 16, but it was not until 1869, when *Little Women* was published, that she became famous.

In 1863, Louisa had a nervous breakdown as a result of nursing soldiers in Union Hospital at Georgetown. SOPHIA HAWTHORNE assisted the Alcott family in caring for her (Stewart, *Hawthorne: A Biography,* 217).

Allen, the Reverend William (1784–1868)   American Congregational clergyman, a native of Pittsfield, Massachusetts, and the son of Thomas Allen, a Revolutionary War hero. He was the president of Dartmouth College from 1817 to 1819 and of BOW-DOIN COLLEGE twice, from 1819 to 1831 and 1833 to 1838.

Upon graduating from Harvard, Allen had compiled the *American Biographical and Historical Dictionary* (1809). When Hawthorne arrived at Bowdoin in October 1821, Allen was only 37, "punctual and strict." In May 1822, Hawthorne was discovered to have played cards for money, and Allen wrote to Mrs. Hawthorne, begging her to persuade her son "to observe the laws of this institution" (Cantwell, *Nathaniel Hawthorne: The American Years,* 71, 87).

Allingham, William A. (1824–1889)   An Irish poet who was also the editor of *Fraser's Magazine* from 1874 to 1879.

In 1854, he visited the American Consulate in Liverpool and presented Hawthorne with a volume of his own poems. Hawthorne pronounced Allingham "not at all John Bullish" and was pleased that a younger literary figure had called on him (Turner, *Nathaniel Hawthorne,* 271). He wrote to the Boston publisher JAMES T. FIELDS, "It seems to me there is good in him, and he is recognized by Tennyson, by Carlisle, by Kingsley, and other of the best people here." He noted that he had left a customs post in Ireland to "cultivate literature in London" and urged Fields to "take him up in America"; someday he might be "glad to have helped a famous poet in his obscurity" (*The Letters, 1853–1856,* 201–202).

American Magazine of Useful and Entertaining Knowledge, The   A picture magazine founded by a group of engravers in September 1834 (Cantwell, *Nathaniel Hawthorne: The American Years,* 176).

The publication was in a state of chaos when, in January 1836, Hawthorne was recruited by the poet Thomas Green Fessenden to take over. Hawthorne boarded with Fessenden; his wife, Lydia; and his niece, Catherine Ainsworth. He was expected to edit and produce the entire magazine while receiving little or no salary.

He wrote much of it until his resignation in August 1836. His own contributions were impressive, ranging from biographical essays to articles on many subjects. These included pieces on the Boston Tea Party, the Chinese Pyramids, the Church of Saint Sophia, the Flathead Indians, and the Schenectady Lyceum (Cantwell, 174–189).

American Monthly Magazine Magazine in which several of Hawthorne's works were published, including "THOMAS GREEN FESSENDEN" (January 1836) and "OLD TICONDEROGA. A PICTURE OF THE PAST" (February 1836).

Androscoggin Leo Club One of three social clubs that Hawthorne joined at BOWDOIN COLLEGE. His friends HORATIO BRIDGE and JONATHAN CILLEY were also members. Bridge reported that the club existed for about two years. The members would take "a keg of wine and a liberal amount of provender . . . for a week end in the forest" (recollection of Mary Touzell Hawthorne, quoted in Turner, *Nathaniel Hawthorne: A Biography*, 40).

Androscoggin River The Androscoggin River flows from New Hampshire into Maine. The village of Brunswick, site of BOWDOIN COLLEGE, is located at the junction of the Androscoggin River and the Kennebec River. It was known for lumbering, and Bowdoin students long recalled the spring floods in which enormous logs were propelled over the rapids and on to the falls at the foot of Maine Street (Turner, *Nathaniel Hawthorne: A Biography*, 34).

Hawthorne and his friend HORATIO BRIDGE often walked along the river and recited poetry. One evening, as they leaned over the river, Bridge quoted a passage from *The Merchant of Venice*. He recalled Hawthorne's responding in "deep musical tones" with verses written before he entered Bowdoin, expressing his sense of loss of the "shadow band, / The dead of other years" (Bridge, *Personal Recollections of Nathaniel Hawthorne* [1893], quoted in Miller, *Salem Is My Dwelling Place*, 70).

Athenaean Society Society at BOWDOIN COLLEGE to which Hawthorne was elected. Other members included FRANKLIN PIERCE, JONATHAN CILLEY, and HORATIO BRIDGE. Hawthorne wrote to his sister Elizabeth ("Ebe") that the club had a library of over 800 volumes (Turner, *Nathaniel Hawthorne: A Biography*, 42).

Atlantic Monthly Hawthorne published regularly in the magazine, especially during his years in England and on the Continent from 1853 to 1860. JAMES T. FIELDS, the editor, welcomed his contributions. He paid $100 for his sketches at first and later increased it to $200 (Turner, *Nathaniel Hawthorne: A Biography*, 359). Among his contributions were "Chiefly about War-matters" (July 1862) and "Leamington Spa" (October 1862). The latter was signed "A Peaceable Man." He also published a number of unsigned pieces, including "Near Oxford" (October 1861), "Pilgrimage to Old Boston" (January 1862), "A London Suburb" (March 1863), and "Outside Glimpses of English Poverty" (July 1863). In 1876, three fictional fragments were published posthumously under the title *THE DOLLIVER ROMANCE*. A full listing of Hawthorne's contributions to the magazine may be found in *Nathaniel Hawthorne: A Descriptive Bibliography*.

Avignon The Hawthorne family, including Hawthorne's mother, concluded their visit to Rome in May 1859 and went by steamer to Marseille. From there, they continued to Avignon by railway, arriving June 1. They stayed at the Hôtel d'Europe, occupying a large suite of rooms. While in Avignon, they explored a number of churches and were most impressed by the Rhone River.

Hawthorne and Julian walked around the city wall, and the family rambled through the narrow streets. Hawthorne went daily to the Rocher des Doms (the Doms Rock), where he admired the view of the "vast mountain girdled plain, illuminated by the far windings and reaches of the Rhone." He found the Palais des Papes "ugly" and "old" but conceded that "no end of historical romances might be made out of this castle of the Popes" (*French and Italian Notebooks*, 540–542). He believed many of the rooms harbored the ghosts of those massacred there over many centuries.

The family went on to Valence, Lyon, and Geneva from Avignon.

B

Bacon, Delia (1811–1859)   An expatriate American writer with whom Hawthorne became acquainted in England. Hawthorne called on her in 1856 in London.

She was the author of *The Philosophy of the Plays of Shakspere Unfolded* and invented the "Baconian" theory of Shakespearean authorship. She argued forcefully that "the man Shakespeare" did not write "Shakespeare's plays" and was sure confirmation of her theory was buried in Shakespeare's grave. Her book was published in London in 1857, with financial assistance from Hawthorne. He disguised his contribution as a publisher's advance. He also contributed a preface to this work, although he regarded her conclusions with considerable skepticism and termed her a "monomaniac." She had a mental breakdown soon after publication. Stewart notes that Hawthorne behaved toward her "with extraordinary tact, patience, and benevolence" (*The English Notebooks by Nathaniel Hawthorne*, 650).

Hawthorne sent a copy of the book to his British friend FRANCIS BENNOCH, explaining that her American countrymen would "feel a certain degree of interest in the book." Delia Bacon, however, returned his preface in a letter with all the words deleted that he had quoted from a previous introduction to it, which she now disavowed. She declared that Hawthorne did not really appreciate her work, since he threw "doubt on the oracle." She considered herself a "priestess of these Nine" (a reference to the nine Muses). She finally accepted his preface, addressed to "Dear Author of this Book" (Turner, *Nathaniel Hawthorne: A Biography*, 284–285).

Delia Bacon's brother, Leonard Bacon, wrote to Hawthorne that he appreciated his assistance to her in England but deplored his encouragement to stay there as her insanity worsened. It remained for her nephew, Theodore Bacon, to gain an appreciation of all Hawthorne had done to assist her. He wrote in his biography of her that nothing Hawthorne had written was "more honorable than the noble generosity, the unwearying patience, the exquisite consideration and delicacy, with which for two years he gave unstinted help . . . to this lonely country-woman" (Bacon, *Delia Bacon*, 170–171, quoted in Turner, *Nathaniel Hawthorne: A Biography*, 285).

For Further Reading

[Nathaniel Hawthorne]. *Delia Bacon: A Biographical Sketch*, Boston and New York: Houghton, Mifflin and Company, 1888. (Previously unpublished material from letter.)

Bancroft, George (1800–1881)   Historian and politician who, as collector of the Port of Boston, offered Hawthorne a post as measurer in the BOSTON CUSTOM-HOUSE, at a salary of $1,100. Bancroft was the author of a much-praised *History of the United States* and an active member of the Democratic Party.

Bennoch, Francis (1812–1890)   Of Scottish descent, Bennoch was a poet, dealer in silk, and friend of many English and American authors.

In 1856, he called on Hawthorne in ROCK FERRY, across the Mersey River from LIVERPOOL, where Hawthorne lived when he was the American consul (1853–57). Hawthorne described him as "a kindly, jolly, frank, off-hand, very good fellow" who was "bounteous" in making Hawthorne's time in England pass pleasantly" (*The English Notebooks by Nathaniel Hawthorne,* ed. Stewart, 282).

When Hawthorne went to London, Bennoch escorted him to Greenwich, Tunbridge Wells, Battle, Hastings, and other historic sites. He invited him to a dinner at the Milton Club in April 1856 and introduced him to other noted Englishmen, who entertained him (Turner, *Nathaniel Hawthorne: A Biography,* 293–294).

Hawthorne's friendship with Bennoch and his wife continued throughout the term of his post as American consul. In 1859, Bennoch wrote a poem, "To Nathaniel Hawthorne. On the Anniversary of his Daughter Una's Birthday" (Turner, *Nathaniel Hawthorne: A Biography,* 348). In 1860, the London photographer Mayall made three portraits of Hawthorne; Bennoch selected the one he thought was best.

For Further Reading

Hawthorne, *The English Notebooks,* passim.

Boboli Gardens Gardens at the Pitti Palace, in Florence, Italy, which was acquired by the powerful Medici family in 1550. They immediately began to lay out the park behind the building, in a scenic setting on the slopes of the Boboli hill.

When Hawthorne and his family were in Florence in June 1858, the gardens were open to the public only on Thursdays and Sundays. They visited on Sunday, June 20. In his notebooks, Hawthorne describes the "embowered walks of box and shrubbery, and little wildernesses of trees . . . and here and there a marble statue, grey with ancient weather-stains" (*French and Italian Notebooks,* 329). He and Sophia toured the Pitti Palace the next day.

Boston Custom-House In 1838, ELIZABETH PEABODY, sister of SOPHIA PEABODY (who would later marry Hawthorne), became convinced that Hawthorne needed a position that would allow him enough time to write. She wrote to her friend ORESTES BROWNSON, who was steward of the Chelsea Marine Hospital, who, in turn, contacted GEORGE BANCROFT. Bancroft, collector of the Port of Boston, had

The Boston Custom-House, where Hawthorne worked as an inspector from 1839 to 1841. *(Courtesy of the Peabody Essex Museum)*

assisted Brownson in obtaining his post. He offered Hawthorne the post of inspector in the Boston Custom-House, at an annual salary of $1,100 (Turner, *Nathaniel Hawthorne: A Biography,* 117).

Hawthorne wrote Bancroft a letter of acceptance in early 1839, although he was uncertain about his qualifications for inspecting incoming vessels and controlling their cargo. He hoped, however, to have time to continue his writing.

He was highly capable in performing his duties and remained in the post until January 10, 1841. He was engaged to Sophia Peabody much of this time and hoped to save enough money to marry her. In November 1840, he and Sophia had decided their future lay in the BROOK FARM communal society that was being established by GEORGE RIPLEY in West Roxbury, just outside Boston (Turner, *Nathaniel Hawthorne: A Biography,* 129–130).

Bowdoin College In March 1820, when Hawthorne was 15, his maternal uncle ROBERT MANNING began preparing him for college. Manning intended to send him to Bowdoin College in Maine. The entrance requirements were an ability to read and write Latin; knowledge of the classics, including some of the works of Cicero and Virgil; and an understanding of arithmetic.

Hawthorne was prepared for college by Dr. BENJAMIN LYNDE OLIVER, a wealthy Salem physician, inventor, and scholar. They worked together early each morning, before Hawthorne reported to work for his uncle, WILLIAM MANNING, who managed the family stagecoach business. At this time, Hawthorne began to harbor thoughts of becoming a writer (Cantwell, *Nathaniel Hawthorne: The American Years,* 54–59).

Robert Manning and Hawthorne went to Brunswick, Maine, on Friday, September 28, 1821; Hawthorne was the first member of his family to attend college. Hawthorne doubted that he would pass the entrance examinations but was admitted at once and given a roommate, Alfred Mason, who had attended Phillips Academy, Exeter, to prepare for college. They lived at first in a room in the home of Professor Samuel Phillips Newman but soon obtained a room in Maine Hall. He and Mason roomed together through their sophomore year; during his junior and senior years, Hawthorne had a single room in the home of Mrs. Downing on Federal Street, near the college.

The curriculum included Greek, Latin, mathematics, and philosophy. There were mandatory recitations and Sabbath services. Turner states that during his first two years, Hawthorne's many infractions of the rules suggested "high spirits and boyish assertiveness" (Turner, *Nathaniel Hawthorne: A Biography,* 38). He had an excellent command of Latin, however, and delivered a dissertation in Latin in the chapel. He concentrated on classical languages and literature, along with biblical studies, although he did attend a series of lectures on anatomy and physiology as a senior. He was described by Prof. Alpheus S. Packard as having a "shy, gentle bearing, black, drooping, full, inquisitive eye, and low, musical voice" (Turner, *Nathaniel Hawthorne: A Biography,* 39).

His closest friends were JONATHAN CILLEY and HORATIO BRIDGE; all three belonged to the ANDROSCOGGIN LEO CLUB. It was at Bowdoin that he met FRANKLIN PIERCE, who was a year ahead of him. Pierce, Hawthorne, Cilley, and Bridge were members of the ATHENAEAN SOCIETY. Pierce would later become president of the United States, and the two were together on a trip at the time of Hawthorne's death, in 1864.

Hawthorne wrote, of his college years, that he was "an idle student, negligent of college rules and the Procrustean details of academic life, rather choosing to nurse my own fancies than to dig into Greek roots and be numbered among the learned Thebans." Turner states, however, that he "formed at college the pattern of imaginative composition that would produce the sketches, tales, and romances of his mature years" (Turner, *Nathaniel Hawthorne: A Biography,* 42–43). At the same time, he made lifelong friends destined to become men of distinction.

For Further Reading

Reed, Richard B., and John D. O'Heru, "Nathaniel Hawthorne at Bowdoin College," *Nathaniel Hawthorne Journal* 2 (1972): 147–157.

Boys' and Girls' Magazine Magazine in which Hawthorne's story "Little Daffydowndilly" was published in August 1843.

Bridge, Horatio (1806–1893) A close friend of Hawthorne, whom he met at BOWDOIN COLLEGE. The son of a banker and lawyer, Bridge was two years younger than Hawthorne but one of the first to perceive that Hawthorne would have a notable future if he were to pursue a writing career (Cantwell, *Nathaniel Hawthorne: The American Years,* 7). Both Hawthorne and Bridge were members of the ATHENAEAN SOCIETY, one of the two literary societies at Bowdoin. When Hawthorne published his first novel, FANSHAWE, anonymously, he gave a copy to Bridge (this was one of the rare surviving copies, as Hawthorne burned all he could locate soon after publication).

Bridge and his brothers invested much of their inheritance in a risky venture, the construction of a dam across the Kennebec River. He still, however, did his best to promote Hawthorne's writing and published an article about his work that would, he insisted, "give him a high place among the scholars of this country" (Cantwell, *Nathaniel Hawthorne: The American Years,* 194). Despite the bleak prospect of success with the Kennebec dam, Bridge guaranteed a subvention to SAMUEL GRISWOLD

GOODRICH if he would publish TWICE-TOLD TALES, which came out on March 17, 1837.

The Kennebec dam eventually failed, but Bridge, meanwhile, had joined the navy and sailed along the coast of Africa on the *Cyane*. He kept a journal, which Hawthorne edited and which EVERT AUGUSTUS DUYCKINCK published as *Journal of an African Cruiser* for the Library of American Books he was editing (Turner, *Nathaniel Hawthorne: A Biography,* 156). About 5,000 copies were sold, but Hawthorne refused to accept the royalties despite Bridge's urging him to do so. He lent Hawthorne and his family money at a time when they were desperately poor, before Hawthorne was offered a post in the Salem Custom-House (Cantwell, *Nathaniel Hawthorne: The American Years,* 380).

Bridge was one of Hawthorne's closest lifelong friends. He was unable to attend Hawthorne's funeral on May 23, 1864, because he had suffered an accident in Washington, D.C.

Bright, Henry (1830–1884) An English writer and university graduate who met Hawthorne during a visit to America. When Hawthorne arrived in LIVERPOOL to take up his duties as American consul in July 1853, Henry Bright and his father called on him immediately. Turner states that their friendship was one of Hawthorne's "most satisfying relationships during his residence in England" (Turner, *Nathaniel Hawthorne: A Biography,* 268).

Bright was highly literate and sometimes contributed to the prestigious *Westminster Review.* He and his father were in the business of foreign trade. At a Christmas celebration in Liverpool in 1855, he composed verses honoring Hawthorne, "Song of Consul Hawthorne," using the meter of the recently published narrative poem "Hiawatha," by HENRY WADSWORTH LONGFELLOW (Turner, *Nathaniel Hawthorne: A Biography,* 289).

Brook Farm On April 12, 1841, Hawthorne moved into the transcendentalist Brook Farm Institute of Agriculture and Education, West Roxbury, Massachusetts, a farm of 200 acres. This was an experiment in utopianism that lasted only until 1847; Hawthorne stayed there less than a year.

His experience figures in his novel *The* BLITHEDALE ROMANCE.

The Brook Farm pilgrims, both young and middle-aged, believed, according to the critic Edwin Miller, that it would be easy to return to a "simple agrarian life and to simple Christian principles." They planned to become self-sufficient and to reject the "money-oriented, industrialized society" they saw developing around them. They would rely on "wisdom and purity" and bestow the "benefits of the highest, physical, intellectual and moral education in the present state of human knowledge" on the community (Miller, *Salem Is My Dwelling Place,* 187–188).

The disillusioned Unitarian clergyman George Ripley was the founder. Other members included Lloyd Fuller, brother of MARGARET FULLER, and the aesthete Charles King Newcomb. Participants bought shares; Hawthorne bought two shares at $500 each, a large sum for him.

RALPH WALDO EMERSON called the experiment a "perpetual picnic, a French Revolution in small, an Age of Reason in a patty pan." Women wore skirts with matching knickerbockers, wide-brimmed hats, and berry, vine, and flower wreaths. The men wore blue frocks, sack trousers, and thick boots. There were eight cows, but Hawthorne was too inexperienced to be allowed to milk them (Miller, 188–191).

Hawthorne departed Brook Farm in November 1841 but kept up his ties. He and Sophia were married on July 9, 1842, a few days after Hawthorne's 38th birthday, and he formally resigned as an associate of the Brook Farm Institute on October 17, 1842. At that time, he wrote that he did not feel "entirely disconnected" from the community but knew that he would not return. He promised, however, to take the "warmest interest" in the progress of the experiment and believed in its ultimate success (Miller, 199).

For Further Reading

Gordon, Joseph T., "Nathaniel Hawthorne and Brook Farm," *ESQ: A Journal of the American Renaissance* 33 (1963): 51–61; Stoehr, Taylor, "Art vs. Utopia: The Case of Nathaniel Hawthorne and Brook Farm," *Antioch Review* 36 (1978): 89–102.

Brown, George Loring (1814–1889) American landscape painter of the Hudson River school. Among the most celebrated of American painters living abroad in the 19th century, he was trained in Paris by Abel Bowen and Eugene Isabey and was inspired and encouraged by Washington Allston. He exhibited frequently at the Boston Athenaeum. He settled in 1839–40 in Italy, where he made a living by painting Italian landscapes to sell to American and European tourists.

The Hawthornes arrived in Rome in February 1858. Hawthorne frequently visited the studios of American artists, including that of Brown. In his notebook for April 22, 1858, he recorded a recent visit the family made to Brown's studio. He pronounced him a "very plain, homely, Yankee sort of a man, quite unpolished by his many years residence in Italy," but "entirely free from affectation in his aspect and deportment." He considered his views of Swiss and Italian scenery "most beautiful and true" and declared that he received "more pleasure from Brown's pictures than from any of the landscapes by old masters." He conceded that Claude was probably "a greater landscape painter than Brown" but declared that Claude's pictures were changed from what he intended them to be by "the effect of time on his pigments" (*French and Italian Notebooks*, 176). Brown returned to the United States in 1859.

Browning, Elizabeth Barrett (1806–1861) A poet and the wife of ROBERT BROWNING.

Hawthorne first met the Brownings in 1856, at the home of RICHARD MONCKTON MILNES, first LORD HOUGHTON. He commented that she was of that "quickly appreciative and responsive order of women, with whom I can talk more freely than with any men . . . I like her very much—a great deal better than her poetry" (Miller, *Salem Is My Dwelling Place: A Life of Nathaniel Hawthorne*, 436). SOPHIA HAWTHORNE also remembered meeting her at that time. Standing in her purple dress, holding a pomegranate blossom plucked for her by Robert Browning, she heard a "delicate sound" she likened to the wings of a hummingbird and discovered his wife, "so weird and fay-like, with a smile gleaming through a cloud of dark curls—summer lightning in shades of light." Hawthorne declared she was a "good and kind fairy with the voice of a grasshopper" (Miller, 437).

They later saw the Brownings a number of times in Rome and Florence, during their continental sojourn in 1858 and 1859.

Browning, Robert (1812–1889) Hawthorne first met the important British poet Robert Browning, along with his wife, ELIZABETH BARRETT BROWNING, in 1856, in London, at the home of RICHARD MONCKTON MILNES, first LORD HOUGHTON. Hawthorne declared he was "very simple and agreeable in manner, gently impulsive, talking as if his heart were uppermost" (Miller, *Salem Is My Dwelling Place: A Life of Nathaniel Hawthorne*, 437).

The Hawthornes moved to the Continent in January 1858; they were not to return to England until the summer of 1859. They met Robert Browning and his wife several times in Florence, at the home of Miss Isabella Blagden, in her villa at Bellosguardo (outside Florence), as well as in Rome.

Robert Browning died in Venice in December 1889 and was buried in Westminster Abbey.

Brownson, Orestes Augustus (1803–1876) A Boston writer, editor, and reviewer. A native of Vermont, he was a leading New England transcendentalist.

He was a friend of ELIZABETH PEABODY, sister of SOPHIA PEABODY HAWTHORNE. Elizabeth was a strong believer in Hawthorne's ability long before he and Sophia were married. In 1838, at a time when Hawthorne was publishing tales and sketches but was unable to support himself as a writer, Elizabeth appealed to Brownson. She hoped he might be able to find a position for Hawthorne that would leave him time for writing. At that time, Brownson was steward of the Chelsea Marine Hospital. He obligingly contacted his friend GEORGE BANCROFT, who had helped secure him his own post at the Chelsea hospital, on behalf of Hawthorne. Bancroft, then collector of the Port of Boston, offered Hawthorne the post of inspector in the Custom-House at an annual salary of $1,100, a position he accepted immediately.

C

"Castle Dismal" Hawthorne's name for the home of his mother's family, the Mannings, on Herbert Street in Salem.

After Hawthorne's father, Captain NATHANIEL HAWTHORNE, SR., died, his mother moved with her three children into the Manning household, where they lived until after Hawthorne and Sophia Peabody were married. In March 1846, while Hawthorne was employed in the Salem Custom-House,

The Manning House (second from left), Herbert St., Salem. After the death of Hawthorne's father, his mother was forced to move the family into this house, home of her parents. Hawthorne referred to it as "Castle Dismal." *(Courtesy of the Peabody Essex Museum)*

he, Sophia, and the infant Una HAWTHORNE moved to 77 Carver Street in Boston, where she would be near her physician before the arrival of their second child (JULIAN HAWTHORNE, born in June 1846). The Hawthornes then moved to 18 Chestnut Street, Salem.

In September 1847, the Hawthornes rented a large house at 14 Mall Street, Salem. His mother and sisters moved to the second floor. On June 7, 1849, Hawthorne lost his position at the Salem Custom-House (Turner, *Nathaniel Hawthorne: A Biography*, passim).

Channing, the Reverend William Ellery (1780–1842)   American clergyman, an ordained Congregationalist minister whose theological beliefs evolved into Unitarianism; he was known as the "Apostle of Unitarianism." He was a leading social reformer and his ideas also led to the emergence of transcendentalism.

Channing was much admired by ELIZABETH PEABODY, whose sister Sophia would marry Hawthorne. Elizabeth served as his secretary and, in 1877, published her reminiscences of him. Her bookstore at 13 West Street, Beacon Hill, Boston, was a center of much transcendentalist discussion, which, eventually led to the establishment of the BROOK FARM community in West Roxbury, Massachusetts (Turner, *Nathaniel Hawthorne: A Biography*, 130).

Channing is thought to have been the model for the Reverend Arthur Dimmesdale in *The SCARLET LETTER*.

Channing, William Ellery (1817–1901)   Ellery Channing was a nephew of the REVEREND WILLIAM ELLERY CHANNING, a poet, and a close friend of Emerson and Thoreau.

Channing's wife, Ellen, was a sister of MARGARET FULLER. When Hawthorne first met him, according to Turner, he "felt little warmth for the 'gnome, yclept Ellery Channing,'" because he believed "the lad" considered himself a genius. SOPHIA HAWTHORNE did like him, however, and wrote in her notebook that he seemed "perfectly to idolize" her husband (Turner, *Nathaniel Hawthorne: A Biography*, 149–150).

The Channings and Hawthornes eventually became family friends. Channing visited the Hawthornes when they lived in the "RED HOUSE" at LENOX, Massachusetts, in the Berkshire mountains. In December 1851, after their residence in England and travels on the Continent, Hawthorne was searching for a permanent home for his family. He learned that the Bronson Alcott house in Concord was for sale. Ellery Channing invited him to visit Concord, stay with him (his family was away), and inspect the house. In February 1852, Hawthorne did make the journey to Concord, accompanied by Sophia and Julian, and quickly completed the purchase.

Chillon, Castle of   In June 1859, the Hawthorne family visited Geneva. The party included Hawthorne's mother and Ada Shepard, the children's companion and tutor. On Sunday, June 12, they took a steamer across Lake Geneva (Lac Léman), getting a distant view of the Castle of Chillon, which at first appeared to be only a "white, ancient-looking group of towers, beneath a mountain." The castle appeared at first to sit on the water, a disappointment since Hawthorne had imagined it as situated upon a high rock. He was impressed, however, to learn that the lake was 800 feet deep at its base.

They stayed at the Hotel de Byron in Villeneuve, "a very grand hotel indeed," and enjoyed an excellent evening meal and a view of the castle by moonlight. The next morning, the party walked to the castle. As they drew closer, Hawthorne recalled Lord Byron's description of "Chillon's snow-white

battlements" in his 1816 poem "The Prisoner of Chillon." This poem was based on the imprisonment in the dungeon of the 16th-century prelate François de Bonnivard and his two brothers, victims of religious persecution. Hawthorne concluded that the battlements made a "fine picture of ancient strength" when seen close up. He persuaded a caretaker to let them see the interior, and they toured the dungeon, chapel, private chambers of the duke of Savoy, and courtyards, where they purchased such souvenirs as napkin rings (*French and Italian Notebooks*, 554–564).

Cilley, Jonathan (1802–1838)   A native of Nottingham, New Hampshire, Cilley was a classmate of Hawthorne's at BOWDOIN COLLEGE. He and Hawthorne, along with HENRY WADSWORTH LONGFELLOW, were all members of the celebrated class of 1825. As seniors, Cilley and Hawthorne each vowed to pay "a barrel of best old Madeira wine" to the other if, in 12 years, he were not married or a widower. Cilley won the bet; he had married and fathered six children long before Hawthorne married in 1842 (Miller, *Salem Is My Dwelling Place*, 71).

After graduation from Bowdoin, Cilley moved to Thomaston, Maine, and began to practice law. He was the editor of the *Thomaston Register* from 1829 to 1831. He then served in the Maine legislature and, in 1836, was elected to the United States House of Representatives.

Matthew Davis, a correspondent for the *New York Courier and Enquirer*, charged that a certain unnamed congressman (William J. Graves of Kentucky) was guilty of a conflict of interest. James Watson Webb, editor of the paper, called for a congressional investigation, but Cilley objected and criticized the editor from the House floor. Graves took offense and, through his spokesman, challenged Cilley to a duel. It took place February 24, 1838, and Cilley was killed.

Hawthorne wrote a eulogy of Cilley for the DEMOCRATIC REVIEW, remarking that he and Cilley had been friends from their earliest youth, and that Cilley had been "almost as an elder brother to him." He described him as having "a thin and thoughtful countenance, which seemed almost stern; but, in the intercourse of society it was brightened with a kindly smile that will live in the recollection of all who knew him." His eulogy, which showed that he was a loyal Democrat, was one reason he was appointed to the Boston Custom-House in 1839 (Miller, *Salem Is My Dwelling Place*, 155–156). He also wrote a "Biographical Sketch of Jonathan Cilley," which was published in the UNITED STATES MAGAZINE AND DEMOCRATIC REVIEW in September 1838.

Cilley once wrote that he loved and admired Hawthorne but did not know him. He considered him to live "in a mysterious world of thought and imagination," which he was not permitted to enter (Miller, *Salem Is My Dwelling Place*, 74).

Civil War   The Civil War years (1861–65) coincided roughly with the final years of Hawthorne's life; he died in May 1864. Terence Martin observes that, whereas for Walt Whitman they were creatively inspiring years, for Hawthorne they were a period of "final imaginative decline." He suggests that the war itself "constituted a staggering problem" for Hawthorne in the writing of fiction (*Nathaniel Hawthorne*, 27).

According to Turner, Hawthorne was ambivalent about the Union, writing to friends that the country should "hold on to the old thing," yet he sympathized and had "no kindred with nor leaning towards the Abolitionists." On the other hand, he wrote to his friend HORATIO BRIDGE after the firing on Fort Sumter that he rejoiced that the Union was "smashed"; it was "unnatural" and he "never loved" the South.

In 1862, Hawthorne visited Washington as part of a Massachusetts contingent and called on President Lincoln. He also visited Alexandria, Harper's Ferry, Manassas, and Newport News; the result was "CHIEFLY ABOUT WAR-MATTERS."

He called the Confederate soldiers he met at Harper's Ferry "peasants, and of a very low order," yet declared they were more respectful "than a rustic New Englander ever dreams of being toward anybody except perhaps his minister." Hawthorne stopped short of advocating retaliation against the Confederate soldiers who were imprisoned or taking of vengeance on the owners of slaves. In 1863, he announced that he hoped New England might be a "nation unto

itself." The war distressed him a great deal, and on the whole he sympathized with the North, yet he saw much that was worth preserving about the South (Turner, *Nathaniel Hawthorne: A Biography*, 350–374, passim). Hawthorne believed the war should have been prevented.

For Further Reading

Aaron, Daniel, *The Unwritten War: American Writers and the Civil War* (New York: Alfred A. Knopf, 1973); Morsberger, Robert E., "Hawthorne: The Civil War as the Unpardonable Sin," *Nathaniel Hawthorne Journal* (1977): 111–122; Yokozawa, Shiro, "Nathaniel Hawthorne's Mental Attitude toward the Civil War," *Journal of the English Institute* 11 (1980): 27–41.

Clark, Lewis Gaylord (1808–1873)   American editor and twin brother of Willis Gaylord Clark. For many years, they were coeditors of the KNICKERBOCKER MAGAZINE. Lewis Gaylord Clark reviewed TWICE-TOLD TALES in the *Knickerbocker Magazine* in April 1837, commenting that "in quiet humor, in genuine pathos, and deep feeling, and in a style equally unstudied and pure, the author . . . has few equals, and with perhaps one or two eminent exceptions, no superior in our country" (Turner, *Nathaniel Hawthorne: A Biography*, 87–88).

Clarke, James Freeman (1810–1888)   American Unitarian clergyman, a native of Hanover, New Hampshire, and the author of several religious books, including *Common Sense in Religion* (1874).

Clarke performed the wedding ceremony for Hawthorne and Sophia Peabody on July 9, 1842, at the Peabody home on West Street, Beacon Hill. No member of the Hawthorne family was present. Sophia was attended by Clarke's sister, Sarah Clarke, and by Cornelia Parks.

Twenty-two years later, on May 23, 1864, Clarke officiated at Hawthorne's funeral, conducting services in the Congregational Church of Concord and at the graveside in Sleepy Hollow.

Concord, Massachusetts   After their wedding in 1842, Hawthorne and his wife, Sophia, rented the

Old Manse in Concord for three years. This house had been built by the clergyman William Emerson, grandfather of RALPH WALDO EMERSON, in 1769 (Turner, *Nathaniel Hawthorne: A Biography*, 144).

A winding path went from the house to the Concord River. Before their arrival, HENRY DAVID THOREAU had planted a large vegetables garden for them, and the orchard gave them plentiful apples, peaches, and pears. Hawthorne and Emerson walked and dined together and skated on the Concord River but never became intimate friends. During the Concord years, Hawthorne was a closer friend of WILLIAM ELLERY CHANNING (Miller, *Salem Is My Dwelling Place*, 208–210). The Hawthornes' first child, a daughter, Una, was born at the Old Manse on March 3, 1844.

Hawthorne kept various journals at the Old Manse, which Turner terms "hardly less finished in plan and execution than those he published" (*Nathaniel Hawthorne: A Biography*, 150). He completed two important essays: "BUDS AND BIRD-VOICES" and "THE OLD MANSE." The latter introduced his collection of tales MOSSES FROM AN OLD MANSE.

While living in Concord, Hawthorne delighted in walking, boating, skating, reading, swimming the river, and writing. Turner observes that during his three and a half years in the Old Manse, he published 20 pieces, including three tales regarded as his best: "The BIRTH-MARK," "The ARTIST OF THE BEAUTIFUL," and "RAPPACCINI'S DAUGHTER."

Hawthorne's writings did not, however, produce an income adequate for the family. He hoped to be offered a postmastership in Salem but was not. In 1845, the Hawthornes learned that the owner of the Manse wanted to return there to live, and they began searching for other accommodations. Economic deprivation finally forced Sophia, again pregnant, to move to 77 Carver Street, Boston, to be near her physician. Hawthorne had moved to Salem, but, as soon as possible, joined Sophia in Boston. Julian was born on June 22, 1846. Meanwhile, Hawthorne had been offered a post in the Salem Custom-House, which he accepted. He was employed there from 1846 to 1849. The Hawthornes rented several houses in Salem while he was at the Custom-House.

In May 1852, on their return from ENGLAND and their travels on the Continent, the Hawthornes purchased the home of AMOS BRONSON ALCOTT and his family, Hillside, in Concord, Massachusetts. They renamed it THE WAYSIDE. This would be the only house they ever owned.

Conolly, Horace Lorenzo (c. 1811–1894) The Reverend Horace Lorenzo Conolly graduated from Yale, where he studied for the ministry. He was adopted by Hawthorne's second cousin, Susanna Ingersoll of Salem, and at one time was Hawthorne's minister.

Hawthorne had ambivalent feelings about Conolly. Although Conolly supported Hawthorne's March 1846 appointment as surveyor of the Salem Custom-House, Hawthorne himself told his sister Louisa that he was a "blackguard." Miller states that Conolly was "pompous, extroverted, alcoholically convivial, and unreliable" (*Salem Is My Dwelling Place: A Life of Nathaniel Hawthorne*, 87–88).

Conolly told Hawthorne the French Canadian tale of a young couple in Acadie. In it, all the men in the province are summoned on the couple's wedding day to hear a proclamation in the local church. They and the new bridegroom are then seized in the church and shipped to various places in New England. The bride searches for him her entire life and finds him on his deathbed when she is very aged. The shock kills her. Longfellow based his poem "Evangeline" on the story, and Hawthorne developed part of it in "The Acadians."

Consul, Hawthorne as American *See* LIVERPOOL.

Curtis, George William (1824–92) An American man of letters, Curtis was a native of Providence, Rhode Island. He was a member of the BROOK FARM community from 1842 to 1843. He was later editor of *Harper's Weekly* and a noted lecturer.

Hawthorne sent him a copy of The BLITHEDALE ROMANCE in July 1852, warning him, "Do not read it as if it had anything to do with Brook Farm (which essentially it has not)." Curtis wrote an essay, "Hawthorne," that appeared in his *Literary and Social Essays* in 1895 (Turner, NATHANIEL HAWTHORNE: A BIOGRAPHY, 422).

D

Dana, Charles Anderson (1819–1897) American newspaper editor, from Buffalo, New York. He was a member of the BROOK FARM Institute from 1841 to 1846 and eventually became editor of the New York *Sun*.

Hawthorne wrote to him on October 17, 1842, saying he ought to have resigned as an associate of the institute but had been "unwilling" to feel himself disconnected from Dana. It was now, however, "proper" for him to take the final step. He assured Dana that he would always "take the warmest interest" in his progress and would "heartily rejoice" at his success, of which he had no "reasonable doubt" (*Letters*, 15, 655).

Democratic Review *See* UNITED STATES MAGAZINE AND DEMOCRATIC REVIEW.

Duomo, Florence, Italy The Hawthornes, accompanied by Ada Shepard, a companion and tutor for the children, stayed in Florence from June to September 1858, at the VILLA MONTAUTO. Hawthorne visited the Duomo (the cathedral) and the nearby Baptistry several times. In his notebook, he described the "dim grandeur" of the interior and of the windows, which he pronounced "worth all the variegated marbles and rich cabinet-work of St. Peter's." He admired the central dome, which rested on three smaller domes, beneath which were three "vast niches" forming the transepts of the cathedral, and the "wreath of circular windows." He remarked that it was a pity anyone should die without seeing an "antique painted window, with the bright Italian sunshine glowing through it" and likened it to Milton's "dim religious light" (*French and Italian Notebooks*, 285–286).

Duyckinck, Evert Augustus (1816–1878) A native of New York City, Duyckinck was editor of the weekly *Literary World* from 1843 to 1853. He also edited the two-volume *Cyclopaedia of American Literature*. He and Hawthorne were friends for a number of years.

Hawthorne's Bowdoin friend HORATIO BRIDGE had kept a journal of a sailing trip along the coast of Africa. In March 1845, Hawthorne edited it and recommended it to Duyckinck, who published it as *Journal of an African Cruiser* in the Library of American Books he was editing for Wiley and Putnam (Turner, *Nathaniel Hawthorne: A Biography*, 156).

The same month, Duyckinck wrote to Hawthorne that he would like to include MOSSES FROM AN OLD MANSE, a collection of tales and sketches, in the Library of American Books. It was published in June 1845.

In 1849, Hawthorne and his wife, SOPHIA HAWTHORNE, were living in poverty, having a difficult time making ends meet. Duyckinck was one of several friends who sent money to enable them to pay household bills. Hawthorne regarded this assistance as a loan, refusing to accept it as a gift, and in 1853, soon after he became consul in Liverpool, repaid it (Turner, *Nathaniel Hawthorne: A Biography*, 190–192).

Duyckinck was one of many friends who visited the "Red House" in Lenox, where the Hawthornes were living, in the summer of 1850. He called Hawthorne "a fine ghost in a case of iron—a man of genius," who "looks it and lives it" (Turner, *Nathaniel Hawthorne: A Biography*, 213).

In 1850, Hawthorne embarked on a campaign biography of his longtime friend FRANKLIN PIERCE, who was hoping to run for president of the United States. Duyckinck approved of this undertaking, stating that it would bring Hawthorne "down from the subtle metaphysical analysis of morbid temperaments . . . to a healthy encounter with living interests." Turner observes that, with this remark, Duyckinck actually attacked the "most characteristic qualities" of Hawthorne's writings (*Nathaniel Hawthorne: A Biography*, 250).

Emerson, Lydia ("Lydian") Jackson (1802–1892)
The second wife of RALPH WALDO EMERSON.
Although her name was Lydia, he renamed her Lydian. The Emersons had four children: Waldo, Ellen,
Edith, and Edward. Waldo died at the age of five.

Lydia was a native of Plymouth, Massachusetts.
A devoted gardener, she planted her favorite flowers, especially tulips and roses, in their garden in
Concord. She was an abolitionist, and on July 4,
1855, she protested the existence of slavery in the
South by draping a black cloth over their gate.

When the Hawthornes returned to Concord after
their stay in Europe and purchased the former home
of AMOS BRONSON ALCOTT (which they renamed
THE WAYSIDE), the Emersons called on them immediately. The two families remained close.

Emerson, Ralph Waldo (1803–1882)   Known as
an essayist, philosopher, and poet, Emerson had also
become a Unitarian minister and was appointed to
the Old Second Church in Boston. His faith in
administering the sacrament of the Lord's Supper
wavered, and he resigned when his first wife, Ellen
Tucker, died.

He traveled to England, where he was influenced by Walter Savage Landor, Thomas Carlyle,
and Samuel Coleridge. While there, he developed
his own philosophy. On his return to New England,
he published his first book, *Nature,* and married
Lydia Jackson. He became known as the "sage of
Concord." His literary circle included MARGARET
FULLER, AMOS BRONSON ALCOTT, HENRY DAVID
THOREAU, and WILLIAM ELLERY CHANNING.

Emerson edited *The Dial,* a transcendentalist journal, and published many books, including
Essays, English Traits, and *Representative Men.* He
refused to believe in the existence of evil, a stance
with which Hawthorne disagreed.

England   Hawthorne's BOWDOIN COLLEGE friend
FRANKLIN PIERCE was elected United States president in 1852. Soon after he took office in 1853, he
appointed Hawthorne United States consul at LIVERPOOL, England. The Hawthornes sailed to England in July 1853 aboard the Cunard Line paddle
wheeler *NIAGARA* and arrived July 17. They were
accompanied by WILLIAM D. TICKNOR. The Hawthornes would live in Europe, principally in England and Italy, until 1860.

In late July, the family moved from the Waterloo Hotel in Liverpool into Mrs. Blodgett's boardinghouse, at 153 Duke Street. In early August,
they moved to the Rock Ferry Hotel, in ROCK
FERRY. Hawthorne took up his duties in early
August. On September 1, they moved once more,
to 26 Rock Park, Rock Ferry. Ticknor returned to
America on October 1.

Hawthorne retained many of the employees
of his predecessors, including the vice-consul,
James Pearce, and the chief clerk, Henry J. Wilding, who provided excellent guidance for him. He
was also assisted by the outgoing consul, Thomas
Crittenden.

Liverpool was the chief portal of trade in England; thus Hawthorne was responsible for dealing
with both commercial and diplomatic matters. He

wrote hundreds of letters, published in two volumes: those to friends, acquaintances, and family (*The Letters,* 1853–1856), and *The Consular Letters,* related to the business of the consulate, problems caused by Americans abroad (deaths, crimes, breakdowns), and other matters. Some of these were drafted by his chief clerk, although Hawthorne approved them before they were sent.

He made many English friends, including HENRY BRIGHT, who was very attentive to the family. Among the highlights of the Hawthornes' lives in England were visits to LONDON, the Lake District, Leamington, Hammersmith, and other places of interest. Before returning to America, the family toured Lincoln, Boston, Peterborough, Nottingham, Manchester, and Scotland. Throughout his time in England, Hawthorne kept an English notebook, later published.

Hawthorne resigned the consulship in February 1857; James Buchanan had become United States president. In 1863, he published *Our Old Home,* a collection of 12 sketches based on his experiences as American consul in Liverpool. He was criticized in Britain for arguing that it was undeniable that an American "was continually thrown upon his national antagonism by some acrid quality in the moral atmosphere of England." He declared that the English thought "so loftily of themselves, and so contemptuously of everybody else" that it was difficult to "stay in a good humor with them." Turner remarks that Hawthorne knew the sketches would "stir resentment" in England (*Nathaniel Hawthorne,* 161).

For Further Reading

Nathaniel Hawthorne, *The English Notebooks,* edited by Randall Stewart (New York: Oxford University Press, 1941).

Essex Institute   Now part of the Peabody Essex Museum, it is located at 132–134 Essex Street, Salem, Massachusetts. The Essex Institute includes the Assembly House, the Gardner-Pingree House, the John Ward House, and the Crowinshield-Bentley House.

It houses many original documents pertaining to the Salem witchcraft trials, in addition to a collection of antiques and historic objects of the colonial, federal, and Victorian periods, and other distinguished historical collections.

One of the treasures of the Essex Institute is a journal kept by Nathaniel Hawthorne's father, NATHANIEL HAWTHORNE, SR., on his homeward voyage from Calcutta to Salem aboard the *America* in the winter of 1795. According to Turner, this journal and two others were once owned by Hawthorne, who read them with much interest. He observes that the owner of the *America,* Elias Hasket Derby, figures in Hawthorne's sketch "The CUSTOM-HOUSE" as "Old King Derby," one of the "princely merchants of Salem" (Turner, *Nathaniel Hawthorne: A Biography,* 6).

The Essex Institute also has account books kept by Richard Manning, Hawthorne's maternal grandfather, who amassed a fortune in real estate in properties on Herbert Street, Union Street, and Derby Street, Salem, as well as nearly 10,000 acres in Maine (Turner, *Nathaniel Hawthorne: A Biography,* 15).

Europe   In late 1857, after Nathaniel Hawthorne resigned his post as United States consul at LIVERPOOL, England, he and his family, accompanied by Ada Shepard, the children's companion and tutor, traveled to the Continent, where they spent the next three years. In 1858, they arrived in Paris, a city they greatly enjoyed for a time despite the cold. They then went on to ITALY, spending several months each in Rome and Florence. UNA HAWTHORNE contracted "Roman fever" in Florence and was seriously ill for six months. This was a dangerous illness at a time when there were no antibiotics; quinine was one of the few available drugs. When she recovered, the Hawthornes went on to Venice, Civitavecchia, Marseille, and back to Italy. They also traveled to Valence, Lyon, Geneva, Villeneuve, Paris, and Le Havre. After returning to Southampton and LONDON, Hawthorne decided to remain in England for another year in order to finish THE MARBLE FAUN. The family returned to THE WAYSIDE, their home in CONCORD, MASSACHUSETTS, in June 1860.

F

Faun of Praxiteles Praxiteles (c. 370–c. 330 B.C.) was one of the more famous of the Greek sculptors. His statue of a Faun, which is in the sculpture gallery in the Capitol at Rome, figures in Hawthorne's novel *The MARBLE FAUN*.

As the novel opens, three young Americans, Miriam, Hilda, and Kenyon, along with Donatello, a young Italian, visit the gallery and gaze at the Faun. The statue represents a young man leaning his right arm on a tree, one hand hanging by his side. In the other he holds a fragment of a pipe, a musical instrument. He wears a lion's skin. The statue, according to Hawthorne, "conveys the idea of an amiable and sensual creature," one who is amoral but whose animal nature is inscrutable and perplexing. He has pointed and furry ears, which, together with the lion's skin, are "the sole indications of his wild, forest nature."

The Americans are struck by the resemblance between the Faun and Donatello. Kenyon asks him to take the "exact attitude" of the statue, and Donatello laughingly does so. Hawthorne remarks that "allowing for the difference of costume, and if a lion's skin could have been substituted for his modern talma, and a rustic pipe for his stick, Donatello might have figured perfectly as the marble Faun, miraculously softened into flesh and blood." The statue depicts a period when "man's affinity with Nature was more strict, and his fellowship with every living thing more intimate and dear."

For Further Reading

Auerbach, Jonathan, "Executing the Model: Painting, Sculpture, and Romance Writing in Hawthorne's *The Marble Faun*," *English Literary History* 47, no. 1 (spring 1980): 103–120; Bentley, Nancy, "Slaves and Fauns: Hawthorne and the Uses of Primitivism," *English Literary History* 57, no. 4 (winter 1990): 901–937; Brodtkorb, Paul Jr., "Art Allegory in *The Marble Faun*," *Publications of the Modern Language Association* 77, no. 3 (June 1962): 254–267.

Fields, Annie Adams (1834–1915) The wife of the publisher JAMES T. FIELDS, Annie Adams Fields was also known as a diarist, literary hostess, biographer, writer, and close friend of the writer Sarah Orne Jewett.

She was the cousin of Fields's first wife, who had died of tuberculosis. She and James T. Fields lived at 148 Charles Street, Boston, transforming their home into a well-known literary salon.

SOPHIA HAWTHORNE met her when the Hawthornes returned from ENGLAND to America in 1860. The Fields had no children, and Annie became very fond of the Hawthorne children. Once the Hawthornes were settled at THE WAYSIDE IN CONCORD, Massachusetts, the Fields visited often. Sophia, in particular, was attached to Annie and, after Hawthorne's death, visited her often in Boston, perhaps more often than Annie Fields would have liked.

After Fields's death in 1881, Annie lived with the poet, novelist, and short-story writer Sarah Orne Jewett for nearly 30 years in what was known as a "Boston marriage," the term given to an arrangement whereby two women lived in close long-term companionship (Miller, *Salem Is My Dwelling Place*, 476–478).

For Further Reading

Fields, Annie, *Authors and Friends* (Boston: Houghton Mifflin, 1897); Fields, James T., *Yesterdays with Authors* (1900; reprint, New York: AMS Press, 1970); Gollin, Rita K., *Annie Adams Fields: Woman of Letters* (Amherst: University of Massachusetts Press, 2002); Gollin, Rita K., "Annie Fields' Nathaniel Hawthorne," in *Hawthorne and Women: Engendering and Expanding the Hawthorne Tradition* (Amherst: University of Massachusetts Press, 1999); Roman, Judith A., *Annie Adams Fields: The Spirit of Charles St.* (Bloomington: Indiana University Press, 1990).

Fields, James T. (1816–1881)   A colorful literary figure in Boston, Fields grew up in Portsmouth, New Hampshire. He left Portsmouth to work at the Old Corner Bookshop in Boston, where he began a long friendship and business association with the publisher WILLIAM D. TICKNOR; they became partners in Ticknor and Company. The firm published the works of Longfellow, Holmes, JOHN GREENLEAF WHITTIER, Tennyson, and Dickens. Fields was also a book promoter, editor, amateur poet, and host to the most distinguished literary salon in America, on Charles Street, Boston.

It is thought that he met Hawthorne at the Old Corner Bookshop while Hawthorne was employed in the Boston Custom-House. Hawthorne had already published FANSHAWE (anonymously, in 1828) and a number of sketches and tales, when, supposedly in 1849, Fields asked him whether he had any manuscripts he might examine. Hawthorne said no at first but then gave him a bulky manuscript from his desk that was later published as *The SCARLET LETTER* (Miller, *Salem Is My Dwelling Place*, 280–281).

For Further Reading

Fields, Annie, *Authors and Friends* (Boston: Houghton Mifflin, 1897); Fields, James T., *Yesterdays with Authors* (1900; reprint; New York: AMS Press, 1970); Tryon, W. S., *Parnassus Corner: A Life of James T. Fields: Publisher to the Victorians* (Boston, Mass.: Houghton Mifflin, 1963).

James T. Fields, Nathaniel Hawthorne, and William D. Ticknor, ca. 1861–1862. Fields and Ticknor were good friends of Hawthorne's, as well as his principal publishers. Photograph by James Wallace Black. *(Courtesy of the Peabody Essex Museum)*

France   In January 1858, en route to Italy, Hawthorne and his family traveled through France. The group also included ADA Shepard, a young graduate of Antioch College who had arrived from America in the fall to serve as tutor and companion to the children. She had been strongly recommended by MARY TYLER PEABODY MANN, who was SOPHIA HAWTHORNE's sister. In Paris, they were joined by the astronomer MARIA MITCHELL, a professor at Vassar College who had discovered a new comet in 1847; she had asked to travel to Rome in their company.

Hawthorne was prepared to dislike France even before they arrived. On January 5, they crossed the English Channel and landed at Boulogne; they continued by train to Amiens, where, the next day, they visited the cathedral. They arrived in Paris on the afternoon of January 6 and registered at the Hôtel du Louvre. They spent a week there, but Hawthorne declared he had a "dreary and desperate feeling," because the sights lasted longer than his capacity for viewing them. He attributed his antipathy to France to having grown too "English" while serving as U.S. consul in LIVERPOOL, as he wrote to his publisher and friend George Ticknor. He did appreciate the food, pronouncing it "very delicate, and a vast change from the simple English system." While in Paris, he called on the American consul, Henry Spencer, who recommended that he get visas for ITALY and Austria from the minister in France, since they would carry more weight than a visa from the consul. He and his son JULIAN HAWTHORNE, walked through the Tuileries gardens, crossed the Seine, and visited the bookstalls, finding the Left Bank livelier and more appealing than the Right Bank. They also toured Nôtre Dame Cathedral, but Hawthorne never warmed to the city and complained of the mud on the pavements (*French and Italian Notebooks*, 3–31).

The Hawthornes went on by train to Lyon and spent three days in Marseille. They then boarded the steamer *Calabrese* and sailed to Genoa and Leghorn; they landed at Civitavecchia on January 20 and traveled on to Rome by carriage.

Fuller, Margaret (Marchesa Ossoli) (1810–1850) American essayist, editor, teacher, and writer. She edited the magazine *The Dial* for two years and was a translator of Goethe. She wrote a number of books, including *Woman in the Nineteenth Century, Papers on Literature and Art,* and *Summer on the Lake.*

In December 1839, Hawthorne was invited to dine with Miss Fuller at the home of GEORGE BANCROFT, but he was unable to accept the invitation because of business (he was employed at the BOSTON CUSTOM-HOUSE at the time). He wrote to Sophia Peabody, to whom he was engaged, that he was relieved not to be able to accept, as he would rather meet "literary lions and lionesses" when she could be with him (*Letters,* 15, 382).

Sophia's sister ELIZABETH PEABODY owned a bookstore at 13 West Street, Boston, where *The Dial* was published and much transcendentalist dis-

cussion and planning occurred. Beginning in 1839, Margaret Fuller gave a series of conversations in the bookstore. She is thought to have been the model for Zenobia in *The BLITHEDALE ROMANCE.* Both Zenobia and Margaret Fuller were writers, gifted conversationalists, and strong advocates of women's rights. Turner suggests, however, that Hawthorne based his description of Zenobia's beauty on another BROOK FARM resident, Mrs. Amelia Barlow (*Nathaniel Hawthorne: A Biography,* 239).

In April 1841, when Hawthorne was living at BROOK FARM, he wrote to Sophia that Margaret Fuller's cow was at the farm, and that she "hooks the other cows, and has made herself ruler of the herd, and behaves in a very tyrannical manner" (*Letters,* 15, 528).

After the Hawthornes were married and living in CONCORD at The Old Manse, in 1842, Margaret Fuller proposed that they take in WILLIAM ELLERY CHANNING (nephew of the famous minister) and his fiancée, Margaret's sister, Ellen Fuller, as boarders, or "inmates of the household." Hawthorne tactfully declined to do so, writing to Margaret that even Adam and Eve would have refused to take two angels into paradise as boarders. It would involve all four of them in an "unnatural relation" and place an undue burden on Sophia. He advised the young couple to seek a farmer's household for such an arrangement; there would be no "nice sensibilities" to worry about, more freedom, and less risk of hurt feelings on either side (*Letters,* 15, 646–647).

In 1846, Margaret Fuller went to Italy, where she became acquainted with a number of leading writers. After meeting the Marchese Ossoli (Giovanni Angelo Ossoli), who was ten years her junior, she became his mistress and gave birth to a son; they married later. In 1850, she and her husband perished in a shipwreck off Fire Island, New York; their bodies were never recovered, although that of the infant son washed ashore.

On the whole, Hawthorne thought Sophia admired Margaret Fuller too much, although they both found Fuller's *Woman in the Nineteenth Century* (1845) disagreeable. Sophia wrote to her mother that she herself had never been interested in women's rights. Hawthorne observed in his notebook that Fuller's marriage to Ossoli proved that she was a "very woman, after all," who "fell as the weakest of her sisters might." He viewed her death as almost inevitable, or, as Turner puts it, "the final step in the working out of inevitable consequences" (*Nathaniel Hawthorne: A Biography*, 324–325).

For Further Reading

Cary, Louise D., "Margaret Fuller as Hawthorne's Zenobia: The Problem of Moral Accountability in Fictional Biography," *American Transcendental Quarterly* 4, no. 1 (March 1990): 31–48; Coffee, Jessie A., "Margaret Fuller as Zenobia in *The Blithedale Romance*," *Proceedings of the Conference of College Teachers of English of Texas* (1973): 23–27; Gilbert, Katherine, "Two Nineteenth-Century Feminists: Nathaniel Hawthorne's Relationship with Margaret Fuller," *Postscript: Publication of the Philological Association of the Carolinas* 13 (1996): 101–111; Kesterson, David B., "Margaret Fuller on Hawthorne: Formative Views by a Woman of the Nineteenth Century," in *Hawthorne and Women: Engendering and Expanding the Hawthorne Tradition*, edited by John L. Idol, Jr. and Melinda M. Ponder, 65–74 (Amherst: University of Massachusetts Press, 1999); Mitchell, Thomas R., "Julian Hawthorne and the 'Scandal' of Margaret Fuller," *American Literary History* 7, no. 2 (summer 1995): 210–233; Young, Virginia Hudson, "Fuller and Hawthorne: The Androgyny of Genius," *Publications of the Missouri Philological Association* 10 (1985): 64–70.

G

Goodrich, Samuel Griswold (1793–1860) The founding editor of *Parley's Magazine*, Goodrich was the author of more than 100 books and played an important role in Hawthorne's early literary career.

In 1829, a year after the anonymous publication of Hawthorne's first novel, FANSHAWE, Goodrich requested a submission from Hawthorne for *The* TOKEN, an annual magazine he edited. He had heard of the "anonymous publication," which indicated "extraordinary literary powers." Hawthorne sent Goodrich several tales, including "The GENTLE BOY" and "My Uncle Molineaux," which would later be published as "MY KINSMAN, MAJOR MOLINEAUX." Goodrich printed several of his tales in the magazine but paid only $108 for eight contributions that appeared in 1837 (Miller, Salem *Is My Dwelling Place*, 93).

In 1836, Hawthorne became editor of the AMERICAN MAGAZINE OF USEFUL AND ENTERTAINING KNOWLEDGE; Goodrich was connected with the publishers and instrumental in his appointment. Hawthorne's friend HORATIO BRIDGE, who always had Hawthorne's best interests at heart, had closely followed Hawthorne's efforts to obtain a reasonable income from editing and writing and was pleased about the editorship. He declared it would provide an introduction to "other and better employment" (Miller, *Salem Is My Dwelling Place*, 94).

Hawthorne commended Goodrich's book *A System of Universal Geography* in the magazine. This connection led to Hawthorne's collaboration with his sister Elizabeth on *Peter Parley's Universal History on the Basis of Geography*, in two volumes, which would appear in many editions in the ensuing years (Turner, *Nathaniel Hawthorne: A Biography*, passim).

For Further Reading

Wadsworth, Sarah A., "Nathaniel Hawthorne, Samuel Goodrich, and the Transformation of the Juvenile Literature Market," *Nathaniel Hawthorne Review* 26, no. 1 (spring 2000): 1–24.

Graham's Lady's and Gentleman's Magazine A literary magazine published in Philadelphia, edited by George R. Graham and EDGAR ALLAN POE. Hawthorne's story "EARTH'S HOLOCAUST" appeared in the magazine in May 1844. At other times, the magazine had different titles, including *Graham's Magazine of Literature and Art* and *Graham's American Monthly Magazine of Literature and Art*.

H

Hathorne This was the original spelling of *Hawthorne*. William Hathorne, Hawthorne's great-grandfather, immigrated to Boston from England with John Winthrop. He was a soldier, legislator, Puritan, and persecutor of Quakers. His son, John Hathorne, became a judge in the famous Salem witchcraft trials. Nathaniel Hathorne, his son, was a ship captain who died of yellow fever in Surinam in 1808, leaving a daughter, Elizabeth, age two, and a son, Nathaniel, age four. A second daughter, Maria Louisa, was born the year her father died. Hawthorne added the *w* to his surname after 1830 (Wineapple, Brenda, *Hawthorne: A Life* (New York: Farrar, Straus and Giroux, 2003), 13–21; Hoeltje, *Inward Sky: The Mind and Heart of Nathaniel Hawthorne* (Durham, N.C.: Duke University Press, 1962), 16–27.

Haworth, Euphrasia Fanny A painter, poet, and writer the Hawthornes knew while living in LIVERPOOL and ITALY. She painted a well-known portrait of Pen Browning, son of ELIZABETH BARRETT BROWNING and ROBERT BROWNING. She was the author of *The Pine Tree Dell, and Other Tales* (London: Andrews, 1827).

Hawthorne, Edith Garregues (1874–1949) The second wife of JULIAN HAWTHORNE, son of Nathaniel Hawthorne and his wife, SOPHIA PEABODY HAWTHORNE. A well-known painter, she was born in Copenhagen, Denmark, the daughter of a surgeon, Dr. Henry Garregues. After moving to San Francisco in 1914, she studied art in Carmel, California, and married Julian Hawthorne in 1925. She painted satyrs and nymphs in sunlit settings, as well as other works, but is primarily known as a landscape painter.

Hawthorne, Elizabeth Clarke Manning (1780–1649) Mother of Nathaniel Hawthorne. She grew up in the large Manning family in their home on Herbert Street, Salem, Massachusetts. When Hawthorne's father died in Surinam, she returned to her childhood family. She was known as "Madame Hawthorne" after her husband's death.

Gloria Erlich observes that because she was widowed with three children and in reduced circumstances, it was natural for her to return home. However, she seems to have had a "lack of vitality and trust in her own competence"; after all, she was "young and strikingly beautiful" and might have remarried. At the same time, she was prone to attacks of "nerves" and headaches. She was also afraid that her son, Nathaniel, might be tempted to become a sailor and go to sea if he were much exposed to the influence of the Hawthornes.

She advised her children to become as helpful and independent as possible within the Manning household, and not to cause their grandparents, aunts, and uncles worry; they were to obey them as they would their mother. Erlich deduces that she was "gentle and affectionate" but lacked confidence in herself and tended to be reclusive (Erlich, Gloria, *Family Themes and Hawthorne's Fiction: The*

Tenacious Web (New Brunswick, N.J.: Rutgers University Press, 1984): 62–68.

Hawthorne, Elizabeth Manning ("Ebe") (1802–1883)

The elder of Hawthorne's two sisters, two years his senior. Turner states that she was "possessively interested in his career" and later in life recorded many recollections of his childhood and early youth (Turner, *Nathaniel Hawthorne: A Biography*, 16–17). Her letters to Hawthorne, combined with many letters about him to friends and relatives, have provided a rich archive of biographical information.

Brenda Wineapple remarks that "Ebe" was the "dazzler" among the three Hawthorne children, walking and talking at nine months and reading Shakespeare at the age of 12. As children, she and her brother read each other's literary efforts, exchanging their writings by sending baskets between their rooms, which were on different floors. Ebe resisted obligatory social calls and never married, probably by choice. Hawthorne termed her "the most sensible woman I ever knew in my life" but feared her ridicule (Wineapple, *Hawthorne: A Life*, 1–44).

Hawthorne, Julian (1846–1934)

Son of Nathaniel Hawthorne, a novelist and biographer of his father. At the time of his birth, Hawthorne wrote to his sister Louisa, "A small troglodyte made his appearance here at ten minutes to six o'clock, this morning, who claims to be your nephew, and the heir to all our wealth and honors" (Turner, *Nathaniel Hawthorne: A Biography*, 172).

Julian was adored by his sisters, Una and Rose, and by his parents. Hawthorne called him "The Black Prince" because his coloring was so much darker than that of his sister Una. Hawthorne read great literature in Latin to the children, and Julian was educated in horseback riding, sword fighting, sketching, and gymnastics. His parents often read Spenser's *The Faerie Queen* aloud (his elder sister Una was, in fact, named after Spenser's heroine).

In 1853, at the age of seven, Julian was taken to LIVERPOOL when his father was appointed United States consul there. The Hawthornes lived in ENGLAND until 1857 and then traveled on the Continent before returning to America in 1860. While on the Continent, the children had a governess, Ada Shepard, who had received a classical education at Antioch College. In 1860, when the family returned to Massachuetts, Julian was sent to a coeducational school in CONCORD, but he was not a distinguished student. He attended Harvard but did not receive a degree.

After his father died in 1864, Julian's mother took her children to Dresden, Germany, where Julian might study engineering. It was in Germany that he met May (Minne) Albertina Amelung, whose family had a prosperous glassworking business. His love sonnets to May were published in *Putnam's*. They were married in 1870, and Julian began writing; he sold a story, "Love and Courtly Love: or, Masquerading," to *Harper's Weekly*. He eventually published a number of books, including *Bressant: A Romance* (1873); *Dust: A Novel* (1883); *American Literature: A Text Book for the Use of Schools and Colleges*, written with Leonard Lemmon (1896); *One of Those Coincidences and Ten Other Stories* (1899); and *Hawthorne and His Circle* (1903).

Julian and May had nine children, but their marriage broke up after the death of their ninth child. He then served a jail term for embezzlement. In 1925, he married the artist Edith Garregues, of Danish descent, who had moved to San Francisco from Copenhagen.

Hawthorne, Maria Louisa (1808–1852)

Nathaniel Hawthorne's younger sister, called Louisa.

Erlich states that she was often described as "fun-loving, amiable, and ordinary." She was a good cook and seamstress and, at the same time, enjoyed hunting and fishing in Raymond, Maine, with Hawthorne. When he published the *Spectator*, as a child, she helped him and was a member of his secret "Pin" society. Erlich concludes that, although she was not as brilliant as her older sister, Elizabeth, she "influenced Hawthorne's conception of the domestic Phoebe type, the fair woman whom the artist may marry" for the purpose of keeping himself "within the bounds of society" (Erlich, Gloria, *Family Themes and Hawthorne's Fiction: The Tenacious Web*, 83–84).

In the summer of 1852, Louisa vacationed in Saratoga Springs with her uncle, John Dike. They decided to return to New York via the Hudson River aboard the steamer *Henry Clay*; from New York, Louisa planned to return to Concord by train. On the afternoon of July 28, the *Henry Clay* and the *Armenia* had a race. The *Clay* ran into the *Armenia*, causing a fire aboard both ships. Louisa was killed when she jumped into the river, trying to escape (Wineapple, *Hawthorne: A Life*, 260). When Pike told the news to Hawthorne and his wife, they were devastated.

Hawthorne, May (Minne) Albertina (Amelong) (1848–1925)   First wife of JULIAN HAWTHORNE. She was born in New Orleans in 1848 and died in 1925 in Redding, Connecticut. She and Julian met in Dresden, Germany. Her father was a member of a wealthy glassmaking family of Germanic stock, and her mother was one of the Randolphs of Virginia. She was said to be witty, intellectually quick, beautiful, and indomitable. They were married in 1871 and had nine children.

Hawthorne, Nathaniel, Sr. (1780–1808)   The father of Nathaniel Hawthorne. The name was spelled HATHORNE at first, but his son changed it to *Hawthorne* after 1830. He was a sea captain who sailed frequently to the Far East. His eldest child, a daughter, Elizabeth, was born in 1802, and his son, Nathaniel, was born in 1804. At the time of his son's birth, he was en route home from the Far East. In 1808, he died in Surinam, at the age of 28. His last child, Hawthorne's younger sister, Mary Louisa, was born the same year.

Hawthorne, Rose (1851–1926)   Youngest child of Nathaniel and SOPHIA HAWTHORNE. *See* LATHROP, ROSE HAWTHORNE.

Hawthorne, Sophia Amelia Peabody (1809–1871)   Sophia Peabody, Hawthorne's wife, was far more independent and talented than his biographers' typical portrayal of her. Her family lived in Boston from 1824 to 1828 and then settled in a large home on Charter Street, in Salem, in 1835. Her father, DR. NATHANIEL PEABODY, was a den-

tist; her mother, ELIZABETH PALMER PEABODY, was a teacher. She was the youngest of three sisters; there were also five brothers in the family, two of whom died prematurely. Educated in her mother's and sister's schools, she was an eager student.

From 1833 to 1835, Sophia's sister MARY TYLER PEABODY MANN (she later married HORACE MANN) was employed as a tutor in a Cuban family. Sophia, who suffered from ill health, accompanied her, keeping a diary while there. When Sophia returned to Salem, she was treated as an invalid and spent part of each day in bed; she was, according to Hawthorne's biographer Arlin Turner, the subject of "medical attention and experimentation."

ELIZABETH PALMER PEABODY, the third sister, had gained a reputation as a member of the Boston intellectual elite. She was once secretary to

Sophia Hawthorne, 1861. Photograph by Silsbee and Case. *(Courtesy of the Peabody Essex Museum)*

WILLIAM ELLERY CHANNING, the Unitarian theologian, and assisted AMOS BRONSON ALCOTT with his experimental school.

Hawthorne noted in an early letter to Sophia that his youthful life at home, in his "haunted chamber," was meaningless, and he wondered whether the world would ever know him. When he began to gain recognition, he found nothing in the outside world preferable to his old "solitude," until a "certain Dove" was revealed to him. He drew nearer and nearer to the Dove and opened his "bosom to her, and she flitted into it, and closed her wings there—and there she nestles now and forever, keeping my heart warm and renewing my life with her own" (Martin, Terence, *Nathaniel Hawthorne*, 27).

Hawthorne's sister ELIZABETH "EBE" MANNING HAWTHORNE was adamantly opposed to the marriage, which many critics attribute to her possessiveness of her brother. On one occasion, she appropriated flowers Elizabeth Peabody sent to Nathaniel, which had been delivered by Sophia. Ebe considered them a gift to herself, pretending that Nathaniel found a love of flowers a "feminine taste." Hawthorne's son, JULIAN HAWTHORNE, writing about the incident many years later, declared that Ebe was jealous, and that his father was certainly "sensible" of the "beauty and charm of flowers." Ebe always felt Hawthorne's writing suffered after the marriage, although Hawthorne himself was firmly convinced that Sophia "rescued him from a life of alienation" (Erlich, Gloria, *Family Themes and Hawthorne's Fiction: The Tenacious Web*, 88–90).

None of the Peabodys attended Sophia's wedding to Hawthorne. By all accounts, she and Hawthorne were extraordinarily happy together. They had three children: UNA HAWTHORNE, JULIAN HAWTHORNE AND ROSE HAWTHORNE. She was a devoted wife throughout his life, arranging their housing, accompanying him on all his travels, and, at one time, helping the family financially by making lampshades.

Sophia was also an excellent painter and a good copyist. She illustrated Hawthorne's story "The GENTLE BOY," which he dedicated to his wife. The story was published in a separate volume by Weeks & Jordan in Boston and by Wiley and Putnam in New York and London in 1839.

Headstone of Sophia Hawthorne in Kensal Green Cemetery, London. Sophia's remains were later transferred to Concord, Massachusetts. *(Photograph by Sarah Bird Wright)*

After her husband's death, in 1864, Sophia was left to deal with her sometimes difficult children alone. Although she was not facing poverty, she was forced to live on a reduced income. In 1870, she and her children moved to Germany so that Julian could study engineering. Later that year, she moved to ENGLAND, where she became ill and died of typhoid pneumonia on February 26, 1871. She was buried in the KENSAL GREEN CEMETERY, north of LONDON.

In June 2006, the remains of Sophia Hawthorne and her daughter Una Hawthorne were removed from Kensal Green Cemetery, London, and reinterred in Sleepy Hollow Cemetery, Concord. The expenses of approximately $15,000 to transport and reinter their remains were covered by the Dominican Sisters of Hawthorne, the Roman Catholic order of nuns that Rose Hawthorne founded. Imogen Howe, now 67, the great-great-granddaughter of Nathaniel and Sophia Hawthorne, remarked that the reinterment was "overwhelming. . . . [I]t's very emotional. They know now in spirit that everyone is reunited" (*New York Times*, June 27, 2006).

For Further Reading

Stewart, Randall, "Recollections of Hawthorne by His Sister Elizabeth," *American Literature* 16 (1945): 316–331; Tharp, Louise Hall, *The Peabody Sisters of Salem* (Boston: Little, Brown, 1950).

Hawthorne, Una (1844–1877)   Elder daughter of Nathaniel and SOPHIA AMELIA PEABODY HAWTHORNE. While the family was in Rome in 1858 and 1859, Una became seriously ill with "Roman fever," a dreaded illness similar to malaria, from which she suffered for six months. She was gravely ill from November 1858 through mid-April 1859. According to Turner, quinine was one of the few medicines available, but it was fatal if given too often. Una finally seemed to have recovered by April 19, although she apparently suffered the aftereffects of the illness as long as she lived; Turner states that Hawthorne "never recovered from the anguish this illness caused him" (Turner, *Nathaniel Hawthorne: A Biography*, 334–335).

In 1867, Una became engaged to Storrow Higginson, a nephew of Thomas Wentworth Higginson, but for reasons that are unclear, the engagement was broken off. Una and Rose met GEORGE P. LATHROP and were both interested in him, but it became clear that he preferred Rose.

After Sophia Hawthorne's death in 1871, Lathrop and Rose became engaged. Apparently, Una had had a "psychotic episode," and Rose married Lathrop in September 1871 for protection from her sister. Their uncle NATHANIEL CRANCH PEABODY wrote that Una had become "dangerously insane, spent great sums of money, [and] nearly took the lives of three people" before being sent to an asylum. She recovered from her depression and later took refuge in an orphanage managed by the Church of England, performing social services there.

Una returned to America and lived with the Lathrops but discovered that their marriage was full of conflicts. She then met and became engaged to Albert Webster Jr., who was already suffering from tuberculosis. While waiting for Webster to return from a voyage, Una moved back to England to live with her brother, JULIAN HAWTHORNE, who was determined to pursue a literary career. When Webster died at sea, Una entered an Anglican convent, where she became ill and died in 1877, at the age of 33. She is buried near her mother in KENSAL GREEN CEMETERY, north of LONDON (Miller, *Salem Is My Dwelling Place*, 525–526).

Una was considered by many to be the model for Pearl in *The* SCARLET LETTER.

Hillard, George   Boston attorney and former schoolteacher whose home was at 54 Pinckney Street, Beacon Hill. He had been a friend of Sophia Peabody and her sisters. While Hawthorne was employed as inspector in the BOSTON CUSTOMHOUSE, he occupied a parlor and bedroom in the Hillard home (Miller, *Salem Is My Dwelling Place*, 169–170).

Hoar, Elizabeth   A young woman who had been engaged to Charles Emerson, brother of RALPH WALDO EMERSON. Charles died early in 1836, at the age of 28. Sophia Peabody (later HAWTHORNE) had commemorated him in a medallion relief, which comforted Elizabeth Hoar. It was she who urged Hawthorne and Sophia to consider renting the parsonage in CONCORD, MASSACHUSETTS, which had become available after the death of the Reverend Ezra Ripley, step-grandfather of Ralph Waldo Emerson (Miller, *Salem Is My Dwelling Place*, 142, 201).

Hosmer, Harriet Goodhue (1830–1908)   American sculptor, born in Watertown, Massachusetts. Her work is represented in a number of institutions, including the Saint Louis Mercantile Library and the Saint Louis Museum of Art.

Hawthorne and his family knew her in ITALY in 1858. He called her statue of Zenobia a "high, heroic ode." She was one of the models for Hilda in *The* MARBLE FAUN; the other was MARIA LOUISA LANDER.

Houghton, Richard Monckton Milnes, first Lord (1809–1885)   Liberal politician, critic, man of letters, and "literary ringmaster of London." He was educated at Trinity College, Cambridge, where he was a friend of Tennyson and Thackeray.

Hawthorne first met him at a dinner in LIVERPOOL at the home of John Heywood in Norris Green, on September 22, 1854. Hawthorne described him in his notebook as "a very agreeable, kindly, man of the world," said to be "a very kind patron of literary men, and to do a great deal of good among young and neglected people of that class." He was considered to be a good conversationalist. He introduced Hawthorne to his wife, one of the daughters of Lord Crewe.

In 1856, Hawthorne was invited to luncheon at the LONDON home of the Milnes on Upper Brook Street, where he met ROBERT BROWNING and ELIZABETH BARRETT BROWNING, the marquess of Lansdown, Florence Nightingale, and other prominent people (*The English Notebooks by Nathaniel Hawthorne*, ed. Stewart, 87, 381–383).

Howitt, Anna Mary *See* WATTS, ANNA MARY HOWITT.

Howitt, William (1792–1879) British writer and author of *Book of the Seasons* (1831), *Rural Life of England* (1838), *History of the Supernatural* (1863), and other books.

In 1856, Hawthorne, then American consul at LIVERPOOL, was invited to dine at the Milton Club in London by FRANCIS BENNOCH, who had been very kind to him. He met Howitt at this dinner and remarked in his notebook that Bennoch knew his books "better than those of any other person there." Hawthorne described him as a "silver headed, stout, firm-looking, and rather puckery-faced old gentleman, whose temper, I should imagine, was not the very sweetest in the world" (*The English Notebooks by Nathaniel Hawthorne*, ed. Stewart, 312).

I

Ingersoll, Susan A distant cousin of Hawthorne, sometimes called "the Duchess," with whom he had a close association. She was the granddaughter of John Hawthorne and Suzannah Touzell. He is supposed to have called on her in 1840 in the home she occupied at the foot of Turner Street in Salem; at that time, she may have furnished the idea for GRANDFATHER'S CHAIR. Hawthorne supposedly inspected the entire house, found five gables, and detected marks where there had been two others. To this day, this is the house shown in Salem as the House of the Seven Gables (Turner, *Nathaniel Hawthorne: A Biography*, 68, 230).

Inman, Henry (1801–1846) An American portrait, genre, and landscape painter, a native of Yorkville, New York. A founder of the National Academy of Design, he was highly esteemed as a portrait painter in the United States and in ENGLAND. He painted Hawthorne's portrait in 1835; it is now in the Peabody Essex Museum, in Salem.

Isle of Man, the In the summer of 1854, while Hawthorne was the American consul at LIVERPOOL, SOPHIA AMELIA PEABODY HAWTHORNE and their children spent a fortnight on the Isle of Man. Hawthorne joined the family on two separate Sundays, which he described in his notebook. He praised the "quiet beauty" and "seclusion" of the little church of Kirk Bradden, remarking that it was "most picturesque in its solitude and bowery environment" (*The English Notebooks by Nathaniel Hawthorne*, ed. Stewart, 70–71).

Isles of Shoals A group of islands off the coast of New Hampshire. The principal one is Appledore Island, which Hawthorne visited in 1852. In April 1864, Hawthorne planned to go there and stay until the tourist season began. Sophia encouraged him, despite the fact that he was clearly ill, since she believed that his health would improve if he could wander on the sea beaches. After a journey to New York, Washington, and Boston, however, he was clearly unable to make such a trip. He died in May 1864.

Italy At the conclusion of his term as American consul in LIVERPOOL, Nathaniel Hawthorne and his family traveled to the Continent. They went to FRANCE and Italy in January 1858, and then back to England in May 1859 so that Hawthorne could rewrite his final novel, *The MARBLE FAUN*, which was set in Italy. They did not return to America until 1860.

Hawthorne's love of the poetry of Dante, Petrarch, and Boccaccio, along with his knowledge of Italian history, made him particularly eager to visit Florence and Rome. Hoeltje remarks that he and Sophia approached Italy "with the heightened sentiments of the time . . . vivified for them, as for many others, by their sympathetic and enthusiastic reading" of Lord Byron's *Childe Harold's Pilgrimage*. They were to spend a total of a year and four months in Italy.

The family went by steamer to Boulogne and on by train to Amiens and PARIS. After a few days, they continued by train to Marseille. The family was accompanied by Ada Shepard, a young college graduate who had been strongly recommended by MARY TYLER PEABODY MANN, Sophia Hawthorne's sister. She acted as companion and tutor to the children. In Paris, they were joined by the astronomer MARIA MITCHELL, a professor at Vassar College who had discovered a new comet in 1847, who had asked to travel to Rome in their company.

The party took the train to Dijon, Lyon, and Marseille. From there, they traveled aboard the Neapolitan steamer *Calabrese* to Genoa, a journey of a week. They toured some of the sights in Genoa, including the Balbi palace, "the stateliest and most magnificent residence" Hawthorne had ever seen (*French and Italian Notebooks,* 49). The family continued to Leghorn and Civita Vecchia by steamer and went on by carriage to Rome, where they arrived in the latter part of January 1858.

They were cold and wretched, being unprepared for the winter weather they encountered. En route to Rome, Hawthorne had caught a cold and had a fever, which marred their first two weeks. They stayed at Spillman's hotel while seeking lodgings, and finally settled at 37, Via Porta Pinciana, where they had a suite of 10 rooms. Wearing all their winter clothes at once, the family shivered but went out sightseeing every day. They were disappointed by Saint Peter's, by the number of pickpockets and beggars, and by the sight of a "shabby population smoking bad cigars" (*French and Italian Notebooks,* 53–59). But it was Carnival time in Rome, and the children, at least, enjoyed themselves.

It was not until the Hawthornes felt better physically that they warmed to the city and began their explorations in earnest. They wrote to and called on people whom they had met, or to whom they had introductions, such as the artists William Wetmore Story, C. G. Thompson, Joseph Mozier, George Loring Brown, and MARIA LOUISA LANDER. They also established social contact with HARRIET HOSMER, William Cullen Bryant, and Fredrika Bremer. By late May 1858, they had had many social invitations and visited all of the major churches, villas, palaces, and art galleries of Rome.

They left Rome on May 24 by carriage. By that time, Hawthorne had become very fond of the city, writing in his notebook, "It is very singular, the sad embrace with which Rome takes possession of the soul" (*French and Italian Notebooks,* 232). They were prevented by rain from viewing the famous Cascade of Terni but saw the town itself.

They continued on to Spoleto, Perugia, Foligno, Assisi, Pasignano, and Arrezzo, where they saw Petrarch's house. The family arrived in Florence in early June. They had been given a letter of introduction to the American sculptor Hiram Powers, who arranged for them to rent the lower floor of the Casa del Bello, for $50 a month. It had many rooms around a courtyard, a terrace, a garden with a fountain, and luxurious furnishings. Hawthorne remarked in his notebook that it was like the "Paradise of cheapness which we were told of" but which they had "vainly sought" in Rome. They engaged a servant and arranged for the delivery of dinner every day from a cook shop. Powers and the family became good friends during the Hawthornes' stay in Florence.

The Hawthornes also saw ROBERT BROWNING and his wife, ELIZABETH BARRETT BROWNING, several times, at the home of Miss Isabella Blagden, in her villa at Bellosguardo (outside Florence). She also introduced them to Thomas Trollope, elder brother of the British novelist Anthony Trollope, who wrote a number of books dealing with Italian life and history.

In Florence, they visited the BOBOLI GARDENS, the UFFIZZI GALLERY, the Cathedral, and the Pitti Palace. Hawthorne declared in his notebook that Julian had passed a "sweeping condemnation upon everything he saw" in the Uffizi Gallery, except a "fly, a snail-shell, a caterpillar, a lemon, a piece of bread, and a wine-glass, in some of the Dutch pictures." Hawthorne recalled that, when young, he himself used to experience a "weary lack of appreciation" in picture galleries (*French and Italian Notebooks,* 350).

One evening, he went with Sophia and Una to the Powers's home, and sat on their terrace at the top of the house. They had a view of the Theatro Goldoni very nearby and heard part of the performance (which may have been a reenactment of one of the plays of the commedia dell' arte, an early form of Italian theater). Before leaving Florence in September 1858, Hawthorne and Sophia visited the Laurentian Library and saw several early manuscripts, including one of Boccaccio's *Decameron*.

From Florence, the family went to Siena, Viterbo, and Sette Vene. They returned to Rome in October 1858 and remained there until May 1859. While they were in Rome, Una became seriously ill with "Roman fever," a dreaded illness similar to malaria, from which she suffered for six months. She was gravely ill from November 1858 through the middle of April 1859. According to Turner, quinine was one of the few medicines available, but it was fatal if given too often. Una finally seemed to have recovered by April 19, although she apparently suffered the aftereffects of the illness as long as she lived; he states that Hawthorne "never recovered from the anguish this illness caused him" (Turner, *Nathaniel Hawthorne: A Biography*, 334–335).

Hawthorne's BOWDOIN COLLEGE classmate and friend General FRANKLIN PIERCE (formerly President Pierce) and his wife arrived in Rome on March 10 and often visited twice a day until April 19. They offered much support. Hawthorne commented in his notebook that Pierce had "undergone so great a sorrow of his own, and has so large and kindly a heart, and is so tender and so strong, that he really

did us good, and I shall always love him the better for the recollection of these dark days" (*French and Italian Notebooks*, 518). The Pierces had seen their only child, an 11-year-old son, killed in a train wreck two months before Pierce took office as president in 1853.

In early April 1859, while the family was still in Rome, Hawthorne began work on a romance about an American journeying to England to claim an ancestral estate. His creative instincts, however, were actually impelling him toward a different theme, inspired by several works of art: Guido's portrait of Beatrice Cenci, the statue *Dying Gladiator* in the Capitoline Museums, and a dancing faun and a copy of the FAUN OF PRAXITELES in the Villa Borghese (he saw another copy of the *Faun of Praxiteles* in the Capitoline Museums). Hawthorne took his family to Florence in the middle of May, for the summer, to avoid the health risks of staying in Rome. After Una improved, he returned to work on his novel. *The MARBLE FAUN* was finished in England and published there in February 1860.

For Further Reading

Boyd, Richard, "The Politics of Exclusion: Hawthorne's Life of Franklin Pierce," *American Transcendental Quarterly* 3, no. 4 (December 1989): 337–351; Buscaroli, Piero, "Hawthorne's Italy," *L'Italia* (Rome) 205 (1965): 26–39; Hawthorne, Nathaniel, *The French and Italian Notebooks*, edited by Thomas Woodson, Centenary Edition 14, passim.

J

James, George Payne Rainsford (1801?–1860) An English novelist Hawthorne first met in 1850, in LENOX, MASSACHUSETTS, where he had engaged the "RED HOUSE" for his family. James was the author of *The King's Highway* and many other works. Hawthorne remarks in his *English Notebooks* that he had found two of James's works in the coffee room at the Lowwood Hotel in the Lake District, where he and his family stayed in 1855 (*The English Notebooks by Nathaniel Hawthorne*, ed. Stewart, 163).

James, Henry (1843–1916) American novelist, short-story writer, and man of letters. He was a member of a distinguished family: He was the grandson of one of the first American millionaires, the son of a well-known Swedenborgian who was a famous writer and lecturer, and the brother of the psychologist William James. His aim as a novelist was to be "one on whom nothing is lost."

James found Hawthorne's 1852 novel *The BLITHEDALE ROMANCE* flawed as satire (Miller, *Salem Is My Dwelling Place*, 368). However, he greatly admired *The MARBLE FAUN*, published in 1860. Two decades later, he remarked that it was a part of the "intellectual equipment of the Anglo-Saxon visitor to Rome, and was read by every English-speaking traveler who arrived there" (Hoeltje, *Inward Sky: The Mind and Heart of Nathaniel Hawthorne*, 501). James lived abroad after 1875, spending a year in Paris and then settling in ENGLAND. In 1879, he published a book called *Hawthorne*, praising him as a writer.

For Further Reading

Gale, Robert L., "*The Marble Faun* and *The Sacred Fount: A Resemblance*," *Studi Americani* 8 (1962): 21–33; Gleckner, Robert F., "James's *Madame de Mauves* and Hawthorne's *The Scarlet Letter*," *Modern Language Notes* 73, no. 8 (December 1958): 580–586; Long, Robert Emmet, "The Society and the Masks: *The Blithedale Romance* and *The Bostonians*," *Nineteenth-Century Fiction* 19, no. 2 (September 1964): 105–122; McCall, Dan, *Citizens of Somewhere Else: Nathaniel Hawthorne and Henry James* (Ithaca, N.Y.: Cornell University Press, 1999).

Journal of an African Cruiser Journal of a cruise along the coast of Africa kept by Hawthorne's BOWDOIN COLLEGE friend HORATIO BRIDGE (1806–93) when he sailed along the coast of Africa aboard the *Cyane*. He was in the U.S. Navy at the time. Hawthorne encouraged him to keep a journal he might later publish, and he did. Hawthorne edited it, and EVERT AUGUSTUS DUYCKINCK published it as *Journal of an African Cruiser* for the Library of American Books he was editing (Turner, *Nathaniel Hawthorne: A Biography*, 155–156).

When it was first published in 1845, it bore the full title of *Journal of an African cruiser: comprising sketches of the Canaries, the Cape de Verds, Liberia, Madeira, Sierra Leone, and other places of interest on the west coast of Africa*. Hawthorne was listed as editor. About 5,000 copies were originally sold. The volume was reprinted in 1853 and again in 1945 and 1968.

K

Kemble, Fanny (1809–1893)   The daughter of the actors Charles and Marie Kemble, Fanny Kemble saved her father's declining Covent Garden Theatre when she began appearing in various roles, including Juliet in *Romeo and Juliet*. In 1833, she toured America with her father. She met and married a southern planter, Pierce Butler, while in New York. She gave up acting at that time but returned to the stage after their divorce, in 1848.

She later retired to LENOX, Massachusetts, where she wrote several autobiographical works, including *Journal of a Residence on a Georgian Plantation in 1838–1839* (1863), *Record of a Childhood* (1878), and *Records of Later Life* (1882).

The Hawthornes met her when they rented an old red farmhouse in Lenox, from 1850 to 1851. According to Hoeltje, Kemble and her father had appeared in Boston together in 1833 in *The School for Scandal* and in *Romeo and Juliet,* and she had given public Shakespearean readings. He believes she sought out the Hawthornes in Lenox. When she returned to ENGLAND during the family's second year there, she offered them her Lenox home, furnished and rent-free. She also wrote to Hawthorne that *The SCARLET LETTER* and *The HOUSE OF THE SEVEN GABLES* were selling extremely well in England. This news prompted him to have his later books copyrighted in England as well as in America (Hoeltje, *Inward Sky: The Mind and Heart of Nathaniel Hawthorne*, 313–314).

Fanny Kemble died in London on January 15, 1893, and was buried in KENSAL GREEN CEMETERY, north of LONDON. SOPHIA AMELIA PEABODY HAWTHORNE and her daughter UNA HAWTHORNE were also buried there.

Kensal Green Cemetery   Cemetery north of LONDON where SOPHIA AMELIA PEABODY HAWTHORNE (1809–71) and her daughter UNA HAWTHORNE (1844–1877) are buried. The actress FANNY KEMBLE is also interred there, as are many members of the nobility.

The cemetery was established by an act of parliament in 1832 and is operated by the General Cemetery Company. It is the longest-surviving English cemetery remaining in private ownership. It extends over 60 acres and has more than 70,000 graves.

The original plan was to create a spacious park to complement the many fine monuments that were expected to be built. In the past, most of London's dead had been buried in very crowded churchyards. Kensal Green, in contrast, would be hygienic as well as a place of recreation. This plan was put into effect, with many imposing monuments and mausoleums built while the owners were still living. There are more freestanding mausolea here than in any other cemetery in England. The cemetery is now a haven for wildlife, and the London Wildlife Trust advises on habitat conservation. Burials are still held today.

The Friends of Kensal Green, formed in 1990, assists with the cleaning of monuments and archival research. In 1997, the Friends restored the 1830s chapel, which had been a ruin, and built a fully equipped Visitors Centre that may be hired for events to benefit the cemetery.

Among the notable people buried in Kensal Green are the writers Anthony Trollope, William Makepeace Thackeray, and Wilkie Collins, as well as two children of King George III and the dramatist Sir Terence Rattigan. The cemetery, on Harrow Road, London, may be reached by tube, rail, or bus from London.

Knickerbocker Magazine, The The outstanding literary periodical of its time, founded in 1833. From 1834 to 1861, it was coedited by LEWIS GAYLORD CLARK (1808–73) and, until his death, by his twin brother, Willis Gaylord Clark (1808–41). Among the noted contributors to the magazine were Washington Irving, William Cullen Bryant, HENRY WADSWORTH LONGFELLOW, Oliver Wendell Holmes, James Russell Lowell, and JAMES T. FIELDS.

Lewis Gaylord Clark reviewed TWICE-TOLD TALES in the *Knickerbocker Magazine* in April 1837, commenting on its "quiet humor," "genuine pathos," and "deep feeling" (Turner, *Nathaniel Hawthorne: A Biography*, 87–88).

Hawthorne's gift book collections, titled *The* TOKEN AND ATLANTIC SOUVENIR: A CHRISTMAS AND NEW YEAR'S PRESENT, were reviewed in the magazine in 1834, 1835, 1836, and 1837. His tales published in the magazine included "The FOUNTAIN OF YOUTH," in January 1837; "A BELL'S BIOGRAPHY," in March 1837; and "EDWARD FANE'S ROSEBUD," in September 1837.

Kossuth, Louis (Lajos) (1802–1894) A champion of Hungarian freedom who visited Boston and Concord in late 1851 and 1852. (His name is pronounced "ko-shoot.")

On November 21, 1851, the Hawthornes went to the Pittsfield railroad station, which was decorated in Kossuth's honor as he passed through en route to Boston. Julian, age five, was introduced to him and showed him a card on which he had printed "God bless you, Kossuth." Hawthorne thought he was "about as enthusiastic as a lump of frozen sand" but went to hear him anyway (Turner, *Nathaniel Hawthorne: A Biography*, 236).

RALPH WALDO EMERSON remarked, in greeting Kossuth on his arrival at CONCORD, MASSACHUSETTS, on May 11, 1852, "[we] have been hungry to see the man whose extraordinary eloquence is seconded by the splendor and the solidity of his actions."

L

Laighton, Thomas B.   Laighton was the father of the poet Celia Thaxter and proprietor of Laighton's Hotel on the ISLES OF SHOALS, off the coast of Portsmouth, New Hampshire, which Hawthorne first visited in 1852. Hawthorne stayed at the hotel at that time, since he had a letter of introduction from FRANKLIN PIERCE. Hawthorne wanted very much to return to the island for another visit, and as late as a few days before his death, SOPHIA AMELIA PEABODY HAWTHORNE hoped to take him there.

Lander, Maria Louisa (1826–1923)   American sculptor, a native of Salem, Massachusetts, whom Hawthorne and his family knew in Rome. She called on the Hawthornes in January 1858, almost as soon as they arrived from ENGLAND. On February 6, the Hawthornes visited her studio, which had once been occupied by the Italian sculptor Antonio Canova (1757–1822). She dined with the Hawthornes several times.

She requested that Hawthorne sit for his bust, and he began doing so on February 15, 1858. He had about 20 sittings, sometimes accompanied by Sophia. On March 31, she told him the clay bust was finished. He and Sophia were both delighted when the stone bust was finished; it was praised by many sculptors in Rome (Turner, *Nathaniel Hawthorne: A Biography*, 322–323).

Lander, along with HARRIET GOODHUE HOSMER, became one of the models for Hilda in *The MARBLE FAUN*. Hawthorne reported that she lived in "almost perfect independence." Her usual dress was a "sort of pea-jacket, buttoned across her breast, and a little foraging-cap, just covering the top of her head," a description used for Hilda.

Lathrop, George Parsons (1851–1898)   American poet and novelist, born in Honolulu, Hawaii, and educated in New York and Dresden, Germany. He was married to ROSE HAWTHORNE in London on September 11, 1871, soon after her mother's death. In 1875, he became associate editor of the *ATLANTIC MONTHLY*. After two years, he left the magazine and took up newspaper work in Boston and New York. Their only child, a son, died of diphtheria. In March 1891, he and his wife became Roman Catholics and were received into the church at New York. He was an alcoholic and reportedly abused his wife. She left him in 1895. In 1900, she took her vows as a Dominican nun.

Lathrop was a prolific writer. Among his works were several novels, including *Spanish Vistas* (1883) and *Dreams and Days* (1892); books of poetry; a travel book, *Newport* (1884); and a history of the Visitation Convent, Georgetown, Washington, D.C. He also edited a complete edition of Hawthorne's works (1883) and adapted *The SCARLET LETTER* for Walter Damrosch's opera of the same name, which was produced in New York in 1896.

Lathrop, Rose Hawthorne (1851–1926)   The youngest daughter of Nathaniel and SOPHIA AME-

LIA PEABODY HAWTHORNE, born while the Hawthornes were living in LENOX, MASSACHUSETTS. It was here, according to Hawthorne's biographer Hubert Hoeltje, that Hawthorne learned, to his astonishment, that British and American critics had "proclaimed him the most eminent writer of prose fiction in America" (Hoeltje, *Inward Sky: The Mind and Heart of Nathaniel Hawthorne*, 299). When Rose was only two, Hawthorne was appointed United States consul at LIVERPOOL, ENGLAND. The family would live in England and on the Continent until 1860.

Rose married the American poet and novelist GEORGE PARSONS LATHROP in 1871, soon after the death of her mother. Their only child, a son, died of diphtheria. In March 1891, the Lathrops became Roman Catholics and were received into the church at New York. He was an alcoholic and reportedly abused his wife. She separated from him in 1895.

In 1898, Rose Lathrop entered a Roman Catholic order. She established one of the first hospices in America, nursing the dying poor in a tenement on Scammel Street on the Lower East Side of Manhattan. She devoted herself to the care of cancer patients, who at that time were treated as lepers. She and Alice Huber opened Sister Rose's Free Home at 426 Cherry Street, New York, in 1897. As Sister Mary Alphonsa Lathrop, she received the Gold Medal of the New York Rotary Club in 1926. She died at the Rosary Hill Home on July 9, 1926. On February 4, 2003, as Mother Alphonsa, Rose Hawthorne was proposed as a candidate for sainthood (Wineapple, *Hawthorne: A Life*, 8–9, 387).

Rose was a diligent writer and published articles in the leading periodicals of the day. Among them were "Hidden History," *Harper's New Monthly Magazine* (January 1884); "Inlet and Shore," *The Century* (January 1888); and "The Lost Battle," *Harper's New Monthly Magazine* (March 1885). In "Memories of Hawthorne," she remarked that she had once been asked to write about her father's "literary methods." She admitted that she scarcely knew what these methods were and wished she did, but she did make a few observations:

One method of obtaining his end was to devote himself constantly to writing, whether it brought him money or not. He might not have seemed to be working all the time, but to be enjoying endless leisure in walking through the country or the city streets. But even a bird would have had more penetration than to make such a mistake as to think this. Another wise provision was to love and pity mankind more than he scorned them, so that he never created a character which did not possess a soul—the only puppet he ever contrived of straw, "Feathertop," having an excellent soul until the end of the story. (*Memories of Hawthorne*, 1897)

Lenox, Massachusetts The Hawthornes rented a farmhouse, the "red house," in Lenox, in the Berkshire mountains of western Massachusetts, from 1850 to 1851. ROSE HAWTHORNE LATHROP was born in Lenox on May 20, 1851.

Hawthorne had been dismissed from the Salem Custom-House in June 1849, and the family was having a difficult time financially. He and Sophia both wished to leave Salem, which Hawthorne called "abominable." Sophia was decorating lampshades to sell and other friends were offering financial gifts, which hurt Hawthorne's pride. Sophia's wealthy friend Caroline Sturgis Tappan and her husband were staying at the estate of Anna and Samuel Ward, in Lenox, and began urging Sophia and her husband to consider a move there. They offered the handyman's small red house at no cost, and the Hawthornes accepted. Hawthorne insisted, however, on paying $50 for rent (Wineapple, *Hawthorne: A Life*, 191–231; Turner, *Nathaniel Hawthorne: A Biography*, 213).

There was a noted literary colony in Lenox and in nearby towns such as Pittsfield, Stockbridge, and Great Barrington. The editor and writer EVERT AUGUSTUS DUYCKINCK was one of many friends who called at the farmhouse in Lenox. Hawthorne also met HERMAN MELVILLE, who lived with his family in Pittsfield; Oliver Wendell Holmes; the actress FANNY KEMBLE; Catharine Maria Sedgwick; and others.

Liverpool In 1853, Hawthorne's classmate and friend from BOWDOIN COLLEGE, President FRANKLIN PIERCE, appointed Hawthorne the American consul in Liverpool. This was a major commercial port and offered many advantages, in addition to the opportunity of seeing England.

The family sailed to Liverpool in July 1853 aboard the Cunard paddle wheeler NIAGARA. Sophia Hawthorne's father and Hawthorne's friend and editor JAMES T. FIELDS saw them off. A salute was fired in honor of Hawthorne as the new consul. He and his family were given places of honor at Captain Leitch's table. The ship reached Liverpool on July 16. At first, the family stayed at a hotel, Waterloo House, but then they moved to Mrs. Blodgett's, a boardinghouse on Duke Street. On August 6, they moved to the Rock Ferry Hotel across the river Mersey, and, somewhat later, they rented a substantial stone house in ROCK PARK, one of the first gated communities in England (Turner, *Nathaniel Hawthorne: A Biography,* 263–265).

Hawthorne took up his duties as consul on Monday, August 1. He kept extensive notebooks throughout his term as consul, some of which were, unfortunately, revised by SOPHIA AMELIA PEABODY HAWTHORNE after his death. The manuscripts are now in the Pierpont Morgan Library; they were edited by Randall Stewart and published by Oxford University Press in 1941.

While he was consul, Hawthorne's duties included interviewing sailors who claimed to be American (he called them rogues); evaluating and assisting other people, including women, who purported to be destitute American citizens; attending formal dinners given in his honor by local officials, including the mayor; assisting with inventories of the personal effects of American citizens who had died in Liverpool; and attending inquests. By 1855, he had become disillusioned with his office. He observed in his notebook that he was leading a "weary life" and was sick of "brutal captains and brutish sailors." He had to deal with "beggars, cheats, simpletons, unfortunates, so mixed up that it is impossible to distinguish one from another"; in self-defense he was forced to distrust them all (*The English Notebooks by Nathaniel Hawthorne,* ed. Stewart, 190).

On the plus side, however, he and his family went sightseeing, visiting the Liverpool Cathedral, Lichfield, Chester, Knowsley-park, Eastham, Birkenhead Park, the ISLE OF MAN, Rhyl (in Wales), Furness Abbey, the Lake District, and many other places of interest. They did not visit LONDON until September 1855.

Among Hawthorne's first callers were HENRY BRIGHT, an English writer and university graduate who had met Hawthorne during a visit to America, and his father. According to Turner, their friendship was one of Hawthorne's "most satisfying relationships during his residence in England" (Turner, *Nathaniel Hawthorne: A Biography* [New York: Oxford University Press, 1980]: 268).

On April 15, 1857, there was a foundation-stone ceremony marking the beginning of construction on the Liverpool Free Public Library. A wealthy citizen of the city, William Brown, donated £40,000 toward construction of the library. Hawthorne was one of the dignitaries in the procession to the site of the ceremony, in what is now William Brown Street. A banquet for 900 guests was held in Saint George's Hall. RICHARD MONCKTON MILNES, later FIRST LORD HOUGHTON, introduced Hawthorne as one of the speakers, praising him as an author. Hawthorne could not hear Milnes's introduction well but responded by paying tribute to Milnes, the spirit of English literature, and William Brown. He reflected later that despite his difficulties, he did not see how he "could have answered it better" (Mays, James O'Donald, *Mr. Hawthorne Goes to England* [Burley, Ringwood, Hampshire: New Forest Leaves], 175–176).

Hawthorne suffered much financial hardship during his tenure as consul. At first, he could retain consular fees and build up some savings, although he had to draw salaries for his clerks and other employees from these fees. The fee-retention system was then abolished, and his salary was barely sufficient to support his family. In 1857, he resigned as consul and took his family to ITALY. They lived in Rome and Florence until 1859 and then returned to England. Hawthorne finished *The MARBLE FAUN* there, and the family moved back to THE WAYSIDE, in CONCORD, MASSACHUSETTS, in 1860.

London During his tenure as American consul in LIVERPOOL, Hawthorne visited London as often as was feasible. The family's first visit was not until September 1855, however. They had been in Shrewsbury and continued by train to London. All three children were with them, in addition to a nurse, Fanny. They had lodgings at 24 George Street, Hanover Square.

Hawthorne's first impression of London was of "stately and spacious streets." He explored the city alone the next day, seeing Hyde Park, Regent's Park, Whitehall, the Houses of Parliament, Saint Paul's, Fleet Street, Whitechapel, and many other sites he had read about. He also crossed the Thames near Charing Cross, had a miserable lunch in the "Albert Dining Rooms," and called on a Mr. Clarke in Regent Street, whom he had met through HENRY BRIGHT.

He, Sophia, and the two eldest children then explored Saint James Park and Hyde Park, after which Hawthorne sent them back to their lodgings by cab and drove to the American Despatch Agency, in Covent Garden. The family visited the Zoological Gardens and on Sunday attended services in Westminster Abbey. The following days included visits to the Tower of London and a cruise to Greenwich on the Thames. The American minister, Mr. Buchanan, called on Hawthorne within a week, and Hawthorne realized he should have paid his respects to him. He found his residence, 56 Harley Street, and did so. Buchanan inquired about Sophia, since he had dined with the family in Liverpool.

Hawthorne returned to Liverpool for a few days to attend to consular business, leaving his family in London, but by September 24 had returned to the city and taken up sightseeing again: Kensington Gardens, the Zoological Gardens, Somerset House, the British Museum, the Houses of Parliament, and other sites. The family then went by train to Southampton and then visited Worcester.

He returned to London several times during his tenure as consul. He was a guest at the Milton Club and the Reform Club, where he met many writers and editors, such as Dr. Charles Mackay and Herbert Ingram, editor and owner, respectively, of the *Illustrated London News*.

One of his biographers, Hoeltje, remarks that Hawthorne was lionized in London. Among those who called on him were the writer Mrs. Gaskell, the poet William Allingham, MONCKTON MILNES (later FIRST LORD HOUGHTON), Harriet Martineau, and the writer Leigh Hunt. Hawthorne found his visits to the city, in which he met many people, "rich in incident and character" (Hoeltje, *Inward Sky: The Mind and Heart of Nathaniel Hawthorne*, 422–426). Milnes later invited him to a breakfast, where he was placed at a table with the historian Thomas B. Macaulay.

Longfellow, Henry Wadsworth (1807–1882) American poet, translator, and professor. He was a descendant of several old New England families and was a classmate and close friend of Hawthorne at BOWDOIN COLLEGE in the celebrated class of 1825. He then studied languages in Europe. His first wife, Mary Potter, died, and he later married Frances Appleton. At that time, her father gave them the beautiful mansion in Cambridge, Massachusetts, called Craigie House. He and Frances lived there until her death, after which Longfellow continued to live in the house. It is now dedicated to his memory.

Hawthorne's volume TWICE-TOLD TALES was published in March 1837. Longfellow wrote a highly favorable review of it for the NORTH AMERICAN REVIEW that appeared in July 1837, helping establish Hawthorne's literary reputation.

Longfellow frequently based his poetry on tales or legends he had read or had heard. Hawthorne also used such tales as material for narratives. Occasionally they created quite different works from the same legends. For example, Longfellow had heard the French Canadian tale of a young couple in Acadie from HORACE LORENZO CONOLLY, at one time Hawthorne's minister. In the story, all the men in the province, including the bridegroom, are seized in the local church and shipped to various places in New England. The bride searches for him her entire life and finds him on his deathbed when she is very aged. The shock kills her. Longfellow based his poem "Evangeline" on the story, while Hawthorne developed part of it in "The OLD FRENCH WAR AND THE ACADIAN EXILES."

At a Christmas celebration in LIVERPOOL in 1855, Hawthorne's English friend HENRY BRIGHT composed verses honoring him, "Song of Consul Hawthorne," using the meter of Longfellow's recently published narrative poem "Hiawatha" (Turner, *Nathaniel Hawthorne: A Biography, 289*).

Lowell, James Russell (1819–1891) American poet and editor, and the author of "The Vision of Sir Launfal," "A Fable for Critics," and other works. In 1857, he became the first editor of ATLANTIC MONTHLY. In 1861, he became coeditor, with Charles Eliot Norton, of *North American Review.*

Hawthorne contributed in 1843 to *The Pioneer,* of which Lowell was editor. In 1844, Lowell called on Hawthorne at THE OLD MANSE, in CONCORD, MASSACHUSETTS. Lowell held a high opinion of Hawthorne and, after his death, wrote to the editor JAMES T. FIELDS, "I don't think people have any kind of true notion yet what a master he was, God rest his soul! Shakespeare, I am sure, was glad to see him on the other side" (*Letters of James Russell Lowell,* edited by Charles Eliot Norton [New York, 1977]).

After Hawthorne's death, HENRY WADSWORTH LONGFELLOW suggested that Lowell write a biography of him. SOPHIA AMELIA PEABODY HAWTHORNE, however, would not allow free use of his notebooks, and Lowell abandoned the idea. Randall Stewart points out that she was, at the time, revising passages from the notebooks for publication and blotting out other passages, causing a monumental loss to Hawthorne scholarship (*The American Notebooks by Nathaniel Hawthorne,* edited by Randall Stewart, preface).

M

Mackay, Charles (1814–1889) Mackay, the son of a navy lieutenant, was employed while a young man as the private secretary to William Cockerill, an ironmaster based in Belgium. At that time, he began writing articles for the local newspaper. In 1832, he returned to Britain and began contributing to newspapers. He eventually became editor of the Glasgow *Argus,* then joined the staff of the *Illustrated London News,* of which he later became editor. He was also a noted poet.

In early April 1856, Hawthorne was invited to Ludgate Hill, LONDON, to dine with his friend FRANCIS BENNOCH at the Milton Club. This club had recently been founded, according to Hawthorne, for "dissenters, nonconformists, and people whose ideas, religious or political, are not precisely in train with the establishment in church and state." He was placed beside Dr. Mackay at dinner. In his *English Notebooks,* he identified him as the "author of the 'Good Time Coming,'" although at the time Mackay was editor of the *Illustrated London News.* Hawthorne termed him a "shrewd, sensible man" (*The English Notebooks by Nathaniel Hawthorne,* ed. Stewart, 311). He saw Mackay on other occasions later.

Mann, Horace (1796–1859) Mann, a native of Franklin, Massachusetts, was a prominent educator and Hawthorne's brother-in-law. He has been called "the father of American Education."

Mann graduated from Brown University, in Providence, Rhode Island, in 1816; entered the Litchfield Law School; and was admitted to the bar in 1823. On April 20, 1837, he left his law practice and accepted the newly established post of secretary of education. During his years as secretary of education, Mann reformed public school organization and teaching and was also instrumental in establishing the first normal school in the United States in 1839. From 1848 to 1853, he was a member of the U.S. House of Representatives. He served as president of Antioch College from 1852 to 1859, the year of his death. He was elected to the American Hall of Fame in 1900.

After the death of his first wife, he married Mary Tyler Peabody, Sophia Amelia Peabody's sister, on May 1, 1843. At the time of their wedding, she was 37 and he was 47 (Miller, *Salem Is My Dwelling Place: A Life of Nathaniel Hawthorne,* 129).

Mann, Mary Tyler Peabody (1806–1887) One of the gifted Peabody sisters of Salem, Mary was the sister of SOPHIA AMELIA PEABODY HAWTHORNE. She was considered the most beautiful of the three Peabody daughters (a fourth sister, Catherine, died when young). In her 20s, she suffered from depression. In 1833, she was employed as a tutor by a Cuban family; Sophia accompanied her.

Mary was in love with HORACE MANN long before she became his second wife, on May 1, 1843; at that time, she was 37 and he was 47 (Miller, *Salem Is My Dwelling Place: A Life of Nathaniel Hawthorne,* 129). Mann, a distinguished educator, took her to investigate educational institutions in ENGLAND and on the Continent.

Mann was then offered the presidency of a new college in Yellow Springs, Ohio, to be named Antioch in honor of "the place where men were first called Christian." Horace, Mary, and their three sons moved to Yellow Springs, where Horace served as president of Antioch College. After his death on August 2, 1859, his friends and schoolchildren contributed money for a bronze statue of him, which was placed on Boston Common. His widow wrote a biography of him, *The Life of Horace Mann*, published in 1865, and edited the five-volume *Life and Works of Horace Mann*, published in 1891, four years after her death in 1887.

Manning, Robert One of five sons of Richard Manning, maternal grandfather of NATHANIEL HAWTHORNE. After the early death of Hawthorne's father, it was Robert Manning who became his guardian. Hawthorne, his mother, and his three sisters lived with the Mannings, and all of the Manning aunts and uncles took a keen interest in them. Miller describes Robert Manning as an "essentially kind man who was constantly being tested by a recalcitrant nephew" (Miller, *Salem Is My Dwelling Place: A Life of Nathaniel Hawthorne*, 29).

When Hawthorne was seven or eight, Robert and his brother SAMUEL MANNING took him on a trip into New Hampshire. Robert began planting trees on the property the Mannings owned in RAYMOND, MAINE, on the shores of Lake Sebago. In December 1816, Uncle Robert took Hawthorne to a boarding school at Stroudwater, Maine, run by the Reverend Caleb Bradley, but Nathaniel was there for only about two months (Turner, *Nathaniel Hawthorne: A Biography*, passim).

Robert Manning later accompanied his nephew to BOWDOIN COLLEGE. On arrival, they called on one of the college trustees, Ebenezer Everett, who went with them to see the president, William Allen. Allen gave Hawthorne an appointment for two o'clock that afternoon to take the entrance examination. He asked his uncle to prepare to take him back home, as he was sure he would fail. However, he returned within an hour, having "been examined, passed, and a roommate or 'chum' selected for him" (Miller, *Salem Is My Dwelling Place: A Life of Nathaniel Hawthorne*, 60). The Manning fam-

ily supported Hawthorne throughout his years at Bowdoin; it seems to have been Robert who paid the bills and maintained frequent contact with Hawthorne.

Hawthorne later assisted his uncle by correcting some of the contributions on horticultural subjects he wrote for Thomas Green Fessenden's *New England Farmer* (Miller, *Salem Is My Dwelling Place: A Life of Nathaniel Hawthorne*, 104).

Manning, Samuel One of Hawthorne's maternal uncles. When Hawthorne was seven or eight, Samuel Manning, along with his brother ROBERT MANNING, took him on a trip into New Hampshire.

Manning, William One of Hawthorne's maternal uncles, the eldest of the nine Manning aunts and uncles. He paid for dancing lessons for Hawthorne's sister Louisa. He also ran the stagecoach office, one of the Manning businesses, in which Hawthorne was employed for a dollar a week.

Melville, Herman (1819–1891) American novelist, short-story writer, and poet. Melville was a member of a formerly prominent but financially unstable New York family. After his father died in 1832, he attempted to earn money for the family, working as a schoolteacher, bank clerk, and seaman. In 1847, he married Elizabeth Shaw and supported his family by writing for magazines. In 1851, he completed *Moby-Dick*, considered his masterpiece.

From 1850 to 1863, Melville and his family lived at Arrowhead, a farmhouse in Pittsfield, near LENOX, MASSACHUSETTS, in the Berkshire mountains. It was here that he met Nathaniel Hawthorne, who had been dismissed from the Salem Custom-House and was having severe financial difficulties. From 1850 to 1851, Hawthorne and his family rented a farmhouse, the "Red House," in Lenox. (Arrowhead is now a house museum interpreting the life of the Melville family; it is owned and operated by the Berkshire County Historical Society.)

In November 1856, Melville traveled to Glasgow on his way to Constantinople. He went on to LIVERPOOL and stayed two nights with the Hawthornes

Herman Melville, a fellow author and good friend of Nathaniel Hawthorne. *(Courtesy of the Library of Congress)*

at Southport. They took a long walk in the sand hills together. According to Hawthorne, Melville began to reason "of Providence and futurity and of everything that lies beyond human ken." He went to Liverpool the next day with Hawthorne, and on Friday Hawthorne's friend HENRY BRIGHT took him sightseeing. On Saturday, Melville and Hawthorne visited Chester; Hawthorne considered Chester "the only place, within easy reach of Liverpool, which possesses any old English interest." They left Chester in the afternoon and parted at Liverpool but saw each other again on Monday. Melville sailed from Liverpool on Tuesday, leaving his trunk behind and taking "only a carpet-bag to hold all his travelling-gear." Hawthorne remarked that this was the "next best thing to going naked"; he declared he did not know "a more independent personage" than Melville (*The English Notebooks by Nathaniel Hawthorne*, ed. Stewart, 432–437). This would be their last visit together.

Michelangelo   During their stay in Florence and Rome from 1858 to 1859, Hawthorne made a point of seeing the works of Michelangelo. In June 1858, in Florence, he went to the Pitti Palace and saw the "Three Fates of Michael Angelo," which was being copied. He learned that it took three years to get an application to copy it approved; this was true of a number of other paintings as well. He comments in his Italian notebook that in a "year's time" he might have "some little knowledge of pictures." He admits that, at present, he knows "nothing" but is grateful that at least he can love "one picture better than another."

His Italian notebooks contain numerous references to the artist. Hawthorne and his family saw Michelangelo's house in Florence and his tomb in Santa Croce. In Rome, they made a point of seeing his paintings, frescoes, and sculptures in the Capitol, Uguccione Palace, Farnese Palace, Saint Peter's, and the Sistine Chapel.

Hawthorne's reactions to the art and architecture of Rome as a whole, copiously recorded in his Italian notebook, were a rich source for his depiction of the city in *The MARBLE FAUN*.

Milnes, Richard Monckton   *See* HOUGHTON, RICHARD MONCKTON MILNES, FIRST LORD.

Mitchell, Maria (1818–1889)   A native of the island of Nantucket, Massachusetts, Mitchell became the first acknowledged woman astronomer in the United States. Her father, William Mitchell, also an astronomer, encouraged her aptitude for science, mathematics, and astronomy. In 1847, she gazed through her telescope at a distant star, and then realized that the faint light was actually a comet. In 1848, Maria became the first woman member of the American Academy of Arts and Sciences and later became a fellow of the society. She served as professor of astronomy at Vassar College from 1865 to 1888. In 1875, Mitchell was elected president of the American Association for the Advancement of Women. She died on June 28, 1889. In 1905, she was elected to the Hall of Fame for Great Americans.

When the Hawthornes journeyed from England to Italy in 1858, Mitchell joined them in PARIS so that she might travel to Rome in their company. She had met them in LIVERPOOL through a letter of introduction while Hawthorne was consul. At that time, he said he and Sophia "readily consented; for she seems to be a simple, strong, healthy-humored woman, who will not fling herself as a burden on our shoulders." He did wonder, though, why "a person evidently so able to take care of herself should care about having an escort" (*French and Italian Notebooks,* 17).

They arrived in Rome on January 20, burdened with a great deal of luggage and unprepared for the cold weather. Their long journey had resulted, apparently, in some friction. Mitchell found Hawthorne indecisive and impractical. She wrote in her journal, "Had Mr. Hawthorne been as agreeable in conversation as he is in writing, it could have made the day pleasant" (Wineapple, *Hawthorne: A Life,* 297).

Mozier, Joseph (1812–1870)   American sculptor, a native of Burlington, Vermont, whom the Hawthornes knew in Rome. His *Wept of Wish-ton-wish* is in New Haven, Connecticut; *Il Penseroso* is in the National Gallery of Art, in Washington, D.C.; and *Rebecca* is in the New York Public Library.

On April 3, 1858, the Hawthornes visited Mozier's studio in Rome. He showed them a figure of Pocahantas, as well as the *Wept of Wish-ton-wish,* a figure of a smiling girl playing with her cat and dog. Hawthorne remarked that at the time Mozier had spent 17 years in Italy, yet was "intensely American in everything but the most external of his manners." He found him "sensible, shrewd, keen, clever, an ingenious workman, no doubt, with tact enough, and not destitute of taste; very agreeable and lively in his conversation, talking as fast and as naturally as a brook runs, without the slightest affectation" (*French and Italian Notebooks,* 154).

Mozier had known MARGARET FULLER Ossoli (who had drowned in 1850) well and told the Hawthornes that the Ossoli family, although "technically noble," really had little rank.

N

Nathaniel Hawthorne: Poems Volume of poems published in 1967 by the Bibliographical Society of the University of Virginia, edited by Richard E. Peck. It contains various poems, many of which were unpublished elsewhere, such as "Moderate Views" (eight lines of untitled verse contained in a letter Hawthorne wrote on February 13, 1817).

Some of the poems were published in the *Salem Gazette,* including "The Ocean" (August 26, 1825), "Moonlight" (September 2, 1825), "Fairies" (August 29, 1826), "To a Cloud" (September 2, 1826), "The Marriage Ring" (June 20, 1826), and "The Consumptive" (December 8, 1826).

Other poems were extracted from Hawthorne's letters to family members, such as his sister Elizabeth. The volume also includes 16 lines of "Nonsense Verse" composed by Hawthorne and his daughter Una.

New-England Magazine Periodical in which some of Hawthorne's stories first appeared. Joseph Tinker Buckingham was the owner and editor when Hawthorne began publishing his fiction and nonfiction in the *Salem Gazette* and *The* TOKEN during the early 1830s. At that time, SAMUEL GRISWOLD GOODRICH, editor of *The Token,* often passed along rejected manuscripts to Buckingham for possible publication. In 1835, Park Benjamin became editor, and at the end of the year the magazine was merged into the *American Monthly Magazine.*

Portions of Hawthorne's collection "The STORY-TELLER" appeared in the magazine, along with "WAKEFIELD"; "The AMBITIOUS GUEST"; "MR. HIGGINBOTHAM'S CATASTROPHE"; "The GRAY CHAM-PION"; "YOUNG GOODMAN BROWN"; "A RILL FROM THE TOWN-PUMP"; "The OLD MAID IN THE WINDING SHEET"; "OLD NEWS. NO. I"; "OLD NEWS. NO. II, The OLD FRENCH WAR"; "OLD NEWS NO. III, THE OLD TORY"; "SKETCHES FROM MEMORY. BY A PEDESTRIAN. NO. 1"; "SKETCHES FROM MEMORY. BY A PEDESTRIAN. NO. 2"; "The DEVIL IN MANUSCRIPT"; "The FOUNTAIN OF YOUTH"; and other short fiction. The sketch called "The VISION OF THE FOUNTAIN" was published in August 1835, and "MY VISIT TO NIAGARA" appeared in the magazine in February 1835. It was signed "By the author of 'The Gray Champion.'"

Newman, Samuel Phillips (1797–1842) Professor at BOWDOIN COLLEGE. He was born in Andover, Massachusetts, and graduated from Harvard College in 1816. From 1816 to 1818, he was a private tutor in Kentucky. He then went to Bowdoin, where he was a professor from 1818 to 1839. He later became principal of the Westfield Normal School and was the author of textbooks on rhetoric and political economy. He died in Brunswick, Maine, in 1842.

When Hawthorne first entered Bowdoin, he boarded, with several other boys, at the home of Newman and his wife. At the end of his first quarter there, however, he ceased boarding with the family and began taking his meals with a Mrs. Adams (Hoeltje, *Inward Sky: The Mind and Heart of Nathaniel Hawthorne,* 60, 65). While Hawthorne was at Bowdoin, Newman was a great admirer of his essays and sometimes asked him to read them aloud. Some critics believe that he helped shape Hawthorne's style. Newman later recalled Hawthorne as a young man of "reluctant step and averted look" who sometimes had an air of "girlish diffidence" (Wineapple, *Hawthorne: A Life*, 52).

By the time of Hawthorne's graduation, his genius was not altogether recognized. Although his essays had been praised by Newman and other professors and were remarkable as the compositions of an undergraduate, Hoeltje observes that his work still lacked the "skill and force of writing capable of competing with mature authors in a literary atmosphere not yet very favorable to any kind of American literature" (Hoeltje, *Inward Sky: The Mind and Heart of Nathaniel Hawthorne*, 92).

Niagara Passenger ship on which the Hawthornes went to ENGLAND in 1853. They sailed from Boston on July 6. They were accompanied by Hawthorne's friend and publisher WILLIAM DAVIS

When Hawthorne was appointed American Consul in Liverpool in 1853, he and his family sailed to England aboard this vessel, the steamship *Niagara*. The Hawthornes spent four years in Liverpool (renting a house at Rock Ferry, across the Mersey River). They then went to Italy, where they spent a year and four months. They returned to England in 1859, remaining there another year. *(Courtesy of the Peabody Essex Museum)*

TICKNOR. As they left the harbor, the ship's guns roared a salute to the author of *The SCARLET LETTER* and new U.S. consul in LIVERPOOL.

Hawthorne had commented in his notebook a few days before sailing, "I burned great heaps of old letters and other papers . . . preparatory to going to England. Among them were hundreds of Sophia's maiden letters." He was proud of this act, unfortunately.

Launched in August 1847, the *Niagara* had a wooden hull, steam engines, and sidewheel paddles. In service until 1875, it was built primarily to assist with the greatly increased mail service between Liverpool and Boston and New York.

The *Niagara* held the eastbound Boston and New York speed records and was a particularly useful means of transport in the Crimean War, carrying a tremendous number of troops with their wives and children. On June 6, 1875, *Niagara* was wrecked near South Stack, Anglesey.

Nineteenth-Century, The   Periodical in which "The GHOST OF DR. HARRIS" was first published, posthumously, in January 1900. It was later reprinted in *The Living Age*, in February 1900, and in *Critic* in April 1900.

Notebooks of Hawthorne   Hawthorne's notebooks offer a view of his daily existence. He first kept a notebook in the summer of 1835. It contained scraps of information and jottings of ideas for tales and sketches. In addition, it constituted a record of his observations on various walks and drives. When he initially began keeping his notebooks, he was still living in Salem and was, for the most part, leading a rather solitary life. He was often in his own room, sometimes going out to the Salem beaches alone. At other times, he traveled to the Beverly seashore or went to Ipswich, Nahant, or Andover.

Woodberry points out that in his observations, he did not have the viewpoint of a naturalist and was not preoccupied with detailed observations of flora and fauna. At the same time, his jottings often contained the seeds of future works of fiction. When he worked as a weigher and gauger in the BOSTON CUSTOM-HOUSE, beginning in January 1839, he began his new job cheerfully. However, it began to pall after a few months. He recorded his frustration in his notebook:

> I have been measuring coal all day, on board of a black little British schooner, in a dismal dock at the north end of the city. Most of the time I paced the deck to keep myself warm. . . . Across the water . . . appeared the Bunker Hill monument, and, what interested me considerably more, a church-steeple, with the dial of a clock upon it, whereby I was enable to measure the march of the weary hours.

He prayed that "in one year more" he might find a way of escaping from the "unblest Custom-House." At the same time, he sometimes felt that even in the Custom-House he was able to "feel and learn things that were worth knowing," and that he would not have learned them unless he had learned them there (Woodberry, *Nathaniel Hawthorne*, 57–58, 94–95).

Old Manse, The *See* CONCORD, MASSACHUSETTS.

Oliver, Benjamin Lynde (1788–1843) A distinguished lawyer who lived in Salem, Massachusetts, Oliver prepared Hawthorne for BOWDOIN COLLEGE. Beginning in the fall of 1820, Hawthorne visited Oliver's home in the early mornings to recite his Latin and Greek lessons. In the afternoons, he worked for his uncle WILLIAM MANNING at the stagecoach office in Salem. Wineapple observes that HORATIO BRIDGE commented that Hawthorne's "timidity prevented him from appearing well as a recitation Scholar; and besides he had but little love for the College Curriculum as a whole." However, he was adept at Latin and Greek and produced "elegant" translations; he was also able to write superb English themes (Wineapple, *Hawthorne: A Life,* 43, 51–52). Oliver wrote a letter of recommendation to the president of Bowdoin; Hoeltje speculates that the letter went far to convince the faculty and administration that Hawthorne was of college caliber (Hoeltje, *Inward Sky: The Mind and Heart of Nathaniel* Hawthorne, 60).

Osgood, Charles (1809–1891) Artist in Salem, Massachusetts, who painted Hawthorne's portrait in 1840. Hawthorne was 36 at the time. His sister MARIA LOUISA HAWTHORNE noted that their mother thought it was "perfect," remarking, "if she is satisfied with the likeness it must be good" (Wineapple, *Hawthorne: A Life,* 140). Many of Osgood's works are now in the Peabody Essex Museum, in Salem.

Charles Osgood's 1840 portrait of Hawthorne at age 36.
(Courtesy of the Peabody Essex Museum)

Ossoli, Giovanni Husband of MARGARET FULLER. In 1846, Miss Fuller, a friend of Hawthorne and his wife, went to Italy, where she met the marquis Ossoli (GIOVANNI OSSOLI), who was 10 years her junior. She became his mistress and gave birth to a son; they married later. In July 1850, she, her husband, and their son all perished when their ship went aground off Fire Island, New York. Their bodies were never recovered, although that of the infant son washed ashore.

The sculptor JOSEPH MOZIER, whom the Hawthornes knew in Rome, had confided to them that Ossoli's family, though technically of the nobility, had "no rank whatever." Ossoli was considered handsome, although Margaret Fuller was said to be afraid he would be ill at ease and out of place in America.

Hawthorne observed in his notebook that Fuller's marriage to Ossoli proved that she was a "very woman, after all," who "fell as the weakest of her sisters might." He viewed her death as almost inevitable, or, as Turner puts it, "the final step in the working out of inevitable consequences" (Turner, *Nathaniel Hawthorne: A Biography*, 324–325).

O'Sullivan, John (1813–1895)   Founder, editor, and publisher of the DEMOCRATIC REVIEW, in which Hawthorne published a number of early pieces. These included "TALES OF THE PROVINCE-HOUSE," "CHIPPINGS WITH A CHISEL," "JOHN INGLEFIELD'S THANKSGIVING," "THE NEW ADAM AND EVE," "EGOTISM: OR, THE BOSOM-SERPENT," "THE PROCESSION OF LIFE," "THE CELESTIAL RAIL-ROAD," "BUDS AND BIRD-VOICES," "FIRE-WORSHIP," "THE CHRISTMAS BANQUET," "THE INTELLIGENCE OFFICE," "The ARTIST OF THE BEAUTIFUL," "A BOOK OF AUTOGRAPHS," "WRITINGS OF AUDÉPINE," "The TOLLGATHERER'S DAY," and "P.'S CORRESPONDENCE."

Hawthorne considered O'Sullivan, who was nine years younger than he, "one of the truest and best men in the world." He was one of Hawthorne's leading editor friends.

O'Sullivan graduated from Columbia College at age 19. In 1837, he launched the *Democratic Review*, which spearheaded the "Young America" movement. He gained admittance to the bar and,

with his brother-in-law, Samuel Langtree, then founded the *Review*. According to Wineapple, O'Sullivan obtained much needed funding for the magazine by winning a suit against the United States government, which had impounded one of the ships owned by his father that been suspected of piracy.

When he launched the magazine, O'Sullivan boasted that he would publish the best writing produced by American authors. Many well-known writers were represented in the pages of the *Democratic Review*, including WILLIAM ELLERY CHANNING, JOHN GREENLEAF WHITTIER, Walt Whitman, EDGAR ALLAN POE, HENRY WADSWORTH LONGFELLOW, Catharine Maria Sedgwick, William Gilmore Simms, GEORGE BANCROFT, and ORESTES AUGUSTUS BROWNSON. Hawthorne's future sister-in-law ELIZABETH PALMER PEABODY reviewed *Nature*, published by RALPH WALDO EMERSON in 1836, although her review was not signed. Hawthorne himself contributed a sketch, "The TOLLGATHERER'S DAY," to the inaugural number of the magazine, which appeared in October 1837. This was the first of many contributions he made to the magazine, including a large number of short stories and a remembrance of his Bowdoin friend JONATHAN CILLEY.

It was O'Sullivan who coined the phrase "Manifest Destiny" in a noted editorial in 1838. Arguing for the admission of Texas to the United States, he asserted that Mexico had released Texas from allegiance. He was thinking of the dissemination of cultural as well as political democratic principles, encompassing literature and other arts, and he rightfully foresaw that California would be the next important state admitted to the Union. Hawthorne once remarked, "The Devil has a smaller share in O'Sullivan than in other bipeds who wear breeches" (Wineapple, *Hawthorne: A Life*, 106).

P

Packard, Prof. Alpheus Spring One of Hawthorne's BOWDOIN COLLEGE professors, who remembered Hawthorne as a "shy, gentle youth who had sat near the end of the first bench in his class." He extended a special invitation to Hawthorne to attend the celebrations connected with the founding of Bowdoin, urging him to contribute "an ode or a tale or a reminiscence, something in his characteristic manner." Hawthorne attended the celebrations, although he did not contribute any writing (Hoeltje, *The Mind and Heart of Nathaniel Hawthorne*, 368–369).

Palazzo Buonarotti Michelangelo's house and museum in Florence, Italy, which the Hawthornes visited. Located in the historical city center, on the Via Ghibellina, it is a typical example of 16th-century Florentine architecture.

The Hawthornes went in search of it on July 2, 1858. Hawthorne termed it an "ordinary-looking, three-story house, with broad-brimmed eaves, a stuccoed front, and two or three windows painted in fresco, besides the real ones." The family had a glimpse of the hills outside Florence while hoping to be admitted. They learned, however, that the house was being repaired and visitors were barred at the time. Hawthorne remarked, "It is a pity; for I wanted to see Michael Angelo's sword, and walking-sticks, and old slippers, and whatever other of his closest little personalities are to be seen" (*French and Italian Notebooks*, 352).

Palfrey, John Gorham American Unitarian clergyman whom Hawthorne met through the lawyer GEORGE HILLARD, in Boston. He saw Palfrey again in LONDON at a breakfast given by RICHARD MONCKTON MILNES. He considered the breakfast his most important literary experience in England, since the other guests were Lady Byron, Thomas Babington Macaulay, ROBERT BROWNING, and the American publisher George Ticknor (Turner, *Nathaniel Hawthorne*, 300–301).

Patmore, Coventry Kersey Dighton (1823–1896) English poet, best known for *Angel in the House*. He became a Roman Catholic in 1864 and wrote *Rod, Root, and Flower*, a volume of prose religious meditations.

Patmore called on the Hawthornes before they left ENGLAND for America, when Hawthorne's tour of duty as consul had drawn to a close. Hoeltje remarks that when the conversation occasionally flagged, it was Hawthorne who "set it afloat again." He observes that Hawthorne's four years in England as consul and as "literary celebrity" had "given him a skill in conversation . . . he had not had before" (Hoeltje, *Inward Sky: The Mind and Heart of Nathaniel Hawthorne*, 424).

Peabody, Elizabeth Palmer (1778–1853) Mother-in-law of Nathaniel Hawthorne. Elizabeth Palmer arrived about 1800 in Andover, Massachusetts, at the age of 23, to take up a post as preceptress of Franklin Academy. She soon met NATHANIEL PEABODY, 27, who had gone to Andover as preceptor of Phillips Andover Academy. They were immediately attracted to each other and were married in November 1802. Nathaniel Peabody trained in a second career and became a dentist, but they were never free of financial struggles. In 1806, they established a school in Cambridge and opened it to boarders.

Elizabeth had eight children—three girls and five boys—at approximately two-year intervals; the last child, a boy, died soon after birth. She published an edition of Spenser's poetry and oversaw the education of her children with great care. She also, according to Miller, "dominated them by her overstrenuous inculcation of religious and moral principles."

Because Dr. Nathaniel Peabody was not an overly successful provider, Elizabeth encouraged her daughters to become teachers. She also instilled strong religious and moral principles in all her children (Miller, *Salem Is My Dwelling Place*, 122–126).

For Further Reading

Tharp, Louise Hall, *The Peabody Sisters of Salem* (Boston: Little, Brown, 1950).

Peabody, Elizabeth Palmer (1804–1894) Sister of SOPHIA AMELIA PEABODY HAWTHORNE and sister-in-law of Nathaniel Hawthorne; the oldest of the Peabody daughters. As a child, she played with the Hawthorne children in Salem, and some people assumed she would marry Hawthorne. The families lived near each other, the Hawthornes on Herbert Street and the Peabodys on Union Street. As a young woman, Elizabeth lived for a time in Boston and became a prominent figure on the intellectual scene. She was secretary to the Unitarian clergyman WILLIAM ELLERY CHANNING and was associated with AMOS BRONSON ALCOTT in his experimental school. Assisted by Sophia, she published the proceedings of the school.

In July 1840, the Peabodys moved to Boston for a few years and lived at 13 West Street, in Beacon Hill. Elizabeth opened a bookstore in their home that specialized in foreign titles; she also published books and *The Dial*, a transcendentalist journal (Turner, *Nathaniel Hawthorne: A Biography*, passim).

Throughout their years in Boston and after the family's return to Salem, Elizabeth was active in promoting Hawthorne's career. Her sister Sophia and Nathaniel Hawthorne were married in Boston on July 9, 1842, at the Peabody home on West Street. Hawthorne's sisters and mother did not attend the ceremony. In many ways, he became as close to the Peabodys as to his own family.

Elizabeth has been characterized as "energetic, dedicated, and tireless." She made many innovations in kindergarden training, and, as publisher of *The Dial*, was at the center of the transcendentalist movement in Boston. RALPH WALDO EMERSON called her bookshop "a private theatre for the exposition of every question of letters, of philosophy, of ethics, and of art." In her old age, she made it a point to attend public lectures and continued to be a good-natured public figure. HENRY JAMES caricatured her as Miss Birdsye in his novel *The BOSTONIANS*.

Sophia once wrote, "I seem to realize with peculiar force that beautiful, fathomless heart of Elizabeth—forever disappointed but forever believing—sorely rebuffed yet never bitter—robbed day by day and giving again from an endless store—more sweet, more tender, more serene as the Hours pass over her" (Miller, *Salem Is My Dwelling Place*, 126–127).

For Further Reading

Stewart, Randall, "Recollections of Hawthorne by His Sister Elizabeth," *American Literature* 16 (1945): 316–331; Tharp, Louise Hall, *The Peabody Sisters of Salem* (Boston: Little, Brown, 1950).

Peabody, George Francis (1813–1839) Brother of SOPHIA AMELIA PEABODY HAWTHORNE. He died at home after a slow and lingering illness.

Peabody, Dr. Nathaniel (1774–1855) Father-in-law of Nathaniel Hawthorne. He went to Andover, Massachusetts, in his late 20s as preceptor of Phillips Andover Academy. After marrying Elizabeth Palmer in 1802, he trained in a second career and became a dentist.

The Peabodys had a difficult life from a financial point of view. In 1806, they established a school in Cambridge and opened it to boarders.

Silhouettes of the Peabody family, 1835. Left to right, top row: Mrs. Elizabeth Peabody, Dr. Nathaniel Peabody, Elizabeth Peabody, and Nathaniel Cranch. Left to right, bottom row: George Peabody, Sophia Peabody, Mary Peabody, and Wellington Peabody. *(Courtesy of the Peabody Essex Museum)*

In 1824, Peabody published a pamphlet titled *The Art of Preserving Teeth*, which sold very well. Over the years, they had eight children—three girls and five boys.

Hawthorne considered his father-in-law charming, but ineffectual and stubborn. Mrs. Peabody once wrote in her journal that her husband suffered because of certain deficiences in his early education and was marked by "constitutional timidity" (Miller, *Salem Is My Dwelling Place*, 126).

Peabody, Nathaniel Cranch (1811–1881) Brother of SOPHIA AMELIA PEABODY HAWTHORNE. The eldest of the Peabody brothers, he became a teacher, a grocer, and finally a pharmacist; he married early and raised a family in Boston that included two children. He wrote to his sister Elizabeth Palmer expressing his doubts about the "*aesthetic* culture" venerated by his sisters, perhaps because he felt this led to a certain distortion in an individual's system of values. He remarked that he had little sympathy with "those who admire and worship brilliant men" because he felt this attitude led to a devaluation in the worth of personal character. Miller believes that Nathaniel Peabody was not as successful as his father, Dr. NATHANIEL PEABODY, who is regarded by many critics as "ineffectual" (Miller, *Salem Is My Dwelling Place*, 134).

Peabody, Wellington (1816–1838) Brother of SOPHIA AMELIA PEABODY HAWTHORNE. The youngest of the Peabody brothers, he was intelligent and handsome. He attended Harvard and left with a certificate of creditable standing. He had acquired many debts, however, and went to sea on a whaling ship based in New Bedford, Massachusetts. He died of yellow fever in New Orleans (Wineapple, *Hawthorne: A Life*, 114).

Pierce, Franklin (1804–1869) President of the United States from 1853 to 1857, Pierce first met Hawthorne at BOWDOIN COLLEGE. Pierce was one class ahead of him, but they met as members of the ATHENEAN SOCIETY. At the time, Pierce was a popular figure on campus—extroverted, sociable, and friendly. That his father had been a hero in the battle of Bunker Hill conferred prestige on him at Bowdoin. Pierce commanded the Bowdoin Cadets, joined the literary society, and was, when first there, a playboy. During his years in college, however, he transformed himself into a serious student and graduated third in his class. Pierce became one of Hawthorne's closest friends. He was elected to the New Hampshire legislature in 1828 and later served in the U.S. Congress, first as representative and then as senator.

After Hawthorne's marriage to Sophia, the young couple had a difficult time financially. In 1845, Pierce visited the Hawthorne home in CONCORD, MASSACHUSETTS, with their mutual Bowdoin friend HORATIO BRIDGE. At the time, Sophia had not yet met Pierce.

Pierce served in the Mexican War and, in 1852, defeated General Lewis Cass to be nominated on the 49th ballot as the Democratic candidate for president. Hawthorne was commissioned to write a campaign biography of him. It had been Pierce who was responsible for Hawthorne's appointment as surveyor of the customs in the Salem Custom-House, a political plum. After Pierce's election as president, he appointed Hawthorne consul to LIVERPOOL, an appointment that presaged a highly significant period in Hawthorne's career as a writer (Hoeltje, *Inward Sky: The Mind and Heart of Nathaniel Hawthorne*, passim).

After his tenure in Liverpool, the Hawthorne family moved to ITALY. Pierce and his wife visited them there. While they were in Rome, Hawthorne's daughter Una became seriously ill with a form of malaria. The Pierces stood by the Hawthornes during Una's slow recovery, just as Hawthorne and Sophia had tried to comfort Pierce and his wife when their only child, an 11-year-old son, was killed in a train accident, two months before he took office as president. Pierce served only one term as president; in 1858, the Democratic Party replaced him with James Buchanan.

The family returned to Concord in 1860, but Hawthorne was not healthy. He grew less robust over the next three years, despite taking recuperative trips to New York and Maine. His work was not going well, and he was despondent. When he became seriously ill in the spring of 1864, Pierce visited him, urging Hawthorne to accompany him in his private carriage to country places such as trout streams and old farmhouses. They would relive their youthful years and escape from their present-day cares. They left on May 16, going north to Lake Winnipesaukee in New Hampshire. Then went on to Plymouth, New Hampshire, where they stayed at the Pemigewasset House. That night, May 18, Hawthorne died in his sleep. Pierce telegraphed Sophia and notified others. It is thought that Hawthorne might have died of a brain tumor, because for weeks before embarking on the carriage trip with Pierce he had suffered pain, weakness, and loss of control over his limbs (Turner, *Nathaniel Hawthorne*, passim).

For Further Reading

Bridge, Horatio, *Personal Recollections of Nathaniel Hawthorne* (New York: Haskell House, 1968); Hoeltje, *Inward Sky: The Mind and Heart of Nathaniel Hawthorne* (Durham, N.C.: Duke University Press, 1962); Nichols, Roy F., *Franklin Pierce* (Norwalk,

Conn.: Easton Press, 1988); Webster, Sidney, *Franklin Pierce and His Administration,* (New York: Appleton, 1892); Turner, Arlin, *Nathaniel Hawthorne,* (New York: Oxford University Press, 1980).

Plymouth, New Hampshire Hawthorne died at the Pemigewasset House, in Plymouth, in May 1864. His friend FRANKLIN PIERCE, former president of the United States, had taken him on a carriage trip, hoping it would restore his strength. They had spent one night at Lake Winnipesaukee in New Hampshire and then had traveled on to Plymouth.

Poe, Edgar Allan (1809–1849) American short-story writer, critic, and poet. Poe was born in Boston but upon the death of his mother was taken into the family of the Richmond, Virginia, merchant John Allan. He studied for one term at the University of Virginia and in later years became a staff writer for the highly regarded *Southern Literary Messenger* and then the literary editor of *Graham's Magazine.* He married Virginia Clemm of Richmond in May 1836, after which he and his wife lived in New York and Philadelphia, supporting themselves on the proceeds of his writing. Virginia later contracted tuberculosis, and Poe himself became an alcoholic. He died in Baltimore, Maryland.

Poe was highly regarded as a literary critic, poet, and author of such stories as "The Fall of the House of Usher" and "The Gold Bug." Among his better-known poems are "Annabel Lee" and "The Raven."

He praised Hawthorne's originality and genius in a review of TWICE-TOLD TALES for *Graham's Magazine* in April and May 1842. He objected to the word *tales,* however, insisting that some of the pieces were essays and not tales. Nevertheless, he stated that he had seen no prose composition by any American that could compare with the best of Hawthorne's. He singled out "The MINISTER'S BLACK VEIL," "DR. HEIDEGGER'S EXPERIMENT," and "The WEDDING-KNELL" for particular praise. He remarked that Hawthorne's style was "purity itself," and his tone "singularly effective—wild, plaintive, thoughtful, and in full accordance with his themes." Poe also wrote an essay about Hawthorne

that appeared in *Godey's Magazine and Lady's Book* in November 1847.

Brenda Wineapple observes that while Poe praised Hawthorne's "precision and fluency," he did not approve of the "hermetic, rarified quality" of his stories. Poe advised him: "'Ger a bottle of visible ink, come out from the Old Manse, cut Mr. Alcott, hang (if possible) the editor of *The Dial,* and throw out of the window to the pigs all his odd numbers of *The North American Review*'" (Wineapple, *Hawthorne: A Life,* 195).

Power, Marguerite Editor of *The Keepsake,* London. She published an essay by Hawthorne on Uttoxeter, England, in the issue for 1857. It was later reprinted in *Harper's New Monthly Magazine* in April 1857.

Puritans Hawthorne once wrote that the "prevailing characteristic" of the Puritan age was gloom, exemplified by the early Puritan governor John Endicott, who was instrumental in expelling the Quaker Anne Hutchinson from Massachusetts. His 1832 story "The GENTLE BOY" depicts the severity of the Puritans against the Quakers. Hawthorne later defended the Puritans, however, saying that the early settlers in Massachusetts believed strict discipline in civic and religious matters was essential for survival.

Hawthorne was descended from Puritans who participated in the Salem witch trials. In ENGLAND, the Hawthornes originated at Bray, in Berkshire, where the landscape featured Hawthorne Hill. William Hathorne, his great-grandfather, was born in England, converted to Puritanism, and arrived in the Massachusetts Bay settlement in 1630. He moved soon afterward to Salem, where he was a prominent and responsible member of county and local governments, and where he pronounced sentences on Quakers. His son John took a notable part in the witch trials of 1692. Hawthorne, according to his biographer Arlin Turner, had a conflicting view of these forebears. He was ashamed of their actions but at the same time considered them men of "station and accomplishment" (Turner, *Nathaniel Hawthorne: A Biography,* 59).

Hawthorne's novel *The* SCARLET LETTER contains his most devastating depiction of the Puritans. Many critics have considered Governor Bellingham and other Puritan characters to be drawn with "eminent fidelity" to history, even though Hawthorne did not claim his writings were "historical tales" (Idol and Jones, *Nathaniel Hawthorne: The Contemporary Reviews,* 119–155, passim).

In *The Scarlet Letter,* Hawthorne uses a physical object as a symbol: the embroidered scarlet letter on a woman's bosom, which he had visualized in the story "ENDICOTT AND THE RED CROSS." This technique focuses the story: We do not have the busy streets, squares, and frenetic crowds of *The* MARBLE FAUN; instead, everything is subordinated to the narrow symbolic emblems of Puritanism embodied in the characters of Hester, Dimmesdale, Chillingworth, and Pearl. The Puritan community is both rigid and forbidding. Hawthorne later remarked, "The spirit of my Puritan ancestors was mighty in me" as he wrote the novel (Wineapple, *Hawthorne: A Life,* 231).

Q

Quakers William Hathorne, Hawthorne's great-grandfather, immigrated to Boston from England in 1630, with John Winthrop. Hathorne was a soldier, legislator, Puritan, and persecutor of Quakers. After 1633, when he lived in Salem, he took a prominent part in colonial affairs. He became a magistrate, and in this capacity he ordered the public whipping of Anne Coleman and four other Quakers. Hawthorne alludes to this event in "The CUSTOM-HOUSE" (Hawthorne, *The American Notebooks*, 288).

In his story "The GENTLE BOY," Hawthorne takes a different view of Quakers. The tale opens in 1656, when members of the Quaker sect began appearing in New England and practicing their religion of peace. Guided by "the command of the spirit," their behavior often struck the Puritans as irrational. A middle-aged Puritan man, Tobias Pearson, thinks he hears wailing as he walks along the road. He finds a small boy of six, Ilbrahim, crying beneath a tree. He offers to take him home and provide supper and a bed for him, but Ilbrahim says his father lies in a nearby grave and he must stay there. The Puritan tells himself he must not leave the child to perish. He finally persuades Ilbrahim, who has not eaten in two days, to go with him. Pearson takes him in his arms and carries him home. His wife, Dorothy, says she wishes to be the boy's mother. The adoption of the child of the "accursed sect" alienates the other Puritans, however, and they begin to persecute the Pearsons and call them "backsliders."

The Pearsons take Ilbrahim to the meeting house, where a Puritan speaks of the danger of pity and the evil of Quakers. Then a woman rises and speaks passionately against the persecution of Quakers. She turns out to be Catharine, Ilbrahim's natural mother. She tells Ilbrahim that his only inheritance from her will be "woe and shame." Dorothy stands and offers to be his mother. The Quaker mother says she is not of their people; which Dorothy agrees, but she argues that if she is allowed to care for him, he will meet his real mother in heaven. She says she will teach him the Puritan faith. The mother asks about Dorothy's husband, and Tobias comes forward. Ilbrahim's mother declares she hears an inner voice addressing her: "'Leave thy child, Catharine, for his place is here, and go hence, for I have other work for thee.'" She entrusts him to Dorothy and leaves; she has already endured persecution by Catholics and Turks.

Pearson and his wife acquire parental rights to Ilbrahim and he becomes "a piece of the immoveable furniture of their hearts." Dorothy nurtures him, and he is "like a domesticated sunbeam" to them. Then the Pearsons temporarily take in a boy two years older, who has been injured in a fall from a tree. Unfortunately, the older boy has a dark nature. This boy later returns to his natural parents, but he and his friends attack Ilbrahim, who survives, but his spirit has been crushed, and he becomes very ill. His natural mother, Catharine, a wild fanatic, returns to the Pearson home to find Ilbrahim on his deathbed. It is as if "Ilbrahim's sweetness yet lingered round his ashes, as if his gentle spirit came down from heaven to teach his parent a true religion." The others in the settlement are, at last, kind to her, and at her death, a "long train of her once bitter persecutors" follows her to her place "by Ilbrahim's green and sunken grave."

For Further Reading

Miller, Edwin Haviland, "'Wounded Love': Nathaniel Hawthorne's 'The Gentle Boy,'" *Nathaniel Hawthorne Journal* 8 (1978): 47–54; Newberry, Frederick, "Hawthorne's 'Gentle Boy': Lost Mediators in Puri-tan History," *Studies in Short Fiction* 21, no. 4 (fall 1984): 363–373.

Quincy, Josiah (1772–1864)   Mayor of Boston from 1823 to 1828 and president of Harvard University from 1829 to 1845. Both Hawthorne and his wife, SOPHIA AMELIA PEABODY HAWTHORNE, had known Quincy and his daughter, Anna Cabot Lowell Quincy Waterston (1812–1899), since the late 1830s.

R

Raymond, Maine Hawthorne's maternal grandfather had bought land in Cumberland County, Maine, on the shores of Lake Sebago. One of Hawthorne's uncles, Richard Manning, began living there and managing the land. He was a justice of the peace, sensitive to the beauty of the landscape, and a collector and reader of books.

Hawthorne, along with his mother and sisters, visited in June 1816. In 1818, they lived there for several months in a home Richard Manning built for them. At one time, the family considered a permanent move to Raymond.

Richard Manning presented his nephew with a diary, inscribed to him "with the advice that he write out his thoughts, some every day, in as good words as he can, upon any and all subjects, as it is one of the best means of his securing for mature years, command of thought and language." Hawthorne later recalled the formative and happy period he spent in Raymond, delighting in nature, shooting, and fishing, but "reading a good deal, too, on the rainy days, especially in Shakespeare and 'The Pilgrim's Progress,' and any poetry or light books within my reach" (Turner, *Nathaniel Hawthorne: A Biography*, 21).

Another uncle, ROBERT MANNING, believed that Hawthorne's education would suffer if he remained in Maine, which he considered unrefined. He insisted that Hawthorne return to Salem. Hawthorne objected, telling Uncle Robert he had caught 18 large brook trout and shot a partridge and a hen hawk. He added that his mother could not spare him. This effort was in vain, however, and he returned to school in Salem. He wrote to his sister Louisa of his nostalgia for Raymond: "How often do I long for my gun, and wish that I could again savagize with you. . . . But I shall never again run wild in Raymond, and I shall never be so happy as when I did." He even wished he had been born a girl so that he would not have to go to school. He wrote to his mother that the "happiest days" of his life were gone." Nevertheless, he did attend school in Salem, read voraciously, and wrote poetry (Wineapple, *Hawthorne: A Life*, 39–40). He went on to BOWDOIN COLLEGE from Salem and never again lived in Raymond.

Ripley, George (1802–1880) The disillusioned Unitarian clergyman who founded the transcendalist BROOK FARM Institute of Agriculture and Education, in West Roxbury, Massachusetts, on 200 acres. He had not been very successful in the capacity of pastor but became convinced that, with his wife to assist him, he could establish a successful experiment in utopian living. This venture would include an educational program that would afford participants "the most complete instruction . . . from the first rudiments to the highest culture" (Miller, *Salem Is My Dwelling Place*, 188). The experiment lasted only until 1847.

SOPHIA AMELIA PEABODY HAWTHORNE's sister ELIZABETH PALMER PEABODY promoted the plan for the West Roxbury community in her magazine, *The Dial.*

In 1841, Hawthorne invested $1,000 in Brook Farm and went there to live. One purpose in so doing was to assess the possibility that he and Sophia might make their home there after they were married; it could be both economical and appealing. Once he became a resident, however, he realized that it would not be suitable and remained less than a year (Martin, *Nathaniel Hawthorne*, 18). Brook Farm is the central subject of Hawthorne's 1852 novel *The BLITHEDALE ROMANCE*.

Roberts, David ("Chancellor") Attorney in Salem, Massachusetts, a longtime friend of Hawthorne.

Roberts gave the Hawthornes half a dozen silver spoons as a wedding gift (Wineapple, *Hawthorne: A Life*, 160). Sophia did not care for Roberts and once called him "an intolerably heavy lump of stupidity & clownishness," although she knew that Hawthorne respected his character and often depended on his judgment (Miller, *Salem Is My Dwelling Place*, 88).

In later years, he wrote books on admiralty law and became mayor of Salem (1866–1867). He supported Hawthorne when he was under consideration for the post of inspector at the BOSTON CUSTOM-HOUSE. At Hawthorne's funeral, he was one of the mourners, a list of whom AMÓS BRONSON ALCOTT kept in his diary (Wineapple, *Hawthorne: A Life*, 128, 178).

Rock Ferry Small town across the Mersey River from LIVERPOOL.

In July 1853, Hawthorne, accompanied by his family, went to Liverpool as the American consul. The Hawthornes first stayed at Waterloo House, a hotel in Liverpool, and then moved to Mrs. Blodgett's boardinghouse on Duke Street, which had long been a favorite of American sea captains.

On August 6, Hawthorne moved his family to the Rock Ferry Hotel across the Mersey River, where he thought the air might be fresher. On September 1, they moved to 26 Rock Park, Rock Ferry, a three-story stone house he had leased. The rent was £160 a year, furnished. Having the large house enabled the Hawthornes to invite friends and acquaintances who were visiting Liverpool to be their houseguests.

Hawthorne commuted to George's Dock, site of the consulate in Liverpool, by steam ferry every day. Ferry service across the river dated back as far as 1660. The Royal Rock Ferry Company was formed in 1836 by a group of businessmen with the aim of extending the Royal Rock Hotel and construction of the Esplanade. In 1891, however, the Mersey Railway was extended to Rock Ferry, and ferry service slowly declined.

According to a history of the community prepared and published in May 2000 by the Rock Park Local History Group, the Rock Park estate was one of the first gated communities in England. It was

Hawthorne home in Rock Park, Rock Ferry, England. In July 1853 Hawthorne accepted the post of American consul in Liverpool, England. He rented this furnished, three-story stone house for £160 per year. Steam ferries crossed the river to Liverpool every half hour. The house stood until an expressway forced its demolition, but Mary and Simon Petris, Hawthorne archivists and devotees, managed to save a gatepost, which is still standing on the site. *(Courtesy of the Peabody Essex Museum)*

designed by Jonathon Bennison in 1836–37 and the houses were built around a serpentine road in a variety of early Victorian styles. Among the buildings were the Royal Mersey Yacht Club, the Royal Rock Hotel with its Olympian Gardens and bowling green, and the Cricket Ground. The community was completed by 1850. The Esplanade was open to the general public as a walk and was popular because of the panoramic views it afforded across to the Liverpool waterfront. The Esplanade is not at present open because of dangerous deterioration, but the Rock Park Local History Group is making a valiant effort to preserve the community's literary and maritime history. Unfortunately, several homes, including the one occupied by the Hawthornes, were demolished in the mid–1970s when the Rock Ferry bypass was constructed.

Local citizens, particularly Mary Petris and Simon Petris of Ferryside, Rock Park, Rock Ferry, recognized the importance of Hawthorne's literary legacy and fought valiantly against the demolition of the Hawthorne home. Through their efforts, a post marking the site of the house was erected, and the Petrises have made an invaluable effort to collect memorabilia and writings about the Hawthornes' residence in Rock Ferry.

Other noted literary and political figures are also associated with Rock Ferry, including King George IV (who stayed at the Rock Ferry Hotel), the poet John Masefield, James Buchanan (later president of the United States), and the celebrated astronomer Isaac Roberts. Although ferry service no longer exists, trains go regularly beneath the Mersey to Rock Ferry, which, even without the house once occupied by the Hawthornes, remains one of the most charming and hospitable communities in England.

For Further Reading

The Rock Park Local History Group, "Rock Park Conservation Area: A Historical Perspective," 2000.

Rome   At the conclusion of his term as American Consul in LIVERPOOL, Nathaniel Hawthorne and his family went to the Continent. They went to FRANCE and had extended stays in several towns and cities in ITALY, returning to England in May 1859.

Lord Byron's *Childe Harold's Pilgrimage* had whetted the Hawthornes' appetite for Italy, as it had that of many other American visitors to the Continent. Hubert Hoeltje observes that the Hawthornes were disillusioned on their arrival in Rome, since Hawthorne was nursing a bad cold and they disliked the beggars, pickpockets, and filth. Within a few days, however, the city "pulled at his heartstrings."

They first stayed at Spillman's Hotel and then settled at 37 Via Porta Pinciana, where they had a suite of 10 rooms. The family slowly warmed to the city and began exploring it. They also wrote and called on people whom they had met or to whom they had introductions, such as the artists WILLIAM WETMORE STORY, C. G. Thompson, Joseph Mozier, George Loring Brown, and Maria Louisa Lander. They had also established social contact with HARRIET HOSMER, William Cullen Bryant, and Fredrika Bremer.

Within four months of their arrival, by late May 1858, they had visited most of the major churches, villas, palaces, and art galleries of Rome. Hawthorne became extremely fond of the city, commenting in his notebook, "It is very singular, the sad embrace with which Rome takes possession of the soul" (*French and Italian Notebooks*, 232).

Soon after their arrival, the Hawthornes visited the Baths of Diocletian and the Fountain of the Termini, with its colossal statue of Moses striking the rock. They were particularly impressed by the church of San Maria dei Angeli. Hawthorne commented that the interior was so "lofty, broad, and airy, that the soul forthwith swells out, and magnifies itself" (*French and Italian Notebooks*, 88–89).

At this time Hawthorne was planning to write an English romance, but he then became preoccupied with the idea of a novel inspired by their visit to the museum of the Roman Capitol, where they saw such famous statues as *Dying Gladiator*. Hawthorne's attention was particularly caught by Praxiteles' statue of a faun; he and his wife also saw other statues of fauns in the Vatican and the Villa Borghese, and gradually he became preoccupied with the images. The Hawthornes departed from Rome in late May 1858, going to Passignano, Perugia, Florence, Siena, Viterbo, Sette Vene, and other towns.   In October 1858 they returned to Rome, remaining there until May 1859.   The Hawthornes' daughter Una was seriously ill with "Roman fever," a dreaded illness similar to malaria, from November 1858 through the middle of April 1859.   At that time, quinine was one of the few known medicines, but it could not be given too often.   Her recovery was slow, but she survived.

Hoeltje remarks that Hawthorne had gone to Italy to write his English romance and to live there economically with his family.   He also wanted to spend time in the country Byron had called "the Mother of Arts."   Hawthorne did attempt to work at the English romance, but eventually he put it aside in favor of a romance set in Italy (Hoeltje,

483, 498).   At the time, it was titled *The Romance of Monte Beni*, but it was eventually renamed *The MARBLE FAUN*.   This novel became his most widely read book.   Distinguished critics praised it as his finest work, and Hawthorne had notes of congratulation and requests for autographs.

Before departing from Rome, Hawthorne went to visit the Pincian Hill, the Borghese grounds, and St. Peter's.   He wrote that they had "never looked so beautiful, nor the sky so bright and blue."   Biographer Arlin Turner states that although Hawthorne had been miserable there, especially in view of Una's illness, "no other place had ever taken so strong a hold on his feelings" (Turner, 343).

S

Salem Custom House Hawthorne's BOWDOIN friend HORATIO BRIDGE was largely responsible for his obtaining the post of surveyor at the Salem Custom House in 1846. Hawthorne was in desperate need of such a permanent post, because he and Sophia were expecting their second child. Una, the eldest, was born in 1844, and Julian, the second, would be born in 1846.

Turner gives a full account of the political machinations behind Hawthorne's appointment and explains Hawthorne's worry that it would not be finalized before the baby's arrival. Hawthorne was finally appointed on April 3, 1846, for four years, and took up work as customs surveyor on April 20. The Hawthornes then moved to 18 Chestnut Street, Salem. In September 1847, the family rented a large house at 14 Mall Street, Salem. His mother and sisters moved to the second floor.

Hawthorne did not expect that all his time would be consumed by his new duties as custom-house surveyor; he assumed he would have time to devote to literature. He was busier than expected, however, and found it difficult to write fiction. He did produce book reviews, one of them written, as he put it, "with an interruption every few sentences."

In June 1849 Hawthorne was removed from his post as surveyor of customs at Salem. He was replaced by Captain Allen Putnam, who was confirmed by the U.S. Senate on September 24, 1850. Hawthorne wrote "The Custom-House," an introduction to his novel The SCARLET LETTER, in March 1850. It was based on his experiences as surveyor.

Salem, Massachusetts Birthplace of Nathaniel Hawthorne on July 4, 1804. His father was NATHANIEL HATHORNE (1780-1808), and his mother was ELIZABETH CLARKE MANNING HATHORNE (1780–1849). He later adopted the spelling of "Hawthorne." His father died in Surinam in 1808, at age 28 (Hoeltje, Inward Sky, 16–27). Most of Hawthorne's 46 years would be spent in Salem. He had an older sister, Elizabeth, and a younger one, Louisa, born the year his father died.

Salem, in Essex County, Massachusetts, about 19 miles northeast of Boston, was founded in 1626. It had been the site of the hysterical persecution of witches and wizards in 1692. At this time a number of young girls accused some older women of bewitching them. Eventually, hundreds of people were accused. Nineteen people were hanged on Gallows Hill, and at least two others died in jail. Fifty-five were forced into false confessions, and at least 150 were imprisoned. Later historians blamed the temperament of the times rather than the influence of Puritanism. The events were aggravated by the spread of an epidemic disease resembling epilepsy in Danvers, then part of Salem. Commentary from the clergyman Cotton Mather incited controversy and the conviction that evil spirits were responsible ("Salem Witchcraft Trials," The Oxford Companion to American Literature, 737–738). An ancestor of Hawthorne's, John Hawthorne (1641–1717), was a magistrate who took part in the witchcraft hearings. Hawthorne's biographer Arlin Turner calls John Hawthorne "earnest and unyielding," but apparently he lacked vindictive harshness and cruelty (64–65).

Salem had been called "Naumberg" by the Indians. It was the second town in New England the Plymouth Company purchased. By the end of the Revolutionary War in 1785 it had a population of 6,665. It was the sixth-largest city in America at that time. Many citizens were widows whose husbands had died in the East India shipping trade that had made Salem prosperous and famous. This trade was mercurial: Fortunes were made overnight but were also lost overnight. The harbor had the disadvantage of being too shallow for vessels drawing more than 12 feet of water. Their wares had to be off-loaded in deeper water at some distance from the wharves.

Wealthy ship captains built magnificent homes on Chestnut Street, many designed by the architect Samuel McIntire. Between 1811 and 1819 40 Salem youths attended Harvard College, making up 10 percent of the student body. Hawthorne's paternal and maternal families were not among the elite Chestnut Street residents, nor did any of the men in the families attend Harvard. Nathaniel Hathorne attended Bowdoin College in Maine; he changed his name to "Hawthorne" after his graduation (Miller, *Salem Is My Dwelling Place*, 11-14, *passim*).

After the death of Hawthorne's father, the family (then consisting of Hawthorne, his mother, and his two sisters) went to live with his maternal grandparents, the Mannings, in their home, which Hawthorne later termed "Castle Dismal," on Herbert Street in Salem. The Mannings were businesspeople, "practical, energetic, and enterprising" (Turner, 14). They owned a stagecoach company, as well as other companies. Hawthorne formed stronger familial allegiances with the Mannings than the Hawthornes. His Manning aunts, however, encouraged him to visit and write his Hawthorne relatives. He remained largely unaware of his distinguished Hawthorne lineage until, as an adult, he began reading New England colonial history in the course of his literary research.

Hawthorne's boyhood in Salem was filled with studies and cultural activities. He learned and delivered orations, took dancing lessons, and formed, with one of his sisters, the "Pin Society," which met on Saturdays and had dues of one pin. They published six numbers of a literary magazine together, the *Spectator*. Hawthorne was tutored for college by a lawyer, Benjamin L. Oliver, learning Latin and Greek. He attended public events, such as a concert by the Handel Society of Salem, and saw the noted Shakespearean actor Edmund Kean play King Lear in Boston. He read widely, from Sir Walter Scott's novels to the travels of Sir John Mandeville.

At that time, Salem still had rural environs. Hawthorne mentions a walk in the grass fields of North Salem he took in 1835. There were "hills and hollows beyond the Cold Spring" shaded with oaks and walnut trees and river vistas. He saw a mare nursing a tiny colt in the grass, "a graceful little beast." He bathed in the cove, overhung with maples and walnuts, and later saw three little girls seated by a fountain, paddling in the water, "light and laughing little figures" (Hawthorne, *American Note-Books*, in *The Complete Works of Nathaniel Hawthorne*, with introductory notes by George Parsons Lathrop, 13 vols. [Boston: Houghton-Mifflin, 1868], 9, 14–16). In his notebooks, Hawthorne describes various houses in detail, apparently as material for later development.

In April 1843 Hawthorne returned to Salem while his wife, Sophia, was visiting her sister in Boston. He gives an ironic description of his homecoming:

> "*Salem.*— . . . Here I am, in my old chamber, where I produced those stupendous works of fiction which have since impressed the universe with wonderment and awe! To this chamber, doubtless, in all succeeding ages, pilgrims will come to pay their tribute of reverence; they will put off their shoes at the threshold for fear of desecrating the tattered old carpets! "There," they will exclaim, "is the very bed in which he slumbered, and where he was visited by those ethereal visions which he afterwards fixed forever in glowing words. . . ."

He then confesses to an "involuntary reserve" on his part that contributes "objectivity" to his writings; anyone wishing to penetrate into his "depths" must find his own way there. "I can neither guide nor enlighten him" (*American Note-Books*, 9, 335–336). Hawthorne's humorous forecast of widespread interest in his works and his origins in Salem, although he discounts it, has certainly been realized more fully than he could ever have imagined.

Hawthorne was offered a post in the Salem Custom House in 1846, which he accepted. He was employed there until 1849. The Hawthornes rented several houses in SALEM while he was at the Custom House.

Today several attractions make up the Salem Maritime National Historic Site, which covers nine acres. The Custom House has become a visitor center, and the Central Wharf Warehouse may be visited. In addition, the Scale House and Bonded Warehouse are open, as well as the Derby House (home of merchant Elias Hasket Derby, the country's first millionaire) and the West India Goods Store, which dates from 1800.

Other important buildings include the House of the Seven Gables (setting for Hawthorne's novel of the same title), Pickering Wharf, and the Essex Institute Museum, which owns and manages a number of other historic houses. The Peabody Museum, founded by sea captains in 1799, depicts the maritime history of New England. There are also the Witch House (where those accused of witchcraft were examined), the Salem Witch Museum, the Witch Dungeon Museum, Pioneer Village (which reproduces a 1630 settlement), and the Stephen Phillips Memorial Trust House, an authentic Federal mansion.

For Further Reading

Baym, Nina, *The Shape of Hawthorne's Career* (Ithaca, N.Y.: Cornell University Press, 1976); Cantwell, Robert, *Nathaniel Hawthorne: The American Years* (New York: Rinehart, 1948); Edwin Miller, *Salem Is My Dwelling Place* (Iowa City: University of Iowa Press, 1991).

San Lorenzo, Church of, Florence, Italy This church was begun by Brunelleschi about 1420. Nathaniel Hawthorne and Sophia visited it on June 19, 1858. He found the facade unattractive;

he explained that providing churches with "an elaborate and beautiful finish" has been delayed in many instances until "the day for spending mines of wealth on churches is gone by." He described the interior, with its nave, high altar, aisles of black and white marble squares, brown worn seats, and marble pulpits. He particularly admired two allegorical statues by Michelangelo, *Morning* and *Evening* (*French and Italian Notebooks*, 325–327).

San Marco, Church of, Florence, Italy On Friday, July 9, 1858, the Hawthornes visited the Church of San Marco and a convent of Dominicans that was connected to the church. In his notebook Hawthorne praised the wooden crucifix by Giotto, with ancient gilding, and a painting of Christ, "considered a wonderful work in its day." The custodian of the church offered to show the Hawthornes some frescoes by Fra Angelico and took them into a large cloister where, under a glass covering, there were pictures of Saint Dominic kneeling at the cross and several other frescoes.

The cloister was of great interest to Hawthorne. He began speculating on where the monks themselves had their burial place and wondered if it might be in the inner cloister, which he did not see. He criticized Fra Angelico's fresco of the Crucifixion, which depicted the crosses of the Savior and the thieves. He wondered whether the multitude of people shown had been martyred after the crucifixion: "some of them had wounds, from which gilded rays shown forth, as if the inner glory and blessedness of the saint burst through the holes in the flesh" (*French and Italian Notebooks*). He considered the painting "ugly" and wished Fra Angelico had "confined himself to miniature-heads, in which his delicacy of touch and minute labour often produce an excellent result."

He learned that he would be admitted into the interior of the convent to see other frescoes, but he was told, unfortunately, that Sophia could not enter. Hawthorne declined to see them also. They did see a shrine hung with offerings of silver, gold, tinsel, and "trumpery." In his opinion, the face of Christ, marked by "pain and grief," looked forth "not a whit comforted" (*French and Italian Notebooks*, 368–370).

Santa Croce, Church of, Florence   In June 1858 the Hawthornes visited the Church of Santa Croce in Florence, which Nathaniel called "the great monumental place of Florentine worthies."

The church and cloisters are located on one of the oldest squares in Florence. The church was begun in 1294 by Franciscans and completed in the second half of the 14th century. Hawthorne was skeptical about whether the church foundations would ever be covered in marble, as originally planned, although he admired the shrines within the church, which have "knightly or priestly figures" in bas-relief. He described a bust of Michelangelo, a monument to Dante, and the tombs of Alfieri and Macchiavelli. He and Sophia explored a number of chapels in the transepts of the church, often finding "an inscrutably dark picture over the altar . . . a marble bust or two, or perhaps a medieval statue of a saint, or a modern monumental bas-relief."

Despite Hawthorne's thorough exploration of the church and his ability to describe the interior in substantial detail, he was implacably Protestant. He remarked that "any little Norman church in England would impress me as much, or more." He concludes, "There is something—I do not know what, but it is in the region of the heart rather than the intellect—that Italian architecture, of whatever age or style never seems to reach" (*French and Italian Notebooks*, 342–345).

Sargent's New Monthly Magazine of Literature, Fashion, and the Fine Arts   Magazine in which Hawthorne's story "The ANTIQUE RING" was published in February 1843. It was signed, "By Nathaniel Hawthorne."

Saturday Club   Prestigious Boston club founded in 1857 for literary discussion. Hawthorne was elected to it while he was serving as American Consul in Liverpool. Meetings were held the last Saturday each month at the Parker House in Boston. Usually Hawthorne would travel to the meetings with RALPH WALDO EMERSON; among the old friends he would see at the club were HENRY WADSWORTH LONGFELLOW, JAMES RUSSELL LOWELL, and OLIVER WENDELL HOLMES (Turner, 351–352). The club still exists.

Shepard, Ada (1834–1874)   In January 1858, at the conclusion of his term as American Consul in LIVERPOOL, Nathaniel Hawthorne and his family travelled to the Continent. They went by steamer to Boulogne and on by train to Amiens and PARIS. After a few days, they continued by train to Marseille. The Hawthornes were accompanied by Miss Ada Shepard. A native of Dorchester, Massachusetts, she had attended the sermons of Theodore Parker in Boston. She graduated from Antioch College at Yellow Springs, Ohio, in 1854 and was a close friend of HORACE MANN, the president. His wife, Mary, was Sophia Hawthorne's sister.

Shepard had been strongly recommended as a companion and tutor. She spoke French well and acted as companion and tutor to the children. She often accompanied Sophia and other members of the family on guided sightseeing trips while they lived in Florence and Rome.

In June 1859 the Hawthorne family and Ada Shepard visited Geneva and made an expedition to the Castle of Chillon. They continued on to Le Havre, where they put Miss Shepard on board the steamer *Vanderbilt* to sail to New York. The Hawthornes returned to London and then continued to Liverpool and sailed back to America.

Siena, Italy   In October 1858 the Hawthornes went to Siena. The American sculptor William Wetmore STORY and his wife greeted them, helped them look for lodgings, and drove them about town in their carriage. They remained in the town for two weeks. Hawthorne pronounced it "far more picturesque" than any other town in Italy, standing as it does in the crater of an extinct volcano and, as he put it, "as uneven as the sea in a tempest." He admired the old stone balconies, arched doorways, and windows set in frames of Gothic architecture. He described the architecture as "massive and lofty, yet minutely interesting when you look at it stone by stone."

They took lodgings in an old palace, where they had the second story (or "piano"). It pleased Hawthorne that they would dwell in "faded grandeur," having a former ballroom for their drawing room. It was ornamented with a large fresco devoted to allegories of Fame and Plenty.

ADA SHEPARD and Hawthorne drove in a carriage to the railway station to oversee the unloading of the luggage-van from Florence; they had 10 trunks, a tin band-box, a leather bag containing Hawthorne's journal, and a "script-book" in which he was "sketching out a Romance" (probably *The MARBLE FAUN*).

While in the town they visited the Piazza del Campo and the Palazzo Publico ("as noble and impressive a Gothic structure [the English cathedrals excepted] as I have ever seen," according to Hawthorne's diary). He also admired the marble antique fountain opposite the Palazzo Publico. He felt the piazza and palace displayed an "antique majesty, in the sunshine and the shadow." The Hawthornes were also drawn to the cathedral, situated on the highest point of the city. Hawthorne later returned to the cathedral to make a watercolor sketch of it (*French and Italian Notebooks*, 442–445).

Stoddard, Richard Henry (1825–1903)   American book reviewer, editor, poet, and man of letters. Throughout his career he held a number of positions in order to support his family.

Hawthorne came to know Stoddard, who had visited his family at the Wayside in Concord, and wanted very much to assist him. Stoddard had published a biographical sketch of Hawthorne in the *National Magazine* for January 1853. When Hawthorne was appointed American consul in Liverpool in 1853, he considered taking Stoddard to England with him to act as his secretary, but he did not do so, finally concluding he did not want to be "bothered with a poet" (Miller, *Salem Is My Dwelling Place*, 391). He later wrote letters on Stoddard's behalf to Senator Charles Gordon Atherton and also to John O'Sullivan, founder, editor, and publisher of the DEMOCRATIC REVIEW, in which Hawthorne published a number of early pieces.

He gave Stoddard some practical advice, to know how to hold his brandy. "Most of these public people are inveterate guzzlers," he warned him; "it would never do to let them see you corned, however" (Miller, *Salem Is My Dwelling Place*, 389).

Story, William Wetmore (1819–1885)   An eminent American sculptor living in ROME when the Hawthornes settled there for a number of months in early 1858. Hawthorne had known Story in Boston and called him "the most variously accomplished and brilliant person, the fullest of social life and fire," he had ever seen. Story and his wife made the Hawthornes welcome and accompanied them on a number of excursions. Hawthorne detected, however, a definite quality of "pain and care" bred out of the "richness of his gifts and abundance of his prosperity" (Turner, 322).

Story was once described as more of an Anglo-Italian than an American. He was the author of *Roba di Roma* and a volume of poems, as well as other works. Three of his well-known poems are "After Long Days of Dull Perpetual Rain," "Human Life," and "Little We Know What Secret Influence / A word, a glance, a casual tone may bring."

On one occasion Story and his wife drove Hawthorne into the outskirts of Rome to see a statue of Venus that had recently been discovered; it would later appear in *The MARBLE FAUN*. Turner remarks that it was Story's "statue of Cleopatra, the artistic theories, speculations, and judgments he encountered in the studios of his friends, the paintings, statues, monuments, buildings, and people that filled his Italian days" (Turner, 329).

T

Teatro Goldoni, Florence, Italy In January 1858, at the conclusion of Hawthorne's term as American consul in LIVERPOOL, he took his family to ITALY. They later went back to ENGLAND and did not return to America until 1860.

In Florence, the Hawthornes met the American sculptor Hiram Powers, to whom they had been given a letter of introduction. He assisted them with their search for an apartment, and they stayed with his family while house hunting. One evening, the Hawthornes went to the Powers's home and sat on their terrace at the top of the house. They had a view of the Teatro Goldoni very nearby and heard part of the performance (which may have been a reenactment of one of the plays of the commedia dell'arte, an early form of Italian theater).

Hawthorne recalled that the Teatro Goldoni had an "open amphitheater, in the ancient fashion, without any roof or other covering on top." They heard the music and applause, and "now and then an actor's stentorian tones" (*French and Italian Notebooks*, 377–378).

Thaxter, Celia Laighton (1835–1894) New Hampshire's best-known poet of the 19th century. Celia Thaxter was a friend of the Hawthornes. She grew up on Appledore Island, in the ISLES OF SHOALS, off the coast of New Hampshire, and spent most of her life there. She depicted the various moods of the islands in her work, publishing *Poems* (1872), *Drift-Weed* (1879), *Idylls and Pastorals* (1886), and many other volumes. Her prose sketch of the island appeared in *Among the Isles of Shoals* (1873) and *An Island Garden* (1891).

The Isles of Shoals were the center of colonial fishing industries and, at one time, the economic hub of New England. Celia Thaxter's father, THOMAS B. LAIGHTON, of Portsmouth, moved his family to the islands when he was appointed lighthouse keeper. He later opened Appledore House, which accommodated more than 500 people. One of the nation's first summer resorts, it attracted artists, philosophers, and writers. In his *American Notebooks,* Hawthorne praised the hotel's "long piazza or promenade . . . so situated that the breeze draws across it from the sea on one side of the island to the sea on the other, and it is the breeziest and comfortablest place in the whole world on a hot day."

Celia and her husband, Levi Thaxter, along with their children, were living in Newtonville, Massachusetts, when her husband discovered one of her poems, "Land-locked," which expressed her longing for Appledore Island. He took it to JAMES RUSSELL LOWELL, then editor of the *Atlantic Magazine.* Lowell published it, launching her career as a poet of nature and the sea. Her "Little Sandpiper and I" was a particular favorite with schoolchildren.

Celia Thaxter became famous, attracting many leading literary and artistic figures of Boston to the family resort. She held literary events and readings each summer; among those attending were JOHN GREENLEAF WHITTIER and JAMES T. FIELDS. She died on Appledore Island at the age of 59.

Thompson, Cephas Giovanni Artist who painted Hawthorne's portrait in 1850, when Hawthorne was 46, after the writing of *The Scarlet Letter*. Sophia Amelia Peabody Hawthorne said the portrait's "sad sweetness" made her catch her breath as she gazed at it. "No one has ever drawn or painted anything of Mr. Hawthorne comparable to this, & Mr. Thompson must have a wondrous perception . . . to have seen all he has there expressed" (Wineapple, *Hawthorne: A Life,* 239).

When the Hawthornes went to Rome in 1858, at the conclusion of his tenure as American consul in Liverpool, Hawthorne was able to renew his acquaintance with Thompson. He became a family friend, and, as Hoeltje puts it, Hawthorne "thought of Thompson as a true artist" (Hoeltje, *Inward Sky: The Mind and Heart of Nathaniel Hawthorne,* 462).

Thoreau, Henry David (1817–1862) Poet, naturalist, and essayist, Thoreau was born in Concord, Massachusetts, and educated at Harvard. He was part of the transcendentalist group, which included Ralph Waldo Emerson, Margaret Fuller, Amos Bronson Alcott, and William Ellery Channing. He edited *The Dial,* a transcendentalist journal.

After Hawthorne and Sophia were married, they moved into The Old Manse in Concord. There they entertained Ralph Waldo Emerson, Margaret Fuller, Henry Wadsworth Longfellow, James Russell Lowell, William Ellery Channing, and Thoreau. Thoreau was living at that time in his solitary cabin at Walden and often spoke to Hawthorne of "pine trees and Indian relics" (Hoeltje, *Inward Sky: The Mind and Heart of Nathaniel Hawthorne,* 209). Hawthorne soon began searching for arrowheads with enthusiasm. During this period, Thoreau dined at the Old Manse; Sophia called him "agreeable & gentle & meek," whereas Hawthorne described him as "ugly as sin, long-nosed, queer-mouthed, and with uncouth and somewhat rustic, although courteous manners." He believed him to be sophisticated, however, in his own way. As was Thoreau, Hawthorne had been regarded as something of a misfit in Concord. He was impressed by Thoreau's "Natural History of Massachusetts,"

which was published in the July issue of *The Dial.* He bought Thoreau's canoe for seven dollars and tried to help him launch his writing career by urging John O'Sullivan to publish his work in the *Democratic Review.* O'Sullivan wisely suggested to Thoreau that he write about nature (Wineapple, *Hawthorne: A Life,* 163–165).

From a literary point of view, Hawthorne was indebted to Thoreau for providing the nucleus of some of his writings. Thoreau had told him of the legend of the "deathless man" who had once lived in the "Wayside," and Hawthorne tried, after Thoreau's death, to incorporate the legend in a short story, although he did not succeed. Hoeltje surmises that neither Thoreau nor Hawthorne read the other's books (Hoeltje, *Inward Sky: The Mind and Heart of Nathaniel Hawthorne,* 208–213).

Ticknor, William Davis (1810–1864) Hawthorne's principal publisher. His business was first established in 1832, when he was in partnership with John Allen; the firm was then called Allen and Ticknor. After Allen retired, Ticknor published books under his own name until 1845, when he was joined by John Reed and James T. Fields. During his lifetime, the firm was called William D. Ticknor and Co. After Reed's retirement, it was known as Ticknor and Fields. Their offices were at the corner of Washington and School streets, in Boston.

Turner terms Hawthorne's relationship with Ticknor one of the most important "author-publisher relationships in the history of American letters" (Turner, *Nathaniel Hawthorne: A Biography,* 192). It endured from about 1843 until Ticknor's death, in April 1864, a few weeks before Hawthorne's own death.

Token, The An annual gift book edited by Samuel Griswold Goodrich that was timed to appear just before Christmas and New Year's each year. Hawthorne wrote a number of pieces for this book, including "Alice Doane's Appeal"; "The Gentle Boy"; "The Haunted Quack"; "The May-pole of Merry Mount"; "The Minister's Black Veil"; "The Man of Adamant"; "Monsieur du Miroir";

"Mrs. Bullfrog"; "My Kinsman, Major Molineux"; "The Prophetic Pictures"; and "Roger Malvin's Burial."

Goodrich described Hawthorne as "unsettled as to his views; he had tried his hand in literature, and considered himself to have met with a fatal rebuff from the reading world. His mind vacillated between various projects, verging, I think, toward a mercantile profession" (Wineapple, *Hawthorne: A Life,* 74).

Hawthorne considered dedicating his early collection of stories, *The Gray Champion, and Other Tales,* to Goodrich. He did not do so, however. His longtime Bowdoin College friend Horatio Bridge considered Goodrich to be "selfish and unscrupulous" and thought he was taking advantage of Hawthorne. He wrote to Hawthorne that "*The Token* was saved by your writing. . . . Unless you are already committed, do not mar the prospects of your *first* book by hoisting Goodrich into favor." The book appeared without a dedication (Turner, *Nathaniel Hawthorne: A Biography,* 85–86).

U

Uffizzi Gallery, Florence, Italy In 1858, when Hawthorne concluded his term as American consul in LIVERPOOL, ENGLAND, he and his family went to the Continent. They would not return to America until 1860.

They arrived in Florence in June 1858. Hawthorne recorded a visit he made to the Uffizzi Gallery on June 8. The Uffizzi is a large U-shaped structure stretching from the Palazzo Vecchio to the river Arno and back. Commissioned by Duke Cosimo, it was designed by Georgio Vasari in 1560, not as a museum but as a series of government offices and workshops for the Medici craftsmen. Among the famous artists represented are Leonardo da Vinci, MICHELANGELO, Botticelli, Piero della Francesco, and Giotto.

Hawthorne described his entire visit in his notebook, elaborating on the various galleries. He was particularly interested in busts of the great men of Rome, antique sculptures, and some of the ceilings with frescoes. He searched for the VENUS DE' MEDICI for some time, finally catching a glimpse of her. He described her face as "so beautiful and intellectual, that it is not dazzled out of sight by her body." He resisted further description, stating that it was best to "leave her standing in chaste and naked grace, as untouched as when I began." Her body, however, had suffered; her arms had been broken off, her head had been snapped off at the neck, and there were "grievous wounds and losses of substance in various tender parts of her body." Hawthorne was reassured, however, by the skill with which the statue had been restored. Also, as he stated in his notebook, "by the skill with which the statue has been restored, and partly because the idea is perfect and indestructible, all these injuries do not in the least impair the effect, even when you see where the dissevered fragments have been reunited" (*French and Italian Notebooks*, 298).

He later took Julian to the Uffizzi but was bemused by his son's lack of appreciation of the works of art. He declared in his notebook that Julian had condemned everything he saw except "a fly, a snail-shell, a caterpillar, a lemon, a piece of bread, and a wine-glass, in some of the Dutch pictures." Hawthorne recalled, however, that he himself used to experience a "weary lack of appreciation" in picture galleries (*French and Italian Notebooks*, 350).

Uncle Tom's Cabin Harriet Beecher Stowe's novel was published in 1852, the same year as Hawthorne's *The BLITHEDALE ROMANCE*. His novel received mixed reviews, and it was compared unfavorably by many reviewers with *Uncle Tom's Cabin*. SOPHIA AMELIA PEABODY HAWTHORNE believed Stowe's novel was overrated, "too much addressed to the movable passions—not to the deeper soul." She predicted that it would do "no good to the slave." Many reviewers agreed. However, it became "wildly popular." Hawthorne's publisher, JAMES T. FIELDS, worried about the sales of *Blithedale* and said to a friend, "'Let us hope there are no more Blithedales. . . . the writer of *Uncle Tom's Cabin* is getting to be a millionaire" (Wineapple, *Hawthorne: A Life,* 254–255).

United States Magazine and Democratic Review   Magazine in which a number of Hawthorne's sketches and tales first appeared. These included "The TOLL-GATHERER'S DAY"; "Legends of the Province-house"; "JOHN INGLEFIELD'S THANKSGIVING"; "The NEW ADAM AND EVE"; "EGOTISM: OR, THE BOSOM-SERPENT"; "The PROCESSION OF LIFE"; "The CELESTIAL RAIL-ROAD"; "BUDS AND BIRD-VOICES"; "FIRE-WORSHIP"; "The CHRISTMAS BANQUET"; "The ARTIST OF THE BEAUTIFUL"; "A BOOK OF AUTOGRAPHS"; "RAPPACCINI'S DAUGHTER"; and "P.'S CORRESPONDENCE."

Upham, the Reverend Charles Wentworth (1802–1875)   Clergyman, lecturer, and author of *Salem Witchcraft* (1867) and a number of other works, including *Memoir of Francis Peabody, President of the Essex Institute, Salem* (1868).

Charles Sumner once called Upham "that oily man of God." Upham did not appreciate Hawthorne and drew up false charges that caused Hawthorne to be relieved of his post as surveyor in the Salem Custom-House in June 1849. Hawthorne had held this post since 1846. He was replaced by Captain Allen Putnam, who was confirmed by the U.S. Senate on September 24, 1850. His reinstatement was blocked by Upham's "Memorial of the Whigs of Salem in regard to Mr. Hawthorne," of which Wineapple gives a full account. Upham was not the only influential citizen of Salem to resent Hawthorne's holding such a post even as he became a successful writer (Wineapple, *Hawthorne: A Life,* 204–205).

Hoeltje suggests that Upham was the prototype of Judge Jaffrey Pyncheon in *The HOUSE OF THE SEVEN GABLES* (Hoeltje, *Inward Sky: The Mind and Heart of Nathaniel Hawthorne,* 346–347).

For Further Reading

Ellis, George Edward, *Memoir of Charles Wentworth Upham* (Cambridge, Mass.: Press of J. Wilson and Son, 1877).

Upham, Thomas Cogswell   One of Hawthorne's most influential teachers at BOWDOIN COLLEGE, although he arrived only a year before Hawthorne graduated. Upham's specialty was "commonsense philosophy" (Wineapple, *Hawthorne: A Life,* 52), but in 1819 he published a book of poems about New England, called *American Sketches.* He also wrote *Elements of Moral Philosophy, Principles of the Interior or Hidden Life,* and *A Treatise on Divine Union* (Miller, *Salem Is My Dwelling Place,* 63–64).

Van Buren, Martin (1782–1862) Van Buren, a native of New York State, was admitted to the bar in 1803. He served as governor of New York from 1828 to 1829. He was the eighth president of the United States, from 1837 to 1841. Hawthorne supported the Democrats throughout the Van Buren administration. Van Buren became the Free-Soil candidate for the presidency in 1848, but Zachary Taylor won the U.S. presidency at that time. This election result caused Hawthorne to lose his very desirable position in the Salem Custom-House.

Venus de' Medici This statue by Cleomenes, son of the Greek artist Apollodorus, who lived in Rome in the first or second century, was discovered in 11 fragments in the Portico of Octavia in Rome. Much of it has been restored, including the right and left arms from the elbows downward. The statue was later moved to the UFFIZZI GALLERY in Florence but was seriously damaged in the process.

While living in Italy, Hawthorne visited the Uffizzi and saw the statue. Beforehand, he had been apprehensive lest he be disappointed; he wrote that he "apprehended the extinction of another of those lights that shine along a man's pathway, and go out in a snuff the instant he comes within eyeshot of the fulfillment of his hopes." He eventually caught a glimpse of her in an octagonal room, surrounded by an iron railing. He wrote that she had a "fresh and new charm . . . unreached by any cast or copy." He felt a "kind of tenderness for her, an affection, not as if she were one woman, but all womanhood in one." The next morning, he returned to the Uffizi and revisited the statue. He saw her as a "being that lives to gladden the world, incapable of decay and death, as young and fair today as she was three thousand years ago."

He and his family then called on the American sculptor Hiram Powers, who began attacking the statue on aesthetic grounds. He felt that her eye looked like a buttonhole, her ear was too low, and her forehead and mouth were wrong. The Hawthornes returned the next day to the Uffizzi and inspected the statue again. He could not see many of the defects observed by Powers and believed ultimately that the original sculptor "intentionally made every feature what it is, and calculated them all with a view to the desired effect." He considered it a "noble and beautiful face" (*Italian Notebook*, 287–311).

Vesta, Temple of Hawthorne and his family visited the erroneously named Temple of Vesta (actually the Temple of Hercules Victor) in March 1858, while they were living in Rome. He called it the "most perfectly preserved Roman ruin" that he had yet seen and described it at length in his *Italian Notebook*. He remarked that it was so small it might well be mistaken for a garden house "rather than an ancient temple." The solid structure of the temple, he reported, was surrounded by a circle of white pillars, "time-worn and a little battered." The roof resembled a round wicker basket cover.

The Corinthian pillars, however, were admirable, and he speculated that when they were new, "and the marble snow-white, and sharply carved and cut, there could not have been a prettier object in all Rome." The interior was a plain marble cylinder, about "ten paces across," and was "fitted up as a Chapel, when the Virgin took the place of Vesta." On the whole, however, Hawthorne felt it was too small to "figure well" as a ruin, unlike the nearby Temple of Fortuna Virilis, which was much better preserved.

Villa Montauto   The Hawthorne family, accompanied by Ada Shepard, a companion and tutor for the children, visited Florence in the summer of 1858. Because the heat was oppressive, the family took the suburban Villa Montauto for two months. It was situated on a hill called Bellosguardo, a mile beyond the Porta Romana. According to Hawthorne's notebook, the villa had an old square tower, "machicolated and battlemented," dating from the Middle Ages. The tower was gray and "venerable of aspect," but the villa itself was covered with modern stucco.

On August 1, the family moved into the villa. As Hawthorne described it in his notebook, there were many "crazy staircases" and dusty rooms. The Hawthornes had heard a story of the imprisonment of Savonarola, the famous friar noted for his reforms, in the villa, although Hawthorne himself was skeptical. The house was of a "bewildering extent," large enough that each member of the family, as

well as Miss Shepard, could have a suite of rooms. Hawthorne himself had a dressing room, a "large vaulted saloon," and a "square writing-closet." The ceilings were ornamented with frescoes of angels, cherubs, temples, pillars, statues, vases, vines, and sunflowers. Una's chamber had its own small oratory with early sacred prints.

There were no carpets on the floors, as these, according to Hawthorne, were traditionally taken up in Italy during the hot summer. The grounds had gravel walks and ornamental shrubbery. There were many laborers on the estate. At night, the Hawthornes faced the difficult task of fastening the iron gate, the ponderous doors, iron-barred windows, and shutters.

The owner was Count Montauto, who, during the summer, let the villa and lived in his palace in Florence. This practice mystified Hawthorne, who had found the city sweltering and the heat intolerable.

While they were in residence in the villa, the sculptor William Story and others often called on them. They would frequently climb up to the tower to see the sunset and on some days go into town to call on people to whom they had been given introductions. Hawthorne made copious entries in his notebook during their stay in the villa, which the entire family much preferred to spending the hot summer in Florence itself.

W

Walden Pond   Once the site of HENRY DAVID THOREAU'S CABIN, WALDEN POND, IN CONCORD, MASSACHUSETTS, is now the Walden Pond State Reservation.

After Hawthorne and Sophia were married in 1842, they moved into THE OLD MANSE in Concord. There they entertained many friends, including Thoreau. Thoreau was living at that time in his solitary cabin at Walden and often spoke to Hawthorne of "pine trees and Indian relics" (Hoeltje, *Inward Sky: The Mind and Heart of Nathaniel Hawthorne,* 209).

One morning, Hawthorne and their houseguest GEORGE HILLARD walked to the pond, stopping for a call at the home of RALPH WALDO EMERSON. Hawthorne described the pond as "embosomed among wooded hills, not very extensive, but large enough for waves to dance upon its surface, and to look like a piece of blue firmament, earth-encircled." It had a bottom of pure white sand. They swam in the pond, and Hawthorne wrote of the experience in his *American Notebook:* It had really seemed as though his "moral self" as well as his "corporeal person" had received a cleansing (*American Notebook,* 157).

In October 1843, Hawthorne recorded a solitary walk to Walden Pond. His sister Louisa, who was visiting them for several days, had stayed home with Sophia, who was expecting a baby in late February or early March (Una Hawthorne was born on March 3 at the Old Manse). Hawthorne swam in the pond, saying the water was "thrillingly cold" and transparent. He felt that "none but angels should bathe there." He stated

that it would be a "fit bathing place" for his "little wife" and expressed the hope that "sometime or other" their "blessed baby shall be dipt into its bosom."

Thoreau went to live at Walden Pond on July 4, 1845, and remained there until September 1847.

Watts, Anna Mary Howitt   Editor of *A Treasury of New Favorite Tales* (1861), in which Hawthorne's story "The CHIMAERA" was reprinted from the first edition of *A WONDER-BOOK FOR BOYS AND GIRLS* (1852).

Wayside, The   Former home of the American transcendentalist philosopher, poet, and teacher AMOS BRONSON ALCOTT, in CONCORD, MASSACHUSETTS. In February 1852, Hawthorne purchased the house, along with nine acres of land, for $1,500 (Turner, *Nathaniel Hawthorne: A Biography,* 241–242). This would be the only house the family ever owned.

Hawthorne wrote to EVERT AUGUSTUS DUYCKINCK that it was "no very splendid mansion" and had been neglected so that it was "the raggedest in the world," but he was convinced it would eventually make "a comfortable and sufficiently pleasant home." Alcott had called it Hillside, but Hawthorne rebaptized it The Wayside, a name possessing a "moral as well as descriptive propriety" (*The Letters,* 16, 548).

According to Brenda Wineapple, the family extended the house upward to three stories and added two stories toward the west. Hawthorne

In February 1852, Hawthorne purchased this home, along with nine acres of land, for $1,500. It would be the only property the Hawthornes ever owned, and they named it "The Wayside." *(Photo courtesy of the Library of Congress)*

used the tower structure for writing. Bronson Alcott, who lived nearby, took an active interest in his former home; he "cut paths and planted gardens in the rear of the house." He also cut tree branches and talked with Hawthorne about "grapes and the consanguinity of people and plants." HENRY DAVID THOREAU surveyed the property for the Hawthornes (Wineapple, *Hawthorne: A Life,* 335).

In 1857, the Hawthornes went to LIVERPOOL; Hawthorne had been appointed American consul there. They remained abroad, on the Continent as well as in England, until 1860 and returned to the Wayside on June 18.

Weal-Reaf, The: A Record of the Essex Institute Fair
A newspaper in eight parts, distributed for the Essex Institute Fair in 1860. The editors pub-

lished a letter from Hawthorne titled "Browne's Folly."

Whipple, Edwin Percy Journalist who reviewed many of Hawthorne's books for the influential periodical GRAHAM'S MAGAZINE, ATLANTIC MONTHLY, the BOSTON DAILY GLOBE, and other publications. He considered THE HOUSE OF THE SEVEN GABLES brilliant in "conception and execution."

Whittier, John Greenleaf (1807–1892) American poet and editor. A Quaker, he was interested in social reform and wrote for a number of abolitionist publications. He became one of the most popular New England poets of his day.

Hawthorne and Whittier were published in many of the same periodicals but never became friends. On September 30, 1854, Hawthorne wrote to his publisher WILLIAM DAVIS TICKNOR, "I like the man, but have no high opinion either of his poetry or prose" (Hawthorne, *The American Notebooks*, note 566, p. 329).

Williams, Roger   A historical figure in Hawthorne's tale "ENDICOTT AND THE RED CROSS." Born in London about 1603, Williams was educated at Cambridge and intended to become a lawyer. He shifted his professional course, however, and by 1629, he had taken orders in the Anglican Church. He was increasingly influenced by the Puritans, and, in 1631, he went to Massachusetts. He then went to Salem as a minister. His views of church government and his espousal of Protestant individualism and human rights soon made him anathema to the Massachusetts theocracy. He disapproved of the expropriation of Indian rights. His church at Salem was considered to be democratic in nature.

In Hawthorne's tale, when the Wanton Gospeller asks Endicott whether his strict vision of the worship of God really represents "liberty of conscience," he depicts Roger Williams as having a "sad and quiet smile" flitting across his "mild visage." Later in Hawthorne's tale, Williams reacts cautiously to John Endicott's fury when he opens the sealed letter from Governor Winthrop. He reminds Endicott that his words are "not meet for a secret chamber, far less for a public street." Endicott, however, silences him, insisting that his own spirit is "wiser" than that of Williams. He then turns to the ominous matter at hand. He warns the colonists that King Charles I and Archbishop Laud want to establish "idolatrous forms of English Episcopacy." Williams, though, takes a longer view and suggests that there should be a separation of spiritual concerns from social and political powers. Williams's role as peace-maker is diminished when Endicott furiously cuts the Red Cross out of the banner of New England, and he takes no further part in the narrative. John Nickel suggests that in this tale, Hawthorne's depiction of Williams actually serves as a vehicle for his own "self-presentation" ("Hawthorne's Demystification of History in 'Endicott and the Red Cross,'" *Texas Studies in Literature and Language*, 42 [Winter 2000]: 347–353).

Witchcraft delusion   Hawthorne's birthplace, Salem, Massachusetts, had been the site of the hysterical persecution of witches and wizards in 1692. A number of young girls accused some older women of bewitching them. Eventually, hundreds of people were accused; more than 140 people were arrested. Nineteen people were hanged on Gallows Hill, and at least two others died in jail. Fifty-five were forced into false confessions. The events were aggravated by the spread of an epidemic disease resembling epilepsy in Danvers, then part of Salem. The clergyman Cotton Mather incited controversy and the conviction that evil spirits were responsible ("Salem Witchcraft Trials," *The Oxford Companion to American Literature*, 737–738). An ancestor of Hawthorne, John Hawthorne (1641–1717), was a magistrate who took part in the witchcraft hearings. He has been termed "earnest and unyielding" but apparently lacking vindictive harshness and cruelty (Turner, *Nathaniel Hawthorne: A Biography*, 64–65).

Cotton Mather was later condemned by CHARLES UPHAM, minister of the First Church, who gave two lectures on the witchcraft delusion; they were published in 1831 as *Lectures on Witchcraft.* He castigated not only Mather, but also Samuel Parris and Nicholas Noyes, as "purveyors of superstition and vindictiveness" (Turner, *Nathaniel Hawthorne: A Biography*, 66). In 1656, the historical figure Mistress Hibbins was hanged in Boston as a witch; Matthew Maule introduces this event into *The HOUSE OF THE SEVEN GABLES.*

The historic witchcraft persecutions are a recurrent theme in the works of Hawthorne. There are allusions to it in "DROWNE'S WOODEN IMAGE," in which an elderly Puritan man accuses Drowne of selling his soul to the devil when his exquisitely carved figurehead of a woman comes briefly to life. The story "EDWARD RANDOLPH'S PORTRAIT," in "LEGENDS OF THE PROVINCE-HOUSE," turns on an ancient, dark picture in the Province-House during the term of Lieutenant-Governor Hutchinson. There is a legend that it depicts the Evil One, taken at a witch meeting near Salem.

The story "YOUNG GOODMAN BROWN" may represent Hawthorne's fullest exploration of witchcraft. Certain witches who were historic figures, hanged in 1692, make appearances in the tale. Hawthorne examines, through Goodman Brown's experiences, the pervasiveness of sin and explores the psychology of the witchcraft frenzy that dominated Salem at the time. Edward Wagenknecht points out that Hawthorne had to "purge himself in his own mind of the sins of his ancestors. . . . The Salem outburst was a 'terrible delusion' . . . in which 'innocent persons' suffered wrongful death" (*Nathaniel Hawthorne: Man and Writer*, 175).

In Salem today, visitors may see the Witch House, where those accused of witchcraft were examined, as well as the Salem Witch Museum and the Witch Dungeon Museum.

For Further Reading

Baym, Nina, *The Shape of Hawthorne's Career* (Ithaca, N.Y.: Cornell University Press, 1976); Bercovitch, Sacvan, "Diabolus in Salem," *English Language Notes* 6 (1969): 280–285; Cantwell, Robert, *Nathaniel Hawthorne: The American Years* (New York: Rinehart, 1948); Miller, Edwin, *Salem Is My Dwelling Place* (Iowa City: University of Iowa Press, 1991).

Worcester, Joseph Emerson (1784–1865) One of Hawthorne's early teachers; he had a school on Federal Street, in Salem, Massachusetts. At the age of nine, Hawthorne ceased going to school for more than a month after an accident that caused a lengthy period of lameness. Worcester went to the home of the Mannings on Herbert Street, where Hawthorne was living with his mother, sisters, and other relatives, to hear his lessons (Turner, *Nathaniel Hawthorne: A Biography*, 18).

Worcester later achieved fame through his writings. Among his most noted works were *Elements of History, Ancient and Modern* (1850), and *A Comprehensive Dictionary of the English Language* (1860).

Wrigley, Fanny Nursemaid whom Hawthorne and his wife, Sophia, engaged for Rose, the youngest of their three children, when they lived in LIVERPOOL, ENGLAND.

X–Z

Xenophon (c. 430–c. 355 B.C.) Athenian writer who assisted in leading 10,000 Greeks through Persia to the Black Sea. He wrote of the expedition in the *Anabasis*. Hawthorne studied the writings of Xenophon at BOWDOIN COLLEGE.

Youth's Keepsake (Youth's Keepsake: A Christmas and New Year's Gift for Young People) Magazine in which "LITTLE ANNIE'S RAMBLE" was published, before it was collected in the first edition of TWICE-TOLD TALES (1837).

PART IV

Appendices

CHRONOLOGY OF NATHANIEL HAWTHORNE'S LIFE

1804

Nathaniel Hathorne is born on July 4, in Salem, Massachusetts, to Nathaniel Hathorne (1780–1808) and Elizabeth Clarke Manning (1780–1849); he later changes his last name to Hawthorne. His elder sister, Elizabeth, had been born in 1802.

1808

Nathaniel Hathorne Sr. dies, at the age of 28. Hawthorne's younger sister, Mary Louisa, is born.

1813

Foot injury forces Hawthorne into a state of semi-invalidism for two years; during this time, his appetite for reading develops.

1816

Hawthorne spends time on Lake Sebago, near Raymond, Maine, where he delights in nature.

1821

Hawthorne's maternal uncle, Robert Manning, sends him to Bowdoin College, near Brunswick, Maine. Fellow students include Henry Wadsworth Longfellow and Franklin Pierce.

1825

Hawthorne graduates from Bowdoin College.

1828

Hawthorne publishes *Fanshawe* anonymously, at his own expense.

1830

The Salem *Gazette* publishes his "The Hollow of Three Hills."

1836

Hawthorne edits the *American Magazine of Useful and Entertaining Knowledge.*

1837

With his sister Elizabeth Hawthorne, Hawthorne publishes *Peter Parley's Universal History,* and *Twice-told Tales.*

1839

Hawthorne becomes engaged to Sophia Amelia Peabody.

1839–1840

Hawthorne is employed in the Boston Custom-House.

1841

Hawthorne lives at the transcendentalist Brook Farm Institute of Agriculture and Education, West Roxbury, Massachusetts. He publishes *Grandfather's Chair* (stories from New England history for children), *Famous Old People,* and *Liberty Tree.*

1842

Hawthorne and Sophia Peabody are married (July 9) at the Peabodys' home on West Street, Boston. They rent the Old Manse, Concord, for the next three years. He publishes *Biographical Stories for Children.*

1844
Una Hawthorne is born March 3 at the Old Manse.

1845
Hawthorne edits and improves the *Journal of an African Cruiser* by Horatio Bridge.

1846–1849
Hawthorne is employed in the Salem Custom-House.

1846
Julian Hawthorne is born June 22 in Boston.

1846
Hawthorne publishes *Mosses from an Old Manse.*

1849
Elizabeth Clarke Manning Hathorne, Hawthorne's mother, dies.

1850
Hawthorne publishes *The Scarlet Letter.*

1850–1851
The Hawthornes rent a farmhouse at Lenox, Massachusetts, in the Berkshires.

1851
Rose Hawthorne is born in Lenox on May 20.

1851–1852
The Hawthornes live in West Newton, Massachusetts.

1851
Hawthorne publishes *The House of the Seven Gables, The Snow Image and Other Twice-*

told *Tales,* and *True Stories from History and Biography.*

1852
The Hawthornes purchase Amos Bronson Alcott's home, Hillside, in Concord, Massachusetts, in May. They rename it The Wayside. This will be the only house they own.

1852
Hawthorne publishes *The Blithedale Romance, A Wonder Book for Girls and Boys,* and *The Life of Franklin Pierce* (a campaign biography).

1853
Hawthorne publishes *Tanglewood Tales for Girls and Boys.*

1853–1857
President Pierce appoints Hawthorne United States consul at Liverpool, England.

1857–1860
The Hawthornes live in Europe, principally in England and in Italy.

1860
Hawthorne returns to The Wayside June 18. He publishes *The Marble Faun.*

1863
Hawthorne's health worsens. He publishes *Our Old Home.*

1864
Hawthorne dies May 19 at Plymouth, New Hampshire. On May 23 he is buried on Author's Ridge, Sleepy Hollow Cemetery, Concord, Massachusetts.

CHRONOLOGY OF MAJOR WORKS BY NATHANIEL HAWTHORNE

1828
Fanshawe

1830
"The Hollow of the Three Hills"

1831
"Dr. Bullivant"

1833
"The Seven Vagabonds"

1835
"The Ambitious Guest," "The Canal Boat," "Alice Doane's Appeal," "The Vision of the Fountain," "The Devil in Manuscript"

1836
(Editor) *The American Magazine of Useful and Entertaining Knowledge*, "Thomas Green Fessenden" (January 1836) and "Old Ticonderoga. A Picture of the Past"

1837
Contributes to *Peter Parley Series for Children*; writes *Peter Parley's Universal History* with his sister Elizabeth; publishes *Twice-told Tales*; "A Bell's Biography," "The Minister's Black Veil," "Dr. Heidegger's Experiment," "Edward Fane's Rosebud," "Sylph Etherege," "David Swan—A Fantasy," "Mrs. Bullfrog"

1838
"Chippings with a Chisel," "Roger Malvin's Burial," "Snow-Flakes," "Howe's Masquerade,"
"Edward Randolph's Portrait," "Lady Eleanore's Mantle"

1839
"Night Sketches under an Umbrella," "Old Esther Dudley," "The Lily's Quest: An Apologue"

1840
"John Inglefield's Thanksgiving"

1841
Grandfather's Chair, "The Provincial Muster," "Famous Old People"

1842
Biographical Stories for Children, "The Village Uncle"

1843
"The Birth-Mark," "Little Daffydowndilly," "Buds and Bird-Voices," "The Antique Ring"

1844
"The Artist of the Beautiful," "Rappaccini's Daughter," "Earth's Holocaust," "The Intelligence Office," "A Book of Autographs," "The Celestial Rail-road" (1844–46), "Drowne's Wooden Image"

1846
Mosses from An Old Manse

1847
American Notebooks

1850
The Scarlet Letter

1851

The House of the Seven Gables, The Snow-Image and Other Twice-told Tales, True Stories from History and Biography

1852

The Blithedale Romance, A Wonder Book for Girls and Boys, "The Canterbury Pilgrims," *The Life of Franklin Pierce* (campaign biography), "The Dragon's Teeth"

1853

Tanglewood Tales for Girls and Boys

1860

The Marble Faun

1861

"Near Oxford"

1862

"Chiefly About War-Matters," "Leamington Spa," "Pilgrimage to Old Boston"

1863

Our Old Home, "A London Suburb," "Outside Glimpses of English Poverty," "Consular Experiences"

1864

[Hawthorne dies at Plymouth, New Hampshire]

1876

The Dolliver Romance (published posthumously)

SELECTED BIBLIOGRAPHY
OF SECONDARY SOURCES

Aaron, Daniel. *The Unwritten War: American Writers and the Civil War.* New York: Alfred A. Knopf, 1973.

Arvin, Newton. *Hawthorne.* Boston: Little, Brown, 1929.

Baym, Nina. "*The Blithedale Romance*: A Radical Reading." *Journal of English and Germanic Philology* 67 (1968): 545–569.

———. "*The Marble Faun*: Hawthorne's Elegy for Art." *New England Quarterly* 44 (1971): 355–376.

———. *The Shape of Hawthorne's Career.* Ithaca, N.Y.: Cornell University Press, 1976.

Beauchamp, Gorman. "Hawthorne and the Universal Reformers." *Utopian Studies: Journal of the Society for Utopian Studies* 13, no. 2 (2002): 38–52.

Bell, Michael Davitt. *Hawthorne and the Historical Romance of New England.* Princeton, N.J.: Princeton University Press, 1971.

Bellis, Peter J. *Writing Revolution: Aesthetics and Politics in Hawthorne, Whitman, and Thoreau.* Athens: University of Georgia Press, 2003.

Benesch, Klaus. "Between Reproduction and Authenticity: The Contested Status of Authorship in Hawthorne's 'The Artist of the Beautiful.'" *Rivista di Studi Anglo-Americani* 10 (1994): 116–123.

Bensick, Carol M. "Dimmesdale and His Bachelorhood: 'Priestly Celibacy' in *The Scarlet Letter.*" *Studies in American Fiction* 21 (1993): 103–110.

Bercovitch, Sacvan. "The A-Politics of Ambiguity in *The Scarlet Letter.*" *New Literary History* 19 (1988): 629–654.

Berthea, Dean Wentworth. "Heat, Light, and the Darkening World: Hawthorne's 'The Artist of the Beautiful.'" *South Atlantic Review* 56 (November 1991): 23–35.

Blythe, Hal, and Charlie Sweet. "Hawthorne's Dating Problem in *The Scarlet Letter.*" *ANQ: A Quarterly Journal of Short Articles, Notes, and Reviews* 16, no. 3 (summer 2003): 35–37.

Bridge, Horatio. *Journal of an African Cruiser.* 1853. Reprint, Detroit: Negro History Press, n.d.

———. *Personal Recollections of Nathaniel Hawthorne.* 1893. Reprint, New York: Haskell House, 1968.

Bruccoli, Matthew J. "A Lost Hawthorne Manuscript: 'Buds and Bird-Voices.'" *The Nathaniel Hawthorne Journal* 1971.

Cantwell, Robert. *Nathaniel Hawthorne: The American Years.* New York: Rinehart, 1948.

Clark, C. E. Frazer, Jr. *Nathaniel Hawthorne: A Descriptive Bibliography.* Pittsburgh: University of Pittsburgh Press, 1978.

Clark, Michael. "Another Look at the Scaffold Scenes in Hawthorne's *The Scarlet Letter.*" *American Transcendental Quarterly* n.s., 1 (1987): 135–144.

Crews, Frederick C. *The Sins of the Fathers: Hawthorne's Psychological Themes.* New York: Oxford University Press, 1966.

Crowley, J. Donald, ed. *Nathaniel Hawthorne: The Critical Heritage.* London and New York: Routledge, 1970.

DeSalvo, Louise. *Nathaniel Hawthorne.* Atlantic Highlands, N.J.: Humanities Press International, 1987.

Dolis, John. "Domesticating Hawthorne: Home Is for the Birds." *Criticism: A Quarterly for Literature and the Arts* 43, no. 1 (winter 2001): 7–28.

Donoghue, Denis. "Hawthorne and Sin." *Christianity and Literature* 52 (winter 2003): 215–234.

Dunne, Michael. "Natural and Imposed Order in Two Sketches by Hawthorne." *Nathaniel Hawthorne Journal* 8 (1978): 197–202.

Elbert, Monika. "Hester on the Scaffold, Dimmesdale in the Closet: Hawthorne's Seven Year Itch." *Essays in Literature* 16 (1989): 234–255.

Emmett, Paul J. "The Murder of Judge Pyncheon: Confusion and Suggestion in *The House of the Seven Gables*." *Journal of Evolutionary Psychology* 24, no. 2–3 (August 2003): 189–195.

Erlich, Gloria. *Family Themes and Hawthorne's Fiction: The Tenacious Web*. New Brunswick, N.J.: Rutgers University Press, 1984.

Fay, Stephanie. "Lights from Dark Corners: Works of Art in 'The Prophetic Pictures' and 'The Artist of the Beautiful.'" *Studies in American Fiction* 13 (spring 1985): 15–29.

Fields, James T. *Yesterdays with Authors*. 1900. Reprint, New York: AMS Press, 1970.

FitzPatrick, Martin. "'To a Practised Touch': Miles Coverdale and Hawthorne's Irony." *American Transcendental Quarterly* 14, no. 1 (March 2000): 28–46.

Fletcher, Angus. *Allegory: The Theory of a Symbolic Mode*. Ithaca, N.Y.: Cornell University Press, 1964.

Folsom, James F. *Man's Accidents and God's Purposes: Multiplicity in Hawthorne's Fiction*. New Haven, Conn.: College and University Press, 1963.

Fossum, Robert H. *Hawthorne's Inviolable Circle: The Problem of Time*. Deland, Fla.: Everett/Edwards, 1972.

Franklin, Rosemary F. "The Seashore Sketches in *Twice-told Tales* and Melville." *English Language Notes* 21, no. 4 (June 1984): 57–63.

Friedman, Thomas. "Strangers Kill: A Reading of Hawthorne's 'The Ambitious Guest.'" *Cuyahoga Review* 1, no. 2 (fall 1983): 129–140.

Gibbens, Victor E. "Hawthorne's Note to 'Dr. Heidegger's Experiment.'" *Modern Language Notes* 60, no. 6 (June 1945): 408–409.

Gordon, Joseph T. "Nathaniel Hawthorne and Brook Farm." *ESQ: A Journal of the American Renaissance* 33 (1963): 51–61.

Grossberg, Benjamin. "'The Tender Passion Was Very Rife among Us': Coverdale's Queer Utopia and *The Blithedale Romance*." *Studies in American Fiction* 28, no. 1 (spring 2000): 3–25.

Hastings, Louise. "An Origin for "Dr. Heidegger's Experiment." *American Literature: A Journal of Literary History, Criticism, and Bibliography* 9, no. 4 (January 1938): 403–410.

Hawthorne, Julian. *Hawthorne and His Circle*. New York: Harder, 1903.

[Hawthorne, Nathaniel]. *Delia Bacon: A Biographical Sketch*. Boston and New York: Houghton, Mifflin and Company, 1888. (Previously unpublished material from letters).

Hawthorne, Sophia. *Notes in England and Italy*. Italy: Putnam and Sons, 1869.

Heilman, Robert B. "Hawthorne's 'The Birth-Mark': Science as Religion." *The South Atlantic Quarterly* 48 (October 1949): 575–583.

Hoeltje, Hubert H. *Inward Sky: The Mind and Heart of Nathaniel Hawthorne*. Durham, N.C.: Duke University Press, 1962.

Hostetler, John. "'Earth's Holocaust': Hawthorne's Parable of the Imaginative Process." *Kansas Quarterly* 7, no. 4 (1975): 85–89.

Idol, John L., Jr., and Buford Jones, eds. *Nathaniel Hawthorne: The Contemporary Reviews*. Cambridge: Cambridge University Press, 1994.

James, Henry. *Hawthorne*. 1879. Reprint, Ithaca, N.Y.: Cornell University Press, 1956.

Johnston, Mark. "'The Canterbury Pilgrims': Hawthorne's Typical Story." *Essays in Arts and Sciences* 12, no. 1 (March 1983): 37–41.

Jordan, Gretchen Graf. "Hawthorne's 'Bell': Historical Evolution through Symbol." *Nineteenth-Century Fiction* 19, no. 2 (September 1964): 123–139.

Kaul, A. N. "*The Blithedale Romance*," in *The American Vision: Actual and Ideal Society in Nineteenth-Century Fiction*. New Haven, Conn.: Yale University Press, 1963.

Kennelly, Laura. "Mark Goldsmith's History in 'The Antique Ring.'" *Nathaniel Hawthorne Review* 15, no. 1 (spring 1989): 24–25.

Kolich, Augustus M. "Miriam and the Conversion of the Jews in Nathaniel Hawthorne's *The Marble Faun*." *Studies in the Novel* 33, no. 4 (winter 2001): 430–443.

Kupsch, Kenneth. "The Modern Tragedy of Blithedale." *Studies in the Novel* 36, no. 1 (spring 2004): 1–20.

Lammers, John. "Powers' Eve Tempted: Sculpture and 'The Birth-mark.'" *Publications of the Arkansas Philological Association* 21, no. 2 (fall 1994): 41–58.

Lauber, John. "Hawthorne's Shaker Tales." *Nineteenth-Century Fiction* 18, no. 1 (June 1963): 82–86.

Lefcowitz, Alan, and Barbara Lefcowitz. "Some Rents in the Veil: New Light on Priscilla and Zenobia in *The Blithedale Romance.*" *Nineteenth-Century Fiction* 21 (1966): 263–276.

Loebel, Thomas. "'A' Confession: How to Avoid Speaking the Name of the Father." *Arizona Quarterly: A Journal of American Literature, Culture, and Theory* 59, no. 1 (spring 2003): 1–29.

Loges, Max. "Hawthorne's *The House of the Seven Gables.*" *Explicator* 60, no. 2 (winter 2002): 64–66.

Magretta, Joan. "The Coverdale Translation: *Blithedale* and the Bible." *Nathaniel Hawthorne Journal* (1974): 250–256.

Martin, Terence. *Nathaniel Hawthorne.* Boston: Twayne, 1983.

Matheson, Neill. "Melancholy History in *The House of the Seven Gables.*" *Literature and Psychology* 48, no. 3 (2002): 1–37.

Matsusaka, Hitoshi. "Hawthorne's 'Egotism' and the Ambiguous Snake." *Chu-Shikoku Studies in American Literature* 26 (June 1990): 1–9.

Matthiessen, F. O. *American Renaissance: Art and Expression in the Age of Emerson and Whitman.* New York: Oxford University Press, 1941.

Mellow, James R. *Nathaniel Hawthorne in His Times.* Boston: Houghton Mifflin, 1980.

Miller, Edwin Haviland. *Salem Is My Dwelling Place: A Life of Nathaniel Hawthorne.* Iowa City: University of Iowa Press, 1991.

Miller, John N. "Eros and Ideology: At the Heart of Hawthorne's Blithedale." *Nineteenth-Century Literature* 55, no. 1 (June 2000): 1–21.

Milliman, Craig. "Hester Prynne as the Artist of the Beautiful." *Publications of the Mississippi Philological Association* (1995): 82–87.

Mills, Angela. "'The Sweet Word,' Sister: The Transformative Threat of Sisterhood and *The Blithedale Romance.*" *American Transcendental Quarterly* 17, no. 2 (June 2003): 97–121.

Monteiro, George. "A Nonliterary Source for Hawthorne's 'Egotism: or the Bosom Serpent,'" *American Literature* 41 (1970): 575–577.

Morsberger, Robert E. "Hawthorne: The Civil War as the Unpardonable Sin." *Nathaniel Hawthorne Journal* (1977): 111–122.

Newberry, Frederick. "'The Artist of the Beautiful': Crossing the Transcendent Divide in Hawthorne's Fiction." *Nineteenth-Century Literature* 50 (June 1995), 78–96.

Newlin, Paul A. "'Vague Shapes of the Borderland': The Place of the Uncanny in Hawthorne's Gothic Vision." *Emerson Society Quarterly* 67 (1972): 83–96.

Normand, Jean. *Nathaniel Hawthorne: An Approach to an Analysis of Artistic Creation.* Cleveland: Case Western Reserve, 1970.

Onderdonk, Todd. "The Marble Mother: Hawthorne's Iconographies of the Feminine." *Studies in American Fiction* 31, no. 1 (spring 2003): 73–100.

Pattison, Joseph C. "'The Celestial Rail-road' as Dream-Tale." *American Quarterly* 20 (1968): 224–236.

Pearce, Colin D. "Hawthorne's 'My Kinsman, Major Molineux.'" *Explicator* 60, no. 1 (fall 2001): 19–22.

Pennell, Melissa. *Student Companion to Nathaniel Hawthorne.* Westport, Conn.: Greenwood Press, 1999.

Plambeck, Vernon L. "Hearth Imagery and the Element of Home in Hawthorne's 'The Ambitious Guest.'" *Platte Valley Review* 9, no. 1 (April 1981): 68–71.

Prochazka, Martin. "Mechanic?-Organic? The Machines of Art in 'The Artist of the Beautiful.'" *Litteraria Pragensia: Studies in Literature & Culture* 10 (2000): 3–15.

Reid, Bethany. "Narrative of the Captivity and Redemption of Roger Prynne: Rereading *The Scarlet Letter.*" *Studies in the Novel* 33 (fall 2001): 247–268.

Rosenberg, Liz. "'The Best That Earth Could Offer': 'The Birth-mark,' a Newlywed's Story." *Studies in Short Fiction* 30, no. 2 (spring 1993): 145–151.

Roulston, C. Robert. "Hawthorne's Use of Bunyan's Symbols in 'The Celestial Rail-road.'" *Kentucky Philological Association Bulletin* (1975): 17–24.

Rucker, Mary E. "Science and Art in Hawthorne's 'The Birth-Mark.'" *Nineteenth-Century Literature* 41, no. 4 (March 1987): 445–461.

Scanlon, Lawrence E. "That Very Singular Man, Dr. Heidegger." *Nineteenth-Century Fiction* 17, no. 3 (December 1962): 253–263.

Schriber, Mary Sue. "Emerson, Hawthorne, and 'The Artist of the Beautiful.'" *Studies in Short Fiction* 8 (1971): 607–616.

Sears, John F. "Hawthorne's 'The Ambitious Guest' and the Significance of the Willey Disaster." *American Literature: A Journal of Literary History, Criticism, and Bibliography* 54, no. 3 (October 1982): 354–357.

Secor, Robert. "Hawthorne's Canterbury Pilgrims." *Explicator* 22 (1963): 8.

Stewart, Randall. *Hawthorne: A Biography.* 1948. Reprint, Hamden, Conn.: Archon, 1970.

Stoehr, Taylor. "Art vs. Utopia: The Case of Nathaniel Hawthorne and Brook Farm." *The Antioch Review* 36 (1978): 89–102.

Swift, Lindsay. *Brook Farm: Its Members, Scholars, and Visitors.* 1900. Reprint, New York: Corinth, 1961.

Tanner, Laura E. "Speaking with 'Hands at Our Throats': The Struggle for Artistic Voice in *The Blithedale Romance.*" *Studies in American Fiction* 21, no. 1 (spring 1993): 1–19.

Tharp, Louise Hall. *The Peabody Sisters of Salem.* Boston: Little, Brown, 1953.

Thornton, Ellen. "Hawthorne's *The Blithedale Romance.*" *The Explicator* (summer 1998): 188–190.

Tuckerman, Henry J. "Nathaniel Hawthorne." *Southern Literary Messenger* 17 (June 1851): 347–348.

Turner, Arlin. *Nathaniel Hawthorne: A Biography.* New York: Oxford University Press, 1980.

Van Doren, Mark. *Nathaniel Hawthorne: A Critical Biography.* 1949. Reprint, New York: Viking, 1966.

Van Leer, David W. "Aylmer's Library: Transcendental Alchemy in Hawthorne's 'The Birth-Mark.'" *American Transcendental Quarterly* 25 (1975): 211–220.

Wagenknecht, Edward. *Nathaniel Hawthorne: Man and Writer.* New York: Oxford University Press, 1961.

Waggoner, Hyatt. *Hawthorne: A Critical Study.* Cambridge, Mass.: Belknap Press of Harvard University Press, 1963.

———. "Hawthorne's 'Canterbury Pilgrims': Theme and Structure." *New England Quarterly* 22 (1949): 373–387.

Walters, C. T. "Ritual, Process and Definition: Hawthorne's 'The Artist of the Beautiful and the Creative Dilemma.'" In *Rituals and Ceremonies in Popular Culture,* edited by Ray B. Browne, ed. (Bowling Green, Ohio: Bowling Green University Popular Press, 1980).

Weber, Alfred, Beth L. Lueck, and Dennis Berthold, eds. *Hawthorne's American Travel Sketches.* Hanover, N.H.: University Press of New England, 1989.

Weinstein, Cindy. "The Invisible Hand Made Visible: 'The Birth-Mark.'" *Nineteenth-Century Literature* 48, no. 1 (June 1993): 44–73.

Williamson, James L. "'Young Goodman Brown': Hawthorne's 'Devil in Manuscript.'" *Studies in Short Fiction* 18, no. 2 (spring 1981): 155–162.

Wilson, Edmund, ed. *The Shock of Recognition.* 2 vols. 1943. Reprint, New York: Grosset & Dunlap, 1955.

Wineapple, Brenda. "The Biographical Imperative; or, Hawthorne Family Values." *Biography and Source Studies.* Vol. 6, edited by Frederick Karl. New York: AMS Press, 1998.

———. *Hawthorne: A Life.* New York: Alfred A. Knopf, 2003.

Yokozawa, Shiro. "Nathaniel Hawthorne's Mental Attitude toward the Civil War." *Journal of the English Institute* 11 (1980): 27–41.

CONTEMPORARY REVIEWS

A review of *Twice-told Tales* by Henry Wadsworth Longfellow, *North American Review*, July 1837

When a new star rises in the heavens, people gaze after it for a season with the naked eye, and with such telescopes as they may find, In the stream of thought, which flows so peacefully deep and clear, through the pages of this book, we see the bright reflection of a spiritual star, after which men will be fain to gaze "with the naked eye, and with the spyglasses of criticism." This star is but newly risen; and ere long the observations of numerous star-gazers, perched up on arm-chairs and editors' tables, will inform the world of its magnitude and its place in the heaven of poetry, whether it be in the paw of the Great Bear, or on the forehead of Pegasus, or on the strings of the Lyre, or in the wing of the Eagle. Our own observations are as follows.

To this little work we would say, "Live ever, sweet, sweet book." It comes from the hand of a man of genius. Every thing about it has the freshness of morning and of May. These flowers and green leaves of poetry have not the dust of the highway upon them. They have been gathered fresh from the secret places of a peaceful and gentle heart. There flow deep waters, silent, calm, and cool; and the green trees look into them, and "God's blue heaven." The book, though in prose, is written nevertheless by a poet. He looks upon all things in the spirit of love, and with lively sympathies; for to him external form is but the representation of internal being, all things having a life, an end and aim. The true poet is a friendly man. He takes to his arms even cold and inanimate things,

and rejoices in his heart, as did St. Bernard of old, when he kissed his Bride of Snow. To his eye all things are beautiful and holy; all are objects of feeling and of song, from the great hierarchy of the silent, saint-like stars, that rule the night, down to the little flowers which are "stars in the firmament of the earth," For he feels that

"The infinite forms of life are bound in one
By Love's eternal band;
The glow-worm and the fire-sea of the sun,
Came from one father's hand."

There are some honest people into whose hearts "Nature cannot find the way." They have no imagination by which to invest the ruder forms of earthly things with poetry. They are like Wordsworth's Peter Bell;

"A primrose by a river's brim,
A yellow primrose was to him,
And it was nothing more."

But it is one of the high attributes of the poetic mind, to feel a universal sympathy with Nature, both in the material world and in the soul of man. It identifies itself likewise with every object of its sympathy, giving it new sensation and poetic life, whatever that object may be, whether man, bird, beast, flower, or star. As in the pure mind all things are pure, so to the poetic mind all things are poetical. To such souls no age and no country can be utterly dull and prosaic. They make unto themselves their age and country; dwelling in the universal mind of man, and in the universal forms of things. Of such is the author of this book.

There are many who think that the ages of Poetry and Romance are gone by. They look upon the Present as a dull, unrhymed, and prosaic translation of a brilliant and poetic Past. Their dreams are of the days of Eld; of the Dark Ages, of the days of Chivalry, and Bards, and Troubadours and Minnesingers; and the times of which Milton says; "The villages also must have their visiters to inquire what lectures the bagpipe, and the rebbec reads even to the ballatry, and the gainmuth of every municipal fidler, for these are the countryman's Arcadia and his Monte Mayors." We also love ancient ballads. Pleasantly to our ears sounds the voice of the people in song, swelling fitfully through the desolate chambers of the past, like the wind of evening among ruins. And yet this voice does not persuade us that the days of balladry were more poetic than our own. The spirit of the past pleads for itself, and time spirit of the present likewise. If poetry be an element of the human mind, and consequently in accordance with nature and truth, it would be strange indeed, if, as the human mind advances, poetry should recede. The truth is, than when we look back upon the Past, we see only its bright and poetic features. All that is dull, prosaic, and commonplace is lost in the shadowy distance, We see the moated castle on the hill, and,

> "Golden and red above it,
> The clouds float gorgeously;"

but we see not the valley below, where the patient bondsman toils like a beast of burden, We see the tree-tops waving in the wind, and hear the merry birds singing under their green roofs; but we forget that at their roots there are swine feeding upon acorns. With the Present it is not so. We stand too near to see objects in a picturesque light. What to others at a distance is a bright and folded summer cloud, is to us, who are in it, a dismal, drizzling rain. Thus to many this world, all beautiful as it is, seems a poor, working-day world. They are ready to exclaim with Göthe;

> "Why so bustleth the people and crieth? would
> find itself victual, Children too would beget,
> feed on the best may be had, Mark in thy note-

books, traveller, this, and at home go do likewise; Farther reacheth no man, make he what stretching he may."

Thus has it been since the world began. Ours is not the only Present, which has seemed dull, commonplace, and prosaic.

The truth is, the heaven of poetry and romance still lies around us and within us. If people would but lay aside their "abominable spectacles," the light of The Great Carbuncle would flash upon their sight with astonishing brightness. So long as truth is stranger than fiction, the elements of poetry and romance will not be wanting in common life. If, invisible ourselves, we could follow a single human being through a single day of its life, and know all its secret thoughts, and hopes, and anxieties, its prayers, and tears, and good resolves, its passionate delights and struggles against temptation,—all that excites, and all that soothes the heart of man,—we should have poetry enough to fill a volume. Nay, set the imagination free, like another Bottle-imp, and bid it lift for you the roofs of the city, street by street, and after a single night's observation you shall sit you down and write poetry and romance for the rest of your life.

We deem these few introductory remarks important to a true understanding of Mr. Hawthorne's character as a writer. It is from this point that he goes forth; and if we would go with him, and look upon life and nature as he does, we also must start from the same spot. In order to judge of the truth and beauty of his sketches, we must at least know the point of view, from which he drew them. Let us now examine the sketches themselves.

The Twice-told Tales are so called, we presume, from having been first published in various annuals and magazines, and now collected together, and told a second time in a volume by themselves. And a very delightful volume do they make; one of those, which excite in you a feeling of personal interest for the author. A calm, thoughtful face seems to be looking at you from every page; with now a pleasant smile, and now a shade of sadness stealing over its features. Sometimes, thought not often, it glares wildly at you, with a strange and painful expression, as, in the German romance, the bronze knocker of the Archivarius Lindhorst makes up faces at the Student Anselmus.

One of the most prominent characteristics of these tales is, that they are national in their character. The author has wisely chosen his themes among the traditions of New England; the dusty legends of "the good Old Colony times, when we lived under a king." This is the right material for story. It seems as natural to make tales out of old tumble-down traditions, as canes and snuff-boxes out of old steeples, or trees planted by great men. The puritanical times begin to look romantic in the distance. Who would not like to have strolled through the city of Agamenticus, where a market was held every week, on Wednesday, and there were two annual fairs at St. James's and St. Paul's? Who would not like to have been present at the court of the Worshipful Thomas Georges, in those palmy days of the law, when Tom Heard was fined five shillings for being drunk, and John Payne the same, "far swearing one oath"? Who would not like to have seen the time, when Thomas Taylor was presented to the grand jury "for abusing Captain Raynes, being in authority, by *thee-ing* and *thou-ing* him"; and John Wardell likewise, for denying Cambridge College to be an ordinance of God; and when some were fined for winking at comely damsels in church ; and others for being common-sleepers there on the Lord's day ? Truly, many quaint and quiet customs, many comic scenes and strange adventures, many wild and wondrous things, fit for humorous tale, and soft, pathetic story, lie all about us here in New England. There is no tradition of the Rhine nor of the Black Forest, which can compare in beauty with that of the Phantom Ship. The Flying Dutchman of the Cape, and the Klabotermann of the Baltic, are nowise superior. The story of Peter Rugg, the man who could not find Boston, is as good as that told by Gervase of Tilbury, of a man who gave himself to the devils by an unfortunate imprecation, and was used by them as a wheelbarrow; and the Great Carbuncle of the White Mountains shines with no less splendor, than that which illuminated the subterranean palace in Rome, as related by William of Malmesbury. Truly, from such a Fortunatus's pocket and wishing-cap, a tale-bearer may furnish

forth a sufficiency of "peryllous adventures right espouventables, bryfefly compyled and pyteous for to here."

Another characteristic of this writer is the exceeding beauty of his style. It is as clear as running waters are. Indeed he uses worth as mere stepping-stones, upon which, with a free and youthful bound, his spirit crosses and recrosses the bright und rushing stream of thought. Some writers of the present day have introduced a kind of Gothic architecture into their style. All is fantastic, vast, and wondrous in the outward form, and within is mysterious twilight, and the swelling sound of an organ, and a voice chanting hymns in Latin, which need a translation for many of the crowd. To this we do not object. Let the priest chant in what language he will, so long as he understands his own mass-book. But if he wishes the world to listen and he edified, he will do well to choose a language that is generally understood.

And now let us give some specimens of the bright, poetic style we praise so highly. Here is the commencement of a sketch entitled "The Vision of the Fountain." What a soft and musical flow of language! And yet all as simple as a draught of water from the fountain itself. . . .

We are obliged to forgo the pleasure of quoting from the Tales. A tale must be given entire, or it is ruined. We wish we had room for "The Great Carbuncle," which is our especial favorite among them all. It is, however, too long for this use. Instead thereof, we will give one of those beautiful sketches, which are interspersed among the stories, like green leaves among flowers. But which shall we give? Shall it be "David Swan"; or "Little Annie's Ramble"; or "The Vision of the Fountain "; or "Fancy's Show-Box"; or "A Rill from the Town Pump"? We decide in favor of the last. . . .

These extracts are sufficient to show the beautiful and simple style of the book before us, its vein of pleasant philosophy, and the quiet humor, which is to the face of a book what a smile is to the face of man. In speaking in terms of such high praise as we have done, we have given utterance not alone to our own feelings, but we trust to those of all gentle readers of the Twice-told Tales. Like children we say, "Tell us more."

A review of *Twice-told Tales* by Edgar Allan Poe, *Graham's Magazine,* May 1842

We said a few hurried words about Mr. Hawthorne in our last number, with the design of speaking more fully in the present. We are still, however, pressed for room, and must necessarily discuss his volumes more briefly and more at random than their high merits deserve.

The book professes to be a collection of *tales* yet is, in two respects, misnamed. These pieces are now in their third republication, and, of course, are thrice-told. Moreover, they are by no means all tales, either in the ordinary or in the legitimate understanding of the term. Many of them are pure essays; for example, "Sights from a Steeple," "Sunday at Home," "Little Annie's Ramble," "A Rill from the Town-Pump," "The Toll-gatherer's Day," "The Haunted Mind," "The Sister Years," "Snow-Flakes," "Night Sketches," and "Foot-Prints on the Sea-Shore." We mention these matters chiefly on account of their discrepancy with that marked precision and finish by which the body of the work is distinguished.

Of the essays just named, we must be content to speak in brief. They are each and all beautiful, without being characterised by the polish and adaptation so visible in the tales proper. A painter would at once note their leading or predominant feature, and style it *repose*. There is no attempt at effect. All is quiet, thoughtful, subdued. Yet this repose may exist simultaneously with high originality of thought; and Mr. Hawthorne has demonstrated the fact. At every turn we meet with novel combinations; yet these combinations never surpass the limits of the quiet. We are soothed as we read; and withal is a calm astonishment that ideas so apparently obvious have never occurred or been presented to us before. Herein our author differs materially from Lamb or Hunt or Hazlitt—who, with vivid originality of manner and expression, have less of the true novelty of thought than is generally supposed, and whose originality, at best, has an uneasy and meretricious quaintness, replete with startling effects unfounded in nature, and inducing trains of reflection which lead to no satisfactory result. The Essays of Hawthorne have much of the character of Irving, with more of originality, and

less of finish; while, compared with the Spectator, they have a vast superiority at all points. The Spectator, Mr. Irving, and Mr. Hawthorne have in common that tranquil and subdued manner which we have chosen to denominate *repose*; but, in the case of the two former, this repose is attained rather by the absence of novel combination, or of originality, than otherwise, and consists chiefly in the calm, quiet, unostentatious expression of commonplace thoughts, in an unambitious, unadulterated Saxon. In them, by strong effort, we are made to conceive the absence of all. In the essays before us the absence of effort is too obvious to be mistaken, and a strong undercurrent of *suggestion* runs continuously beneath the upper stream of the tranquil thesis. In short, these effusions of Mr. Hawthorne are the product of a truly imaginative intellect, restrained, and in some measure repressed, by fastidiousness of taste, by constitutional melancholy and by indolence.

But it is of his tales that we desire principally to speak. The tale proper, in our opinion, affords unquestionably the fairest field for the exercise of the loftiest talent, which can be afforded by the wide domains of mere prose. Were we bidden to say how the highest genius could be most advantageously employed for the best display of its own powers, we should answer, without hesitation—in the composition of a rhymed poem, not to exceed in length what might be perused in an hour. Within this limit alone can the highest order of true poetry exist. We need only here say, upon this topic, that, in almost all classes of composition, the unity of effect or impression is a point of the greatest importance. It is clear, moreover, that this unity cannot be thoroughly preserved in productions whose perusal cannot be completed at one sitting. We may continue the reading of a prose composition, from the very nature of prose itself, much longer than we can persevere, to any good purpose, in the perusal of a poem. This latter, if truly fulfilling the demands of the poetic sentiment, induces an exaltation of the soul which cannot be long sustained. All high excitements are necessarily transient. Thus a long poem is a paradox. And, without unity of impression, the deepest effects cannot be brought about. Epics were the offspring of an imperfect sense of Art, and their reign is no more. A poem *too* brief may produce a vivid, but never an intense or enduring impression. Without a certain continuity of effort—without a certain duration or repetition of purpose—the soul is never deeply moved. There must be the dropping of the water upon the rock. De Béranger has wrought brilliant things—pungent and spirit-stirring—but, like all immassive bodies, they lack *momentum*, and thus fail to satisfy the Poetic Sentiment. They sparkle and excite, but, from want of continuity, fail deeply to impress. Extreme brevity will degenerate into epigrammatism; but the sin of extreme length is even more unpardonable. *In medio tutissimus ibis.*

Were we called upon, however, to designate that class of composition which, next to such a poem as we have suggested, should best fulfil the demands of high genius—should offer it the most advantageous field of exertion—we should unhesitatingly speak of the prose tale, as Mr. Hawthorne has here exemplified it. We allude to the short prose narrative, requiring from a half-hour to one or two hours in its perusal. The ordinary novel is objectionable, from its length, for reasons already stated in substance. As it cannot be read at one sitting, it deprives itself, of course, of the immense force derivable from *totality*. Worldly interests intervening during the pauses of perusal, modify, annul, or counteract, in a greater or less degree, the impressions of the book. But simple cessation in reading, would, of itself, be sufficient to destroy the true unity. In the brief tale, however, the author is enabled to carry out the fullness of his intention, be it what it may. During the hour of perusal the soul of the reader is at the writer's control. There are no external or extrinsic influences—resulting from weariness or interruption.

A skilful literary artist has constructed a tale. If wise, he has not fashioned his thoughts to accommodate his incidents; but having conceived, with deliberate care, a certain unique or single effect to be wrought out, he then invents such incidents— he then combines such events as may best aid him in establishing this preconceived effect. If his very initial sentence tend not to the outbringing of this effect, then he has failed in his first step. In the whole composition there should be no word writ-

ten, of which the tendency, direct or indirect, is not to the one pre-established design. And by such means, with such care and skill, a picture is at length painted which leaves in the mind of him who contemplates it with a kindred art, a sense of the fullest satisfaction. The idea of the tale has been presented unblemished, because undisturbed; and this is an end unattainable by the novel. Undue brevity is just as exceptionable here as in the poem; but undue length is yet more to be avoided.

We have said that the tale has a point of superiority even over the poem. In fact, while the *rhythm* of this latter is an essential aid in the development of the poet's highest idea—the idea of the Beautiful—the artificialities of this rhythm are an inseparable bar to the development of all points of thought or expression which have their basis in *Truth*. But Truth is often, and in very great degree, the aim of the tale. Some of the finest tales are tales of ratiocination. Thus the field of this species of composition, if not in so elevated a region on the mountain of Mind, is a table-land of far vaster extent than the domain of the mere poem. Its products are never so rich, but infinitely more numerous, and more appreciable by the mass of mankind. The writer of the prose tale, in short, may bring to his theme a vast variety of modes or inflections of thought and expression—(the ratiocinative, for example, the sarcastic, or the humorous) which are not only antagonistical to the nature of the poem, but absolutely forbidden by one of its most peculiar and indispensable adjuncts; we allude, of course, to rhythm. It may be added here, *par parenthèse*, that the author who aims at the purely beautiful in a prose tale is laboring at great disadvantage. For Beauty can be better treated in the poem. Not so with terror, or passion, or horror, or a multitude of such other points. And here it will be seen how full of prejudice are the usual animadversions against those *tales of effect*, many fine examples of which were found in the earlier numbers of Blackwood. The impressions produced were wrought in a legitimate sphere of action, and constituted a legitimate although sometimes an exaggerated interest. They were relished by every man of genius: although there were found many men of genius who condemned them without just ground. The true critic will but demand that the design intended be accomplished, to the fullest extent, by the means most advantageously applicable.

We have very few American tales of real merit—we may say, indeed, none, with the exception of "The Tales of a Traveller" of Washington Irving, and these "Twice-told Tales" of Mr. Hawthorne. Some of the pieces of Mr. John Neal abound in vigor and originality; but in general, his compositions of this class are excessively diffuse, extravagant, and indicative of an imperfect sentiment of Art. Articles at random are, now and then, met with in our periodicals which might be advantageously compared with the best effusions of the British Magazines; but, upon the whole, we are far behind our progenitors in this department of literature.

Of Mr. Hawthorne's Tales we would say, emphatically, that they belong to the highest region of Art—an Art subservient to genius of a very lofty order. We had supposed, with good reason for so supposing, that he had been thrust into his present position by one of the impudent *cliques* which beset our literature, and whose pretensions it is our full purpose to expose at the earliest opportunity; but we have been most agreeably mistaken. We know of few compositions which the critic can more honestly commend than these "Twice-told Tales." As Americans, we feel proud of the book.

Mr. Hawthorne's distinctive trait is invention, creation, imagination, originality—a trait which, in the literature of fiction, is positively worth all the rest. But the nature of originality, so far as regards its manifestation in letters, is but imperfectly understood. The inventive or original mind as frequently displays itself in novelty of *tone* as in novelty of matter. Mr. Hawthorne is original at *all* points.

It would be a matter of some difficulty to designate the best of these tales; we repeat that, without exception, they are beautiful. "Wakefield" is remarkable for the skill with which an old idea—a well-known incident—is worked up or discussed. A man of whims conceives the purpose of quitting his wife and residing *incognito*, for twenty years, in her immediate neighborhood. Something of this kind actually happened in London. The force of Mr. Hawthorne's tale lies in the analysis of the motives

which must or might have impelled the husband to such folly, in the first instance, with the possible causes of his perseverance. Upon this thesis a sketch of singular power has been constructed.

"The Wedding Knell" is full of the boldest imagination—an imagination fully controlled by taste. The most captious critic could find no flaw in this production.

"The Minister's Black Veil" is a masterly composition of which the sole defect is that to the rabble its exquisite skill will be *caviare*. The *obvious* meaning of this article will be found to smother its insinuated one. The *moral* put into the mouth of the dying minister will be supposed to convey the *true* import of the narrative; and that a crime of dark dye (having reference to the "young lady"), has been committed, is a point which only minds congenial with that of the author will perceive.

"Mr. Higginbotham's Catastrophe" is vividly original and managed most dexterously.

"Dr. Heidegger's Experiment" is exceedingly well imagined and executed with surpassing ability. The artist breathes in every line of it.

"The White Old Maid" is objectionable, even more than the "Minister's Black Veil," on the score of its mysticism. Even with the thoughtful and analytic, there will be much trouble in penetrating its entire import.

"The Hollow of the Three Hills" we would quote in full, had we space;—not as evincing higher talent than any of the other pieces, but as affording an excellent example of the author's peculiar ability. The subject is commonplace. A witch subjects the Distant and the Past to the view of a mourner. It has been the fashion to describe, in such cases, a mirror in which the images of the absent appear; or a cloud of smoke is made to arise, and thence the figures are gradually unfolded. Mr. Hawthorne has wonderfully heightened his effect by making the ear, in place of the eye, the medium by which the fantasy is conveyed. The head of the mourner is enveloped in the cloak of the witch, and within its magic folds there arise sounds which have an all-sufficient intelligence. Throughout this article also, the artist is conspicuous—not more in positive than in negative merits. Not only is all done that should be done, but (what perhaps is an end with more difficulty attained) there is nothing done which should not be. Every word *tells* and there is not a word which does *not* tell.

In "Howe's Masquerade" we observe something which resembles plagiarism—but which *may be* a very flattering coincidence of thought. We quote the passage in question.

> "*With a dark flush of wrath* upon his brow they saw the general *draw his sword* and *advance to meet* the figure *in the cloak* before the latter had stepped one pace upon the floor.
>
> "'*Villain, unmuffle yourself,*' cried he. 'you pass no farther!'
>
> "The figure, without blenching a hair's breadth from the sword which was pointed at his breast, made a solemn pause, and *lowered the cape* of the cloak from his face, yet sufficiently for the spectators to catch a glimpse of it. But Sir William Howe had evidently seen enough. The sternness of his countenance gave place to a look of wild amazement, if not horror, while he recoiled several steps from the figure, *and let fall his sword* upon the floor."—See vol. 2, page 20.

The idea here is, that the figure in the cloak is the phantom or reduplication of Sir William Howe; but in an article called "William Wilson," one of the "Tales of the Grotesque and Arabesque," we have not only the same idea, but the same idea similarly presented in several respects. We quote two paragraphs, which our readers may compare with what has been already given. We have italicized, above, the immediate particulars of resemblance.

> "The brief moment in which I averted my eyes had been sufficient to produce, apparently, a material change in the arrangement at the upper or farther end of the room. A large mirror, it appeared to me, now stood where none had been perceptible before: and as I stepped up to it in extremity of terror, mine own image, but with features all pale and dabbled in blood, *advanced* with a feeble and tottering gait to meet me.
>
> "Thus it appeared I say, but was not. It was Wilson, who then stood before me in the agonies of dissolution. Not a line in all the marked and singular lineaments of that face which was not even

identically mine own. *His mask and cloak lay where he had thrown them, upon the floor.*"—Vol. 2, p. 57.

Here it will be observed that, not only are the two general conceptions identical, but there are various *points* of similarity. In each case the figure seen is the wraith or duplication of the beholder. In each case the scene is a masquerade. In each case the figure is cloaked. In each, there is a quarrel—that is to say, angry words pass between the parties. In each the beholder is enraged. In each the cloak and sword fall upon the floor. The "villain, unmuffle yourself," of Mr. H. is precisely paralleled by a passage at page 56 of "William Wilson."

In the way of objection we have scarcely a word to say of these tales. There is, perhaps, a somewhat too general or prevalent *tone*—a tone of melancholy and mysticism. The subjects are insufficiently varied. There is not so much of *versatility* evinced as we might well be warranted in expecting from the high powers of Mr. Hawthorne. But beyond these trivial exceptions we have really none to make. The style is purity itself. Force abounds. High imagination gleams from every page. Mr. Hawthorne is a man of the truest genius. We only regret that the limits of our Magazine will not permit us to pay him that full tribute of commendation, which, under other circumstances, we should be so eager to pay.

An anonymous review of *Twice-told Tales* and *Mosses from an Old Manse,* in *New Englander* and *Yale Review,* January 1847

The works of Nathaniel Hawthorne place him, in our judgment, in the first rank of American authors, in the department of imaginative literature.

A curiosity to know something of the history of those who instruct or interest us, and honor our country, by their writings, is quite natural. Our readers, doubtless, would be gratified to know more of Mr. Hawthorne's history than we are able so give: for our knowledge of it is very limited, He is, as we are informed, a native of Salem, Massachusetts, a graduate of Bowdoin College, and about forty years of age. Instead of entering on the active duties of either of the learned professions to which a liberal education is usually preparatory, he has led a singularly quiet and retired life, partly at Salem, and partly at Boston as an officer in the custom-house, partly at Concord in the old mansion of the late venerable Dr. Ripley, whence the title of his last volumes, "Mosses from an old Manse," and now, by the appointment of the present administration of our national government, of which he is a noiseless supporter, he is an officer of the customs in the port of his native town.

His residence at Concord was, perhaps, either cause or effect of his sympathy with the amiable and highly cultivated, but misty and groping, philanthropists of the "Concord sect" and the "Roxbury Phalanx." This sympathy, we regret to see and to say, appears, here and there, in his last volumes. It seems however, to be more a sympathy of heart and sentiment, than of intellect and conviction. For his native good sense evidently distrusts, and declines to adopt, their loose doctrines, and their unsubstantial plans and theories.

The volumes before us are four; two entitled Twice Told Tales, first and second series, of about 350 pages each, published in 1842; and two entitled Mosses from an Old Manse, part first and second, of about 210 pages each, published in 1846. They consist of various Tales, Essays, Allegories, and *Pieces*—we know of no term more specific which will answer our purpose.

Mr. Hawthorne's style of writing greatly pleases us. While it is lively, graphic, and picturesque, and occasionally forcible, it is very natural and quiet. There is nothing strained, and no painfully manifest aim and effort to be brilliant and effective. We have become so wearied with these faults in modern writers, that it is really refreshing to read one who writes unambitiously, and without this apparent labor—one who tells us his thoughts and emotions, without a manifest consciousness of himself, and naturally, "like the outbreaking of a fountain from the earth." Much of the writing of these times aims to be piquant, striking and astonishing, such us will arrest men amid the characteristic haste and bustle of the times. And this ambitious aim to be pointed is too apparent. If there must be so much labor and art in writing, there should be also the *"summa ars, ariem celare."* We are made to see, not so much the subject as the author. Our impression is not, here is an author who has something to say, and who says

it, but here is an author who is ambitious to say something very rhetorically and impressively, and who thinks less of his subject than of himself as seen through his subject. We feel, when reading such an author, as we do, when hearing a choir who sing ambitiously—whose selection of tunes and style of singing are plainly more for self-exhibition than for music; or as we do, when conversing with a person, whose object seems to be, not so much to entertain us, or to be entertained by us, as to impress us with an admiring sense of his conversational powers; or as we do, when talking with a person, who seems to be chiefly attentive to his face and figure in a mirror which happens to be opposite to him.

There is none of this diseased self-consciousness and this laborious self-display in Hawthorne's writing. His pleasant, truthful and earnest thoughts come forth noiselessly, and pass quietly on, as the clear water rises from the wellspring, and flows on in a gentle stream, His style is the simple clothing of his thought. There is nothing to draw our attention to it as style—to make us think of it, rather than of the thought which it communicates. It well illustrates Dr. Emmons' remark, "Style is only the frame to hold our thoughts. It is like the sash of a window; a heavy sash will obscure the light. The object is to have as little sash as will hold the lights, that we may not think of the frame, but have the most light." Mr. Hawthorne's style reminds us of Addison's, and of Charles Lamb's, and also of Scott's: though his simplicity is not so majestic and rich as Scott's, whose narration seems to us unequalled.

Mr. Hawthorne is a very minute observer. His eye seems to take in, at once, the whole, and each of the parts; and his narratives and pictures have often a particularity, which gives them a charming completeness and individuality—revealing minute traits, which we immediately and pleasantly recognize, but should not ourselves have thought of recording. He shows, in his descriptions of natural scenery, the quick and accurate and comprehensive eye of the true painter. And, then, mingled with his narrative or description, there is a kind of thinking aloud, or talking to himself, very truthful and pleasant—a sort of practical commentary on nature. We will give an illustration. Take this from his Buds and Bird-Voices. . . .

The same minuteness and accuracy of observation, and picturesque expression are seen in Mr. H's representations of the scenery of human life and character. He sees deeply into the interior of human character. He observes particularly and exactly its outward manifestations. And he sketches many varieties of it, in his usual easy and quiet style, but with great liveliness, and, indeed, dramatic skill and power. His personages are not all the same, with different names and in different circumstances, but they preserve their individuality, and so stand out upon the canvass that we immediately recognize them. He is fond of seeing a great variety of characters. He frequently takes a position, whence he can see, at a glance, or in quick succession, a great many persons, as they actually appear. As, for instance, in his "Sights from a Steeple," whence he can see, not only the clouds, which he makes as full of varied life as the earth below, and, in the distance, on the one side, the cultivated fields, villages, white country Seals, the waving lines of rivulets, little placid lakes, and the knolls and hills, and, on the other side, the sea stretching away to a viewless distance, and the broad harbor on which is the town—but can also see the varied persons that appear to the eye and to the pocket spy-glass—here a fine young man of twenty, with a pensive air, either in doubt, or in debt, or in love—there, in another but not distant street, coming from an aristocratic looking edifice, two ladies, swinging their parasols and lightly arrayed for a summer ramble, both young and both pretty, whom, era long, the aforesaid pensive youth *happens* to meet, and turns, after a recognition and a little shyness, to walk with them—there, upon the wharf amid the bustle of business, tho wealthy merchant, watching the unloading of his ships, the clerks, diligent with their paper and pencils, the sailors, plying the block and tackle, and accompanying their toil with cries long drawn and roughly melodious, while, at a little distance, a group of grave seniors are gathered round the door of n warehouse, thinking of their distant ships and rich freights—hero, in two streets converging at right angles, appear three different processions; one a proud array of voluntary soldiers,

in bright uniform and with stirring martial music; another, close to the rear of the first, a battalion of school-boys, ranged in crooked and irregular platoons, shouldering sticks, and thumping a harsh and unripe clatter from an instrument of tin, and ridiculously aping the intricate manœuvres of the foremost band; and the third, a funeral procession, which, as soon as seen, hushes the music of the soldiers and the mirthful clamor of the boys. Or, as in his "Toll-Gatherer's Day," he takes his position at a toll-gate, on a frequently traveled road, and there observes all who pass from morning till night, reading their minds and hearts and condition, in their faces and general appearance and few passing words. Or, as in his "Chippings with a Chisels," he spends day after day in the workshop of a carver of tomb-stones, noting and reading the various persons who come to employ him. He is especially fond of bringing out the inward character. He loves to paint what he or some one else has called "the moral picturesque," and makes his accurate and lively description of the outward but the medium of vision into the inward.

Mr. Hawthorne has a very pleasant and good natured, yet successful and effective way of hitting off, or satirizing the faults and foibles and errors of individuals and cliques, of schools, and communities, and ages. And, while he looks with a kindly eye on human nature, and appreciates all its good qualities, ho seems to be aware of its dark depths and its universal fountain of corruption. As illustrations of this trait, we would refer to The New Adam and Eve, The Intelligence Office, P. S. Correspondence, The Hall of Fantasy, The Procession of Life, Chippings with a Chisel, Peter Goldthwaite's Treasure, The Artist of the Beautiful—indeed we might go through the whole catalogue. But that which, in this respect, surpasses all his other writings, and we were about to say the writings of all but John Bunyan, is "The Celestial Rail-road:" which in respect to ease and rapidity, bears a relation to the road of John Bunyan's Pilgrim, like to that which a modern railroad bears to an old fashioned turnpike or county road—a pleasant but keen and truthful satire on modern easy modes of getting to heaven. . . .

We are greatly pleased with a gentle yet earnest humanity—a true interest in man and whatever pertains to him—which pervades all that Hawthorne writes. Its manifestations, however, are all of the indirect kind. There is no parade of it. There is no declamation about it. There is no manifest aim nor self-conscious effort, to be, and appear a philanthropist. His writings are instinct with a love of man as man, which appears, not because it desires to be seen, but because it is there and naturally comes forth toward its object. It speaks, not because it wishes to be heard, but because it has something pertinent and weighty to say. While Mr. H. has no hostility or envy toward the great and the opulent, and recognizes and appreciates their real manhood and worth, he is, evidently, most fond of the lowly and mediocrat scenes and characters of life. He prefers to penetrate the humble externals of poverty, and to admire, or sympathize with, and picture, what is within, rather than to linger in marble halls and gorgeous dwellings, and amid the garniture and appliances and indulgences of luxury. And yet, there is in his writings nothing of mawkish sympathy with the poor, no philanthropic cant, no hobby-riding upon humanity.

Of course Mr. H. has no favor to bestow upon that feeling of caste, to which the human heart is, in prosperity, so prone—the pride, which prompts its possessor to place himself above the sympathies of our common nature, above the sympathies of all except a select circle or class; which fills him with the thought that he is of better clay or mould than the mass of men, and can mingle with them only by condescension. A spirit of indirect, but decided, hostility to it, pervades all his writings. And some of his tales (for instance Lady Eleanore's Mantle) have a moral, which visits it with skillful and forcible rebuke. Mr. hawthorne s said to belong to the democratic party. He certainly has that sympathy with every thing human which belongs to the true men of all parties. And he is very unlike many, who, with "equal and exact justice to all men" and "the largest liberty" on their lips, are the most inveterate haters of a particular class of men, the most obstinate withholders of "equal and exact justice" from them, and the apologists, or advocates, or guardians of a system of their bitter oppression.

There is an unfavorable criticism which we feel bound to make on one of Hawthorne's tales. It is respecting a fault which offends our reverence and affection for the early New Englanders. This occurs in his story entitled "The Gentle Boy," founded on the persecutions of the Quakers—a tale, which, as a work of imagination, is excellent—varied, graphic, and surpassingly tender and beautiful. He exaggerates, in his story, the spirit of hostility, among the New England Puritans, to the Quakers. And he fails to make a very obvious and just distinction between persecution of the Quakers for heresy, and their punishment for civil offenses—for absolute breaches of the peace—for publicly vilifying the magistracy, for open and boisterous disturbance of worshiping congregations on the Sabbath, and for violent and abusive interruptions of clergymen in their discourses. It is true, indeed, that the utterance of heretical opinions was accounted, in the colonies of New England, (as it was in the parent country, in a greater degree, especially by those attached to the Episcopal hierarchy,) a civil crime. This was an error. It is to be acknowledged and regretted. But it was an error of the age; and one from which the Puritans were more free than most of their contemporaries. Oliver Cromwell, for example, was almost two hundred years in advance of his age, in respect to intellectual and religious tolerance. The early New Englanders ought to be admired for going so far toward entire freedom of opinion, in an age of ecclesiastical establishments, and of intellectual and religious servitude, rather than blamed for not going on to the perfection of toleration and spiritual freedom, which, by gradual steps, their posterity have attained. Many of the Quakers, in the wildness of their enthusiasm, felt called to be, and actually were, serious disturbers of the peace. And they were punished, with the severity of those rigid times towards offenders against good order and good manners, more for those breaches of the peace, than for the utterance of heresy. Though we do not deny that there were cases, where the utterance of heresy was made, partly at least, matter of accusation and of punishment. This was a stain upon the age, and upon our fathers, in that age. Let it not be denied. But, in the name of all that is worthy of reverence in any ancestry, let it not be magnified and blackened.

We regret this injustice by Mr. Hawthorne towards the New England Puritans. We are somewhat surprised at it. For he has shown, in other parts of his works, that he highly appreciates their character. True, the plan of the story of "The Gentle Boy" was quite a temptation to exaggerate the persecution of the Quakers. But an author of Mr. H.'s genius has no need of the aid of exaggeration.

Hawthorne is generally quite successful, when he employs the supernatural. But, sometimes, he makes the lesson he would teach thereby so obscure, that it is not apprehended by many readers, who, to say the least, are not obtuse. For instance. His story of "Young Goodman Brown" is designed to teach a moral lesson. But the design fails of accomplishment by the obscurity of execution. The lesson is not apprehended by nine out of ten of intelligent readers. The story is to them unintelligible. They do not know what the writer would be at. They can, perhaps, see the lesson, after some fortunate one has discovered and explained it. But such an explanation should be unnecessary. An allegory with crutches is a poor affair. An illustration, that needs to be illustrated, may well be spared.

But we have little except praise to offer respecting Hawthorne. We hope that he will write and publish often. For it is pleasant to observe, that the more he writes the better he writes. Mosses from an Old Manse—his last volumes—are decidedly superior to his Twice Told Tales.

Involuntarily, while we have been reading Hawthorne, Washington Irving comes up in our mind in comparison with him. Irving has labored successfully in a department of literature which Hawthorne has not entered. They can not, therefore, be compared, except in that kind of imaginative literature, which they have cultivated in common; and therein, we think Hawthorne quite equal to Irving. While he is not inferior to him in easy, graceful style of expression, and scarcely inferior in that exquisite gentleness and sensibility which is Irving's forte, he has a wider and deeper insight into human character, a greater fondness and capability for the moral picturesque, more dramatic power, and is a profounder thinker on the subjects of which he treats.

We hope Mr. Hawthorne will quit the custom house, and devote himself wholly to literature. His pen, now that it has won for him so high a reputation, will doubtless yield him an ample support, and in a way more congenial to his taste, and far more useful and honorable to his country. There are many hungry politicians who are competent to perform the duties of his office in the port of Salem, who have no great gift for benefiting the country in any other way. It is a waste of a kind of genius, which we can not well spare, to shut up Nathaniel Hawthorne in a custom house.

S. W. S. D.

An anonymous review of *The Scarlet Letter* in *The North American Review,* July 1850

That there is something not unpleasing to us in the misfortunes of our best friends, is a maxim we have always spurned, as a libel on human nature. But we must be allowed, in behalf of Mr. Hawthorne's friend and gossip, the literary public, to rejoice in the event—a "removal" from the office of Surveyor of the Customs for the port of Salem,—which has brought him back to our admiring, and, we modestly hope, congenial society, from associations and environments which have confessedly been detrimental to his genius, and to those qualities of heart, which, by an unconscious revelation through his style, like the involuntary betrayal of character in a man's face and manners, have won the affection of other than personal friends. We are truly grieved at the sayage "scratches" our phoenix has received from the claws of the national eagle, scratches gratuitous and unprovoked, whereby his plumage remains not a little ruffled, if his breast be not very deeply lacerated. We hope we do not see tendencies to *self immolation* in the introductory chapter to this volume. It seems suicidal to a most enviable fame, to show the fine countenance of the sometime denizen of Concord Parsonage, once so serene and full of thought, and at the same time so attractively arch, now cloudy and peevish, or dressed in sardonic smiles, which would scare away the enthusiasm of less hearty admirers than those he "holds by the button." The pinnacle on which the "conscience of the beautiful" has placed our author's graceful image is high enough, however, to make slight changes from the wear and tear of out-door elements, highway dust, and political vandalism, little noticed by those accustomed to look lovingly up to it. Yet they cannot be expected to regret a "removal," which has saved those finer and more delicate traits, in which genius peculiarly manifests itself, from being worn away by rough contact, or obliterated by imperceptible degrees through the influence of the atmosphere.

Mr. Hawthorne's serious apprehensions on this subject are thus candidly expressed:—

> "I began to grow melancholy and restless; continually prying into my mind, to discover which of its poor properties were gone, and what degree of detriment had already accrued to the remainder. I endeavored to calculate how much longer I could stay in the Custom House, and yet go forth a man. To confess the truth, it was my greatest apprehension,—as it would never be a measure of policy to turn out so quiet an individual as myself, and it being hardly in the nature of a public officer to resign,—it was my chief trouble, therefore, that I was likely to grow gray and decrepit in the Surveyorship, and become much such another animal as the old Inspector. Might it not, in the tedious lapse of official life that lay before me, finally be with me as it was with this venerable friend,—to make the dinner hour the nucleus of the day, and to spend the rest of it, as an old dog spends it, asleep in the sunshine or the shade? A dreary lookforward this, for a man who felt it to be the best definition of happiness to live throughout the whole range of his faculties and sensibilities! But, all this while, I was giving myself very unnecessary alarm. Providence had meditated better things for me than I could possibly imagine for myself."

A man who has no rare an individuality to lose may well shudder at the idea of becoming a soulless machine, a sort of official scarecrow, having only so much of manly semblance left as will suffice to warn plunderers from the property of "Uncle Sam." Haunted by the horror of mental annihilation, it is not wonderful that he should look askance at the drowsy row of officials, as they reclined uneasily in tilted chairs, and should measure their mental torpidity by the length of time they had been subjected to the soul-exhaling process in which he

had not yet got beyond the conscious stage. It was in pure apprehension, let us charitably hope, and not in a satirical, and far less a malicious, mood, that he describes one of them as retaining barely enough of the moral and spiritual nature to keep him from going upon all fours, and possessing neither soul, heart, nor mind more worthy of immortality than the spirit of the beast, which "goeth downward." Judging his aged colleagues thus, well might the young publican, as yet spiritually alive, stand aghast! A man may be excusable for starving his *intellect*, if Providence has thrown him into a situation where its dainty palate cannot be gratified. But for the well being of his *moral nature,* he is more strictly responsible, and has no right, under any circumstances, to remain in a position where, from causes beyond his control, his conscience is deprived of its supremacy over the will, and policy or expediency, whether public or selfish, placed upon its throne. "Most men," says our honest author, "suffer moral detriment from this mode of life," from causes which, (having just devoted four pages to a full-length caricature,) he had not space to hint at, except in the following pithy admonition to the aspirants after a place in the Blue Book.

> "Uncle Sam's gold—meaning no disrespect to the worthy old gentleman—has, in this respect, a quality of enchantment, like that of the Devil's wages. Whoever touches it should look well to himself, or he may find the bargain to go hard against him, involving, if not his soul, yet many of his better attributes; its sturdy force, its courage and constancy, its truth, its self-reliance, and all that gives the emphasis to manly character."

It was great gain for a man like Mr. Hawthorne to depart this truly unprofitable life; but we wish that his demise had been quiet and Christian, and not by violence. We regret that any of the bitterness of heart engendered by the polical battle, and by his subsequent decapitation without being judged by his peers, should have come with him to a purer and higher state of existence. That a head should fall, and even receive "an ignominious kick," is but a common accident in a party struggle, and would be of no more consequence to the world in Mr. Hawthorne's case than any other, (the metaphorical head not including brains,) provided the spirit had suffered no material injury in the encounter. Of that, however, we have no means of judging, except by comparing this book of recent production with his former writings. Of the "stern and sombre" pictures of the world and human life, external and internal, found in the Scarlet Letter, we shall speak anon. The preface claims some farther notice.

One would conclude, that the mother on whose bosom the writer was cherished in his urchinhood had behaved herself like a very step-mother towards him, showing a vulgar preference of those sons who have gathered, and thrown into her lap, gifts more substantial than garlands and laurel wreaths. This appears from his reluctant and half ashamed confession of attachment to her, and his disrespectful remarks upon her homely and commonplace features, her chilly and unsocial disposition, and those marks of decay and premature age which needed not to be pointed out. The portrait is like, no doubt; but we cannot help imagining the ire of the ancient dame at the unfilial satire. Indeed, a faint echo of the voice of her indignation has arrived at our ears. She complains, that, in anatomizing the characters of his former associates for the entertainment of the public, he has used the scalpel on some subjects, who, though they could not defend themselves, might possibly wince; and that all who came under his hand, living or dead, had probably relatives among his readers, whose affections might be wounded.

Setting this consideration apart, we confess that, to our individual taste, this naughty chapter is more piquant than any thing in the book; the style is racy and pungent, not elaborately witty, but stimulating the reader's attention agreeably by original turns of expression, and unhackneyed combinations of words, falling naturally into their places, as if of their own accord, and not obtained by far seeking and impressment into the service. The sketch of General Miller is airily and lightly done; no other artist could have given so much character to each fine drawn line as to render the impression almost as distinct to the reader's fancy as a portrait drawn by rays of light is to the bodily vision. Another

specimen of his word painting, the lonely parlor seen by the moonlight melting into the warmer glow of the fire, while it reminds us of Cowper's much quoted and admired verse, has truly a great deal more of genuine poetry in it. The delineations of wharf scenery, and of the Custom House, with their appropriate figures and personages, are worthy of the pen of Dickens; and really, so far as mere style is concerned, Mr. Hawthorne has no reason to thank us for the compliment; he has the finer touch, if not more genial feeling, of the two. Indeed, if we except a few expressions which savor somewhat strongly of his late unpoetical associations, and the favorite metaphor of the guillotine, which, however apt, is not particularly agreeable to the imagination in such detail, we like the preface better than the tale.

No one who has taken up the Scarlet Letter will willingly lay it down till he has finished it; and he will do well not to pause, for he cannot resume the story where he left it. He should give himself up to the magic power of the style, without stopping to open wide the eyes of his good sense and judgment, and shake off the spell; or half the weird beauty will disappear like a "dissolving view." To be sure, when he closes the book, he will feel very much like the giddy and bewildered patient who is just awaking from his first experiment of the effects of sulphuric ether. The soul has been floating or flying between earth and heaven, with dim ideas of pain and pleasure strangely mingled, and all things earthly swimming dizzily and dreamily, yet most beautiful, before the half shut eye. That the author himself felt this sort of intoxication as well as the willing subjects of his enchantment, we think, is evident in many pages of the last half of the volume. His imagination has sometimes taken him fairly off his feet, insomuch that he seems almost to doubt if there be any firm ground at all,—if we may so judge from such mistborn ideas as the following.

"But, to all these shadowy beings, so long our near acquaintances,—as well Roger Chillingworth as his companions,—we would fain be merciful. It is a curious subject of observation and inquiry, whether hatred and love be not the same thing at bottom. Each, in its utmost development, supposes a high degree of intimacy and heart-knowledge; each renders one individual dependent for the food of his affections and spiritual life upon another; each leaves the passionate lover, or the no less passionate hater, forlorn and desolate by the withdrawal of his object. Philosophically considered, therefore, the two passions seem essentially the same, except the one happens to be seen in a celestial radiance, and the other in a dusky and lurid glow. In the spiritual world, the old physician and the minister—mutual victims as they have been—may, unawares, have found their earthly stock of hatred and antipathy transmuted into golden love."

Thus devils and angels are alike beautiful, when seen through the magic glass; and they stand side by side in heaven, however the former may be supposed to have come there. As for Roger Chillingworth, he seems to have so little in common with man, he is such a gnome-like phantasm, such an unnatural personification of an abstract idea, that we should be puzzled to assign him a place among angels, men, or devils. He is no more a man than Mr. Dombey, who sinks down a mere *caput mortuum*, as soon as pride, the only animating principle, is withdrawn. These same "shadowy beings" are much like "the changeling the fairies made o' a benweed." Hester at first strongly excites our pity, for she suffers like an immortal being; and our interest in her continues only while we have hope for her soul, that its baptism of tears will reclaim it from the foul stain which has been east upon it. We see her humble, meek, self-denying, charitable, and heartwrung with anxiety for the moral welfare of her wayward child. But anon her humility catches a new tint, and we find it pride; and so a vague unreality steals by degrees over all her most humanizing traits—we lose our confidence in all—and finally, like Undine, she disappoints us, and shows the dream-land origin and nature, when we were looking to behold a Christian.

There is rather more power, and better keeping, in the character of Dimmesdale. But here again we are cheated into a false regard and interest, partly perhaps by the associations thrown around

him without the intention of the author, and possibly contrary to it, by our habitual respect for the sacred order, and by our faith in religion, where it has once been rooted in the heart. We are told repeatedly, that the Christian element yet pervades his character and guides his efforts; but it seems strangely wanting. "High aspirations for the welfare of his race, warm love of souls, pure sentiments, natural piety, strengthened by thought and study, and illuminated by revelation—all of which invaluable gold was little better than rubbish" to Roger Chillingworth, are little better than rubbish at all, for any use to be made of them in the story. Mere suffering, aimless and without effect for purification or blessing to the soul, we do not find in God's moral world. The sting that follows crime is most severe in the purest conscience and the tenderest heart, in mercy, not in vengeance, surely; and we can conceive of any cause constantly exerting itself without its appropriate effects, as soon as of a seven years' agony without penitence. But here every pang is wasted. A most obstinate and unhuman passion, or a most unwearying conscience it must be, neither being worn out, or made worse or better, by such a prolonged application of the scourge. Penitence may indeed be life-long; but as for this, we are to understand that there is no penitence about it. We finally get to be quite of the author's mind, that "the only truth that continued to give Mr. Dimmesdale a real existence on this earth, was the anguish in his inmost soul, and the undissembled expression of it in his aspect. Had he once found power to smile, and wear an aspect of gayety, there had been no such man." He duly exhales at the first gleam of hope, an uncertain and delusive beam, but fatal to his misty existence. From that time he is a fantasy, an opium dream, his faith a vapor, his reverence blasphemy, his charity mockery, his sanctity impurity, his love of souls a ludicrous impulse to teach little boys bad words; and nothing is left to bar the utterance of "a volley of good, round, solid, satisfactory, heaven-defying oaths," (a phrase which seems to smack its lips with a strange *gout!*) but good taste and the mere outward shell, "the buckramed habit of clerical decorum." The only conclusion is, that the shell never possessed any thing real,—never was the Rev. Arthur Dimmesdale, as we have foolishly endeavored to suppose; that he was but a changeling, or an imp in grave apparel, not an erring, and consequently suffering human being, with a heart still upright enough to find the burden of conscious unworthiness and undeserved praise more intolerable than open ignominy and shame, and refraining from relieving his withering conscience from its load of unwilling hypocrisy, if partly from fear, more from the wish to be yet an instrument of good to others, not an example of evil which should weaken their faith in religion. The closing scene, where the satanic phase of the character is again exchanged for the saintly, and the pillory platform is made the stage for a triumphant *coup de théatre,* seems to us more than a failure.

But Little Pearl—gem of the purest water— what shall we say of her? That if perfect truth to childish and human nature can make her a mortal, she is so; and immortal, if the highest creations of genius have any claim to immortality. Let the author throw what light he will upon her, from his magical prism, she retains her perfect and vivid human individuality. When he would have us call her elvish and implike, we persist in seeing only a capricious, roguish, untamed child, such as many a mother has looked upon with awe, and a feeling of helpless incapacity to rule. Every motion, every feature, every word and tiny shout, every naughty scream and wild laugh, come to us as if our very senses were conscious of them. The child is a true child, the only genuine and consistent mortal in the book; and wherever she crosses the dark and gloomy track of the story, she refreshes out spirit with pure truth and radiant beauty, and brings to grateful remembrance the like ministry of gladsome childhood, in some of the saddest scenes of actual life. We feel at once that the author must have a "Little Pearl" of his own, whose portrait, consciously or unconsciously, his pen sketches out. Not that we would deny to Mr. Hawthorne the power to call up any shape, angel or goblin, and present it before his readers in a striking and vivid light. But there is something more than imagination in the picture of "Little Pearl." The heart takes a part in it, and puts in certain inimitable touches of nature here and there, such as fancy never dreamed of, and only a

long and loving observation of the ways of childhood could suggest. The most characteristic traits are so interwoven with the story, (on which we do not care to dwell,) that it is not easy to extract a paragraph which will convey much of the charming image to our readers. The most convenient passage for our purpose is the description of Little Pearl playing upon the sea-shore. We take in the figure of the old man as a dark back-ground, or contrast, to heighten the effect.

"In fine, Hester Prynne resolved to meet her former husband, and do what might be in her power for the rescue of the victim on whom he had so evidently set his gripe. The occasion was not long to seek. One afternoon, walking with Pearl in a retired part of the peninsula, she beheld the old physician, with a basket on one arm, and a staff in the other hand, stooping along the ground, in quest of roots and herbs to concoct his medicines withal.

"Hester bade little Pearl run down to the margin of the water, and play with the shells and tangled seaweed, until she should have talked awhile with yonder gatherer of herbs. So the child flew away like a bird, and, making bare her small white feet, went pattering along the moist margin of the sea. Here and there, she came to a full stop, and peeped curiously into a pool, left by the retiring tide as a mirror for Pearl to see her face in. Forth peeped at her, out of the pool, with dark, glistening curls around her head, and an elf-smile in her eyes, the image of a little maid, whom Pearl, having no other playmate, invited to take her hand and run a race with her. But the visionary little maid, on her part, beckoned likewise, as if to say,"'This is a better place! Come thou into the pool!' And Pearl, stepping in, mid-leg deep, beheld her own white feet at the bottom; while, out of a still lower depth, came the gleam of a kind of fragmentary smile, floating to and for in the agitated water.

"Meanwhile, her mother had accosted the physician.

"'I would speak a word with you,' said she,— 'a word that concerns us much.'"

Here follows a dialogue in the spirit of the idea that runs through the book,—that revenge may exist without any overt act of vengeance that could be called such, and that a man who refrains from avenging himself, may be more diabolical in his very forbearance than he who in his passionate rage inflicts what evil he may upon his enemy; the former having that spirit of cold hate which could gloat for years, or forever, over the agonies of remorse and despair, over the anguish bodily and mental, and consequent death or madness, of a fellow man, and never relent—never for a moment be moved to pity. This master passion of hatred, swallowing up all that is undevilish and human in Roger Chillingworth, makes him a pure abstraction at last, a sort of mythical fury, a match for Alecto the Unceasing. . . .

We know of no writer who better understands and combines the elements of the picturesque in writing than Mr. Hawthorne. His style may be compared to a sheet of transparent water, reflecting from its surface blue skies, nodding woods, and the smallest spray or flower that peeps over its grassy margin; while in its clear yet mysterious depths we espy rarer and stranger things, which we must dive for, if we would examine. Whether they might prove gems or pebbles, when taken out of the fluctuating medium through which the sun-gleams reach them, is of no consequence to the effect. Everything charms the eye and ear, and nothing looks like art and pains-taking. There is a naturalness and a continuous flow of expression in Mr. Hawthorne's books, that makes them delightful to read, especially in this our day, when the fear of triteness drives some writers, (even those who might otherwise avoid that reproach,) to adopt an abrupt and dislocated style, administering to our jaded attention frequent thumps and twitches, by means of outlandish idioms and forced inversions, and now and then flinging at our heads an incomprehensible, break-jaw word, which uncivilized missile stuns us to a full stop, and an appeal to authority. No authority can be found, however, which affords any remedy or redress against determined outlaws. After bumping over "rocks and ridges, and gridiron bridges," in one of these prosaic latter-day omnibuses, how pleasant it is to

move over flowery turf upon a spirited, but properly trained Pegasus, who occasionally uses his wings, and skims along a little above *terra firma*, but not with an alarming preference for cloudland or rarefied air. One cannot but wonder, by the way, that the master of such a wizard power over language as Mr. Hawthorne manifests should not choose a less revolting subject than this of the Scarlet Letter, to which fine writing seems as inappropriate as fine embroidery. The ugliness of pollution and vice is no more relieved by it than the gloom of the prison is by the rose tree at its door. There are some palliative expressions used, which cannot, even as a matter of taste, be approved.

Regarding the book simply as a picture of the olden time, we have no fault to find with costume or circumstance. All the particulars given us, (and he is not wearisomely anxious to multiply them to show his research,) are in good keeping and perspective, all in softened outlines and neutral tint, except the ever fresh and unworn image of childhood, which stands out from the canvas in the gorgeously attired "Little Pearl." He forbears to mention the ghastly gallows-tree, which stood hard by the pillory and whipping-post, at the city gates, and which one would think might have been banished with them from the precincts of Boston, and from the predilections of the community of whose opinions it is the focus. When a people have opened their eyes to the fact, that it is not the best way of discountenancing vice to harden it to exposure and shame, and make it brazen-faced, reckless, and impudent, they might also be convinced, it would seem, that respect for human life would not be promoted by publicly violating it, and making a spectacle, or a newspaper theme, of the mental agony and dying struggles of a human being, and of him least fit, in the common belief, to be thus hurried to his account. "Blood for blood!" We are shocked at the revengeful custom among uncivilized tribes, when it bears the aspect of private revenge, because the executioners must be of the kindred of the slain. How much does the legal retribution in kind, which civilized man exacts, differ in reality from the custom of the savage? The law undertakes to avenge its own dignity, to use a popular phrase; that is, it regards the community as one great family, and constitutes itself the avenger of blood in its behalf. It is not punishment, but retaliation, which does not contemplate the reform of the offender as well as the prevention of crime; and where it wholly loses the remedial element, and cuts off the opportunity for repentance which God's mercy allows, it is worthy of a barbarous, not a Christian, social alliance. What sort of combination for mutual safety is it, too, when no man feels safe, because fortuitous circumstances, ingeniously bound into a chain, may so entangle Truth that she cannot bestir herself to rescue us from the doom which the judgment of twelve fallible men pronounces, and our protector, the law, executes upon us?

But we are losing sight of Mr. Hawthorne's book, and of the old Puritan settlers, as he portrays them with few, but clearly cut and expressive, lines. In these sketchy groupings, Governor Bellingham is the only prominent figure, with the Rev. John Wilson behind him, "his heard, white as a snowdrift, seen over the Governor's shoulder."

> "Here, to witness the scene which we are describing, sat Governor Bellingham himself, with four sergeants about his chair, bearing halberds as a guard of honor. He wore a dark feather in his hat, a border of embroidery on his cloak, and a black velvet tunic beneath; a gentleman advanced in years, and with a hard experience written in his wrinkles. He was not ill-fitted to be the head and representative of a community, which owed its origin and progress, and its present state of development, not to the impulses of youth, but to the stern and tempered energies of manhood, and the sombre sagacity of age; accomplishing so much, precisely because it imagined and hoped so little."

With this portrait, we close our remarks on the book, which we should not have criticized at so great length, had we admired it less. We hope to be forgiven, if in any instance our strictures have approached the limits of what may be considered personal. We would not willingly trench upon the right which an individual may claim, in common courtesy, not to have his private qualities or personal features discussed to his face, with everybody

looking on. But Mr. Hawthorne's example in the preface, and the condescending familiarity of the attitude he assumes therein, are at once our occasion and our apology.

An anonymous review of *The House of Seven Gables* in "Notices of New Books," *The United States Democratic Review,* May 1851

The reputation of Mr. Hawthorne is sufficiently established and widely known, to procure for any stories of his production a large and eager circle of readers. His delineations of New-England manners, conversations and language, are governed by good taste in avoiding to adulterate the conversations of ordinary people with idioms and barbarisms.

An anonymous review of *The Blithedale Romance* in *American Whig Review,* November 1852

Every work which proposes to develop a new phase of human character, or philosophize upon an assumption of original responsibilities, derives a species of adventitious interest from the novelty of its subject, independent of any artistic ability by which it may be accompanied. When it was publicly understood that Mr. Hawthorne was engaged in the composition of a romance, having for its origin, if not its subject, a community which once had a brief existence at Brook Farm, speculation was awakened, anticipations grew vivid, and the reading public awaited anxiously the issue of book which it was hoped would combine in itself the palatable spices of novelty and personality. A portion of these expectations were doomed to disappointment. In the preface to the Blithedale Romance, Mr. Hawthorne distinctly disavowed any intention of painting portaits. To his sojourn at Brook Farm he attributes his inspiration, but that is all. Blithedale is no caligraph of Brook Farm. Zenobia first sprang into actual existence from the printing press of Ticknor, Reed and Fields, and the quiet Priscilla is nothing more than one of those pretty phantoms with which Mr. Hawthorne occasionally adorns his romances.

We believe that if Mr. Hawthorne had intended to give a faithful portrait of Brook Farm and its inmates, he would have signally failed. He has no genius for realities, save in inanimate nature. Between his characters and the reader falls a gauze-like veil of imagination, on which their shadows flit and more, and play strange dramas replete with second-hand life. An air of unreality enshrouds all his creations. They are either dead, or have never lived, and when they pass away they as leave behind them an oppressive and unwholesome chill.

This sluggish antiquity of style may suit some subjects admirably. When, as in the Scarlet Letter, the epoch of the story is so far removed from the present day as to invest all the events with little more than a reminiscent interest; when characters and customs were so different to all circumstance that jostles us in the rude, quick life of today, and when we do not expect to meet, in the long corridors of Time down which the author leads us, any company beyond the pale, shadowy ancestry with whose names we are faintly familiar, but with whom we have no common sympathies. Mr. Hawthorne's genius, if we may be permitted to use so extravagant a simile, reminds us forcibly of an old country mansion of the last century. It seems as if it had been built a very long time. It is but half inhabited, and throbs with only a moiety of life. The locks and bolts are rusty, and the doors creak harshly on their hinges. Huge twisted chimneys branch out of every gable, and in every chimney is lodged some capricious, eccentric old rook, who startles us unexpectedly with his presence. Great wings, and odd buttresses, jut out from all the corners, the phrenological bumps of architecture; while here and there, in warm sheltered nooks, sweet climbing flowers, dewy roses, and jessamine prodigal of its perfume, cling lovingly to the old moss-grown walls, and strive, but with ill success, to conceal the quaint deformity of the building.

In the House of the Seven Gables this dreary beauty is eminently prominent. The poetry of desolation, and the leaden vapors of solitude are wreathed around the scene. The doings of the characters awaken only a faint, dream-like interest in our hearts. We seem to hear the hollow echoes of their footsteps in the silence, and follow them with our fingers as if we expected them each moment to melt and mingle with the surrounding air. This sad

and unsubstantial painting is no doubt excellently well achieved. Mr. Hawthorne deals artistically with shadows. There is a strange, unearthly fascination about the fair spectres that throng his works, and we know no man who can distort nature, or idealize abortions more cleverly than the author of the Scarlet Letter. But we question much, if we strip Mr. Hawthorne's works of a certain beauty and originality of style which they are always sure to possess, whether the path which he has chosen is a healthy one. To us it does not seem as if the fresh wind of morning blew across his track; we do not feel the strong pulse of nature throbbing beneath the turf he treads upon. When an author sits down to make a book, he should not alone consult the inclinations of his own genius regarding its purpose or its construction. If he should happen to be imbued with strange, saturnine doctrines, or be haunted by a morbid suspicion of human nature, in God's name let him not write one word. Better that all the beautiful, wild thoughts with which his brain is teeming should moulder for ever in neglect and darkness, than that one soul was overshadowed by stern, uncongenial dogmas, which should have died with their Puritan fathers. It is not alone necessary to produce a work of art. The soul of beauty is Truth, and Truth is ever progressive. The true artist therefore endeavors to make the world better. He does not look behind him, and dig out of the graves of past centuries skeletons to serve as models for his pictures; but looks onward for more perfect shapes, and though sometimes obliged to design from the defective forms around him, he infuses, as it were, some of the divine spirit of the future into them, and lo! we love them with all their faults. But Mr. Hawthorne discards all idea of successful human progress. All his characters seem so weighed down with their own evilness of nature, that they can scarcely keep their balance, much less take their places in the universal march. Like the lord mentioned in Scripture, he issues an invitation to the halt, the blind, and the lame of soul, to gather around his board, and then asks us to feast at the same table. It is a pity that Mr. Hawthorne should not have been originally imbued with more universal tenderness. It is a pity that he displays nature to us so shrouded and secluded, and that he should be afflicted with such a melancholy craving for human curiosities. His men are either vicious, crazed, or misanthropical, and his women are either unwomanly, unearthly, or unhappy. His books have no sunny side to them. They are unripe to the very core.

We are more struck with the want of this living tenderness in the Blithedale Romance than in any of Mr. Hawthorne's previous novels. In the Scarlet Letter and the House of the Seven Gables, a certain gloominess of thought suited the antiquity of the subjects; but in his last performance, the date of the events, and the nature of the story, entitle us to expect something brighter and less unhealthy. The efforts of any set of hopeful, well-meaning people to shame society into better ways, are deserving of respect, as long as they do not attempt to interfere with those sacred foundation-stones of morality on which all society rests. It was a pure, fresh thought, that of flying from the turmoil of the city, and toiling in common upon the broad fields for bread. With all their fallacies, there is much that is good and noble about the American communists. It is a sad mistake to suppose them stern exponents of the gross and absurd system laid down by Fourier. They are not, at least as far as our knowledge goes, either dishonest or sensual. They do not mock at rational rights, or try to overturn the constitution of society. We believe their ruling idea to be that of isolating themselves from all that is corrupt in the congregations of mankind called cities, and seek in open country and healthy toil the sweets and triumphs of a purer life. One would imagine that dealing with a subject like this would in some degree counteract Mr. Hawthorne's ascetic humor. One would have thought that, in narrating a course of events which, acted on as they were by the surrounding circumstances, must have been somewhat buoyant and fresh, he would have burst that icy chain of puritanical gloom, and for once made a holiday with Nature. No such thing! From the beginning to the end, the Blithedale Romance is a melancholy chronicle, less repulsive, it is true, than its predecessors, but still sad and inexpressibly mournful. Not that the author has intended it to be uniformly pathetic. It is very evident that he sat down with the intention of writing a strong, vigorous book, upon a strong, vigorous subject; but his own baneful spirit hovered over the pages, and turned the ink into bitterness and tears.

Let us review his characters, and see if we can find any thing genial among them. Hollingsworth in importance comes first. A rude fragment of a great man. Unyielding as granite in any matters on which he has decided, yet possessing a latent tenderness of nature that, if he had been the creature of other hands than Mr. Hawthorne's, would have been is redemption. But our author is deeply read in human imperfection, and lets no opportunity slip of thrusting it before his readers. A horrid hump of unappeasable egotism is stuck between Hollingsworth's shoulders. He is depicted as a sort of human Maëlstrom, engulfing all natures that come within his range, and relentlessly absorbing them in his own vast necessities. He is selfish, dogmatic, and inhumanly proud, and all these frightful attributes are tacked on to a character that, in the hands of a Dickens or a Fielding, would have loomed out from the canvas with sufficient imperfection to make it human, but with enough of heart and goodness to compel us to love it.

Readers will perchance say that Mr. Hawthorne has a right to deal with his characters according to his pleasure, and that we are not authorized to quarrel with the length of their noses, or the angularities of their natures. No doubt. But, on the other hand, Mr. Hawthorne has no right to blacken and defame humanity, by animating his shadowy people with worse passions and more imperfect souls than we meet with in the world.

Miles Coverdale, the narrator of the tale, is to us a most repulsive being. A poet, but yet no poetry in his deeds. A sneering, suspicious, inquisitive, and disappointed man, who rejects Hollingsworth's advances because he fears that a connection between them may lead to some ulterior peril; who allows Zenobia to dominate over his nature, because she launches at him a few wild words, and who forsakes the rough, healthy life of Blithedale, because he pines for Turkey carpets and a sea-coal fire. Such is the man upon whose dictum Mr. Hawthorne would endeavor covertly to show the futility of the enterprise in whose favor he was once enlisted.

Zenobia, the character on which he has probably bestowed the most pains, is no doubt true to nature. Women that thrust themselves out of their sphere must inevitably lose many of those graces which constitute their peculiar charm. Looked upon by their own sex with dismay, and by ours with certain mingled feelings of jealousy and pity, they voluntarily isolate themselves from the generality of the world, and fancy themselves martyrs. They are punished with contempt, and to reformers of their fiery nature, contempt is worse than death. They blaspheme God by stepping beyond the limits. He has assigned to them through all ages, and seem to fancy that they can better laws which are eternal and immutable.

The Zenobia of our author does not command our interest. Her character, though poetically colored, is not sufficiently powerful for a woman that has so far outstridden the even pace of society. She has a certain amount of courage and passion, but no philosophy. Her impulses start off in the wrong direction, nor does she seem to possess the earnestness necessary to induce a woman to defy public opinion. She is a mere fierce, wild wind, blowing hither and thither, with no fixity of purpose, and making us shrink closer every moment from the contact.

In truth, with the exception of Priscilla, who is faint and shadowy, the dramatis personae at Blithedale are not to our taste. There is a bad purpose in every one of them—a purpose, too, which is neither finally redeemed nor condemned.

Notwithstanding the faults which we have alluded to, and which cling to Mr. Hawthorne tenaciously in all his works, there is much to be admired in the Blithedale Romance. If our author takes a dark view of society, he takes a bright one of nature. He paints truthfully and poetically, and possesses a Herrick-like fashion of deducing morals from flowers, rocks, and herbage, or any other little feature in his visionary landscape. . . .

On the socialist theory Mr. Hawthorne says little in the Blithedale Romance. That he is no longer a convert is evident, but he does not attempt to discuss the matter philosophically. Judging from many passages in the book, we should say that he had been sadly disappointed in the experiment made at

Brook Farm, and sought thus covertly and incidentally to record his opinion. One of the most curious characteristics of the book is, that not one of the persons assembled at Blithedale treat the institution as if they were in earnest. Zenobia sneers at it—Coverdale grumbles at it—Hollingsworth condemns—Priscilla alone endures it. We know not if this is a feature drawn from realities. If it is not, Mr. Hawthorne is immediately placed in the position of having created a group of fictitious hypocrites, not true to human nature, merely for the sake of placing them in a novel position and surrounding them with fresh scenery. . . .

With the last paragraph we cannot agree. The mind depends for healthy action upon the health and soundness of the flesh, and in no way can the physical constitution be developed better than by hard work; that is, work, not for hours, days or weeks, but constant, unremitting employment. Mr. Hawthorne writes this passage very much like a man to whom labor was a new thing, and who, though he may have worked hard during the day, at night found himself from sheer exhaustion almost incapable of thought. But the man who habitually works feels no after lassitude. Were the laborer in the fields, or the blacksmith at the anvil, to the gifted with purer intellect or higher mental culture than is usually allotted to such men, they would not find their labor interfering with their inspiration. After working hours, such men do not experience any lassitude. They surrender themselves to a pleasing sensation of tranquillity, but would be as fit for any new physical or mental occupation as they ever were. But with the experimentalist in toil it is different. The muscles, that from their first maturity have been accustomed to lie at ease, are not so readily brought into play. The gentleman whose days have been spent in sedentary occupations, no matter how powerful his physical frame may be, will find that on his first initiation into the school of labor, he is unfit for any task save one. His nature is suddenly worked against the grain, and refuses to act beyond a certain time. But if these tasks were continued for any period, if day after day the gentleman were to go out into the fields and make fences or plough cornfields, the mental sluggishness complained of by Mr. Hawthorne would wear off, and he would find that hardened muscles were not at all incompatible with the struggles of philosophic thought, or the play of imagination.

In Priscilla, Mr. Hawthorne has essayed a delicate character, but in his portraiture he has availed himself of an ingenious expedient, which we know not whether to rank as intentional or accidental. In drawing a portrait, there are two ways of attaining delicacy of outline. One is by making the outline itself so faint and indistinct that it appears as it were to mingle with the surrounding shadow; the other and more difficult one is, to paint, and paint detail after detail, until the whole becomes so finished a work of art, so harmoniously colored, that one feature does not strike us more forcibly than another; so homogeneous in its aspect that outline, background and detail are all painted perfectly on our perceptions in a manner that defies analysis. Now, there is no question that the man who employs the first means has infinitely easier work than the last. He has nothing to do but conjure you up a pretty-looking ghost, and lo! the work is done. Mr. Hawthorne is fond of these ghosts. Priscilla is a ghost; we do not realize her, even to the end. Her connection with Westervelt is shadowy and ill–defined. Zenobia's influence over her nature is only indistinctly intimated. Her own mental construction is left almost an open question; and even when, in the crowning of the drama, we find her the support, the crutch of the rugged. Hollingsworth, there is no satisfactory happiness wreathed about her destiny. This is not artistic or wholesome. We all know that a certain fascination springs up in every breast when the undefined is presented. The love of spectral stories, and superhuman exhibitions, all have their root in this, and Mr. Hawthorne appears to know well how to play upon this secret chord with his fantastic shadows. We do not look upon his treatment of character as fair. He does not give it to us in its entirety, but puts us off with a pleasant phantasmagoria. We should attribute this to inability in any other man, but we feel too well convinced of Mr. Hawthorne's genius to doubt his capability for an instant to furnish us with a perfect picture. But we doubt his will. This sketchy painting is easy and rapid. A very few lines will indicate a spectre, when it would take

an entire month to paint a woman; and Mr. Hawthorne finds this unsubstantial picture-making suit his own dreamy and sometimes morbid fancy. For Heaven's sake, Mr. Hawthorne, do not continue to give us shadows, even if they be as sweet and loveable as Priscilla! Recollect that you have earned a great name as a writer of romance, and will necessarily have many followers. Cease then, good sir; for if you continue to give us shadows, in another year your imitators will inundate their books with skeletons!

That Mr. Hawthorne can paint vividly when he likes it, few who have read his novels can doubt. He possesses all the requisites for the task—power of language, felicity of collateral incident, and a certain subdued richness of style which is one of his greatest charms. The following description of the death of Zenobia is exquisitely managed. . . .

This is powerful—sadness and strength mingled into a most poetical and vivid deathscene. A thought crosses us, whether Mr. Hawthorne would paint a wedding as well as a death; whether he could conjure as distinctly before our vision the bridal flowers, as he has done the black, damp weeds that waved around the grave of Zenobia. We fear not. His genius has a church-yard beauty about it, and revels amid graves, and executions, and all the sad leavings of mortality. We know no man whom we would sooner ask to write our epitaph. We feel assured that it would be poetical, and suitable in the highest degree.

Since the publication of his book, it grieved us to learn that a severe domestic affliction has overtaken Mr. Hawthorne, through the terrible calamity that befell the Henry Clay. It was a sad coincidence that death by the waves should overtake a member of his family so soon after his fictitious tragedy of Zenobia. It was a bitter thing for the secluded author to be forced to entwine with his newly acquired laurel-wreaths so melancholy a leaf as that of cypress.

An anonymous review of *The Marble Faun, North American Review,* April 1860

On the publication of Mr. Hawthorne's last romance, his writings were made the subject of an extended article in this journal; and we need not therefore enter into any discussion now of his general characteristics, for they remain unchanged except by the modifications arising from moral and intellectual growth. The greater part of the interval which has since elapsed has been passed by Mr. Hawthorne in England and in Italy, and the book before us is the first fruit of his residence abroad,— to be followed, we hope, by many other productions of equal merit. As a work of art, we are inclined to place it above either of his previous books. Its style has a harmony and beauty of expression and a warmth of coloring which are seen in none of his other writings, and there are passages in which criticism cannot suggest even the alteration of a word. Though it owes much of its interest to the mystery surrounding its principal character, and is deeply penetrated by the tragic element in which the author delights, its tone is far more healthful than is that of his other romances. Its plot, however, has the intricacy which is a prominent fault in all his romances; and the book leaves on the mind of the reader an impression of incompleteness. Its scene is laid in Italy, and the first draft of the story was made there, though it was written out for the press in England. Its inspiration indeed comes wholly from Italy, and some of its most delightful pages record the impression produced on the author by the masterpieces of ancient and modern art in Rome, in by Italian scenery and life. Never obtrusively introduced, these descriptions spring naturally out of the narrative, and give to the volumes much of the interest belonging to a book of travels. Two of the characters are American artists, one a sculptor and the other a painter; and among the descriptive passages is an enthusiastic mention of Story's statue of Cleopatra.

There are only four personages brought prominently into notice; but they have great individuality, and their characters are drawn with even more than Mr. Hawthorne's accustomed skill. Nothing, indeed, can be more finely delineated than the beautiful and sinless life of Hilda, while its striking contrast with the dark and guilt-stained career of Miriam gives added force to the representation. As is the case in his previous romances, Mr. Hawthorne has thrown all his strength into the delineation of his women; but the characters of Kenyon, the speculative sculptor, and of Donatello, in whom so great a transformation is wrought, are both delineated with much power. As a work of the imagination, and as a picture of modern Italian life, the book is equally deserving of praise; and its fascination is such, that the reader will scarcely close the volumes until he has turned the last page.

MELVILLE AND HAWTHORNE

The following is from Melville's letter to Hawthorne, April 1851

My Dear Hawthorne,—Concerning the young gentleman's shoes, I desire to say that a pair to fit him, of the desired pattern, cannot be had in all Pittsfield,—a fact which sadly impairs that metropolitan pride I formerly took in the capital of Berkshire. Henceforth Pittsfield must hide its head. However, if a pair of *bootees* will at all answer, Pittsfield will be very happy to provide them. Pray mention all this to Mrs. Hawthorne, and command me.

"The House of the Seven Gables: A Romance. By Nathaniel Hawthorne. One vol. 16mo, pp. 344." The contents of this book do not belie its rich, clustering, romantic title. With great enjoyment we spent almost an hour in each separate gable. This book is like a fine old chamber, abundantly, but still judiciously, furnished with precisely that sort of furniture best fitted to furnish it. There are rich hangings, wherein are braided scenes from tragedies! There is old china with rare devices, set out on the carved buffet; there are long and indolent lounges to throw yourself upon; there is an admirable sideboard, plentifully stored with good viands; there is a smell as of old wine in the pantry; and finally, in one corner, there is a dark little black-letter volume in golden clasps, entitled "Hawthorne: A Problem" It has delighted us; it has piqued a reperusal; it has robbed us of a day, and made us a present of a whole year of thoughtfulness; it has bred great exhilaration and exultation with the remembrance that the architect of the Gables resides only six miles off, and not three thousand miles away, in England, say. We think the book, for pleasantness of running interest, surpasses the other works of the author. The curtains are more drawn; the sun comes in more; genialities peep out more. Were we to particularize what most struck us in the deeper passages, we would point out the scene where Clifford, for a moment, would fain throw himself forth from the window to join the procession; or the scene where the judge is left seated in his ancestral chair. Clifford is full of an awful truth throughout. He is conceived in the finest, truest spirit. He is no caricature. He is Clifford. And here we would say that, did circumstances permit, we should like nothing better than to devote an elaborate and careful paper to the full consideration and analysis of the purport and significance of what so strongly characterizes all of this author's writings. There is a certain tragic phase of humanity which, in our opinion, was never more powerfully embodied than by Hawthorne. We mean the tragicalness of human thought in its own unbiassed, native, and profounder workings. We think that into no recorded mind has the intense feeling of the visable truth ever entered more deeply than into this man's. By visable truth, we mean the apprehension of the absolute condition of present things as they strike the eye of the man who fears them not, though they do their worst to him,—the man who, like Russia or the British Empire, declares himself a sovereign nature (in himself) amid the powers of heaven, hell, and earth. He may perish; but so long as he exists he insists upon treating with all Powers upon an equal basis. If any of those other Powers choose to withhold certain secrets, let them; that does not impair my sovereignty in myself; that does not make me tributary. And perhaps, after all, there is *no* secret. We incline to think that the Problem of the Universe is like the Freemason's mighty secret, so terrible to all children. It turns out, at last, to consist in a triangle, a mallet, and an apron,—nothing more! We incline to think that God cannot explain His own secrets, and that He would like a little information upon certain points Himself. We mortals astonish Him as much as He us. But it is this *Being* of the matter; there lies the knot with which we choke ourselves. As soon as you say *Me*, a *God*, a *Nature*, so soon you jump off from your stool and hang from the beam. Yes, that word is the hangman. Take God out of the dictionary, and you would have Him in the street.

There is the grand truth about Nathaniel Hawthorne. He says No! in thunder; but the Devil himself cannot make him say yes. For all men who say yes, lie; and all men who say *no*,—why, they are in the happy condition of judicious, unincumbered travellers in Europe; they cross the frontiers into Eternity with nothing but a carpet-bag,—that is to say, the Ego. Whereas those *yes*-gentry, they travel with heaps of baggage, and, damn them! they will never get through the Custom House. What's the reason, Mr. Hawthorne, that in the last stages of metaphysics a fellow always falls to *swearing* so? I could rip an hour. You see, I began with a little criticism extracted for your benefit from the "Pittsfield Secret Review," and here I have landed in Africa.

Walk down one of these mornings and see me. No nonsense; come. Remember me to Mrs. Hawthorne and the children.

                                         H. Melville.

P.S. The marriage of Phoebe with the daguerreotypist is a fine stroke, because of his turning out to be a *Maule*. If you pass Hepzibah's cent-shop, buy me a Jim Crow (fresh) and send it to me by Ned Higgins.

Melville's essay "Hawthorne and His Mosses," from *Literary World*, August 17 and 24, 1850

By a Virginian Spending July in Vermont

A papered chamber in a fine old farm-house—a mile from any other dwelling, and dipped to the eaves in foliage—surrounded by mountains, old woods, and Indian ponds,—this, surely is the place to write of Hawthorne. Some charm is in this northern air, for love and duty seem both impelling to the task. A man of a deep and noble nature has seized me in this seclusion. His wild, witch voice rings through me; or, in softer cadences, I seem to hear it in the songs of the hill-side birds, that sing in the larch trees at my window.

Would that all excellent books were foundlings, without father or mother, that so it might be, we could glorify them, without including their ostensible authors. Nor would any true man take exception to this;—least of all, he who writes,—"When the Artist rises high enough to achieve the Beautiful, the symbol by which he makes it perceptible to mortal senses becomes of little value in his eyes, while his spirit possesses itself in the enjoyment of the reality."

But more than this, I know not what would be the right name to put on the title-page of an excellent book, but this I feel, that the names of all fine authors are fictitious ones, far more than that of Junius,—simply standing, as they do, for the mystical, ever-eluding Spirit of all Beauty, which ubiquitously possesses men of genius. Purely imaginative as this fancy may appear, it nevertheless seems to receive some warranty from the fact, that on a personal interview no great author has ever come up to the idea of his reader. But that dust of which our bodies are composed, how can it fitly express the nobler intelligences among us? With reverence be it spoken, that not even in the case of one deemed more than man, not even in our Saviour, did his visible frame betoken anything of the augustness of the nature within. Else, how could those Jewish eyewitnesses fail to see heaven in his glance.

It is curious, how a man may travel along a country road, and yet miss the grandest, or sweetest of prospects, by reason of an intervening hedge, so like all other hedges, as in no way to hint of the wide landscape beyond. So has it been with me concerning the enchanting landscape in the soul of this Hawthorne, this most excellent Man of Mosses. His "Old Manse" has been written now four years, but I never read it till a day or two since. I had seen it in the book-stores—heard of it often—even had it recommended to me by a tasteful friend, as a rare, quiet book, perhaps too deserving of popularity to be popular. But there are so many books called "excellent," and so much unpopular merit, that amid the thick stir of other things, the hint of my tasteful friend was disregarded; and for four years the Mosses on the Old Manse never refreshed me with their perennial green. It may be, however, that all this while, the book, like wine, was only improving in flavor and body. At any rate, it so chanced that this long procrastination eventuated in a happy result. At breakfast the other day, a mountain girl, a cousin of mine, who for the last two weeks has every morning helped me to strawberries and raspberries,—which like the roses and pearls in the fairy-tale, seemed to fall into the saucer from those strawberry-beds her cheeks,—this delightful crature, this charming Cherry says to me—"I see you spend your mornings in the hay-mow; and yesterday I found there 'Dwight's Travels in New England'. Now I have something far better than that,—something more congenial to our summer on these hills. Take these raspberries, and then I will give you some moss."—"Moss!" said I—"Yes, and you must take it to the barn with you, and good-bye to 'Dwight.'"

With that she left me, and soon returned with a volume, verdantly bound, and garnished with a curious frontispiece in green,—nothing less, than a fragment of real moss cunningly pressed to a fly-leaf.—"Why this," said I, spilling my raspberries, "this is the 'Mosses from an Old Manse.'" "Yes," said cousin Cherry, "yes, it is that flowery Hawthorne."—"Hawthorne and Mosses," said I, "no more: it is morning: it is July in the country: and I am off for the barn."

Stretched on that new mown clover, the hillside breeze blowing over me through the wide barn door, and soothed by the hum of the bees in the meadows around, how magically stole over me this Mossy Man! And how amply, how bountifully, did he redeem that delicious promise to his guests in the Old Manse, of whom it is written—"Others could give them pleasure, or amusement, or instruction—these could be picked up anywhere—but it was for me to give them rest. Rest, in a life of trouble! What better could be done for weary and world-worn spirits? what better could be done for

anybody, who came within our magic circle, than to throw the spell of a magic spirit over them?"—So all that day, half-buried in the new clover, I watched this Hawthorne's "Assyrian dawn, and Paphian sunset and moonrise, from the summit of our Eastern Hill."

The soft ravishments of the man spun me round in a web of dreams, and when the book was closed, when the spell was over, this wizard "dismissed me with but misty reminiscences, as if I had been dreaming of him."

What a mild moonlight of contemplative humor bathes that Old Manse!—the rich and rare distilment of a spicy and slowly-oozing heart. No rollicking rudeness, no gross fun fed on fat dinners, and bred in the lees of wine,—but a humor so spiritually gentle, so high, so deep, and yet so richly relishable, that it were hardly inappropriate in an angel. It is the very religion of mirth; for nothing so human but it may be advanced to that. The orchard of the Old Manse seems the visible type of the fine mind that has described it. Those twisted, and contorted old trees, "that stretch out their crooked branches, and take such hold of the imagination, that we remember them as humorists and odd-fellows." And then, as surrounded by these grotesque forms, and hushed in the noon-day repose of this Hawthorne's spell, how aptly might the still fall of his ruddy thoughts into your soul be symbolized by "the thump of a great apple, in the stillest afternoon, falling without a breath of wind, from the mere necessity of perfect ripeness"! For no less ripe than ruddy are the apples of the thoughts and fancies in this sweet Man of Mosses.

"Buds and Bird-Voices"—What a delicious thing is that!—"Will the world ever be so decayed, that Spring may not renew its greenness?"—And the "Fire-worship." Was ever the hearth so glorified into an altar before? The mere title of that piece is better than any common work in fifty folio volumes. How exquisite is this:—"Nor did it lessen the charm of his soft, familiar courtesy and helpfulness, that the mighty spirit, were opportunity offered him, would run riot through the peaceful house, wrap its inmates in his terrible embrace, and leave nothing of them save their whitened bones. This possibility of mad destruction only made his domestic kindness the more beautiful and touching. It was so sweet of him, being endowed with such power, to dwell, day after day, and one long, lonesome night after another, on the dusky hearth, only now and then betraying his wild nature, by thrusting his red tongue out of the chimney-top! True, he had done much mischief in the world, and was pretty certain to do more, but his warm heart atoned for all. He was kindly to the race of man."

But he has still other apples, not quite so ruddy, though full as ripe:—apples, that have been left to wither on the tree, after the pleasant autumn gathering is past. The sketch of "The Old Apple Dealer" is conceived in the subtlest spirit of sadness; he whose "subdued and nerveless boyhood prefigured his abortive prime, which, likewise, contained within itself the prophecy and image of his lean and torpid age." Such touches as are in this piece can not proceed from any common heart. They argue such a depth of tenderness, such a boundless sympathy with all forms of being, such an omnipresent love, that we must needs say, that this Hawthorne is here almost alone in his generation,—at least, in the artistic manisfestation of these things. Still more. Such touches as these,—and many, very many similar ones, all through his chapters—furnish clews, whereby we enter a little way into the intricate, profound heart where they originated. And we see, that suffering, some time or other and in some shape or other,—this only can enable any man to depict it in others. All over him, Hawthorne's melancholy rests like an Indian summer, which, though bathing a whole country in one softness, still reveals the distinctive hue of every towering hill, and each far-winding vale.

But it is the least part of genius that attracts admiration. Where Hawthorne is known, he seems to be deemed a pleasant writer, with a pleasant style,—a sequestered, harmless man, from whom any deep and weighty thing would hardly be anticipated:—a man who means no meanings. But there is no man, in whom humor and love, like mountain peaks, soar to such a rapt height, as to receive the irradiations of the upper skies;—there is no man in whom humor and love are developed in that high form called genius; no such man can exist without also possessing, as the indispensable complement of these, a great, deep intellect, which drops down into the universe like a plummet. Or, love and humor are only the eyes, through which such an intellect views this world. The great beauty in such a mind is but the product of its strength. What, to all readers, can be more charming than the piece entitled "Monsieur du Miroir"; and to a reader at all capable of fully fathoming it, what at the same time, can possess more mystical depth of meaning?—Yes, there he sits, and looks at me,—this "shape of mystery," this "identical Monsieur du Miroir."—"Methinks I should tremble now, were his wizard power of gliding through all impediments in search of me, to place him suddenly before my eyes."

How profound, nay appalling, is the moral evolved by the "Earth's Holocaust"; where—beginning with the hollow follies and affectations of the world,—all vanities and empty theories and forms, are, one after another, and by an admirably graduated, growing comprehensiveness, thrown into the allegorical fire, till, at length, nothing is left but the all-engendering heart of man; which remaining still unconsumed, the great conflagration is naught.

Of a piece with this, is the "Intelligence Office," a wondrous symbolizing of the secret workings in men's souls. There are other sketches, still more charged with ponderous import.

"The Christmas Banquet," and "The Bosom-serpent" would be fine subjects for a curious and elaborate analysis, touching the conjectural parts of the mind that produced them. For spite of all the Indian-summer sunlight on the hither side of Hawthorne's soul, the other side—like the dark half of the physical sphere—is shrouded in a blackness, ten times black. But this darkness but gives more effect to the evermoving dawn, that forever advances through it, and cirumnavigates his world. Whether Hawthorne has simply availed himself of this mystical blackness as a means to the wondrous effects he makes it to produce in his lights and shades; or whether there really lurks in him, perhaps unknown to himself, a touch of Puritanic gloom,—this, I cannot altogether tell. Certain it is, however, that this grat power of blackness in him derives its force from its appeals to that Calvinistic sense of Innate Depravity and Original Sin, from whose visitations, in some shape or other, no deeply thinking mind is always and wholly free. For, in certain moods, no man can weigh this world, without throwing in something, somehow like Original Sin, to strike the uneven balance. At all events, perhaps no writer has ever wielded this terrific thought with greater terror than this same harmless Hawthorne. Still more: this black conceit pervades him, through and through. You may be witched by his sunlight,—transported by the bright gildings in the skies he builds over you;—but there is the blackness of darkness beyond; and even his bright gildings but fringe, and play upon the edges of thunder-clouds.—In one word, the world is mistaken in this Nathaniel Hawthorne. He himself must often have smiled at its absurd misconceptions of him. He is immeasurably deeper than the plummet of the mere critic. For it is not the brain that can test such a man; it is only the heart. You cannot come to know greatness by inspecting it; there is no glimpse to be caught of it, except by intuition; you need not ring it, you but touch it, and you find it is gold.

Now it is that blackness in Hawthorne, of which I have spoken, that so fixes and fascinates me. It may be, nevertheless, that it is too largely developed in him. Perhaps he does not give us a ray of his light for every shade of his dark. But however this may be, this blackness it is that furnishes the infinite obscure of his background,—that background, against which Shakespeare plays his grandest conceits, the things that have made for Shakespeare his loftiest, but most circumscribed renown, as the profoundest of thinkers. For by philosophers Shakespeare is not adored as the great man of tragedy and comedy.—"Off with his head! so much for Buckingham!" this sort of rant, interlined by another hand, brings down the house,—those mistaken souls, who dream of Shakespeare as a mere man of Richard-the-Third humps, and Macbeth daggers. But it is those deep far-away things in him; those occasional flashings-forth of the intuitive Truth in him; those short, quick probings at the very axis of reality:—these are the things that make Shakespeare, Shakespeare. Through the mouths of the dark characters of Hamlet, Timon, Lear, and Iago, he craftily says, or sometimes insin-

uates the things, which we feel to be so terrifically true, that it were all but madness for any good man, in his own proper character, to utter, or even hint of them. Tormented into desperation, Lear the frantic King tears off the mask, and speaks the sane madness of vital truth. But, as I before said, it is the least part of genius that attracts admiration. And so, much of the blind, unbridled admiration that has been heaped upon Shakespeare, has been lavished upon the least part of him. And few of his endless commentators and critics seem to have remembered, or even perceived, that the immediate products of a great mind are not so great, as that undeveloped, (and sometimes undevelopable) yet dimly-discernible greatness, to which these immediate products are but the infallible indices. In Shakespeare's tomb lies infinitely more than Shakespeare ever wrote. And if I magnify Shakespeare, it is not so much for what he did do, as for what he did not do, or refrained from doing. For in this world of lies, Truth is forced to fly like a scared white doe in the woodlands; and only by cunning glimpses will she reveal herself, as in Shakespeare and other masters of the great Art of Telling the Truth,—even though it be covertly, and by snatches.

But if this view of the all-popular Shakespeare be seldom taken by his readers, and if very few who extol him, have ever read him deeply, or, perhaps, only have seen him on the tricky stage, (which alone made, and is still making him his mere mob renown)—if few men have time, or patience, or palate, for the spiritual truth as it is in that great genius;—it is, then, no matter of surprise that in a contemporaneous age, Nathaniel Hawthorne is a man, as yet, almost utterly mistaken among men. Here and there, in some quiet arm-chair in the noisy town, or some deep nook among the noiseless mountains, he may be appreciated for something of what he is. But unlike Shakespeare, who was forced to the contrary course by circumstances, Hawthorne (either from simple disinclination, or else from inaptitude) refrains from all the popularizing noise and show of broad farce, and blood-besmeared tragedy; content with the still, rich utterances of a great intellect in repose, and which sends few thoughts into circulation, except they be arterialized at his large warm lungs, and expanded in his honest heart.

Nor need you fix upon that blackness in him, if it suit you not. Nor, indeed, will all readers discern it, for it is, mostly, insinuated to those who may best undersand it, and account for it; it is not obtruded upon every one alike.

Some may start to read of Shakespeare and Hawthorne on the same page. They may say, that if an illustration were needed, a lesser light might have sufficed to elucidate this Hawthorne, this small man of yesterday. But I am not, willingly, one of those, who as touching Shakespeare at least, exemplify the maxim of Rochefoucauld, that "we exalt the reputation of some, in order to depress that of others";—who, to teach all noble-souled aspirants that there is no hope for them, pronounce Shakespeare absolutely unapproachable. But Shakespeare has been approached. There are minds that have gone as far as Shakespeare into the universe. And hardly a mortal man, who, at some time or other, has not felt as great thoughts in him as any you will find in Hamlet. We must not inferentially malign mankind for the sake of any one man, whoever he may be. This is too cheap a purchase of contentment for consious mediocrity to make. Besides, this absolute and unconditional adoration of Shakespeare has grown to be a part of our Anglo Saxon superstitions. The Thirty-Nine Articles are now Forty. Intolerance has come to exist in this matter. You must believe in Shakespeare's unapproachability, or quit the country. But what sort of belief is this for an American, an man who is bound to carry republican progressiveness into Literature, as well as into Life? Believe me, my friends, that men not very much inferior to Shakespeare, are this day being born on the banks of the Ohio. And the day will come, when you shall say who reads a book by an Englishman that is a modern? The great mistake seems to be, that even with those Americans who look forward to the coming of a great literary genius among us, they somehow fancy he will come in the costume of Queen Elizabeth's day,—be a writer of dramas founded upon old English history, or the tales of Boccaccio. Whereas, great geniuses are parts of the times; they themselves are the time; and possess an cor-

respondent coloring. It is of a piece with the Jews, who while their Shiloh was meekly walking in their streets, were still praying for his magnificent coming; looking for him in a chariot, who was already among them on an ass. Nor must we forget, that, in his own life-time, Shakespeare was not Shakespeare, but only Master William Shakespeare of the shrewd, thriving business firm of Condell, Shakespeare & Co., proprietors of the Globe Theater in London; and by a courtly author, of the name of Chettle, was hooted at, as an "upstart crow" beautified "with other birds' feathers." For, mark it well, imitation is often the first charge brought against real originality. Why this is so, there is not space to set forth here. You must have plenty of sea-room to tell the Truth in; especially, when it seems to have an aspect of newness, as American did in 1492, though it was then just as old, and perhaps older than Asia, only those sagacious philosophers, the common sailors, had never seen it before; swearing it was all water and moonshine there.

Now, I do not say that Nathaniel of Salem is a greater than William of Avon, or as great. But the difference between the two men is by no means immeasurable. Not a very great deal more, and Nathaniel were verily William.

This too, I mean, that if Shakespeare has not been equalled, give the world time, and he is sure to be surpassed, in one hemisphere or the other. Nor will it at all do to say, that the world is getting grey and grizzled now, and has lost that fresh charm which she wore of old, and by virtue of which the great poets of past times made themselves what we esteem them to be. Not so. The world is as young today, as when it was created, and this Vermont morning dew is as wet to my feet, as Eden's dew to Adam's. Nor has Nature been all over ransacked by our progenitors, so that no new charms and mysteries remain for this latter generation to find. Far from it. The trillionth part has not yet been said, and all that has been said, but multiplies the avenues to what remains to be said. It is not so much paucity, as superabundance of material that seems to incapacitate modern authors.

Let American then prize and cherish her writers, yea, let her glorify them. They are not so many in number, as to exhaust her good-will. And while she has good kith and kin of her own, to take to her bosom, let her not lavish her embraces upon the household of an alien. For believe it or not England, after all, is, in many things, an alien to us. China has more bowels of real love for us than she. But even were there no strong literary individualities among us, as there are some dozen at least, nevertheless, let America first praise mediocrity even, in her own children, before she praises (for everywhere, merit demands acknowledgment from every one) the best excellence in the children of any other land. Let her own authors, I say, have the priority of appreciation. I was very much pleased with a hot-headed Carolina cousin of mine, who once said,—"If there were no other American to stand by, in Literature,—why, then, I would stand by Pop Emmons and his 'Fredoniad,' and till a better epic came along, swear it was not very far behind the 'Iliad.'" Take away the words, and in spirit he was sound.

Not that American genius needs patronage in order to expand. For that explosive sort of stuff will expand though screwed up in a vice, and burst it, though it were triple steel. It is for the nation's sake, and not for her authors' sake, that I would have America be heedful of the increasing greatness among her writers. For how great the shame, if other nations should be before her, in crowning her heroes of the pen. But this is almost the case now. American authors have received more just and discriminating praise (however loftily and ridiculously given, in certain cases) even from some Englishmen, than from their own countrymen. There are hardly five critics in America, and several of them are asleep. As for patronage, it is the American author who now patronizes the country, and not his country him. And if at times some among them appeal to the people for more recognition, it is not always with selfish motives, but patriotic ones.

It is true, that but few of them as yet have evinced that decided originality which merits great praise. But that graceful writer, who perhaps of all Americans has received the most plaudits from his own country for his productions,—that very popular and amiable writer, however good, and self-reliant in many things, perhaps owes his chief reputation to the self-acknowledged imitation of a foreign model, and to the studied avoidance of all topics but smooth ones. But it is better to fail in originality, than to succeed in imitation. He who has never failed somewhere, that man can not be great. Failure is the true test of greatness. And if it be said, that continual success is a proof that a man wisely knows his powers,—it is only to be added, that, in that case, he knows them to be small. Let us believe it, then, once for all, that there is no hope for us in these smooth pleasing writers that know their powers. Without malice, but to speak the plain fact, they but furnish an appendix to Goldsmith, and other English authors. And we want no American Goldsmiths, nay, we want no American Miltons. It were the vilest thing you could say of a true American author, that he were an American Tompkins. Call him an American, and have done, for you can not say a nobler thing of him.—But it is not meant that all American writers should studiously cleave to nationality in their writings; only this, no American writer should write like an Englishman, or a Frenchman; let him write like a man, for then he will be sure to write like an American. Let us away with this leaven of literary flunkyism towards England. If either we must play the flunky in this thing, let England do it, not us. While we are rapidly preparing for that political supremacy among the nations, which prophetically awaits us at the close of the present century; in a literary point of view, we are deplorably unprepared for it; and we seem studious to remain so. Hitherto, reasons might have existed why this should be; but no good reason exists now. And all that is requisite to amendment in this matter, is simply this: that, while freely acknowledging all excellence, everywhere, we should refrain from unduly lauding foreign writers, and, at the same time, duly recognize the meritorious writers that are our own,—those writers, who breathe that unshackled, democratic spirit of Christianity in all things, which now takes the practical lead in the world, though at the same time led by ourselves—us Americans. Let us boldly contemn all imitation, though it comes to us graceful and fragrant as the morning; and foster all originality, though, at first, it be crabbed and ugly as our own pine knots. And if any of our authors fail, or seem to fail, then, in the words of my enthusiastic

Carolina cousin, let us clap him on the shoulder, and back him against all Europe for his second round. The truth is, that in our point of view, this matter of a national literature has come to such a pass with us, that in some sense we must turn bullies, else the day is lost, or superiority so far beyond us, that we can hardly say it will ever be ours.

And now, my countrymen, as an excellent author, of your own flesh and blood,—an unimitating, and perhaps, in his way, an inimitable man—whom better can I commend to you, in the first place, than Nathaniel Hawthorne. He is one of the new, and far better generation of your writer. The smell of your beeches and hemlocks is upon him; your own broad prairies are in his soul; and if you travel away inland into his deep and noble nature, you will hear the far roar of his Niagara. Give not over to future generations the glad duty of acknowledging him for what he is. Take that joy to yourself, in your own generation; and so shall he feel those grateful impulses in him, that may possibly prompt him to the full flower of some still greater achievement in your eyes. And by confessing him, you thereby confess others, you brace the whole brotherhood. For genius, all over the world, stands hand in hand, and one shock of recognition runs the whole circle round.

In treating of Hawthorne, or rather of Hawthorne in his writings (for I never saw the man; and in the chances of a quiet plantation life, remote from his haunts, perhaps never shall) in treating of his works, I say, I have thus far omitted all mention of his "Twice Told Tales," and "Scarlet Letter." Both are excellent, but full of such manifold, strange and diffusive beauties, that time would all but fail me, to point the half of them out. But there are things in those two books, which, had they been written in England a century ago, Nathaniel Hawthorne had utterly displaced many of the bright names we now revere on authority. But I content to leave Hawthorne to himself, and to the infallible finding of posterity; and however great may be the praise I have bestowed upon him, I feel, that in so doing, I have more served and honored myself, than him. For at bottom, great excellence is praise enough to itself; but the feeling of a sincere and appreciative love and admiration towards it, this is relieved by utterance; and warm, honest

praise ever leaves a pleasant flavor in the mouth; and it is an honorable thing to confess to what is honorable in others.

But I cannot leave my subject yet. No man can read a fine author, and relish him to his very bones, while he reads, without subsequently fancying to himself some ideal image of the man and his mind. And if you rightly look for it, you will almost always find that the author himself has somewhere furnished you with his own picture. For poets (whether in prose or verse), being painters of Nature, are like their brethren of the pencil, the true portrait-painters, who, in the multitude of likenesses to be sketched, do not invariably omit their own; and in all high instances, they paint them without any vanity, though, at times, with a lurking something, that would take several pages to properly define.

I submit it, then, to those best acquainted with the man personally, whether the following is not Nathaniel Hawthorne,—to himself, whether something involved in it does not express the temper of this mind,—that lasting temper of all true, candid men—a seeker, not a finder yet:—

A man now entered, in neglected attire, with the aspect of a thinker, but somewhat too rough-hewn and brawny for a scholar. His face was full of sturdy vigor, with some finer and keener attribute beneath; though harsh at first, it was tempered with the glow of a large, warm heart, which had force enough to heat his powerful intellect through and through. He advanced to the Intelligencer, and looked at him with a glance of such stern sincerity, that perhaps few secrets were beyond its scope.

"'I seek for Truth,' said he."

Twenty-four hours have elapsed since writing the foregoing. I have just returned from the hay mow, charged more and more with love and admiration of Hawthorne. For I have just been gleaning through the "Mosses," picking up many things here and there that had previously escaped me. And I found that but to glean after this man, is better than to be in at the harvest of others. To be frank (though, perhaps, rather foolish), notwithstanding what I wrote yesterday of these Mosses, I had not then culled them all; but had, nevertheless, been sufficiently sensible of the subtle essence, in them, as to write as I did. to what infinite height of loving wonder and admiration I may yet be borne, when by repeatedly banquetting on these Mosses, I shall have thoroughly incorporated their whole stuff into my being,—that, I can not tell. But already I feel that this Hawthorne has dropped germinous seeds into my soul. He expands and deepens down, the more I contemplate him; and further, and further, shoots his strong New-England roots into the hot soil of my Southern soul.

By careful reference to the "Table of Contents," I now find, that I have gone through all the sketches; but that when I yeterday wrote, I had not at all read two particular pieces, to which I now desire to call special attention,—"A Select Party," and "Young Goodman Brown." Here, be it said to all those whom this poor fugitive scrawl of mine may tempt to the purusal of the "Mosses," that they must on no account suffer themselves to be trifled with, disappointed, or deceived by the triviality of many of the titles to these Sketches. For in more than one instance, the title utterly belies the piece. It is as if rustic demjohns containing the very best and costliest of Falernian and Tokay, were labeled "Cider," "Perry," and "Elderberry Wine." The truth seems to be, that like many other geniuses, this Man of Mosses takes great delight in hoodwinking the world,—at least, with respect to himself. Personally, I doubt not, that he rather prefers to be generally esteemed but a so-so sort of author; being willing to reserve the thorough and acute appreciation of what he is, to that party most qualified to judge—that is, to himself. Besides, at the bottom of their natures, men like Hawthorne, in many things, deem the plaudits of the public such strong presumptive evidence of mediocrity in the object of them, that it would in some degree render them doubtful of their own powers, did they hear much and vociferous braying concerning them in the public pastures. True, I have been braying myself (if you please to be witty enough, to have it so) but then I claim to be the first that has so brayed in this particular matter; and therefore, while pleading guilty to the charge, still claim all the merit due to originality.

But with whatever motive, playful or profound, Nathaniel Hawthorne has chosen to entitle his pieces in the manner he has, it is certain, that some of them are directly calculated to deceive—egregiously deceive—the superficial skimmer of pages. To be downright and candid once more, let me cheerfully say, that two of these titles did dolefully dupe no less an eagle-eyed reader than myself, and that, too, after I had been impressed with a sense of the great depth and breadth of this American man. "Who in the name of thunder," (as the country-people say in this neighborhood), "who in the name of thunder, would anticipate any marvel in a piece entitled "Young Goodman Brown"? You would of course suppose that it was a simple little tale, intended as a supplement to "Goody Two Shoes." Whereas, it is deep as Dante; nor can you finish it, without addressing the author in his own words— "It is yours to penetrate, in every bosom, the deep mystery of sin." And with Young Goodman, too, in allegorical pursuit of his Puritan wife, you cry out in your anguish,—

"Faith!" shouted Goodman Brown, in a voice of agony and desperation; and the echoes of the forest mocked him, crying—"Faith! Faith!" as if bewildered wretches were seeking her all through the wilderness.

Now this same piece, entitled "Young Goodman Brown," is one of the two that I had not all read yesterday; and I allude to it now, because it is, in itself, such a strong positive illustration of that blackness in Hawthorne, which I had assumed from the mere occasional shadows of it, as revealed in several of the other sketches. But had I previously perused "Young Goodman Brown," I should have been at no pains to draw the conclusion, which I came to, at a time, when I was ignorant that the book contained one such direct and unqualified manifestation of it.

The other piece of the two referred to, is entitled "A Select Party," which in my first simplicity upon originally taking hold of the book, I fancied must treat of some pumpkin-pie party in Old Salem, or some Chowder Party on Cape Cod. Whereas, by all the gods of Peedee! it is the sweetest and sublimest thing that has been written since Spenser wrote. Nay, there is nothing in Spenser that surpasses it, perhaps, nothing that equals it. And the test is this: read any canto in "The Faery Queen," and then read "A Select Party," and decide which pleases you the most,—that is, if you are qualified to judge. Do not be frightened at this; for when Spenser was alive, he was thought of very much as Hawthorne is now—was generally accounted just such a "gentle" harmless man. It may be, that to common eyes, the sublimity of Hawthorne seems lost in his sweetness,—as perhaps in this same "Select Party" his; for whom, he has builded so august a dome of sunset clouds, and served them on richer plate, than Belshazzar's when he banquetted his lords in Babylon.

But my chief business now, is to point out a particular page in this piece, having reference to an honored guest, who under the name of "The Master Genius" but in the guise "of a young man of poor attire, with no insignia of rank or acknowledged eminence," is introduced to the Man of Fancy, who is the giver of the feast. Now the page having reference to this "Master Genius", so happily expresses much of what I yesterday wrote, touching the coming of the literary Shiloh of America, that I cannot but be charmed by the coincidence; especially, when it shows such a parity of ideas, at least, in this one point, between a man like Hawthorne and a man like me.

And here, let me throw out another conceit of mine touching this American Shiloh, or "Master Genius," as Hawthorne calls him. May it not be, that this commanding mind has not been, is not, and never will be, individually developed in any one man? And would it, indeed, appear so unreasonable to suppose, that this great fullness and overlowing may be, or may be destined to be, shared by a plurality of men of genius? Surely, to take the very greatest example on record, Shakespeare cannot be regarded as in himself the concretion of all the genius of his time; nor as so immeasurably beyond Marlowe, Webster, Ford, Beaumont, Johnson, that those great men can be said to share none of his power? For one, I conceive that there were dramatists in Elizabeth's day, between whom and Shakespeare the distance was by no means great. Let anyone, hitherto little acquainted with those neglected old authors, for the first time read them thoroughly, or even read Charles Lamb's Specimens of them, and he will be amazed at the wondrous ability of those Anaks of men, and shocked at this renewed example of the fact, that Fortune has more to do with fame than merit,—though, without merit, lasting fame there can be none.

Nevertheless, it would argue too illy of my country were this maxim to hold good concerning Nathaniel Hawthorne, a man, who already, in some minds, has shed "such a light, as never illuminates the earth, save when a great heart burns as the household fire of a grand intellect."

The words are his,—in the "Select Party"; and they are a magnificent setting to a coincident sentiment of my own, but ramblingly expressed yesterday, in reference ot himself. Gainsay it who will, as I now write, I am Posterity speaking by proxy—and after times will make it more than good, when I declare—that the American, who up to the present day, has evinced, in Literature, the largest brain with the largest heart, that man is Nathaniel Hawthorne. Moreover, that whatever Nathaniel Hawthorne may hereafter write, "The Mosses from an Old Manse" will be ultimately accounted his masterpiece. For there is a sure, though a secret sign in some works which proves the culmination of the power (only the developable ones, however) that produced them. But I am by no means desirous of the glory of a prophet. I pray Heaven that Hawthorne may yet prove me an impostor in this prediciton. Especially, as I somehow cling to the strange fancy, that, in all men, hiddenly reside certain wondrous, occult properties—as in some plants and minerals—which by some happy but very rare accident (as bronze was discovered by the melting of the iron and brass in the burning of Corinth) may chance to be called forth here on earth, not entirely waiting for their better discovery in the more congenial, blessed atmosphere of heaven.

Once more—for it is hard to be finite upon an infinite subject, and all subjects are infinite. By some people, this entire scrawl of mine may be esteeemed altogether unnecessary, inasmuch, "as years ago" (they may say) "we found out the rich and rare stuff in this Hawthorne, whom you now parade forth, as if only yourself were the discoverer of this Portuguese diamond in our Literature."—But even granting all this; and adding to it, the assumption that the books of Hawthorne have sold by the five-thousand,—what does that signify?—They should be sold by the hundred-thousand, and read by the million; and admired by every one who is capable of Admiration.

Henry James on Hawthorne

The following excerpts are from Henry James's book-length study *Hawthorne* (London: Macmillan, 1879).

The following are the opening pages to *Hawthorne*

It will be necessary, for several reasons, to give this short sketch the form rather of a critical essay than of a biography. The data for a life of Nathaniel Hawthorne are the reverse of copious, and even if they were abundant they would serve but in a limited measure the purpose of the biographer. Hawthorne's career was probably as tranquil and uneventful a one as ever fell to the lot of a man of letters; it was almost strikingly deficient in incident, in what may be called the dramatic quality. Few men of equal genius and of equal eminence can have led on the whole a simpler life. His six volumes of Note-Books illustrate this simplicity; they are a sort of monument to an unagitated fortune. Hawthorne's career had few vicissitudes or variations; it was passed for the most part in a small and homogeneous society, in a provincial, rural community; it had few perceptible points of contact with what is called the world, with public events, with the manners of his time, even with the life of his neighbours. Its literary incidents are not numerous. He produced, in quantity, but little. His works consist of four novels and the fragment of another, five volumes of short tales, a collection of sketches, and a couple of story-books for children. And yet some account of the man and the writer is well worth giving. Whatever may have been Hawthorne's private lot, he has the importance of being the most beautiful and most eminent representative of a literature. The importance of the literature may be questioned, but at any rate, in the field of letters, Hawthorne is the most valuable example of the American genius. That genius has not, as a whole, been literary; but Hawthorne was on his limited scale a master of expression. He is the writer to whom his countrymen most confidently point when they wish to make a claim to have enriched the mother-tongue, and, judging from present appearances, he will long occupy this honourable position. If there is something very fortunate for him in the way that he borrows an added relief from the absence of competitors in his own line and from the general flatness of the literary field that surrounds him, there is also, to a spectator, something almost touching in his situation. He was so modest and delicate a genius that we may fancy him appealing from the lonely honour of a representative attitude—perceiving a painful incongruity between his imponderable literary baggage and the large conditions of American life. Hawthorne on the one side is so subtle and slender and unpretending, and the American world on the other is so vast and various and substantial, that it might seem to the author of *The Scarlet Letter* and the *Mosses from an Old Manse,* that we render him a poor service in contrasting his proportions with those of a great civilization. But our author must accept the awkward as well as the graceful side of his fame; for he has the advantage of pointing a valuable moral. This moral is that the flower of art blooms only where the soil is deep, that it takes a great deal of history to produce a little literature, that it needs a complex social machinery to set a writer in motion.

American civilization has hitherto had other things to do than to produce flowers, and before giving birth to writers it has wisely occupied itself with providing something for them to write about. Three or four beautiful talents of trans-Atlantic growth are the sum of what the world usually recognizes, and in this modest nosegay the genius of Hawthorne is admitted to have the rarest and sweetest fragrance.

His very simplicity has been in his favour; it has helped him to appear complete and homogeneous. To talk of his being national would be to force the note and make a mistake of proportion; but he is, in spite of the absence of the realistic quality, intensely and vividly local. Out of the soil of New England he sprang—in a crevice of that immitigable granite he sprouted and bloomed. Half of the interest that he possesses for an American reader with any turn for analysis must reside in his latent New England savour; and I think it no more than just to say that whatever entertainment he may yield to those who know him at a distance, it is an almost indispensable condition of properly appreciating him to have received a personal impression of the manners, the morals, indeed of the very climate, of the great region of which the remarkable city of Boston is the metropolis. The cold, bright air of New England seems to blow through his pages, and these, in the opinion of many people, are the medium in which it is most agreeable to make the acquaintance of that tonic atmosphere. As to whether it is worth while to seek to know something of New England in order to extract a more intimate quality from *The House of Seven Gables* and *The Blithedale Romance,* I need not pronounce; but it is certain that a considerable observation of the society to which these productions were more directly addressed is a capital preparation for enjoying them. I have alluded to the absence in Hawthorne of that quality of realism which is now so much in fashion, an absence in regard to which there will of course be more to say; and yet I think I am not fanciful in saying that he testifies to the sentiments of the society in which he flourished almost as pertinently (proportions observed) as Balzac and some of his descendants—M M. Flaubert and Zola—testify to the manners and morals of the French people. He was not a man with a

literary theory; he was guiltless of a system, and I am not sure that he had ever heard of Realism, this remarkable compound having (although it was invented some time earlier) come into general use only since his death. He had certainly not proposed to himself to give an account of the social idiosyncrasies of his fellow-citizens, for his touch on such points is always light and vague, he has none of the apparatus of an historian, and his shadowy style of portraiture never suggests a rigid standard of accuracy. Nevertheless he virtually offers the most vivid reflection of New England life that has found its way into literature. His value in this respect is not diminished by the fact that he has not attempted to portray the usual Yankee of comedy, and that he has been almost culpably indifferent to his opportunities for commemorating the variations of colloquial English that may be observed in the New World. His characters do not express themselves in the dialect of the *Bigelow Papers*—their language indeed is apt to be too elegant, too delicate. They are not portraits of actual types, and in their phraseology there is nothing imitative. But none the less, Hawthorne's work savours thoroughly of the local soil—it is redolent of the social system in which he had his being.

James on *Twice-told Tales* and *Mosses from an Old Manse* (from *Hawthorne,* chapter 3)

As for the *Twice-told Tales* themselves, they are an old story now; every one knows them a little, and those who admire them particularly have read them a great many times. The writer of this sketch belongs to the latter class, and he has been trying to forget his familiarity with them, and ask himself what impression they would have made upon him at the time they appeared, in the first bloom of their freshness, and before the particular Hawthorne-quality, as it may be called, had become an established, a recognized and valued, fact. Certainly, I am inclined to think, if one had encountered these delicate, dusky flowers in the blossomless garden of American journalism, one would have plucked them with a very tender hand; one would have felt that here was something essentially fresh and new; here, in no extraordinary force or abundance, but in a degree distinctly appreciable, was an original element in literature. When I think of it, I almost envy Hawthorne's earliest readers; the sensation of opening upon *The Great Carbuncle, The Seven Vagabonds,* or *The Threefold Destiny* in an American annual of forty years ago, must have been highly agreeable.

Among these shorter things (it is better to speak of the whole collection, including the *Snow Image,* and the *Mosses from an Old Manse* at once) there are three sorts of tales, each one of which has an original stamp. There are, to begin with, the stories of fantasy and allegory—those among which the three I have just mentioned would be numbered, and which on the whole, are the most original. This is the group to which such little masterpieces as *Malvin's Burial, Rappaccini's Daughter,* and *Young Goodman Brown* also belong—these two last perhaps representing the highest point that Hawthorne reached in this direction. Then there are the little tales of New England history, which are scarcely less admirable, and of which *The Gray Champion, The May-pole of Merry Mount,* and the four beautiful *Legends of the Province-House,* as they are called, are the most successful specimens. Lastly come the slender sketches of actual scenes and of the objects and manners about him, by means of which, more particularly, he endeavoured "to open an intercourse with the world," and which, in spite of their slenderness, have an infinite grace and charm. Among these things *A Rill from the Town-pump, The Village Uncle, The Toll-gatherer's Day,* the *Chippings with a Chisel,* may most naturally be mentioned. As we turn over these volumes we feel that the pieces that spring most directly from his fancy, constitute, as I have said (putting his four novels aside), his most substantial claim to our attention. It would be a mistake to insist too much upon them; Hawthorne was himself the first to recognize that. "These fitful sketches," he says in the preface to the *Mosses from an Old Manse,* "with so little of external life about them, yet claiming no profundity of purpose—so reserved even while they sometimes seem so frank—often but half in earnest, and never, even when most so, expressing satisfactorily the thoughts which they profess to image such trifles, I truly feel, afford no solid basis for a literary reputation." This is very becom-

ingly uttered; but it may be said, partly in answer to it, and partly in confirmation, that the valuable element in these things was not what Hawthorne put into them consciously, but what passed into them without his being able to measure it—the element of simple genius, the quality of imagination. This is the real charm of Hawthorne's writing—this purity and spontaneity and naturalness of fancy. For the rest, it is interesting to see how it borrowed a particular colour from the other faculties that lay near it—how the imagination, in this capital son of the old Puritans, reflected the hue of the more purely moral part, of the dusky, overshadowed conscience. The conscience, by no fault of its own, in every genuine offshoot of that sombre lineage, lay under the shadow of the sense of sin. This darkening cloud was no essential part of the nature of the individual; it stood fixed in the general moral heaven under which he grew up and looked at life. It projected from above, from outside, a black patch over his spirit, and it was for him to do what he could with the black patch. There were all sorts of possible ways of dealing with it; they depended upon the personal temperament. Some natures would let it lie as it fell, and contrive to be tolerably comfortable beneath it. Others would groan and sweat and suffer; but the dusky blight would remain, and their lives would be lives of misery. Here and there an individual, irritated beyond endurance, would throw it off in anger, plunging probably into what would be deemed deeper abysses of depravity. Hawthorne's way was the best, for he contrived, by an exquisite process, best known to himself, to transmute this heavy moral burden into the very substance of the imagination, to make it evaporate in the light and charming fumes of artistic production. But Hawthorne, of course, was exceptionally fortunate; he had his genius to help him. Nothing is more curious and interesting than this almost exclusively imported character of the sense of sin in Hawthorne's mind; it seems to exist there merely for an artistic or literary purpose. He had ample cognizance of the Puritan conscience; it was his natural heritage; it was reproduced in him; looking into his soul, he found it there. But his relation to it was only, as one may say, intellectual; it was not moral and theological. He played with it and used it as a pigment; he treated it, as the metaphysicians say, objectively. He was not discomposed, disturbed, haunted by it, in the manner of its usual and regular victims, who had not the little postern door of fancy to slip through, to the other side of the wall. It was, indeed, to his imaginative vision, the great fact of man's nature; the light element that had been mingled with his own composition always clung to this rugged prominence of moral responsibility, like the mist that hovers about the mountain. It was a necessary condition for a man of Hawthorne's stock that if his imagination should take licence to amuse itself, it should at least select this grim precinct of the Puritan morality for its play-ground. He speaks of the dark disapproval with which his old ancestors, in the case of their coming to life, would see him trifling himself away as a story-teller. But how far more darkly would they have frowned could they have understood that he had converted the very principle of their own being into one of his toys!

It will be seen that I am far from being struck with the justice of that view of the author of the *Twice-told Tales,* which is so happily expressed by the French critic to whom I alluded at an earlier stage of this essay. To speak of Hawthorne, as M. Emile Montégut does, as a *romancier pessimiste,* seems to me very much beside the mark. He is no more a pessimist than an optimist, though he is certainly not much of either. He does not pretend to conclude, or to have a philosophy of human nature; indeed, I should even say that at bottom he does not take human nature as hard as he may seem to do. "His bitterness," says M. Montégut, "is without abatement, and his bad opinion of man is without compensation. . . . His little tales have the air of confessions which the soul makes to itself; they are so many little slaps which the author applies to our face." This, it seems to me, is to exaggerate almost immeasurably the reach of Hawthorne's relish of gloomy subjects. What pleased him in such subjects was their picturesqueness, their rich duskiness of colour, their chiaroscuro; but they were not the expression of a hopeless, or even of a predominantly melancholy, feeling about the human soul. Such at least is my own impression. He is to a considerable degree ironical—this is part of

his charm—part even, one may say, of his brightness; but he is neither bitter nor cynical—he is rarely even what I should call tragical. There have certainly been story-tellers of a gayer and lighter spirit; there have been observers more humorous, more hilarious—though on the whole Hawthorne's observation has a smile in it oftener than may at first appear; but there has rarely been an observer more serene, less agitated by what he sees and less disposed to call things deeply into question. As I have already intimated, his Note-Books are full of this simple and almost childlike serenity. That dusky preoccupation with the misery of human life and the wickedness of the human heart which such a critic as M. Emile Montegut talks about, is totally absent from them; and if we may suppose a person to have read these Diaries before looking into the tales, we may be sure that such a reader would be greatly surprised to hear the author described as a disappointed, disdainful genius. "This marked love of cases of conscience," says M. Montegut, "this taciturn, scornful cast of mind, this habit of seeing sin everywhere and hell always gaping open, this dusky gaze bent always upon a damned world and a nature draped in mourning, these lonely conversations of the imagination with the conscience, this pitiless analysis resulting from a perpetual examination of one's self, and from the tortures of a heart closed before men and open to God—all these elements of the Puritan character have passed into Mr. Hawthorne, or to speak more justly, have *filtered* into him, through a long succession of generations." This is a very pretty and very vivid account of Hawthorne, superficially considered; and it is just such a view of the case as would commend itself most easily and most naturally to a hasty critic. It is all true indeed, with a difference; Hawthorne was all that M. Montegut says, minus the conviction. The old Puritan moral sense, the consciousness of sin and hell, of the fearful nature of our responsibilities and the savage character of our Taskmaster—these things had been lodged in the mind of a man of Fancy, whose fancy had straightway begun to take liberties and play tricks with them—to judge them (Heaven forgive him!) from the poetic and aesthetic point of view, the point of view of entertainment and irony. This absence of conviction makes the difference; but the difference is great.

Hawthorne was a man of fancy, and I suppose that in speaking of him it is inevitable that we should feel ourselves confronted with the familiar problem of the difference between the fancy and the imagination. Of the larger and more potent faculty he certainly possessed a liberal share; no one can read *The House of the Seven Gables* without feeling it to be a deeply imaginative work. But I am often struck, especially in the shorter tales, of which I am now chiefly speaking, with a kind of small ingenuity, a taste for conceits and analogies, which bears more particularly what is called the fanciful stamp. The finer of the shorter tales are redolent of a rich imagination.

> Had Goodman Brown fallen asleep in the forest and only dreamed a wild dream of witch-meeting? Be it so, if you will; but, alas, it was a dream of evil omen for young Goodman Brown! a stern, a sad, a darkly meditative, a distrustful, if not a desperate, man, did he become from the night of that fearful dream. On the Sabbath-day, when the congregation were singing a holy psalm, he could not listen, because an anthem of sin rushed loudly upon his ear and drowned all the blessed strain. When the minister spoke from the pulpit, with power and fervid eloquence, and with his hand on the open Bible of the sacred truth of our religion, and of saint-like lives and triumphant deaths, and of future bliss or misery unutterable, then did Goodman Brown grow pale, dreading lest the roof should thunder down upon the gray blasphemer and his hearers. Often, awaking suddenly at midnight, he shrank from the bosom of Faith; and at morning or eventide, when the family knelt down at prayer, he scowled and muttered to himself, and gazed sternly at his wife, and turned away. And when he had lived long, and was borne to his grave a hoary corpse, followed by Faith, an aged woman, and children, and grandchildren, a goodly procession, besides neighbours not a few, they carved no hopeful verse upon his tombstone, for his dying hour was gloom.

There is imagination in that, and in many another passage that I might quote; but as a general thing I should characterize the more metaphysical of our author's short stories as graceful and felicitous conceits. They seem to me to be qualified in this manner by the very fact that they belong to the province of allegory. Hawthorne, in his metaphysical moods, is nothing if not allegorical, and allegory, to my sense, is quite one of the lighter exercises of the imagination. Many excellent judges, I know, have a great stomach for it; they delight in symbols and correspondences, in seeing a story told as if it were another and a very different story. I frankly confess that I have as a general thing but little enjoyment of it and that it has never seemed to me to be, as it were, a first-rate literary form. It has produced assuredly some first-rate works; and Hawthorne in his younger years had been a great reader and devotee of Bunyan and Spenser, the great masters of allegory. But it is apt to spoil two good things—a story and a moral, a meaning and a form; and the taste for it is responsible for a large part of the forcible feeble writing that has been inflicted upon the world. The only cases in which it is endurable is when it is extremely spontaneous, when the analogy presents itself with eager promptitude. When it shows signs of having been groped and fumbled for, the needful illusion is of course absent and the failure complete. Then the machinery alone is visible, and the end to which it operates becomes a matter of indifference. There was but little literary criticism in the United States at the time Hawthorne's earlier works were published; but among the reviewers Edgar Poe perhaps held the scales the highest. He at any rate rattled them loudest, and pretended, more than any one else, to conduct the weighing-process on scientific principles. Very remarkable was this process of Edgar Poe's, and very extraordinary were his principles; but he had the advantage of being a man of genius, and his intelligence was frequently great. His collection of critical sketches of the American writers flourishing in what M. Taine would call his *milieu* and *moment,* is very curious and interesting reading, and it has one quality which ought to keep it from ever being completely forgotten. It is probably the most complete and exquisite specimen of *provincialism* ever prepared for the edification of men. Poe's judgments are pretentious, spiteful, vulgar; but they contain a great deal of sense and discrimination as well, and here and there, sometimes at frequent intervals, we find a phrase of happy insight imbedded in a patch of the most fatuous pedantry. He wrote a chapter upon Hawthorne, and spoke of him on the whole very kindly; and his estimate is of sufficient value to make it noticeable that he should express lively disapproval of the large part allotted to allegory in his tale—in defence of which, he says, "however, or for whatever object employed, there is scarcely one respectable word to be said. . . . The deepest emotion," he goes on, "aroused within us by the happiest allegory as allegory, is a very, very imperfectly satisfied sense of the writer's ingenuity in overcoming a difficulty we should have preferred his not having attempted to overcome. . . . One thing is clear, that if allegory ever establishes a fact, it is by dint of overturning a fiction"; and Poe has furthermore the courage to remark that the *Pilgrim's Progress* is a "ludicrously overrated book." Certainly, as a general thing, we are struck with the ingenuity and felicity of Hawthorne's analogies and correspondences; the idea appears to have made itself at home in them easily. Nothing could be better in this respect than *The Snow-Image* (a little masterpiece), or *The Great Carbuncle*, or *Doctor Heidegger's Experiment*, or *Rappaccini's Daughter*. But in such things as *The Birthmark* and *The Bosom-Serpent*, we are struck with something stiff and mechanical, slightly incongruous, as if the kernel had not assimilated its envelope. But these are matters of light impression, and there would be a want of tact in pretending to discriminate too closely among things which all, in one way or another, have a charm. The charm—the great charm—is that they are glimpses of a great field, of the whole deep mystery of man's soul and conscience. They are moral, and their interest is moral; they deal with something more than the mere accidents and conventionalities, the surface occurrences of life. The fine thing in Hawthorne is that he cared for the deeper psychology, and that, in his way, he tried to become familiar with it. This natural, yet fanciful familiarity with it, this air, on the author's part, of being a confirmed habitue of

a region of mysteries and subtleties, constitutes the originality of his tales. And then they have the further merit of seeming, for what they are, to spring up so freely and lightly. The author has all the ease, indeed, of a regular dweller in the moral, psychological realm; he goes to and fro in it, as a man who knows his way. His tread is a light and modest one, but he keeps the key in his pocket.

James on *The Scarlet Letter* (from *Hawthorne,* chapter 5)

His publisher, Mr. Fields, in a volume entitled *Yesterdays with Authors,* has related the circumstances in which Hawthorne's masterpiece came into the world. "In the winter of 1849, after he had been ejected from the Custom-house, I went down to Salem to see him and inquire after his health, for we heard he had been suffering from illness. He was then living in a modest wooden house. . . . I found him alone in a chamber over the sitting-room of the dwelling, and as the day was cold he was hovering near a stove. We fell into talk about his future prospects, and he was, as I feared I should find him, in a very desponding mood." His visitor urged him to bethink himself of publishing something, and Hawthorne replied by calling his attention to the small popularity his published productions had yet acquired, and declaring that he had done nothing and had no spirit for doing anything. The narrator of the incident urged upon him the necessity of a more hopeful view of his situation, and proceeded to take leave. He had not reached the street, however, when Hawthorne hurried to overtake him, and, placing a roll of MS. in his hand, bade him take it to Boston, read it, and pronounce upon it. "It is either very good or very bad," said the author; "I don't know which." "On my way back to Boston," says Mr. Fields, "I read the germ of *The Scarlet Letter;* before I slept that night I wrote him a note all aglow with admiration of the marvellous story he had put into my hands, and told him that I would come again to Salem the next day and arrange for its publication. I went on in such an amazing state of excitement, when we met again in the little house, that he would not believe I was really in earnest. He seemed to think I was beside myself, and laughed sadly at my enthusiasm." Hawthorne, however, went on with the book and finished it, but it appeared only a year later. His biographer quotes a passage from a letter which he wrote in February, 1850, to his friend Horatio Bridge. "I finished my book only yesterday; one end being in the press at Boston, while the other was in my head here at Salem, so that, as you see, my story is at least fourteen miles long. . . . My book, the publisher tells me, will not be out before April. He speaks of it in tremendous terms of approbation, so does Mrs. Hawthorne, to whom I read the conclusion last night. It broke her heart, and sent her to bed with a grievous headache—which I look upon as a triumphant success. Judging from the effect upon her and the publisher, I may calculate on what bowlers call a ten-strike. But I don't make any such calculation." And Mr. Lathrop calls attention, in regard to this passage, to an allusion in the English Note-books (September 14, 1855). "Speaking of Thackeray, I cannot but wonder at his coolness in respect to his own pathos, and compare it to my emotions when I read the last scene of *The Scarlet Letter* to my wife, just after writing it—tried to read it rather, for my voice swelled and heaved as if I were tossed up and down on an ocean as it subsides after a storm. But I was in a very nervous state then, having gone through a great diversity of emotion while writing it, for many months."

The work has the tone of the circumstances in which it was produced. If Hawthorne was in a sombre mood, and if his future was painfully vague, *The Scarlet Letter* contains little enough of gaiety or of hopefulness. It is densely dark, with a single spot of vivid colour in it; and it will probably long remain the most consistently gloomy of English novels of the first order. But I just now called it the author's masterpiece, and I imagine it will continue to be, for other generations than ours, his most substantial title to fame. The subject had probably lain a long time in his mind, as his subjects were apt to do; so that he appears completely to possess it, to know it and feel it. It is simpler and more complete than his other novels; it achieves more perfectly what it attempts, and it has about it that charm, very hard to express, which we find in an artist's work the first time he has touched his highest mark—a sort of straightness and naturalness of execution,

an unconsciousness of his public, and freshness of interest in his theme. It was a great success, and he immediately found himself famous. The writer of these lines, who was a child at the time, remembers dimly the sensation the book produced, and the little shudder with which people alluded to it, as if a peculiar horror were mixed with its attractions. He was too young to read it himself, but its title, upon which he fixed his eyes as the book lay upon the table, had a mysterious charm. He had a vague belief indeed that the "letter" in question was one of the documents that come by the post, and it was a source of perpetual wonderment to him that it should be of such an unaccustomed hue. Of course it was difficult to explain to a child the significance of poor Hester Prynne's blood-coloured A. But the mystery was at last partly dispelled by his being taken to see a collection of pictures (the annual exhibition of the National Academy), where he encountered a representation of a pale, handsome woman, in a quaint black dress and a white coif, between her knees an little girl, fantastically dressed and crowned with flowers. Embroidered on the woman's breast was a great crimson A, over which the child's fingers, as she glanced strangely out of the picture, were maliciously playing. I was told that this was Hester Prynne and little Pearl, and that when I grew older I might read their interesting history. But the picture remained vividly imprinted on my mind; I had been vaguely frightened and made uneasy by it; and when, years afterwards, I first read the novel, I seemed to myself to have read it before, and to be familiar with its two strange heroines. I mention this incident simply as an indication of the degree to which the success of *The Scarlet Letter* had made the book what is called an actuality. Hawthorne himself was very modest about it; he wrote to his publisher, when there was a question of his undertaking another novel, that what had given the history of Hester Prynne its "vogue" was simply the introductory chapter. In fact, the publication of *The Scarlet Letter* was in the United States a literary event of the first importance. The book was the finest piece of imaginative writing yet put forth in the country. There was a consciousness of this in the welcome was given it—a satisfaction in the idea of America having produced a novel that belonged to literature, and to the forefront of it. Something might at last be sent to Europe as exquisite in quality as anything that had been received, and the best of it was that the thing was absolutely American; it belonged to the soil, to the air; it came out of the very heart of New England.

It is beautiful, admirable, extraordinary; it has in the highest degree that merit which I have spoken of as the mark of Hawthorne's best things—an indefinable purity and lightness of conception, a quality which in a work of art affects one in the same way as the absence of grossness does in a human being. His fancy, as I just now said, had evidently brooded over the subject for a long time; the situation to be represented had disclosed itself to him in all its phases. When I say in all its phases, the sentence demands modification; for it is to be remembered that if Hawthorne laid his hand upon the well-worn theme, upon the familiar combination of the wife, the lover, and the husband, it was after all but to one period of the history of these three persons that he attached himself. The situation is the situation after the woman's fault has been committed, and the current of expiation and repentance has set in. In spite of the relation between Hester Prynne and Arthur Dimmesdale, no story of love was surely ever less of a "love story." To Hawthorne's imagination the fact that these two persons had loved each other too well was of an interest comparatively vulgar; what appealed to him was the idea of their moral situation in the long years that were to follow. The story indeed is in a secondary degree that of Hester Prynne; she becomes, really, after the first scene, an accessory figure; it is not upon her the denoument depends. It is upon her guilty lover that the author projects most frequently the cold, thin rays of his fitfully-moving lantern, which makes here and there a little luminous circle, on the edge of which hovers the livid and sinister figure of the injured and retributive husband. The story goes on for the most part between the lover and the husband—the tormented young Puritan minister, who carries the secret of his own lapse from pastoral purity locked up beneath an exterior that commends itself to the reverence of his flock, while he sees the softer partner of his guilt standing

in the full glare of exposure and humbling herself to the misery of atonement—between this more wretched and pitiable culprit, to whom dishonour would come as a comfort and the pillory as a relief, and the older, keener, wiser man, who, to obtain satisfaction for the wrong he has suffered, devises the infernally ingenious plan of conjoining himself with his wronger, living with him, living upon him, and while he pretends to minister to his hidden ailment and to sympathise with his pain, revels in his unsuspected knowledge of these things and stimulates them by malignant arts. The attitude of Roger Chillingworth, and the means he takes to compensate himself—these are the highly original elements in the situation that Hawthorne so ingeniously treats. None of his works are so impregnated with that after-sense of the old Puritan consciousness of life to which allusion has so often been made. If, as M. Montégut says, the qualities of his ancestors filtered down through generations into his composition, *The Scarlet Letter* was, as it were, the vessel that gathered up the last of the precious drops. And I say this not because the story happens to be of so-called historical cast, to be told of the early days of Massachusetts and of people in steeple-crowned hats and sad coloured garments. The historical colouring is rather weak than otherwise; there is little elaboration of detail, of the modern realism of research; and the author has made no great point of causing his figures to speak the English of their period. Nevertheless, the book is full of the moral presence of the race that invented Hester's penance—diluted and complicated with other things, but still perfectly recognisable. Puritanism in a word, is there, not only objectively, as Hawthorne tried to place it there, but subjectively as well. Not, I mean, in his judgment of his characters, in any harshness of prejudice, or in the obtrusion of a moral lesson; but in the very quality of his own vision, in the tone of the picture, in a certain coldness and exclusiveness of treatment.

The faults of the book are, to my sense, a want of reality and an abuse of the fanciful element—of a certain superficial symbolism. The people strike me not as characters, but as representatives. very picturesquely arranged, of a single state of mind; and the interest of the story lies, not in them, but in the situation, which is insistently kept before us, with little progression, though with a great deal, as I have said, of a certain stable variation; and to which they, out of their reality, contribute little that helps it to live and move. I was made to feel this want of reality, this over-ingenuity, of *The Scarlet Letter,* by chancing not long since upon a novel which was read fifty years ago much more than to-day, but which is still worth reading—the story of *Adam Blair,* by John Gibson Lockhart. This interesting and powerful little tale has a great deal of analogy with Hawthorne's novel—quite enough, at least, to suggest a comparison between them; and the comparison is a very interesting one to make, for it speedily leads us to larger considerations than simple resemblances and divergences of plot.

Adam Blair, like Arthur Dimmesdale, is a Calvinistic minister who becomes the lover of a married woman, is overwhelmed with remorse at his misdeed, and makes a public confession of it; then expiates it by resigning his pastoral office and becoming a humble tiller of the soil, as his father had been. The two stories are of about the same length, and each is the masterpiece (putting aside of course, as far as Lockhart is concerned, the Life of Scott) of the author. They deal alike with the manners of a rigidly theological society, and even in certain details they correspond. In each of them, between the guilty pair, there is a charming little girl; though I hasten to say that Sarah Blair (who is not the daughter of the heroine but the legitimate offspring of the hero, a widower) is far from being as brilliant and graceful an apparition as the admirable little Pearl of *The Scarlet Letter.* The main difference between the two tales is the fact that in the American story the husband plays an all-important part, and in the Scottish plays almost none at all. Adam Blair is the history of the passion, and *The Scarlet Letter* the history of its sequel; but neverthelss, if one has read the two books at a short interval, it is impossible to avoid confronting them. I confess that a large portion of the interest of Adam Blair, to my mind, when once I had perceived that it would repeat in a great measure the situation of *The Scarlet Letter,* lay in noting its difference of tone. It threw into relief the passionless quality of Hawthorne's novel its element of

cold and ingenious fantasy, its elaborate imaginative delicacy. These things do not precisely constitute a weakness in *The Scarlet Letter;* indeed, in a certain way they constitute a great strength; but the absence of a certain something warm and straightforward, a trifle more grossly human and vulgarly natural, which one finds in Adam Blair, will always make Hawthorne's tale less touching to a large number of even very intelligent readers, than a love-story told with the robust, synthetic pathos which served Lockhart so well. His novel is not of the first rank (I should call it an excellent second-rate one), but it borrows a charm from the fact that his vigorous, but not strongly imaginative, mind was impregnated with the reality of his subject. He did not always succeed in rendering this reality; the expression is sometimes awkward and poor. But the reader feels that his vision was clear, and his feeling about the matter very strong and rich. Hawthorne's imagination, on the other hand, plays with his theme so incessantly, leads it such a dance through the moonlighted air of his intellect, that the thing cools off, as it were, hardens and stiffens, and, producing effects much more exquisite, leaves the reader with a sense of having handled a splendid piece of silversmith's work. Lockhart, by means much more vulgar, produces at moments a greater illusion, and satisfies our inevitable desire for something, in the people in whom it is sought to interest us, that shall be of the same pitch and the same continuity with ourselves. Above all, it is interesting to see how the same subject appears to two men of a thoroughly different cast of mind and of a different race. Lockhart was struck with the warmth of the subject that offered itself to him, and Hawthorne with its coldness; the one with its glow, its sentimental interest—the other with its shadow, its moral interest. Lockhart's story is as decent, as severely draped, as *The Scarlet Letter;* but the author has a more vivid sense than appears to have imposed itself upon Hawthorne, of some of the incidents of the situation he describes; his tempted man and tempting woman are more actual and personal; his heroine in especial, though not in the least a delicate or a subtle conception, has a sort of credible, visible, palpable property, a vulgar roundness and relief, which are lacking to the dim and chastened image of Hester Prynne. But I am going too far; I am comparing simplicity with subtlety, the usual with the refined. Each man wrote as his turn of mind impelled him, but each expressed something more than himself. Lockhart was a dense, substantial Briton, with a taste for the concrete, and Hawthorne was a thin New Englander, with a miasmatic conscience.

In *The Scarlet Letter* there is a great deal of symbolism; there is, I think, too much. It is overdone at times, and be-comes mechanical; it ceases to be impressive, and grazes triviality. The idea of the mystic A which the young minister finds imprinted upon his breast and eating into his flesh, in sympathy with the embroidered badge that Hester is condemned to wear, appears to me to be a case in point. This suggestion should, I think, have been just made and dropped; to insist upon it and return to it, is to exaggerate the weak side of the subject. Hawthorne returns to it constantly, plays with it, and seems charmed by it; until at last the reader feels tempted to declare that his enjoyment of it is puerile. In the admirable scene, so superbly conceived and beautifully executed, in which Mr. Dimmesdale, in the stillness of the night, in the middle of the sleeping town, feels impelled to go and stand upon the scaffold where his mistress had formerly enacted her dreadful penance, and then, seeing Hester pass along the street, from watching at a sickbed, with little Pearl at her side, calls them both to come and stand there beside him—in this masterly episode the effect is almost spoiled by the introduction of one of these superficial conceits. What leads up to it is very fine—so fine that I cannot do better than quote it as a specimen of one of the striking pages of the book.

But before Mr. Dimmesdale had done speaking, a light gleamed far and wide over all the muffled sky. It was doubtless caused by one of those meteors which the night-watcher may so often observe burning out to waste in the vacant regions of the atmosphere. So powerful was its radiance that it thoroughly illuminated the dense medium of cloud, betwixt the sky and earth. The great vault brightened, like the dome of an immense lamp. It showed the familiar scene of the street with the distinctness of mid-day, but also with the awfulness that is always imparted to familiar objects by an unaccustomed light. The wooden houses, with their jutting stories and quaint gable-peaks; the doorsteps and thresholds, with the early grass springing up about them; the garden-plots, black with freshly-turned earth; the wheel-track, little worn, and, even in the market-place margined with green on either side;—all were visible, but with a singularity of aspect that seemed to give another moral interpretation to the things of this world than they had ever borne before. And there stood the minister, with his hand over his heart; and Hester Prynne, with the embroidered letter glimmering on her bosom; and little Pearl, herself a symbol, and the connecting-link between these two. They stood in the noon of that strange and solemn splendour, as if it were the light that is to reveal all secrets, and the daybreak that shall unite all that belong to one another.

That is imaginative, impressive, poetic; but when, almost immediately afterwards, the author goes on to say that "the minister looking upward to the zenith, beheld there the appearance of an immense letter—the letter A—marked out in lines of dull red light," we feel that he goes too far and is in danger of crossing the line that separates the sublime from its intimate neighbour. We are tempted to say that this is not moral tragedy, but physical comedy. In the same way, too much is made of the intimation that Hester's badge had a scorching property, and that if one touched it one would immediately withdraw one's hand. Hawthorne is perpetually looking for images which shall place themselves in picturesque correspondence with the spiritual facts with which he is concerned, and of course the search is of the very essence of poetry. But in such a process discretion is everything, and when the image becomes importunate it is in danger of seeming to stand for nothing more serious than itself. When Hester meets the minister by appointment in the forest, and sits talking with him while little Pearl wanders away and plays by the edge of the brook, the child is represented as at last making her way over to the other side of the woodland stream, and disporting herself there in a manner which makes her mother feel herself, "in some indistinct and tantalising manner, estranged from Pearl; as if the child, in her lonely ramble through the forest, had strayed out of the sphere in which she and her mother dwelt together, and was now vainly seeking to return to it." And Hawthorne devotes a chapter to this idea of the child's having, by putting the brook between Hester and herself, established a kind of spiritual gulf, on the verge of which her little fantastic person innocently mocks at her mother's sense of bereavement. This conception belongs, one would say, quite to the lighter order of a story-teller's devices, and the reader hardly goes with Hawthorne in the large development he gives to it. He hardly goes with him either, I think, in his extreme predilection for a small number of vague ideas which are represented by such terms as "sphere" and "sympathies." Hawthorne makes too liberal a use of these two substantives; it is the solitary defect of his style; and it counts as a defect partly because the words in question are a sort of specialty with certain writers immeasurably inferior to himself.

I had not meant, however, to expatiate upon his defects, which are of the slenderest and most venial kind. *The Scarlet Letter* has the beauty and harmony of all original and complete conceptions, and its weaker spots, whatever they are, are not of its essence; they are mere light flaws and inequalities of surface. One can often return to it; it supports familiarity and has the inexhaustible charm and mystery of great works of art. It is admirably written. Hawthorne afterwards polished his style to a still higher degree, but in his later productions—it is almost always the case in a writer's later productions—there is a touch of mannerism. In *The Scarlet Letter* there is a high degree of polish, and at the same time a charming freshness; his phrase is less conscious of itself. His biographer very justly calls attention to the fact that his style was excellent from the beginning; that he appeared to have passed through no phase of learning how to write, but was in possession of his means from the first of his handling a pen. His early tales, perhaps, were not of a character to subject his faculty of expression to a very severe test, but a man who had not Hawthorne's natural sense of language would certainly have contrived to write them less well. This natural sense of language—this turn for say-

ing things lightly and yet touchingly, picturesquely yet simply, and for infusing a gently colloquial tone into matter of the most unfamiliar import, he had evidently cultivated with great assiduity. I have spoken of the anomalous character of his Note-Books—of his going to such pains often to make a record of incidents which either were not worth remembering or could be easily remembered without its aid. But it helps us to understand the Note-Books if we regard them as a literary exercise. They were compositions, as school boys say, in which the subject was only the pretext, and the main point was to write a certain amount of excellent English. Hawthorne must at least have written a great many of these things for practice, and he must often have said to himself that it was better practice to write about trifles, because it was a greater tax upon one's skill to make them interesting. And his theory was just, for he has almost always made his trifles interesting. In his novels his art of saying things well is very positively tested, for here he treats of those matters among which it is very easy for a blundering writer to go wrong—the subtleties and mysteries of life, the moral and spiritual maze. In such a passage as one I have marked for quotation from *The Scarlet Letter* there is the stamp of the genius of style.

Hester Prynne, gazing steadfastly at the clergyman, felt a dreary influence come over her, but wherefore or whence she knew not, unless that he seemed so remote from her own sphere and utterly beyond her reach. One glance of recognition she had imagined must needs pass between them. She thought of the dim forest with its little dell of solitude, and love, and anguish, and the mossy tree-trunk, where, sitting hand in hand, they had mingled their sad and passionate talk with the melancholy murmur of the brook. How deeply had they known each other then! And was this the man? She hardly knew him now! He, moving proudly past, enveloped as it were in the rich music, with the procession of majestic and venerable fathers; he, so unattainable in his worldly position, and still more so in that far vista in his unsympathising thoughts, through which she now beheld him! Her spirit sank with the idea that all must have been a delusion, and that vividly as she had dreamed it, there could be no real bond betwixt the clergyman and herself. And thus much of woman there was in Hester, that she could scarcely forgive him—least of all now, when the heavy footstep of their approaching fate might be heard, nearer, nearer, nearer!—for being able to withdraw himself so completely from their mutual world, while she groped darkly, and stretched forth her cold hands, and found him not!

James on *The House of the Seven Gables* (from *Hawthorne,* Chapter 5)

The House of the Seven Gables was written at Lenox, among the mountains of Massachusetts, a village nestling, rather loosely, in one of the loveliest corners of New England, to which Hawthorne had betaken himself after the success of *The Scarlet Letter* became conspicuous, in the summer of 1850, and where he occupied for two years an uncomfortable little red house which is now pointed out to the inquiring stranger. The inquiring stranger is now a frequent figure at Lenox, for the place has suffered the process of lionisation. It has become a prosperous watering-place, or at least (as there are no waters), as they say in America, a summer-resort. It is a brilliant and generous landscape, and thirty years ago a man of fancy, desiring to apply himself, might have found both inspiration and tranquillity there. Hawthorne found so much of both that he wrote more during his two years of residence at Lenox than at any period of his career. He began with *The House of the Seven Gables*, which was finished in the early part of 1851. This is the longest of his three American novels, it is the most elaborate, and in the judgment of some persons it is the finest. It is a rich, delightful, imaginative work, larger and more various than its companions, and full of all sorts of deep intentions, of interwoven threads of suggestion. But it is not so rounded and complete as *The Scarlet Letter;* it has always seemed to me more like a prologue to a great novel than a great novel itself. I think this is partly owing to the fact that the subject, the *donnée,* as the French say, of the story, does not quite fill it out, and that we get at the same time an impression of certain complicated purposes on the author's part, which seem to reach beyond it. I call it larger and more various than its companions, and it has indeed a

greater richness of tone and density of detail. The colour, so to speak, of *The House of the Seven Gables* is admirable. But the story has a sort of expansive quality which never wholly fructifies, and as I lately laid it down, after reading it for the third time, I had a sense of having interested myself in a magnificent fragment. Yet the book has a great fascination, and of all of those of its author's productions which I have read over while writing this sketch, it is perhaps tine one that has gained most by re-perusal. If it be true of the others that the pure, natural quality of the imaginative strain is their great merit, this is at least as true of *The House of the Seven Gables,* the charm of which is in a peculiar degree of the kind that we fail to reduce to its grounds—like that of the sweetness of a piece of music, or the softness of fine September weather. It is vague, indefinable, ineffable; but it is the sort of thing we must always point to in justification of the high claim that we make for Hawthorne. In this case of course its vagueness is a drawback, for it is difficult to point to ethereal beauties; and if the reader whom we have wished to inoculate with our admiration inform us after looking a while that he perceives nothing in particular, we can only reply that, in effect, the object is a delicate one.

The House of the Seven Gables comes nearer being a picture of contemporary American life than either of its companions; but on this ground it would be a mistake to make a large claim for it. It cannot be too often repeated that Hawthorne was not a realist. He had a high sense of reality—his Note-Books super-abundantly testify to it; and fond as he was of jotting down the items that make it up, he never attempted to render exactly or closely the actual facts of the society that surrounded him. I have said—I began by saying—that his pages were full of its spirit, and of a certain reflected light that springs from it; but I was careful to add that the reader must look for his local and national quality between the lines of his writing and in the indirect testimony of his tone, his accent, his temper, of his very omissions and suppressions. *The House of the Seven Gables* has, however, more literal actuality than the others, and if it were not too fanciful an account of it, I should say that it renders, to an initiated reader, the impression of a summer afternoon in an elm-shadowed New England town. It leaves upon the mind a vague correspondence to some such reminiscence, and in stirring up the association it renders it delightful. The comparison is to the honour of the New England town, which gains in it more than it bestows. The shadows of the elms, in *The House of the Seven Gables,* are exceptionally dense and cool; the summer afternoon is peculiarly still and beautiful; the atmosphere has a delicious warmth, and the long daylight seems to pause and rest. But the mild provincial quality is there, the mixture of shabbiness and freshness, the paucity of ingredients. The end of an old race—this is the situation that Hawthorne has depicted, and he has been admirably inspired in the choice of the figures in whom he seeks to interest us. They are all figures rather than characters—they are all pictures rather than persons. But if their reality is light and vague, it is sufficient, and it is in harmony with the low relief and dimness of outline of the objects that surround them. They are all types, to the author's mind, of something general, of something that is bound up with the history, at large, of families and individuals, and each of them is the centre of a cluster of those ingenious and meditative musings, rather melancholy, as a general thing, than joyous, which melt into the current and texture of the story and give it a kind of moral richness. A grotesque old spinster, simple, childish, penniless, very humble at heart, but rigidly conscious of her pedigree; an amiable bachelor, of an epicurean temperament and an enfeebled intellect, who has passed twenty years of his life in penal confinement for a crime of which he was unjustly pronounced guilty; a sweet-natured and bright-faced young girl from the country, a poor relation of these two ancient decrepitudes, with whose moral mustiness her modern freshness and soundness are contrasted; a young man still more modern, holding the latest opinions, who has sought his fortune up and down the world, and, though he has not found it, takes a genial and enthusiastic view of the future: these, with two or three remarkable accessory figures, are the persons concerned in the little drama. The drama is a small one, but as Hawthorne does not put it before us for its own superficial sake, for the dry facts of the case, but for something in it which he holds to be symbolic and of large application,

something that points a moral and that it behoves us to remember, the scenes in the rusty wooden house whose gables give its name to the story have something of the dignity both of history and of tragedy. Miss Hephzibah Pyncheon, dragging out a disappointed life in her paternal dwelling, finds herself obliged in her old age to open a little shop for the sale of penny toys and ginger-bread. This is the central incident of the tale, and, as Hawthorne relates it, it is an incident of the most impressive magnitude and most touching interest. Her dishonoured and vague-minded brother is released from prison at the same moment, and returns to the ancestral roof to deepen her perplexities. But, on the other hand, to alleviate them, and to introduce a breath of the air of the outer world into this long unventilated interior, the little country cousin also arrives, and proves the good angel of the feebly distracted household. All this episode is exquisite—admirably conceived, and executed with a kind of humorous tenderness, an equal sense of everything in it that is picturesque, touching, ridiculous, worthy of the highest praise. Hephzibah Pyncheon, with her near-sighted scowl, her rusty joints, her antique turban, her map of a great territory to the eastward which ought to have belonged to her family, her vain terrors and scruples and resentments, the inaptitude and repugnance of an ancient gentlewoman to the vulgar little commerce which a cruel fate has compelled her to engage in—Hephzibah Pyncheon is a masterly picture. I repeat that she is a picture, as her companions are pictures; she is a charming piece of descriptive writing, rather than a dramatic exhibition. But she is described, like her companions too, so subtly and lovingly that we enter into her virginal old heart and stand with her behind her abominable little counter. Clifford Pyncheon is a still more remarkable conception, though he is perhaps not so vividly depicted. It was a figure needing a much more subtle touch, however, and it was of the essence of his character to be vague and unemphasised. Nothing can be more charming than the manner in which the soft, bright, active presence of Phoebe Pyncheon is indicated, or than the account of her relations with the poor dimly sentient kinsman for whom her light-handed sisterly offices, in the evening of a melancholy life, are a revelation of lost possibilities of happiness. "In her aspect," Hawthorne says of the young girl, "there was a familiar gladness, and a holiness that you could play with, and yet reverence it as much as ever. She was like a prayer offered up in the homeliest beauty of one's mother-tongue. Fresh was Phoebe, moreover, and airy, and sweet in her apparel; as if nothing that she wore—neither her gown, nor her small straw bonnet, nor her little kerchief, any more than her snowy stockings—had ever been put on before; or if worn, were all the fresher for it, and with a fragrance as if they had lain among the rose-buds." Of the influence of her maidenly salubrity upon poor Clifford, Hawthorne gives the prettiest description, and then, breaking off suddenly, renounces the attempt in language which, while pleading its inadequacy, conveys an exquisite satisfaction to the reader. I quote the passage for the sake of its extreme felicity, and of the charming image with which it concludes.

But we strive in vain to put the idea into words. No adequate expression of the beauty and profound pathos with which it impresses us is attainable. This being, made only for happiness, and heretofore so miserably failing to be happy—his tendencies so hideously thwarted that some unknown time ago, the delicate springs of his character, never morally or intellectually strong, had given way, and he was now imbecile—this poor forlorn voyager from the Islands of the Blest, in a frail bark, on a tempestuous sea, had been flung by the last mountain-wave of his shipwreck, into a quiet harbour. There, as he lay more than half lifeless on the strand, the fragrance of an earthly rose-bud had come to his nostrils, and, as odours will, had summoned up reminiscences or visions of all the living and breathing beauty amid which he should have had his home. With his native susceptibility of happy influences, he inhales the slight ethereal rapture into his soul, and expires!

I have not mentioned the personage in *The House of the Seven Gables* upon whom Hawthorne evidently bestowed most pains, and whose portrait is the most elaborate in the book; partly because he is, in spite of the space he occupies, an accessory figure, and partly because, even more than the others, he is what I have called a picture rather than a character. Judge Pyncheon is an ironical portrait,

very richly and broadly executed, very sagaciously composed and rendered—the portrait of a superb, full-blown hypocrite, a large-based, full-nurtured Pharisee, bland, urbane, impressive, diffusing about him a "sultry" warmth of benevolence, as the author calls it again and again, and basking in the noon-tide of prosperity and the consideration of society; but in reality hard, gross, and ignoble. Judge Pyncheon is an elaborate piece of description, made up of a hundred admirable touches, in which satire is always winged with fancy, and fancy is linked with a deep sense of reality. It is difficult to say whether Hawthorne followed a model in describing Judge Pyncheon; but it is tolerably obvious that the picture is an impression—a copious impression—of an individual. It has evidently a definite starting-point in fact, and the author is able to draw, freely and confidently, after the image established in his mind. Holgrave, the modern young man, who has been a Jack-of-all-trades and is at the period of the story a daguerreotypist, is an attempt to render a kind of national type—that of the young citizen of the United States whose fortune is simply in his lively intelligence, and who stands naked, as it were, unbiased and unencumbered alike, in the centre of the far-stretching level of American life. Holgrave is intended as a contrast; his lack of traditions, his democratic stamp, his condensed experience, are opposed to the desiccated prejudices and exhausted vitality of the race of which poor feebly-scowling, rusty-jointed Hephzibah is the most heroic representative. It is perhaps a pity that Hawthorne should not have proposed to himself to give the old Pyncheon-qualities some embodiment which would help them to balance more fairly with the elastic properties of the young daguerreotypist—should not have painted a lusty conservative to match his strenuous radical. As it is, the mustiness and mouldiness of the tenants of the House of the Seven Gables crumble away rather too easily. Evidently, however, what Hawthorne designed to represent was not the struggle between an old society and a new, for in this case he would have given the old one a better chance; but simply, as I have said, the shrinkage and extinction of a family. This appealed to his imagination; and the idea of long perpetuation and survival always appears to have filled him with a kind of horror and dis-approval. Conservative, in a certain degree, as he was himself, and fond of retrospect and quietude and the mellowing influences of time, it is singular how often one encounters in his writings some expression of mistrust of old houses, old institutions, long lines of descent. He was disposed apparently to allow a very moderate measure in these respects, and he condemns the dwelling of the Pyncheons disappear from the face of the earth because it has been standing a couple of hundred years. In this he was an American of Americans; or rather he was more American than many of his countrymen, who, though they are accustomed to work for the short run rather than the long, have often a lurking esteem for things that show the marks of having lasted. I will add that Holgrave is one of the few figures, among those which Hawthorne created, with regard to which the absence of the realistic mode of treatment is felt as a loss. Holgrave is not sharply enough characterised; he lacks features; he is not an individual, but a type. But my last word about this admirable novel must not be a restrictive one. It is a large and generous production, pervaded with that vague hum, that indefinable echo, of the whole multitudinous life of man, which is the real sign of a great work of fiction.

James on *The Blithedale Romance* (from *Hawthorne*, chapter 5)

This work, as I have said, would not have been written if Hawthorne had not spent a year at Brook Farm, and though it is in no sense of the word an account of the manners or the inmates of that establishment, it will preserve the memory of the ingenious community at West Roxbury for a generation unconscious of other reminders. I hardly know what to say about it save that it is very charming; this vague, unanalytic epithet is the first that comes to one's pen in treating of Hawthorne's novels, for their extreme amenity of form invariably suggests it; but if on the one hand it claims to be uttered, on the other it frankly confesses its inconclusiveness. Perhaps, however, in this case, it fills out the measure of appreciation more completely than in others, for *The Blithedale Romance* is the lightest, the brightest, the liveliest, of this company of unhumorous fictions.

The story is told from a more joyous point of view—from a point of view comparatively humorous—and a number of objects and incidents touched with the light of the profane world—the vulgar, many-coloured world of actuality, as distinguished from the crepuscular realm of the writer's own reveries—are mingled with its course. The book indeed is a mixture of elements, and it leaves in the memory an impression analogous to that of an April day—an alternation of brightness and shadow, of broken sun-patches and sprinkling clouds. Its denoument is tragical—there is indeed nothing so tragical in all Hawthorne, unless it be the murder of Miriam's persecutor by Donatello, in *Transformation*, as the suicide of Zenobia; and yet on the whole the effect of the novel is to make one think more agreeably of life. The standpoint of the narrator has the advantage of being a concrete one; he is no longer, as in the preceding tales, a disembodied spirit, imprisoned in the haunted chamber of his own contemplations, but a particular man, with a certain human grossness.

Of Miles Coverdale I have already spoken, and of its being natural to assume that in so far as we may measure this lightly indicated identity of his, it has a great deal in common with that of his creator. Coverdale is a picture of the contemplative, observant, analytic nature, nursing its fancies, and yet, thanks to an element of strong good sense, not bringing them up to be spoiled children; having little at stake in life, at any given moment, and yet indulging, in imagination, in a good many adventures; a portrait of a man, in a word, whose passions are slender, whose imagination is active, and whose happiness lies, not in doing, but in perceiving—half a poet, half a critic, and all a spectator. He is contrasted, excellently, with the figure of Hollingworth, the heavily treading Reformer, whose attitude with regard to the world is that of the hammer to the anvil, and who has no patience with his friend's indifferences and neutralities. Coverdale is a gentle sceptic, a mild cynic; he would agree that life is a little worth living—or worth living a little; but would remark that, unfortunately, to live little enough, we have to live a great deal. He confesses to a want of earnestness, but in reality he is evidently an excellent fellow, to whom one might look, not for any personal performance on a great scale, but for a good deal of generosity of detail. "As Hollingsworth once told me, I lack a purpose," he writes, at the close of his story. "How strange! He was ruined, morally, by an overplus of the same ingredient the want of which, I occasionally suspect, has rendered my own life all an emptiness. I by no means wish die. Yet were there any cause in this whole chaos of human struggle, worth a sane man's dying for, and which my death would benefit, then—provided, however, the effort did not involve an unreasonable amount of trouble—methinks I might be bold to offer up my life. If Kossuth, for example, would pitch the battle-field of Hungarian rights within an easy ride of my abode, and choose a mild sunny morning, after breakfast, for the conflict, Miles Coverdale would gladly be his man, for one brave rush upon the levelled bayonets. Further than that I should be loth to pledge myself."

The finest thing in *The Blithedale Romance* is the character of Zenobia, which I have said elsewhere strikes me as the nearest approach that Hawthorne has made to the complete creation of a person. She is more concrete than Hester or Miriam, or Hilda or Phoebe; she is a more definite image, produced by a greater multiplicity of touches. It is idle to inquire too closely whether Hawthorne had Margaret Fuller in his mind in constructing the figure of this brilliant specimen of the strong-minded class and endowing her with the genius of conversation; or, on the assumption that such was the case, to compare the image at all strictly with the model. There is no strictness in the representation by novelists of persons who have struck them in life, and there can in the nature of things be none. From the moment the imagination takes a hand in the game, the inevitable tendency is to divergence, to following what may be called new scents. The original gives hints, but the writer does what he likes with them, and imports new elements into the picture. If there is this amount of reason for referring the wayward heroine of Blithedale to Hawthorne's impression of the most distinguished woman of her day in Boston, that Margaret Fuller was the only literary lady of eminence whom there is any sign of his having known, that she was proud, passionate, and

eloquent, that she was much connected with the little world of Transcendentalism out of which the experiment of Brook Farm sprung, and that she had a miserable end and a watery grave—if these are facts to be noted on one side, I say; on the other, the beautiful and sumptuous Zenobia, with her rich and picturesque temperament and physical aspects, offers many points of divergence from the plain and strenuous invalid who represented feminine culture in the suburbs of the New England metropolis. This picturesqueness of Zenobia is very happily indicated and maintained; she is a woman, in all the force of the term, and there is something very vivid and powerful in her large expression of womanly gifts and weaknesses. Hollingsworth is, I think, less successful, though there is much reality in the conception of the type to which he belongs—the strong-willed. narrow-hearted apostle of a special form of redemption for society. There is nothing better in all Hawthorne than the scene between him and Coverdale, when the two men are at work together in the field (piling stones on a dyke), and he gives it to his companion to choose whether he will be with him or against him. It is a pity, perhaps, to have represented him as having begun life as a blacksmith, for one grudges him the advantage of so logical a reason for his roughness and hardness.

Hollingsworth scarcely said a word, unless when repeatedly and pertinaciously addressed. Then indeed he would glare upon us from the thick shrubbery of his meditations, like a tiger out of a jungle, make the briefest reply possible, and betake himself back into the solitude of his heart and mind. . . . His heart, I imagine, was never really interested in our socialist scheme, but was for ever busy with his strange, and as most people thought, impracticable plan for the reformation of criminals through an appeal to their higher instincts. Much as I liked Hollingsworth, it cost me many a groan to tolerate him on this point. He ought to have commenced his investigation of the subject by committing some huge sin in his proper person, and examining the condition of his higher instincts afterwards.

The most touching element in the novel is the history of the grasp that this barbarous fanatic has laid upon the fastidious and high-tempered Zenobia, who, disliking him and shrinking from him at a hundred points, is drawn into the gulf of his omnivorous egotism. The portion of the story that strikes me as least felicitous is that which deals with Priscilla and with her mysterious relation to Zenobia—with her mesmeric gifts, her clairvoyance, her identity with the Veiled Lady, her divided subjection to Hollingsworth and Westervelt, and her numerous other graceful but fantastic properties—her Sibylline attributes, as the author calls them. Hawthorne is rather too fond of Sibylline attributes—a taste of the same order as his disposition, to which I have already alluded, to talk about spheres and sympathies. As the action advances, in *The Blithedale Romance,* we get too much out of reality, and cease to feel beneath our feet the firm ground of an appeal to our own vision of the world, our observation. I should have liked to see the story concern itself more with the little community in which its earlier scenes are laid, and avail itself of so excellent an opportunity for describing unhackneyed specimens of human nature. I have already spoken of the absence of satire in the novel, of its not aiming in the least at satire, and of its offering no grounds for complaint as an invidious picture. Indeed the brethren of Brook Farm should have held themselves slighted rather than misrepresented, and have regretted that the admirable genius who for a while was numbered among them should have treated their institution

mainly as a perch for starting upon an imaginative flight. But when all is said about a certain want of substance and cohesion in the latter portions of *The Blithedale Romance* the book is still a delightful and beautiful one. Zenobia and Hollingsworth live in the memory, and even Priscilla and Coverdale, who linger there less importunately, have a great deal that touches us and that we believe in. I said just now that Priscilla was infelicitous; but immediately afterwards I open the volume at a page in which the author describes some of the out-of-door amusements at Blithedale, and speaks of a foot-race across the grass, in which some of the slim young girls of the society joined. "Priscilla's peculiar charm in a foot-race was the weakness and irregularity with which she ran. Growing up without exercise, except to her poor little fingers, she had never yet acquired the perfect use of her legs. Setting buoyantly forth therefore, as if no rival less swift than Atalanta could compete with her, she ran falteringly, and often tumbled on the grass. Such an incident—though it seems too slight to think of—was a thing to laugh at, but which brought the water into one's eyes, and lingered in the memory after far greater joys and sorrows were wept out of it, as antiquated trash. Priscilla's life, as I beheld it, was full of trifles that affected me in just this way." That seems to me exquisite, and the book is full of touches as deep and delicate.

INDEX